Third Edition

FREEDOM AND CRISIS

AN AMERICAN HISTORY
Volume One – To 1877

Third Edition
FREEDOM

AND CRISIS

AN AMERICAN HISTORY
Volume One – To 1877

Allen Weinstein
Smith College

Frank Otto Gatell
University of California, Los Angeles

Random House  New York

Third Edition
987654321
Copyright © 1974, 1978, 1981 by Random House, Inc.

Library of Congress Cataloging in Publication Data

Weinstein, Allen
  Freedom and crisis.

  Includes bibliographies and index.
  CONTENTS: v. 1. To 1877. — v. 2 Since 1860.
  1. United States — History. I. Gatell, Frank Otto,
joint author. II. Title.
E178.1.W395 1981   973   80-39866
ISBN 0-394-32611-3

Cover Photograph: © Susan Lapides 1980/Design Conceptions
Picture Research: Mary Jenkins
Photo Editor: R. Lynn Goldberg

Text design: Dana Kasarsky Design and Infield/D'Astolfo Associates
Cover Design: Dana Kasarsky Design

Project Researcher: Susan Sherer Osnos

Manufactured in the United States of America. Composed by Ruttle, Shaw & Wetherill,
Inc., Philadelphia, Pa. Printed and bound by Von Hoffmann Press, St. Louis, Mo.

To Andrew and David, with love

Contents

EXPANDING AMERICA UNIT
212 THREE

DIVIDED AMERICA UNIT FOUR

Maps and Charts

Author's Introduction

Freedom and Crisis is a book of discovery about the American past. The reader will quickly recognize, by glancing at the table of contents or by flipping through the pages, that this book is different from the ordinary "text." The difference is embodied in the way that *Freedom and Crisis* organizes the American experience.

Units are arranged in pairs of chapters. Every pair opens with a dramatic narrative of a significant episode in the American past. Each episode was chosen not only because it conveys an exciting story but also because it introduces many aspects of American life during the period under investigation. The chapter that follows then locates the episode within its appropriate historical context, interpreting the major forces that shaped the actions described in the episode.

This remains the book's basic format: a narrative chapter on a single episode, based on fresh documentary research, followed by an explanatory chapter linking historical fact and interpretation to the episode itself. The account of Jamestown in Chapter 3, for example, is followed by a chapter on seventeenth-century plantation colonies. Similarly, the Watergate drama serves as the basis for examining American politics and society during the 1970s in the accompanying chapter.

I have employed this novel approach to an introductory book on American history because my primary concern from the start has been to write a book that would hold the interest of today's students, perhaps the most inquisitive but skeptical generation of students ever. To do this, I felt that a book had to be readable and realistic. *Freedom and Crisis* is both. The book dramatizes critical moments in the American democratic experience and deals candidly with both the extension and the denial of liberty at those times.

Freedom and Crisis, then, is not a traditional book on United States history. Often such traditional books are written in the belief that there exists a certain body of data (election results, dates and outcomes of wars, treaties, major laws, and so forth) that comprises American history. I accept this idea only to the extent that most of the data of conventional texts can be found somewhere in this book. Sometimes, however, the information is located in maps, charts, and special features rather than in the text itself.

Frequently overlooked by students (and even by some teachers) is the point that this central body of data, the "facts," emerges only after a certain selection on the part of historians. There exists, after all, an almost infinite number of facts that could be chosen to represent the history of the human experience. In writing this book, I simply carried the usual selection process a step farther. Half the book is devoted to selected dramatic episodes. When linked to the accompanying chapters, the episodes form my bedrock of factual material. Using this foundation, students can then inquire into the fundamental questions of American history.

Most episodes can be read simply as absorbing stories. Thus readers will discover much about the country's past merely by studying such vivid incidents as the Boston massacre, the Lewis and Clark expedition, the Nat Turner revolt, the Custer massacre, the Triangle fire, the Philippines revolt, the attack on Pearl Harbor, and Watergate. But by using the interpretative chapter accompanying each episode, students will develop the ability to extract greater meaning from the facts in these dramas and, at the same time, acquire an understanding of related historical events.

Freedom and Crisis moves chronologically through the American experience, but certain themes recur and receive particular attention. The book devotes several episodes, for example, to patterns of race and ethnic relations, especially the treatment of blacks, Indians, immigrants, and other oppressed minorities. The struggle for political liberties and economic betterment, class conflicts, territorial expansion, technological change, and basic ideological and cultural disputes are also treated.

The constant interplay of factual drama and careful interpretation is the book's distinctive feature. Facts and concepts cross paths on each page, thereby avoiding the usual unhappy classroom extremes of concentrating either on what happened or on why it happened. *Freedom and Crisis* has no room for empty historical abstractions that leave students without a factual anchor. Nor does an uncontrolled flood of rampaging facts lacking solid conceptual boundaries spill endlessly off the printed pages. The paired-chapter format, I believe, avoids both these extremes.

The episode–explanatory chapter pairs present a concise but comprehensive introduction to the history of the United States. Yet although the book covers the American experience, I wrote with less urgent concern for coverage than for concreteness, drama, and interpretative depth. Almost every detail included in the narrative episodes has a larger meaning, so that students and instructors must work outward in this text from concrete detail to generalized understanding.

History as an act of inquiry involves putting great questions to small data, discovering general significance in particular events. *Freedom and Crisis* evolved from my belief that students are both willing and able to engage in the same process of inquiry as professional historians. In this manner each incident in the American odyssey, from the earliest European discoveries to our generation's exploration of the moon, can become a personal act of discovery for the reader, risky but rewarding.

The first two editions of *Freedom and Crisis* involved the joint efforts of myself and my collaborator, R. J. Wilson of Smith College, whose subtle intelligence contributed meaningfully to the book's success. This edition includes eighteen new chapters and thoroughly updates the others, so that it represents an entirely fresh attempt to make the paired-chapter format even more effective and useful to teachers and students. The popular short biographies of earlier editions have been supplemented with a series of "American profiles." Pictures and maps have also been revamped.

In the third and subsequent editions of *Freedom and Crisis*, Frank Otto Gatell joins me as co-author. Professor Gatell had contributed significantly, though without prior acknowledgment at his own request, to the book's first two editions.

The chapters that follow chart the authors' personal roadmap through American experience. This book will achieve its purpose only if it helps the reader begin his or her own private journey through the national past.

Allen Weinstein

Third Edition

FREEDOM AND CRISIS

AN AMERICAN HISTORY

T he European conquest of the American continents was, like most momentous events in human history, a confused and complicated experience punctuated by a measure of greed, cruelty, and violence. The first pair of chapters in this unit of *Freedom and Crisis,* third edition, deals in general with the initial European discoveries, explorations, and attempts at colonization. For its specific example, it focuses in detail on the Spanish conquest of the elaborate and advanced Aztec civilization in Mexico.

From a modern perspective, the European triumph seems to have been an inevitable result of superior technology. But from the perspective of the sixteenth and seventeenth centuries, the European foothold in the New World appears to have been the precarious result of advantages won through daring exercises in ruthless desperation.

When the English managed to establish their first successful settlement in North America, they did not encounter Native American civilizations as advanced as those the Spanish found in Latin America. Nor did they find gold and silver. What they found was land—land that sometimes seemed impossible to conquer.

The early English settlements held on by a thread just as thinly stretched as the one that enabled Cortez and his men to survive in Mexico. They, too, encountered blood and suffering. Gradually, in the course of the seventeenth century, two successful centers of colonization developed, one in Virginia and the other in Massachusetts. Then, from these initial centers, English settlement fanned out into Maryland and the Carolinas, into Connecticut and Rhode Island, and into New York and Pennsylvania.

The two initial areas of English success—Virginia and Massachusetts—faced comparable problems of survival, although Virginia's were far more agonizing in the early years. Both colonies confronted the basic matters of feeding and sheltering their settlers, dealing with the native Americans they wished to displace, and ensuring an economic base with which to survive.

In the end, however, important economic and social differences developed between the plantation colonies of the South and the English settlements in New England and the "middle colonies." Differences in climate and soil reinforced settler preferences concerning the economic basis of colonization. By the century's end, Southern agriculture had become dependent upon slaves imported from Africa rather than upon the labor force of Europeans—free settlers or indentured servants—who dominated the remaining colonies. In Massachusetts and other New England colonies, moreover, variants of English Puritan society shaped colonial life for most of the century. Elsewhere in the Northern settlements, non-Puritan societies evolved displaying far greater religious and social tolerance.

This complex mosaic of English colonial existence emerges in the second and third pairs of chapters. Chapter 3 describes the Jamestown settlers' ordeal, while the accompanying chapter studies life in the Southern plantation colonies. Chapter 5 provides a vivid portrait of the Salem, Massachusetts, witchcraft trials, followed in Chapter 6 by a general discussion of seventeenth-century developments in Puritan New

COLONIAL
AMERICA

UNIT
ONE

England and the middle colonies. All three stories—the Aztec conquest, the founding of Jamestown, and the witchcraft trials—dramatize the lives of the men and women, European and native American, who helped to shape the first centuries of American settlement. They provide insight into the overall question of the European encounter, whether Spanish or English, with New World realities.

Cortez and Montezuma: I The Conquest of the Aztecs

For days Emperor Montezuma had eaten and slept badly. He feared for the safety of his kingdom. Strange ships had been sighted on the coast, and Montezuma anxiously awaited the return of messengers he had sent to greet the strangers, to present them with gifts of gold and precious jewels, and to urge them to leave Mexico at once. Montezuma believed the new-comers might be ancient Aztec gods, returning—as foretold in a prophecy—to claim his empire for their own. As a deeply religious man and a cautious ruler, the emperor wished neither to offend his gods nor to lose his throne.

Following Aztec religious practice at times of great crisis, the emperor ordered that upon the messengers' return, two Indian captives be brought to the city's largest temple and sacrificed to the supreme Aztec god, Huitzilopochtli. Montezuma's priests tore open the breasts of the captives, and the messengers were sprinkled with their blood. This was necessary because the messengers had completed a dangerous and difficult mission: their eyes had looked upon the gods' faces. They had even talked to the gods!

The messengers had sighted the white sails of gigantic ships on the coast of the Gulf of Mexico. Armed strangers had led them before a light-skinned but sunburned man, stocky and heavily bearded, who wore the armor of a warrior. This was the "god" himself, the returning Aztec deity Quetzalcoatl, god of learning and of the wind, whose sign was that of a serpent.

The messengers told the god that his vassal Montezuma, who ruled the kingdom for him, had sent them to pay homage. They dressed the god in Quetzalcoatl's vestments: a serpent's mask, armor, and other "divine adornments" heavy with jewels and gold. The other strangers—also light-skinned and bearded like the god himself, armor-clad and armed with swords—crowded around Montezuma's brown-skinned, clean-shaven envoys. Only when the messengers had completed their

On the portrait banner:
TO
RITR·DI·MOTEZVMA
CAVATO·DALL·ORIGINA
VENVTO·DAL·MESSICO
AL·SER:·G·D·DI·TOSCA

A stylized portrait of Montezuma, emperor of the Aztecs, before his humiliation by Cortez and the first conquistadores. (Library of Congress)

ceremonial presentation did the god finally speak: "And is this all? Is this your gift of welcome? Is this how you greet people?"

The god ordered them chained by the neck and feet. The frightened messengers submitted without protest. They then watched several of the strangers walk toward a long iron cylinder tipped upward near the ship's edge. At the god's command, his men lit the cylinder with burning sticks, and the noise of the explosion that followed sent the messengers fainting onto the deck.

The Conquest of the Aztecs **5**

When they recovered, they were unchained, and once again the god spoke: "I have heard that you Mexicans are very great warriors, very brave and terrible. Supposedly one Mexican can pursue, overpower, conquer, and rout ten, even twenty, of his foes. I want to find out if you are truly that strong and brave."

The god next handed them swords, spears, and leather shields, ordering them to return at daybreak to fight his own men. The envoys protested strongly. If they fought with the strangers, Montezuma would surely put them to death. The god seemed amused by the frightened Aztecs. "No," he said, "it must take place. I want to see for myself." He dismissed the messengers and sent them back to their canoes. They paddled furiously away from the ship, some with oars and others with only their hands, fleeing from the god's command.

The messengers did not return. Instead, they hurried westward from the coast to report to Montezuma in the Aztec capital, Tenochtitlán (now Mexico City). From time to time they paused for food and water in villages or cities inhabited by Indians previously conquered by the Aztecs. Thus Montezuma's own messengers spread word among the conquered tribes about the arrival of strangers more powerful than the Aztecs themselves!

Once they had washed in the blood of the two sacrificed captives, the messengers told the emperor all about "Quetzalcoatl." Montezuma displayed evident fear when they mentioned the explosive weapon: "If the cannon is aimed against a mountain, the mountain splits and cracks open." But their description of the god and his followers was no less terrifying.

How fearsome, for example, did the god's companions dress!: Their trappings and arms are all made of iron. They dress in iron and wear iron cover-

An Indian view of Cortez on his march to Mexico City. The eagle perched on the cactus, at right, was the Aztec national symbol and today forms the Mexican coat of arms. (American Museum of Natural History)

ings on their head. Their swords are iron; their spears are iron. Their deer carry them on their backs wherever they wish to go.

And how strange their appearance!

Their skin is white, as if it were made of lime. They have yellow hair, although some of them have black. Their beards are long and yellow, and their moustaches are also yellow.

Montezuma hung on the messengers' every word. They confirmed all the earlier omens and signs, all the predictions of Aztec priests and magicians. His own messengers testified to the emperor's greatest fear: the return of Quetzalcoatl himself.

At once Montezuma began preparing himself for the arrival of Quetzalcoatl, much as one of his own fearful vassals would prepare himself for Montezuma's appearance. The sacred Aztec texts stated clearly that Quetzalcoatl's return meant the end of Montezuma's reign and the destruction of the Aztec Empire. It had taken several hundred years for Montezuma's ancestors to extend their control from their original home on the small island fortress of Tenochtitlán in the great interior Lake Texcoco, one of five interconnected lakes, until they ruled all of Mexico. Most of the other tribes feared them. The few villages or cities that continued to resist had to fight constant and generally losing battles against the Aztecs, battles aimed not at killing the enemy but at taking as many prisoners as possible: a constant supply of human sacrifices for the insatiable Aztec gods.

Now in their calendar year "13-Rabbit" (A.D. 1518), Aztec dominance over Mexico faced its major challenge. Montezuma brooded:

> What will happen to us? Who will outlive it? Ah, in other times I was contented, but now I have death in my heart! Will our lord Quetzalcoatl come here?

At the same time, Montezuma began to search for means of determining whether or not the strangers were *truly* gods. "Strangers as powerful as gods" — but still human beings — might be dealt with more easily than Quetzalcoatl himself.

In the usual fashion of Aztec diplomacy, the emperor first sent magicians, along with his own personal wizards, to confront the strangers. He provided them with food for the visitors and with "captives to be sacrificed, because the strangers might wish to drink their blood." Traveling east, his magicians linked up with the gods moving westward from the coast. Immediately Montezuma's envoys began to sacrifice their captives, but as the strangers watched the Aztec ritual,

> they were filled with disgust and loathing. They spat on the ground, or wiped away their tears, or closed their eyes and shook their heads in abhorrence. They refused to eat the food that was sprinkled with blood, because it reeked of it; it sickened them, as if the blood were rotted.

Montezuma's wizards had failed him: they had no magic powerful enough to turn the strangers back. And all along the route to Tenochtitlán, scores of Indians paid homage to the god and his few hundred com-

A sixteenth-century map presents a stylized view of Tenochtitlán. At the center stands the plaza with a great pyramid temple where important sacrifices took place. Causeways lead across Lake Texcoco to "suburbs"—here depicted as European fortresses. One Spaniard wrote on entering the city: "Gazing on such wonderful sights, we did not know what to say. Some of our soldiers even asked whether the things we saw were not a dream."

panions. Thousands joined the march, until it stretched out for miles along the royal road. Several times, the strangers fought against hostile tribes whom they encountered along the way. Each time, the god and his men triumphed.

One tribe in particular resisted ferociously. The Tlaxcalans, whose lands were to the east of those controlled by Montezuma and the Aztecs, had alternately fought with the Aztecs or lived in a state of uneasy alliance with them. Now, they battled the strangers three times before finally surrendering and pledging their friendship and alliance. After defeating the Tlaxcalans, the strangers marched on toward the Aztec capital, stopping at the town of Cholula. The Cholulans feigned friendship but planned to attack the strangers (acting at the direct orders of Montezuma). Through Doña Marina, his interpreter,[1] the god learned of this plan and launched an attack of his own. The Cholulans were defeated and, like the Tlaxcalans, joined the ranks of Indian tribes supporting the strangers' march toward Tenochtitlán.

---

[1] During his travels Cortez acquired several "interpreters." One such person was Jerónimo de Aquilar, a Spanish castaway who lived among the natives of Cozumel—an island off Mexico's Yucatan coast. The "god's" other chief interpreter was an Indian woman whom the Spaniards named Doña Marina. She was a "gift" from one of the first Indian tribes he and his men conquered. Doña Marina became Cortez's main interpreter with Indian messengers such as those from Montezuma.

One final time the emperor tried to appease the approaching strangers and to induce them to depart. He sent Aztec war chiefs rather than wizards this time, warriors who presented them with golden feathers and necklaces, at which point the gods began grinning.

They picked up the gold and fingered it like monkeys; they seemed to be transported by joy. . . . For in truth they lusted for gold. Their bodies swelled with greed, and they hungered like pigs for that gold.

The strangers asked through their Indian interpreters whether the leading Aztec envoy was the emperor himself, to which that man replied, "I am your servant. I am Montezuma." The Indians who accompanied the strangers knew better. When they informed the gods of this lie, Quetzalcoatl himself shouted at the Aztec impersonator:

You fool! Why try to deceive us? Who do you take us for? You can not fool, nor mock us, nor deceive us, nor flatter us, nor trick us, nor misguide us, nor turn us back, nor destroy us, nor dazzle us, nor throw dust in our eyes! You are not Montezuma, but he cannot hide from us either. Where can he go? . . . We are coming to see him, to meet him face to face.

As the god drew ever closer to the city, Montezuma abandoned all efforts to halt his progress. Many Indians were eager for the god's arrival, especially tribes like the Tlaxcalans, who had chafed under Aztec rule for two centuries. One such Indian was the prince of the city of Texcoco, who led his people not only in joining the strangers' army but in accepting their religion as well. Although the prince did not understand why Quetzalcoatl pretended to worship an even greater god, he listened as the god explained that "the emperor of the Christians had sent him here, so far away, in order that he might instruct them in the law of Christ." Upon hearing Quetzalcoatl describe the mysteries of this "Christ," the Texcocoan prince and most of his noblemen asked to be converted to the new religion. Thus the two strongest subject tribes of the Aztecs, the Texcocoans and the Tlaxcalans, had joined the strangers' small band on its inexorable march to Montezuma's city.

The strangers and their sprawling columns of Indian allies strode across one of the three causeways that led over the lake to the Aztec capital. This normally bustling, noisy thoroughfare was almost deserted. On most days, tens of thousands of tradesmen, nobles, priests, and commoners used the causeway. That day, however, "all lay quiet: the people did not go out or venture forth. . . . The people retired to their houses . . . and the common folk said: '. . . Now we shall die; we shall perish.' "

Across this deserted, water-borne highway strode a remarkable caravan: the pale-skinned strangers themselves—armed, iron-clad, many riding their strange "deerlike" animals, some carrying iron crossbows, still others pulling the dreaded cannon; the thousands of Indians who had joined the procession during its trip across Mexico; and the god himself, Quetzalcoatl, directing the entire operation from a position between his own companions and his Indian subjects.

When the god and his huge army entered Tenochtitlán, they were the first armed and possibly hostile force in centuries to walk unopposed through the elaborate and complex defenses that the Aztecs had constructed around their capital. "We entered Tenochtitlán," one of the soldiers later wrote,

> over a causeway wide enough for three or four or more horsemen to ride comfortably abreast. The causeway was built across the lake and had wooden bridges that could be raised or removed. The water was [so] full of canoes loaded with people who were watching us that it was frightening to see such multitudes.
>
> As we approached the city we could see great towers and churches of the kind they build, and large palaces and dwellings. There were over one hundred thousand houses in this city, each house built over the water on wooden piles, with nothing but a beam connecting one house to another, so that each one was a fortress in itself.

Montezuma, dressed in his imperial finery and attended by scores of Aztec princes, chieftains, and knights, awaited the god. The emperor himself presented gifts of flowers and precious ornaments to the visitors. Finally the god spoke: "Are you Montezuma? Are you the king?" The emperor replied that he was and then came forward, head bowed low, and made a welcoming speech:

> Our lord, you are weary. The journey has tired you, but now you . . . have come to your city, Mexico. No, it is not a dream. . . . I have seen you at last! I was in agony . . . [but] now you have come out of the clouds and mists to sit on your throne again.
>
> This was foretold by the kings who governed your city. . . . You have come back to us; you have come down from the sky. Rest now, and take possession of your royal houses. Welcome to your land, my lords!

The god ordered his Indian translator to respond to the emperor:

> Tell Montezuma that we are his friends. There is nothing to fear. We have wanted to see him for a long time, and now we have seen his face and heard his words.

Turning to Montezuma directly, Quetzalcoatl continued:

> We have come to your home in Mexico as friends. There is nothing to fear.

The strangers then took Montezuma by the hand and patted him on the back to demonstrate their affection. Dismounting from their horses, they entered the royal palace, accompanied by Montezuma and his chiefs. The god had arrived.

"Quetzalcoatl" was known to his troops as Hernando Cortez, no "god" but a Spanish soldier and adventurer who had sailed to the Mexican coast from Cuba with a small fleet. Cortez had been ordered by Cuba's Spanish governor, Velazquez, to explore for precious metal, which could then be divided among the king of Spain, the Cuban governor, Cortez, and his men.

Cortez learned from the coastal Indians that the many tribes of the Mexican peninsula had been formed into an empire by the Aztecs. The process resembled the recent Christian reconquest of Spain itself. But the Aztecs worshiped natural forces that the Spaniard and his men consid-

ered pagan deities. Cortez was particularly offended by the Aztec ritual of human sacrifice. From the moment he first learned of these Indian religious practices, Cortez determined not only to search for treasure, but to substitute Christian rituals for the Aztec forms of placating the gods.

Very early in the expedition, Cortez decided *not* to share any of the Aztec gold, silver, or precious stones with Governor Velazquez but, instead, to deal directly with the king of Spain. That way, Cortez would solicit his own royal honors while dividing up wealth and a new territory. Most of his men agreed. To keep those who remained loyal to the Cuban governor from returning to Havana and disclosing his treachery, Cortez resorted to a simple but drastic expedient. Once he and his men landed on the shores of Mexico, he burned his ships. From that moment on, he was legally a traitor to the Spanish king's representative, the governor of Cuba. Cortez realized that if he failed to stuff the king's coffers with Aztec gold, he would return to Spain in chains or be executed as a traitor in America.

Although his troops did not consider their captain a god, as Montezuma did, they rallied to Cortez's almost godlike self-confidence. The Spaniards fought few battles before reaching the halls of Montezuma. Yet they managed to force most of the Indian towns and villages they passed into submission. Upon their arrival in Tenochtitlán, they were welcomed as gods and escorted into the palace.

Although Montezuma soon realized that the strange warriors were not deities but mere men, the Aztec emperor continued to believe the ancient prophecies concerning the destruction of his kingdom. He became a prisoner in his own palace, and his power over the people of Mexico weakened at once. The Aztecs had offered no resistance to the white-skinned visitors, partly because of their own fears and partly because of Montezuma's commands. Their fears increased as they watched their own leaders either hiding from or bowing to "Quetzalcoatl." For several months the strangers ruled Mexico City by issuing their orders through Montezuma. Thus without shedding any Mexican blood, a mere three hundred heavily armed soldiers gained temporary control over an empire of millions.

When the Spaniards retired to their quarters on their first evening in the emperor's palace, they accidentally discovered the main Aztec treasure room, filled (as one Spaniard later wrote) with "a large quantity of idols, featherwork, jewels, precious stones, silver, and an astonishing amount of gold, as well as so many lovely things that I was amazed." For the moment Cortez decided to leave the treasure undisturbed. He ordered the secret room sealed. One of Montezuma's servants, who had watched the scene, reported to the emperor that "the Spaniards grinned like little beasts and patted each other in delight. When they entered the hall of treasures, it was if they had arrived in Paradise."

To placate his captor, Montezuma informed Cortez that he offered the contents of the room to the Spanish king, along with whatever else remained of his own personal treasure. Cortez and his men, "amazed at the great liberality of Montezuma," proceeded to divide the gold according to the custom of such expeditions: one-fifth for King Charles; one-fifth for Cortez, "captain general" of the band; a large portion to cover the expenses of mounting the expedition in Cuba and another substantial sum to pay for Governor Velazquez's destroyed ships; smaller shares for the various captains and officers who served under Cortez; and finally, shares for the ordinary troops, which were "so little that many of the soldiers did not want to take it and Cortez was left with it all."

At first, Cortez proved less successful in changing Aztec religious practice than he had been in obtaining Aztec gold. During his early days in Tenochtitlán, he urged Montezuma several times to forbid human sacrifice in the Aztec temples, but to no avail. Montezuma did grant Cortez's "request" for permission to erect a separate Christian place of worship, with a cross and a statue of Christ and the Virgin Mary, but he refused to abandon his own gods. Because the Spanish captain general hoped to dominate the Aztecs by using Montezuma as a figurehead emperor, he compromised for the moment. Cortez realized that an all-out fight within Tenochtitlán would find three hundred Spaniards and their Indian allies surrounded by three million Aztecs.

Once it became clear that Montezuma had been placed under "house arrest," his Aztec nobles began plotting to drive out the Spaniards. The emperor, however, observed his pledge of loyalty to Cortez and revealed their schemes. Montezuma even ordered the chief Aztec plotter, his nephew Cacama, seized and delivered to Cortez. Next Montezuma called a council of Aztec nobles, priests, and chief vassals, urging them all to submit to Cortez and to the Spanish king. Although they protested, the nobles obeyed, at least nominally, and pledged their loyalty.

Cortez was so confident of Montezuma's continued influence over his people by this time that he ordered the closing of Aztec religious shrines. For days thereafter, the Spaniards and their Indian converts to Christianity destroyed statues of Aztec gods, drove the native priests from their temples, cleansed the altars used for human sacrifices, and erected Christian shrines throughout Tenochtitlán.

Finally, the captain general decided to strengthen his authority over the Mexicans by completing the humiliation of Montezuma. First, Cortez displayed before the emperor two Aztec nobles who (according to Cortez) had confessed that Montezuma had ordered them to lead a revolt against the Spaniards. Then he ordered Montezuma placed in irons and forced the emperor to watch as the two Aztec prisoners were burned to death before his eyes.

If Cortez hoped to terrify the Aztecs and Montezuma by this action, he miscalculated badly. Even Montezuma now threw his support behind the secret plans of Aztec nobles and priests to organize armed resistance to the Spaniards. The emperor's uncertainty and fear of his captors disappeared; he began to recover his strength and resolve. At a private meeting, he warned the captain general to leave Mexico immediately because "the gods are very angry with me for entertaining you here." Montezuma indicated clearly to Cortez that he could no longer guarantee the Spaniards' safety against an Aztec attack.

Cortez stalled for time. For several weeks, Montezuma, reconfirmed in his authority, and Cortez, quietly encircled by hostile Aztecs, skirted each other uneasily. Both men waited for some decisive break in this contest of wills. The "break," like Cortez himself, came from the coast. A new expedition of nineteen ships arrived at Vera Cruz, a small settlement Cortez had founded. These ships brought soldiers from Cuba, sent by Governor Velazquez to destroy Cortez and his party. "Now you will not need to build ships," Montezuma told Cortez blandly. The emperor's agents had been in touch with the expedition's commander, Pánfilo de Narváez, and knew of its purpose.

Cortez left Tenochtitlán within days, taking most of his soldiers and Indian allies to confront Narváez. He left behind a small Spanish contingent under the command of one of his captains, Pedro de Alvarado. Montezuma remained a hostage, and most Aztecs seemed willing to wait, hoping that the soldiers of Cortez and Narváez would destroy one another. Then there would be time to deal with Alvarado's small rear guard.

But Alvarado proved restless as the appointed caretaker of Tenochtitlán, and shortly after Cortez departed, the pent-up conflict between Spaniard and Aztec, which seemed almost like a struggle between a bee and an elephant, broke into warfare. It was the bee that went on the attack.

The occasion for battle came when Aztec priests requested Montezuma's permission to celebrate the feast of their chief god, Huitzilopochtli. This major harvest festival in Aztec religious life included an elaborate, exhausting dance-and-song ceremony which Aztec warriors performed at night in the temple courtyard. Alvarado heard rumors that

This woodcut recon-struction of the great temple at Tenoch-titlán and surround-ing area suggests the extraordinary achieve-ment of Aztec archi-tecture, building de-sign, and decorative arts. The great pyra-mid temple, site of Aztec human sacri-fices, towers over the various subsidiary temples, government buildings, and fortress walls, suggesting the gigantic scale of Mon-tezuma's capital city. (American Museum of Natural History)

the Aztecs planned to attack his troops once the dance ended. The hostil-ity that Cortez's soldiers now encountered throughout Tenochtitlán, combined with the drum beatings, trumpet blarings, and frenzied dancing of the festival, struck fear in the Spaniards. Alvarado lacked Cortez's cool composure at such moments, and he mistakenly believed that the car-nival-like ceremony foreshadowed a Mexican assault on his troops.

Alvarado ordered his men to block the temple's entrances. Then the Spaniards moved into the courtyard and massacred all those within. An Aztec narrative described the scene:

> They attacked all the celebrants, stabbing them, spearing them, striking them with their swords. They attacked some of them from behind, and these fell instantly to the ground with their entrails hanging out. Others they beheaded: they cut off their heads, or split their heads in pieces. . . . No matter how they tried to save themselves, they could find no escape.

When news of the slaughter spread through Tenochtitlán, the entire com-munity exploded in anger and grief. Montezuma's captains assembled thousands of warriors within hours, and armed with only spears and jave-lins, they attacked. Alvarado and his men immediately took refuge in the palace. The first siege of Tenochtitlán had begun.

Alvarado ordered Montezuma shackled again, and his soldiers opened fire with cannon and muskets to defend themselves against a bliz-zard of Aztec spears. The Aztecs, enraged at the unprovoked slaughter of their temple dancers, scorned an emissary from Montezuma, who pleaded with them to return to their homes. "Who is Montezuma to give us orders?" they shouted at the envoy. "We are no longer his slaves!" Aztec captains and warriors denounced Montezuma himself for collabo-ration with their enemies. They put the emperor's servants to death, prevented food and supplies from entering the palace, and seized anyone attempting to enter. At the same time they watched closely the roads and causeways leading to the city, to guard against Cortez's return.

While Alvarado brought war to Tenochtitlán, Cortez managed to capture Narváez's expedition with a minimum of bloodshed. He first sent gifts of gold to Narváez's men and promised them more treasures if they joined him. Then he led his forces in a night attack on Narváez's camp. After some brief, half-hearted resistance, most of the eight hundred soldiers (Cortez had half that number) surrendered and swore loyalty to Cortez. Twelve days later, Cortez received a message from Alvarado describing his desperate situation. Cortez and his soldiers, now numbering perhaps a thousand, began a second march on the Aztec capital.

The Mexican siege had proved effective. By the time Cortez arrived in Tenochtitlán, Alvarado's men had almost exhausted their food and water. Cortez's column entered the city without resistance, since the Mexicans apparently hoped to trap *all* the Spaniards inside the royal palace. By this time, the Aztec nobles had deposed Montezuma as emperor in favor of his brother Cuitlahuac, a man long committed to total destruction of the white strangers. The Aztecs renewed their attack on the palace, opening a raging, four-day struggle.

During the battle, while still a Spanish captive, Montezuma died. The Spaniards later claimed that he had been fatally wounded by rocks thrown by his own people while pleading for peace from the palace roof. Aztecs insisted that he had been killed by the Spaniards.

The fierce bloodletting went badly for the Spaniards, and the royal palace, no longer a fortress, was fast becoming a death trap. Cortez decided to abandon Tenochtitlán and withdraw at night. By the time he fled the city, only four of the eight bridges on the causeway that led to safety were still in Spanish hands. Even these were under attack by Aztec warriors.

The captain general apparently hoped to surprise his opponents, but it proved impossible to hide from Aztec sentries the movement of a thousand Spaniards, several thousand "loyal" Indians, horses, cannon, and baggage. Cortez and his men also tried to cart away the *entire* Aztec treasure horde, most of it by then melted into ingot bars—a total of eight tons in gold. By the time this cumbersome procession reached the causeway's second bridge, the alarm had been sounded; thousands of Aztec warriors encircled the fleeing Spaniards. The lake was thick with canoes full of Indians, who swarmed over Cortez's retreating company. "The canal was soon choked with the bodies of men and horses," ran one Aztec account of the episode. "They filled the gap in the causeway with their own drowning bodies."

When the armies had finished hacking and slashing at one another in the dark, at least six hundred of Cortez's thousand men lay dead, while his Indian allies (chiefly the Tlaxcalans) numbered over two thousand fatalities. At least that many Aztecs also perished in the battle, an episode that Cortez's men referred to later as *la noche triste*, the night of sorrows.

Cortez's decimated army found itself harried mercilessly during the retreat that followed. Thousands of Aztec warriors remained behind in Tenochtitlán, many of them scouring the canals for gold and equipment abandoned by the Spaniards, but an even greater number marched north in pursuit of Cortez. They massed for a final attack, which occurred the following day (July 7, 1520) on a plain outside the village of Otumba. The battle ended indecisively, with the outnumbered Spanish and Tlaxcalan contingents still intact. The next day they reached the safety of the Tlaxcalans' own territory. The Aztecs pursued them but did not attack again, and for the moment "Quetzalcoatl" and his depleted company could rest.

"When the Spaniards left Tenochtitlán," wrote a Mexican chronicler, "the Aztecs thought they had departed for good and would never return. Therefore they repaired and decorated the temple of their god" and began again to hold traditional Aztec religious celebrations. Yet life in Tenochtitlán never returned to normal. Cortez proved a persistent and "mortal" enemy. He sent immediately to the Spanish coastal settlement at Vera Cruz for additional powder, weapons, and soldiers. Even more important, he managed to persuade his dispirited band of 400 survivors that they could reconquer the Aztecs and regain their gold.

The captain general and his men, several badly wounded (Cortez himself had lost two fingers on his left hand), marched after only three weeks' rest against the nearby Mexican town of Tepeaca. The defenders were easily overcome and most of them sold into slavery, a fate that Cortez decreed would await any Indian allies of the Spaniards who reneged on their promises of loyalty. The victory at Tepeaca had its desired effect. Indian tribes that had deserted the Spaniards after their flight from Tenochtitlán quickly rejoined their ranks, especially once they saw that Cortez was willing to allow his allies to continue their religious practice of ritual sacrifice.

Cortez prepared methodically for the assault on Tenochtitlán. He spent months gathering his Indian forces while constructing thirteen fortified sloops, known as brigantines, for use on Lake Texcoco during the coming battle.

Events in Tenochtitlán itself during this period worked to his advantage. Smallpox, a disease new to Mexico, spread quickly through the city, killing thousands (a fair return, one Spanish writer insisted, for the syphilis that the Indians had first transmitted to the Spaniards). Among those who died was the Aztec emperor, Cuitlahuac, who was replaced by one of Montezuma's sons-in-law, Cuauhtemoc. In the months from August 1520 to April 1521, the Spaniards and their Tlaxcalan allies raided a number of Mexican garrisons surrounding Lake Texcoco, seeking mainly gold and slaves while awaiting Cortez's order to begin the main assault.

By May 1521, Cortez's preparations were complete. He launched his brigantines on Lake Texcoco and sent messengers to his various Indian allies summoning them to battle. That month his entire force moved out, an impressive contrast to the scruffy band of stragglers that had taken refuge in Tlaxcala territory the previous year. Now, with new recruits from ships that had landed on the coast, Cortez had again managed to muster almost a thousand Spaniards, as well as eighty-six horses and plenty of powder for his cannon. Marching alongside the Spaniards were more than seventy-five thousand Indian soldiers.

Cortez directed the battles that followed from the deck of a brigantine, dividing the land forces into mixed Spanish-Indian units, each commanded by a Spanish captain. Soon after arriving at Lake Texcoco, his ships destroyed more than a thousand Aztec canoes. "We killed and drowned many of the enemy — the greatest sight to see in the world," Cortez later wrote to the Spanish king. More important, this early victory over the Aztecs assured the Spaniards control of the lake itself and thus helped seal the Aztecs inside Tenochtitlán, away from their allies and sources of supply across the lake.

The Aztecs, now encircled, were forced into an unfamiliar defensive role. The defenders of Tenochtitlán fought as bravely and ferociously to preserve their city as the Spaniards had fought the previous year to leave it. Several times Cortez himself nearly lost his life. He probably would have been killed if his Aztec pursuers had not been trying (unsuccessfully) to capture him alive for use as a sacrifice.

The Spaniards, while waging continuous battle against the warriors of Tenochtitlán, at the same time tried to starve out the city. Cortez's forces blockaded all the land and canal approaches to Tenochtitlán and seized relief supplies. For every Spaniard or Indian sacrificed to the Aztec gods, a thousand Mexicans perished through a longer, although not less painful, process, as the Aztec chronicles describe:

> The only food was lizards, swallows, corncobs, and the salt grasses of the lake. The people also ate water lilies and seeds, and chewed on deerhides and pieces of leather. . . . They ate the bitterest weeds and even dirt.

Several times the new Aztec emperor, Cuauhtemoc, and his chief nobles rejected Spanish demands for the city's surrender, while day by day Cortez and his army fought closer and closer toward the center of Tenochtitlán. At Cortez's orders, his Indian vassals systematically destroyed every building and structure they captured, choking off all possibility of Aztec ambush and escape. They leveled entire streets, turning the lake city of Tenochtitlán — only months before, the most majestic city in the Western Hemisphere — into a desolate island wilderness. In the last days of the battle, Cortez's forces slaughtered thousands of Mexico's army, now penned into less than one-eighth the city's area at its very center.

The battle ended on August 13, 1521, almost two years to the day after Cortez had begun his original march from the coast to Tenochtitlán. That day, over 15,000 Indians perished during a final assault by Cortez's troops. The remaining Aztec troops and nobles, including the emperor, fled by canoe into the city's maze of canals, but Cuauhtemoc was captured by a brigantine crew. With his surrender the independence and empire of the Aztecs ended.

> We found the houses full of corpses [wrote the Spaniard Bernal Diaz], and some poor Mexicans still in them who could not move away. Their excretions were the sort of filth that thin swine pass which have been fed on nothing but grass. The city looked as if it had been ploughed up. . . .

Of the 300,000 Aztec warriors who had begun the defense of Tenochtitlán, only 60,000 remained. Still the Spaniards' Indian allies continued killing indiscriminately, looting for gold, and taking Aztec captives, either as slaves or as victims for eventual sacrifice. Cortez himself acquired many Aztec nobles as his personal prisoners and ordered the entire city—which was strewn with unburied corpses—cleansed by fire.

Within days after his victory, Cortez and his Indian allies exchanged parting gifts. The bulk of their 200,000 troops marched homeward from Tenochtitlán, laden with gold and captives. The Spaniards, after celebrating a Thanksgiving Mass, began a systematic search for the Aztec gold lost during *la noche triste.* Despite the torture to which they subjected Aztec captives, however, only two of the original eight tons of gold were recovered. Much of that went to the coast for shipment to Spain as "the royal fifth," the share owed to King Charles.

Once the pillage and slaughter in Tenochtitlán ended, many of Cortez's men received not gold but Aztec slaves as compensation. Those who managed to survive the destruction of their nation faced a future as slaves, either to the Spaniards or to their own former Indian subjects. Cortez appointed himself Governor of Mexico. With Tenochtitlán destroyed and its population homeless, the last expression of Aztec culture came from poems written to mourn this monumental defeat:

> Broken spears lie in the roads,
> we have torn our hair in our grief.
> The houses are roofless now, and their walls
> are red with blood. . . .
>
> We have pounded our hands in despair
> against the adobe walls,
> for our inheritance, our city, is lost and dead.
> The shields of our warriors were its defense,
> but they could not save it. . . .
>
> Weep, my people; know that with these disasters
> we have lost the Mexican nation.
> The water has turned bitter, our food is bitter!
> These are the acts of the Giver of Life. . . .

Three ships left Vera Cruz for Spain in December 1522. Their cargo consisted of gold—"the royal fifth"—and of exquisite Aztec jewelry sent by the acting governor of Mexico, Hernando Cortez, to His Most Catholic Majesty, King Charles V. The ships never reached Spain. They were attacked and seized by a French privateer, who delivered their contents to his own sovereign, Francis I. But the real prize—the Aztec Empire and not the remnants of Montezuma's treasure house—would remain in Spanish hands for almost three centuries after Montezuma's messengers had first sighted the returning "Quetzalcoatl."

2 Exploring and Conquering the Americas

Cortez arrived in the New World more than twenty thousand years after the North American Indians. For hundreds of years, European scholars tried to demonstrate that the Indians were the survivors of the sunken continent of Atlantis or the ten lost tribes of Israel. But nothing so spectacular had happened. Instead, roving Mongolian hunters had slowly wandered through Siberia, across the prehistoric land bridge of the Bering Strait, and into Alaska.

It took several thousand years for them to spread throughout the entire Western Hemisphere—past the Mississippi and the Great Lakes, down along the Rockies and the Andes, and on to the islands of the Caribbean.

Only when they had settled at various points did these nomads begin acquiring traits linked with a sedentary life, such as agriculture and the domestication of animals. They then slowly developed complex civilizations varying in sophistication and size from the Aztecs to the Patagonians. None of them, however, could withstand the onslaught of the Europeans. Not all Indian states fell as quickly or as painfully as Montezuma's, and some would not have to contend with the whites for many years. But the Indians' control of the continents they had discovered had passed. Within two centuries of the first landing, the newcomers had divided up nearly fifteen million square miles among themselves.

DEVELOPMENT OF THE AZTEC EMPIRE

Since the Aztecs were perhaps as highly organized as any society the Europeans encountered, the building of their civilization deserves examination. The Aztecs borrowed freely from earlier cultures in the area. First came the people of Teotihuacán, who constructed a great city near the later site of Tenochtitlán. Teotihuacán flourished during the fourth and fifth centuries A.D. Here the Indians built pyramids, palaces, and temples.

A later people in the Valley of Mexico, the Toltecs, built another great city, Tula, just north of Teotihuacán. Under the leadership of a strong king named Quetzalcoatl, the Toltecs conquered a sizable territory, built beautiful palaces, and erected huge stone sculptures. Although Toltec rule collapsed, Indians in the Valley of Mexico retained Toltec cultural patterns. For example, they began worshiping Quetzalcoatl as a god. They believed that he had departed to the East, abandoning his people, but that one day he would return by ship from the other end of the world. This legend was the basis for Montezuma's initial fear that Cortez and his men were returning deities.

The Aztecs, initially bands of warriors, came into the Valley of Mexico from the north around 1215. Neighboring peoples helped to educate them in the fine arts and skills that had been handed down from the Toltecs. The Aztecs needed little training in the art of warfare, however. Within decades of their arrival in the valley, they had conquered every major city-state in the area.

The new overlords built upon the achievements not only of local peoples, but also of those in nearby regions, notably the Mayas. Mayan culture surpassed that of both the Aztecs and the Toltecs. Mayan civilization in Central America reached its height between A.D. 200 and 700. The people were not united under one government, but they lived clustered around such ceremonial cities as Tikal and Palenque.

THE INCAS

Because of their cultural achievements, the Mayas have sometimes been thought of as the Greeks of pre-Columbian America. Similarly, the Incas have been compared to the Romans because of their imperial political and administrative organization. The Inca Empire sprawled over the western part of South America. It covered large portions of modern Ecuador, Peru, Bolivia, and Chile—in other words, most of the land available for cultivation on the Andean Plateau. In the eleventh century, at roughly the same time the Toltecs were invading the Mayan region, the Incas began extending their control along the Pacific slope of the southern continent. At its peak in the sixteenth century, the Inca Empire stretched 1500 miles down the coast and 300 miles inland. It surpassed the Aztec state in communications and organization, as well as in size.

The Incas considered their emperor, known himself as "the Inca," to be divine. He ruled from the capital city of Cuzco, high in the Andes Mountains. An excellent system of roads and runners connected Cuzco to every part of the empire.

Superb Inca roads made it easy to move troops. "Not an insurrectionary movement could occur, not an invasion on the remotest frontier," wrote an American historian, "before the tidings were conveyed to the capital, and the imperial armies were on the march along the magnificent roads of the country to suppress it."

Although the Incas had a more efficient war machine than the Aztecs, they too were unsuccessful in resisting the Europeans. An adventurer named Francisco Pizarro had first heard of a rich inland kingdom while voyaging along the Pacific coast during the 1520s. In 1531 he led a group of Spaniards into the Inca domain. They found the empire in the throes of a civil war between two sons of the previous emperor. The more successful imperial contender, Atahualpa, had recently won control.

Because of this civil war, Inca forces were weakened and divided. They could not muster effective resistance when Pizarro attacked. The climax of Pizarro's campaign came in a scene resembling the episode in Tenochtitlán, when the Spaniards slaughtered the Aztecs at worship. Pizarro lured Atahualpa to a meeting, where he ordered Spanish troops to cut down thousands of poorly armed, unsuspecting Inca soldiers. Pizarro promised to release the Inca emperor after payment of a fantastic ransom in gold and silver worth an estimated ten million dollars. Once the Indians had delivered the ransom, Pizarro had Atahualpa executed, and the Incas (like the Aztecs) fell under Spanish rule.

NORTH AMERICAN CULTURES

The complex societies developed by the Aztecs, Mayas, and Incas contrasted with the simpler cultures of most North American Indians at the time of the European influx. On the one hand, the Indian population in Latin America was large; there were probably over fifteen million Indians south of the Rio Grande when the whites came. Societies were stable; people built cities and made a living by farming settled areas. Corn, the staple crop for almost all American Indians, was probably first cultivated in Mexico.

Probably no more than a million Indians, on the other hand, lived in what eventually became the United States and Canada. Instead of large civilizations like the Aztecs or the Incas, North American Indians formed small tribal groupings. Tribal societies in North America reflected the wide variety of climates and geographic features of the world's third largest continent. Alaska, Florida, the Great Plains, and the Rockies produced a striking diversity of lifestyles.

Remnants of some relatively advanced Indian cultures still exist in several regions of North America. One such culture flourished in southern Arizona, where an Indian-built complex of irrigation canals dating to the eighth century suggests highly sophisticated farming techniques. The Pueblos, the oldest inhabitants of the Southwest, lived in adobe villages built on high mesas. More warlike and nomadic tribes like the Navajos and the Apaches moved into the region later.

In the Mississippi Valley, early Indians known as Mound Builders heaped earth and rubble into pyramids and other structures used as temples

These Mayan buildings are among several at Chichen Itzá. At left is a temple to Kulkulcan, the Mayan counterpart of Quetzalcoatl. The round structure at right is an astronomical observatory, no longer standing. (George Halton/ Photo Researchers)

High in the Andes lies the Inca town of Macchu Picchu. Undiscovered by Spanish conquerors, it remained hidden in the mountains until an American explorer stumbled across it in 1911. (George Halton/ Photo Researchers)

THE FIRST AMERICANS

or burial mounds; these have yielded many beautiful works of art.

In the large area to the north between the Rockies and the Mississippi River lived the Plains Indians: the Cheyenne, the Pawnee, and the Sioux. Although these tribes did some farming, hunting was the main source of their livelihood and the basis of their social organization. After the coming of the whites—and with them the horse—the Plains Indians happily gave up farming altogether and lived entirely by hunting the buffalo, which filled the plains in vast numbers.

Small tribes like the Shoshoni and the Ute roamed the bleak lands between the Rockies and the Pacific Ocean. They made a poor living gathering wild plants and eating small animals such as rabbits and snakes. In California—home of the Pomos, Hupas, and others—acorns were a staple food. Life was easier there, and people had time to make some of the finest basketwork in the world.

Tribes such as the Kwakiutl, Nootka, and Tlingit lived in what is now Oregon, Washington, and British Columbia. They based their economy on salmon and other fish available in the rivers, and on lumber from the great forests of cedars, using the wood to create handsome canoes and totem poles (many of which survive today).

Explorers landing on the East Coast encountered settled tribes living by a combination of fishing and hunting. Most of them dressed in deerskin and lived in bark-covered wigwams. The famous Iroquois confederacy occupied the New York State region. This league of five tribes consisted of the Mohawks, Oneidas, Onondagas, Cayugas, and Senecas. In the Southeast, Seminoles, Cherokees, and Creeks greeted the Spaniards coming up through Florida.

THE INDIAN WAY

Indian life clearly differed a great deal from group to group and place to place. But certain traits were common to almost all Indians and set them apart from other peoples — especially from the Europeans who settled in America. One of these characteristics was the Indian attitude toward land. Although a tribe might have hunting rights to a certain territory, its members no more owned this territory than the sky above it. Even among the complex farming societies of Latin America, land generally belonged to the community or perhaps to a god or spirit. Indians, in short, held a different concept of land ownership than did the Spanish invaders.

Indians also had different attitudes about warfare. For them battle was as much a ceremony as a conflict. Even in the Aztec Empire, where territory and tribute were important, the basic goal of war was to capture prisoners for religious sacrifice. To many North American tribes, war was almost a game. Plains fighters, for example, achieved as much glory for touching an enemy in battle as for killing him.

The first Europeans who came to America were accustomed to powerful monarchs, but even a ruler of Montezuma's importance did not possess *absolute* power. He was, in fact, elected to his post, and many of his duties were merely ceremonial. Few chiefs of North American tribes had the au-

Indians of a vanished era scratched these mysterious figures on a cliff wall in Wyoming. They may represent priests or perhaps gods held sacred by the tribe. (American Museum of Natural History)

thority to rule by themselves. When there was an issue to be decided, all the respected elders of a band would gather together and, after lengthy deliberations, try to reach a unanimous decision or, at least, a consensus.

Indian religious concepts differed greatly from those of Christianity. The idea of an afterlife was, at most, vague. They prayed not to one God but often to a multitude of gods or spirits. (The Aztecs worshiped more than 300 deities.) Indians were believed to have their own guardian spirits that helped them through life. Such spirits were also thought to inhabit trees, animals, rivers, and mountains. The Indians trusted in what we would call magic, but they soon found out that their magic could not make the white man disappear.

In America north of the Rio Grande, Indians created a number of distinctive styles. Typical of the Mound Builder culture is the kneeling stone figure at left, found in Tennessee. From New York State is the Cayuga Iroquois mask above, braided from corn husks. Masks like this were worn by members of the so-called False Face Societies—secret organizations whose members performed dances and other rituals to heal the sick. Below is a slate canoe sculpted by a Haida Indian of the Northwest. The figure in front is a shaman, or medicine man. He wears a crown of bear claws set in a rope of twisted cedar bark. The reclining figure at the back, with closed eyes, probably represents a dead person. (top left and bottom—Museum of Primitive Art; top right—American Museum of Natural History)

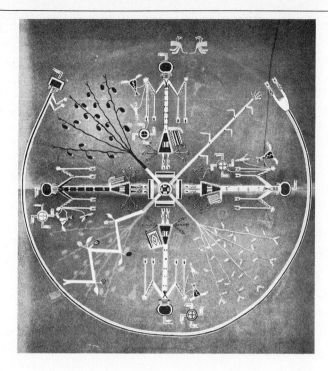

Navajo Indians of the Southwest are noted for their sand paintings, like the one above. Each one, combining sacred symbols and used as part of a healing ceremony, is formed by a priest in the morning and destroyed before nightfall. At right above are blanket bands woven by the Sioux Indians of the Great Plains. These were made after the white man came with beads for trade; in the early days, women fashioned similar designs using dyed porcupine quills or wampum (beads drilled from clam shells). The whale statuette at left was carved by a Chumash Indian of California. (top left—Bureau of Ethnology; top right—American Museum of Natural History; bottom—Museum of Primitive Art)

FIRST CONTACTS

Five hundred years before Cortez, in the far northeastern corner of the New World, Indians had in fact driven off the first European settlers. After raiding Ireland, France, and Italy, the red-bearded Vikings (or Norsemen) from Scandinavia also sailed far out into the North Atlantic. In the ninth century they established a settlement in Iceland. From this base of operations they conducted daring voyages of exploration farther westward.

Vikings led by Eric the Red discovered and settled Greenland during the tenth century. Around the year 1000, Eric's son Leif anchored his ship off the coast of what is now Newfoundland. He called the place Vineland the Good, and he and his men spent the winter there before returning to Greenland. A decade later, other Vikings sailed from Iceland to found a colony of farmers and tradesmen in Vineland. After spending two or three years fighting hostile Indians, however, they abandoned their settlement and returned to their Greenland base.

Cortez knew as little of his Scandinavian predecessors as Montezuma did. His knowledge that a New World existed came, of course, from much later visitors such as the Italian Christopher Columbus, who explored under the Spanish flag. In 1492 Columbus, with ninety men in three small ships, landed on a small island in the Caribbean, and promptly returned to Spain to announce that he had found China.

SPANISH AND PORTUGUESE EXPLORATION

Lacking the Vikings' pure thirst for adventure, the Spanish had a specific reason for sending out Columbus and the many Spanish explorers who followed him. For centuries, luxury products such as spices, jewels, and silk had come from Asia overland or across the Indian Ocean. In either case, the Italian middlemen transported the goods from the eastern end of the Mediterranean into western Europe. They had a monopoly on the trade, so they charged high prices. Nations on the Atlantic—Portugal and Spain, for example—decided to bypass the Mediterranean (and the Italians) and do their own trading with the East.

The Portuguese concentrated mainly on finding a route around Africa and then eastward to India and China. In the early fifteenth century, Prince Henry the Navigator sponsored a school of navigation on his country's southwestern coast. He devoted his life to sending out fleets of ships to explore the west coast of Africa. Year by year the Portuguese sailed farther south along the African coast. In 1488 Bartholomew Diaz voyaged as far as the Cape of Good Hope, at the tip of Africa. Vasco da Gama sailed around the cape and reached India in 1498, returning to Portugal with a rich cargo the following year. In 1500 Pedro Cabral, headed for India, was blown off course by trade winds and landed in what is now Brazil. This region of South America, claimed by Portugal, was the only area in the Western Hemisphere that the Portuguese exploited.

The Spanish, pursuing a different strategy, sent Columbus west to reach Asia. Although the admiral found only a scraggly village of naked Indians, he remained convinced that he had reached, if not China, certainly the outlying areas of Asia. On Columbus's three subsequent voyages, mainly to the Caribbean islands of Cuba and Hispaniola, the Spanish monarchs Ferdinand and Isabella sent along everybody needed to duplicate Spanish society in the New World. The ships carried missionaries, artisans, knights, soldiers, and field laborers. Unfortunately, even all this support could not establish a successful colony when the expected riches of the East failed to materialize. At one point the impatient Spanish rulers had Columbus brought back to Madrid in chains. Despite Columbus's lack of material success, he did set a pattern for future settlers.

The honor of having two continents named after him went not to Columbus but to a Florentine bank manager, Amerigo Vespucci. He claimed to have sailed to America several times. In widely read letters, he described his experiences in what he called the New World. In 1507 a geographer named Martin Waldseemüller suggested naming the new land "America, because Americus discovered it." (*Americus* is the Latin form of Vespucci's first name.)

In 1519 the Portuguese explorer Ferdinand Magellan, with Spanish backing, sailed around the southern tip of South America. He crossed the Pacific and thus found the westward route to the East. Magellan was killed by natives in the Philippine Islands. But his navigator, Sebastian del Cano, continued westward in the only ship that remained of the original five. He returned to Lisbon in 1522, having completed the first voyage around the world. The people of Europe then realized what many scholars had already known—namely, that the world is round. And they realized, too, that a whole "New World" lay to the west between Europe and Asia.

EARLY SPANISH EXPLORERS

In the fifty years after Columbus's first voyage, a host of Spanish explorers and conquerors performed incredibly daring and profitable feats all over America. Like Columbus, they dreamed of fame, of winning converts to the Christian faith, and of wealth; Spanish goals have been described as "glory, God, and gold."

For every Cortez or Pizarro who found the riches he had dreamed of, there were many who discovered only dusty, impoverished villages, bitter disappointment, and sometimes violent death. No Spaniard appears to have gotten rich exploring what is now the United States. Juan Ponce de León (who sailed to America on Columbus's second voyage) failed to find either gold or the legendary fountain of youth when he explored Florida in 1513. After trying unsuccessfully to found a settlement on the peninsula in 1521, he was wounded by Indians and died on his return voyage to Cuba. Searching for the legendary "Seven Cities of Cibola," said to be full of riches, Francisco Vasquez de Coronado explored much of the Southwest in 1540–42. When found, the "Seven Cities" turned out to be nothing more fabulous than the simple adobe villages of the Pueblo Indians. Hernando de Soto, leading a large military expedition from Cuba, wandered from Florida and the Carolinas to Texas and became the first white man to look upon the Mississippi. After finding only bloody battles with Indians, he died of disease and

disappointment in Louisiana. Not wanting the Indians to find a white body, his men wrapped and weighted his corpse and threw it into the river he had discovered.

CREATING AN EMPIRE

In spite of all these setbacks, the Spanish continued to come to the New World in tremendous numbers. They formed political units and appointed Spanish rulers. They built missions, military outposts, and towns, thereby creating an overseas empire.

By 1600, a quarter of a million Spaniards had settled in the Western Hemisphere. Here they introduced crops previously unknown in America—among them wheat, rye, oats, and barley. They found that bananas, peaches, and citrus fruits would grow well in America, too. Sugar cane became an especially important crop in tropical regions. The Spanish also brought draft animals—horses, mules, and oxen—and livestock, including cattle, hogs, and sheep. And the newcomers quickly learned to grow native American crops: corn, tomatoes, potatoes, beans, cacao, and tobacco.

Spanish civilization in the Americas prospered on gold and silver acquired from the Aztec and Inca empires. Fabulously rich silver mines were discovered in Mexico and Peru in 1545. Silver and to a lesser extent gold were for many decades Spain's chief exports from the New World.

SPANIARDS, INDIANS, AND AFRICANS

After the Spanish conquests of America, those Indians who survived war and epidemic diseases were virtually enslaved by their conquerors. Thousands labored in the mines digging and smelting silver and gold; others farmed and tended livestock.

Some Spanish friars and priests protested against mistreatment of the Indians. In time, the Spanish crown passed laws designed to limit the abuse of native labor. These efforts, however, were not notably successful in preventing cruelty and

Christopher Columbus

(Metropolitan Museum of Art—Gift of J. Pierpont Morgan, 1900)

We know more about the deeds of the adventurous, obstinate, and visionary mariner Christoper Columbus than about the man himself, especially his earliest years. Born the eldest son of an Italian wool weaver in 1451, possibly a weaver himself for a time, Christopher Columbus (the English version of a name which began as "Cristoforo Colombo" in Genoa and became "Cristobal Colon" during later years in Spain) left his native Genoa to become a sailor in about 1472.

The popular literature on Columbus, written after he became famous, described the young sailor as engaged in numerous adventures. It was said that when his ship caught fire in battle off the Portuguese coast, Columbus swam to safety. We know that he lived in Portugal—when not on voyages—for most of the period between 1476 and 1486. He married there, and studied navigation and geography among the circle of interested scholars and seamen who seemed almost too numerous in that maritime kingdom. Columbus knew about the Portuguese discoveries elsewhere in the world and he absorbed an idea, familiar to the more expert sailors of his day, that it might prove possible to reach the Far East by sailing westward across the uncharted ocean. Columbus was fascinated by the accounts which the Italian traveler Marco Polo wrote in the thirteenth century of his visit to Kublai Khan, the Mongol ruler of China ("Cathay"), and to other Far Eastern kingdoms. Columbus began dreaming of an ocean voyage westward to the Far East and, in the mid-1480s, set out in search of royal support and money to finance the voyage.

After being rebuffed by King Joao of Portugal from 1483–84, Columbus turned his attention to the devout Catholic rulers of Spain, Ferdinand and Isabella, then busily engaged in military campaigns to drive the remaining Moors from the Iberian peninsula and reunite their kingdom under Christian overlordship. Columbus emigrated to Spain and followed Ferdinand and Isabella from town to town, petitioning them to sponsor his expedition. Although impressed by the Italian's evident religious faith and dynamic personality, the king and queen of Spain persistently rejected his proposals over the next six years while waging war against the Moors. Finally in 1492, just as Columbus was preparing to leave Spain to try his luck with the king of France, Isabella summoned him and agreed to finance the voyage.

The forty-one-year-old Columbus set sail westward from Palos for "the Indies" on August 3, 1492, with three ships and less than a hundred men. After stopping at the Canary Islands in September, the ships proceeded across the ocean. On October 12, only two days after a near-mutinous crew had debated throwing "Admiral" Columbus overboard, the Spaniards sighted land, a small island in the Bahamas which Columbus named San Salvador (Spanish for "Holy Savior"). Convinced that he had arrived in the East Indies, he named the island's inhabitants "Indians." Columbus continued sailing through the *West* Indies, however, mistakenly naming islands he came to after places in Marco Polo's chronicle: Cuba became "Cathay" and Hispaniola, later Santo Domingo, "Cipango" (Polo's Japan). When Columbus set sail for Spain, he persisted in believing he had reached his original goal and left behind a small settlement of sailors on Hispaniola to wait for his return.

All of Europe rejoiced with the news that Columbus had discovered the "Indies" (albeit the

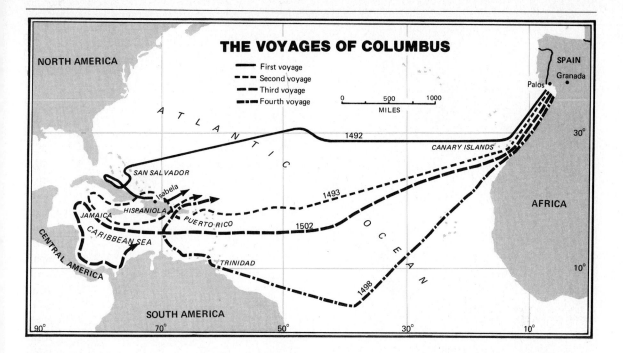

THE VOYAGES OF COLUMBUS

—— First voyage
– – – Second voyage
– · – Third voyage
–··– Fourth voyage

wrong ones, West and not East, though he never admitted that fact). His *second* voyage took place in 1493 with seventeen ships and 1500 men intent upon gaining quick profits for Ferdinand and Isabella from discoveries of gold, jewels, and other treasures. Missionaries intent upon converting the Indians to Christianity accompanied the adventurers, and the ships contained a social microcosm of Imperial Spain: knights, artisans, courtiers, and field laborers. By the time they reached Hispaniola —where they established the framework of a Spanish town—no trace of the garrison left behind remained. Columbus discovered Puerto Rico, Jamaica, and other New World islands on this voyage, but his more ambitious plans never materialized. His men found neither precious metals (except in small supply) nor the great Asian cities that Columbus believed were just over the horizon. Cruel treatment of the Indian tribes led to a rebellion in which, after three years of sporadic warfare, the Spaniards wiped out two-thirds of the native population and enslaved the rest.

Columbus returned to Spain in 1496 without substantial treasure but persuaded Ferdinand and Isabella to sponsor a third voyage in 1498. This time, he discovered Trinidad and the coast of South America. Because of a revolt against Columbus's rule in Hispaniola, the Spanish rulers dispatched an investigator who ordered Columbus returned to Spain in chains. After convincing the king and queen of his innocence, Columbus obtained his release and made a fourth and last voyage to America from 1502 to 1504, on which he sailed along the eastern coast of Central America before returning home.

The "Admiral of the Ocean Seas," as he was called in his agreement with the Spanish rulers, found little tangible wealth for Spain on his voyages. The slave trade became the only consistent source of revenue during the decade he ruled Hispaniola, and Columbus shipped hundreds of Indians to Spain. Few Spaniards appeared grateful for his labors, and once when his two children walked through the streets of Granada, mobs of townspeople reportedly pursued them shouting, "There go the sons of the Admiral of the Mosquitoes, who has found lands of vanity and delusion, the grave and misery of Castilian gentlemen!" Still persuaded that he had discovered some fringe territories of Asia, not a new and unsuspected world to the west, Christopher Columbus died in 1506 at Valladolid. His death went virtually unnoticed.

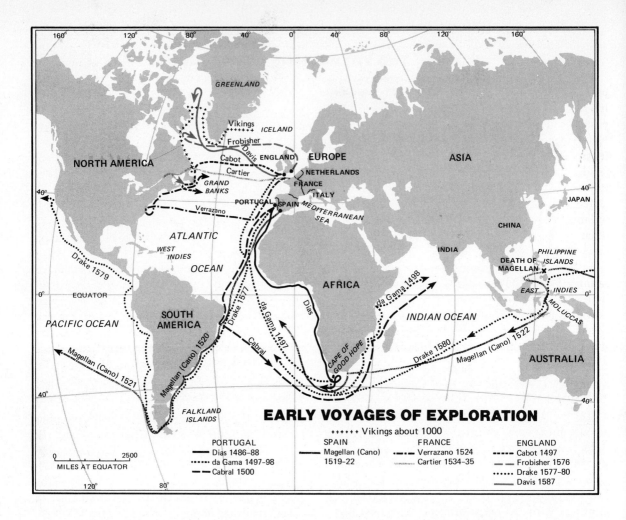

EARLY VOYAGES OF EXPLORATION

+ + + + + Vikings about 1000

PORTUGAL	SPAIN	FRANCE	ENGLAND
—— Dias 1486–88	—— Magellan (Cano)	—·—·— Verrazano 1524	– – – Cabot 1497
········ da Gama 1497–98	1519–22	·········· Cartier 1534–35	— — Frobisher 1576
– — Cabral 1500			············ Drake 1577–80
			—— Davis 1587

0   2500
MILES AT EQUATOR

Map labels: GREENLAND, Vikings, ICELAND, Frobisher, Davis, ENGLAND, EUROPE, ASIA, Cabot, Cartier, NETHERLANDS, FRANCE, ITALY, JAPAN, NORTH AMERICA, GRAND BANKS, PORTUGAL, SPAIN, MEDITERRANEAN SEA, CHINA, Verrazano, ATLANTIC, WEST INDIES, OCEAN, INDIA, PHILIPPINE ISLANDS, DEATH OF MAGELLAN, Drake 1579, Drake 1577, da Gama 1497, da Gama 1498, AFRICA, EAST INDIES, MOLUCCAS, EQUATOR, Dias, INDIAN OCEAN, PACIFIC OCEAN, SOUTH AMERICA, Cabral, Drake 1580, Magellan (Cano) 1522, Magellan (Cano) 1520, Drake 1577, CAPE OF GOOD HOPE, AUSTRALIA, Magellan (Cano) 1521, FALKLAND ISLANDS

---

exploitation. Cortez, Pizarro, de Soto, and other Europeans of that time regarded Indians as barely human. After a century of Spanish rule, the Indian population of Mexico, through maltreatment and white men's diseases, had been reduced from five million to one million. The Mexican experience was not unique. Elsewhere in the New World—in Peru and on the Caribbean islands, for example— the Indian population decreased at comparable rates and for similar reasons.

Since many Indians died or fled from Spanish settlements, another steady source of cheap labor was necessary, for raising crops like sugar cane required a large labor force. So the Spanish began importing black slaves from Africa. The first slaves came as early as 1510. Later, Europeans kidnapped and bought hundreds of thousands of Africans to ship to the New World.

Packed tightly into cramped cargo spaces, on ships called "floating coffins," some blacks preferred to jump overboard rather than accept slavery. Many more died of disease on board. Only a fraction of the slaves survived the journey, but enough reached America to make the trade profitable, and their numbers increased. They were more resistant to the diseases of the whites than the Indians were, since they had already been exposed to them in Africa. Due to their previous experience with agriculture, the blacks also proved to be better at it than the Indians, many of whom— especially those in the Caribbean and in North America—had done relatively little farming.

THE SPANISH EMPIRE: THEORY AND REALITY

Spain dominated sixteenth-century European politics, diplomacy, warfare, and economic life as gold and silver flowed in from its American possessions. This vast influx of precious metals had serious consequences for the Spanish economy. It caused an enormous rise in prices and a decline in the real value of money—that is, inflation. Prices rose about 400 percent in Spain during the sixteenth century—a tremendously high rate of inflation for those times. The Spanish government often found it impossible to collect enough tax revenue to pay its debts.

Furthermore, inflation made it difficult for Spanish farm or manufactured goods to compete with cheaper foreign imports. Thus the same harvest of gold and silver that gave Spain temporary dominance in Europe also helped cripple her long-range chances as a food-producing, manufacturing nation.

Spain's overwhelming desire for precious metals grew out of a certain view of economic life held by most European governments. According to this view, the true measure of any nation's economic prosperity and power was the amount of gold and silver it controlled. Later economic writers gave the name *mercantilism* to this set of ideas, which had generally governed the economic behavior of European nations since the fifteenth century. Spain's New World possessions, and the gold and silver found there, allowed Madrid to put such ideas into practice.

Spain alone had the mines from which to acquire gold and silver directly. Every other European power turned to foreign commerce to increase its stock of precious metals. The goal was to maximize exports and minimize imports from other countries; this was known as a favorable *balance of trade*. Mercantilists believed that gold and silver could best be kept within a country by achieving such a favorable balance of trade. To this end, the ships of Portugal, Holland, England, France, and other European nations crossed and recrossed the oceans in search of new opportunities for trade. Spain, by contrast, never developed a strong commerce, partly because of her smug certainty that

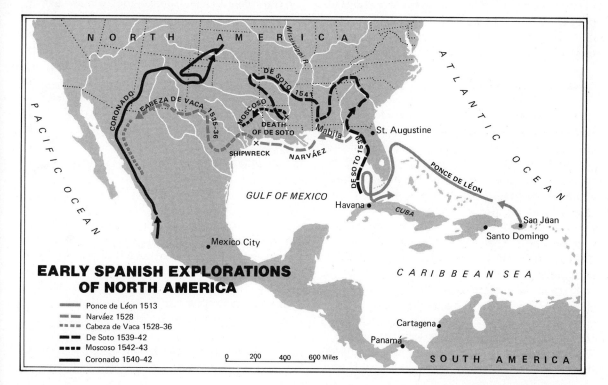

EARLY SPANISH EXPLORATIONS OF NORTH AMERICA

Ponce de Léon 1513
Narváez 1528
Cabeza de Vaca 1528–36
De Soto 1539–42
Moscoso 1542–43
Coronado 1540–42

0 200 400 600 Miles

New World mines would eternally provide all the gold and silver she needed.

Unfortunately for Spain, those sources ran dry in the seventeenth century. Her great period of national prosperity soon waned, as did her political and military influence in Europe. What endured from decades of Spanish conquest and exploitation was not the treasure itself. Instead, there remained a vast imperial domain studded with great plantations, ranches, and orchards. Through it ran an equally impressive network of Catholic missions and churches, strung like rosary beads along the Spanish-American countryside. And over all lay the veneer of Spanish language and culture.

FRANCE IN THE NEW WORLD

King Ferdinand of Spain, the patron of Columbus, called himself "His Most Catholic Majesty." Therefore, when he wished to have his claims to the new discoveries made legitimate, he knew exactly whom to consult. In 1494, Pope Alexander VI, strongly influenced by the Spanish and Austrian ruling family of Hapsburg, drew a line down the Atlantic from north to south, cutting along the western border of Brazil, with all of North America to the west of it. He proclaimed that all new lands east of the line belonged to Portugal; west of it, to His Most Catholic Majesty of Spain.

Predictably, other European nations did not accept this division as happily as Spain and Portugal did. Francis I, who became king of France in 1515, reacted strongly. "Show me the will of Adam," he demanded, "dividing the world between Spain and Portugal." In challenging Spain's claim to the New World, Francis was only opening a new front in his European war with the Hapsburgs. From 1521 to 1559, France fought a perpetual battle with Charles V and his heirs. In hopes of bringing in some badly needed revenue, Francis sent Giovanni de Verrazano, a Florentine navigator, across the ocean in 1523. He told Verrazano to find a water route through North America to China. This idea of a "northwest passage" would fascinate explorers for the next century.

Unlike the first Spanish explorers, Verrazano had a fairly good idea of what he would find.

For twenty years, French fishermen had sailed to Newfoundland to gather codfish. Verrazano navigated along the eastern coast of the continent from the Carolinas to Newfoundland, establishing a French claim to North America, but he found no route to China.

Distracted by civil war, France did not attempt to develop her claim for sixty-five years; then Henry IV sent out his friend Samuel de Champlain. Champlain founded Quebec and reached the Great Lakes, but he failed to establish anything comparable to Spanish colonization in Mexico or Peru. Instead, French exploration continued at a leisurely pace. It was not until almost the end of the seventeenth century that René Robert Cavelier, sieur de La Salle, reached the foot of Lake Michigan and then journeyed down the length of the Mississippi to New Orleans. After one hundred and fifty years of fitful efforts, with long periods of neglect, France could claim an enormous North American empire — half of modern Canada plus the valley of the Mississippi.

The society of New France differed greatly from that of New Spain. The Spanish took the Aztecs' gold and land, destroying the Indians in the process. The French never found gold, and very few Frenchmen wanted to come to Canada to take the Indians' land. Thirty years after Champlain had founded Quebec, only two French farmers had immigrated. The only economic value Canada had for the French was the fur trade, which required amicable relations with the Indians.

THE PROTESTANT POWERS IN AMERICA

After the Protestant Reformation had swept across Europe in the first half of the sixteenth century, Spain and France, the western European superpowers, remained Catholic. But others nations that had adopted various types of Protestantism now had new reason to challenge the Spanish domination of the New World. As would often happen in the future, European conflicts extended overseas.

After a long and hard-fought war of rebellion, the Netherlands by 1600 had won their in-

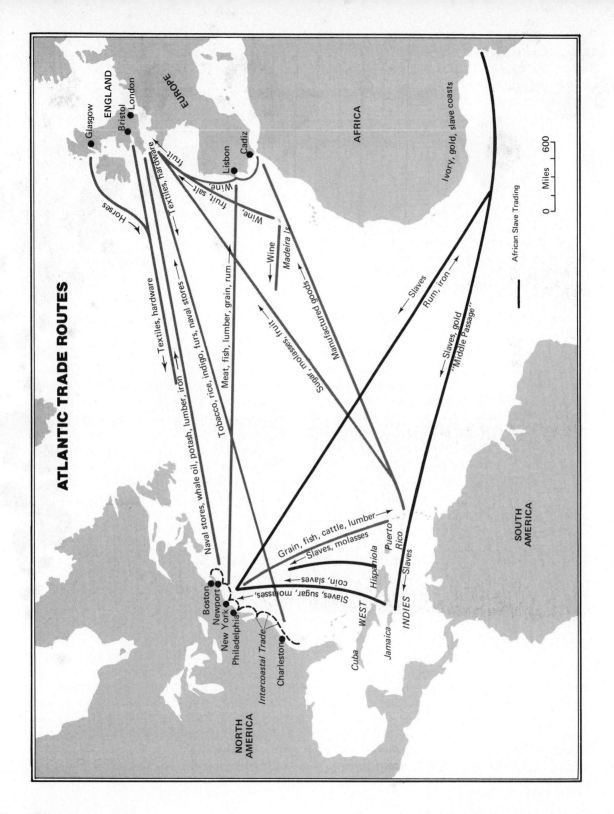

ATLANTIC TRADE ROUTES

EUROPE

ENGLAND

Glasgow

Bristol
London

Lisbon

Cadiz

AFRICA

Ivory, gold, slave coasts

Madeira Is.

Wine

Wine

Wine, fruit, salt

fruit

Textiles, hardware

Horses

Textiles, hardware

Manufactured goods

Sugar, molasses, fruit

Tobacco, rice, indigo, furs, naval stores

Meat, fish, lumber, grain, rum

Naval stores, whale oil, potash, lumber, iron

Slaves

Rum, iron

Slaves, gold
"Middle Passage"

African Slave Trading

0   Miles   600

NORTH
AMERICA

Boston
Newport
New York
Philadelphia

Charleston

Intercoastal Trade

Slaves, sugar, molasses,

coin, slaves

Grain, fish, cattle, lumber

Slaves, molasses

Slaves

Puerto
Rico

Hispaniola

WEST
INDIES

Cuba

Jamaica

SOUTH
AMERICA

dependence from Spain. During the struggle, the Spanish had attempted to destroy the Dutch Reformed Church. The Dutch, who had won largely by virtue of their superior seamanship, preyed profitably upon Spanish shipping before actually attempting their own overseas colonization.

In 1609 the Dutch sent an Englishman named Henry Hudson to try to reach Asia around the top of Europe. Turned back by ice, Hudson instead sailed to America, up the New York river that now bears his name. His sailors brought the story of a rich land back to the Netherlands. A dozen years later, the Dutch founded the Dutch West India Company, largely as a weapon against the Spanish. While concentrating on the plunder of the Spanish and Portuguese colonies, the company established a small colony on Manhattan Island, as well as some nearby forts.

But Dutch farmers proved no more eager to cross the Atlantic than French farmers. New Amsterdam rapidly became a polyglot colony with residents from all nations, especially after the Dutch annexed a small Swedish colony on Delaware Bay. The company lost interest, and the colonists exhausted themselves in a long war with the Algonquin Indians. Forty years after its founding, New Amsterdam was itself annexed by the greatest Protestant power, England. (See Chapter 6, p. 118.)

BACKGROUND OF ENGLISH COLONIZATION

As early as 1497, the English crown had sent an exploratory expedition to the New World. Henry VII sent John Cabot, a Genoese born Giovanni Caboto, to discover an English northwest passage to Asia. Like Columbus, Cabot had kept company with a wide circle of Italian geographers and believed that Asia could be reached by sailing west across the Atlantic. By sailing over the old Norse westward routes (Cabot believed the Vikings had reached the Asian coast centuries earlier), Cabot expected to establish the precise locations of Japan and China. Instead his voyage took him to a landing somewhere in the rich fishing grounds of what is now Newfoundland or Canada's Maritime Provinces. Convinced he had reached the Asian mainland, Cabot coasted for several hundred miles along the shoreline before returning to the English port of Bristol, whose merchants had helped finance the trip.

On a second voyage from Bristol in May 1498, Cabot had five ships, the merchants of both Bristol and London having competed in assembling cargo for him to trade with the "Asians." A number of English adventurers joined Cabot, hoping to share in the expected wealth. One ship put in at Ireland for repairs. History does not record the fate of Cabot or of four of his ships, however. Presumably if Cabot reached "New Found Land" (as he called it), he confirmed the plentiful presence of fish and the disappointing absence of Chinese. We shall never know. But given the failure of Cabot's second expedition, Henry VII, a tight man with a shilling in the best of times, refused to finance future voyages.

His son, Henry VIII, was too busy getting married and unmarried, and forming a new Protestant Church of England, to support colonial ventures. Eventually the English Reformation would serve to populate Massachusetts, but under Henry it prevented any colonization at all. Henry's elder daughter, Queen Mary, was a Catholic who had married King Philip II of Spain and had no interest in encroaching upon her husband's domains. She channeled English adventuring around the top of Europe, and chartered the Muscovy Company to trade with Russia in 1555. Although English merchants and sailors profited from such dealings, they hungered for the richer (and warmer) trade with America.

Their opportunity came with the succession to the throne of Henry's younger daughter, Elizabeth I, one of the most remarkable women of history. The red-haired Virgin Queen was as strong a Protestant as her sister had been a Catholic, and had little respect for Spanish claims or property. She also cared little for the Pope's division of the New World, especially when the papacy had declared her an illegitimate and illegal occupant of the English throne. Soon after she became queen in 1558, English ships again turned west and once more began to make voyages across the Atlantic.

In some ways England seemed an unlikely candidate to challenge Spain's power in the New World. A relatively small country on the fringes of Europe, England did not even control the entire island of Great Britain (Scotland remained independent until 1603). England had about as many people as the Netherlands, half as many as Spain, and one-quarter as many as France. Finally, parliamentary control of the purse strings greatly limited the moneys available to Elizabeth, preventing the kind of explorations that kings of Spain had financed personally. From Cabot's initial voyage, therefore, to the subsequent centuries of New World settlement, English efforts in America depended to a considerable extent upon the financial investments of its merchant class, and consequently upon the uneasy collaboration of the British monarchy, adventurous aristocrats, and ambitious middle-class entrepreneurs.

Hundreds of thousands of black-faced sheep grazing quietly in the English countryside lay behind the largest European migration to America. For centuries English merchants had carried on a large and lucrative trade in wool across the Channel. Consequently, private citizens, when gathered together in joint stock companies (the forerunners of modern corporations), possessed enough capital to underwrite settlements in Massachusetts and Virginia.

The sheep had also helped produce settlers for the new land. For several decades, landowners had been involved in the process of *enclosure*— fencing in what had been common farmland — in order to raise more sheep, a more profitable endeavor than simple crop growing. The process forced many farm laborers off the land, resulting in an extremely high rate of unemployment in sixteenth-century England. In some places, as much as one-third of the population lived on poor relief.

Finally, England's long history of shipping wool to Europe involved the development of a large fleet of ships and men who knew how to sail them. In what would essentially be a naval contest with Spain in the Atlantic, England's skilled and experienced — if somewhat informal — navy might prevail even over Spain's greater resources in gold and population.

EARLY ELIZABETHAN EXPLORATION

The idea of a northwest passage to the Orient fascinated Elizabeth as much as it had her grandfather Henry VII. Starting in 1576, she dispatched Martin Frobisher on three voyages over the top of Canada. Frobisher explored Labrador and became the first European to encounter the Eskimos, but found no shortcut to China.

Some English sailors set their goals beyond the ice floes of Hudson's Bay. Although England had not officially declared war against Spain, the rich Spanish treasure fleets were tempting targets. English captains also kidnapped slaves from Africa and smuggled them into Spanish America, which tried to limit the number of slaves brought in. Elizabeth's sailors believed strongly in an aggressive Protestantism, which allowed them to rationalize dealing in slaves not only for quick profits but also as a means of Christianizing blacks, and permitted them to justify anything done against Catholic Spain.

Queen Elizabeth supported and encouraged this slave dealing and semiofficial piracy. She hoped to add funds to her royal coffers while reducing Spanish power. From 1562 to 1568, Sir John Hawkins made three voyages, smuggling slaves from Sierra Leone and returning to England with ginger, sugar, and pearls. In 1570 Elizabeth commissioned Hawkins's cousin, Sir Francis Drake, as a *privateer*— essentially a pirate who split his booty with the crown. The following year Drake led a group of seventy sailors in an ambush of a Spanish mule train lumbering across the Isthmus of Panama with a cargo of silver from Peru. After pillaging a Spanish town on the Panama coast in mid-1573, Drake returned safely to England with his prizes.

DRAKE SAILS AROUND THE WORLD

In 1577 Drake set out with five ships and 164 officers and men to break Spain's monopoly in the Pacific. His squadron sailed near the Cape

Drake's campaign of the 1580s was his first act of open warfare against the Spanish. He commanded a fleet of twenty-nine ships. One successful episode was the sack of Santo Domingo, above. While the fleet lay at anchor, foot soldiers—their ranks bristling with spears—attacked the walled city from the left. Drake was a daring man who much enjoyed what the English of his day called "singeing the king of Spain's beard." (NYPL/Rare Book Collection)

Verde Islands, where he captured Spanish and Portuguese ships. Proceeding southward along the east coast of South America, Drake beat back an attempted mutiny, losing ships and men along the way. He rounded Cape Horn and reached the Pacific in September 1578 with only one remaining vessel, the *Pelican*, which was later renamed the *Golden Hind*.

Drake then turned north, seizing treasure and provisions from Spanish ships and towns along the way. To escape enemy attack he kept heading north—sailing, he wrote, "on the backside of America." Along the coast of California he stopped at a "fair and good bay"—what may be the San Francisco Bay of today. Finding no northwest passage to take him back to England, he crossed the

Pacific (taking on a valuable cargo of pepper in what is now Indonesia), rounded the Cape of Good Hope, and sailed up the west coast of Africa to reach Plymouth in September 1580.

Drake reached England uncertain of his reception. Spain was demanding the return of Drake's booty and his execution as a pirate, and hinted at war if Elizabeth refused. After a time of uncertainty, the queen, influenced by Drake's new status as a popular hero (and the estimated twenty-five-million-dollar value of his prizes), knighted Drake and allowed him to continue his raids on Spanish America.

ENGLISH VENTURES

The voyages of her "sea dogs" made the New World appear so attractive to Elizabeth that she took yet another step. In the 1580s she began to authorize other English adventurers—not pirates this time, but enterprising businessmen among the nobility—to explore and to found settlements.

Sir Humphrey Gilbert, attracted by the profits and glory of dealing with the New World, now persuaded Elizabeth to give him a charter to discover and settle such lands. Gilbert made two attempts at colonization. In 1578 he was either forced back by bad weather or diverted by the more attractive possibilities of piracy (historical accounts differ on this point). He tried again in 1583 with a larger expedition. This time he reached Newfoundland and took possession of a surprised international colony of summer fishermen. Soon afterward, however, he perished in a storm.

The dream of an English colony in America was carried further by Gilbert's half brother, Sir Walter Raleigh. He took over Gilbert's charter in 1584 on even more favorable terms than those granted his relative. Raleigh sent out an advance party that year to search for a suitable place. After Gilbert's misadventures in the chilly climate of Newfoundland, Raleigh decided to look farther south. His scouting party found a promising site, which it called Roanoke Island, along the Atlantic coast south of Chesapeake Bay. Raleigh named the entire coastal region Virginia, in honor of Elizabeth, England's Virgin Queen.

THE INVINCIBLE ARMADA

Spain, the most powerful nation in Europe, would not tolerate activities like Raleigh's—or like Drake's—forever. In 1588 King Philip II of Spain, hoping to ensure Spanish control of the Americas and the Atlantic, and to reclaim England for the Catholic Church, sent a large fleet against his sister-in-law Elizabeth. Hundreds of ships departed from the same port Columbus had used, carrying soldiers for invasion and priests for reconversion.

The sailors who had ravaged Spain on the oceans now rallied to the defense of their homeland. Drake, Hawkins, Frobisher, and other veteran captains moved their ships into the Channel, bringing a new idea of naval warfare. According to the traditional stategy, as used by the Spanish, ships were mainly transportation for soldiers, who would capture enemy ships by hand-to-hand fighting. Accordingly, the Spanish galleys were large and cumbersome, and were propelled largely by oarsmen. Expertly sailing their smaller ships in and out of the Armada, Drake and the English destroyed many of the invading ships. Others, heading northward, went down in a series of furious storms off the Scottish and Irish coasts.

Although the Armada came to grief thousands of miles from America, the battle proved crucial for future English settlement. England now controlled the Atlantic and could establish and supply projected colonies without fear of Spanish blockades.

Soon after the defeat of the Armada, England established its first permanent colonies in the New World. "He who rules the sea," proclaimed Raleigh jubilantly, "rules the commerce of the world, and to him that rules the commerce of the world belongs the treasure of the world and indeed the world itself." If England did not yet rule the world, it would soon rule a large part of North America.

THE ROANOKE SETTLEMENT

Raleigh's enthusiasm for English commercial expansion had taken tangible shape even before the Armada's destruction. In 1585 he dispatched an expedition of settlers to the recently

The mysterious end of the Roanoke or "lost" colony reached the awareness of other British explorers only in 1591, when they returned to the settlement to find all of its inhabitants missing without having left any indication of their whereabouts except for the word "CROATOAN" (the name given to a nearby island) carved on a doorpost. This later sketch shifts the location to a tree. (NYPL/Picture Collection)

explored Roanoke Island. The members of the group devoted most of their energy to roaming the countryside in search of gold. They also explored nearby rivers seeking the Pacific Ocean. They failed at both, of course, and since they had no interest in colonizing the area, most of the participants returned the following year.

In 1587 Raleigh sponsored yet a third expedition, this time commanded by an artist, John White, a veteran of the previous expedition. This group contained the first women and children to come to America, further evidence that the expedition anticipated a more permanent settlement in the Chesapeake Bay area than earlier expeditions. Although their English sponsors expected them to establish a "Citie of Ralegh in Virginia" elsewhere in the region, White's band disembarked at Roanoke Island. They searched vainly for fifteen men who had remained behind after the 1585 expedition and, finding their houses "standing unhurt," remained on the island. White helped the 118 settlers organize their colony, but a month later, in August 1587, he returned to England for supplies.

The Armada's assault and disorders within England prevented his immediate return, but White finally sailed back to America in 1590.

When he reached Roanoke, he found the settlement in ruins. The entire colony had vanished without a trace, except for the single word CROATOAN—the name of a nearby island and site of an Indian village—carved on a doorpost. White's own daughter and his granddaughter, the first English child born in America, were among the missing. A storm forced White to abandon the search, return to his ships, and leave Roanoke without solving the mystery of its "Lost Colony." A subsequent expedition by Raleigh in 1602 shed no further light on the settlers' fate. It was not until 1607 that the English attempted another settlement in the area, this time along a river named (along with the town itself) for England's new monarch, Elizabeth's successor, James I. While exploring the James River, one of the colony's first settlers described his encounter with "a Savage Boy about the age of ten yeeres, which had a head of haire of a perfect yellow and a reasonable white skinne, which is a Miracle amongst all Savages." Was the "Miracle Savage Boy" the belated child of an ill-fated Roanoke settler? None of the subsequent English colonists, either at Jamestown or elsewhere on the North American coastal mainland, could ever resolve that mystery.

Suggested Readings
Chapters 1-2

Cortez and Montezuma

Charles Gibson, *The Aztecs Under Spanish Rule* (1964); Hammond Innes, *The Conquistadors*; Miguel Leon-Portilla, *Broken Spears: The Aztec Account of the Conquest of Mexico* (1962).

Discoveries and Explorations

John B. Brebner, *The Explorers of North America*; Samuel Eliot Morison, *Admiral of the Ocean Sea* (1942), *The European Discovery of America: The Northern Voyages, A.D. 500-1600* (1971), and *The European Discovery of America: The Southern Voyages: A.D. 1492-1616* (1974); John H. Parry, *The Age of Reconnaissance* (1963).

Indian Cultures

Woodrow Borah, and Sherburne F. Cook, *The Aboriginal Population of Central Mexico on the Eve of the Spanish Conquest* (1963); H. E. Driver, *Indians of North America* (2nd ed., 1970); J. A. Hester, Jr., and Kenneth MacGawan, *Early Man in the New World*; Alvin M. Josephy, Jr., *The Indian Heritage of America* (1969); G. R. Nash, *Red, White and Black: The Peoples of Early America* (1974); Carl O. Sauer, *Sixteenth-Century North America: The Land and People As Seen by Europeans* (1971); George C. Vaillant, *Aztecs of Mexico*; W. E. Washburn, *The Indian in America* (1975).

Spanish America

C. R. Boxer, *The Portuguese Seaborne Empire* (1969); A. W. Crosby, Jr., *The Columbian Exchange: Biological and Cultural Consequences of 1492* (1972); Charles Gibson, *Spain in America* (1966); Lewis Hanke, *The Struggle for Justice in the Conquest of America* (1949); Clarence H. Haring, *The Spanish Empire in America* (1947); James Lang, *Conquest and Commerce: Spain and England in the Americas* (1975); James Lockhart, *Spanish Peru, 1532-1560* (1968); John H. Parry, *The Spanish Seaborne Empire* (1966).

England and the New World

Wallace Notestein, *The English People on the Eve of Colonization, 1603-1630* (1954); David B. Quinn, *England and the Discovery of America, 1481-1620* (1974) and *Roanoke Voyages, 1584-1590* (1955); A. L. Rowse, *The Elizabethans and America* (1959) and *The Expansion of Elizabethan England* (1955); J. A. Williamson, *Voyages of the Cabots and the English Discovery of North America Under Henry 7th and Henry 8th* (1929).

3 Death and Survival: The Founding of Jamestown

The Indian king refused to kneel and receive the cheap copper "crown" brought to his village by the band of armed and unwelcome Englishmen. The visitors in turn kept careful watch on Powhatan's hundreds of warriors, who crowded in to watch the coronation. Finally, several of the English shoved Powhatan's shoulders down slightly to allow one of them to place the crown upon the unwilling Indian's head. Not to be outdone, Powhatan presented his cloak and moccasins to a surprised "guest." The ceremony was over.

Led by Captains John Smith and Christopher Newport, the Englishmen had come from the nearby settlement of Jamestown, which had been founded a year before, in 1607. The survival of Jamestown remained in doubt when Smith and Newport brought their men, bearing gifts, through the forest to Powhatan's village of Werowocomoco, home of the Pamunkey Indians. Powhatan, undisputed leader of the area's Indians, had refused Smith's invitation to come to Jamestown. He suspected that the English would lay a trap for him: "If your king has sent me presents," Powhatan had told Smith, "I also am a king and this is my land."

The gifts came not from James I of England, in fact, but from the London Company, the settlement's sponsor in England. Newport had recently arrived from there with fresh supplies for Jamestown and a curious assortment of presents designed to please Powhatan's fancy and thereby reduce the threat of Indian attack on the colony's outnumbered whites.

But what could Powhatan do with a wooden bed, several pieces of furniture, cutlery, and fashionable European clothing? Did the English expect Powhatan to move to Jamestown and imitate their ways?

The Indian leader remained unappeased and distrustful, although he accepted the gifts and admired the bravery (and resourcefulness) of John Smith, who had even taken pains to learn the Indian language. When asked after the coronation ceremony to allow Newport to explore the sur-

POWHATAN

Held this state & fashion when Capt. Smith was deliuered to him prisoner 1607

Appamatuck

When the Englishmen first arrived in Virginia, Powhatan was the powerful chief of an informal confederation of Indian tribes along the coast. His actions toward the English in the years that followed showed him to be a brave and politically astute leader. (Granger Collection)

rounding countryside, Powhatan refused. He did give his guests some corn, a most welcome present, since Jamestown residents rarely had enough food. In the end, Smith and Newport left Werowocomoco with their followers, uncertain whether their actions had made Powhatan into a friend or had placed Jamestown's future in even greater jeopardy.

The first voyage to Jamestown had taken more than four months. Three ships sailed from England in mid-December 1606, reaching the entrance to Chesapeake Bay by late April 1607. The London Company had placed Newport in command of the vessels, a 100-ton flagship, *Susan Constant,* and two smaller escort vessels, the *Godspeed* and *Discovery.* Surprisingly, the long winter ocean passage proved fatal to only one of the more than one hundred men who shipped out. They achieved this in part by making long island stopovers, first at the Canaries and then in the Caribbean, where they took on fresh food and water.

About a third of those who sailed with Newport were considered "gentlemen," according to prevailing English standards, enjoying some measure of either wealth, influence, or position through birth into a leading family or through personal achievement. Such gentlemen often saw their role in the new settlement as *supervisors* rather than *followers,* overseers and not workers. This ambitious crowd of "captains," minor noblemen, and lesser gentry found it easier to give orders than to take them. Unfortunately, this left an extremely large number of potential "leaders" for the work of colonization which lay ahead. The London Company further complicated the problem by keeping secret the names of those who would form Jamestown's governing council. These were listed in a sealed envelope given to Newport with instructions to open the envelope only *after* the ships had reached America.

Fortunately the *Susan Constant* and her two escort ships also carried a number of craftsmen: blacksmiths, carpenters, bricklayers, masons, laborers, and even a surgeon. These would prove far more valuable in building a *permanent* English colony in North America, the company's goal, than would many of the gentlemen, who schemed to dominate the settlement even before the ships left port.

Why did these people come? Reasons varied with each person. Most of them probably shared hopes, nurtured by the London Company, of wealth and glory in America, just as similar goals had driven the first Spanish *conquistadores* more than a century earlier. Surely the land contained exploitable minerals, possibly even gold. Many of the adventurers, John Smith included, had often sailed against the Spaniards in voyages and sea battles in the Caribbean and South America that aided their own fortunes while bolstering English power in the New World.

Smith, a short muscular man, lived an adventurous life even before leaving for America. While still in his teens, he fought for Austria against the Turks. A fearless self-promoter, Smith later wrote vivid accounts of his experiences, claiming that once he actually chopped off a Turkish commander's head. But the Turks captured and enslaved Smith. Eventually he escaped and wandered across Europe, Asia, and North Africa before returning to England in 1603. After this sort of warrior's life on three continents, Smith, at the age of twenty-six, cast his fortunes with Newport and the others, sailing to Virginia in December 1606 to become one of its "first planters."

On reaching Chesapeake Bay in April 1607, Newport began exploring the countryside for a site on which to build the colony, while trying to

John Smith seizes the Indian chief Openchancanough during a struggle between the English and the Indians in the first years of Jamestown's settlement. The illustration comes from one of Smith's own books on his Virginia adventures. (The Granger Collection)

C Smith taketh the King of Pamavnkee prisoner 1608

make contact with Indians. The land proved more agreeable than the Indians, who attacked a landing party. The incident reminded Newport and the others that the London Company had instructed them to build a fort and town at some *inland* point, not on the coast. A new colony hugging the shoreline might attract Spanish warships only too eager to emulate the raids of people like Walter Raleigh, who had attacked *Spanish* outposts in the New World.

After sailing thirty miles up the largest of the rivers emptying into Chesapeake Bay, the vessels reached a peninsula. Though marshy and low-lying, the site afforded good visibility of both the river and the countryside. They named both the river and the town they began building after England's King James I.

Who would run Jamestown? The London Company's charter virtually guaranteed an initial period of disorder in the colony, since a company council, which remained in England, supposedly governed Jamestown. In Virginia, actual authority fell to a *local* council appointed by the parent body in England. Most Jamestown settlers, therefore, had no voice in choosing their leaders, for seven men had already been selected by the company. Newport and Smith were named to the council.

The settlers faced grave problems. They had to build up the town's defenses, stockpile enough food to last through the winter, and explore the countryside to find "exports" which Newport could take back to England. But council members bickered endlessly, neglecting the work

A contemporary mural depicts Jamestown in the early years. In the foreground is the James River. Farmers beyond the town would take refuge inside the palisade in case of attack. (Photo by Thomas L. Williams, mural by Sidney King—Jamestown Foundation)

that had to be done. The situation got so bad that one of the councillors was executed as a mutineer. Newport finally sailed for England in June. While uneasily awaiting his return and continuing their struggle for personal power, the remaining leaders managed somehow to mobilize the settlement against Indian attack.

The Paspahegh Indians living near Jamestown attacked only a few days after the English colonies built their first shelters. They were led by a *werowance* (an Indian captain) named Wowinchopunk, who owed no loyalty to Powhatan. Wowinchopunk was understandably angered over a white man's settlement on the Paspaheghs' traditional hunting grounds. Three days after the ships unloaded, Wowinchopunk and a hundred armed warriors appeared outside Jamestown. The Indians proposed that the whites drop *their* weapons and join in a feast, but Wowinchopunk's band fled hurriedly after one Englishman killed a warrior who tried to take a hatchet.

Soon many more Indian soldiers surrounded Jamestown. They waited until Smith, Newport, and several dozen heavily armed whites boarded one of the ships to explore land farther upriver. Then, in late May, the Indians attacked in force, taking the remaining colonists completely by surprise. As unsuspecting Englishmen worked in the field outside the town's primitive palisades, the Indians, as Smith later described the scene, "came up almost into the fort, shot [arrows] through the tents, [and] appeared in this skirmish, which lasted hot for about an hour, a very valiant people."

At first it seemed as if the attackers would overrun the settlement. Suddenly a blast of cannon shot came from the two remaining ships, and the tide of battle turned. Wowinchopunk and his warriors knew nothing of the wonders and terrors of artillery. The Indians collected their dead and wounded, and faded into the forests. Two settlers had been killed and ten more wounded, but for the moment, Jamestown had avoided extinction, the fate of Raleigh's earlier Roanoke colony.

Jamestown's troubles had only begun. The Indians who surrounded the settlement attacked sporadically, though now without the element of surprise. Newport's exploring party returned after the big battle, and the settlers fought off the Indians for the next three weeks while steadily reinforcing the town's fortifications. When Wowinchopunk's raids stopped, the English continued to scan nearby forests. The colony remained on alert for weeks expecting new attacks.

Newport, having sailed back to England in late June 1607, had supervised the loading of *Susan Constant* and *Godspeed* with whatever could be sold in England. He hoped to demonstrate Jamestown's economic potential and carried clapboard, ore samples for testing (since gold and other precious metals remained an obsession of Jamestown's founders), and sassafras roots. Englishmen of that day believed sassafras would heal and cure venereal disease.

Within weeks of Newport's departure, most of the hundred men still at Jamestown had to contend with a malaria and yellow fever epidemic, for the low and marshy ground, a virtual swampland, encouraged the diseases. The settlers' relentless work schedule left them exhausted, and they were unnerved by the strain of anticipated Indian attacks.

That first summer, only a half dozen or fewer men were normally available to patrol the palisades or perform other essential work. One of them, Captain George Percy, later wrote of those agonizing months:

> There were never Englishmen left in a foreign country in such miserie as we were in this new discouvered Virginia. Wee watched every three nights, lying on the bare-ground, what weather soever came; . . . which brought our men to bee most feeble wretches . . . [We heard] the pitifull murmurings and outcries of our sick men without reliefe, every night and day for the space of six weeks; in the morning their bodies being trailed out of their cabines like Dogges, to be buried.

Half of the original one hundred settlers in April were dead by September. By the time Newport returned in January 1608, the company had been further reduced to thirty-eight survivors.

One of these was John Smith. Although ill that first summer, Smith managed to recover and bring some order to the colony's desperate search for food. Shortly after the Paspaheghs' attack, friendlier Indians from other villages came near the fort to trade beans and corn. By then,

Newport had returned to England again seeking fresh supplies, and Smith became the settlement's chief trade negotiator. Not content to await the arrival of Indian goods, Smith led expeditions up the James River and its tributaries seeking out Indians willing to barter food for English-made items such as hatchets, household utensils, and copperware. Smith refused to supply the Indians, however, with guns and ammunition. That fall he returned from several boat trips into the country of the Chickahominy Indians bearing bargeloads of corn and beans, obviously increasing his influence in Jamestown.

During one expedition, Smith's luck ran out. He had journeyed into the territory of normally friendly Chickahominy Indians. Smith left seven of his nine white followers guarding the barge, while he, two Indian guides, and two companions went upstream by canoe. An Indian ambush wiped out all seven members of Smith's rearguard, while a second surprise assault by Powhatan's Pamunkey warriors cut down one of the whites in Smith's canoe. Smith's guide, whom he had been using as a shield, cried out to the surrounding Pamunkey Indians that Smith was a *werowance* of the whites. The Indians let him live, although Smith had already shot down two of the attackers. Smith's captors brought him to Powhatan. Ever resourceful, Smith had managed to persuade the leader of his captors, Powhatan's brother Opechancanough, that unless news of his capture was delivered to Jamestown, Englishmen (whose numbers Smith exaggerated) would seek revenge on the Pamunkeys. Opechancanough agreed to have his men carry the news.

Ever the survivor, Smith managed to keep his captors entertained by performing tricks with an ivory pocket compass and with his endless supply of adventure stories (and tall tales) translated by the Indian guide (at this point, Smith had not yet mastered Indian speech). After passing through a series of Indian villages, Smith carefully observing customs and ceremonies, the prisoner and the Pamunkeys finally reached Powhatan's village, Werowocomoco. A year after the encounter, Smith wrote that he had first seen Powhatan

> proudly lying upon a bedstead a foot high, upon ten or twelve mats, richly hung with many chains of great pearls about his neck, and with a great covering of [raccoon skins]. At his head sat one woman, at his feet another. On each side, sitting upon a mat upon the ground, were ranged his chief men on each side of the fire, ten in a rank, and behind them as many young women, each with a great chain of white beads over their shoulders, their heads painted in Red.

Surprised to discover such regal bearing "in a naked savage," Smith described his host as "grave and majestic."

Although he probably did not expect to leave Powhatan's camp alive, Smith tried to reassure the great chief that Jamestown people were friendly, denying that the London Company intended to establish permanent settlements on Powhatan's land. When the Indian chief asked him "the cause of our comming," Smith replied that the English "being in fight with the Spaniards our enemie, being over powred, [sic] neare put to retreat," came ashore. Then, because their ships had supposedly leaked,

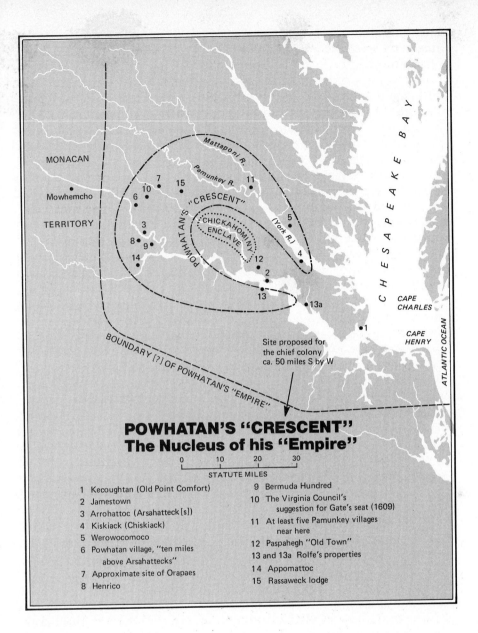

POWHATAN'S "CRESCENT"
The Nucleus of his "Empire"

Site proposed for
the chief colony
ca. 50 miles S by W

0   10   20   30
STATUTE MILES

1 Kecoughtan (Old Point Comfort)
2 Jamestown
3 Arrohattoc (Arsahatteck [s])
4 Kiskiack (Chiskiack)
5 Werowocomoco
6 Powhatan village, "ten miles
      above Arsahattecks"
7 Approximate site of Orapaes
8 Henrico

9 Bermuda Hundred
10 The Virginia Council's
      suggestion for Gate's seat (1609)
11 At least five Pamunkey villages
      near here
12 Paspahegh "Old Town"
13 and 13a Rolfe's properties
14 Appomattoc
15 Rassaweck lodge

"wee were inforced to stay to mend her, till Captaine Newport my father came to conduct us away."

Why, then, asked Powhatan, had Smith and his friends continued to explore so close to Indian villages? Again, John Smith answered deceitfully. The English, he explained, were searching for a great sea on the other side of the mountains (a clear reference to the continuing European pursuit of a westward passage to China). Despite the fact that Powhatan probably did not believe much of Smith's explanation, in the end, he welcomed Smith as a friend, "appointed" him the *werowance* of a nearby village, and agreed to provide guides who would deliver him safely back to Jamestown.

Powhatan exerted great power throughout the region, although Smith could not have known how much. As the chief of thirty Indian tribes spread along the coast of Virginia, Powhatan ruled a loosely knit kingdom, which would be dubbed a "confederacy" by Thomas Jefferson a century and a half later. But his authority, like Montezuma's in Mexico, was roughly equivalent to that of European monarchs such as James I. The Indian tribes spoke a common language, Algonkian, and shared common cultural beliefs and practices as well as Powhatan's leadership. In the years before Jamestown's settlement, Powhatan had expanded and consolidated control over many Virginia tribes. Thus, although he came to respect the military power commanded by the gun-carrying white newcomers, Powhatan displayed no apparent sense of inferiority. He welcomed John Smith as a potential ally against his remaining Indian enemies, especially the tribes that had escaped his domination by remaining in the mountainous Piedmont region beyond the coast. Powhatan evidently liked the notion of trading food (his tribes had plenty) for European weapons and military support.

When, seventeen years later, Smith wrote of his captivity at Powhatan's village, he mentioned for the first time an episode involving the Indian's favorite daughter, twelve-year-old Pocahontas. While eating a meal prepared by guards, according to Smith's 1624 account, he was abruptly bound and tied to boulders, presumably as the prelude to execution. Suddenly, although the Indians were "ready with the clubs, to beate out his braines, *Pocahontas* the King's dearest daughter . . . got his head in her armes, and laid her owne upon his to save him from death: whereat the Emperour was contented he should live. . . ." The tale of Pocahontas's rescue of Smith, whether or not it happened, has survived in myth and memory.

Several days after his alleged brush with death, Smith and Indian guides bearing gifts of food returned to Jamestown. He showed the Indians the fort and demonstrated the power of its cannons by firing a load of stones at nearby icicle-laden trees, terrifying them much as Cortez's demonstrations had struck fear in Montezuma's envoys.

But things were not well at Jamestown. Having survived probable death at the hands of Indians, Smith now faced the wrath of his English peers. His opponents held Smith responsible for the deaths of those on the exploratory trip. They tried and convicted Smith, and prepared for a hanging. Only Newport's arrival from London on January 2, 1608, saved Smith's life. Newport backed him against his enemies on the council.

The squabble over Smith's behavior receded days later, on January 7, when the attention of all settlers turned to putting out a major fire in the town, which destroyed buildings and supplies. Food and equipment were now even scarcer, at a time when the fresh recruits Newport had brought from England increased the colony's ranks to over a hundred mouths to feed. But Smith's "friendship" with Powhatan came in handy.

Twice in the days after the fire, gifts of food and raccoon skins arrived from the Indian monarch. Powhatan evidently sought a truce, although not an alliance, with the English intruders.

During the next few years, relations between the region's Indian tribes and the English remained tense and uncertain. Smith and his fellow settlers continued to explore the Chesapeake Bay region, striving always to forge friendly ties with Indians, especially those who opposed Powhatan's dominance. Smith traded beads and other European-made goods for food wherever he could, and he searched unsuccessfully for precious metals.

The Jamestown settlers, however, never dropped their guard against the Indians. Powhatan, for his part, appeared content to postpone a full-fledged assault on the English, possibly because of a fear of their superior weaponry, but he remained just as cautious in dealing with Jamestown as the English were with him. In 1609, for example, Powhatan moved his headquarters from Werowocomoco, only fifteen miles from Jamestown, to a more distant village. Nevertheless, in the early years of white settlement, Powhatan carefully avoided breaking off relations with Smith, even sending occasional delegations with gifts of food to Jamestown. These delegations sometimes included Pocahontas, Powhatan's impressionable daughter, who openly expressed her delight with life at the English settlement.

Pocahontas's preference for "city life" aside, the rhythm of relations between the two groups often became discordant. When Indians came upon whites exploring tribal lands, the intruders were often attacked. Such incidents inevitably led to English reprisals. When the Indians proved unwilling to "trade" food for the cheap goods bartered by the English, their towns and possessions were burned. In daily practice, both sides behaved as harshly toward one another as circumstances allowed, despite the London Company's instructions that the American settlers should be fair and friendly toward the natives (even this happened a few times, as when young Indians were brought to Jamestown to study white customs). It galled the colonists that, despite their superior arms and farming methods, even despite their *moral* status as Christians and cultural virtues as Englishmen, they depended upon the Indians for food with which to survive. If the Indians were indeed "savages," as many at Jamestown believed, how did they manage to keep the colony at bay so easily? Irritation at this inability to dominate and master the Indians turned easily to anger and, from there, to bloody killings and torture by the whites on many occasions. One thing, however, is certain: without the continuing supply of native corn and beans and other food over the years, the colony would have perished.

Having failed to hang John Smith, council members elected him their president. In September 1608, Smith clearly embodied the colony's best hope for surviving the coming winter. He ordered storehouses built to hold food supplies; he conducted military drills; and he ordered greater vigilance to prevent surprise attacks, all previously neglected measures.

To the unruly colonists, Smith offered a simple choice: cooperate or suffer the punishment. No work, in short, no food.

Newport's ship had finally arrived bringing much needed supplies as well as additional settlers: fourteen artisans, fourteen laborers, two women, and a less helpful resupply of twenty-eight gentlemen recruits. Several Polish and German craftsmen came to develop a glass factory and other manufacturing projects. These schemes had no realistic place in the desperate condition of Jamestown that winter, where food remained scarce and workmen had to stay inside the fort because of possible Indian attacks.

Newport had received still another series of unhelpful orders from the company's council, directives even more foolish than the notion that tiny Jamestown could become a manufacturing center overnight. The London Company wanted the search for gold stepped up and thus gave Newport a gold refiner—just in case. The captain was also to resume the impossible search for a westward passage to Asia, using a monstrously unwieldy five-section barge, which was to be carried across the mountains and reassembled on some westward-flowing river for the journey to the "South Seas." Finally, the search for the lost Roanoke colony was to be continued. Later that fall, Newport led 120 men up the James River. He found neither gold nor a South Sea passage, and other exploratory parties failed to turn up the Roanoke settlers.

Once Newport had returned empty-handed, Smith and the other council members set about, more practically, loading Newport's vessel for its return to England with *something—anything*—available near Jamestown that might please their English sponsors. They hoped that additional timber, loads of clapboard, and samples of glass (also pitch and tar) might suggest to the London Company that such goods—if produced in large quantity—would repay their investments in Virginia.

As winter approached, Smith also tried to increase trade with nearby tribes. But the Indians now proved more reluctant to part with corn and beans in exchange for English tradegoods, possibly (Smith suspected) following Powhatan's orders. John Smith then used an iron fist, menacing Indian villages until they agreed to "trade" their food supplies. Newport sailed for England in December, leaving behind a hungry community of two hundred people, half of them sick or disabled even before the start of winter.

Smith ruled Jamestown dictatorially for the next several months, imposing stern discipline despite his frequent absences while he foraged for food. He divided the colony into work details of ten to fifteen men and maintained constant patrols at the palisades. He staged weekly drills and frequent musket firings to impress watchful Indians, who lurked on the outskirts of Jamestown.

In January 1609, Smith traveled to Powhatan's village, at the Indian monarch's request, to build him an "English-style" wooden house (possibly to hold the earlier gifts, although Powhatan may have hoped to lure Smith into an ambush). Eventually, Smith cajoled and pressured Powhatan into agreeing to load his boat with corn. After that, Smith and

9. their Danceing.

(8) the manner of Praying to their Idol.

9. the Town of Pomeioc

his men left abruptly because Pocahontas supposedly provided another timely warning that her father's warriors planned to kill him.

Smith sailed off with his corn. At Opechancanough's village Smith, never at a loss for adversaries, challenged the *werowance* to hand-to-hand combat, the winner to rule the other's troops. When Opechancanough hesitated, Smith grabbed his hair, stuck a pistol against his chest, and shoved him out in front of all his warriors. The Englishman then threatened the Indian captain and his people with bloody reprisals unless they supplied more corn. The shaken Indians delivered their supplies, and Smith left hastily for yet another "trade."

Thanks largely to Smith's stern rules within the fort and to his effective, if unusual, methods of strong-arming bargeloads of corn from the Indians, almost none of the settlers perished because of starvation or disease during the winter. When spring came, Indians again began arriving at the fort to trade corn, beans, and newly killed game. Smith had intimidated them, and now the Indians even delivered over to him those tribal members accused of stealing goods from Jamestown, usually weapons. Smith punished them sternly.

Governing partly through clever bluffs and partly through an extremely harsh but effective system of personal justice, Smith proved a master at dealing both with the Indians and with his own people. He ruled Jamestown arbitrarily but well until the end of his one-year term as president of the council. Despite obvious achievements, Smith received no second term. Complaints about his harsh dealings with the Indians had reached London when Newport arrived there early in 1609. By that time, the company had already decided to revise its plans for Jamestown. The struggling settlement on Chesapeake Bay received a new charter in 1609, a new president, a new local council, and most important of all, a new supply of a most vital resource—manpower.

The new charter came first, handed down by King James to the

London Company, assigning more powers to the company's leading figures and promising less royal interference. In exchange, the charter abolished the Jamestown council and appointed, instead, a governor to be advised by a *new* council and by other appointed officials, all of whom would be under the governor's absolute authority. The company named an able figure as Jamestown's first governor, Lord Thomas de la Warr, with Sir Thomas Gates as his lieutenant governor. De la Warr could not leave immediately, so Gates—who had sailed to America with Sir Francis Drake in 1585—went instead to assume command.

With the new charter and the new frame of government, enthusiasm for Jamestown's future soared in England. Excitement over the future prospects for developing America led more than 650 individuals and 56 city companies to subscribe stock in the reorganized London Company. This outpouring of support for England's experiment in American colonization was most amazing because Smith, Newport, and the other settlers had failed either to discover valuable metals or to find a new passage to Asia.

Six hundred new settlers joined the nine-ship fleet that sailed from England to Jamestown in June 1609. But it was not simply the larger numbers that distinguished the fleet. This "supply" expedition also differed from the earlier ones in qualitative ways. It included more than a hundred women, children, and servants, indicating clearly that the company had decided on a permanent venture in America. Jamestown as a virtually all-male preserve of "adventurers," gentlemen, and skilled craftsmen was dead.

Most of the vessels arrived at Jamestown in August, but the crossing was perilous. Gates's ship was wrecked in Bermuda, so that the new governor did not reach Jamestown for ten more months. The newcomers informed Smith and the old settlers of the revised London Company charter and its altered frame of government. Still Smith declined to quit as president until he had met with Gates. Once it became known that Smith's rule would soon end, however, the factionalism that had been firmly checked for the past year quickly reappeared.

Old enemies and long-standing grievances surfaced. The bickering Jamestown settlers, now tripled in number with the new arrivals, neglected the vital tasks of food collecting and town building, which Smith had directed so smoothly though harshly. At one point, Smith claimed that his enemies on the council, some of whom had returned with the new settlers, tried to murder him. Enough was enough. He decided to leave for England in October. Although John Smith kept in touch with events in Virginia, and although he later wrote several short books on his experiences, he never returned to America.

Winter was coming. Smith had sailed for England, and Governor Gates remained stranded in Bermuda. The Jamestown settlers lacked legitimate, effective leadership. An English nobleman named George Percy took over temporarily, but Smith's departure increased Indian confidence. Powhatan promptly resumed attacks on the white intruders. Thus when Captain John Martin, an original settler, left with seventeen men to trade for food, the entire party disappeared without a trace. Elsewhere, the bodies of several recently slaughtered whites were found. Percy sent Captain John Ratcliffe to negotiate with Powhatan for food. Ratcliffe went up the James River with fifty armed men and two Indians ("Powhatan's son and daughter," according to one account) as hostages. After reaching the Indian village, Ratcliffe succumbed to the type of false welcome from Powhatan that had never fooled John Smith. When Ratcliffe released the hostages, Powhatan's soldiers killed two-thirds of the Englishmen before the rest escaped.

Powhatan saved a special fate for Ratcliffe. According to George Percy, the luckless and trusting captain was

> bound unto a tree, naked, with a fire before [him]. And by women his flesh was scraped from his bones with mussel shells, and before his face thrown into the fire. And so for want of circumspection [he] miserably perished.

Discipline among the desperately hungry settlers quickly deteriorated. Percy had sent a few colonists to an outpost given the hopeful name Point Comfort. There, thirty miles from the fort, they eked out a tolerable existence that winter eating shellfish and boar meat. But the Point Comfort settlers never provided supplies for their starving brethren in Jamestown. On another occasion, Percy ordered Captain Francis West and three dozen men to trade for food with the Potomac tribe. West did well for himself, stocking the boat with corn, after handling the Indians savagely, even cutting off the heads of two Potomac warriors. West and his men then brazenly set sail for England, to the amazement and horror of Percy and his hungry colonists.

"A world of miseries ensued," Percy wrote after that agonizing winter, ". . . in so much that some to satisfy their hunger have robbed the store, for the which I caused them to be executed. Then, having fed upon horses and other beasts as long as they lasted, we were glad to make shift with [such] vermin as dogs, cats, rats, and mice."

Life in Jamestown during the winter of 1609–10 later came to be called "the starving time," a period of almost unbearable misery for those who endured it. John Smith, though himself far from the scene, collected accounts of the period from survivors, and described those grisly months when suffering and hunger could be alleviated at times only by munching upon "roots, herbes, acornes, walnuts, berries, now and then a fish . . . yea, even the very skinnes of our horses":

> Nay, so great was our famine, that a Salvage [an Indian] we slew and buried, the poorer sort took him up again and eat him; and so did divers one another boyled and stewed with roots and herbs. And one amongst the rest did kill his wife, powdered [i.e., salted] her, and had eaten part of her before it was knowne, for which he was executed, as he well deserved: now whether she was better roasted, boyled, or carbonado'd [i.e., grilled], I know not, but of such a dish as powdered wife I never heard of.

Such cases of cannibalism were not unique, not if George Percy is to be believed. He later recalled "things which seem incredible, as to dig up corpses out of graves and to eat them—and some have licked up the blood which hath fallen from their weak fellows." As for the man who murdered his wife for food, Percy had him tortured to obtain a confession before executing him by the slow and agonizing method of burning him alive, a clear enough warning to other settlers.

Some colonists simply ran off into the woods, apparently hoping to find friendly Indians willing to share their food, with unknown but probably fatal results. Others were killed by Indian attacks while wandering through the forests and riverbeds searching for food. A number of settlers died inside the fort, not only from starvation but also from the many diseases that had plagued Jamestown since its earliest days. Others relapsed into numbness, seemingly incapable of working or searching for food, although not actually sick. John Smith's iron discipline had been effective the previous winter at snapping the lethargic settlers out of such stupors. But many in the winter of 1609–10 wandered through their days at Jamestown in a deathlike trance, unable to function.

When Thomas Gates, Christopher Newport, and the others who had spent a relatively comfortable winter shipwrecked in Bermuda finally reached Jamestown in May 1610, they found the settlement close to total starvation. Gates and his 150 settlers had not brought much food with them, expecting to encounter a prosperous colony. What they saw left them stunned. The previous fall's six hundred colonists had been reduced to fewer than sixty survivors; most of the remainder had died, although some had fled to England with West, and others kept their distance at Point Comfort. As for Jamestown, it appeared (in John Smith's words) "rather as the ruins of some ancient fortification, then that any people living might now inhabit it."

It seemed evident to Gates that the colony could not be maintained as it stood. Food remained scarce, and with 150 additional people to feed, Gates decided to abandon Jamestown in favor of an English outpost far to the north, Newfoundland. Available grain would be rationed, and from Newfoundland, the party hoped to make its way back to England.

More than two hundred people boarded the four fragile boats on June 7, 1610, for yet another long journey. Many wanted to burn Jamestown to the ground, a fitting end to so much misery. Gates refused. Even without a fiery finale, it seemed evident that this ambitious English experiment in America had ended as miserably, though not so tragically, as Roanoke.

But the Jamestown refugees never reached open seas, thanks to what their more devout members considered Divine intervention and even the less reverent considered a miracle in timing. The colony's governor, Lord de la Warr, had succeeded in wrapping up his affairs in England and had sailed for Virginia in April 1610 with three ships, several hundred immigrants, and plenty of food and other supplies. De la Warr reached Point Comfort first, and he learned of Gates's plans to leave Virginia for Newfoundland. Lord de la Warr immediately dispatched a ship up the James River to alert Gates and scotch the project. Gates promptly and happily complied. Once again, the recently abandoned town throbbed with excitement and anticipation, preparing for the arrival of de la Warr's new recruits—and his food.

The new governor quickly asserted his authority and set the colonists to rebuilding Jamestown. Sounding remarkably like John Smith in earlier days, de la Warr addressed the community, denouncing their previous "idleness" and promising to restore both internal discipline and a strict work schedule. Every able-bodied person in Jamestown, including the gentlemen, would spend at least six hours a day at hard labor in repairing fortifications, planting crops, and constructing new buildings. Twice daily, the entire colony paused for communal prayers. The new governor also brought with him a new set of tough laws to deal with every breach of behavior and decorum. Killing an animal without permission, for example, was punishable by death; washing filthy items near the village well—chief source of the colony's fresh water supply—punished by whipping; cursing or fighting by being "tied head and feete together" every night for a month. Although de la Warr did not enforce the new code rigidly, the lawful threat of such extreme punishment helped to maintain peace at Jamestown, much as John Smith had done earlier.

But even under the sternest administration, Jamestown retained its nasty climate. Another muggy and unhealthy summer season arrived, undermining de la Warr's plans for recovery. At least 150 people died during that "sickly season" of 1610 from diseases such as dysentery, malaria, and scurvy. The Bermuda newcomers proved especially vulnerable to the spread of sickness and to that lethargic weakening of the will to live (and to work) that had always bedeviled the colony.

The most prominent casualty was de la Warr himself. Soon after arriving at Jamestown, the governor later wrote, he was "welcomed by a hot and violent Ague which . . . disease had not long left mee, till . . . I began to be distempered with other greevous sickness, which successfully & severally assailed me. . . ." After suffering bouts of what he described as "the Flux," "the Gout," more "Ague," and finally scurvy, de la Warr fled Virginia to escape sure death, leaving Jamestown in the far less competent hands of George Percy. Another "supply" arrived from England in March 1611, commanded by Sir Thomas Dale and carrying three hundred more settlers, and Dale soon replaced Percy as deputy governor.

Under Dale's leadership, de la Warr's earlier efforts to strengthen the colony continued. Work parties scurried around the settlement, planting crops and repairing buildings while organizing for winter. Sensitive to the decimation continually wrought at Jamestown, Dale directed a search for a new and healthier site for colonizing. Eventually, he supervised the development of a site fifty miles upstream, which Dale called Henrico (after Henry, the Prince of Wales), near the point at which the

Sir Thomas Dale was a successor to Lord de La Warr as governor of Virginia. He continued de La Warr's system of rigid control and strict discipline. Under his leadership, the colony expanded up and down the James River and into the surrounding area. (Virginia State Library)

James and Appomattox rivers meet. Henrico became Virginia's most important community for a time, better fortified and in a healthier location than Jamestown itself.

But Dale became known chiefly for his attempt to enforce a legal code even more stringent than earlier ones, a code that became known as the "Laws Divine, Moral and Martial." Dale's laws seemed designed to coerce a colony that consisted largely of rebellious or lethargic settlers into behaving responsibly; in short, the laws were savage and probably appropriate to Jamestown.

Trial by jury and other rights that the Jamestown settlers had known back in England were denied under Dale. Persons convicted of crimes were dealt with in an extraordinarily brutal manner—some burned at the stake, others hanged or shot, still others lashed to wheels to be broken into pieces. When the Virginia assembly (which did not exist in the time of Smith and Dale) issued a description in 1624 of the bad old days under Dale's rule, the details defied belief. Many settlers fled to the Indians in order to escape being punished for minor infractions of the "Laws Divine, Moral and Martial." If recaptured, they were normally put to death or subjected to punishments such as these: "one for steeling . . . 2 or 3 pints of oatmeal had a bodkin [dagger] thrust through his tongue and was tyed with a chain to a tree untill he starved. . . . Many through these extremities, being weary of life, digged holes in the earth and there hid themselves till they famished." When Thomas Gates replaced Dale in August 1611, the change did not noticeably lighten the burdens of ordinary Virginians.

Throughout the years of stern leadership under Dale, de la Warr, and Gates, the threat of English–Indian hostilities never abated. Both sides raided back and forth. Neither side displayed much pity toward the other. On one campaign, George Percy's men raided a Paspahegh village, cutting off the heads of several Indians and later throwing captured children overboard from their ship, shooting out their brains in the water. Rarely did the English take prisoners. Powhatan encouraged his warriors and subject tribes to attack, especially small, relatively defenseless groups of Englishmen caught outside the fortifications of Jamestown or Henrico. These forays, in turn, interrupted tobacco and corn cultivation. Both Dale and Gates had successfully encouraged the latter for winter food supplies. Tobacco, which King James I (an ardent opponent of smoking) called that "noxious weed," had rapidly become Virginia's leading hope for economic stability.

A kidnapping, and the semi-dynastic marriage that followed, brought Jamestown eight years of relative peace with most of the Chesapeake Bay Indian tribes. In the spring of 1613, when Powhatan refused to surrender eight white prisoners and some captured English weapons, the English took his daughter Pocahontas hostage. Pocahontas, now practically a woman, had always been friendly toward the Jamestown settlers. Early in 1613, Captain Samuel Argall was sailing along the Rappahannock River, seeking corn supplies, when he came upon Pocahontas visiting the king of the Potomac Indians, a tribe that wanted to be friendly with the English. Argall demanded and got Pocahontas, who then became a pawn in negotiations between Powhatan and the Virginians.

Shortly afterward, Dale and Argall took her up the James River, well-guarded. The English demanded that Powhatan either fight or return his cache of captured supplies, and they set a ransom for Pocahontas: five hundred bushels of corn. When Powhatan refused both demands, the English returned to Jamestown with their prisoner, warning the Indian king to comply by harvest time or else.

Events soon passed out of Dale's control, however, when a gentleman of Jamestown, a widower named John Rolfe, asked the leaders of the colony for permission to marry Pocahontas. The government approved the request after the Indian princess agreed to become a Christian. She

Pocahontas went to England as Rebecca Rolfe in 1616 and was presented to King James I. She died not long after, at the beginning of her return voyage to Virginia. (Library of Congress)

and Rolfe were married in April 1614. Powhatan refused to attend, but one of Pocahontas's uncles represented him, bringing her father's reluctant approval for the wedding.

In the eight years that followed, until Powhatan's death, the Virginia settlements enjoyed peace largely because of Pocahontas's marriage and Powhatan's subsequent pledge to avoid further conflict. Old by then, tiring of the constant struggle against the English, and deeply disappointed in his daughter's decision to join the company of his enemies, Powhatan had no heart for further battle. His decision encouraged tribes hostile to Powhatan's confederacy to make separate peace with the English, lest the full force of Jamestown's weaponry be turned against them. A number of treaties with tribes such as the Chickahominy turned most of the neighboring Indians into English vassals, who agreed to furnish regular tributes of corn and—when required—even warriors to fight for the English.

Pocahontas did not live to watch the years of peace descend upon the Chesapeake Bay region. She and John Rolfe toured England in 1616 before admiring crowds. She was received by the king in court, became celebrated by London society, and made several sentimental visits to her old friend, John Smith. Shortly after boarding a ship to return to Virginia with her husband in March 1617, "Rebecca Rolfe," born Pocahontas, died after a brief illness. She left as her legacy a grieving husband, a two-year-old child, and a moment of amity between Virginia's whites and Indians, which lasted for another five years.

When Powhatan died the following year, 1618, and his brother, Opechancanough, succeeded him as head of the confederation, Jamestown had yet another governor, Captain George Yeardley. Barely half a decade from the time Gates prepared to abandon the settlement, Jamestown had grown rapidly. Hundreds of new recruits came each year from

England; and despite a fearfully high death toll from disease, the population continued to increase. Newer tracts in the countryside came under corn and tobacco cultivation. Fear of Indian attack had receded after 1613, more a bad memory than a present reality. Tobacco, meanwhile, ensured the colony's growth and future.

The English had purchased most of their tobacco from Spanish colonies before the settlement of Virginia. By importing seeds of tobacco varieties planted in Spanish America, John Rolfe experimented to improve the unpopularly strong tobacco grown by Indians near Jamestown. Rolfe's mixture soon captured the English market with some help from King James, who craved additional revenue more than he despised tobacco. Thus, in 1612, the king granted the London Company a seven-year exemption from customs duties on its imports from America.

A tobacco boom was under way, especially after settlers began acquiring land privately in 1614 to grow crops. Governor Dale found himself forced to *order* all planters to grow at least two acres of *corn* to ensure an adequate food supply. If they did not, they risked having their tobacco crop forfeited. Still, tobacco production soared. In 1615, Virginians shipped only 2000 pounds of tobacco back to England, but by 1620, exports exceeded 40,000 pounds, and by 1622, 60,000. Only four years later, in 1626, the amount reached 500,000 pounds, and by 1629, a record 1.5 million pounds! Despite periodic declines in the English market in the decades ahead, either because supply outpaced demand or times were hard, the emergence of tobacco as its major export crop guaranteed the future of Virginia.

The newer immigrants from England spread out across the territory, surrounding Jamestown and other recently fortified towns. But despite the tobacco prosperity, the incidence of disease remained high. It proved as difficult for most new immigrants to adjust to unhealthy Virginian conditions as it had a decade earlier. Thus, although over 1000 settlers flocked to the colony each year from 1619 to 1622 (the population in 1618 had been about 700), the London Company complained that massive migration to Virginia had become little more than a "regulated kind of killing of men." The company estimated that over 3000 people died in Virginia between 1618 and 1622. Almost none of the fatalities could be blamed on Indians. The culprits remained disease in its usual varieties, hunger, malnutrition, and that extreme passivity that often afflicted otherwise healthy persons at Jamestown.

Powhatan's successor, Opechancanough, finally broke the peace in 1622 in a last desperate effort to force the whites from Indian lands before they themselves were completely driven off. The slaughter of English settlers that followed, although significant, involved only a tenth of the number that had perished from supposedly "natural" causes over the preceding three years.

The attack came suddenly, without warning. On March 22, some Indians paid their usual visits to English plantations and homes throughout the area to trade. Occasionally the Indians completed their exchanges, sat down for meals with their white hosts—and only then began the bloodletting, "not sparing either age or sex, man, woman, or childe." The killing assumed a special horror, even by Virginian standards, because often the whites and Indians involved had known one another well and lived peacefully alongside one another for almost a decade. Bodies were butchered, heads chopped off, and extremities defaced. That single day's carnage cost 347 white settlers their lives. Most of the atrocities occurred on farms spread out at a good distance from the fortified towns. Jamestown, warned of the impending attack by friendly Indians, mobilized its forces. Other communities, less fortunate and unsuspecting, suffered costly surprise assaults.

The reprisals taken by white settlers over the next several years proved even more terrible than the events of March 22. The English abandoned all efforts at friendship with the Indians. The colony's governor declared at Jamestown that there existed an "irreconcilable" conflict between the two cultures: "All trade with them must be forbidden, and without doubt either we must cleere them or they us out of the Country." Several expeditions, led by the colony's leaders, left from Jamestown to wipe out all tribes in the region.

Although Opechancanough himself escaped capture, the English exacted fearful retribution against the Indians whom they managed to track down: burning villages, slaughtering their inhabitants indiscriminately, and setting the torch to nearby cornfields after confiscating whatever food could be found. Throughout the region, white Virginians set up a series of fortifications to protect the outlying plantations. Bloody warfare between Indians and whites in the Chesapeake Bay area persisted for decades, with the English forcing out the remaining tribes and enlarging their territories bit by bit each year.

The Massacre of 1622 had another immediate effect, this one in England. It helped to stir opposition by many influential persons to the way in which the London Company had managed its American settlement under *both* old and new charters. Company critics complained about the shockingly high death rates (especially among new immigrants), the company's failure to diversify its economic base (where was the *gold* so confidently predicted by the "first settlers"?), and the obvious mismanagement by most of the colony's presidents and governors from the start. Finally, in May 1624, responding to a crescendo of complaints about the company, a royal court annulled and recalled its charter. Virginia fell under direct supervision of the crown.

By then, however, the defunct company's most important contribution to the growth of Virginia was already half a decade old. Governor Yeardley had been instructed in 1619 to summon a "general assembly," which would then meet annually, so that settlers "might have a hand in the governing of themselves." Although the governor and his advisory council would attend the assembly's meetings, two representatives (to be called "burgesses") would be elected from each plantation "freely . . . by the inhabitants thereof; this assembly to have power to make and ordain whatsoever lawes and orders should by them be thought good and proffittable for our subsistence."

The first Negroes were brought to Virginia in 1619 by Dutch traders. Slaves would form the basis of the Southern economy for more than two centuries, though at first, the legal and personal status of the Negro arrivals remained unclear. (The Bettmann Archive)

Yeardley's instructions also abolished Dale's "cruel laws by which we had so long been governed," substituting instead "those free laws which his Majesty's subjects live under in Englande. . . ." Apparently most adult males in the colony, except for indentured servants, could meet the qualifications and vote for burgesses.

The first general assembly met in the Jamestown church on July 20, 1619, convened after June elections had chosen twenty-two burgesses.

The assembly sat in session for almost a week debating many problems. It devised a new and milder criminal code to replace Dale's draconian sentences. Acting as the colony's supreme court, it also sentenced quite leniently a number of lawbreakers. The burgesses petitioned members of the London Company to resolve a series of land disputes within Virginia. Most important, the assembly showed from the start that it intended to assert the *exclusive* power to pass tax measures in Virginia. Although the governor could veto its actions, and although the London Company could also disallow its existence, the general assembly proved surprisingly aggressive even at its initial meeting in 1619.

Despite more than a decade of starvation and warfare, Jamestown colony managed to survive. By the time the first assembly met in 1619, tobacco planting had guaranteed the Virginians a steady source of income. The Indian tribes that had once dominated the region had been pushed back. The general assembly brought representative government to the New World for the first time in a form that would serve as a model for other English colonies.. The fragile roots set down at Jamestown had taken hold in spite of mismanagement from England and inept actions by leaders in Virginia itself.

When the general assembly adjourned on August 4, 1619, it noted "the intemperature of the Weather, and the falling sick of diverse of the Burgesses." That same month, Pocahontas's again-widowed husband, John Rolfe, wrote a letter, published later by John Smith in his *Generall Historie of Virginia*, which mentioned in passing the following news item: "About the last of August came in a dutch man of warre that sold us twenty Negars. . . ." Those "twenty Negars," the first Africans to reach the English colonies, arrived almost at the very moment that representative government began. Both came upon the scene at Jamestown during the worst disease-ridden weeks of midsummer. So preoccupied were Virginians with the problems of death and survival that the coincidence passed without comment. Although unnoticed then, the origins of both slavery and freedom converged in Virginia during the summer of 1619, inextricably bound together in time and place. Thus began the ordeal that would harness them together for the next 250 years.

4 American Origins: The Plantation Colonies

T he English investors in the London Company's venture at Jamestown had hoped for a quick and substantial profit. A ship had been sent back to England with its hold full of New World soil. Yet there were no minerals or precious metals to be found in all that dirt, no gold or silver as the Spaniards had found in Mexico and Peru. If there were profits to be made, they would have to come from more prosaic sources, and a government that would encourage and protect new sources of wealth would have to be created.

Tobacco did not make the Virginia company's investors immediately wealthy, but it eventually gave rise to a class of wealthy planters in Virginia itself. Some of the idle Englishmen who had so resentfully performed the manual labor needed to grow food after the first ships landed in Jamestown now began enthusiastically to cultivate the profitable crop of tobacco to meet the increased European demand. Tobacco leaves would even serve as currency in early Virginia.

The success and expansion of the tobacco crop helped heighten a problem already present in Jamestown—internal divisions within the settlement. Virginia had been regarded as a land where English gentlemen might make fortunes for themselves and, also, as a place where the poor and unemployed could be sent to ease the economic stress caused by the depression in England's textile industry. Would there be enough land to make both gentleman and laborer wealthy tobacco planters? If not, how would government and society react to the formation of distinct economic and social classes in England's first successful mainland settlement? The answers were defined over the next half-century of settlement and dramatized in a revolt against the colonial governor in 1676.

TOBACCO AND EXPANSION

The Virginia colonists had sent their first exports of tobacco back to England in 1615; by 1626 they were shipping over 500,000 pounds, and three years later, the figure had reached 1.5 million pounds. King James had granted huge areas of land to the Virginians' English sponsors. Those Englishmen who wanted land were willing to work as sharecropping tenants on the land of wealthier planters for several years if, at the end of their service, they could obtain land of their own. As the price of tobacco rose in the 1620s, the colonists continued to grow more and more of the crop, but they still would not grow enough corn to feed themselves. By 1624, in the midst of an economic boom, white Virginians were still dependent on Indian corn to stay alive.

New immigrants with their eyes on land often did not survive even with sufficient corn to eat. Ship captains would overload their Virginia-bound vessels, causing food shortages and deaths during the voyage. Those who survived the journey frequently died of scurvy shortly after reaching port. Although from 1625 to 1640, a period of significant migration from England, the population increased from 1300 to 8100, thousands (especially the newcomers) died of malaria, typhoid fever, and other diseases. One man observed that 1800 people perished in 1635 alone. In 1638, when the king proposed that tobacco production be limited, the House of Burgesses questioned the proposal because the burgesses could not estimate precisely what the population's current or future size might be.

Widespread disease helped create a feeling that everything was temporary. One was not quite certain what the next year, or even the next

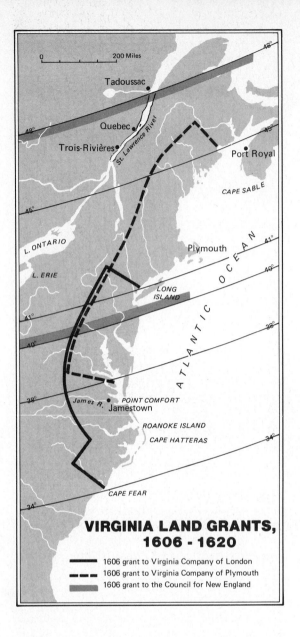

VIRGINIA LAND GRANTS,
1606 - 1620

——— 1606 grant to Virginia Company of London
- - - 1606 grant to Virginia Company of Plymouth
▬▬▬ 1606 grant to the Council for New England

change location soon. Masters purchasing servants, who were usually white and agreed to be "indentured," that is, to work for a period of years in exchange for their passage and the hope of land, often found that the servants did not survive long enough for a profit to be made from their labor. Since land was so abundant and cheap, and servants' life spans so uncertain, few planters were able to acquire huge fortunes during those early decades.

Yet, despite heavy death rates and declining tobacco prices in the 1630s, white servants remained cheap enough for planters to continue to purchase them. During the 1640s and 1650s, a combination of elements worked to make many master planters rich. For one thing, large planters adopted better methods of tobacco cultivation. Also, diseases that had killed so many newcomers began to decline in intensity, and Virginia's population increased sharply beginning in 1644. For Virginia's first half-century of settlement, the vast majority of indentured servants were whites, the major source of labor in the colony during those decades. Since servants now normally lived to fulfill their obligations, planters enjoyed additional profits that could help them purchase still more servants and plant still more tobacco. The cycle continued yearly. The growth of a class of wealthy planters, once it occurred, would have a profound impact upon Virginia society and the government that reflected the society.

BURGESSES AND PLANTERS

The London Company had paved the way for representative government by revising its charter in 1618. It instructed the new governor sent from England to call an assembly each year, and the House of Burgesses had met for the first time in 1619. The governor and the council which he appointed, however, clearly exercised greater power during the colony's early years. They often appropriated the labor of men the company sent to Virginia for themselves, thus furthering their own private fortunes. After hearing rumors regarding the exploitation of newcomers, King James I appointed an investigating committee that con-

month, might bring. Small planters often spent their tobacco profits on liquor, expensive clothing, or other luxuries. In many recorded cases, rather than invest their return from tobacco in building a substantial house, men continued to live in the shacks they had thrown up in the belief they might want to abandon them should the soil become exhausted or simply because they might want to

firmed the rumors. In 1624 he abolished the company's control and declared the settlement a royal colony under his officials' supervision. Although the king did not provide for the House of Burgesses to continue its meetings, the assembly was revived in 1629.

Some of the very first acts of the House of Burgesses were designed to secure the rights of planters to "own" servants. The members established a registration of all servants in the colony, noting the date of the expiration of their terms of service. The governor's council was composed of men with many servants. Even after the king had dissolved the London Company, its of-

ficials continued to hold many of the privileged positions that allowed them to control the labor of others. Since laws had been designed to protect the masters' property in servants, the poorer newcomers had few, if any, rights. Planters holding the transportation contracts of servants sold, hired out, lent, and even gambled away their human chattels. Servants could be shuffled from one master to another without their consent. The government refused to restrict the right of a master to punish a servant, and severe beatings of Englishmen by other Englishmen were seemingly condoned.

As the privileges of planters in the House of Burgesses grew, so did the power of this represen-

The 1622 Indian attack on Virginians, as imagined by an artist. Gory pictures of Indian atrocities appealed to Europeans, who held contradictory views of native Americans as either *violent brutes or noble savages untouched by the vices of civilization. (Bry, America, Part XIII— NYPL/Rare Book Collection/Astor, Lenox, and Tilden Foundations)*

tative assembly within the colonial government. Even before the London Company's abolition, the governor's council and the House of Burgesses had declared that the governor, appointed by the king, would have no power to levy taxes without the consent of the assembly. After 1629, a new governor, John Harvey, made peace with the Indians, questioned the illegal bargains of council members, and tried to persuade Virginians to raise crops other than tobacco. For his efforts, he was unceremoniously (although temporarily) shipped back to England in 1635. When the colonists defied an English law prohibiting trade with the Dutch, Parliament sent an armed force to Virginia in 1652. The governor, William Berkeley, persuaded the English authorities that the colonists required a certain amount of free trade to ensure their prosperity. Meanwhile the members of the Burgesses drew large salaries paid by their constituents, making them more powerful than ever.

PRELUDE TO DISASTER

With most indentured servants living out their terms of obligation, which usually ran up to seven years, it seemed that the dreams of poorer English immigrants might eventually be fulfilled. By 1660, however, developments that had created a wealthy class of planters were also restricting the hopes of the poor. The increase in population had enlarged the labor force and, thus, the output of tobacco. With the increase in tobacco production and the passage, in 1660, of the Navigation Act, which outlawed direct sales to the Dutch, the price of the crop fell, requiring the planting of additional acres. Land now became still more expensive, making it increasingly difficult for a newly freed servant to become a tobacco planter on his own.

Wealthy planters saw the profits to be made by speculating on the best remaining lands in the colony and quickly began to buy them up. The largest of these planters also became merchants, loaning goods to smaller farmers and exercising their role as creditors to increase their privileged standing in society. Many of them became tax collectors, keeping a handsome share of the government's revenue for themselves. Governor Berke-

ley compiled an impressive private fortune, for example, receiving 200 pounds of tobacco for every marriage license issued and 350 pounds annually from taverns that held a liquor license.

The new freeman, the former servant, found it increasingly difficult to prosper. He normally had to pay between 100 and 200 pounds of tobacco in taxes each year. If he could not afford to buy his own land and remained a tenant, the landlord still might require him to pay the tobacco tax. Since the wealthy were buying up the best lands, the smaller farmer often had to pay expensive transportation costs to market his crop. It was often easier and less expensive to sell his crop to a wealthy neighbor, who would then market it. If the recently freed farmer could not afford or find new land, he sometimes had to sell his labor again to another farmer and return to servitude. The decline of social mobility in those years is illustrated by the fact that no servant who arrived in Virginia after 1640 ever became a member of the House of Burgesses.

Wealthy planters in the Burgesses enacted laws making it even more unlikely that servants would ever rise too high. If former servants were allowed to acquire land and grow tobacco, they would be competing with their former masters and add to the excessive volume of tobacco production, further lowering the market price. Thus large planters passed laws increasing the length of indenture for servants, often by as much as three years beyond the original indenture agreement.

Sir William Berkeley— shown here before the time of Bacon's Rebellion— was not always a harsh ruler. But after his bloody revenge on the insurgents, King Charles II remarked, "The old fool has killed more people in that naked country than I have done for the murder of my father." (Berkeley Castle— Courtesy, Virginia Historical Society)

They also provided for longer terms as punishments for servants who ran away, stole, or violated the society's strict moral codes.

Freed servants with no land, and small farmers who could not maintain their freehold, were anything but happy over this situation. These young men increasingly joined the wandering poor who traveled from county to county, avoiding the tax collector while hunting and stealing to stay alive. Discontent grew in the plantation counties among the large number of new freemen, but their unrest was not directed solely against the government in Jamestown. The counties with the largest numbers of ex-servants also contained the highest number of Indians. Like the poorer whites, Indians had been pushed inland by the wealthy planters, who had come to dominate the better lands near the shoreline, the Tidewater. By the 1670s, the wandering whites had grown desperate. Some action needed to be taken, but would they strike against the colony's ruling elite and Jamestown— or against their more immediate competitors for land, the Indians?

BACON'S REBELLION

Governor William Berkeley of Virginia was well aware that these angry white men posed a threat to the colony's existing social order. When the Dutch attacked along the James River in 1673, Berkeley and many large planters refused to arm servants and even feared to leave them behind when the Virginia militia went into battle. The militia itself contained a large percentage of landless freemen whom Berkeley distrusted as potential rebels.

After the king made large land grants to two of his friends the next year, 1674, outraged Virginia land speculators sent a representative to England to protest, taxing every planter in the colony 100 pounds of tobacco to pay for the mission. There was no question that an entrenched elite was running Virginia. The last election for the House of Burgesses had been held in 1661; thus the same men had held office nearly fifteen years.

The tension between Indians and the encroaching poor whites led to violence in 1675. A group of Doeg Indians took some hogs from a white planter, claiming that he had not paid them for goods purchased earlier. The planter then gathered some men who recovered the hogs after some fighting with the Indians. When the Doegs struck back in a raid on nearby settlements, the county militia killed fourteen Susquehannah Indians whom they had mistaken for Doegs. Eventually settlers began to believe that all Indian tribes had banded together to destroy the whites, and hysteria swept through Tidewater and backcountry Virginia alike.

The reaction or, more appropriately, the inaction of Governor Berkeley and the assembly angered settlers. Just as Berkeley was ready to dispatch a large force against the Indians, he suddenly recalled them, deciding instead on defensive measures. Berkeley ordered whites to withdraw from areas near Indian land and locate behind a line of forts at the falls of the rivers. The governor offered good pay to farmers to enroll as soldiers, probably more than a small tobacco farmer could make in a year, and decided to build frontier forts. But security came with a high price tag: imposing a large tax for the construction of these forts. Moreover, wealthy members of the assembly intended to build the forts on *their* land, helping to increase its worth.

These decisions from Jamestown disgusted Nathaniel Bacon, a twenty-eight-year-old planter of aristocratic background who had come from England several years earlier. Governor Berkeley, his cousin by marriage, had given Bacon a seat on the council. He had also received a land grant of a thousand acres up the James River in the frontier interior. Here, Bacon could see the discontent of the wandering poor embittered with Virginia's self-absorbed ruling oligarchy. As an official, Bacon saw the advantages of leading these men against Indians as a way of satisfying their craving for land of their own.

Berkeley continued to maintain his defensive strategy, perceiving his young cousin as merely a troublemaker and a possible threat to his authority. When Bacon applied for a commission to lead a force against the Indians, the governor turned him down. Bacon intended to carry out his plan in any case, although he wrote a conciliatory

Nathaniel Bacon demanded permission from Governor Berkeley to make wholesale war on the Indians of the region. When denied this, he led unsanctioned settler warfare against both the Indians and the governor, throwing the entire Virginia colony into turmoil. (Culver Pictures)

letter to the governor explaining the need for independent action. In May 1676, Berkeley denounced Bacon and expelled him from the council. Then, for the first time in fifteen years, the governor called for a new election of burgesses. The new representatives, he explained, could air their grievances to him in a proper legal manner.

But Bacon's forces were already on the march. They no longer discriminated between tribes that had been friendly toward the colonists and those that had been hostile. After friendly Oceaneechees captured a number of Susquehannahs for them, Bacon's men turned on the friendly Indians and promptly massacred them. When Bacon returned to Jamestown, Berkeley urged him to repent his actions and offered to allow him to sail to England if he wished to ask for a king's pardon. Bacon refused to apologize, however, renewing his request for a commission. Berkeley finally denounced Bacon and all of his followers as rebels, calling for a militia to be raised to suppress the entire group.

In a situation where the discontent of landless colonists had become widespread, Berkeley's action proved unwise. Now, many humble Virginians focused their anger not only upon the Indians along the frontier, but upon the Jamestown government as well. Even the new elections brought a majority of representatives sympathetic to Bacon. Elected himself, Bacon arrived in Jamestown to take his seat in the Burgesses, surrounded by fifty armed men. Berkeley managed to capture him, however, and to extract a confession. Surprisingly, then, the governor decided to placate the group of wealthy Virginians who thought Indian fighting a perfectly appropriate activity for discontented poor whites such as many of Bacon's followers. Berkeley pardoned Bacon, restored his seat on the council, and promised him a commission. He warned cousin Nathaniel, however, to stay out of New Kent County, center of the discontented poor.

Meanwhile the new representatives passed badly needed reforms designed to reduce the level of discontent. The right to vote in Virginia was granted to landless freemen. Members of the council were no longer exempt from taxes, and tax collectors, sheriffs, and other officials were now forbidden to take a percentage of the government revenues they received. The burgesses dropped the proposal to build frontier forts for defense, voting to raise a thousand troops instead. They offered attractive pay for soldiers and guaranteed them the plunder of all Indian goods they could carry, including the right to enslave captive Indians.

Bacon, who had disobeyed Berkeley's orders to stay away from New Kent, now appeared in Jamestown with 500 frontiersmen demanding his promised commission. At gunpoint, Bacon obtained the commission and the authority to raise as many volunteers as he wanted to lead. When eight whites were killed by Indians in New Kent, Bacon's men responded by entering prosperous Gloucester County and taking whatever horses and supplies they could find to avenge the deaths. Berkeley's supporters, meanwhile, were able to draw up a petition, signed by Gloucester landholders, protesting Bacon's high-handed action and requesting protection from the man. Berkeley then declared that Bacon's commission was void and marched to the county himself. He found that al-

though the inhabitants were willing to fight Indians under his command, they were hesitant to attack their fellow Virginians led by Bacon. When the latter learned that Berkeley was gathering a force to use against him, he marched after the governor, forcing him to retreat by ship.

The young Bacon was now ready to challenge Berkeley for leadership in Virginia. In a "Declaration of the People," he condemned the levying of taxes for public projects that would create fortunes for certain officeholders. As an English aristocrat, Bacon was also convinced that many of the men who had accumulated these fortunes were upstarts socially inferior to true gentlemen like himself. He saw himself now as a person determined to curb the oligarchy's power and influence, as a kind of Robin Hood who would redistribute their wealth. Bacon's forces thus began to pillage large estates and to attack Indians in the backcountry. His cause was first dealt a blow when his top two assistants, sent out to capture Berkeley, were themselves caught by the governor's men. Berkeley now issued an appeal for support, promising Virginians the plunder of the estates of Bacon's supporters. To prevent landholders from supporting Bacon, he even promised freedom to the servants of those who had signed an oath of support for Bacon.

Bacon and his followers were now at the height of their power. After more Indian fighting in New Kent, they had captured both Indians and their possessions. As a show of strength, Bacon marched his prisoners through Jamestown. Servants and slaves of those loyal to Berkeley now joined the rebellion, greatly adding to Bacon's forces. With the governor and his following in retreat aboard ships, Nathaniel Bacon's troops burned Jamestown to the ground. The rebels spent the next weeks looting their wealthy opponents' homes.

But the rebellion lacked any positive program of reform or revolutionary goals, as was soon evident following Bacon's sudden death from the "bloody flux" (probably dysentery). With no real direction, men gradually began to switch sides or lay down their arms. Significantly, the last of the rebel forces to surrender were slaves and twenty English servants. Governor Berkeley hanged the remaining leaders, even though the king had sent a pardon for all those who had engaged in the rebellion.

Had the uprising decided anything? Servants continued to arrive, live out their terms of indenture, and seek land, which would provide a better life, in the New World. Large planters, eager to maintain their privileged status, still required a labor force to produce massive quantities of tobacco. The labor problem, present in Jamestown when the first English ships reached North America, remained a dilemma in 1676. Bacon's Rebellion, however, had taught the ruling planter class that some changes were necessary to avert another violent conflict. That next outburst might not only disrupt their political and social standing in the colony, as Bacon had managed to do, but cost them their lives as well.

SLAVERY AND PLANTATIONS

By the time of Bacon's Rebellion, the idea of enslaving Africans to create a steady supply of forced labor was hardly new. Spanish and Portuguese slave traders had begun bringing African slaves to Latin America in the early sixteenth century. The Dutch, and then the English, had been drawn into the trade. In 1671, black slaves made up less than 5 percent of Virginia's population, while there were three times as many white indentured servants. But in the English colony of Barbados in the Caribbean, where a sugar-producing settlement required back-breaking work that discouraged the immigration of English indentured servants, many thousands of African slaves toiled and died under the tropical sun. Slavery had also been introduced into England's other colonies along the Atlantic coast but on a smaller scale.

When Negroes first arrived in Virginia, it was not assumed that they would all become

Slaves gather for festivities on a Carolina plantation. According to one expert, both the drum and the dance depicted are of Yoruba origin. (Many American slaves were descended from the Yoruba people, whose home is near the coast of West Africa.)

slaves. From the time when a Dutch ship arrived with twenty black captives, in 1619, to the middle of the century, all Africans *arrived* without fixed legal or social status. In the early decades, they achieved different destinies: some became slaves; some became servants for a term of years; and others became free. Some slaves were allowed to buy their freedom, and black servants and freemen were often treated comparably to their white indentured counterparts. Black and white servants worked and lived together, although firm evidence of racial practices in early Virginia remains incomplete. Early Virginia society *seemed* to make little distinction between those of different color, though we may never be certain of this point.

Economic trends, however, soon led wealthy white planters to favor black slaves over white indentured servants. Initially, because of the heavy death rate in the colony, it had not been advantageous to spend the extra money to purchase more expensive black slaves for life instead of buying the labor of white servants for a period of years. As life expectancy began to increase, however, the lower mortality rate of white servants gave planters more money and more confidence in buying the labor of a Negro for life. There is evidence, also, that blacks proved healthier than whites in the Southern climate and more immune to diseases such as malaria and yellow fever because of their African experiences. Also, an improving English economy induced fewer laborers to emigrate to the colonies. Bacon's Rebellion, moreover, helped induce the planter class to stop relying primarily upon a white indentured labor force. A black labor force, which could be kept *permanently* enslaved, seemed both safer and more reliable. Now such investors arrived in the New World, bought slaves, and settled on immense plantations. By 1700 half of Virginia's labor force was enslaved.

Just as they had passed laws before to lower the status and mobility of white servants, Virginia aristocrats now enacted legislation that discriminated between whites and blacks, demeaning Negroes and leading to a policy of permanent enslavement. Actions of the assembly that lowered the status of Negroes helped to reinforce feelings of racism, which apparently characterized large and small white planters alike. In 1662, the assem-

This leaflet advertising an upcoming slave auction illustrates the concern of potential owners for the health of their investments. (Library of Congress)

bly decided that even with Christian baptism, a slave remained a slave, and that all offspring of slave mothers automatically became slaves. All blacks were declared slaves in 1682, just six years following Bacon's Rebellion. In 1691 the assembly set strict penalties for miscegenation (interracial sexual relations). The same phrases that wealthy Englishmen had used to describe the supposed "natural" inferiority of the white poorer classes were now ascribed to African slaves.

The development of racist feelings was strongly aided by the rising opportunities for small white farmers. Bacon's battles with the Indians and subsequent campaigns greatly weakened the power of coastal tribes, and whites drove the natives farther and farther into the interior. This, along with the decline of immigration, allowed poorer whites to move into new areas and become landowners. In 1705, the Virginia assembly, now fearing that the greater threat came from black slaves rather than from poor whites, voted to provide freed indentured servants with money, clothes, and firearms. Small farmers also enjoyed a reduction of the poll

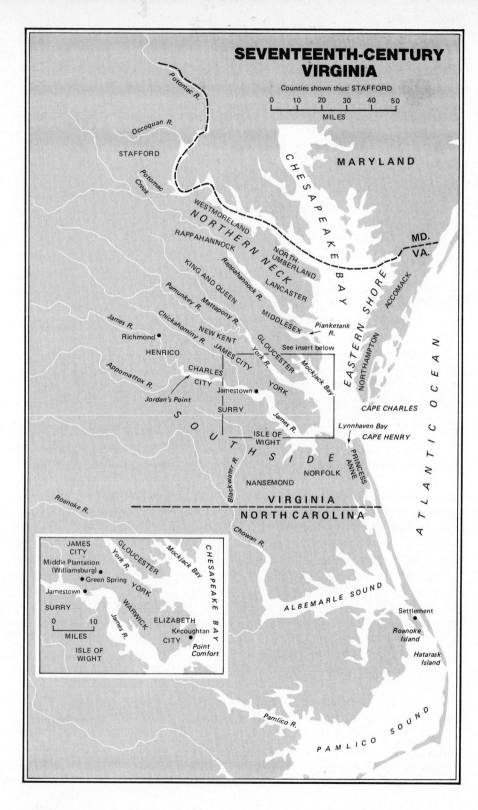

SEVENTEENTH-CENTURY VIRGINIA

Counties shown thus: STAFFORD

0 10 20 30 40 50
MILES

tax and, by the eighteenth century, had begun prospering with growth in the international tobacco market. Small white farmers no longer represented the bottom rung of Virginia's social ladder now that black enslavement had become institutionalized. Large and small planters both used the same racist rationalizations to justify the exploitation of the African peoples who now provided the bulk of plantation society's steady but unwilling labor supply.

PLANTATIONS AND SOCIETY

Despite the oppression inherent in racial slavery, black slaves in colonial Virginia fared better than those in other areas of the New World. Unlike the British West Indies, where staggering profits in sugar growing led planters to work slaves to death in order to increase their yields, the relatively less strenuous task of raising tobacco, and the prudence with which Virginia planters viewed their human "investment," created conditions under which black slaves could survive, procreate, and to an extent, experience stable family life. Beginning with the second generation of slaves, black women began to have more children, and more survived to adulthood. Nowhere else in the Western Hemisphere did the black slave population reproduce more than in the British colonies along the Atlantic coast. Still sexual exploitation of slave women by their white masters, and forced separation of women from their husbands and children, placed enormous stresses on the black family. Oppression, however, may also have driven black people into closer personal ties; when planters refused to provide enough food for slaves, they supplemented their meager rations by growing food near the cabin, involving all family members in the process.

The introduction of African slaves on a large scale, more than a half-century after Jamestown's founding, made the existence of huge, almost self-sufficient plantations possible. Wealthy planters often bought up the crops of smaller farmers, selling them retail goods, repairs, home manufactures, and slaves. Some powerful slaveholders built up their own individual "kingdoms." They were able

to offer services from their flour mills, textile-weaving centers, blacksmith shops, and even iron foundries. White indentured servants, and increasingly black slaves, were taught the skills of tailor, carpenter, or blacksmith. The relative ease with which white farmers obtained land created opportunities for slaves to fill these roles as artisans, and the situation meant that they, along with the house servants, had close associations with the planter or his assistants. This closer proximity often earned slaves privileges, inside information, and perhaps an opportunity to become literate. It might also intensify the frustrations of enslavement and leave those slaves feeling deeply alienated from the larger number of blacks who labored more routinely and rigorously as field hands.

Most plantations did not contain mills or clothing manufactures but existed almost solely for the production of tobacco and, sometimes, other crops. The planter's large house usually faced a river, with the slave cabins in the distance. The Westmoreland County mansion that had thirty-three buildings around it, including a brewery and a spinning center, was indeed an exception. Few plantations contained more than a thousand acres or more than one hundred slaves.

Yet leadership in Virginia society remained dominated by a small elite group of large planters. Aristocratic families such as the Carters, Lees, Byrds, and Randolphs maintained their power through close association and intermarriage. By the eighteenth century the grandeur of their Georgian-style mansions overshadowed the humbler dwellings of their predecessors. The most stylish and expensive European furniture was imported to fill their huge stately rooms. If the appropriate articles could not be found, artisans could be employed to create worthy imitations. The atmosphere of wealth and a life of ease led this ruling class to pursue pleasures of the present, although (superficially, at least) in a more dignified manner than had its predecessors when tobacco had first brought easy riches. By the eighteenth century, the Virginia elite's days were filled with horse racing, fox hunting, and partying. Even after the founding of the College of William and Mary in Williamsburg in 1693, few planters' sons ever gave more thought to serious studies than had their fathers.

Although they might live on self-sufficient plantations, needing only to sell tobacco to England in return for the much-demanded luxury items, the planters' association with one another and their elevated social position above other farmers required that they assume active leadership in directing the colony. The interest of large planters in buying the crops of smaller farmers, selling them goods in turn and lending their less prosperous neighbors money, moved the tobacco elite toward directing politics within Virginia, both through the local county courts and as members of the House of Burgesses. These few great families also held themselves responsible for managing the religious life of the colony, usually through the appointment of Anglican ministers. The supreme irony of the Virginia planters' world occurred in the mid-eighteenth century when, out of this social context of elitism and slavery, there emerged the greatest champions of freedom and liberty in the American Revolution: men such as George Washington, Thomas Jefferson, James Madison, James Monroe, and Patrick Henry. But earlier in the eighteenth century, these "gentlemen freeholders" and their families held no particular thoughts of rebellion from the comforts of provincial society and benign English rule.

THE LATER SOUTHERN COLONIES

Maryland

Unlike Virginia, the colony of Maryland was founded when King Charles I gave a grant of land to a *single* proprietor and not a company. Initially the grant was made to Sir George Calvert, the first Lord Baltimore, who had been a stockholder of the London Company and had made an unsuccessful earlier effort to establish his own colony in Newfoundland. He had then emigrated to Virginia, but was ordered out for maintaining his Roman Catholic faith. Baltimore died before the Maryland charter received final approval in 1632, but his son, Leonard,[1] led the first group of Catholic settlers to

---

[1] Leonard's older brother, Cecelius, the second Lord Baltimore and first proprietor of Maryland, remained in England to defend his charter against Protestant attacks.

St. Mary's at the mouth of the Potomac River in 1634. They did not suffer through any period of starvation as their southern neighbors had at Jamestown; the Virginia settlement was near, and the newcomers maintained friendly relations with the coastal Indian tribes (unlike Virginia's more brutal experiences).

Despite its Catholic origins, the colony eventually allowed Protestants to settle there as well. Maryland provided a haven for English and Irish Catholics who faced oppression at home, but once Protestants began settling, the Baltimore proprietors urged that they be treated civilly. During the English Civil War in the 1640s, Virginia's loyalty to the crown helped spur anti-Puritan feelings in that colony, but Maryland allowed hundreds of Puritan immigrants to seek refuge there. This influx of Protestants led Baltimore to introduce his Toleration Act in 1649 to protect what had become, by then, a Catholic *minority* in the colony. Although the act required belief in Christianity, the document set a standard of religious tolerance for the Southern colonies of North America by endorsing the coexistence of different Christian sects —no small achievement in that age of religious warfare in England itself. Only Rhode Island further north practiced comparable religious tolerance toward dissenters.

After Oliver Cromwell and the Puritans triumphed in England in 1650, Puritans eventually came into power in Maryland, repealing the Toleration Act and helping to precipitate a small-scale religious war. Baltimore had summoned an assembly, since the royal charter guaranteed that all freemen should have a role in the making of laws. But the proprietor allowed the assembly little power, while awarding most of the important offices to relatives and Catholic friends. The outbreak of hostilities in Maryland in 1654 reflected the antagonism between Protestant small farmers and Catholic larger planters and lords. By 1657, Baltimore had recovered control of the colony, which again served as the tolerant home of Catholics and Protestants alike. At the same time, Maryland became prosperous, growing tobacco in the same soil and climate that Virginians had for decades—and growing wealthy like their neighbors across Chesapeake Bay.

William Byrd

I n the beginning, all America was Virginia." The author of those words, William Byrd of Westover (1674–1744), was an archetypal member of Virginia's plantation aristocracy: farmer, writer, colonial official, businessman, surveyor, and bibliophile (among his many interests). Byrd's life spanned the transforming decades in provincial American society—from Bacon's Rebellion to the mid-eighteenth century. As a leading member of the colonial elite, Byrd lived within the orbit of an Anglo-Virginian cultural world that would produce, one generation later, many of the leaders of the American Revolution. In his own time, however, politics lacked any focus beyond Virginia's borders. Gentlemen such as Byrd consumed their energies in a wide variety of economic, literary, and personal pursuits.

Raised on a plantation in frontier territory, son of a wealthy planter also named William Byrd, he was shipped off to relatives in England for education while still a boy. Eventually he studied law at the Middle Temple in London while also cultivating a taste for the literary life. Byrd became friendly with famous playwrights such as Congreve and Wycherley before returning to Virginia in 1692. Already a widely-known figure in the colony because of his father's economic position and his own large circle of influential friends, Byrd was elected to the House of Burgesses the year he returned from England. He became active in the colony's political life and, in 1697, again traveled to England where, the following year, he became Virginia's agent. (Byrd served two periods as colonial agent in England, 1697–1705 and 1715–26.) When the elder Byrd died in 1705, his son returned to the family estate at Westover and married within his class the following year.

Byrd resumed his political career and became a member of the Virginia Council of State in 1709. Over the next decade, Byrd and other members of the plantation gentry battled with the Lieutenant-Governor, Alexander Spotswood, who unsuccessfully attempted to assert royal prerogative against the interests of the leading planters. In 1718, Spotswood failed in an attempt to have Byrd removed from the Council and, in 1720, himself lost his post.

Turning increasingly to economic interests, Byrd pursued a relentless policy of land accumulation and speculation, increasing his acreage from 26,000 to 180,000 before his death. Like other Virginia planters, he was, at the same time, sometimes forced to sell slaves and land to pay his debts. He was a commissioner or surveyor of boundary lands between colonies, owned much land in frontier regions, and was committed to Virginia's expansion westward both for strategic reasons (to deny the French access to the territory) and economic ones. Byrd's *History of the Dividing Line* (between North Carolina and Virginia), a book first published in 1841, several other manuscripts, and voluminous private correspondence revealed Byrd's urbane and lively imagination. A Fellow and corresponding member of the Royal Society of London, Byrd owned what was probably the largest private collection of books (over 4,000 volumes on all subjects) in the American colonies at the time.

Byrd pursued his energetic and varied interests virtually to the time of his death in August 1744. Only with the posthumous publication of his manuscripts and letters, however, has the full measure of William Byrd of Westover—Virginia patrician—finally emerged. "A library, a garden, a grove, and a purling stream are the innocent scenes that divert our leisure," Byrd wrote of his Westover, Virginia, mansion. He might as easily have added his *outdoor* pursuits to the list: planter, councillor, speculator, surveyor, entrepreneur, and unofficial one-man cultural ambassador between the American and English Enlightenments.

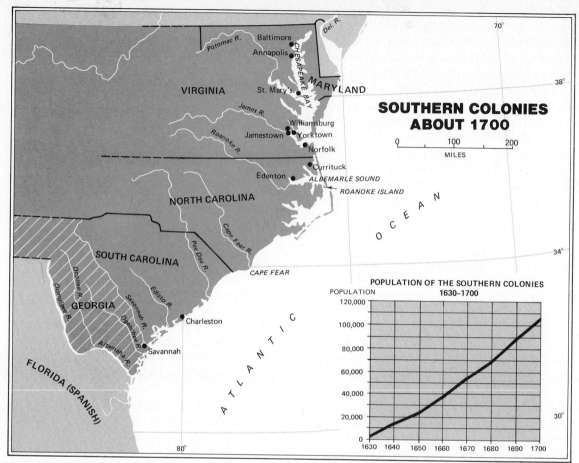

SOUTHERN COLONIES ABOUT 1700

0   100   200
MILES

POPULATION OF THE SOUTHERN COLONIES 1630–1700

Permanent English settlement in the Southern colonies began after the Virginia grant of 1606. From then on, English kings carved big chunks of land out of Virginia to form the four other Southern colonies.

Land north of the Potomac River was given in proprietorship to Lord Baltimore in 1634. Land south was given to eight noblemen as proprietors by King Charles II in two separate grants in 1663 and 1665. The king hoped that this new colony, Carolina, would serve as a buffer state, protecting Virginia from Indian and Spanish attack. The first settlers to Carolina came in 1653 from Virginia. They settled in the northeast, along Albemarle Sound. Carolina was treated as one colony until 1712, when it became known as North Carolina and South Carolina.

The last mainland colony to be claimed was the land southwest of Carolina, between the Savannah and Altamaha rivers. Georgia was founded not as a proprietory nor as a corporate colony, but rather under the trusteeship of a group of Englishmen. The most famous of these trustees was James Oglethorpe. Oglethorpe's goal was to create a refuge for worthy Englishmen imprisoned for debt. The founding of this new colony delighted South Carolinians, who saw Georgia as a bulwark against the Spanish in Florida. By 1700 the population of the Southern colonies (excluding Georgia) was 104,588. Virginia was the most populous.

The Carolinas

After the death of Oliver Cromwell and the restoration of royal authority in England in 1660, interest in New World settlement revived. Just as his father before him had done with Lord Baltimore, Charles II made a large grant of land to eight of his noble friends in 1663. All of the eight had been extremely helpful in assisting Charles to recover the throne, and their reward was "Carolina," an enormous grant that included the area between Virginia and Spanish Florida, extending theoretically to the Pacific Ocean.[2] Some of these men had made fortunes in sugar plantations on the Caribbean colony of Barbados, and they now needed more land to expand their American ventures. Early Carolina, therefore, has been aptly described as the colony of a colony.

Even before Barbadians established the first permanent settlements along the Atlantic coast, the northern area of the colony, in the region of Albemarle Sound, had already been partially settled (without any land tenure rights) by poor Virginia farmers, criminals, and runaway slaves. They grew some tobacco but mainly dealt in subsistence farming. The new Carolina proprietors gave them a separate governor in 1664, and a popularly elected assembly sat for the first time in 1665. The region contained only about four or five thousand small farmers by 1700, but in 1729, King George II took control from the proprietors. The area became the royal colony of North Carolina.

The first expedition sponsored by the eight proprietors was undertaken in 1670 when English colonists from the Barbados as well as from the mother country established themselves at Charles Town (later Charleston) near the confluence of the Ashley and Cooper rivers on the Atlantic coast. There, the new settlers engaged in a thiving trade with local Indian tribes, acquiring furs and hides, as well as Indians captured from other tribes, which they sold as slaves to the Caribbean. By the early eighteenth century, there were over a thousand Indian slaves in the Carolina colony.

In Barbados, wealthy planters had created a society in which the vast majority of the population were Negro slaves, and by the early 1700s, blacks outnumbered whites in Carolina as well. In that colony, neither Barbados sugar nor Chesapeake tobacco became the colony's staple and primary source of wealth; that place was reserved for rice plantations. As in Virginia, high initial costs had kept down the number of slaves in the beginning, but Carolina's close ties with Barbados reinforced the idea of slave ownership as a source of social prestige. With the length of the white indentured servants' terms declining by the 1680s, black slaves became increasingly involved in all facets of the colony's economy: guiding ships through the river marshes, herding cattle, trading with the Indians, and serving as blacksmiths. African slaves helped to teach the English colonists how to plant, tend, and harvest rice—the key to Carolina's survival.

The ruling whites of South Carolina faced challenges from both red and black, Indians and Africans, as they expanded their economy during the first half of the eighteenth century. Whites insisted that the Yamasees, a tribe with whom they frequently traded, had fallen into debt to them, and therefore began seizing Indian women and children to be sold as slaves as partial repayment. The Yamasees were then able to forge alliances with other tribes and mount an impressive attack in 1715 against the whites, who survived, first, because they had taken the risk of arming their black slaves against the Indians and second, because they persuaded the Cherokees to fight with them against the Yamasees and the latter's allies, the Creeks (ancient enemies of the Cherokees).

By the 1730s, the colony's elite took steps to encourage the immigration of more whites, while passing laws that took skilled jobs away from blacks and assigned them to more menial duties. Fear of a black uprising remained when expansion of rice cultivation required the importation of large numbers of West African slaves. In 1739, a rebellion near Charleston of newly arrived blacks brought death to twenty-five whites in a region where rice cultivation was intensive and the black population highly concentrated. As a result, white South Carolinians passed a Comprehensive Negro Act reducing slave importations and outlawing private manumissions (freeing) of slaves. As in Virginia, the labor force needed to be secure and reliable for South Carolina's white planters, whatever the human cost to African slaves and local Indians.

Georgia

In 1732 George II made a grant of land that became the last colony founded on the North American mainland under English royal auspices.

---

[2] Carolina was named for King Charles, whose name in Latin is "Carolus." The Carolina proprietors included Sir William Berkeley, Governor of Virginia during Bacon's Rebellion.

Charles Calvert (child), the third Lord Baltimore, was governor of Maryland during a period of traumatic upheaval both in England and in the colony. His Catholic co-religionists had become Maryland's minority by then. Despite Calvert's efforts, his family's charter was abandoned after the Glorious Revolution in England in 1689. (Courtesy, Enoch Pratt Free Library)

He gave the unsettled southernmost part of Carolina to James Oglethorpe, who hoped to use the new settlement to create a home for thousands of the English poor and imprisoned. (Many of Georgia's earliest settlers came directly from English prisons.) Oglethorpe and the first hundred colonists arrived in 1733 and founded the city of Savannah near the South Carolina border. The founders of Georgia hoped that the new colony would also serve as protection against Spanish incursions, from Florida outposts, into England's more northerly provinces, while producing badly needed silk to export to the mother country.

The trustees of Georgia, led by Oglethorpe, hoped to reach their humanitarian goals by creating a society of small, hardworking farmers not unlike those in the New England colonies and in Pennsylvania. Capital for this project came from Parliament and from private donations by the trustees themselves. With the Spanish close by and always threatening, settlements in Georgia were kept small and compact. Land sales were prohibited to avoid speculation and expansion. Slavery was outlawed at first, landholdings limited to 500 acres, and the settlers forced to grow silk which was less profitable than tobacco or rice. Alcohol was also prohibited to encourage both greater productivity and an elevated moral level in the colony. The controls exercised by the trustees discouraged migration and private investment.

Pressure from newcomers and South Carolinians soon forced the abandonment of Oglethorpe's noble experiment, however. Farmers within Georgia were discontented with their compulsory military service, restrictions upon expanding their land holdings, and the paternalistic bureaucratic controls exercised by the Georgia proprietors. By 1742, the ban on rum had been removed, and by 1750, slavery was permitted. This led, in turn, to an increase in the number of rice plantations and in the size of estates. When Georgia finally became a royal colony in 1752, it had already acquired the social structure common to neighboring provinces, including slavery and a racist caste structure, which would separate its interests and those of the other Southern colonies from the patterns that characterized English settlements farther to the north. Nor must it be forgotten that the whole process of English settlement in the Southern colonies stretched out over more than a century, with Georgia being established a century-and-a-quarter after Jamestown. The arc of settlement in the South from Jamestown to Georgia had its Northern counterpart in the more than half-century of colonization running from Pilgrim Plymouth to Quaker Philadelphia.

Suggested Readings
Chapters 3-4

Jamestown

Philip L. Barbour, *Pocahontas and Her World* (1969) and *The Three Worlds of Captain John Smith* (1964); Carl Bridenbaugh, *Jamestown, 1544-1699* (1980); E. H. Campbell, *Jamestown: The Beginning* (1974); Frances Mossiker, *Pocahontas: The Life and the Legend* (1976); Bernard Sheehan, *Savagism and Civility: Indians and Englishmen in Colonial Virginia* (1980); Alden T. Vaughan, *American Genesis: Captain John Smith and the Founding of Virginia* (1975).

Colonial Virginia and English Backgrounds

C. M. Andrews, *The Colonial Period in American History*, (Vols I-III, 1934-1937); Carl Bridenbaugh, *Vexed and Troubled Englishmen, 1590-1642* (1968); Verner Crane, *The Southern Frontier, 1670-1732* (1977); W. F. Craven, *The Southern Colonies in the Seventeenth Century, 1607-1689* (1949); Hugh Honour, *The New Golden Land* (1975); Edmund S. Morgan, *American Slavery, American Freedom* (1975); Richard L. Morton, *Colonial Virginia* (2 vols., 1960); J. E. Pomfret and F. M. Shumway, *Founding the American Colonies* (1970); David B. Quinn, *England and the Discovery of America, 1481-1620* (1974); A. L. Rowse, *Elizabethans and America* (1959); James M. Smith, ed., *Seventeenth Century America* (1959); Clarence L. Ver Steeg, *The Formative Years, 1607-1763* (1964); Wilcomb E. Washburn, *The Governor and the Rebel* (1957); G. F. Willison, *Behold Virginia* (1951); Louis B. Wright, *The Cultural Life of the American Colonies, 1607-1763* (1964).

Southern Colonies

Carl Bridenbaugh, *Myths and Realities: Societies of the Colonial South* (1963); L. C. Gray, *History of Agriculture in the Southern United States to 1860* (2 vols., 1933); Marcus W. Jernegan, *Laboring and Dependent Classes in Colonial America, 1607-1783* (1931); Hugh T. Lefler and Albert R. Newsome, *North Carolina* (1954); T. R. Reese, *Colonial Georgia* (1963); M. Eugene Sirmans, *Colonial South Carolina* (1966); A. E. Smith, *Colonists in Bondage* (1974).

Indians, Blacks, and the Problem of Slavery

Philip D. Curtin, *The Atlantic Slave Trade* (1970); David Brion Davis, *The Problem of Slavery in Western Culture* (1966); Carl Degler, *Neither Black Nor White* (1971); H. R. Driver, *Indians of North America* (2nd ed., 1970); John Hope Franklin, *From Slavery to Freedom* (1980 ed.); Eugene D. Genovese, *The World the Slaveholders Made* (1970); Wilbur R. Jacobs, *Dispossessing the American Indian* (1972); Winthrop D. Jordan, *White Over Black: American Attitudes Toward the Negro, 1550-1812* (1968); A. L. Kroeber, *Cultural and Natural Areas of Native North America* (1939 and later eds.); Edmund S. Morgan, *American Slavery, American Freedom* (1975); Gary Nash, *Red, White, and Black: The Peoples of Early America* (1974); Wilcomb E. Washburn, *The Indian in America* (1975); Peter Wood, *Black Majority* (1974).

5 The Witches of Salem

The charge: witchcraft. Dragged from her sickbed to be questioned at the Salem Village meeting house on March 23, 1692, seventy-three-year-old Rebecca Nurse calmly awaited her accusers. Ailing and nearly deaf, she could barely hear herself charged with "suspicion of having committed . . . acts of witchcraft and thereby having done much hurt and injury to the bodies of Ann Putnam, the wife of Thomas Putnam of Salem Village, and Ann Putnam, the daughter of said Thomas Putnam, and Abigail Williams, etc."

Twelve-year-old Abigail Williams had been the first to name Goodwife Nurse[1] as a witch four days earlier when, at the Putnam home, Abigail suddenly broke into what one observer described as a "grievous fit":

> sometimes makeing as if she would fly, stretching up her arms as high as she could and crying "Whish, Whish, Whish" several times; Presently after she said there was Goodw. N [Nurse] and said "Do you not see her? Why, there she stands!" And then said Goodw. N offered her The Book, and she was resolved she would not take it, saying Often, "I won't, I won't, I won't take it. I do not know what Book it is; I am sure it is none of God's Book, it is the Devil's Book, for ought I know." After that she run to the Fire, and begun to throw Fire Brands about the house. . . .

Another twelve-year-old, Ann Putnam, supported Abigail's charges two days later at the examination of Martha Cory, another Salem woman accused of witchcraft. "She thought Goodw. N. Praying . . . to the Devil," Ann told a meeting house "thronged with spectators." Although "she was not sure it was Goodw. N., she thought it was."

By the time Rebecca Nurse appeared before Magistrates John Hathorne and Jonathan Corwin on March 24, the lists of her accusers had grown. Ann Putnam's mother, also named Ann, had gone into a fit the previous day, which she blamed on a visit from Rebecca Nurse's "apparition." When Deodat Lawson, a former minister of Salem Village, saw

---

[1] "Goodwife" was the favored term of respect for married women in Puritan New England.

Salem was caught in a frenzy of witchcraft accusations and denials. The painting is a late-nineteenth-century artist's attempt to capture the hysterical quality of the proceedings. One of the young accusers writhes in apparent agony on the floor before the examining magistrates while an accused witch defends herself. (Library of Congress)

Goodwife Putnam that day, she "was so stiff, she could not be bended . . . [then] quickly began to strive violently with her Arms and Legs . . . and as it were to Converse personally with Goodw. N., saying, 'Goodw. N. Be gone! Be gone! Be gone! Are you not ashamed . . . to afflict a poor Creature so?'" During her examination by the magistrates, a pair of seventeen-year-olds, Mary Walcott and Elizabeth Hubbard, chimed in accusing Rebecca's apparition of having hurt them "most grievously."

But to her large family and her many friends in the village, Rebecca Nurse seemed a most unlikely witch. She and her husband Francis Nurse were among Salem's most respected figures, tilling a prosperous three-hundred-acre farm alongside their four sons and four daughters. A deeply religious woman, Rebecca differed from most of the unsavory or unpopular women in Salem Village who had recently been charged with witchcraft (for Rebecca was not the first person to be so accused). Thus, when the magistrates questioned Rebecca on March 24 to decide whether she should stand trial, even they seemed uncertain. "If you have confessed and give Glory to God," commented one a bit confusingly, "I pray God clear you, if you are innocent. And if you be guilty, discover you."

The examination proved a bedlam. Shrieks from Rebecca's "afflicted" accusers frequently punctuated the questions that Salem Village's minister, the Reverend Samuel Parris, dutifully recorded:

MR. HATHORNE: What do you say (speaking to one afflicted), have you seen this woman hurt you?

Yes, she beat me this morning.

Abigail, have you been hurt by this woman?

Yes.

Ann Putnam, in a grievous fit, cried out that she hurt her.

[HATHORNE]: Goody Nurse, here are two—Ann Putnam the child and Abigail Williams—complain of your hurting them. What do you say to it?

N. [NURSE]: I can say before my Eternal Father, I am innocent, and God will clear my innocency . . . I never afflicted no child, never in my life.

[H.]: You see these accuse you. Is it true?

[N.]: No

[H.]: Are you an innocent person, relating to this witchcraft?
Here Tho. Putnam's wife (Ann) cried out: Did you not bring the Black man with you? Did you not bid me tempt God and die? How oft have you eat and drunk your own damnation? What do you say to them?

Suddenly the "afflicted" girls and woman began howling as if stirred by Ann Putnam Senior's shouted question, screaming out that Rebecca Nurse's apparition was pursuing them. Hathorne complained to the witness: "It is very awful for all to see these agonies, and you, an old professor, this charged with contracting with the devil by the effects of it, and yet to see you stand with dry eyes when there are so many wet."

Rebecca snapped back: "You do not know my heart . . . I am as clear as the child unborn." She denied having caused her accusers any pain. Yet, at virtually every movement of Rebecca's hands or body, "the afflicted persons were seized with violent fits of torture." Rebecca agreed with Hathorne that the afflicted females appeared "bewitched," but she could not explain the cause of their suffering: "I cannot help it," she finally conceded; "the Devil may appear in my shape."

Exhausted by the questioning, Rebecca hung her head down to one side. Immediately, Elizabeth Hubbard's neck drooped to the same position, while Abigail Williams screamed: "Set up Goody Nurse's head, [or] the maid's neck will be broke." Those closest to Rebecca raised her neck to an unright position, after which Elizabeth Hubbard's neck also straightened out at once.

With such strong evidence, the magistrates ordered Rebecca Nurse imprisoned to await trial. Their indictment charged her with having committed against Ann Putnam Junior, Mary Walcott, Elizabeth Hubbard, and Abigail Williams "certain detestable arts called Witchcraft and Sorceries." According to the charges, Rebecca had allegedly "hurt, tortured, afflicted, consumed, pined, wasted, and tormented" all of the accusing girls. Her apparition had appeared before them a number of times, moreover, pummeling and otherwise injuring them by "Biting, Pinching, Bruising, Tormenting, at their Breasts, by her Leaning, and when, bended Back, as if their Backs were Broken." The afflicted girls also claimed that Rebecca had confessed to them a variety of murders (with six children among the alleged victims). Most of the accusers also mentioned the presence of a black man hovering near Rebecca and occasionally whisper-

A fragment of the "Examination of Rebecca Nurse" at Salem Village in the handwriting of Rev. Mr. Parris. (Courtesy, Essex Institute, Salem, Mass.)

ing instructions to her, presumably a reference to the Devil images associated with "blackness" in that era among Englishmen and other Europeans.

When Rebecca's trial took place on June 30, her accusers repeated their earlier statements: Goody Nurse's apparition had tormented them. Again, Rebecca protested her innocence. Other witnesses linked Rebecca to various deaths in the Salem community. A neighbor's widow even claimed that Rebecca had caused her husband's sudden death after an argument they had had because his pigs had accidentally strayed into the Nurses's fields.

Possibly the strangest (yet in a sense the most *tangible*) "evidence" presented for Rebecca Nurse's alleged witchery came from a local physician, one "J. Barton, Surgeon," who had inspected five women then being tried for witchcraft — including Rebecca Nurse — assisted by several other women of Salem. According to their deposition, the group found on Nurse and two others "a preternatural excrescence of flesh between the pudendum and anus, much like to teats, and not usual in women" — in short, "witches' tit" markings considered "proof" of devilish connection. More startling still, according to this account, when inspected three or four hours later, Rebecca's skin was "dry," free, and clear of any "preter-

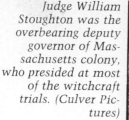

Judge William Stoughton was the overbearing deputy governor of Massachusetts colony, who presided at most of the witchcraft trials. (Culver Pictures)

natural excrescence." The evidence of "J. Barton, Surgeon" suggested some supernatural tampering with Rebecca's body, but the accused woman protested the conclusion. Any marks upon her ancient flesh, Rebecca avowed, came from a simple and *natural* cause—aging.

The jury brought back an unexpected verdict of "*not* guilty" for Rebecca, a tribute to her reputation within Salem considering the array of witnesses against her. Unfortunately, the nearly deaf woman failed to hear the verdict. Nor, though she watched the scene, could she hear the commotion which followed when her small group of accusers reacted to it:

> Immediately all the accusers in the Court, and suddenly all the afflicted out of Court, made a hideous out-cry, to the amazement, not only of the Spectators, but the Court also seemed strangely surprised; one of the Judges expressed himself not satisfied, another of them as he was going off the Bench, said they would have her Indicted anew.

Through all this, Rebecca stood patiently awaiting the court's instructions. But the accusers' shrieks and Rebecca's own flawed hearing now doomed her.

Massachusetts Bay's newly arrived governor, Sir William Phips, had assigned Chief Justice William Stoughton, the colony's lieutenant governor, to try the witchcraft cases. Stoughton asked whether jury members had "considered one Expression of the Prisoner's, when she was upon Tryal, viz. That one Hobbs, who had confessed her self to be a Witch, was brought into court to testify against her, the Prisoner turning her head to her, said 'What, do you bring her? she is one of us,' or to that effect."

The jury withdrew to reconsider its verdict, stirred by Stoughton's question and by the "Clamours of the Accused." They came to no agreement, returned to court, and repeated the allegedly offensive words to Rebecca Nurse for an explanation. By "one of us," had she meant another witch? Had this been an inadvertent confession of guilt? But Rebecca failed to hear the jury's question and, therefore, failed to reply. Again the jury left the court, this time returning with a verdict of "guilty." (Later, when the matter was finally explained to her, Rebecca Nurse insisted that she had referred to Deliverance Hobbs only as another *defendant* — "one of us" — but by then the damage was done.)

Several days later, the ailing woman was carried in a chair from prison to the meeting house to "hear" both her death sentence and her excommunication from the Salem church. Forty Salem residents petitioned Govenor Phips on Rebecca's behalf, and at first, Phips granted a reprieve of her death sentence. But upon learning of this, "the Accusers renewed their dismal outcries against her," and the governor withdrew his reprieve. Rebecca Nurse and four other women convicted of witchcraft were hanged on Salem's Gallows Hill on July 19. The five bodies were cut down from the gallows and thrown into a barely covered grave on the spot.

Rebecca appears to have gone to her death as quietly and uncomplainingly as she had lived with her ordeal from the beginning. Not so for another of her companions that day. When the Reverend Nicholas Noyes asked Sarah Good one last time to confess and save her soul by admitting her witchcraft, Sarah shouted, back: "You're a liar. I am no more a witch than you are a wizard! If you take my life away, God will give you blood to drink."

Why did Nurse, Good, and the others have to die? How had witchcraft first become an issue in the apparently peaceful Massachusetts Bay colony community of Salem? The trouble started two months before Rebecca Nurse was accused, in January 1692, in the home of Salem Village's minister, Samuel Parris, with the strange illness of his nine-year-old daughter Betty. The child would suddenly lapse into uncontrollable fits of weeping or, on other occasions, would wander distractedly through the house without any thought of those around her. Sometimes Betty sat quietly for hours oblivious to the world, as if in a trance, and when shaken out of the mood, she would scream frantically. The minister and his wife prayed intently for their daughter. But Parris tried to keep Betty's bizarre behavior secret until her cousin, Abigail Williams (age twelve), began displaying similar and even more alarming signs of affliction.

By then it was February, and the sickness, however caused, had spread to other young women in Salem: Elizabeth Hubbard (age seventeen), Mary Walcott (age sixteen), Mercy Lewis (age nineteen), Ann Putnam, Junior (age twelve), and Mary Warren (age twenty). Their behavior began to terrify the entire Salem community. The girls appeared prey to hysterical and abrupt convulsions. "Their arms, necks, and backs," wrote the Reverend John Hale, who had been summoned to witness and pray for the afflicted, "were turned this way and that way, and returned back again, so it was impossible for them to do of themselves, and beyond the power of any epileptic fits, or natural disease to effect."

All of the young women hallucinated regularly and complained about apparitions which bit and pinched them. Sometimes the victims displayed physical evidence of bites and punctures on their bodies. Often the girls could be found, according to one description, "getting into Holes, and creeping under Chairs and Stools, and [using other] Odd Postures and Antick Gestures, uttering foolish, ridiculous Speeches, which neither they themselves nor any others could make sense of."

To New England Puritans of the 1690s, the signs seemed unmistakable. But the Reverend Parris, possibly because his own daughter and niece were involved, tried to avoid thinking about them at first. "When these calamities first began," Parris later wrote, "which was in my own family, the affliction was several weeks before such hellish operations as witchcraft were suspected."

Ministers from nearby Massachusetts Bay towns rode into Salem, summoned for their opinions. On March 11, Parris invited several of his godly colleagues from neighboring parishes to join him for a day of public prayer and fasting. The spectacle must have unnerved the ministers. During the prayer sessions, the afflicted girls kept silent. Between prayers, however, "they would Act and Speak strangely and Ridiculously." Abigail Williams would lapse into occasional convulsions, "her Limbs being twisted several ways, and very stiff" before her fits ended. Even before that day, one Salem doctor, William Griggs, had pronounced to Parris his personal judgment: Griggs "was afraid they were Bewitched." Sometime later that month, Samuel Parris sent his daughter Betty out of Salem Village to stay in nearby Salem Town, and the child never figured in the terrible events that followed.

Like most Europeans in the seventeenth century, Protestant or Catholic, the New England Puritans believed devoutly in the existence of evil supernatural forces, which often affected daily life, either directly or through malevolent "apparitions." These forces could change the behavior or warp the minds of *apparently* good and innocent Christians. The *reality of* witches and wizards (their male counterparts) seemed as obvious to those in the deeply religious towns of Massachusetts Bay as the existence of the Devil himself. They believed also that the Devil and his helpers often worked their "black magic" through the youngest and most innocent members of a community, a useful conviction since it served to bolster their belief that young people had to be severely controlled.

A crude English drawing of 1655 shows the hanging of witches. A hangman climbs up to check the bodies. Below stand three condemned women and various officers of the law. (R. Gardiner, England's Grievance Discovered, 1655)

Nor had Salem escaped the problem in earlier days. Massachusetts Bay's great early governor John Winthrop had written of one Dorothy Talbie, a Salem woman hanged in 1638 for murdering her three-year-old daughter, Difficult Talbie. The mother, according to Winthrop, "was so possessed with Satan, that he persuaded her (by his delusions, which she listened to as revelations from God), to break the neck of her own child...." But New England's history of punishing suspected witches had been remarkably mild when compared with Europe's. Thousands of accused persons were burned at the stake or hanged as convicted witches in seventeenth-century Europe, and in "old" England at the time, numerous "witches" lost their lives. But in the New England Puritan colonies, excepting Salem in 1692, fewer than twenty persons died on the gallows as witches during the entire century, while many more than this number were acquitted of witchcraft at their trials.

Yet the *scent* of witches may have first reached Salem from the larger and more influential neighboring city of Boston, where, in 1688, a

A very influential minister in Boston during the Salem trials, Cotton Mather was also the author of numerous books, among them a "study" of witchcraft. (NYPL/Picture Collection)

Gaelic-speaking old Irish woman, Goodwife Glover, was executed after confessing to having "afflicted" four young girls. The distinguished minister Cotton Mather had followed the case closely and even taken one of the girls into his home afterward in order to "cure" her affliction. Mather wrote extensively on the episode in a 1689 book, *Memorable Providences,* restating the accepted Puritan belief in an "invisible world" of witchcraft. Later, in 1692, Mather would be drawn to Salem, fascinated by its unfolding drama of that world. *If* the afflicted girls were telling the truth, it seemed evident almost from the start of the troubles that Salem Village harbored a massive "coven" (or group) of witches.

First to be named, according to most accounts, was a West Indian slave, Tituba. The Reverend Parris had brought her to Salem from the British island of Barbados, where he had lived as a merchant prior to becoming a minister. Parris had also brought Tituba's husband, another Caribbean native whom Salem residents called John Indian, and the couple both served the Parris household. Tituba later admitted to the magistrates that she had entertained young people with tales of the occult and with magical experiments recalled from her Caribbean youth, both undoubtedly influenced strongly by African cultural survivals in the West Indies. Tituba's first "circle" of listeners included Betty Parris and her cousin, Abigail Williams, but the group's size grew as word of Tituba's wondrous tales spread.

Late in February, at the request of Mary Siblet, "afflicted" Mary Walcott's aunt, Tituba and John Indian prepared a "witch's cake," a popular test at the time in England for exposing the presence of devilish behavior. They mixed rye meal with the afflicted children's urine, baked the "cake," and fed it to the Parrises' dog, which, considering Betty's initial involvement, had been considered a prime suspect as a possible "familiar" (an agent of the Devil who worked closely with the responsible witch). Apparently the dog survived and thus proved its innocence.

Although Samuel Parris complained bitterly, when he learned about the "witch's cake" test, that it smacked of "going to the Devil for help against the Devil," the problem was now clearly viewed by Parris and other village leaders as a virtual epidemic of witchcraft in their community, affecting by then almost a dozen of Salem's young women. After sharp and relentless questioning, the afflicted girls finally had named as the witches responsible for their suffering three people, all women of poor reputation in Salem: Tituba, the West Indian slave; a sharp-tongued young mother named Sarah Good; and Sarah Osborne, an old woman well-known for lying and a poor record of church attendance.

The afflicted girls had chosen well, since almost no one in Salem Village could be expected to step forward to defend the innocence of any in this trio of suspected witches. All of these unfortunate women were arrested on March 1.

To examine the three women, two members of the Massachusetts Bay legislature who lived in nearby Salem Town (five miles from Salem Village), John Hathorne and Jonathan Corwin, came for what would be the first of many pretrial questioning sessions. Hathorne, who handled most of the examination, usually assumed the accused guilty, and acted like a prosecutor seeking confessions:[2]

> HATHORNE: Sarah Good, what evil spirit have you familiarity with?
>
> GOOD: None.
>
> HATHORNE: Have you made no contract with the devil?
>
> GOOD: No.
>
> HATHORNE: Why do you hurt these children?
>
> GOOD: I do not hurt them. I scorn it.
>
> . . . HATHORNE: What creature do you employ then?
>
> GOOD: No creature. But I am falsely accused.

At that point, Hathorne ordered Good's accusers to look at her directly and confirm that Sarah had been the one who hurt them: "and so they all did look upon her and said this was one of the persons that did torment them. Presently they were all tormented." The shrieking and apparently agonized behavior of the afflicted girls while confronting the accused became one of the major proofs of a witch's guilt.

But Sarah Good persisted in her denials. When asked who was responsible, then, she replied, "It was Osborne." But naming Sarah Osborne only confirmed the magistrates' belief that Good herself was a witch. How else would she *know* another one? Nor did the testimony of William Good, Sarah's husband, help her case. Of his wife, a petulant woman whom Magistrate Hathorne said had answered his questions "in a very wicked, spiteful manner . . . with base and abusive words," William noted only that she "either was a witch or would be one very quickly." Although William denied having seen Sarah behave in a supernatural manner (an admission that would have led the trial directly to him), he described Sarah's "bad carriage to him" and, apparently with no pun intended, ended by observing: "I may say with tears that she is an enemy to all good." Even Sarah's four-year-old daughter Dorcas gave evidence against her mother, claiming that Sarah had used as familiars three birds that "hurt the children and afflicted persons." Dorcas, herself, though only four, was arrested on suspicion of witchcraft later in March and held chained in a dungeon for eight months before being released!

Of the three women originally arrested, only Tituba confessed her guilt. She tried in her testimony to divert the magistrates' and the girls' attention from her husband, John Indian, who might easily have faced arrest as the likeliest local candidate for the role of mysterious "black man" whom the possessed young women often mentioned in their narratives. Not only did Tituba implicate Sarah Good as her accomplice in evil (indeed, Tituba's testimony left no doubt that Good was the groups' ringleader), but more importantly, she confirmed for the magistrates what

---

[2] John Hathorne's great-great-grandson, Nathaniel, would change the spelling of the family name to "Hawthorne." Nathaniel wrote brilliantly of the Puritan mentality in his novel *The Scarlet Letter.*

Tituba was a slave in the house of Samuel Parris where the first two "afflicted" girls lived. She had come from the West Indies, and her exotic stories and "magic" tricks contributed to the emotional tension that underlay the girls' early seizures. (Library of Congress)

they evidently most wanted to hear: that the pain and suffering of the afflicted girls was *real* and caused by the presence of witches and at least one wizard.

"The devil came to me and bid me serve him," Tituba swore, adding that she had seen "four women sometimes hurt the children" along with a single man. The man was white-haired and clothed in black, a "tall man from Boston" — in short, a white stranger and *not* Salem's own John Indian! The man sometimes brought two other female witches with him from Boston, hence the *four* women. Always, the group forced Tituba to join their devilish work *against her will.* The "tall man from Boston" was evidently Tituba's description of the Devil, who also appeared on occasion in the shape of an animal: "a thing all over hairy, all the face hairy, and a long nose." He had brought the obligatory "Devil's book" with him, in which the names of witches such as Sarah Good were written and Good's mark signed (a symbol used as a signature by those unable to read and write).

Tituba described the Devil's procedures vividly. She included sketches of familiars used by Sarah Good, such as a yellow bird and a cat. The Caribbean slave also recalled riding on "a stick or pole and Good and Osborne behind me . . . taking hold of one another. . . ." And again, Tituba: "Sarah Good appeared like a wolf to [Elizabeth] Hubbard. . . . Good caused her to pinch the children. . . ."

Tituba's examination had sent the afflicted girls into convulsions inside the meeting house. When Hathorne demanded to know the tormenter's name, Tituba once more volunteered the news that she had seen Sarah Good's apparition at work. The young women agreed, and soon Tituba herself began convulsing: "I am blind now. I cannot see." The magistrates were persuaded. All three women were held for later trial, though only Sarah Good ever faced one. (Osborne died in jail, and Tituba was eventually sold by her jailer when the Reverend Parris refused to pay the jailer his fees.)

Without Tituba's startling testimony, the pursuit of witchcraft at Salem Village might have ended as inconclusively as had most earlier alleged outbreaks of the "invisible world" in New England. Even without her confession, the affair might have been blamed only on the three women—Tituba, Good, and Osborne—whose reputations set them apart from more respectable citizens. But the girls continued to experience fits and hysterical outbursts of even greater intensity. When Samuel Parris held his day of prayer and fasting on March 11, for example, they punctuated every pause in the proceedings with shrieks. At some level, conscious or otherwise, the afflicted youngsters—joined by some older women who also professed to be tormented—had begun to recognize that they enjoyed an extremely powerful hold upon the adults in their fear-ridden community. Naming someone as a witch or wizard could taint that person forever in the eyes of other Salem residents, even if the person managed to "prove" her or his innocence. And the girls' behavior was not only tolerated but encouraged by the examining magistrates and attending ministers (by the colony's traditional sources of authority, in short), supported also by the Parris and Putnam families, which (between them) accounted for a majority of the afflicted persons.

The hysterical girls soon found additional targets for their deadly accusations. The first three women named had been outcasts of questionable reputation. Many in Salem Village now wondered whether the charge of witchcraft could be sustained against more prominent churchgoing people.

The answer came on March 20. At Sunday prayer meeting, the afflicted girls found a new target, an articulate and respected woman named Martha Corey. The girls began their usual fits that day without first naming any tormenter, until Abigail Williams shouted out: "Look where Goodwife Corey sits on the Beam suckling her Yellow bird betwixt her fingers." Ann Putnam and others took up the cry about a yellow bird (Tituba had described such a bird as one of *Sarah Good*'s familiars), and the following day, Martha Corey found herself being examined at the crowded meeting house as a suspected witch.

When Martha entered the room, the afflicted girls began their full performance, screaming out that Martha was torturing them with bites and pinches. One Salem woman (claiming that Corey was "tearing out" her bowels) threw her muff and shoe at the accused witch, scoring a direct hit on Corey's head. When Goodwife Corey told the magistrates at the start that she wished to pray (and not *immediately* answer the allegations), the several hundred assembled townspeople murmured at her insolence.

Corey denied having afflicted the girls and protested that she was a God-fearing "Gospel woman," at which her accusers shouted back: "Ah! She was a Gospel witch." The girls followed each movement of Corey's with a physical display of pain, producing marks on their bodies which they alleged Corey was inflicting upon them even at that very moment. One witness, Deodat Lawson, later provided this description of the way in which the magistrates often allowed afflicted girls to direct the examination (Corey persisted in denying all charges):

They affirmed, she [Corey] had a Yellow-Bird, that used to suck betwixt her Fingers, and being asked about it, if she had any Familiar Spirit, that attended her, she said, She had no Familiarity with any such thing . . . The afflicted persons asked her why she did not go to the company of Witches which were before the Meeting house mustering? Did she not hear the Drum beat? They accused her of having Familiarity with the Devil, in the time of Examination, in the shape of a Black man whispering in her ear . . . They told her, she had Covenanted with the Devil for ten years, six of them were gone, and four more to come.

The most startling piece of news to those at Martha Corey's hearing was the "company of Witches" supposedly mustering directly outside the meeting house while beating on drums. That drum beat, more than any previous accusations by the afflicted, signaled the escalation of the girls' assault upon respectable members of the church and village with accusations of complicity in witchcraft. It was also at Martha Corey's interrogation that Ann Putnam first raised Rebecca Nurse's name as another witch. After Corey was held for trial, Rebecca was summoned from her sickbed to begin her long ordeal to the gallows.

Thus even the most prominent, wealthy, and respected figures in Salem Village were no longer safe from the screams of the afflicted girls. The matter had become a colony-wide concern, in fact, and the examinations that followed Nurse's, on April 11, were moved to Salem Town's larger meeting house. Those hearings were not only attended by Magistrates Hathorne and Corwin but were also observed by Deputy Governor Thomas Danforth (who would be replaced by William Stoughton later that year), half a dozen additional magistrates, and a number of concerned ministers.

The "company of witches" grew with each feverish outburst by the afflicted girls. Thus Abigail Williams found on March 31 that "she saw a great number of Persons in the Village at the Administration of a Mock Sacrament, where they had Bread as red as raw Flesh, and red Drink"—a kind of black mass linked to witchcraft ceremonies. No longer was it even safe to be related to an accused person, as Sarah Cloyce, Rebecca Nurse's sister, discovered on April 3, when she suddenly stood up and walked out of The Reverend Parris's "Sacrament Day" sermon after Parris named his Text: "6. John, 70. *Have I not chosen you Twelve, and one of you is a Devil.*" When the wind shut the meeting house door with a long bang behind Sarah, suspicions spread immediately: "she was soon after complain'd of, examin'd and Committed" to arrest on witchcraft charges.

Those courageous enough to challenge the genuineness of the afflicted girls' torments found themselves immediately suspect. John Proctor, a prosperous Salem Village farmer, discovered this when he came

to take home his servant, Mary Warren, one of the accusers, the day after Rebecca Nurse's examination. Proctor did not bother hiding his contempt for the witch hunt or for what he considered the shameful gullibility of the magistrates who believed the young women: "If they were let alone, we should all be devils and witches quickly," Proctor stated according to one account. "They should rather be had to the whipping post. But he would fetch his jade [that is, Mary Warren] home and thrash the Devil out of her." Within days of this incident, John Proctor's *wife* Elizabeth had been denounced as a witch and arrested.

One of Elizabeth Proctor's chief accusers (he also denounced Sarah Cloyce as a witch) was Tituba's husband, John Indian, who had joined the girls as a prime witness for the examining magistrates. Stories of witches' conclaves at Salem had become even more elaborate by this time. Mary Walcott and Abigail Williams, for example, now identified those attending one such gathering as Rebecca Nurse, Martha Corey, Sarah Good, and Sarah Cloyce. The combinations seemed ever more expandable as "old" witches and newly accused ones shared the spotlight in the revised tales of the invisible world.

When Elizabeth Proctor's turn came to deny the accusations on April 11, the girls went through their usual repertoire of convulsions and fits timed to coincide with Elizabeth's movements, John Indian joining in the ranks of tormented ones this time. Elizabeth, who was then pregnant, denied their charges: "I take God in heaven to be my witness that I know nothing of it, no more than the child unborn."

Not content to denounce Goodwife Proctor alone, Abigail Williams and Ann Putnam Junior suddenly cried out that *John* Proctor's apparition floated above them on a high beam in the meeting house along with his wife's, which meant that Proctor was a wizard. Proctor's arrest and jailing provoked the first recantation among the afflicted girls. His "jade," the impressionable Mary Warren, evidently infatuated with Proctor, began retracting her own earlier testimony. Mary now insisted that she and the other young women had been making false charges from the beginning. Even their fits, she asserted to a stunned meeting house audience, had been false and contrived. After this, Mary Warren confronted the magistrates next on April 19, not as one of the afflicted but—given the twisted logic of the examining magistrates—herself accused of witchcraft.

Hathorne asked the inevitable question: "You were a little while ago an afflicted person. Now you are an afflicter. How comes this to pass?" Mary Warren: "I look up to God and take it to be a great mercy of God." Hathorne: "What! Do you take it to be a great mercy to afflict others?" When the remaining group of afflicted girls greeted Mary's testimony with the inevitable convulsions and hysteria, Mary lost her nerve. Apparently confused beyond words about what to say or believe, she began to babble: "I will speak. . . . Oh! I am sorry for it, I am sorry for it . . . Oh Lord help me! Oh good Lord save me!" Shaking with seizures herself by this time, which alternated with minutes of stony silence, Mary Warren finally blurted out "I will tell, I will tell," only to "tell" nothing. Then she indicated the latest direction of her mind by screaming, "I will tell! They did! They did! They did! . . . I will tell! They brought me to it!"

Days later, Mary Warren returned quietly to the ranks of the afflicted, not only confirming for the magistrates that John and Elizabeth Proctor were guilty but also denouncing several others as witches within Salem. As for the Proctors, once they went to prison, the sheriff of Essex County (of which Salem Village formed a part) followed the letter of the law, which allowed confiscation of property in such cases. He

> came to Proctor's house and seized all the Goods, Provisions, and Cattle that he could come at, and sold some of the Cattle at half price, and killed others, and put them up for the West-Indies; threw the Beer out of a Barrel, and carried away the Barrel; emptied a Pot of Broath, and took away the Pot, and left nothing in the House for the support of the Children: No part of the said Goods are known to be returned. . . .

Over two dozen people at Salem Village *confessed* to some complicity in witchcraft during 1692, either as "afflicted" persons or as accused witches and wizards. Many of them suffered from the same psychological pressures that had turned young persons like Mary Warren into fearful hysterics. Many of the "confessions," therefore, must be considered (for whatever reason) voluntary ones *up to a point*. Others came only through coercion. Magistrates such as Hathorne browbeat terrified witnesses into bargaining for their lives by making false and extravagant statements about their lives as witches or wizards (and about the complicity of others in the community). Those who confessed a role in the in-

visible world usually lived to survive those terrible months, while accused persons who claimed to be innocent and challenged the afflicted girls' reliability often paid with their lives.

Some confessions were coerced by barbaric means. Thus John Proctor wrote from Salem prison in July 1692 to a group of Boston ministers (who had expressed concern over the events at Salem Village) about five of his fellow prisoners whose confessions "we know to be Lies":

> Two of the 5 are [Martha] Carrier's [Sons], Young-men, who would not confess any thing till they tyed them Neck and Heels till the Blood was ready to come out of their Noses. . . . My son William Proctor, when he was examin'd, because he would not confess that he was Guilty, when he was Innocent, they tyed him Neck and Heels till the Blood gushed out at his Nose. . . .

One stubborn victim of the witchcraft craze, Martha Corey's husband Giles, "stood mute" and refused to stand formal trial. Huge boulders were placed on Gile's chest as punishment in an effort to force him to testify against Martha or himself. But Corey, "pressed" to death, went to his grave unrepentant, his last words of contempt reportedly: "More weight!"

Despite the many accusations, inquisitors remained unpersuaded that the young women had identified the *leader* of this local "company of witches." Then, on April 20, Ann Putnam Junior "discovered" him. The news could not have been worse.

As her father and others watched Ann lapse into one of her seizures, she suddenly shouted out: "Oh, dreadful, dreadful! Here is a minister come. What, are ministers witches too? . . . Oh dreadful, tell me your name that I may know who you are." By this time, according to Ann, "Dreadful" had begun choking and hurting her in the usual fashion of witches and wizards. Surprisingly, the apparition proceeded to identify himself to Ann Putnam and to catalog his iniquities.

It took only a few days for Ann's intimate cohorts—among them Abigail Williams, Mary Walcott, Mary Warren, Mercy Lewis, and the confessed witches Abigail and Deliverance Hobbs—to confirm the devilish presence of this ministerial apparition. Ann Putnam Junior later described her initial encounter with "Dreadful":

> . . . he told me that his name was George Burroughs, and that he had had three wives, and that he had bewitched the first two of them to death, and that he killed Mistress Lawson because she was so unwilling to go from the village [with him], and also killed Mr. Lawson's child . . . and that he had bewitched a great many soldiers to death . . . and that he had made Abigail Hobbs a witch, and several witches more. And he has continued ever since, by times tempting me to write in his [Devil's] book and grievously torturing me by beating, pinching, and almost choking me several times a day. And he also told me that he was above a witch, he was a conjurer.

The Reverend George Burroughs seemed to many at Salem a likely candidate for the role of "conjurer" or even chief wizard. Burroughs had served as Salem Village's minister from 1680 to 1683 before leaving for a frontier congregation in the Maine wilderness. Reports of his cruelty toward his first two wives, and of somewhat mysterious personal habits while at Salem, fueled the hostility toward him. From the start, the magistrates were willing to believe the accusations made by Putnam and the others against Burroughs. On April 30 they ordered the minister arrested and returned to Salem for questioning. When examined on May 9, Burroughs denied the charges. Throughout the hearing, Ann Putnam Junior and the other girls performed their fits at appropriate moments. Burroughs's testimony that he had not received the sacrament of the Lord's Supper for "so long . . . he could not tell" weighed heavily against him. The magistrates sent him off to prison to join the four dozen other accused witches and wizards of Salem, who now crowded the dungeons of Boston's jail awaiting trial.

The delay in bringing this accused "company of witches" to trial stemmed from the fact that Massachusetts Bay lacked a legal government or governor for much of the period. James II, the last Stuart king of England, had revoked the old Puritan charter in 1684, declared Massachusetts a *royal* colony, and appointed Sir Edmund Andros as governor. Andros ruled despite the opposition of most Puritan ministers and political figures until overthrown peacefully early in 1689 following England's Glorious Revolution, which deposed James II and placed William and Mary of Orange on the throne.

Although the Puritans behaved briefly as if the old charter had been restored, few people in Massachusetts were surprised when the new governor, Sir William Phips, reached Boston in mid-May 1692, confirming a previously announced new charter that maintained *royal* supremacy in the colony. The thirty-nine-year-old Phips was a New Englander himself, born to a humble family, who rose to wealth and prominence after a romantic career fighting Spaniards as a Caribbean "sea dog." Phips then married a rich English noblewoman.

When Phips arrived in Boston, the witchcraft controversy at Salem topped his agenda of unresolved problems. The new governor decided to skirt direct involvement, but, before leaving to organize a military campaign against the French in Canada, he appointed the lieutenant governor, William Stoughton, as chief justice of a special seven-man "Court of Oyer and Terminer" to dispose of the backlog of trials involving accused witches. Stoughton began the trials at Salem Town on June 2.

First to be judged was Bridget Bishop, a woman reputed to have a "smooth and flattering manner" with Salem's more flirtatious men and notorious for her extravagant habits of dress. Bridget had been suspected of witchcraft much earlier, in 1679 at the time of her second marriage, but had gained release after trial without punishment. Now, even her current spouse, tavern owner Edward Bishop, denounced her as a witch when the afflicted girls renewed their accusations. Also, several reputable men of Salem testified that they had seen Bridget employ spells and charms in making advances toward them, claiming that their loved ones had been injured after they rebuffed her proposals. Bridget's movements in the courtroom provoked the usual round of shrieks and complaints from the afflicted, who were joined now by a confessed witch, Deliverance Hobbs, in denouncing Bridget's devilish activities.

Evidently Magistrates Hathorne and Corwin selected Bishop to lead off the trials in order to make the strongest possible case at the start. The *new* judges had to be convinced concerning the validity of their earlier examinations. Thus not only were statements that had been made by accusers and accused prior to trial admitted in evidence (in this and all subsequent trials), but a "medical" examination of Bridget turned up the obligatory testimony concerning a witch's tit that subsequently disappeared. Also, a search of her house produced rag dolls in the cellar allegedly stuck with pins. "There was little occasion to prove the witchcraft, this being evident and notorious to all beholders," the Reverend Cotton Mather observed of Bridget's trial. Mather's comments probably reflected the views of most orthodox Puritan ministers in Massachusetts Bay.

Although the jury found Bridget guilty and the judges sentenced her to hang, they paused before carrying out the sentence until the Massachusetts General Court (the colony's legislature) on June 8 restored an earlier law that made witchcraft punishable by death. Bridget then became the first convicted witch of Salem Village to walk to her doom on Gallows Hill (which Salem residents began calling "Witches Hill") on June 10.

Despite pressures to begin new trials quickly, Stoughton delayed matters for over two weeks. All the judges were important figures in the colony, but only one came from Salem, and a majority of the others were

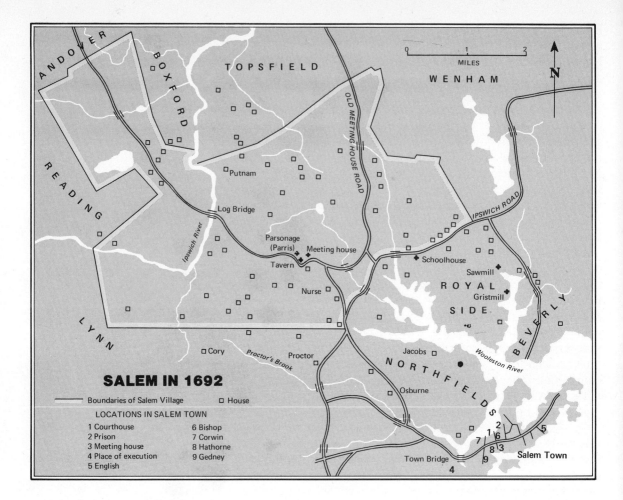

SALEM IN 1692

Boundaries of Salem Village □ House

LOCATIONS IN SALEM TOWN

1 Courthouse 6 Bishop
2 Prison 7 Corwin
3 Meeting house 8 Hathorne
4 Place of execution 9 Gedney
5 English

from Boston. They believed in the reality of witches and their invisible world, to be sure, but as shrewd and practical men, they also recognized the problem of dealing with testimony that might be tainted by Salem's family feuds and town quarrels.

The judges were particularly concerned with evaluating "spectral evidence," in other words, the afflicted girls' testimony that they had witnessed apparitions of witches commiting dreadful acts or apparent indications of "spectral" influence on the girls' behavior in court. Without such spectral evidence, one member of the court pointed out, it would not have been possible to convict even as mischievous a woman as Bridget Bishop. But by allowing admission of such evidence, the court had already weighted the scales heavily against *all* accused persons. Stoughton and his colleagues also accepted as fact the pretrial depositions of the afflicted, and they promised not to punish witches who confessed, thereby possibly encouraging false admissions even from the innocent.

Should such spectral evidence have been allowed? To resolve the question before starting trials, the court relied on a conference of twelve leading Bay colony ministers summoned in Boston on June 15 and presided over by Cotton Mather. The document produced there apparently cautioned against accepting spectral evidence of witchcraft from afflicted persons, at least against accepting it *uncritically* and without additional proof, especially when the accused "have been persons formerly of unblemished reputations." By such restraint, the ministers seem to have thought that a number of those awaiting trials could be cleared. Mather and his colleagues urged "a very critical and exquisite caution [in using spectral evidence] lest by too much credulity of things received only upon the devil's authority there be a door opened for a long train of miserable consequences." The ministers thus evidently agreed with a point made earlier by the doomed Rebecca Nurse, namely that the "demon may assume the shape of the innocent."

Despite these reservations, the ministers' statement praised the previous efforts by Parris, Hathorne, Corwin, Stoughton, and the others involved in pretrial examinations and trial of accused witches. Yet these men had relied heavily, often exclusively, and most certainly "uncritically" upon the spectral testimony of afflicted girls like Ann Putnam Junior and Abigail Williams, or on similar evidence by confessed witches like Tituba and Deliverance Hobbs. Moreover, Mather and his colleagues went on to "humbly recommend the speedy and vigorous prosecution of those as have rendered themselves obnoxious."

Thus the ministers straddled the issue of spectral evidence, leaving its admissibility in the hands of Stoughton and his fellow judges. Since the ministerial recommendations remained secret at the time in any event, accused witches could not even refer to the explicit warnings against careless use of such evidence. In the trials that followed, therefore, when the afflicted girls cried out against their tormenters' apparitions, such spectral presences remained *hard proof* of witchcraft for the judges. One of them, Nathaniel Saltonstall, resigned from the court because he refused to believe such evidence, but he was promptly replaced by Magistrate Jonathan Corwin, who had no doubts on the matter. (As might be expected, after Saltonstall's resignation, some of the afflicted began complaining that *his* apparition had been pursuing them.)

When the court resumed on June 29, it tried five cases in a single day, among them that of Rebecca Nurse. The jury found all five guilty, although only Stoughton's intervention caused its change of decision on Nurse. All five were hanged on July 19. The Reverend George Burroughs came up for trial on August 5, along with John and Elizabeth Proctor and three others. One of them, John Willard, the former Salem Village constable, had been accused only after expressing doubts about the charges raised by the afflicted girls. Another, a lame old man named George Jacobs, who swung about the courtroom aided by two canes, ridiculed the proceedings. He called one of his accusers, Sarah Churchill, his house servant and a new recruit to the ranks of the afflicted, a "witch bitch." Jacobs complained that his granddaughter, Margaret, who had been ar-

Witchcraft victims on their way to the gallows. (Painting by F. C. Yohn. Courtesy, Essex Institute, Salem, Mass.)

rested and thrown into prison, had been tricked into testifying against him. (Margaret later recanted her confession in court.) And Jacobs told the judges: "You tax me for a wizard; you might as well tax me for a buzzard!"

All six were convicted and sentenced to hang, although Elizabeth Proctor, pregnant at the time, had her sentence stayed until after she gave birth. The others went to their deaths on Gallows Hill on August 19. Most of the crowd's attention that day went to George Burroughs, the "chief wizard," who spoke briefly and again declared his innocence before climbing the ladder to the scaffold. Burroughs apparently shook the confidence in his guilt of many of those present. A number of them wept as Burroughs concluded his oration with a flawless recital of the Lord's Prayer, something that no agent of the Devil supposedly could accomplish. There even seemed a possibility that the crowd would try to stop the execution, when Cotton Mather, who had been mounted on a horse as he watched the event, suddenly called for everyone's attention. He declared that Burroughs was not even an ordained minister, that "the Devil has often been transformed into an Angel of Light," and that Burroughs was surely guilty. The mood of uncertainty dissolved, and without further interruption, George Burroughs and the four others were dispatched, after which their bodies were thrown into a two-foot-deep hole between the nearby rocks.

The trials continued. Within the next several weeks, fifteen more accused witches were convicted. Eight of these were hanged on September 22. Of the remainder, five had confessed and therefore escaped execution; the sixth had her sentence delayed because of pregnancy; and the final one, Mary Bradbury, escaped from prison with the help of friends.

Strife within the Salem Village community increased after each execution. Despite the hysteria, twenty-one of John Proctor's Salem neighbors had signed a petition affirming their belief in his religious piety. Ninety-three of Mary Bradbury's Salem friends and associates had petitioned on her behalf. Thus even in Salem and the surrounding towns, not everyone trusted the spectral revelations made by afflicted young women as devoutly as did William Stoughton and his fellow judges. The hangings themselves—and especially the sight of Giles Corey's body crushed to death on September 19—also helped persuade many that the *real* afflicters were the girls who had leveled charges of witchcraft upon so many innocent persons.

The eight hanged on September 19 included Giles Corey's wife, Martha; another sister of Rebecca Nurse's, Mary Easty; and a man named Samuel Wardwell, who had confessed but recanted at his trial. Wardwell's previous confession, supported by spectral evidence from the afflicted girls, doomed him. While making a final speech from the scaffold protesting his innocence, Wardwell began choking on the tobacco smoke from the Executioner's pipe, which had been blown into his face. The afflicted girls then cried delightedly that "the Devil hindred him with smoak." As all eight bodies dangled from the gibbet, the Reverend Nicholas Noyes, an early supporter of the hunt for witches, intoned to all who would listen: "What a sad thing it is to see Eight Firebrands of Hell hanging there." Although neither Noyes nor anyone else in the crowd knew this at the time, there would be no further executions.

Witchcraft had ceased to be a local problem by then. It affected virtually every town in Essex County and other communities in the Massachusetts Bay colony. The jails of Boston alone held over one hundred accused witches and wizards in September 1692, all awaiting trial, while other suspects were being examined each day. At first, the afflicted young women had made their charges only against those who lived in or near Salem Village. But after the initial dozen accusations, the net broadened to involve others outside the vicinity of the village. Joined by accusations from "afflicted" persons elsewhere in Essex County, they soon spread to towns over a wide area, and of those awaiting trial in September for witchcraft, barely a dozen came from Salem itself.

As the spring and summer of 1692 wore on, each fresh burst of accusations were aimed at more highly placed figures in the colony. Prominent persons in Massachusetts Bay affairs were now cried out against and joined the ranks of accused witches and wizards, although most of these people managed to avoid arrest or imprisonment.

One who did not was Captain John Alden of Boston, the son of neighboring Plymouth's best known couple, John and Priscilla Alden. Ordered to appear for questioning by Deputy Governor Stoughton himself, Alden confronted the afflicted girls—whom he called the "Salem wenches"—in that town on May 28. The girls had identified Alden as another plausible candidate for the role of chief wizard. They had described him in seizures as a "tall man from Boston" following Tituba's initial statement. Unfortunately for Alden, George Burroughs, also high up the Devil's ladder in the girls' eyes, was a short, stubby man from back-country Maine.

Alden arrived in Salem furious at having been dragged into the whole affair, and he quarreled intemperately with both the girls and the judges. The magistrates, still uncertain about the identification of Alden, ordered the accusers to form a ring around him and identify the accused, at which point one of the girls cried out: "There stands Alden, a bold fellow with his Hat on before the Judges, he sells Powder and Shot to the Indians and French, and lies with the Indian Squaws, and has Indian Papooses." Alden was arrested on the spot and brought to the meeting house to be examined. He denied the girls' charges that he had tormented them. He also bickered with one of the judges, Bartholemew Gedney, an old friend who now seemed to accept his accusers' account. Taken back to Boston under arrest, Alden was confined for the next fifteen weeks to his house (and not in Boston prison, where less influential "wizards" were kept) until he finally escaped, fleeing the colony for safety in New York, where he remained for the next year.

Other important personages in Massachusetts Bay found themselves and their loved ones under threat of similar imprisonment and death. One wealthy Salem man, Philip England, and his wife Mary, friends of Governor and Lady Phips, were also placed under house arrest in Boston and fled to New York as Alden had done. Nathanial Cary, a rich shipowner from Charlestown, arranged the escape of his wife from prison. Both went first to Rhode Island and then to New York.

No one, no matter how powerful, appeared to be safe from the afflicted girls' accusations. George Burroughs paid with his life, and another minister, John Hale, who had originally championed Abigail Williams and her cohorts, found his own wife accused of witchcraft. Wealthy members of Boston's mercantile and political "first families" found their names dragged into the "Devil's mud." There seemed no end to it. After Nathaniel Saltonstall withdrew as a judge in disbelief at spectral evidence, the girls cried out against him. One of them went to the top, implicating Cotton Mather. Several named Lady Mary Phips, the governor's wife! But by now—nine months, nineteen hangings, and one crushed body later—the afflicted young women of Salem had finally overreached themselves.

Again the ministers took the lead, this time in bringing the witchcraft trials to a halt. As early as mid-August, Cotton Mather had written John Foster, a member of the governor's council, repeating even more strongly his earlier assertion that spectral evidence alone from afflicted persons "is not enough to convict . . . of witchcraft" and that "devilish presences" sometimes could enter innocent bodies—even his own. The point was made with still greater authority by Mather's father, Increase Mather, the colony's most respected minister. In a sermon preached to a conclave of ministers at Cambridge on October 3, Increase Mather denounced categorically the use of spectral evidence. In that sermon, soon published as *Cases of Conscience Concerning Evil Spirits Per-*

sonating Men, he also criticized as inadequate most other types of "evidence" used in the Salem witchcraft trials and argued: "It were better that ten suspected witches should escape, than that one innocent person should be condemned."

Most of Mather's ministerial audience evidently agreed with him. They shared by then a widespread consensus among Massachusetts Bay's civil and religious authorities that matters at Salem had gotten out of hand. Nine days after Mather's sermon, Governor Phips issued instructions banning any further arrests or trials for witchcraft. Later that month, the Massachusetts legislature passed a bill calling for a ministerial meeting to advise civil authorities on the best way to handle cases involving the accused witches who remained in jail. A short time later, Phips abolished the special Court of Oyer and Terminer which had been appointed to try the cases and freed on bond many of those in prison awaiting trial.

Another special court met at Salem early in 1693 to deal with the imprisoned persons. Stoughton was again its chief judge, but this time Governor Phips instructed the judges that no accused witch could be convicted *solely* on spectral evidence. Only three of the fifty-two cases tried ended in conviction, and in all three cases, the "witch" had confessed. The remaining forty-nine accused witches were acquitted. Stoughton sentenced all three found guilty to hang along with five others, including Elizabeth Proctor, who had been convicted earlier but spared because of her pregnancy. Governor Phips promptly reprieved all eight, giving obvious vent to his displeasure with Stoughton's attempt to salvage one final act of bloody retribution from the Salem tragedy. The lieutenant governor could hardly contain his outrage at Phips's action: "We were in a way to have cleared the land of the witches!" he complained. "Who is it that obstructs the course of justice I know not. The Lord be merciful to the country!"

Stoughton knew perfectly well who had "obstructed" the "justice" of spectral evidence. When his court resumed hearing witchcraft cases in Boston that April, others accused of the crime were also cleared, including one mentally ill woman who had confessed. Meanwhile, Governor Phips proclaimed John Alden innocent of the charges against him and, in May 1693, decisively ended the episode by freeing those who remained in jail on witchcraft charges.

Phips also proclaimed a general pardon for the fortunate people who had fled the colony when accused. The governor had written to the earl of Nottingham in February 1693 defending his belated decisiveness in terminating the witch hunt as necessary in order to dissipate "the black cloud that threatened this Province with destruction" and to relieve the threats against innocent victims of the afflicted girls, including "some of the principal persons here." Even Phips's pardon did not free some of those in jail, since payment of prison fees was then a prisoner's responsibility and not the state's. Only when the jailer had been reimbursed for expenses could the accused buy their way out of jail, a costly procedure that kept a number of them in jail long after their pardons.

Slowly Salem Village regained its earlier peaceable state. But supporters and opponents of the Reverend Samuel Parris, in whose house the affair had germinated, continued to bicker for several years. The afflicted young women returned to their homes, subdued finally by fear of the governor's displeasure. Pro-Parris and anti-Parris factions in the Village fought so fiercely within the church that, in April 1695, a special conference of neighboring clergymen met at Salem to mediate. Their conclusions gave Parris little comfort, since the ministers agreed (in a model of understatement) that Parris had taken "unwarranted and uncomfortable steps" against those of his parishioners accused of witchcraft. Still, the visiting ministers pleaded with survivors of the ordeal to display "compassion" toward Parris and toward his followers, presumably including the afflicted girls. Parris eventually agreed to resign as minister and leave the community, *if* he received his unpaid back salary (approximately £79 or $4000 by today's standard). Raising the money proved easy, so badly did even those who had supported Parris yearn to close the wounds that he had opened in Salem Village.

Samuel Parris resigned in July 1696 and left the village forever in the following year to become a schoolmaster and merchant in another town. By then, Parris had come to recognize the enormity of his responsibility for the events that had taken place. So had others involved in stirring up the witchcraft craze (including the "afflicted" Ann Putnam Junior, who later begged forgiveness for her actions). "To see a dear friend torn, wounded, and the blood streaming down his face and body, will much affect the heart," Parris had preached in an August 1693 sermon. "But much more when those wounds we see, and that streaming blood we behold, accuseth *us* as the vile actors . . . much more when our consciences tell us that we, our cruel hands, have made those wounds, and the bloody instruments by which our dearest friend was gored, were of our own forging."

When he left Salem, Samuel Parris took with him his daughter Betty, whose strange sickness had begun the events of 1692 in the village, and his younger son Noyes, born during those hysterical months and named after the Reverend Nicholas Noyes, a prime supporter of the Salem witchcraft trials. No record tells us whether Betty Parris ever recovered from her afflictions. As for Noyes Parris, he grew to adulthood only to become insane and to die in that unfortunate condition.

6 Puritan New England and the Middle Colonies

The *Speedwell* leaked so badly that it could not be trusted to cross the Atlantic. The ship had made two unsuccessful starts from Plymouth, England. The twice-disappointed passengers, thirty-five Pilgrims, as they later called themselves, were members of a small sect of religious dissenters who had sailed to Plymouth on the *Speedwell* from the Dutch city of Leyden. Several hundred Pilgrims had taken refuge at Leyden years earlier. Now the thirty-five joined dozens of other passengers, Pilgrims and non-Pilgrims alike, aboard a larger vessel, the *Mayflower,* which sailed for the Virginia colony on September 16, 1620. The 102 passengers had accepted an offer made by London merchants to settle in Virginia and exchange their hard work in return for the chance to build new lives in the wilderness.

The uncomfortable trans-Atlantic voyage lasted nine weeks. Men, women, children, chickens, pigs, and goats all jostled for room on the overcrowded *Mayflower.* Although illnesses struck passengers and crew, all but one person survived the crossing, and two babies were born during the voyage. Somehow the ship managed to drift hundreds of miles northward and off course, far to the north of Virginia, anchoring first near the tip of Cape Cod on November 11. Although they lacked legal title to the land, the group determined to sail no farther. They would build their community somewhere in the vicinity, but less exposed to storms than at the ocean's edge on Cape Cod.

Even before the Pilgrims found a town site, and in the absence of either a royal charter or authority from their merchant sponsors, those aboard ship committed themselves to organizing a government. Forty-one of the forty-four men on the *Mayflower* signed a document, the Mayflower Compact, in which they agreed to form a colony and to obey its laws and its officials. There were no other English settlements in the region (such as those in Virginia, whose assembly had met for the first time the previous year) for the Pilgrims to associate with. The signers of the Mayflower Compact promised to "combine ourselves together into a civill body politick, for our better ordering and preservation and . . . to enacte, constitute, and frame such just and equall laws."

The *Mayflower* weighed anchor again and sailed up the coast, arriving on December 21 at another harbor, which the group named Plymouth. There they went ashore to build their colony, not knowing that only half the hundred or so settlers would survive that winter. The death toll mounted for reasons already familiar at Jamestown: disease, hunger, passivity, and the exhausting ocean voyage. In addition, the Pilgrims had not been prepared for the long and harshly cold New England winter. Those who survived gratefully accepted help from friendly local Indians as they learned to plant the local corn, trade for furs, and explore the surrounding forests and rivers of that unfamiliar countryside, soon to be called New England. In the fall of 1621, after harvest, the Pilgrims held a three-day festival of thanksgiving to which ninety Indians were invited.

The devout Pilgrims were simple and modest people who dealt fairly, both with the Indians and with their merchant sponsors back in England. Their colony—which existed independently until it was absorbed into the Massachusetts Bay colony in 1691—struggled for decades to repay debts owed in England, colonists working hard but without notable success to become solvent, and the colony expanded only slowly within the area. The population of Plymouth never increased, not

even in irregular spurts as it did at Jamestown; after a decade of settlement, there were still fewer than four hundred people. Nevertheless, William Bradford, the colony's first governor, wrote truly in his chronicle of the Pilgrim experiment, *Of Plymouth Plantation:* "as one small candle may light a thousand, so the light here kindled hath shone unto many . . ."

Portrayals of the Pilgrims praying together shortly before they disembarked at Plymouth (or earlier on Cape Cod) became a mythic part of America's colonial heritage during the nineteenth century, when this one was painted. (NYPL/Picture Collection)

William Bradford became governor of the Pilgrim's Plymouth colony in 1621 and was re-elected a number of times. His life was inseparable from that of the Pilgrim settlement, and he later became its most famous chronicler with Of Plymouth Plantation. *(Culver Pictures)*

THE PURITAN MIGRATION: ORIGINS OF THE "BIBLE COMMONWEALTH"

Beginning in the late 1620s another much larger group of English religious dissenters, the Puritans, migrated to New England to found another colony. They proved more aggressive, better organized, more expansionist, and wealthier than the Pilgrims. Leading Puritans (including John Winthrop, later first governor of the Massachusetts Bay colony) managed to gain a royal charter from Charles I in 1629. The charter provided for a governor and a number of "assistants" whom "freemen" or shareholders of the Massachusetts Bay Company would elect while meeting in a general assembly four times each year. These company officials were to manage the colony's affairs, make its laws, punish wrongdoers, assign lands, and otherwise run matters in Massachusetts Bay.

The company organized an advance expedition of "old planters" during the summer of 1629, five ships bearing several hundred colonists, cattle, supplies and Indian trade goods. They sailed to New England and took over a small settlement founded the previous year on the Naumkeag River, calling the new community "Salem" or "house of peace." It was at Salem, where witches would be pursued so avidly six decades later, that New England Puritan civilization first took root.

The following year, 1630, seventeen ships from England brought the Puritans' new governor, John Winthrop, and another thousand settlers. Because of religious persecution, Winthrop and his colleagues had decided to transfer the company's charter and government to the New World, safely out of the grasp of unfriendly royal officials.

Stopping first at Salem, where the older Puritan migrants struggled to survive in crude surroundings (many living in tents or Indian huts), the group's leaders judged the community a poor location for their chief settlement. Food and land capable of decent cultivation were in short supply, considering the many new settlers already on the way from England. Winthrop and his advisers decided to shift the center of Puritan control from Salem farther south, landing this time in Boston harbor where a new string of towns quickly developed in the surrounding bay area—foremost among them Boston itself. Within little more than a decade, over 20,000 additional settlers joined this Puritan "exodus" from Old England. This "Great Migration" gave New England by 1640 a population more than twice that of the Virginia colony, despite the latter's far longer history of settlement.

The Puritans came to create a society organized for God's purposes as they understood them. It would be a "covenanted community" in the American wilderness fit to serve as a model for Europeans to follow in completing the Protestant Reformation. Even before landing in America, John Winthrop had preached such a sermon aboard his

John Winthrop was a man of refinement and sensitivity. Though some questioned his arbitrary rulings (he had no faith in democracy), none doubted his integrity. (American Antiquarian Society)

ship, the *Arbella*. He defined the religious purposes for which Puritans had come to America. Their community would be "as a City set upon a hill, in the open view of all the earth; the eyes of the world are upon us . . ." Solving the problems of survival that had bedeviled the Jamestown colony became, if not easy, at least simpler than it had been for the Virginians because the Puritans had clearly stated goals. No massive search for gold or other treasures preoccupied Massachusetts Bay; nor did its settlers pursue imaginary inland routes to Asia, unrealistic manufacturing ventures, or unknown sites of "lost colonies"—all of which had been done at Jamestown.

The Puritans, like the Pilgrims before them, fished and farmed and sought after practical, easily developed sources of export trade (primarily lumber, furs, and fish). Nor did they suffer from a shortage of needed laborers or an excess of "gentlemen at leisure." Puritan immigrants, apart from hardworking farmers and cattle herders, included a variety of artisans, merchants, lawyers, ministers, and other groups which quickly gave each Puritan town a rich mixture of occupations. Nor was money or administrative talent in short supply, either in New England or among the English backers of the Puritan experiment. Thus the permanent settlements that spread out quickly along the coastline and inland sections of Massachusetts Bay never underwent the perilous *early* years of imminent disaster so familiar to the older settlers of Jamestown. Above all else, New England settlers of the 1630s shared common religious beliefs and values.

THE ENGLISH REFORMATION AND PURITAN BELIEFS

Most of those who settled the Virginia colony in its founding decades were members of the Church of England, itself a relatively recent creation of Henry VIII. Christians throughout Europe had lived for over a thousand years within the unifying orbit of Roman Catholicism, when, in 1517, a German Augustinian monk named Martin Luther began his world-shaking denunciations of papal rule, church corruption, and overly elaborate church ritual and hierarchy. Luther's Reformation received the backing of several German princes and, later, of rulers elsewhere in Europe, such as England's Henry VIII, who were anxious to staunch the flow of local wealth to Rome, to gain church lands for themselves, and to increase their authority over the populace—and their support within their countries—at the Papacy's expense. Henry's immediate concern was to ensure a legal divorce from

his then-wife, Catherine, who had failed to produce a male offspring as heir to the throne, so that he could remarry.

Protestantism, as the general movement for church reformation became known, gained powerful allies in the rising monarchs of nation-states such as England and among groups within society most affected by the social instability that religious upheaval both reflected and reinforced. Rising merchant classes, entrepreneurial landowners, professional classes, such as the new body of lawyers allied to monarchs in court or parliamentary roles—all of these "middle-class" elements within European society contributed meaningfully to the different Protestant sects.

Nothing distinguished the web of reformist doctrine more fully than conflicts between Protestant and Catholic views of "sin." Although all Christians believed (and believe) that mankind's "original sin" derived initially from the fall of Adam in the Garden of Eden, in practice Catholicism by the sixteenth century had come to view human decline with relative tolerance. So long as an individual relied regularly upon the authority of the church, his or her sins could be alleviated without extraordinary exertions.

But for Protestants, especially those who followed the stern teachings of the Swiss lawyer and theologian John Calvin, human beings were obliged to strive relentlessly against every manifestation of sin in their behavior and thoughts. Neither priests nor rituals could replace, in this view, the obligation of each person to pursue *actively* his or her own spiritual salvation. Like their Calvinist brethren on the Continent, English "Puritans"[1] believed that God had "predestined" some for eternal salvation and others for damnation. God's grace had determined the "elect" or "company of saints" from the beginning of time, not because of any intrinsic goodness on their part but of His own volition. Most human beings were to try and live devout lives, *as if* they had been chosen one of God's elect, while searching for signs of Gods grace (or the opposite). Nothing that occurred at Salem in 1692 during the witchcraft trials could have

---

[1] The term "Puritan" was used to describe individuals intent upon "purifying" the Church of England during the Protestant Reformation in that country.

surprised believing Puritans, at least with regard to the examining magistrates presenting "evidence" that persons considered moral pillars of the community were in reality agents of the Devil. For all true Puritans believed that only God knew with assurance which people *really* lived among the "invisible" company of the saved—or the damned.

Among Puritans, then, there existed an obligation to conduct at every moment a spiritual accounting. Only those who had undergone actual "conversion" experiences, those who had personally experienced God's grace, entered into the first ranks of Puritan society during the early seventeenth century. Since Puritans did not believe in the exoneration of sins by absolution, the pursuit of their own moral impurities offered constant activity for the Puritan conscience. The events at Salem in 1689, therefore, involving constant calibration of moral behavior and assessments of individual sinfulness that might have been deemed excessive in many *non*-Puritan communities at the time, seemed only the normal pattern of life within Puritan society.

Since, for the Puritans, individuals and not whole groups achieved salvation, freely given and predestined by God, the role of priests or churches underwent fundamental change. Puritan ministers devoted themselves to providing moral and theological guides by examining the Bible and sermonizing. Exact and comprehensive understanding of the Old and New Testaments replaced ritualized worship that Puritans thought extraneous to determining God's will and obeying it.

When Henry VIII broke with Catholicism, he hoped to minimize the changes in doctrines and rituals that his Church of England would follow, a policy continued by Henry's daughter, Queen Elizabeth. But Puritan attacks on the monarchy and on the Church of England intensified under James I (1603–25). The reformers demanded that all vestiges of Catholicism be abolished and that each congregation be considered self-governing (that is, Congregationalist).

Some dissenters dismissed the idea of reforming the Church of England. Among those "purifiers" who wanted *complete* separation were the Pilgrims or "Separatists." Others, non-separating Congregationalists, remained in England to battle for church and political reform, among them the Puritans, though thousands of these "*non*-separating congregationalists" would later migrate to America. Thus the chief distinction between *Separatist* Pilgrims and *non-separatist* Puritans concerned a theological argument over whether to try and purify the Church of England from within or, as the Pilgrims believed, to abandon the effort entirely and *separate* from the "impure" English mother church to found an entirely separate sect.

James's son, Charles I, came to the throne in 1625. Charles attempted to extend royal authority by ruling and taxing without Parliament. His appointee as Archbishop of Canterbury, William Laud, began a full-scale campaign against the Puritans, demanding that all conform to the Church of England's practices. As the persecution continued, both on religious and political grounds, John Winthrop and the other leading Puritans of the Massachusetts Bay Company finally decided on a transfer of their colony's government and charter to New England, where distance alone would ensure less interference in religious and political practices by royal authority.

PURITAN SOCIETY IN NEW ENGLAND: THE PURSUIT OF PERFECTION

The transfer decision ensured that Puritanism in the New World would retain significant freedom from English restraints. Unlike Jamestown, where the Virginia Company had interfered continuously, Massachusetts Bay could devise its own laws and governing proceedings. This remarkable measure of independence allowed the Puritan communities of New England to evolve free from English restraints for more than a half-century.

Puritans based their government on a set of political ideas derived from religion. In this view, government represented a God-given mechanism for restraining man's innate sinfulness. *All* government derived from what Puritans considered a formal agreement—a "covenant"—between rulers and ruled under God. Those Puritans who made the Atlantic crossing to New England believed that their society had a *special* covenant with God to build their holy "City upon a Hill." All of Europe would turn to Massachusetts Bay as a model in time, or so they reasoned. Even aboard the *Arbella,* John Winthrop spoke for other Puritan leaders when he warned in a sermon that God "will expect a strict performance" from the new arrivals, since His covenant with Massachusetts Bay had "given us leave to draw our own Articles."

Political leadership in Puritan Massachusetts fell naturally into the hands of church members, those "visible saints" who could provide some evidence of genuine conversion experiences and of model Christian behavior. To consider oneself "converted" meant, for the Puritans, to have undergone a transforming personal religious experience which signaled—both to the individual in question and to other members of his church—apparently "visible" evidences of God's grace. Those who underwent such experiences continued testing themselves and their moral behavior most strenuously for continual confirmation of their position among the "saved."

Inevitably the Puritan ministers played a major role, not simply in church life but in the political lives of the towns as well (though not through holding elective office). Despite the close relations between church and state in Massachusetts Bay, never could the colony have been termed a genuine "theocracy," where ministers exercise political power by virtue of their *church* offices. Rather, the relation between ministers and the governing officials in Puritan New England, though intimate, clearly provided for distinct realms of authority. Moreover, many of the colony's leaders—from the 1630s to the witch trial period—from Winthrop to Phips—were vigorous and aggressive secular figures and not ministers: lawyers, landowners, merchants, and teachers among them.

When Winthrop and other members of the company gathered to organize their society, the structure of government emerged directly from the charter. It provided for the members or freemen of the company to meet four times yearly in a "General Court" which, once a year, would select a governor, deputy governor, and eighteen assistants. These officials would run the company—that is,

the colony—for a year until the next election by the company's full membership.

The General Court met for the first time in October 1630 in the newly founded community of Charlestown. At that time, "Company" formally became "Colony." In May 1631, most of the colony's church members—116 in all—became freemen, and the number expanded steadily in the years ahead. In order to keep control of the government in the hands of believing Puritans, church membership became a fixed condition for being made a freeman. Within the next few years, each town in Massachusetts Bay's commonwealth gained the right to elect representatives to the General Court, which had evolved into a representative colonial legislature comparable to Virginia's House of Burgesses.

But the Bay colony's affairs remained in the hands of a Puritan elite, despite constant pressure from freemen or those who wished to become freemen for a greater share of power. Thus John Winthrop served as governor for eleven years, although not continuously. His periodic ouster at election time by Puritan rivals showed that even the most respected leaders in the colony could not hope to rule continuously.

Puritans brought with them not simply a set of religious ideals but also English patterns and beliefs that often mixed uneasily in the new colony. Demands for a written legal code, for example, quickly arose among dissatisfied settlers, and the earliest Puritan efforts to create such a body of laws combined biblical injunctions, English common law, and statutes passed by the Massachusetts General Court. Finally, in 1648, a revised code known as the Laws and Liberties of Massachusetts—mixing all these elements—became the colony's fundamental legal code. Punishments were generally harsh by today's standards but not by those of the seventeenth century. In every town and county, a local court system had taken root, with the governor's council of assistants serving as Massachusetts's highest court of appeals. Special courts were also established for extraordinary occasions similar to the court that Governor Phips created to try accused witches.

Within each town, the Puritan church exercised remarkable influence and control. Both re-

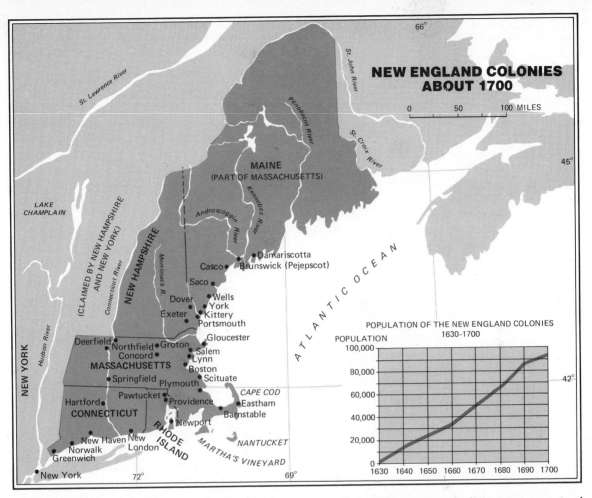

NEW ENGLAND COLONIES
ABOUT 1700

0 · 50 · 100 MILES

MAINE
(PART OF MASSACHUSETTS)

ATLANTIC OCEAN

POPULATION OF THE NEW ENGLAND COLONIES
1630–1700

POPULATION

By 1700, the New England colonies had a population of 92,763. Over three-fourths of this total lived in Massachusetts and Connecticut. Northern New England, as can be seen, had not yet taken on the form familiar to us today.

Maine's English beginnings went back to a grant to proprietors Sir Ferdinando Gorges and John Mason. In 1622 they received the land between the Merrimac and Kennebec rivers. They did little to build up a colony. Most early settlers came from Massachusetts, and the region remained part of that state until 1820.

In 1629 Gorges and Mason divided their lands. Mason received the region between the Piscataqua and Merrimac rivers, which he named New Hampshire. Like Maine, it had many ties to Massachusetts. The colony became a separate royal province in 1679. Both New Hampshire and New York claimed it, but there were no English settlements until the eighteenth century.

ligious worship and the monitoring of moral behavior were normal aspects of *daily* behavior for every churchgoer—not only church "members" but all residents—in Puritan New England. Although each congregation chose its own minister and particular pattern of worship without interference from other churches, every resident of a town had an obligation to attend services regularly, contribute money or goods toward a minister's support, and accept whatever scrutiny and criticism other church members might provide. Rarely have the members of a society watched one another as closely as in seventeenth-century Puritan New England. Rarely have members of a community

Harvard College was founded in 1636 in large measure to train ministers. The middle of the three halls pictured here was named for Judge William Stoughton of the Salem trials. (NYPL/ Stokes Collection)

been bound by such intricate networks of religious, moral, and economic attitudes and regulations as those that affected the Puritan towns of New England.

Puritans placed high value on education. How else could a Christian know the Bible? Many Puritan leaders were university-educated, and Puritans determined to preserve this background in the American wilderness. Village schools were established in most towns, and parents were required by law to make certain that their children (and others in the household) learned to read. Secondary schools modeled after those in England also appeared, and Harvard College was established in 1636, using the same curriculum as that employed at the best English colleges. Massachusetts Bay had the first printing press in the English settlements; it published not only sermons but also almanacs, schoolbook primers, and psalms. The first book published in Massachusetts was the Bay Psalm Book in 1636.

New England Puritans led a communal existence compressed into towns sprinkled neatly across the landscape. From the early establishment of communities such as Salem and Boston along the seacoast to the development of town sites inland, the migrants to Massachusetts Bay often passed quickly through the older settlements only long enough to lay groundwork for newer towns of their own. All groups of freemen had the right to request from the Massachusetts General Court a grant of land upon which to establish a new town. Once settlers reached the site of their new community, they took pains to lay out a full plan for the town, complete with a central commons and a location for the church. By reserving a large portion of land as "common" land for grazing animals, they often achieved a combination of personal landholding and communal agriculture. The town pattern provided an effective compromise between the Puritan concern for a structure sufficiently closed to ensure supervision of religious and moral life and a structure sufficiently flexible to allow room for individual economic and social enterprise. Anyone dissatisfied with a specific town could always pack up and either move to another community or hope to find enough other malcontents to establish a town more to one's liking.

In later periods of communal stress, such as the one that preceded the Salem witchcraft trials, New England Puritans searched relentlessly for external, "visible" signs of God's disapproval to explain the *internal* turbulence. Indian wars, famines, plagues, foreign invasions, and political setbacks were usually seen as tokens of divine judgment. In the early decades, however, the ministers and governors of Massachusetts Bay had found more signs of divine *approval* than rejection.

A prosperous economic life seemed only the most notable of these signs. From the beginning of migration, New England Puritans practiced a mixture of economic pursuits that ensured self-sufficiency for most communities. Farming the rocky land adjacent to the New England coast proved less profitable than agriculture in the valleys farther inland in Massachusetts Bay and in the Connecticut Valley. Those who preferred not to farm often fished or traded with the Indians for furs, and an abundance of forest woods and plants served as additional staples of the export trade from earliest years. African and Indian slaves came to the colony by mid-century, but slavery itself never became as economically or socially important as in the Southern colonies. A number of merchants—men such as Salem's Philip England and Charlestown's Nathaniel Cary—grew wealthy, and such entrepreneurs became an increasingly significant element in the political and even religious life of Massachusetts Bay, not always to the satisfaction of the older ministerial class.

On the whole, however, the society that evolved under Puritan rule in New England held more freemen than servants, more craftsmen than merchants, and still more farmers and fishermen. There were far fewer gradations in rank and prosperity than in England or in the plantation colonies to the south. The bedrock of Puritan New England society seemed at all levels to be characterized by a remarkable measure of independence, self-sufficiency, and self-confidence. Only when all three had declined profoundly could an event as horrendous as the Salem witch trials have occurred. Had any such disorder threatened the colony's peace in their lifetime, the founders of New England would undoubtedly have moved swiftly to bring matters under stern control.

The Ben Franklin hand press. (Eliot Elisofon, Life Magazine © 1959 Time, Inc.)

NEW ENGLAND MIGRATIONS

Puritans seemed forever poised to move again. As wave after wave of migrants arrived in Massachusetts Bay from England during the 1630s, the "older" townships of the earliest settlers— Salem, Boston, Charlestown, Newton, Watertown, Dorchester, and Roxbury—often served mainly as departure points into newer communities. The movement went not only up the coast toward

Maine or south, impinging upon the Plymouth townships, but inland toward the forests and river-beds to the west. With the founding of each town, as the population spread out over the colony, the central authority of Massachusetts Bay's General Court became less binding. By the mid-1630s, Puritans had begun moving beyond the lands and authority of the commonwealth itself. Some had private visions of God's purpose in New England. Others wished greater authority both to enlarge their own lands and to practice variations of the doctrines that ruled in Massachusetts Bay.

The Founding of Connecticut

Expeditions by traders from Plymouth and Massachusetts Bay had reached the lush farming lands of the Connecticut Valley as early as 1632, and small groups of settlers began trickling into the valley by mid-decade. One of the Massachusetts Bay colony's leading ministers, Thomas Hooker, petitioned the General Court in 1635 to allow him to take his congregation there in order to found a new settlement, still nominally under the control of Massachusetts Bay. Political and religious disagreements figured in Hooker's unhappiness. He felt that ties between church and state were too close in Massachusetts and believed that participation in town affairs should not be limited to church members alone. During the next few years, other groups of migrants from Massachusetts joined Hooker's band and founded towns at Hartford, Wethersfield, Windsor, and additional points in the Connecticut Valley. Representatives from these towns issued in 1639 the "Fundamental Orders of Connecticut," a compact that served as a frame of government similar to that of Massachusetts Bay in many ways but different in one "fundamental": there was no religious test for town "freemenship," and all men acceptable to the majority of town householders would be "freemen" and voters. Unlike Massachusetts, then, the Puritan society of Connecticut would not be ruled by "visible saints," even in its earliest year. The colony finally obtained a charter from King Charles II in 1662 that confirmed its control over the Connecticut Valley towns.

Anne Hutchinson and Puritan Dissent

Two leading dissenters, Roger Williams (see p. 116) and Anne Hutchinson, migrated to the Narragansett Bay area. Anne Hutchinson, like Williams, had directly challenged the authority and beliefs of orthodox New England Puritans. Hutchinson showed, among other things, that a religiously trained and imaginative woman could effectively dispute theology with the major Puritan ministers of the period. The matter under contention went to the heart of Puritan concerns in the Bible Commonwealth. Hutchinson challenged the view that proper conduct, moral behavior, and Christian piety—visible evidence of what Puritans called "sanctification"—necessarily foreshadowed "justification" or the divine infusion of the Holy Spirit. Good "works," in short, did not determine divine "grace," according to Hutchinson. Puritans called this heresy (which had antecedents in the history of Christianity) "antinomianism." Anne Hutchinson had begun holding Tuesday meetings in her home where she and her friends would

Anne Hutchinson, who immigrated to Boston in 1634, soon became a figure of controversy within orthodox Puritan circles. Tried for blasphemy in 1637, she was exiled from the colony.

discuss orthodox theology and then her own views. Her arguments appeared to threaten the established order as too "individualistic," encouraging above all else personal communion with God and individual alertness to such divine "infusion." At a trial conducted by the General Court, Anne Hutchinson defended herself brilliantly but sealed her fate in the colony when she asserted an awareness of the deity through "immediate" personal revelation and not through the normal church practices. Hutchinson was ordered banished from Massachusetts Bay. She settled with her family and a number of followers on an island in Narragansett Bay (Aquidneck) in 1638. Five years later, having moved to what is now New York, she fell victim to a band of attacking Indians.

Both Roger Williams and Anne Hutchinson showed to orthodox Puritan leaders in Massachusetts Bay what effects *excessive* zeal could have on talented individuals. John Winthrop's "City upon a Hill" could handle the religiously lax more easily than it could absorb overenthusiastic believing spirits intent upon pursuing private religious truths. Such visions, Winthrop and his colleagues feared, might just as easily come from the Devil as from the Lord, which made first-generation Puritans extremely cautious, for example, when the occasional church member complained of "witches" or "evil presences" in their midst. Puritans guarded against such disruptions within the community during the earlier decades because they threatened to untangle the carefully maintained structure of religious and civil authority within Massachusetts Bay. For several generations, the colony's leaders proved confident and successful when handling such menacing signs. Communal pressures, jailings, banishments, and even executions could deal with those who chose direct communion with God in place of properly channeled church worship.

Catholic "New France"

From earliest settlement, the Puritans at Massachusetts Bay found themselves coming into contact with French traders and seamen from the North. At various times during the seventeenth century, the Puritans engaged in wary but amicable contacts with French officials in the area which came to be known as Canada, but the Puritans remained deeply suspicious of these occasional links to the Catholic foreigners so close to their borders.

The original European settlers in Canada were the French, who first came in the early seventeenth century. Like the English in Virginia, these colonists were sent by a trading company operating under royal charter. The stockholders were allowed to set up a fur trade, but they were also committed to establish colonies in Canada.

Once in Canada, however, men were lured from the stern task of hacking out pioneer farms by the free life of the forest and by dreams of a quick fortune made in the fur trade. They became hunters and trappers—often living with the Indians—rather than settling down to raise large broods of children. By 1660 there were only 2000 inhabitants in New France, compared with 75,000 in the thirteen English colonies. This scant population did not produce enough food to support itself, nor was it a match for hostile Indians. The French government took over the colony in 1663.

During the next hundred years the government made a systematic effort to people New France. Population did increase, but in 1760 the colony fell to the British in the French and Indian War. By 1763, the British controlled the four chief regions of Canada—Quebec, Nova Scotia, Newfoundland, and Rupert's Land. (See Chapter 8, p. 163.)

THE MIDDLE COLONIES: ORIGINS AND PATTERNS

From their earliest days of settlement, the Puritans considered themselves an embattled society. Not only did they suffer from *internal* strains but non-English colonial outposts hemmed them in on both the north and south. Thus, during the seventeenth century, Massachusetts Bay had at times to trade or negotiate with the authorities of Catholic "New France" along the St. Lawrence River. There was less contact with the Dutch Protestants of "New Netherland," although in some ways, this colony remained the most direct threat

Roger Williams

(Brown Brothers)

Salem symbolized not only the beginning but the end of Puritan control of the Massachusetts Bay colony. In 1692, the witchcraft trials and their aftermath signaled the death knell both of Puritan religious authority and of the colony's independence from royal control. More than a half-century earlier, however, the most explosive challenge to domination of Massachusetts Bay by its founding ministers and magistrates also began, appropriately, at Salem. Provoking the controversy with John Winthrop and the other Puritan leaders was a heretical minister and self-professed "Separatist" named Roger Williams.

Williams arrived in New England in 1631, age twenty-eight. He promptly stirred tempers in the colony by declining to fill temporarily the vacant post of minister in Boston. That church, he asserted, had not truly separated itself from the Church of England.

After a stint as a minister in Plymouth, marked as usual by controversies concerning religious "purity," Williams departed for Salem, where he was elected pastor in April 1635. By then, Roger Williams had managed to confront the authorities on other questions as well. He challenged the legitimacy of Massachusetts Bay's title to its lands, arguing that the English king had no right to grant lands owned by the Indians. Williams even suggested that the Puritans either return to England or confirm their land title properly with the Indians. He opposed laws enforcing taxes to pay for church expenses and those that made church attendance mandatory.

Ironically, Roger Williams arrived at an acceptance of virtual religious *tolerance* precisely because of his uncompromising spiritual *intolerance.* Thus Williams believed in the complete *separation* of church and state because of the overriding importance he attached to *individual* pursuit of true faith. Spokesman for a vision of religious "purity" far more personal than the communal faith of Massachusetts Bay, Williams opposed strongly the oligarchical control exercised by the Puritan leaders. On virtually every fundamental issue, from church membership to political rights and from land titles to religious conscience, then, Williams disagreed. Small wonder that the colony's General Court tried him during the fall of 1635 and ordered him banished.

The dissenter fled Massachusetts Bay in midwinter and took refuge among the Narragansett Indians. In their midst, Williams and his few supporters established a new settlement, which he called Providence Plantation. Lacking a royal charter, Williams devised a "compact," which did not require church membership or any other religious test for voting in town affairs. It recognized no ecclesiastical role in civil matters whatsoever, demanding instead that laws be made simply "by the major consent of the present inhabitants." All sects were welcomed without prejudice to the community, and church and state were entirely separate, with the right to worship according to one's own creed guaranteed. Several other towns were founded in the Narrangansett Bay area by additional groups of Puritan dissenters and by other Protestants including Baptists and Quakers. In 1642, Williams traveled to England and obtained from Parliament in 1644 a charter for the "Incorporation of Providence Plantations." The four towns of Providence, Newport, Warwick, and Aquidneck (later Portsmouth) united formally under the charter in 1647, and the colony of Rhode Island, which evolved from this union, continued to reflect the representative and libertarian ideals of its founder, Roger Williams, who died in 1683.

to the cohesion of Puritan New England. Still, the relatively brief sea war between England and Holland (1652–54) did not greatly affect either Massachusetts Bay or New Netherland. England remained a land in turmoil for most of the decade preceding and the decade following the execution of Charles I in 1649. The English Civil War and Oliver Cromwell's Puritan Revolution affected life in New England more directly than any Dutch merchant colony on its borders.

The Puritan leaders in Massachusetts Bay found immigration drying up after the 1640s, and they also learned to their dismay that the City upon a Hill did not appeal to Cromwell, who regarded New Englanders' pretensions to a measure of political or religious leadership in *his* England as grotesque and absurd. By the end of Cromwell's Protectorate, the New Englanders' early notion of returning in triumph to a transformed England had been thoroughly shattered. New England Puritanism, as one historian wrote, had been "left alone with America." In some ways, therefore, the beginning of the end for New England Puritanism came *not* with the return of Charles II to England in 1660 but with the emergence of Oliver Cromwell's Protectorate two decades earlier. It was Cromwell's imposition of a degree of religious tolerance within England, not restoration of Anglican control two decades later, that dealt the first major blow to the values of Puritan New England, which treated its own dissenters less forgivingly.

New Netherland Becomes New York

The decision by a number of highly placed Massachusetts Bay residents accused of witchcraft during the Salem hysteria of 1692 to flee to New York for safety continued a pattern begun in the earliest years of Puritan rule. As early as the 1630s, Dutch New Netherland served as a refuge for religious dissenters. From its inception, the tolerance of the Dutch colony contrasted vividly with Puritan repressiveness. New Netherland allowed members of all Protestant sects to settle there, and even accepted Jews. At the beginning, however, the Dutch viewed their activites on the North American mainland as a part of more important trading concerns elsewhere. The Englishman Henry Hudson sailed up the large river that now bears his name as agent of the Netherland East Indies Company, seeking an American passage to Asia. Hudson had traded with the local Indians for furs, and more than a decade later, Dutch merchants founded the Netherland *West* India Company in order to develop American trade.

The company founded small trading posts from as far south as the Delaware Valley north to Long Island Sound on the Connecticut River. New Amsterdam on Manhattan Island's tip was established as a trading post in 1624, one of the Dutch outposts, which together came to be known as New Netherland. (In 1626, one of the early governors or "director generals," Peter Minuit, "bought" Manhattan Island from Indians for an amount estimated at from twenty-four to forty dollars in this century's money.)

New Netherland was ruled by its governor and council. There was no popular representation, a typical state of affairs given the status of the colony as a commercial joint stock company. The company's bylaws provided for worship in the Calvinist Dutch Reformed Church but explicitly allowed members of *all* Protestant groups to live in New Netherland without fear of persecution. A number of farmers emigrated along with merchants to New Amsterdam, the chief town within New Netherland, and more than a dozen languages were spoken in this cosmopolitan community. In 1629, the company further encouraged immigration by creating a Charter of Privileges for "Patroons" (great landowners), who were given huge tracts of land in return for bringing over fifty families of farm tenants. Within a few years, the Hudson Valley north of New Amsterdam had been divided into "patroonships" virtually under the feudal control of their owners. (When the English occupied New Netherland, they confirmed these land titles, thereby keeping the patroon system of estate ownership.)

The Dutch colony's most important governor was a soldier named Peter Stuyvesant, who came in 1647, and who extended the control of New Netherland over a Swedish settlement on the Delaware River ("New Sweden"). If religious life remained tolerant during these years, political

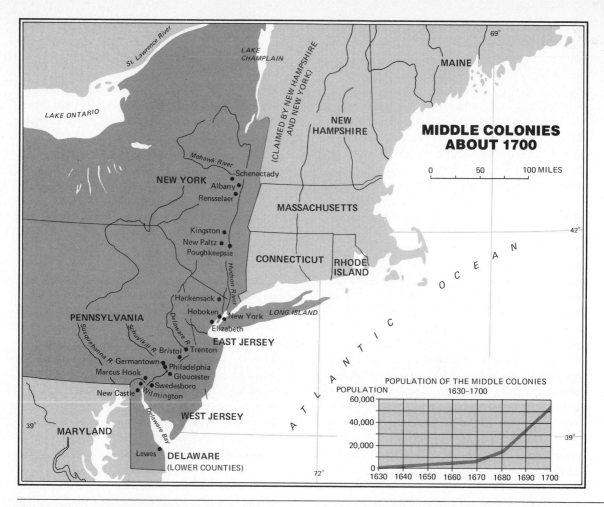

MIDDLE COLONIES
ABOUT 1700

0   50   100 MILES

POPULATION OF THE MIDDLE COLONIES
1630–1700

The land between the Southern colonies and the New England colonies was known as the Middle Colonies. This region early attracted settlers from many different countries in Europe, and from other colonies.

The Dutch staked one of the first claims in the Middle Colonies on the basis of explorations by Henry Hudson in 1609. Dutch merchants established fur trading posts at Fort Orange (Albany), on the Connecticut River, and on the Delaware River. They called the land they claimed New Netherland. Dutch merchants negotiated a famous real estate deal with the Indians. They purchased Manhattan Island for twenty-four dollars' worth of goods, and changed its name to New Amsterdam.

The Dutch were also responsible for the settlement of Delaware. A Dutchman obtained a charter that organized a company headed by Swedes and Dutchmen. Fifty Swedes sailed up the Delaware River in 1638 and established Fort Christina, on the site of present-day Wilmington. Sev-eral Finnish families joined them later. The colony was called New Sweden.

In 1655 the Dutch strengthened their hold on this region by seizing Fort Christina. But New Sweden did not remain in Dutch hands long. King Charles II of England did not like having Dutch settlements wedged in between the English colonies. In 1664 he declared that all the territory between the Connecticut and Delaware rivers belonged to his brother James, the Duke of York. The Dutch, realizing they were in no position to fight, surrendered when an English fleet sailed into New Amsterdam. Thus ended Dutch colonial power in mainland America. The new proprietor, the Duke of York, promptly renamed the colony New York.

Included in James' grant was the region of New Jersey, which had been settled by Swedish and Dutch pioneers. James gave the land to two of his friends, Lord John Berkeley and Sir George Carteret. The province was soon divided into East Jersey and West Jersey. In 1702 England claimed all

life was arbitrary and economic affairs firmly in the hands of an oligarchy of merchants and patroons. Popular government never reached New Netherland. Tensions between Stuyvesant's regime and the English settlers to his north, including those Puritans who had migrated into various Long Island towns, remained serious. During the English Civil Wars of the 1640s and 1650s, however, it proved impossible to extend English control over New Amsterdam and the other Dutch possessions.

Once the monarchy was restored and Charles II took the throne in 1660, however, he began rewarding his favorite supporters with grants of titles and land. One of the largest went to the Duke of York, who received a grant in March 1664 of all the land between the Connecticut and Delaware rivers (including Long Island), most of which happened to belong to the Dutch at the time. The duke dispatched four ships and several hundred soldiers, many of them recruited at Puritan Boston, to New Amsterdam harbor, where they demanded the fort's surrender. Recognizing the futility of resisting the far superior English force, Governor Stuyvesant capitulated on September 8, 1664, and New Amsterdam became New York that same day. Shortly thereafter the British occupied the former Swedish settlements on the Delaware, and the Dutch ceased to be a factor in North America.

New Jersey as a royal colony. There is still a Board of Proprietors for East Jersey and one for West Jersey.

The most successful of the Middle Colonies was Pennsylvania. William Penn, a Quaker, received the land from Charles II in 1681. He envisioned his colony as a refuge for fellow Quakers. Arriving in Pennsylvania in 1682, he carefully studied his property before selecting the site of Philadelphia. Attracted by the prospect of good land, political liberty, and religious tolerance, people flocked to Pennsylvania. By 1700 Philadelphia had 10,000 people. It would eventually outstrip Boston as the largest city in colonial America.

In 1682 Penn convinced the Duke of York to grant him control of the southern portion of the Delaware River. This area, already inhabited by Swedes and Dutch, was known as "the lower counties." It became the colony of Delaware in 1704.

Puritan New England could not take heart from this transfer of power. If anything, it made the task of enforcing religious conformity more difficult, because the Duke of York's agents confirmed their intention to maintain the same standard of religious tolerance as the Dutch within the newly acquired domains. Now there were *two* English colonies on New England's borders—Rhode Island and New York—prepared to receive those who rejected the coercion of Puritan society. Another colony, New Jersey, would later emerge from a portion of the Duke of York's grant assigned to a pair of English proprietors, Sir George Carteret and Lord John Berkeley, although New Jersey became a *royal* province in 1702. But sales of land along the Delaware to various Quaker purchasers during the 1670s and 1680s, including a major purchase in 1682 by that sect's most well-connected and aristocratic young leader, William Penn, led to creation of *another* non-Puritan Northern colony, Pennsylvania. All of these circumstances confirmed both the growing importance of religiously "tolerant" provinces within English North America and the increasing isolation of that survivor from a more *intolerant* period in colonial affairs, Puritan New England.

Quakerism and Puritan Massachusetts

Although few Quakers tried to settle in Massachusetts Bay during the seventeenth century, the sect proved especially irritating to Puritan leaders. They reacted mercilessly to Quaker infiltration. The Quakers, also known as the Society of Friends, had emerged as a significant dissenting movement in England. Its leader, George Fox, advocated a form of spiritual individualism even greater than the variety that had caused Anne Hutchinson's banishment. Fox and the other Quakers challenged the notion that ministers stood apart from ordinary believers in any respect, thereby denying the hierarchy that even Puritan churches accepted as legitimate. The Quakers also denied the primacy of biblical authority, believing that Christ's "inner light" entered every human being. Elaborate church ceremonies and even formal preaching seemed without basic spiritual significance to the Quakers, who were also pacifists and egalitarian believers in universal brotherhood. Practically every basic tenet of Quakerism contradicted orthodox doctrine, whether Puritan or Anglican. Although thousands of Quakers were jailed in England, Quakerism became the most dynamic faith within English Protestantism in the second half of the seventeenth century.

Massachusetts Bay passed statutes banning Quakers, and when two Quaker women arrived there from Barbados in 1656, the authorities responded drastically. They had just hanged a local woman for witchcraft. Now the Quaker ladies were undressed and subjected to demeaning bodily examinations comparable to those given at Salem in 1692 in search of witches' tits and similar malign evidences. None were found, so the women were jailed and deported rather than hanged.

The laws governing Quaker intrusion at Massachusetts Bay were then made even more stern. One imprisoned Quaker was beaten unconscious for his beliefs. A Quaker couple failed to pay their fines and, as a consequence, witnessed their two children sold into slavery outside the colony. An old man who tried to help a pair of Quaker women starving in prison found himself banished to Rhode Island in midwinter. In 1658, the General Court approved the death penalty for Quakers who returned after banishment. The following year, two Quakers were hanged and a third, Mary Dyer, banished. When she returned to Boston in 1660, she too went to the gallows.

Quaker Pennsylvania

It was evident to Quakers in England that they needed more hospitable areas to settle in English America, and hundreds drifted into the colonies south of New England even before acquiring their own refuge. The person responsible for providing Quakers with a colony of their own, William Penn, was the son of Admiral Sir William Penn, a leading figure both in the Cromwellian era and during the Restoration period when Charles II "restored" the Stuart monarchy. Young William, born in 1644, converted to Quakerism in 1667 and became passionately devoted to the notion of beginning a colony in America that would receive all groups persecuted for political or religious reasons, not simply Quakers alone. Penn, although a Quaker, remained on good terms with prominent figures in the Stuart Restoration such as the Duke of York, whose troops had conquered New Netherland. With the duke's support, Penn managed to obtain a charter from Charles II (1681) for an area roughly the size of England itself around York's Delaware River territories. Penn and his heirs would hold the land in feudal tenure from the king (a situation that continued up to 1776) and would serve as sole proprietor and ruler, paying Charles only "two Beaver skins" and a fifth share of any precious metals found.

The arrangement was a colossal bargain for Penn and a boon to his fellow Quakers. The king ordered the territory named Pennsylvania, and its proprietor began immediately advertising both in England and on the European continent for farmers and artisans. Settlers were promised generous land grants for farms as well as complete freedom to worship and some political influence through a representative assembly.

Thousands of settlers quickly followed Penn to the new colony during the 1680s. Many came from other English colonies in the New World, while others migrated from Germany, Wales, Ireland, and Holland as well as from England. Penn-

---

Each colonial government had a governor and a legislature. All the legislatures except that of Pennsylvania had two houses. The upper house was usually called the council. The lower house was generally known as the assembly.

There were three main types of colonial governments—royal, proprietary, and self-governing. In a royal colony, the governor and council were appointed by the crown; the assembly was elected by freemen. In a proprietary colony, the proprietor (or his appointee) was appointed by the crown. He in turn named the council, while freemen elected the assembly. In a self-governing colony, freemen elected the governor, the council, and the assembly. In a self-governing corporate colony, directors of the corporation appointed the governor and council; freemen elected the assembly.

For additional information on the original thirteen colonies, see maps on pp. 76, 111, and 118.

Founding of the Thirteen English Colonies

Colony	Early Settlements	Year Founded	Type of Colonial Government
Connecticut	Windsor	1633	Self-governing corporate
	Wethersfield	1634	
	Hartford	1636	
	New Haven	1638	
Delaware	Zwaanedael (Lewes) (settled by Dutch)	1631	Proprietary to 1682/Part of Pennsylvania, 1682–1703/Self-governing corporate
	Fort Christina (Wilmington) (settled by Swedes)	1638	after 1703
Georgia	Darien	1721	Proprietary 1732–54/Royal after 1754
	Savannah	1733	
	Augusta	1735	
Maryland	St. Mary's	1634	Proprietary 1632–91/Royal 1691–1715/
	Annapolis	1648	Proprietary after 1715
Massachusetts	Plymouth	1620	Self-governing corporate 1620–91/Royal
	Gloucester	1623	after 1691
	Salem	1626	
	Boston	1630	
New Hampshire	Rye	1623	Proprietary 1622–41/Part of Massachu-
	Portsmouth	1624	setts, 1641–80/Royal after 1680
New Jersey	Glucester	1623	Proprietary 1664–1702 (divided into
	Hoboken	1630	East Jersey and West Jersey 1676)/
	Hackensack	1639	Royal after 1702
	Swedesboro	1641	
	Elizabeth	1664	
New York	New Amsterdam (New York) (settled by Dutch)	1609	Colony of Dutch West India Company, 1624–64/Proprietary 1664–85/Royal
	Kingston (settled by Dutch)	1615	after 1685
	Fort Orange (Albany) (settled by Dutch)	1623	
North Carolina	Edenton	1658	Part of Carolina proprietary colony 1670–
	Currituck	1672	1712/Separate proprietary colony
	Bath	1705	1712–29/Royal after 1729
	New Bern	1710	
Pennsylvania	Marcus Hook (settled by Swedes)	1640	Proprietary
	Bristol	1681	
	Philadelphia	1682	
	Germantown	1683	
Rhode Island	Providence	1636	Self-governing 1636–44/Self-governing
	Portsmouth	1638	corporate 1644–63/Royal after 1663
	Newport	1639	
	Warwick	1643	
South Carolina	Charleston	1670	Part of Carolina proprietary colony
	Beaufort	1711	1670–1712/Separate proprietary colony 1712–29/Royal after 1729
Virginia	Jamestown	1607	Self-governing corporate 1607–24/Royal
	Hampton	1610	after 1624
	Newport News	1611	

William Penn was granted land on both sides of the Delaware River by Charles II in repayment for a debt owed Penn's father. The younger Penn established a Quaker society, guaranteeing an unusual amount of self-government and religious tolerance. In dealing with the Indians, he was consistently fair. (Colonial Williamsburg)

sylvania quickly became a cosmopolitan haven for dissenters from many countries. That suited the proprietor, who considered the venture his "Holy Experiment" in establishing religious freedom within a colony devoted to a belief in man's essential goodness.

Penn wrote a "Frame of Government" for the colony that provided for a governor (he served himself while in the colony from 1682 to 1684), an appointed council, and an elected assembly whose role remained largely advisory until 1701. Penn also supervised the work of engineers and architects who laid out the plan for his capital city of Philadelphia (the "City of Brotherly Love"), and he personally met with Indian chieftains to confirm through purchase from the Indians the land already granted him by the English king. (Roger Williams would have approved.)

Despite the goodness of man, quarrels broke out. Penn's representatives in the colony fought for power with assembly members demanding the right to *initiate* laws. Penn himself returned in 1699 to help devise "A New Charter of Privileges," which served as the colony's constitution until the revolution. Pennsylvania flourished economically from the start. Farmers spread out over the rich inland riverbed fields, while merchants traded for furs with the Indians and engaged in a variety of other commerce with England, the West Indies, and the other mainland colonies.

By the time he died, Penn recognized that his colonial experiment had become more prosperous than holy. A Quaker elite arose among Pennsylvania's merchants and large landholders and used the assembly as a base to contend for power with those representing the proprietor's interests. Still, Penn's efforts to guarantee religious liberty in his province served as a model for other mainland colonies, spreading the gospel of toleration that Roger Williams had preached without success when battling Puritan orthodoxy earlier in the century.

TOWARD THE WITCHCRAFT TRIALS: THE PARADOX OF PURITAN DECLINE

It is hard to imagine disillusioned Puritans, a scholar of Puritanism once wrote, if only because the group was conditioned to expect disappointment and suffering while obeying God. Nevertheless, from the mid-seventeenth century on, ministers preached constantly on the theme of "declension" or *decline* from the expectations of the founding generation. Even within their own churches, by the 1660s, the Puritans began watering down their stringent standards for membership. Rather than risk antagonizing a large body of believers, whose moral behavior was admirable but who had not undergone religious conversion, the churches of New England agreed in 1662 to a "halfway covenant" membership. Those who practiced high standards of personal behavior could now achieve a "halfway" status within the church, a status normally sufficient to allow freemanship and voting within the town as well as maintenance of their Puritan identity.

The founders had passed from the scene by that time. England had restored the monarchy under Charles II, and Puritanism was a declining faith in the mother country. Second- and third-generation New Englanders could not escape recognizing that their "errand into the wilderness" had been successful—but irrelevant as an example of a City upon a Hill. New England retreated even before the Restoration period into a defensiveness about its virtues, proudly independent from practically any English control and groping toward a new identity.

"I write the Wonders of the Christian Religion," Cotton Mather proclaimed in his *Magnalia Christi Americana*, "flying from the Depravations of Europe, to the American strand." Although Mather stressed the theme of declension—berating his own generation for failing to measure up to their revered fathers—the dilemma faced by late-seventeenth-century Puritans such as Mather reflected a problem of cultural transition. Committed to a set of beliefs that appeared increasingly archaic within their own environment, observing their religion even as faith gave way to economic activity or secular achievement, Puritan leaders like Mather and Stoughton in the 1680s and 1690s found no adequate way to reconcile their society's past and present.

Even the once humbled Indians of New England revived themselves for a final outburst that Puritans viewed as yet another evidence of declension and of God's disfavor. New England had not known a major Indian uprising since the Pequot War of 1636–37, which ended with the bloody suppression of the Pequots and the opening to settlement of the eastern Connecticut region. During the next four decades, white settlers—Puritans and non-Puritans—had driven New England's Indians from their lands, from Maine and New Hampshire south to the New York border. In 1661, Massasoit, king of the Wampanoag Indians who had befriended the Pilgrims, died and his son, Metacom, whom the whites called Philip, took charge. After years of trying to maintain friendly relations with English settlers only to be humiliated in return, Philip and his outnumbered subjects undertook a desperate final stand against the English. It began in June 1675 with an attack on the town of Swansea. Within months, frontier settlements in western Massachusetts had been attacked and destroyed. Philip's Wampanoags were joined by Maine's Abenaki Indians and by the normally peaceful Narragansett tribe from Rhode Island, so that the uprising spread throughout New England.

The Indians managed to wipe out entire settlements in Maine and Massachusetts over the next year, but the English gradually regained the initiative aided by thousands of loyal Indians. They began tracking down the rebellious warriors. Then

Philip's death in 1676 took the steam out of the war, which ended with the almost complete destruction of Indian culture in New England. By the time peace returned to the frontier, one out of every sixteen whites in the region had been killed along with a huge but uncounted number of Indians.

King Philip's war was only a temporary menace, but the English government's decision to revoke the Massachusetts Bay charter in 1684 proved a permanent disaster from which Puritan society never recovered. Massachusetts Bay authorities had alienated Charles II and his advisers almost from the moment he returned to the throne. First, the colony declined to enforce the Navigation Acts (see Chapter 8, p. 154), arguing that England could not regulate trade in its waters because Massachusetts Bay had no representatives in Parliament. Second, the Puritans would not allow other religious groups, including Anglicans, to practice their faith freely. In a number of other ways, the colony displayed its evident belief that it enjoyed freedom from English control in all but name. Massachusetts coined money without permission from the crown, and it refused to allow appeals to English courts. An official of the Lords of Trade, which supervised the colonies, Edward Randolph, toured New England in 1676, reporting back these and other offenses against English authority.

The following year, Massachusetts sent two agents to England to defend its rights, one of them being William Stoughton (later the magistrate at Salem's witch trials). The agents accomplished little, since the Puritan commonwealth could count on few defenders in England by then. Finally, after years of continued resistance by Massachusetts Bay to the Navigation Acts, the Lords of Trade persuaded the Court of Chancery to declare Massachusetts's charter forfeit in October 1684. By 1687, the charters of Connecticut and Rhode Island had also been annulled, thus clearing the ground for imposing direct royal control over New England.

The frustrations of Puritan leaders in Massachusetts Bay grew daily as they watched the old order crumble. Shortly after revocation of the charter in 1684, the first Anglican congregation began holding services in Boston. What would

Winthrop, John Cotton, and the other founders have thought had they witnessed the Anglican parson obtain permission to conduct services in the Puritan's historic Old South Church—while those who had come to attend regular Congregational services waited outside for the Anglicans to conclude their prayers? Adding to this *religious* humiliation came political subordination; that same year, 1686, brought a new royal governor to Massachusetts, Sir Edmund Andros. He ruled a "Dominion of New England"—Massachusetts Bay, Connecticut, Rhode Island, New York, and New Jersey—without a representative assembly. The dominion government also began enforcing the Navigation Acts, imposing taxes without assembly approval. Andros's council also challenged earlier New England land titles as part of the governor's campaign to break the power of the old Puritan oligarchy.

When Bostonians learned in the spring of 1689 that William and Mary of Orange had assumed the throne in England after the Glorious Revolution of 1688, ending the last Stuart king's rule, they promptly arrested Andros and shipped him back to England. There were revolts against Andros's rule in the other dominion colonies, and in New York, rebellious militia led by Jacob Leisler threw the province into a state of civil war for a time before a new royal governor arrived.

Puritan leaders promptly sent Increase Mather, whose ministerial authority would later help terminate the witchcraft agitation, to England on a desperate mission: gaining permission from William and Mary to restore the old Massachusetts Bay charter. Mather failed, and the new charter, which he brought back in 1691, left Massachusetts a crown colony, although with some aspects of limited self-rule. (The assembly, for example, and not the governor, would choose the members of the governor's council.)

By the time the first royal governor under the new regime, William Phips, reached Massachusetts in the midst of the witchcraft crisis in 1692, the end of the old Puritan order seemed complete. Because of Andros, Anglicans worshiped freely in the heart of Congregationalist Boston. Many of Massachusetts Bay's new *economic* elite, especially the merchant princes of Salem Town,

Sir Edmund Andros served in the closing years of James II's reign as governor of the "Dominion of New England," which stretched from New Jersey to Massachusetts. Andros became widely unpopular and was overthrown as a result of the Glorious Revolution in England. (NYPL/Picture Collection)

Boston, and other leading seaports, were either Anglicans or otherwise alienated from traditional Puritan dogma. The political disturbances of the Andros period had reduced the previously unchecked *local* authority of Puritan ministers and town officials throughout the commonwealth. Even before the first witchcraft outbreak at Salem, a general mood of uncertainty and foreboding prevailed in Massachusetts Bay. Teetering between the final collapse of *all* Puritan authority and the beginning of its new status under royal control, the leaders of Massachusetts in 1692 were ill-tempered and ill-prepared. They had difficulty in coping, therefore, with that final assault upon *local* patterns of authority represented by the temporary triumph of the "afflicted" teenagers and their supporters at Salem. With the end of the the witchcraft trials, the Puritan ideal no longer dominated New England's political and social developments as had been the case up to then. The passing of the old Puritan order went unmourned by most New Englanders on the eve of the eighteenth century. They appeared more concerned with the processes of economic growth and social change than with any lingering allegations of spiritual "declension."

Suggested Readings
Chapters 5-6

The Salem Witch Trials

Paul Boyer and Stephen Nissenbaum, *Salem Possessed: The Social Origins of Witchcraft* (1974) and *Salem-Village Witchcraft: A Documentary History* (1972); Sanford J. Fox, *Science and Justice: The Massachusetts Witchcraft Trials* (1968); Chadwick Hansen, *Witchcraft in Salem* (1969); David Levin, *What Happened in Salem?* (1960); Marion L. Starkey, *The Devil in Massachusetts* (1949); C. W. Upham, *Salem Witchcraft* (reprinted, 1959).

Puritanism in New England

James Axtell, *The School Upon a Hill: Education and Society in Colonial New England* (1976); Bernard Bailyn, *The New England Merchants in the Seventeenth Century* (1955); Viola Barnes, *The Dominion of New England* (1923); Emery Battis, *Saints and Sectaries: Anne Hutchinson and the Antinomian Controversy* (1962); Sacvan Bercovitch, *The Puritan Origins of the American Self* (1975); Timothy H. Breen, *The Character of the Good Ruler* (1970); C. E. Clark, *The Eastern Frontier: The Settlement of Northern New England, 1610–1763* (1970); Lawrence A. Cremin, *American Education: The Colonial Experience* (1969); John Demos, *A Little Commonwealth* (1970); R. S. Dunn, *Puritans and Yankees: The Winthrop Dynasty of New England* (1962); Kai Erikson, *Wayward Puritans* (1966); D. H. Flaherty, *Privacy in Colonial New England* (1972); Charles Grant, *Democracy in the Connecticut Frontier Town of Kent* (1961); P. J. Greven, *Four Generations* (1969); David Hall, *The Faithful Shepherd* (1972); Michael Hall, *Edward Randolph and the American Colonies, 1676–1703* (1960); G. H. Haskins, *Law and Authority in Early Massachusetts* (1960); Sydney V. James, *Colonial Rhode Island* (1975); Mary J. A. Jones, *Congregational Commonwealth* (1968); George Langdon, *Pilgrim Colony: A History of New Plymouth, 1620–1691* (1966); Kenneth Lockridge, *A New England Town* (1970); Robert Middlekauff, *The Mathers* (1971); Perry Miller, *Errand Into the Wilderness* (1956), *The New England Mind: From Colony to Province* (1953), *The New England Mind: The Seventeenth Century* (1954), and *Orthodoxy in Massachusetts*

(1959); Edmund S. Morgan, *The Puritan Dilemma* (1958), *The Puritan Family* (1966), *Roger Williams: The Church and the State* (1967), and *Visible Saints* (1963); Samuel E. Morison, *Builders of the Bay Colony* (1930), *The Founding of Harvard College* (1935), and *Harvard in the Seventeenth Century* (2 vols., 1936); Sumner C. Powell, *Puritan Village* (1963); Darrett B. Rutman, *American Puritanism* (1970) and *Winthrop's Boston 1630–1649* (1965); Alan Simpson, *Puritanism in Old and New England* (1955); R. E. Wall, *Massachusetts Bay: The Crucial Decade, 1640–1650* (1972); Ola Winslow, *Master Roger Williams* (1957) and *Meetinghouse Hill* (1952); Larzer Ziff, *Puritanism in America* (1973).

Indians and Puritans

Francis Jennings, *The Invasion of America* (1975); Douglas Leach, *Flintlock and Tomahawk: New England in King Philip's War* (1958) and *The Northern Colonial Frontier, 1607–1763* (1966); Richard Slotnick, *Regeneration Through Violence* (1973); Alden T. Vaughan, *New England Frontier: Puritans and Indians, 1620–1675* (1965); Anthony F. C. Wallace, *The Death and Rebirth of the Seneca* (1970).

The Middle Colonies

Charles M. Andrews, *The Colonial Period of American History* (Vols. I and III, 1934–1937); Van Cleaf Bachman, *Peltries or Plantations* (1969); Daniel J. Boorstin, *The Americans: The Colonial Experience* (1958); Charles Boxer, *The Dutch Seaborne Empire, 1600–1800* (1965); Carl Bridenbaugh, *Cities in the Wilderness, 1625–1742* (1938); E. B. Bronner, *William Penn's "Holy Experiment": The Founding of Pennsylvania* (1962); Thomas J. Condon, *New York Beginnings* (1968); Wesley F. Craven, *The Colonies in Transition, 1660–1713* (1968) and *New Jersey and the English Colonization of North America* (1964); Mary M. Dunn, *William Penn: Politics and Conscience* (1967); M. B. Endy, *William Penn and Early Quakerism* (1973); Rufus Jones, *Quakers in the American Colonies* (1911); Michael Kammen, *Colonial New York* (1975); L. H. Leder,

Robert Livingston and the Politics of Colonial New York, 1654–1728 (1961); David S. Lovejoy, *The Glorious Revolution in America* (1972); Gary B. Nash, *Quakers and Politics: Pennsylvania, 1681–1726* (1968); J. E. Pomfret, *The Province of East New Jersey, 1609–1702* (1962) and *The Province of West New Jersey, 1609–1702* (1956); Ellis L. Raesley, *Portrait of New Netherland* (1945); J. R. Reich, *Leisler's Rebellion* (1953); F. B. Tolles, *Meeting House and Counting House: The Quaker Merchants of Colonial Philadelphia* (1963) and *Quakers and the Atlantic Culture* (1960); Allen W. Trelease, *Indian Affairs in Colonial New York: The Seventeenth Century* (1960); Thomas J. Wertenbaker, *The Founding of American Civilization: The Middle Colonies* (1938); H. E. Wildes, *William Penn* (1974).

The British colonies in North America at the time of Bacon's Rebellion and the Salem trials had been little more than a series of isolated settlements scattered along the eastern coast. The planters of Virginia and the Puritans of Massachusetts, like other early colonists, were still basically Europeans. They continued to identify with the European concepts of home, family, culture, and government. Royal authority remained almost unchallenged, and when social crises occurred, more often than not, they were resolved by the exercise of British power. Thus Governor Berkeley in Virginia, backed by English soldiers, put an end to Bacon's rebels, and in similar fashion, Governor Phips in Massachusetts clamped a final lid on the Salem hysteria.

By the mid-eighteenth century, two generations after the fateful events described in the previous episodes, all this had changed. With remarkable speed, the British colonists and other settlers in English North America had created a distinctly new and American society. From Georgia to Maine, the settlement line was almost solid, as population expanded along with agriculture and commerce. Cities like Boston, Philadelphia, and New York became almost as large and as wealthy as many European urban centers.

Culturally, the new society remained mostly British, while it absorbed large clusters of German, Dutch, and Swedish immigrants (among others) who settled along the seaboard. But as it grew, British North America became increasingly conscious of its identity and style as distinctly American rather than English. The events that moved the thirteen colonies toward their fateful decision to break with England in the mid-1770s came at the end of two decades during which a multiplicity of actions had engraved American patterns of family life, religious and cultural values, economic behavior, and—most importantly—political autonomy upon the older British fabric of this society. The chapters that follow describe this process of "Americanization," the political strife that ensued from it, and the creation of a new nation from the turmoil of revolution.

Chapter 7 describes the background and drama of that March 5, 1770, event that occurred in Boston when a squad of British soldiers fired their weapons into a noisy and threatening crowd of Bostonians. One of a series of such conflicts that grew during the 1760s and 1770s between the American colonies and British authorities, the Boston Massacre symbolized the evolving separation of mother country and colonies. Chapter 8 details the chain of events leading to American independence.

But the winning of independence and the creation of a loosely connected confederation of thirteen distinct "nation-states" proved only the first part in a two-phase drama of nation building. To the surprise of many, including a number of their own leaders and citizens, the Americans managed to win the Revolutionary War. The hero of that war, General George Washington, retired to his Virginia plantation after directing American military efforts. Soon, he and many of his revolutionary associates came to believe that the new government they had brought into existence had not succeeded in consolidating the political society for which they had fought. After long and thoughtful deliberation, they concluded

REVOLUTIONARY AMERICA

UNIT
TWO

that the Confederation had to be replaced. The culmination of the slow, painful process by which the revolutionary leaders reached this conclusion occurred at the Constitutional Convention held in 1787 at Philadelphia, the subject of Chapter 9. The new Constitution and frame of government for the United States of America is described in Chapter 10. Having entered the eighteenth century a small, weak, European, and divided people, Americans began their first century as an independent people in 1800 with a host of problems but also (with resources as a new country born of their three-decade-long struggle for survival) independence and nationhood.

7 The Boston Massacre

Some called the eleven-year-old boy Christopher Seider, others, Christian Snider. Whatever his real name, Christopher Seider (let us call him that) stood in a crowd outside Ebenezer Richardson's home in Boston's North End on the windy morning of February 22, 1770. Seider was one of several hundred Bostonians gathered there, many of them youngsters like himself. They had penned Richardson and his family inside, and now they pelted the house with eggs, fruit peelings, sticks, and stones. The crowd broke most of the house's glass windowpanes. One rock struck Richardson's wife. Others barely missed his two daughters. Richardson took an unloaded musket to the window and aimed it at the mob outside. The crowd broke down his front door, but continued to stand outside—probably because of its healthy respect for the gun—and bombard the house with stones.

Richardson loaded his musket with small birdshot pellets. He fired and hit several people in the crowd, some of whom were injured slightly. Christopher Seider less fortunate than others, fell to the ground with eleven pellets in his chest and abdomen. He died that evening.

The angry crowd surged into the house after the boy fell. It cornered Richardson, who surrendered without further resistance. The mob prepared to lynch the unfortunate man and doubtless would have except for the timely appearance of William Molineux, one of Boston's leading "radical" opponents of British authority. Molineux persuaded the angry crowd to turn Richardson over to the law officials. Within the hour Richardson appeared before four justices of the peace and a thousand onlookers in Faneuil Hall. Witnesses were heard at the open hearing, and Richardson was held in jail until the next session of the Massachusetts Superior Court, charged with "giving Christopher Seider a very dangerous wound." After Seider died, the charge became murder.

Before his death Seider had been unknown to most of Boston's 16,000 residents. On February 26, however, he received the "largest funeral perhaps ever known in America" up to that time. Several thousand Bostonians braved snow-clogged streets to pay tribute to his memory.

The funeral was organized by one of Boston's leading radicals, Samuel Adams, a lawyer and former town official with a reputation as an effective political agitator.

Seider's death provided Adams, and the cause of colonial resistance, with a perfect juvenile martyr to British tyranny. It was disclosed that Richardson had served in previous years as an informer for the British customs commissioners, who had been sent to Boston in 1767 to collect duties on colonial imports. These duties had been set by Parliament in the Townshend Acts.

A few days later, after Christopher Seider's death, Boston's townspeople poured into the streets again, this time not as a mob but as a funeral procession. The following opinion appeared in the *Gazette*, the unofficial newspaper of the Sons of Liberty: "Young as he was, [Seider] died in his Country's Cause, by the Hand of an execrable Villain, directed by others, who could not bear to see the enemies of America made the Ridicule of Boys."

Boston merchants, along with merchant groups throughout the North American colonies of Great Britain,[1] viewed the taxes imposed upon them by Parliament as both unfair and illegal. In an attempt to force Parliament to repeal the Townshend Acts, they organized a boycott of all British-manufactured goods, which was referred to as the nonimportation agreement. Those merchants and other colonists who protested against the taxes levied upon them by the king and Parliament came to be known as Whigs (a term used earlier for *English* opponents of royal tyranny) or Patriots; the more militant among them organized themselves into the Sons of Liberty. Their opponents, those colonists who believed Great Britain did have the right to tax them, were known as Loyalists or Tories.

After passage of the Townshend Acts, increasingly large and unruly crowds of Patriots began to roam the streets of Boston at night, intimidating Tories or crown officials with threats of violence—and with violence itself. British officials claimed that such mobs were directed by radical leaders like Samuel Adams and William Molineux, and some of them were. On occasion, a town meeting[2] could transform itself into a mob simply by moving from its usual meeting place in Faneuil Hall into the streets, where it had been summoned to help enforce the decisions of the town leaders, most of whom were Patriots. Crowds like these often included the city's most respectable merchants and politicians. Mobs also gathered spontaneously, their numbers swelled by the presence in that port city of sailors, itinerant workers and artisans, jobless teenagers, and local bullyboys. More often than not, the more spontaneous crowds were dominated by those with powerful lungs or muscles. The mob that

---

[1] In 1707 England was united with Scotland. After this date the governmental unit as a whole is usually referred to as Great Britain. Its overseas possessions together became known as the British Empire.

[2] Boston was governed by a town meeting consisting mostly of voters. It met whenever the need arose. It could bring as many as 3000 people together for several days running.

stormed Ebenezer Richardson's house had gathered in this fashion. They were reacting to Richardson's attempt, that same night, to keep another, more organized mob from interfering with a merchant who was reported to be violating the nonimportation agreement.

During the two years preceding this incident, the Patriots and the colony's royal government had struggled bitterly to control Boston's economic and political life. Patriots like Samuel Adams used the easily aroused mobs to exert pressure on even Tory merchants to endorse the nonimportation agreement. The royal governor of Massachusetts, Francis Bernard, troubled by the Patriots' effective economic boycott and their control of the city's streets, encouraged the British army commander in North America, Major General Thomas Gage, to send troops from the large garrison at Halifax, Nova Scotia, to help restore the authority of the crown in Boston. But Bernard himself could not directly request troops. He had first to secure the consent of the governor's council, the upper house of the Massachusetts legislature. This council, which was elected by the citizens, generally sided with the opponents of British taxation and control. Bernard outlined his dilemma, one shared in some measure by most royal governors in the American mainland colonies, in a letter written in July 1768 to an official in Great Britain:

> General Gage has now informed me that his orders to Halifax are that the Troops shall be collected & kept in readiness, but are not to move till I require them. I answer that then they will never move: for I shall not make such a requisition without the Advice of Council: & I never expect to obtain that: neither their popular Constitution nor the present intimidation

British soldiers disembark at Boston's Long Wharf in October 1768. According to engraver Revere's caption, the troops then marched up King Street "with insolent parade." (Henry Francis DuPont Winterthur Museum)

will permit it. . . . In short, my Lord, Troops are not wanted here to quell a Riot or a Tumult, but to rescue the Government out of the hands of a trained mob & to restore the activity of the Civil Power, which is now entirely obstructed. And if an open Defiance of the Authority of Great Britain: a persecution of all those who are supposed to be maintainers of that authority . . . are not sufficient to show the Expedience of quartering Troops at Boston, we must wait till it becomes more apparent.

But if Bernard could not order troops, the authorities in London could. In October 1768 Boston witnessed the arrival of the first redcoats from the two regiments to be stationed there—the Fourteenth and the Twenty-ninth. After a lengthy struggle with Boston's local officials to obtain adequate quarters for the soldiers (one regiment spent its first night in Faneuil Hall), the troops began regular patrols. Overnight, Boston became a garrisoned town; the center of colonial opposition to parliamentary and royal authority had been "occupied." But the presence of troops failed to check the townspeople's "mobbish disposition"; it succeeded only in helping to unify the various local factions that opposed British attempts to tax and govern. Before the soldiers came, these factions had few visible symbols of British authority to complain about. Neither the ineffective Governor Bernard, nor the talented but unpopular Lieutenant Governor Thomas Hutchinson—not even the customs commissioners—had managed to rally patriotic sentiment among the people as effectively as did the presence of the British troops, whose numbers ranged from 600 to 1000 men. In the months between the arrival of the troops and the death of Christopher Seider, tempers flared repeatedly on both sides.

During these months the troops controlled their sentry posts. The Patriots controlled the merchants and the town meeting. Crown officials controlled Boston by day. The mobs, when they appeared, controlled the streets at night. The royal governor controlled only his temper. He resigned in 1770 in favor of Thomas Hutchinson. As far as anyone could judge, however, none of the authorities controlled Boston itself with any certainty. Both royal officials and Patriot leaders freely predicted that any major incident could trigger an open rebellion against British authority in that edgy community.

Relations between Bostonians and the British troops were sometimes friendly, sometimes hostile. Two groups among the unwanted soldiers made them even less welcome to townspeople than they would otherwise have been. These were the many Irish Catholics, whose presence offended the town's Protestant citizens, and a number of black troops, an affront to those Bostonians who kept black slaves or servants.

Any occupying army, of course, must expect hostility from those whose territory it controls. The British army was no exception. From the moment the troops arrived, the town's Patriot newspapers filled their columns with accounts of friction involving townspeople. There were numerous fights (invariably begun by the soldiers, according to townspeople), many minor acts of harassment, and endless arguments as the red-

Thomas Hutchinson, a loyal servant to the crown, moved to England in 1774 and never returned to America. But he loved Boston and was homesick for it until he died in 1780. (Massachusetts Historical Society)

coats attempted to patrol the community. Soldiers who searched for quarters for their families in the town were overcharged shamelessly if they managed to obtain quarters at all, and few Boston merchants resisted the temptation to raise their normal prices for British customers. But what proved particularly galling to the troops and their officers was not the understandable bitterness of private citizens. It was the hostility of public officials, especially the magistrates of Boston's court system. Sentries who were instructed to challenge passersby at fixed guard posts throughout Boston, especially after dark, found that civilians could and often did swear out warrants against the sentries themselves for disturbing the peace! The civil magistrates generally fined harshly any soldiers on guard duty whom townspeople accused of rude behavior. "We are in a pleasing Situation," wrote one British officer, "who are ordered here to Aid & assist the Civil Magistrate in preserving the peace & protecting his Majesty's subjects, when those very magistrates are our Oppressers." Ordinary soldiers complained about unfair treatment at the hands of American justices of the peace with the same kind of outrage voiced by colonial merchants at their treatment by British customs commissioners. Each side believed that justice could rarely be gained in the other's courts. Both sides were usually correct.

By late 1769 it had become clear that both the Townshend Acts and the dispatch of troops to Boston had failed to enforce British taxation. The struggle to assert royal authority in Boston had ended in a political stalemate between crown officials and the city's Patriot leadership—neither the troops nor the mobs managed to control the streets unopposed. Bernard and Hutchinson were reluctant to risk a general uprising by trying to enforce the customs laws, which merchant signers of the nonimportation agreement continued to ignore. Samuel Adams and his fellow radical Patriots, for their part, proved equally reluctant to provoke outright rebellion against all British authority. British officials and most American Tories believed, however, that the Patriots wanted not only to abolish the onerous customs duties but to end British rule entirely. They viewed the Patriots, in General Gage's words, as "an illegal combination of people" conspiring to stir popular feeling against Britain as a first step along the road to revolution.

The Patriots did not consider themselves conspirators. But they did view the British authorities and Tories as schemers trying to deprive provincial America both of its traditional liberties and of its hard-earned income. "There was a cursed cabal [group of plotters], principally residing in this town," Samuel Adams wrote in 1769 of Boston's Loyalists, "who . . . were perpetually intriguing to bring about another parliamentary tax act; for no other purpose than that they might feast and fatten themselves upon the spoils and plunder of the people." Adams added:

> One man has as good reason to affirm that a few, in calling for a military force under pretense of supporting civil authority, secretly intended to introduce a general massacre, as another has to assert, that a number of loyal subjects, by calling upon one another to be provided with arms, according to law, intended to bring on an insurrection.

Although at times Adams argued the existence of this British–Tory "conspiracy," he also acknowledged his opponents' belief in a comparable Bostonian plot against British rule. That the 600 harassed British soldiers who occupied Boston in early 1770 "secretly intended to introduce a general massacre" against Boston's 16,000 residents seems improbable. But at the time many Bostonians believed it, and they acted accordingly. Tensions ran high in the early months of 1770. Each group feared an attack that it believed its opponents had plotted well in advance. More often than not, however, the violence that actually flared up was unplanned and disorganized.

The British troops recognized by 1770 that their role in Boston had little to commend it. The job was lonely. The soldiers were shunned by the town's Patriot majority, abused in the courts, challenged boldly on the streets, and threatened regularly by mobs—all this for extremely low wages. To supplement their pay, many soldiers braved local hostility and sought jobs during their off-duty hours. Unfortunately, there were few part-time jobs available in Boston; there had been a grave depression in local commerce because of the enforcement of the nonimportation agreement. Bostonians were worried about their own unemployed, whose numbers increased daily. Competition between off-duty soldiers and unemployed townsmen for the few available jobs provoked a number of noisy arguments and minor fights.

One such incident took place on March 2, 1770, only four days after Christopher Seider's funeral. With emotions still running high in the town, this minor flurry brought Bostonians and redcoats to the brink of major civil conflict. The trouble began at John Gray's "ropewalk,"[3] a large plant where a number of workers produced rope and cable. Temporary laborers' jobs were often available there. These attracted unemployed townspeople and British troops. On this particular day a British soldier named Thomas Walker of the Twenty-ninth Regiment entered the plant and asked for work. Ropemaker William Green, a Bostonian, asked him: "Soldier, do you want work?" "Yes, I do," replied Walker. Green responded with an amused smirk, "Well, then go and clean my outhouse." The other ropemakers roared with laughter, but Walker's face turned red with fury. "Empty it yourself!" he shouted at Green. The pair exchanged hard words for a moment longer. Then the fight began.

The ropemakers pounced on Walker and pummeled the unfortunate soldier badly before he managed to get away. He returned shortly with eight or nine other redcoats, and the slugfest resumed. Both sides fought mainly with wooden clubs, although the soldiers also slashed away at times with their swords. The Bostonians managed to chase Walker and his cohorts from the ropeworks. But the soldiers returned within minutes, bringing with them nearly thirty reinforcements. By then, the number of civilians had also grown. Soon Gray's ropewalk was jammed with troops and ropeworkers, cracking their clubs against all

---

[3] At this time rope was made in a long, low building. A ropemaker walked backward from one end to the other, paying out fiber from a bundle at his waist and braiding it as he walked.

comers. Both sides suffered casualties, some quite severe, until the soldiers were once more driven from the factory.

The following day, Saturday, March 3, a trio of redcoats returned to the ropewalk, where they renewed the battle against workers on the scene. This time, one of the soldiers suffered a fractured skull and arm before he and his friends withdrew. Sunday, March 4, seemed more peaceful, although a group of British officers visited the ropewalk searching for a missing British sergeant, whose comrades had reported him killed by the townspeople.

The sergeant's body was never found, but rumors spread among the troops that the Bostonians planned some larger dramatic gesture of revenge against the British soldiers. One private "remembered some ropemakers asking where the Twenty-ninth [Regiment] planned to bury its dead." A Bostonian later swore that he heard four soldiers from the regiment say that "there were a great many townspeople who would eat their dinners on Monday next [March 5], who would not eat any on Tuesday."

The day of Monday, March 5, passed without incident. A foot of snow covered the ground. Bostonians who braved the cold, windswept city walked cautiously over the ice sheets that covered most of the streets. Boston had no street lamps then. As darkness fell, people had only a first-quarter moon to light their way. Snow covered King Street, which housed both the Custom House and the Main Guard, British army headquarters.

No one in Boston knew then that in London, earlier in the day, the British Parliament had repealed most of the controversial Townshend Acts (all but the one on tea). This was a stunning victory for colonial protesters, but the news of repeal reached Boston only in late April. By that time Bostonians were preoccupied with the events that had occurred on King Street on the bitter cold evening of March 5. It was then that the fragile structure of civic peace in Boston finally collapsed.

The incident began as had similar ones in the past—with a nervous British soldier, a sharp-tongued young Bostonian, and a fight. The soldier, Private Hugh White of the Twenty-ninth Regiment, was on guard duty at a sentry box on the corner of King Street and Shrimton's Lane, down the street from both the Main Guard and the Custom House. Along came a young wigmaker's apprentice named Edward Garrick. Garrick spotted a British officer named Goldfinch, and shouted within earshot of Private White: "There goes the fellow that won't pay my master for dressing his hair." Joined by another apprentice, Garrick strolled through the King Street area, later returning to White's sentry post, where he resumed his criticism of Captain Goldfinch. At this point, Private White defended the officer as a gentleman who would pay all his debts. "There are no gentlemen in the Twenty-ninth Regiment," shouted Garrick, whereupon White left his post and joined Garrick in the street.

"Let me see your face," ordered White. Garrick obliged, and White immediately smashed his musket into the young wigmaker's head. Garrick cried out in pain, and his companion began exchanging curses with the angry sentry. Within minutes a crowd of some fifty townspeople had gathered in the street, surrounding the lone sentry, shouting at him to fight them. White loaded his musket, retreated down the block to the steps of the Custom House, fixed his bayonet, and faced the angry crowd.

The mob began throwing large chunks of ice at White, screaming as they flung their missiles: "Kill him, kill him, knock him down. Fire, damn you, fire, you dare not fire." The town watchman suddenly appeared on the scene and urged the sentry to restrain himself, pleading that most people in the mob were youths who would not hurt him. As the crowd continued nevertheless to pelt him with ice, White responded: "Damn them; if they molest me I will fire." Finally, he shouted for assistance from the nearby regimental headquarters: "Turn out, Main Guard!"

Meanwhile, similar mobs had appeared elsewhere in Boston. Just a few blocks from King Street, soldiers strolled along Brattle Street carrying clubs, bayonets, and other weapons, while a solitary Bostonian ran up and down the immediate area shouting the usual call for a mob to gather: "Town born, turn out! Town born, turn out!" A crowd collected quickly at a regimental encampment called Murray's Barracks near Brattle Street. Soon volleys of snowballs hurled at the soldiers accompanied the shouts of bystanders. Several British officers, including Captain Goldfinch, ordered the soldiers back into the barracks to forestall bloodshed. More than once, officers knocked their own troops to the ground to prevent them from shooting into the onrushing crowd.

Another throng gathered in Dock Square, only two blocks from Private White's sentry post on King Street. Several hundred townspeople poured into the empty stalls of Boston's town market. They ripped the legs off produce and butcher tables and shouted "Fire!" to attract additional recruits from the neighborhood.

The cry of "Fire!" sounded repeatedly through the dark Boston streets and attracted a number of sleepy townspeople. Boston depended on volunteer firefighting companies. So groups of such firefighters carrying buckets joined the three separate crowds of agitated Bostonians spoiling for a fight with the soldiers. At some point, church bells began tolling an additional call for firefighters.

Bostonians of all ages converged on King Street—some with buckets, others with sticks. Many ran from the Dock Square and Murray's Barracks fracases once those incidents had quieted down. The crowd in King Street varied in size from several dozen to several hundred over the next hour, as men and boys moved along the town's cramped lanes and alleys. "There is no fire," shouted one youth to a bystander. "It is the soldiers fighting." "Damn it, I am glad of it," came the response. "I will knock some of them on the head." A number of Bostonians left the sidewalks to join the unruly scene in the streets.

The mob that gathered in King Street surrounded White's sentry post but made no immediate attempt to overwhelm him. Meanwhile, the British officer of the guard that evening, Captain Thomas Preston, had

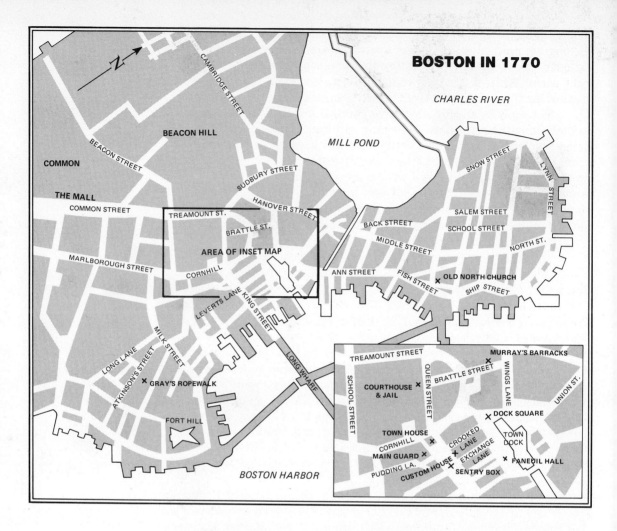

Boston in 1770

been summoned from his dinner table by White's urgent request for reinforcements. He went to the Main Guard on King Street, and he surveyed the crowd. By now it had grown to at least several hundred (accurate estimates were difficult). After deciding to help the beleaguered White, Preston ordered up a relief party of sentries—six privates and a corporal. This group then marched toward the menacing crowd, their muskets empty and shouldered—but their bayonets fixed.

Preston's few soldiers managed to push through the crowd, loading their muskets after reaching White's empty sentry box. White still confronted the large throng from a position on the Custom House steps. At Preston's orders and without interference from the bystanders, he joined the other soldiers.

Preston had ordered the sentries out primarily to relieve White. Having done so, the captain tried to march his soldiers back toward the Main Guard. The surrounding mob either would not or could not allow the troops through, so great was the press of bodies. Some people in the throng began shouting at the redcoats: "Damn you, fire. You can't kill us all." Within moments Preston found himself and his men cut off from assistance. He ordered his soldiers to form a curved line with their backs to the Custom House. Although they tried to keep the crowd from encircling them, some Bostonians managed to slip behind the soldiers.

The crowd, obviously leaderless, shuffled angrily yet uneasily around the nervous redcoats, uncertain whether to attack or withdraw. To add to the confusion, the church bells kept tolling. Every few moments, more bucket-carrying Bostonians arrived at the scene. Many exchanged their buckets quickly for clubs or ice chunks when they understood the situation. Preston shouted for the crowd to disperse, but received in return only laughter, hooting, and a pelting with snowballs. The crowd taunted the soldiers to shoot, and the small company of British troops clenched their weapons tightly.

The only town official to brave the mob scene was one James Murray, a Tory justice of the peace, who arrived at King Street to read the Riot Act. By law, the statute forbidding riotous gatherings had to be read to a mob before it took effect. The crowd knew this. They knew, therefore, that Preston and his men would be on questionable legal ground if they fired without having first ordered the mob to disperse by a reading of the Riot Act.

The mob wanted to prevent the reading. A volley of snowballs and ice chunks soon sent Murray scurrying toward safety. The mob's anger increased when some of its members recognized at least two of the sentries, Privates Matthew Kilroy and William Warren, as participants in the battle at the ropewalk four days earlier. At the same time, Private White himself spotted a familiar face in the crowd, a young woman named Jane Whitehouse, whose home was near his own Boston living quarters. "Go home," he cried, taking her arm and pushing her toward the corner. "Go home, or you'll be killed."

The mob soon abandoned all restraint short of directly assaulting the soldiers. Individuals began pushing forcefully against Preston's troops, daring them to fire, denouncing them as cowards and scoundrels, challenging them to fistfights. "Why do you not fire? Damn you, you dare not fire. Fire and be damned," they continued to shout. There were small duels, as townsmen carrying clubs beat them against the guardsmen's musket barrels and bayonets. Preston continued to shout demands that the crowd disperse, at the same time restraining his frightened band of soldiers from opening fire. Several times the captain was approached by Patriot leaders in the crowd who asked whether he intended to fire. Each time he responded, "By no means, by no means."

A Tory dignitary urged the captain to disperse the unruly rioters with a warning volley of musket shot. At this, stressing his desire to prevent bloodshed, Preston placed himself directly in front of the muskets so that he would be the first victim of any shooting. The crowd cheered at Preston's predicament, which at the moment seemed an almost perfect reflection of the overall British situation in Boston — incapable either of maintaining public order or of withdrawing gracefully.

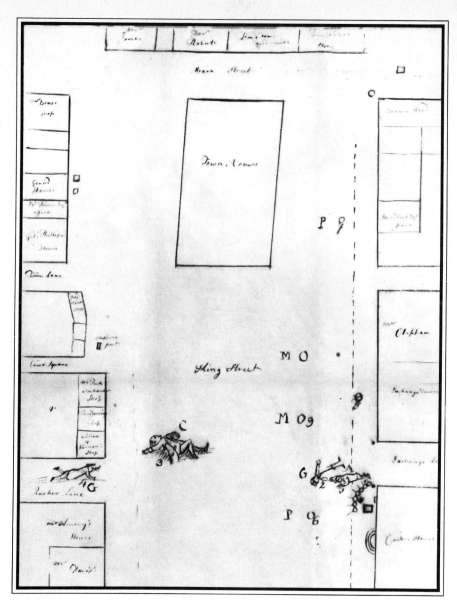

No more than a foot or two separated the line of soldiers from the nearest rioters. Suddenly a club went sailing from the midst of the crowd into the dimly lit street, hitting Private Hugh Montgomery. The private fell to the ground and dropped his musket on the ice. No one knows what triggered that particular act of violence, or what emotions Private Montgomery felt as he staggered to his feet and recovered his musket. But matters had reached the breaking point. Montgomery shouted, "Damn you, fire," and proceeded to pull his trigger. Within seconds, members of the crowd lunged at Preston and his troops, swinging their clubs wildly.

The soldiers managed to fight off these blows, but in an interval of from fifteen seconds to two minutes (the exact time remains unclear), the other troops also fired their weapons.

Preston neither ordered the shooting, nor did he—stunned at Montgomery's impulsive action—order it to stop. When the shooting finally ceased, the crowd continued to advance on the small group of soldiers, although few people got close enough to swing their clubs. The soldiers parried blows while reloading their muskets. They fired another round. Again the firing took place sporadically, with single shots being fired over a period of minutes. This time, several people in the crowd were wounded, and some fell to the ground. Finally, the crowd began to disperse, although it regrouped quickly once the firing had stopped, this time to recover the bodies of those who lay dead or wounded. The soldiers, fearing another attack, raised their muskets to fire a third round. By now, Preston had regained his composure and personally shoved down his soldiers' gun barrels before they could shoot, shouting, "Stop firing! Do not fire!"

The mob drew back for the moment, carrying the bodies of those hit by the troops. Preston's soldiers began to explain to their agitated captain that they had fired only after hearing what they believed to be *his* command. While emergency hospitals for the wounded were being set up in nearby homes, Preston marched his company back to the Main Guard. He then turned out the entire guard and placed it in formation on King Street between the Main Guard and Boston's Town House (the Old State House). The troops were drawn up in street-firing position, an eighteenth-century tactic for controlling urban riots in narrow streets. Rows of soldiers stood in single-file formation. The man at the head of the line would shoot, then move to the back of the line. There he reloaded and waited his turn to shoot once more.

In front of the Custom House, small groups of Bostonians passed grimly along King Street and stared at the bloodstains splattered on the icy thoroughfare. Word had spread quickly through town that, as a result of the shooting, five men lay dead or dying. Among the dead was one who would soon become the most famous martyr of the evening's bloodshed, Crispus Attucks. (Accounts differ as to whether he was a free black, a runaway slave, or an Indian of the Natick tribe.) Four others also died—an Irish Catholic immigrant named Patrick Carr; Samuel Gray, the son of the ropewalk owner; seventeen-year-old Samuel Maverick; and a young apprentice sailor named James Caldwell.

The withdrawal of Preston's men did not dispel the threat of further bloodshed that very night, as angry Bostonians filled the streets, hurling curses at the British troops and crying "To arms!" Every church bell in Boston began pealing. Even the town's official drums—which generally summoned the militia to combat—beat solemnly to announce the tragedy. Within an hour after the "massacre" itself, more than a thousand citizens crowded King Street. Rumors spread quickly among the townspeople that the soldiers planned a wholesale slaughter of the inhabitants. Local Tories were attacked and beaten in the streets. British officers and

Although only a mediocre artist, Paul Revere was a fine silversmith in addition to being an ardent Patriot. As a skilled craftsman, he cast cannon for the army, printed the first Continental money, and designed the state seal still used by Massachusetts. (Museum of Fine Arts, Boston— Gift of Joseph W., William B., and Edward H. R. Revere)

soldiers also found it dangerous to walk through Boston without armed escorts that night.

Moderate Patriot leaders pleaded with Lieutenant Governor Hutchinson, the leading civil official in town, to remove Preston's troops from King Street before their presence provoked further retaliation from the crowd. Hutchinson approached the troops and exchanged some harsh words with Preston. But he declined to order the soldiers back to quarters. Instead, he addressed the people from a balcony of the Town House. He urged them to retire peacefully, promising that he would do everything possible to ensure a full inquiry into the shooting. "The law shall have its course," he shouted. "I will live and die by the law." Apparently, this was also the view of the many Bostonians in the crowd who left quietly. The hundreds who remained demanded both immediate action against the British soldiers and removal of the troops from Boston's streets. Preston's superior officer, Lieutenant Colonel Maurice Carr, feared a renewed confrontation between the crowd and the troops. He ordered the soldiers on King Street to abandon street-firing formation and return to their barracks. As the troops marched off, the crowd—now silent and somber—dispersed.

At 2 A.M. on March 6 the town sheriff served a warrant on Captain Preston for his role in the episode. Preston surrendered an hour later. A few hours afterward, the eight redcoats in Preston's sentry party were also imprisoned. All nine were charged with murder.

After the arrest of Preston and his men, Boston drew back from the brink of civil disorder. Hutchinson and Carr were not the only ones who feared a bloodbath. Most responsible Patriot leaders shared their anxieties. They believed that the continued presence of troops among angry townspeople would only provoke violence on an uncontrollable scale. So they urged the removal of British troops from the town itself to Castle William, an island fort in Boston harbor.

Bostonians were still outraged over the massacre. At a town meeting on March 6, which was dominated by Samuel Adams and other Patriots, the people demanded removal of the British troops. Hutchinson tried to compromise between his loyalty to the crown and his recognition of the town's anger. He ordered only Preston's regiment, the Twenty-ninth, to Castle William.

The town meeting remained dissatisfied. On March 10 it sent a committee led by Samuel Adams to see Hutchinson. The group demanded that the remaining British regiment be ordered out of town. Hutchinson and his advisers had no choice but to submit. They ordered the Fourteenth Regiment, the last British troops in Boston, to depart the following day for Castle William. Boston now returned to the control of its own, Patriot-dominated town meeting. The remaining loyal dignitaries—Hutchinson, the customs commissioners, and lesser officials—could not direct the course of events without assistance from troops. The Patriots had no further need for nightly mobs to confront crown authority. Thus the immediate threat of civil disorder ended.

With the troops gone from Boston, the Patriots turned their attention to settling accounts with the imprisoned soldiers. On March 12 the *Gazette* employed the term "massacre" in connection with the events of March 5. This was the first public use of the term. A week later, on March 19, Boston's town meeting approved printing a version of the events that justified the behavior of the rioters and condemned the British soldiers. Entitled *A Short History of the Horrid Massacre at Boston,* the pamphlet was dispatched on fast ships to England to soften British anger at the Bostonians' conduct toward the troops. The Patriots decided not to distribute the pamphlet in Boston itself, lest it prejudice the soldiers' trials.

Also on March 19, the town meeting petitioned Hutchinson for an early trial of the prisoners. The lieutenant governor and other Loyalists resisted, considering the aroused state of emotions in Boston regarding Preston and his men. "I have assurances from the court," Preston wrote General Gage on April 1, "that they will continue [postpone] the trial . . . until the last week in May [although] great pain is being taken to intimidate the judges and compel them to bring it on sooner." Hutchinson's concern for a fair trial seemed even more understandable after the conclusion of Ebenezer Richardson's trial. On April 21 a Boston jury found Richardson guilty of the murder of Christopher Seider. They did so despite the judge's instruction from the bench that Richardson had clearly committed justifiable homicide in self-defense.

Soon after the "massacre," both Tories and Patriots began arguing that the incident had been part of a prearranged scheme of wholesale murder on the part of their opponents. Such assertions appeared in versions of the incident prepared by the British military authorities and in the town meeting's *Short History.* A town meeting on May 15 issued statements that referred to "a deep-laid and desperate plan of imperial despotism . . . for the extinction of all civil liberty" in the American colonies. On the other hand, Hutchinson viewed the behavior of Adams and the Patriots as simply the "designs of particular persons to bring about a revolution, and to attain to independency." In the aftermath of the massacre, belief in conspiratorial plots hardened into obsessions on both sides. Loyalists and Patriots seemed worlds apart, and Boston was split irrevocably into two camps. "They call me a brainless Tory," said one local gentleman. "But tell me . . . which is better—to be ruled by one tyrant three thousand miles away, or by three thousand tyrants not one mile away?" Aware of this tension, Hutchinson and other crown dignitaries employed various legal devices to delay proceedings against Preston and his soldiers. They were finally indicted in September.

Preston's trial began on October 24. Ironically, one of his prosecutors was a well-known Tory, Samuel Quincy. And his defense was undertaken by two of the colony's leading Patriot lawyers, John Adams (Samuel Adams's cousin) and Josiah Quincy (Samuel Quincy's brother). There is some evidence that Samuel Adams and other Patriot leaders encouraged John Adams and Josiah Quincy to act as defense counsel, not wishing the British to feel that Boston had failed to provide a fair trial.

John Adams was forty-one when this drawing was made, in 1776. His grandson later described him as "grave and imposing, but not unbending" and as one who "delighted in social conversation." (Massachusetts Historical Society)

Whatever their motives, Adams and Quincy performed brilliantly. Actually, Preston's chances for acquittal seemed good from the start, especially since five acknowledged Tories were among the jury. The failure or inability of Patriot leaders to pack the jury with hostile Bostonians suggests that the Patriots were less concerned with convicting Preston and his men than with exploiting the trial as propaganda.

A parade of prosecution and defense witnesses testified to the different British and Bostonian versions of the events on King Street. James Brewer's testimony for the prosecution summarized the claim that the soldiers had lacked sufficient provocation to fire into the crowd.

Q. Did you see anything thrown at the soldiers?

A. No.

Q. Did you hear anybody call them names?

A. No.

Q. Did you hear any threatening speeches?

A. No, except that the people cried "Fire! Fire!" The word "fire" was on everybody's mouth.

Q. Did you take that to be the cry of fire, or bidding the soldiers fire?

A. I cannot tell now what I thought then.

Q. Did you see anything extraordinary, to induce them to fire that gun?

A. Nothing, but a short stick was thrown, which seemed to go clear over all [the soldiers'] heads.

A typical statement for the defense came in the testimony of Newton Prince:

I ran to the door [of my house] and heard the cry of fire. I went out and asked where the fire was; somebody said it was something better than fire. I met some with clubs, some with buckets and bags, and some running before me with sticks in their hands . . . there were a number of people by the west door of the Townhouse; they said let's go and attack the main guard. . . . After a while they huzzaed and went down King Street; they went down to the Custom-house, and I went down . . . There were people all round the soldiers . . . I saw people with sticks striking on the guns.

Q. Did you hear at that time they were striking, the cry of fire, fire?

A. Yes, [the crowd] said fire, damn you, fire, fire you lobsters,[4] fire you dare not fire.

At several points during Captain Preston's trial—and later during the other soldiers' trial—John Adams threatened to resign as defense attorney because his co-counsel, Josiah Quincy, wished to introduce evidence that Bostonians had triggered the violence. Adams felt that the

---

[4] "Lobsters" was a slang term for British soldiers because of the red coats they wore.

British soldiers could be acquitted without putting Boston and the Patriot cause itself on trial.

From the manner in which they dealt with Boston itself, the closing arguments by prosecution and defense lawyers used at the soldiers' trial illustrated the basic issues of Preston's case as well. The chief prosecutor, Robert Treat Paine, tried to absolve the mob itself of blame for the shooting. He answered "yes" to his own questions: "Was it lawful for the inhabitants of Boston to walk the streets that evening with sticks? Was it lawful for them to run on the cry of 'fire!'?" And he responded "no" to this critical question: "Must they be answerable for the rude speech of every person that happens to be near them, when it does not appear they assented to them and joined in putting them in execution?" In other words, Paine thundered, Preston's company of sentries had no lawful right to fire into the crowd. They were, therefore, guilty of murder.

While Paine defended the radical mob's behavior, lawyer Josiah Quincy (defense lawyer for the sentries as well as for Preston) denied the importance, perhaps even the existence, of such a mob. He insisted that

> Boston and its inhabitants have no more to do with this cause than you or any other two members of the community. . . . The inhabitants of Boston, by no rules of law, justice, or common sense, can be supposed answerable for the unjustifiable conduct of a few individuals hastily assembled in the streets.

In other words, Quincy argued that the crowd's responsibility for provoking the incident was essentially different from the soldiers' guilt or innocence of the murder charge itself. Yet Quincy went on to defend the soldiers' innocence of murder, at the same time defending Boston against those who would criticize it.

Who, then, was to blame for the massacre? The prosecutor pointed to outside agitators who had provoked the violence, and he mentioned two such groups in his summation. One was "sailors and foreigners of the lower Class . . . who are fond of mingling with such Commotions and pushing on a disorder of which they feel not the Consequences." The other was the British army. The crowd's threatening words and hostile stirrings were only natural "among a free People Oppressed and galled with the ravagings of an ungoverned Soldiery [and were not] to be construed as Evidence of an Insurrection or a design to put in Execution the Supposed threats." John Adams picked up the outsider theme and made it the pivotal argument of his defense summation. Although the British did not come out unscathed, the soldiers' defender obviously directed his eloquence against the mob itself. But *what* mob? Composed of *whom*?

> The plain English is, gentlemen [that] most [of the mob] was probably a motley rabble of saucy boys, Negroes and mulattos, Irish teagues,[5] and outlandish jack tarrs [sailors]. . . . There was a mob in Boston on the 5th of

---

[5] "Teague," from the Irish name "Tadhg," was a nickname for an Irishman.

March that attacked a party of soldiers. . . . And indeed, from the nature of things, soldiers quartered in a populous town will always occasion two mobs where they prevent one. They are wretched conservators of the peace!

As for the role of Boston's citizens in the episode, Adams continued:

> A Carr from Ireland, and an Attucks from Framingham, happening to be here, shall sally out upon their thoughtless enterprises, at the head of such a rabble . . . as they could collect together, and then there are not wanting, persons to ascribe all their doings to the good people of the town.

Judge Edmund Trowbridge, shrewdest of the three-judge panel that presided at both trials, told the jury that if they were satisfied "that the sentinel was insulted and that Captain Preston and his party went to assist him, it was doubtless excusable homicide, if not justifiable." Trowbridge went on to deny the conspiracy theories of the massacre. He stated that there had been "no concerted plan on either side," only the provocative actions of an angry crowd and the nervous reaction of frightened soldiers. In that situation "any little spark would kindle a great fire—and five lives were sacrificed to a squabble between the sentry [Private White] and Piemont's barber's boy [Edward Garrick]." The jury at Preston's trial agreed with the judge. On October 30 it found the officer not guilty.

The second trial began on November 27 and ended on December 5. Six of the eight soldiers were also found not guilty. The two others, Matthew Kilroy and Hugh Montgomery, were found guilty of manslaughter. Both soldiers later used a legal technicality to avoid imprisonment. Nine months from the day of the massacre itself, the eight men who had fired their weapons into the King Street crowd had all returned to their military posts. As for the massacre, its fame was only beginning.

Boston was peaceful for a brief period after repeal of the Townshend Acts. In colony after colony during 1770 merchants repudiated their nonimportation agreements. They swiftly resumed trade with Great Britain so that competitors from other provinces would not take over their business. In the rush to resume business as usual, only Boston held firm, demanding that England repeal the remaining duty on tea and renounce similar taxes in the future. Finally, even Boston had to accept the inevitable and abandon nonimportation.

By the end of 1770 the Patriot movement had lost momentum throughout British North America. The spark of rebellion that had flared momentarily at the time of the massacre now flickered low. Samuel Adams confessed in a letter of April 1771:

> The Generality are necessarily engaged in Application to private Business for the Support of their own families, and when at a lucky Season the publick are awakened to a Sense of Danger [and] a manly resentment is enkindled, it is difficult, for so many separate Communities as there are in all the colonies, to agree in one consistent plan of Opposition.

Boston, as Samuel Adams recognized, was the symbol and center of colonial resistance. The game of rebellion would continue to be played first in that throbbing seaport town, where so many prominent political, economic, and intellectual leaders resided. As part of their campaign to rekindle colonial resistance to Great Britain, Boston's Patriots produced a number of posters, pamphlets, engravings, and poems. Many of them dealt with the massacre. The events of March 5 began filtering into the daily language of patriotic protest as American Patriots drew appropriate lessons from the massacre—namely, that the proper response to tyranny was resistance, and that true resistance usually meant the sacrifice of life as well as property. The following appeared in the Boston *Gazette:*

Let THESE Things be told to Posterity!

And handed down
From Generation to Generation
'Til time shall be no more!
Forever may AMERICA be preserved,

Crispus Attucks dies a martyr in the Boston Massacre. (The Bettmann Archive)

From weak and wicked monarchs,
Tyrannical Ministers,
Abandoned Governors,
Their Underlings and Hirelings!
And may the
Machinations of artful, designing wretches,
Who would ENSLAVE THIS People
Come to an end.

Every March 5, in the years that followed the King Street killings, Boston remembered. On that anniversary day a major speech was given to commemorate the five martyrs. The speeches were highly emotional in tone. They evoked the images of blood-stained streets and dying victims more than they asserted political and constitutional arguments for freedom. Leading Patriots delivered the orations. John Hancock spoke in 1774. The 1775 oration was given by Joseph Warren, whose heated remarks stirred a large audience in Faneuil Hall. When Warren cried out the words "Bloody Massacre" for the first time, an irreverent listener, presumably a Tory, shouted back, "Oh fie!" Many of those in the gallery, believing that the speaker had shouted "Fire!" began jumping out the windows. They collided on the ground with a passing regiment of parading British soldiers, whose fife and drum contingent blared so noisily that some of those inside the hall began to suspect another massacre. The incident amused bystanders and participants alike. But New England had no further humorous moments in connection with the annual observances of the massacre. On March 5 of the following year, Peter Thatcher addressed the gathering with a passionate plea for American independence. It concluded simply: "O God, let America be free!"

8 Eighteenth-Century America: From Provinces To Independence

The crisis of the 1770s in Massachusetts had actually been brewing for many decades throughout the British North American provinces. The troubles of Governors Bernard and Hutchinson had been experienced earlier by many other royal officials in other colonies. At least as far back as the days of Sir William Berkeley in Virginia, the relationship between American colonists and royal officials had been a troubled one. Powerful stresses and strains were built into the very structure of the British Empire. Many royal governors had complained about how the colonists tried to escape, bypass, or limit British control of colonial life and trade.

What had changed in the years since Berkeley had less to do with the type of quarrel between governors and colonists than with the context of their argument. Conflicts in Boston and elsewhere grew heated in the 1760s. They stemmed from rapidly changing views on both sides of the Atlantic as to the rights and obligations of American subjects under the British crown.

Before the 1760s, traditionally and in theory, colonists swore—and felt—loyalty to the British crown. But in practice they gave their own colony first allegiance. Politically, a colonial American's "country" was his province, and his public life centered in the towns, counties, and cities of that province. Intercolonial political contacts were rare before the 1760s. Within each province, colonists had always taken certain rights and privileges for granted. Among these were the common law, the protection of private property, the right to representative legislatures, and the privilege of trial by jury.

Colonial obligations to the mother country seemed equally clear. Many of these involved trade and its regulation.

A CENTURY OF "SALUTARY NEGLECT"

Mercantilism

In general, the British government followed a mercantilist policy in relation to its American colonies. The British believed that all their colonies existed mainly to bring benefits to the mother country. Mercantilism, in theory, represented a reasonable division of economic labor between colonies and mother country. The mother country would produce most of the manufactured goods needed by the empire. The colonies would produce raw materials. In some cases Britain even paid bounties (for example, on naval stores[1] and indigo) to encourage colonial production. With other products, such as tobacco, Englishmen living at home were forbidden to compete with colonial producers.

In carrying out its mercantilist policies, England passed a number of trade regulations known as the Navigation Acts. Their purpose was to ensure that American commerce would "terminate in the advantage of the Mother State, unto whom it owes its being and protection." Another purpose was to limit the amount of colonial produce car-

---

[1] Naval stores were certain products needed to operate British navy and merchant ships; they included hemp, tar, and resin.

149

ried to Europe in foreign ships, especially those of the Dutch.

The Navigation Act of 1660 was a major trade law affecting the American colonies. It declared that goods from the American colonies could be transported in English ships only. The English crown also wanted to limit profits made by colonial shippers from the sale of American produce. So the 1660 Navigation Act enumerated certain commodities such as tobacco, sugar, indigo, and cotton (most of English America's leading exports). These commodities could only be shipped to points outside the empire from England and not directly from American colonies. Later acts added to the enumerated list new sources of trade almost as fast as Americans developed them—molasses, naval stores, rice, and furs.

It was easier to pass such laws than to enforce them. Smuggling was common. It was not difficult for a colonial merchant to ship enumerated goods to French colonies in America or even to mainland Europe. Breaking the law was all the easier because British colonial administration during the seventeenth and eighteenth centuries was badly disorganized. Several different royal agencies in the British government helped to set early policies for the mainland colonies.[2] In 1696 an agency known as the Board of Trade was created to bring some degree of order to colonial administration. Throughout the eighteenth century the Board of Trade had primary responsibility for shaping royal policy in America. (It was the Board of Trade, for example, that approved the dispatch of troops to Boston in 1768.)

Administrative reorganization did not solve Britain's major colonial problems. For one thing, political conflicts, both internal and external, often preoccupied the mother country. Those responsible for colonial regulation were generally too busy with other concerns to worry about widespread smuggling in America. Even if British officials had wished to enforce the laws more rigorously, they had few customs officers and few ships for coastal patrol. Thus, from the viewpoint of British imperial control, the century after 1660 was accurately called a period of "salutary neglect."

---

[2] That is, British North American colonies other than those in the West Indies.

As far as the colonists were concerned, they had relatively few complaints about the imperial system during this period. It seemed to meet the needs of a largely undeveloped, labor-scarce group of provinces that specialized in producing raw materials. Colonial commerce and agriculture matured under mild royal supervision. Successive Board of Trade members rarely interfered when American merchants violated the Navigation Acts with regularity.

Colonial Government

From his distant London office, a British administrator may easily have winked at American violations of the law. It was much more difficult, however, for a royal governor stationed in one of the colonies to keep his good humor.

By 1760, eight of the thirteen colonies were under direct royal control. In these colonies, governors like Francis Bernard or Thomas Hutchinson received their appointments directly from the king. In every royal colony except Massachusetts (where the council was elective), the governor appointed a council, which usually included the wealthiest and most distinguished citizens in the colony.

On paper a royal governor looked unbeatable. His duties were numerous. He enforced royal legislation. He summoned and adjourned colonial assemblies—or dissolved them whenever their actions threatened royal authority. He vetoed colonial statutes if they conflicted with British law. He also commanded the provincial militia and appointed local judges. Despite these impressive powers, the governors often found themselves isolated among unfriendly colonists and lacking the means to enforce royal authority against colonial assemblies.

Few royal governors had an easy time in dealing with the colonial assemblies. For although the king appointed the colonial governors, the assemblies paid their salaries. And they did so irritably, ungenerously, and on a year-to-year basis. Each mainland British colony had an assembly that controlled the colony's purse strings. The assemblies had the right to initiate legislation, levy taxes, and appropriate money—including the governor's salary—on a yearly basis. Except for Pennsylvania, all the colonies had two-house (bicameral) assemblies. The elected lower house passed laws, assessed taxes, and dispensed funds. The upper house, appointed by the king in royal colonies, advised the governor.

By passing tax measures that had only limited duration, the colonial assembly ensured that it would be called into session regularly by any royal governor who needed more revenue quickly. By stating how money raised by specific taxes should be spent, an assembly limited the governor's freedom of action. In extreme cases of conflict with crown officials, the assembly resorted to the effective practice of withholding salaries. The assembly was powerful not only because it was elected by the people. Voters and nonvoters alike were kept aware of its actions by means of newspapers, political meetings, and even sermons.

Estimates differ concerning the number of colonists who met the requirements for voting in the mid-eighteenth century. Voters had to be Christians, though in a number of colonies not of any particular religious denomination. They were required to own a certain amount of property, but the amount of land or its monetary equivalent required was not unreasonably high. In almost every colony property qualifications for voting were met by a large majority of the *white, free, male* population. (These were, of course, important and massive restrictions, since they excluded free blacks, slaves, and women.) The exact proportion of voters probably ranged from 50 to 75 percent in most colonies. In Massachusetts, for example—a colony composed mainly of small, family-owned farms—more than 80 percent of the male population could have voted at the time of the Revolution.

Whatever royal governors or imperial legislation might have said on the matter, every colonial assembly already exercised the functions of local self-government by 1750. The assemblies had been generally successful in asserting their claims for colonial autonomy. Supporting the assemblies' actions were majorities of each colony's qualified voters. Even most leading Tories—men such as Thomas Hutchinson, for example—argued for a greater measure of internal self-government in the American provinces.

From their earliest days, the mainland English settlements had waged almost continuous warfare against the Indian tribes and European settlements along their borders. As the seventeenth century drew to a close, England's chief European rival for control of North America was France. Her trading posts and fortified settlements ringed the British colonies like a vise from the eastern tip of Canada to the mouth of the Mississippi River. Aiding the French were thousands of Indians—great tribes like the Algonquins and the Hurons—with whom they traded furs. The powerful tribes of the Iroquois Confederation, however, were allies of the British.

France and Britain fought a series of four wars between 1689 and 1763. At stake were territories in Europe and possessions throughout the overseas empires of the two nations. In America, British troops were aided by American militia and their Indian allies in their fight against combined French and Indian forces.

The first of these wars, known in America as King William's War (1689–97), ended inconclusively. In the next war, Queen Anne's War (1702–13), the British won most of the battles, both in Europe and America. As a result, Britain acquired Nova Scotia, Newfoundland, and the Hudson Bay region of Canada. The third conflict, called King George's War (1740–48) in America, ended as indecisively as King William's War. But the French and Indian War, the fourth and last round of fighting, proved decisive. It began in the spring of 1754.

The Albany Congress

At the start of war, the American colonies displayed in dramatic fashion their divided condition and mutual suspiciousness. What made the display even more striking was the fact that this first attempt to achieve intercolonial unity was organized by none other than the British Board of Trade.

The Board of Trade wanted the colonists to meet with Britain's Iroquois allies. The purpose of the meeting was to discuss defense measures to be taken against the French and their Indian allies.

Jonathan Edwards

(Culver Pictures)

Jonathan Edwards, the most influential religious teacher and writer in eighteenth-century America, spent most of his life concerned with the problem of spiritual decline and possible regeneration of the faith—and the faithful—in what was once Puritan New England. Edwards was America's most subtle and original student of religious psychology and modes of thought. Born in Windsor, Connecticut, in 1703, he was descended from influential Puritan ministers on both sides of his family, among whom his grandfather Solomon Stoddard of Northampton was probably the most famous.

He proved an intellectual prodigy, studying at home with his highly educated parents before entering Yale College when he was almost thirteen. Even before then, he had written brilliant essays on aspects of natural history. After graduating from Yale in 1720, Edwards studied theological subjects for two years, briefly held a ministry in New York, and, in 1726, joined his grandfather, Solomon Stoddard, in the Northampton church. Although he later wrote of the deep religious feelings he had as a child, Edwards underwent a transforming conversion experience in 1721 which reinforced his pivotal belief in God's utter omnipotence and control over human affairs and persuaded him that he had been "saved" by an infusion of divine grace. Edwards associated this experience of salvation with an intuited moment of religious rapture quite distinct from any more pallid and rational "proofs" of salvation.

Solomon Stoddard did not share his grandson's fascination with the process of achieving personal redemption. In Stoddard's Northampton church, membership had been extended to all those interested in becoming church members, including any "morally sincere" persons who had not been converted. But Edwards had come to believe that *true* church members experienced an inner transformation prior to becoming saved through God's freely given grace, and he disapproved strongly of Stoddard's practice of admitting the entire congregation to the sacrament of the Lord's Supper as a method for converting the unregenerate. When Stoddard died in 1729, Edwards became Northampton's only pastor and almost immediately began tightening requirements for church membership.

Edwards stressed to his parishioners their inability to influence through personal efforts or moral behavior alone God's sovereign decisions over saving or damning individual human beings. Images of hell and divine punishment filled Edwards's sermons and terrified many of his audiences into a shocked awareness of their own helplessness before the deity. As for the unregenerate: "The

---

The British also wanted to encourage cooperation among the various colonial militias, which had been sadly lacking up to this time. The result was the Albany Congress, which met in June and July of 1754. Seven colonies sent delegates. Among them were Thomas Hutchinson of Massachusetts and Benjamin Franklin of Pennsylvania.

Once the meeting began, Franklin went beyond the British agenda and proposed instead a general plan of intercolonial union. According to

devil is waiting for them, hell is gaping for them, the flames gather and flash about them, and would fain hold on them and swallow them up. . . . All that preserves them every moment is the mere arbitrary will and unconvenanted, unobliged forbearance of an incensed God."

Edwards's inspired preaching and fearsome admonitions led to the announced "conversions," in 1735, of dozens of his parishioners, especially young people, and a revival of religious enthusiasm which spread throughout the Connecticut Valley—the first such "revival" in American history—making Edwards famous on both sides of the Atlantic. His *Faithful Narrative* of the revival, published in 1737, was quickly translated into German and Dutch and served as a model for John Wesley, founder of the Methodist church. Edwards's activity in Northampton helped to prepare New England churches for the outburst of religious evangelism and spread of conversion experiences which attended George Whitfield's preaching in 1740–42. In the wake of Whitfield's tour of the colonies, evangelical ministers stirred up highly emotional conversion scenes throughout the American provinces. The infusion of divine grace often reached communicants in a profoundly dramatic manner. Screaming and writhing, fainting, and weeping accompanied many of the conversions during the "Great Awakening." And although Jonathan Edwards decried many of these emotional excesses for their possibly "devilish" origins, he welcomed the renewed stress on genuine spiritual transformations which the Awakening appeared to bring. His most significant analysis of the psychology of religion, *A Treatise Concerning Religious Affections,* was published in 1746. Among other points, Edwards defended the notion of man's necessary and total subordination to divine moral perfection, stressed the role played by emotions in apprehending God's holiness, but cautioned against excessive dependence on the intensity of emotions alone among truly devout persons.

Edwards's two decades as minister in Northampton had often seen stormy battles between pastor and parishioners. After one such dispute involving standards of church membership, the congregation dismissed him in 1750. The following year, Edwards settled with his wife and children in the frontier outposts of Stockbridge where he served both as pastor of the small church and as missionary to the Indians (the church itself included both white settlers and Indian parishioners). Although deeply in debt and virtually impoverished for the next seven years, Edwards remained in Stockbridge and wrote many of his most important religious treatises. The two most extraordinary works which further developed his uncompromising perspective on Godly control of human destiny appeared in 1754 (*A Careful and Strict Enquiry into the Modern Prevailing Notions of . . . . Freedom of* (the) *Will . . .*) and 1758 (*The Great Christian Doctrine of Original Sin Defended*). Edwards ended his Stockbridge isolation in January 1758, when he traveled to Princeton, New Jersey, to become president of the College of New Jersey. There he preached and taught theology for the next two months before dying of a fever on March 22, 1758, after receiving a smallpox inoculation.

Few subsequent theologians could match the rigor of Edwards's logic and theoretical rebuilding of Calvinist doctrine. His major legacy, however, remains a tradition of evangelical religious revivalism which Jonathan Edwards helped first to create and then to weave into the central tapestry of American Protestant belief.

Franklin's plan of union, the king would appoint a president-general, a kind of supergovernor, presumably with the usual lack of enforcement authority. The provincial assemblies would be represented in proportion to their tax payments in a grand council, a kind of superassembly somewhat like our present-day Congress. Taxes on each colony would support the grand council's control of intercolonial defense, Indian relations, and westward expansion. The central body would be allowed to raise an army and navy and build forts and settlements. The president-general, however (like the royal governors), could veto any laws in the king's name.

The Albany Congress approved the essential outlines of Franklin's plan and submitted it to the colonial assemblies. Three of these simply ignored the proposal. The other four rejected it, agreeing with the Boston town meeting that the Albany Plan endangered popular liberties. Throughout the French and Indian War, each colony preferred to protect itself. Whatever common defense did exist in British North America was led and staffed largely by regular units of the British army. None of the colonial assemblies was willing to surrender its taxing powers; nor, for that matter, did any assembly wish to allow any "grand council" to divide the unclaimed lands in the interior that some colonies hoped to acquire by driving out the French.

The French and Indian War

In the beginning, this conflict (also known as the Seven Years' War) went badly for the British. Colonial assemblies were reluctant to contribute men and money to the fight. The result was a series of British defeats along the frontier line with French Canada.[3] Not until William Pitt became prime minister in 1757 did the British war effort begin to take shape. For one thing, Pitt shifted the war's main emphasis from Europe (on which it had been centered during the earlier three Anglo-French conflicts) to the empire. Here Pitt assigned most of Britain's military strength. Pitt bankrupted the national treasury to pay for additional regiments of British troops to send to America.

In order to win over the colonial assemblies, Pitt directed British military officials to assume the cost of feeding and arming colonial militia. The British also promised to repay the assemblies for money they spent to supply additional volunteers. Such generosity swelled the ranks of colonial regi-

ments that fought alongside British redcoats in subduing the French.

The British won a series of military victories under aggressive new commanders such as James Wolfe and Jeffrey Amherst. In 1759 they captured Quebec from the French, who were led by the Marquis de Montcalm. Within a year all of French Canada lay in British hands. In the Treaty of Paris in 1763, France surrendered all of her North American possessions east of the Mississippi from Canada to Florida. The exception was Louisiana, which France had earlier ceded to its ally Spain.

During the war all did not go smoothly between Britain and her colonies. For one thing, Pitt insisted on rigorously enforcing the Navigation Acts in America. British warships patrolled in force to choke off trade with the enemy.

Northern colonial merchants were also outraged by Britain's intensified hunt for smuggled goods through the use of so-called general writs of assistance. These were unlimited search warrants good for the entire period of a king's reign. They allowed customs officers to enter and search any building in daytime, without having prior knowledge of allegedly imported goods.

After the death of King George II in 1760, Boston merchants (many of whom later led the nonimportation campaign) retained James Otis, one of the colony's best lawyers, to argue the illegality of the writs in order to prevent their renewal under the new king, George III. Otis lost his case, and the writs were upheld. Often during the following decade, royal customs officials barged unannounced into Boston warehouses and homes searching for smuggled goods.

INCREASED BRITISH CONTROL

After the French and Indian War, it became clear that the British intended to regulate their American provinces much more closely and thoroughly in the future than they had in the past. One important decision involved the new trans-Appalachian territories recently acquired from the French. Even before 1754, settlers had begun moving into the rich Ohio Valley. Land companies were organized to take control of the region's fur

---

[3] One American who got his first taste of battle in this conflict was George Washington. As a young officer with British General Edward Braddock, he took part in an unsuccessful campaign against the French near what is now Pittsburgh.

trade and to explore other opportunities. Then the British government issued the Proclamation of 1763, banning, for an indefinite time, settlement and land grants beyond the crest of the Appalachian Mountains. Land speculators (among them George Washington) denounced British efforts to close off the West. Unofficially and in violation of British law, American settlement and land speculation continued.

Another problem was financial. Who would pick up the tab for Britain's costly victory over France? Pitt's war strategy had succeeded, but in the process England had spent £82 million, virtually bankrupting the treasury. Despite heavy wartime taxation, the British national debt had run up to £130 million by 1764. Every leading British minister during the 1760s and 1770s agreed that it was only fair for the American colonies to share in paying off the war debts. After all, they reasoned, the mainland provinces had achieved almost complete security on their borders at practically no cost to themselves.

Americans disagreed with the British argument that Parliament had the right to tax colonists along with other British subjects. This dispute over taxation, brought on by the British government's search for revenue, quickly became the major source of colonial unrest during the 1760s. Throughout the eighteenth century most Americans had accepted Parliament's right to legislate for the colonies. But they denied its right to tax them. Most Americans would probably have agreed with the Virginia legislature that, "Laws imposing taxes on the People ought not to be made without the Consent of Representatives chosen by themselves." Colonial assemblies believed that they had won the exclusive right to initiate taxes within their own provinces. Yet in April 1764, George Grenville, Britain's first lord of the treasury, steered through Parliament a law that challenged this right and, in the process, stirred up colonial resistance from New England to Georgia.

The Sugar Act

When George Grenville became British finance minister in 1763, he made an embarrassing discovery: the customs service in America cost the

George III, long thought to have become insane in later life, probably suffered from a rare inherited disease. (Colonial Williamsburg)

British government four times as much in salaries as it collected in revenues! Grenville's solution was a revenue-raising bill that came to be known as the Sugar Act.

Earlier in the century the British had taxed foreign molasses at the rate of sixpence a gallon in order to encourage colonials to purchase this product from the British West Indies. The regulation was largely ignored. American rum distillers found it much cheaper to bribe customs officials (at one penny or "pence" a gallon) so they could smuggle in cheaper molasses from the French West Indies. Grenville's Sugar Act of 1764 was designed to eliminate such colonial trading freedom.

The new statute lowered the molasses duty from six to three pence, thereby making payment of the duty more competitive with payment of the bribe—and much safer. The new duty applied to both British and foreign molasses entering the colonies. This provision transformed a trade-regulating device into a revenue-producing tax. The Sugar Act also placed new tax duties on such commodities as sugar, indigo, wine, and textiles.

More upsetting to the colonists than the taxes themselves was Parliament's obvious determination to enforce their collection. Colonial shipowners now had to file official papers for every vessel leaving and entering American harbors. Moreover, accused violators of the Sugar Act would be tried in admiralty (naval) courts distant from their hometowns or cities. Such courts operated without juries and under rules according to which a defendant was considered guilty until proved innocent. Provincial merchant-smugglers had come to depend on sympathetic local juries or judges (men like Boston's justice of the peace William Molineux, who had persuaded a mob to surrender Ebenezer Richardson). Local jurors and judges generally gave violators of British trade regulations what the defendants wished—freedom, not justice.

A storm of protest over the Sugar Act spread quickly through the colonies. It was sparked by commercial cities like Boston, which reminded their rural countrymen of the stake all Americans had in the new British policies. "If our Trade may be taxed, why not our Lands?" asked the Boston town meeting in a thumping denunciation of the Sugar Act. "Why not the produce of our Lands and every Thing we possess or make use of?" Similar complaints filled newspapers from Massachusetts to the Carolinas. Widespread smuggling continued. Yearly collections of revenue from the Sugar Act averaged a ridiculously small £20,000.

Grenville (and many other British officials) failed to realize that, to provincial Americans, their idea of freedom as British subjects included the right of their assemblies alone to levy taxes over them. Americans were as much concerned with the *precedent* set by the Sugar Act as with its actual enforcement. The rights of Englishmen, colonists argued, depended upon a person's right—as James Otis put it—to be "free from all taxes but what he consents to in person, or by his representative." Actually, although the colonists lacked rep-

Paying taxes to England became one of the most galling aspects of life for an American colonial in the 1770s. Often the tax man bore the brunt of communal anger, as portrayed in this 1774 British print, "The Bostonians Paying the Excise-Man, or Tarring & Feathering." (The Henry Francis DuPont Winterthur Museum)

resentation in Parliament, by and large they did not want it. They recognized that this would lead to tighter and costlier English control of provincial affairs—taxation *with* representation.

Additional Regulations

Colonial protests over the Sugar Act did not lessen Grenville's interest in squeezing additional revenue out of North America. In March 1765 Parliament passed the Stamp Act. It required Americans to buy tax stamps for newspapers, legal documents, and other types of printed matter. Englishmen had paid such a tax for decades. Grenville made certain to mention that revenues raised from the new tax, which was to take effect in

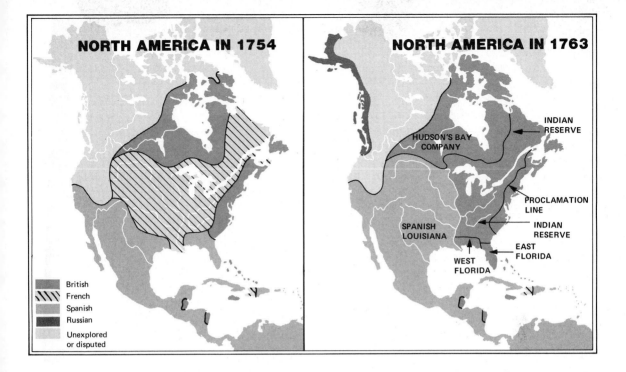

NORTH AMERICA IN 1754

NORTH AMERICA IN 1763

INDIAN RESERVE

HUDSON'S BAY COMPANY

PROCLAMATION LINE

SPANISH LOUISIANA

INDIAN RESERVE

EAST FLORIDA

WEST FLORIDA

British
French
Spanish
Russian
Unexplored or disputed

November 1765, would be applied entirely to "the Defense of the Colonies."

A related measure also sponsored by Grenville was the Quartering Act, passed by Parliament in March 1765. It obliged colonial assemblies to furnish British troops stationed in their colonies with adequate living quarters and provisions. Many colonists considered the timing strange. Britain had kept almost no royal troops garrisoned in America when the French, the Spanish, and the Indians menaced the western borders of almost every colony. Now, after this threat had been removed, she planned to station soldiers there. Americans realized that the troops were actually being sent to enforce royal authority – which they did with such mixed results in Boston three years later.

The Stamp Act and the Quartering Act fed a growing suspicion of England among knowledgeable Americans. Had the British government deliberately set out to deny them freedoms they had previously exercised? Some of these might be called *negative* freedoms – the absence of British taxation, the lack of a British army in their midst,

lax enforcement of the Navigation Acts. Others were more *positive* – trial by local juries, the liberty to expand westward.

None of the king's ministers would have denied that Britain meant to change its permissive ways in North America. They would have argued, though, that Parliament did not wish to deny *legitimate* colonial rights. It wanted only to remind the mainland colonies of their equally legitimate responsibilities toward the mother country. In practice, however, Britain's sudden effort to tighten the parental screws triggered an immediate protest from her fully grown New World children.

American Opposition

The Stamp Act generated the first successfully organized intercolonial opposition to British policy. It took the form of almost complete resistance to buying the required stamps. For a lawyer, merchant, newspaper editor, small businessman, or even a planter, the stamps represented both a costly expense and an illegal parliamentary attack on colonial liberties. As usual, resistance centered in the commercial cities and towns, to which Britain had sent most of the stamps and tax collectors. For the first (but hardly the last) time in the struggle, Boston became the center of both legal and violent protest.

The Massachusetts assembly took the lead in June 1765, when it proposed an intercolonial meeting to unify opposition to parliamentary taxation. Boston mobs—often organized by the same Sons of Liberty who would prove so effective later in the decade—ransacked the homes of several British officials, including the chief royal stamp collector. The mobs also burned Lieutenant Governor Thomas Hutchinson's elegant mansion to the ground, destroyed important government records, and forced several stamp distributors to resign their offices. Riotous Sons of Liberty played a similar role in New York City and elsewhere.

Meanwhile, peaceful forms of protest were having an even more unsettling effect on British policy. As early as May 1765, a young lawyer named Patrick Henry introduced a series of resolutions in the Virginia House of Burgesses. They asserted that this body alone had the right to tax Virginians. The House of Burgesses adopted the more moderate of Henry's resolutions, but it rejected his call for outright resistance to collection of stamp taxes. Most other colonial assemblies followed Virginia's lead and passed similar resolutions, all of which Parliament ignored.

But the British government could hardly overlook the resolutions passed by an intercolonial Stamp Act Congress, first proposed by Massachusetts. The assemblies of nine colonies were represented when this congress convened in October 1765 in New York City. Although the congress assured Parliament of "all due subordination," the phrase was negligible, since it went on to deny that Britain had the right either to tax the colonists or to try Americans in admiralty courts. Furthermore, the delegates demanded immediate repeal of both the Sugar Act and the Stamp Act.

In order to put teeth into these demands, more than a thousand colonial merchants from all the major trading cities quickly organized an effective boycott of British manufactured goods. This was the first of several times that colonial economic pressures through such nonimportation agreements were to force changes in British policy. The merchants played a crucial role in the struggle with Britain—so crucial that the strength of colonial resistance at any given moment depended to a large degree on the extent of merchant support, or lack of support.

The most important long-term result of the Stamp Act protests was that Americans of all classes and backgrounds began to learn the habit of resistance. Some Americans—including militants like Samuel Adams—even began to advocate independence and revolution. They argued that, both historically and legally, a people had the right to change or overthrow a government that systematically violated people's rights and exceeded its authority. Such opinions frightened members of Parliament. William Pitt urged repeal of the Stamp Act on the grounds that doing so would restore the loyalty to England of most *moderate* Americans and isolate the minority of *radicals:* "If we repeal the Act, we shall have all the sober part of America on our side, and we shall easily be able to chastize the few hot-headed republicans among them." Pitt might also have reminded his colleagues that the Stamp Act had proved a total failure. It earned no revenue, since no Americans could be found who were brave enough to collect the tax. American business continued as usual, while British manufacturers suffered from the boycott of their goods in America. Responding finally to economic and political pressures, Parliament repealed the Stamp Act in March 1766.

A DEEPENING CRISIS

Americans might have celebrated the repeal of the Stamp Act a bit more heartily had not Parliament coupled its repeal with passage of another measure. This was the Declaratory Act, which reaffirmed colonial subordination. It also asserted Parliament's right to pass any law it wished (presumably, therefore, any *tax* law), "to bind the colonies and people of America."

In 1767 a new British finance minister, Charles Townshend, exercised this dangerous option. He secured a new program of colonial duties, to be placed on imports of items such as paper, tea, lead, paint, and glass. Townshend believed somewhat naïvely that his move would produce much-needed revenue. Instead, he succeeded only in reopening the unsettled issues of the Stamp Act crisis.

Once more, Massachusetts led intercolonial resistance. This time its assembly sent a Circular Letter to the other colonial legislatures urging some form of united opposition similar to the Stamp Act Congress. The Circular Letter denied that Massachusetts advocated independence. Still, the British government considered the letter dangerous enough to demand that the assembly rescind it. When the assembly refused, Governor Bernard, on orders from London, prevented the legislators from meeting in 1768. Special town meetings summoned delegates to an extralegal convention to discuss the matter. It was at this point that two regiments of British troops were sent to occupy Boston in order to protect the unpopular customs commissioners.

The civic turmoil that ensued over the next two years would lead directly to the Boston Massacre. New York City was also the scene of protests and mob violence after Parliament dissolved the New York assembly for refusing to obey the Quartering Act.

As with the Stamp Act, however, the peaceful boycott of British goods by colonial merchants proved more effective with Parliament than threats or violence. Boston's nonimportation agreement was followed by other cities, among them Providence, Newport, and New York. In the Virginia assembly a set of resolutions sponsored by George Washington supported Massachusetts' Circular Letter. When the royal governor dissolved the assembly, its leaders regrouped informally and endorsed a nonimportation campaign. Throughout the colonies unrest died down only after Parliament had repealed all the Townshend duties except the tax on tea. The king's new prime minister, Lord North, had insisted that this tax remain in order to uphold the "supremacy of Parliament" in America.

Lacking a dramatic rallying point against Britain, many American Patriots lapsed back easily into provincial disunity. Even dogged fighters like Samuel Adams were hard-pressed to keep alive much bitterness toward royal authority during the few relatively quiet years that followed repeal of the Townshend Acts. Customs commissioners went about their business. British troops remained quartered in the colonies. And royal governors began to act more confidently.

To counteract this apathy, Samuel Adams and other Sons of Liberty in Boston created a Committee of Correspondence to publicize complaints against the British. The idea spread throughout the colonies and revived intercolonial cooperation. The committees found a convenient *cause célèbre* when Rhode Islanders burned a British customs patrol boat, the *Gaspée,* after it ran aground in Narragansett Bay in June 1772. This led to a royal investigation. To the Patriots' delight, the investigators could find no sign of the culprits. The incident also probably served as a model for another one, involving a shipload of tea, which took place in Boston harbor in December 1773.

The Boston Tea Party

Tea was the colonists' most popular beverage, and few Americans liked Lord North's decision in May 1773 to aid the financially ailing British East India Company by granting it a monopoly in America. Previously, the company had sold its tea to British wholesalers. They in turn sold to Americans wholesalers, who distributed the tea to local merchants. The British government now proposed to allow the East India Company to sell tea directly through its own agents in America. This step would eliminate both British and colonial middlemen.

The immediate effect was to *reduce* the retail price of tea considerably. But Americans grasped almost immediately the long-term effect of this action. In return for cheaper tea, they were being asked to accept a new royal interference in normal patterns of colonial commerce. If Parliament could so easily dispose of a profitable, long-standing colonial tea trade, then no portion of America's commerce would be safe from British interference.

Public protests against the Tea Act spread quickly throughout the colonies. They were fueled by passionate letters exchanged among the Com-

In December 1773, a group of Boston townspeople dressed as Indians dumped an entire cargo of tea into Boston harbor. The "Tea Party" was a reaction to the Tea Act, a British effort to by-pass colonial merchants in the highly profitable tea trade. The Tea Party stirred the imagination of those colonials intent upon resisting British authority at all costs. (The Bettmann Archive)

mittees of Correspondence and by the almost unanimous opposition of colonial newspapers. Once again the British government had unintentionally revived the colonial resistance movement. In New York and Philadelphia royal authorities, fearing violence, ordered the first East India Company tea ships back to Britain without attempting to unload them. In Charleston the tea was simply locked in a warehouse and not offered for sale.

Bostonians, as usual, thought of a more direct and effective way to rally patriotic sentiment and provoke royal anger. On December 16, 1773, a ship called the *Dartmouth* lay at dockside waiting for her captain to decide whether to try to unload her cargo of tea. That night, led by the Sons of Liberty, a band of townspeople disguised as Indians boarded the *Dartmouth*. A huge crowd of Bostonians cheered as the "Indians" dumped the cargo overboard.

Aftermath: The Intolerable Acts

Parliament responded to this "tea party" by passing a series of laws designed to punish Boston. These so-called Coercive Acts took away the city's remaining liberties. One of them closed the port to all commerce until its residents had paid for the spoiled tea. Another authorized the transfer of cases involving British officials from Massachusetts to England in order to escape the hostility of local judges and juries. A third act revised the fundamental structure of Massachusetts' government to strengthen royal authority in the colony. The upper house (governor's council) would now be appointed by the king and no longer elected. Town meetings, in which the Sons of Liberty engaged in their most effective organizing, could be held only once a year. Once more British troops appeared in Boston. General Gage, commander-in-chief of all British troops in America, became military governor of Massachusetts. For Bostonians, British occupation and interference with normal political and economic life was far more sweeping than it had been during the controversy over the Townshend duties.

Another statute passed by Parliament at this time was the Quebec Act, which applied to the recently conquered French territory that Americans had already begun settling. The law recognized the practice of Roman Catholicism and

French civil law in that area — both unpopular with the largely Protestant and largely English colonists of the thirteen colonies. They dubbed the Coercive Acts and the Quebec Act the Intolerable Acts.

Supplies and pledges of support from all over the provinces flowed into Boston. The Intolerable Acts achieved something that had previously eluded Samuel Adams and the Sons of Liberty — the unification of colonial resistance to Britain.

OUTBREAK OF THE REVOLUTION

In June 1774 the Massachusetts assembly asked other colonies to send delegates to a congress where they could agree on common action against the Intolerable Acts. Fifty-five delegates from twelve colonies attended the First Continental Congress, which met at Philadelphia in September. (Georgia was unrepresented at this time, but later sent delegates.) The Congress rejected by one vote a compromise proposal for a new scheme of colonial government similar to Franklin's 1754 Albany Plan. The Congress then endorsed a set of resolutions proposed originally by a convention in Suffolk County, Massachusetts. These Suffolk Resolves demanded direct resistance to the Intolerable Acts. The Congress also adopted John Adams's Declaration of Rights and Resolves, a statement of the colonists' constitutional arguments.

The most practical step taken by the Continental Congress was to create an association to enforce a complete boycott against Britain. Delegates vowed not to import, export, or consume British goods until the crisis had been settled. Before adjourning in October 1774, the delegates also decided to meet again in May 1775.

King George and his ministers had erroneously believed that colonial resistance was confined largely to Massachusetts, and their reaction to the First Continental Congress reflected this mistaken judgment. They convinced themselves that stern measures in *that* colony would dampen unrest elsewhere. "The New England governments are in a state of Rebellion," George III remarked in November 1774. "Blows must decide whether they are to be subject to this country or independent."

General Gage, ordinarily as stubborn as George III himself about punishing colonial resistance, had been sobered by his new role as governor of Massachusetts. He tried to warn London of what lay ahead. The provincial militia was then gathering on the outskirts of Boston. To subdue it and reassert parliamentary authority in Massachusetts, Gage wrote Lord North, would require 20,000 additional troops. Until their arrival, Gage recommended that Britain suspend the Coercive Acts in order to reduce tensions in America. But his superiors responded by declaring Massachusetts to be in a state of rebellion. They sent Gage an additional 3500 men. They directed the general to suppress the rebellion and arrest "the principal actors in the provincial Congress." Gage attempted to obey this order on April 19, 1775, and, in the process, began the American Revolution.

Open Hostilities in Massachusetts

Not suprisingly, the conflict began in Boston. Massachusetts Patriots had been drilling for months, organized into extralegal militia companies sometimes called Minutemen. Gage had been informed that the Patriots were storing arms at Concord, west of Boston, and that Samuel Adams and John Hancock were also in the vicinity. The British general sent a force of some 700 regulars to confiscate the arms and arrest the Patriot leaders.

On April 19, arriving at Lexington on their way to Concord, the British found about seventy Minutemen assembled on the town common. The British commander ordered the Americans to disperse. Then someone — whether British or American remains unclear — fired a shot. Just as had happened six years earlier during the Boston Massacre, a single shot led to additional firing and a state of general confusion. When the smoke cleared, the Minutemen had fled, leaving eight dead and ten wounded. The British continued to Concord only to find that most of the colonial arms stored there had already been removed. The British destroyed what supplies they could find and fought several skirmishes with small groups of Minutemen.

Meanwhile, colonial militia had converged on Lexington and Concord throughout the day, the alarm having been spread the previous night by a

"Give Me Liberty, or Give Me Death!" This 1870 rendering of Patrick Henry's March 23, 1775, oration to the Virginia assembly shows vividly how later Americans viewed his famous "war cry of the Revolution." (Culver Pictures)

few Boston Sons of Liberty, including Paul Revere. Some 900 British reinforcements joined the first detachment at Lexington for the march back to Boston. But they found themselves outnumbered and outvolleyed by more than 4000 colonial marksmen, who fired from behind stone walls and other cover. The colonists peppered the British troops with musket fire along their 20-mile retreat. Even the 1500 additional redcoats sent by Gage to protect the retreat failed to prevent it from turning into a chaotic stampede.

By the time the British straggled back to safety in Boston, they had lost 73 men and suffered 149 wounded, compared to American casualties of 49 killed and 39 wounded. More ominously still, the Minutemen did not return to their homes. They began instead to surround Boston, and their ranks grew. First they came from other Massachusetts towns. Then, within days, volunteers began arriving from other colonies as well. Gage and his undermanned British garrison now found themselves under siege from all sides.

Two months later, reinforced by only 1100 troops, Gage attempted to break the colonial lines ringing Boston. He fought colonial militia entrenched on two strategic high points, Breed's Hill and Bunker Hill. After a furious day's fighting, on June 17, the British cleared both hills of American soldiers. The cost was high. The British suffered more than 1000 killed or wounded out of an attacking force of 2000 men. The Americans counted fewer than 450 men killed, wounded, or captured. As one of Gage's officers aptly remarked, "another such victory would have ruined us."

The Second Continental Congress

In May 1775, while 16,000 colonial militia penned the British garrison in its uncomfortable quarters among Boston's hostile townspeople, the Second Continental Congress met at Philadelphia. Its members now confronted not merely the older pattern of colonial grievances but also the new reality of armed revolt. After the British "victory" at Bunker Hill, George III had relieved Gage of his command and formally declared the colonies to be "in open rebellion." The Continental Congress endorsed the description and began the difficult job of trying to make the rebellion succeed.

One of the Congress's first acts was to appoint one of the delegates, George Washington of Virginia, as commander-in-chief of Continental forces. Delegates also prepared to requisition men and supplies for the new army.

Some of the men at Philadelphia still considered the revolt a *temporary* break with Britain. They believed that the grievances that had inspired it could be resolved by compromise. In deference to these moderates, the Continental Congress, in July 1775, adopted a conciliatory document that came to be known as the Olive Branch Petition. The delegates, "as faithful subjects," requested the repeal of all oppressive legislation and an end to tyranny.

The Second Continental Congress also passed a Declaration of the Causes and Necessities of Taking up Arms. This document was drafted by John Dickinson of Pennsylvania and a new delegate from Virgina, Thomas Jefferson. It defended colonial resistance as the only alternative to "unconditional submission to the tyranny of irritated ministers." It also denied that the American aim was complete independence and promised to lay down arms once Britain ceased its abusive behavior.

The declaration was a response to the so-called Conciliatory Act, passed by Parliament the previous February. The act had promised to exempt from British taxes those colonies that paid for royal expenses voluntarily. The declaration rejected this idea, however, and signaled the colonists' continued opposition to British policies.

Canada Remains Loyal

Renewed imperial controls, which followed the British victory of 1763, ran counter to a rising desire for independence in the thirteen colonies. Americans hoped that Nova Scotia and Quebec would sympathize with their grievances against Britain. (They did not consider Newfoundland or Rupert's Land, as they were too far away.)

Although part of the same empire, Nova Scotia and Quebec did not cast their lot with the thirteen colonies. Few of the American protests applied to Nova Scotia. The closing of the western lands did not affect the colony, which had many empty acres of its own. Nor was Nova Scotia a Massachusetts, ready to stand on its own feet in world trade.

In Quebec support for the colonies to the south was not forthcoming either. The Catholic Canadians had little love for the Protestant Americans, nor much interest in English traditions of government. In Quebec the French were a majority. But if Quebec combined with the other colonies, the French would be a minority. In addition, because of decades of warfare, the colonists of France and those of Britain still regarded each other more as enemies than as friends.

Despite Canadian neutrality, the American Revolution had a profound influence on Canada. She became a refuge for supporters of the crown — Tories to the Americans, United Empire Loyalists to the British. Over 40,000 moved north to Canada. Their descendants live there still.

SEVERING TIES WITH BRITAIN

All the actions taken to strengthen intercolonial resistance reinforced Lord North's belief, shared by George III, that the Americans wanted complete independence. Various proposals for compromise were defeated by Parliament. The British government's answer to the Olive Branch Petition was to send 25,000 additional troops to America. Britain also began to hire foreign mercenary soldiers. In August 1775 the king had declared the colonies to be in rebellion. In December Parliament outlawed trade with the colonies and declared American ships and cargoes subject to confiscation.

As far as Britain was concerned, she was at war with rebellious subjects in a conflict that permitted only one solution: the colonists' submission as dutiful subjects of the mother country and the king. As far as a growing number of Americans were concerned, the colonies had no choice left but to fight. This involved taking a more serious step toward independence: repudiating the basic symbol of British power — the British monarchy — and colonial allegiance to it.

Normal people do not surrender their customary loyalties easily or without overwhelming reasons. Many of the delegates at Philadelphia shrank from defying the king himself. To strike such a blow at the symbol of monarchy required someone who hated more bitterly than did most Americans, even in 1776, *both* the British crown and the ruler on whose head it now rested. The man who struck the blow was a recently arrived immigrant from England named Thomas Paine.

Thomas Paine had left England in 1774 for the colonies. He was a failure in marriage and a failure in business. More important, however, he was an ardent republican who believed in rule by the people rather than by a monarch. He made an enormous impact in America with his anonymously printed pamphlet, *Common Sense,* which first appeared in January 1776. Paine's pamphlet sold 150,000 copies in the critical months from January to July 1776.

Common Sense contained outspoken attacks on George III as "the royal brute of Britain." Paine assailed the idea of monarchy itself. He wrote: "Of more worth is one honest man to society and in the sight of God, than all the crowned ruffians that ever lived." Through Paine's influence enthusiasm for republican government spread quickly throughout the colonies.

In May 1776 the Continental Congress adopted John Adams's proposal urging all provincial assemblies to suppress any remaining vestiges of royal government, to establish constitutions, and to create new state governments based upon popular consent. Royal authority had already collapsed throughout the colonies by this time, as British officials fled to safety and American Tories retreated into silence. Colonial assemblies began functioning as independent, provisional state legislatures.

The Second Continental Congress had already begun acting as a provisional national government. It sought diplomatic and military assistance abroad. It authorized Americans to attack English shipping in retaliation for the British embargo on American trade. In addition, it opened American ports to foreign shipping, thus formally ending further pretense at recognizing England's right to regulate American trade.

The decisive step in the move toward independence came on May 15. Virginia's new revolutionary legislature instructed its delegates to the Congress to introduce a resolution proposing both independence *and* an intercolonial confederation. Many Virginians were already convinced that Britain was indifferent to colonial interests. This belief grew stronger after the efforts made by Virginia's last royal governor, Lord Dunmore, to recruit slaves into the British army by promising them freedom. Rumors of a British scheme to stir up a slave rebellion swept the South in 1776. Such rumors probably helped some fearful Southerners to overcome their reluctance and endorse a complete break with the mother country.

The Declaration of Independence

On June 7 Richard Henry Lee introduced Virginia's independence resolution into the Congress. A five-man committee was assigned the task of preparing an appropriate document defending colonial actions. The committee consisted of John Adams, Benjamin Franklin, Thomas Jefferson, Roger Sherman of Connecticut, and Robert Livingston of New York. The thirty-three-year-old Jefferson, the youngest man in the Congress, became chairman of the committee. Adams and Franklin made suggestions, but the draft was largely Jefferson's.

By late June more moderates had accepted the idea of a complete break. On July 2 Congress finally voted to approve Richard Henry Lee's earlier motion "that these united colonies are, and of right ought to be, free and independent states." Jefferson's Declaration of Independence was then submitted to the full membership of the Congress. Delegates altered some of the wording, but they made few substantial changes except to strike out a rather questionable passage blaming George III for the existence of slavery in America.

Most of Jefferson's draft had a familiar ring to the delegates. Perhaps most original was its attempt to attribute colonial oppression to *royal* rather than *parliamentary* tyranny. Much of the Declaration consisted of a list of the alleged "injuries and usurpations" by George III that had forced America to resort to rebellion. Some of the complaints were reasonable: the king's interference with representative assemblies, his abuse of civil rights, his use of an army of occupation without colonial consent, and his allowing Parliament to tax the colonies and restrain their trade. Other grievances had plainly been designed to arouse American fears, not to gain foreign support, especially charges that the king had incited slave and Indian insurrections, "plundered our seas, ravaged our coasts, burnt our towns, and destroyed the lives of our people."

Jefferson's preamble to the Declaration attempted to justify a people's right to rebel and to alter their form of government. He employed concepts that were thoroughly familiar to his associates in Congress and to his American readers. These included (1) the duty of a government to protect a people's unalienable "natural rights"—among which are "Life, Liberty, and the Pursuit of Happiness"; and (2) government's origin in the consent of those governed. The preamble also spoke of the obligation of a people to alter or abolish their government whenever their rights were persistently violated—in other words, it defended the right to revolution. (For the complete text of the Declaration of Independence, see the back of this volume.)

John Adams later said that there was "nothing new" in Jefferson's Declaration. Its author would have agreed. Most of these ideas had been included in earlier statements of colonial grievances against England. What *was* new about the Declaration, which Congress adopted on July 4, 1776, was its suggestion that Americans had become a single, separate people, and the "united colonies" a single, separate nation. The president of the Continental Congress, John Hancock, reportedly said as he signed the Declaration (the first to do so): "We must be unanimous; there must be no pulling different ways; we must all hang together." To which Benjamin Franklin supposedly replied: "Yes, we must indeed all hang together, or most assuredly we shall all hang separately." The exchange probably never occurred, but it suggests an important symbolic truth. During the previous decade, colonists had come to define their loyalties as *national* as well as provincial. They had begun to see themselves as Americans, not merely as Massachusetts people, New Yorkers, or Virginians.

From a sense of shared grievances and from efforts at common action, a broader definition of national loyalty had begun to evolve. This pattern of allegiance would be strengthened immeasurably in the revolutionary struggle that loomed ahead. Even for many of those who had hoped for a compromise settlement, there seemed to be no choice but to acknowledge their mutual peril as *Americans* in revolt.

THE WAR FOR INDEPENDENCE

War followed and continued throughout the next five years. Despite a number of defeats in battle and a variety of difficulties which plagued him and his officers, Washington managed to keep an army in the field—and thereby to keep the Revolution alive. The Continental Army he commanded rarely exceeded 5,000–10,000 men, although it was periodically reinforced by units of state militia, whose lack of discipline or zeal often exasperated the general. George Washington, a professional soldier by training and inclination, had served with valor and distinction during the Seven Years' War, and he had little fondness for the Minute Men and other citizen soldiers he now commanded.

Still he understood how effective such volunteers could be in battle, especially when fighting

An American cartoon satirizes the British retreat from Concord. British troops, portrayed with jackass heads, stop to burn and plunder in this distorted but lively drawing. (John Carter Brown Library)

on familiar ground against British troops unaccustomed to the terrain or the vastness of America's thirteen independent "nations." Thus, in May 1775, hardly a month after the initial clashes at Lexington and Concord, a force of patriotic Vermont irregulars known as "Green Mountain Boys," led by Ethan Allen, captured Fort Ticonderoga and Crown Point from the British. That fall, however, Americans led by Richard Montgomery and Benedict Arnold launched an unsuccessful assault against Canada in an effort to force Quebec to join the rebellion (See p. 163.)

By the time Washington took command of the Massachusetts militiamen who were confronting General Thomas Gage's troops near Boston, he had a clear notion of the difficulties that awaited him, especially the inequality in numbers and training between his own Continental Army and his British adversaries. Gage's replacement as British commander, General William Howe, decided

to evacuate the unfriendly city of Boston in March 1776 and shift the base of his military operations southward to New York. He sailed into its harbor that summer with a fleet carrying 30,000 troops, and for the next several years, Howe and other British generals pursued a logical—but eventually unsuccessful—strategy of attempting to sever and isolate New England from the other rebellious colonies. Although the British defeated Washington's army at the Battle of Long Island (August 1776) and later at the Battle of White Plains (October 1776), forcing him to abandon Manhattan Island and retreat southward with his bedraggled troops, Howe failed to obtain a single, decisive victory, as he had hoped, that would terminate the revolution by wiping out the American army. On December 26, 1776, Washington routed German mercenaries, employed by the British at Trenton, New Jersey (during the war, the British hired more than 30,000 such mercenaries), and eight days later, he defeated a force led by Charles, Lord Cornwallis, at Princeton.

Farther southward in 1776, patriots were victorious against a group of Loyalists at Moore's Creek Bridge, North Carolina, and Americans also repulsed a British naval attack on Charleston. (The British navy was then the largest in the world, and

at times, about half its ships participated in the effort to crush the American rebellion.) Howe's army proved more successful that year in pacifying insurgent areas of New Jersey and other Northern states, and thousands of Americans initially rushed to affirm their allegiance to the king, a process aborted in New Jersey only by Washington's victory at Princeton.

The two chief campaigns in 1777 took place in the North, involving British efforts to isolate New England. In June General John Burgoyne invaded upstate New York from Quebec, recapturing Fort Ticonderoga but allowing his supply lines and troops to become badly overextended in the process. Burgoyne was stopped at Bennington, Vermont, on August 16 by New Hampshire militiamen, and after savage fighting during September and October and subsequent defeats at Saratoga, he surrendered on October 19. Burgoyne's capitulation has often been called a turning point in the American struggle for independence, since it helped to persuade the French government to form an overt alliance with the revolutionaries. (Royalist France, England's traditional enemy, had been supplying the Americans with arms and other assistance even earlier.) Meanwhile, General Howe left New York by sea, intent upon capturing Phila-

delphia, seat of the Continental Congress. The British occupied Philadelphia, but their defeats of Washington at the nearby battles of Brandywine in September and Germantown in October came at the cost of any sustained effort to assist the unfortunate Burgoyne. Washington's army quartered at Valley Forge, Pennsylvania, where they spent an anguished and ill-supplied winter. Although the moment seemed desperate for the American cause, in retrospect, time had already begun to work against the British.

Early the following year, in February 1778, the French signed both military and commercial treaties with the Americans, shrewdly negotiated by Benjamin Franklin, our envoy in Paris. Franklin held over the heads of Louix XVI's ministers the threat that the "United States" might rejoin England under the terms offered by the so-called Carlisle Commission earlier that year. That body, appointed by the British government, conceded the

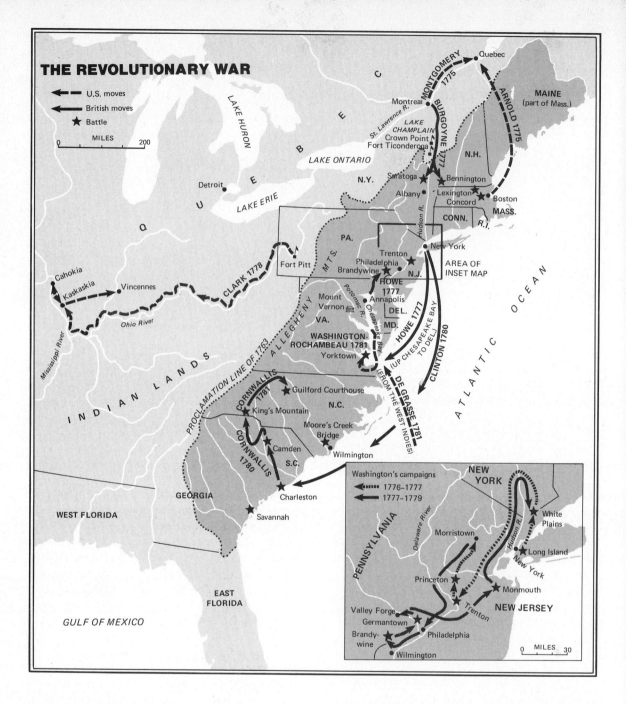

THE REVOLUTIONARY WAR

U.S. moves

British moves

★ Battle

MILES
0 — 200

LAKE HURON

LAKE ONTARIO

LAKE ERIE

Detroit

Cahokia

Kaskaskia

Vincennes

CLARK 1778

Ohio River

Mississippi River

INDIAN LANDS

PROCLAMATION LINE OF 1763

ALLEGHENY MTS.

Fort Pitt

PA.

Mount Vernon

VA.

WASHINGTON-ROCHAMBEAU 1781

Yorktown

CORNWALLIS 1781

King's Mountain

Guilford Courthouse

N.C.

Moore's Creek Bridge

Camden

Wilmington

CORNWALLIS 1780

S.C.

Charleston

GEORGIA

Savannah

WEST FLORIDA

EAST FLORIDA

GULF OF MEXICO

QUEBEC

MONTGOMERY 1775

Montreal

St. Lawrence R.

LAKE CHAMPLAIN

Crown Point

Fort Ticonderoga

BURGOYNE 1777

ARNOLD 1775

MAINE (part of Mass.)

N.H.

N.Y.

Saratoga

Bennington

Albany

Lexington

Concord

Boston

MASS.

R.I.

CONN.

Hudson R.

New York

AREA OF INSET MAP

Trenton

Philadelphia

Brandywine

HOWE 1777

N.J.

Annapolis

DEL.

Chesapeake Bay

MD.

Potomac R.

HOWE 1777 (UP CHESAPEAKE BAY TO DEL.)

CLINTON 1780

DE GRASSE 1781 (FROM THE WEST INDIES)

ATLANTIC OCEAN

Washington's campaigns

1776–1777

1777–1779

NEW YORK

White Plains

Long Island

New York

Hudson R.

Morristown

Princeton

Monmouth

Trenton

NEW JERSEY

PENNSYLVANIA

Delaware River

Valley Forge

Germantown

Brandywine

Philadelphia

Wilmington

MILES
0 — 30

rebellious colonies terms—a return to the pre-1763 status of noninterference by the mother country—that might have been acceptable as late as 1775 but had been overtaken by events since then. The following year, Spain joined with France in alliance against England, so that the Americans now had strong and reliable European patrons in their continuing struggle. The British, in turn, found themselves increasingly preoccupied with their disadvantageous position in the European struggle against France. Their tactics in America became increasingly defensive. Sir Henry Clinton, who replaced Howe in command of the British army, evacuated Philadelphia in 1778, and the British forces retired into strongholds in New York, Rhode Island, and the West Indies. Their only significant victory that year was Clinton's successful attack on Savannah beginning in December. But that summer, George Rogers Clark, a Kentucky militiaman under orders from Virginia, had pushed westward with 175 men and seized three British forts.

Neither side made significant gains in 1779, an indecisive period which ended the next year with a series of major British victories. After the surrender of 5500 American troops under General Benjamin Lincoln in May 1780, the British captured Charleston. Lord Cornwallis defeated another American force under General Gates at Camden, South Carolina, in mid-August, but an American victory at King's Mountain, North Carolina, in October kept Cornwallis from progressing farther in his avowed aim of pacifying the Southern states. American guerrilla bands under the famous "Swamp Fox," Francis Marion, also impeded British movements throughout the region.

The energetic Cornwallis went on the attack again the following spring, 1781, engaging a patriot army led by General Nathanael Greene in the Battle of Guilford Courthouse in March. Heavy losses forced Cornwallis's troops to retreat to Wilmington, North Carolina, while American units reoccupied most of the inland South that summer. Cornwallis withdrew his troops to Yorktown, Virginia, on the coast where he was trapped between the American and French army commanded by Washington and Comte de Rochambeau and a French fleet in the harbor commanded by the Comte de Grasse. Cornwallis surrendered his 8000 troops on October 19, 1781, in the last major engagement of the war. The military phase of the Revolution had ended.

It remained to conclude arrangements for peace. Negotiations for a treaty of peace began among commissioners of the three nations primarily involved in the war—the British, the French, and the Americans—in Paris in April 1782. Meanwhile, the British began evacuating their re-

Washington's army spent a freezing and hungry winter at Valley Forge in 1777. His ultimate triumph has inspired American patriots for more than two centuries. (NYPL/Prints Division)

maining garrisons in the coastal cities, although they remained in New York until November 1783, seven months after Congress (in April) ratified the terms of the peace treaty. Washington—the country's hero and easily its most popular choice for chief magistrate in any American government—gave up his command in December 1783, bidding farewell to his officers in an emotional scene at Fraunces' Tavern in New York on December 4. He traveled south toward his plantation home at Mt. Vernon, receiving tumultuous receptions from his grateful countrymen at Philadelphia and elsewhere. Finally, on December 23, he spoke to Congress, then meeting in Annapolis, and announced his retirement—however temporary— from "all public employments."

Washington's departure symbolized the shift in attention among Americans from the uppermost problem of survival during the Revolution's military phase to the political tasks of consolidating a system of government that would prove itself worthy of the hopes and ideals for which so many Americans had sacrificed.

Suggested Readings
Chapters 7-8

Boston Massacre

Richard B. Morris, *Government and Labor in Early America* (1946); Carl Bridenbaugh, *Cities in Revolt, 1743–1776* (1955) and *Mitre and Sceptre* (1962); Edmund S. Morgan and Helen M. Morgan, *The Stamp Act Crisis* (1953); Hiller B. Zobel, *Boston Massacre* (1976).

Economic Life

Lewis C. Gray, *History of Agriculture in the Southern United States to 1860* (2 vols., 1933); Arthur L. Jensen, *Maritime Commerce of Colonial Philadelphia* (1963); Richard Pares, *Yankees and Creoles* (1950).

Social and Cultural Life

J.T. Adams, *Provincial Society, 1690–1763* (1927); Bernard Bailyn, *Education in the Forming of American Society* (1960); Sacvan Berkovitch, *The Puritan Origins of the American Self* (1975); Daniel J. Boorstin, *The Americans: The Colonial Experience* (1958); Carl Bridenbaugh, *Cities in the Wilderness, 1625–1742* (1938) and *Myths and Realities: Societies of the Colonial South* (1952); Lawrence A. Cremin, *American Education: The Colonial Experience, 1607–1783* (1970), Alan Heimert, *Religion and the American Mind From the Great Awakening to the Revolution* (1966); James A. Henretta, *The Evolution of American Society, 1700–1815* (1973); Michael Kraus, *The Atlantic Civilization: Eighteenth Century Origins* (1949); Henry F. May, *The Enlightenment in America* (1976); Richard Slotkin, *Regeneration Through Violence* (1973); R. P. Stearns, *Science in the British Colonies of America* (1970); Louis B. Wright, *The Cultural Life of the American Colonies, 1607–1763* (1957); Michael Zuckerman, *Peaceable Kingdoms* (1970).

Politics and Government

Charles M. Andrews, *The Colonial Period in American History,* (vol. IV, 1938); Bernard Bailyn, *Origins of American Politics* (1968); Robert B. Brown, *Middle-Class Democracy and the Revolution in Massachusetts, 1691–1780* (1955); Robert B. Brown and B. Katherine Brown, *Virginia, 1705–1780: Aristocracy or Democracy?*

(1964); Lawrence H. Gipson, *The British Empire Before the American Revolution,* (15 vols., 1936–1970); Jack P. Green, *The Quest For Power* (1963); Michael Kammen, *Empire and Interest* (1969); Leonard W. Labaree, *Royal Government in America* (1930); Edmund S. Morgan, *The Birth of the Republic, 1763–1789* (rev. ed., 1977); Howard H. Peckham, *The Colonial Wars, 1689–1762* (1964).

Origins of the Revolution

John R. Alden, *The American Revolution, 1775–1783* (1969); Charles M. Andrews, *Colonial Background of the American Revolution* (1924, rev. ed., 1931); Bernard Bailyn, *Ideological Origins of the American Revolution* (1967) and *The Ordeal of Thomas Hutchinson* (1974); Thomas C. Barrow, *Trade and Empire: The British Customs Service in Colonial America, 1660–1775* (1967); John Brooke, *King George III* (1972); Robert M. Calhoon, *The Loyalists in Revolutionary America* (1973); Ian R. Christie and Benjamin W. Labaree, *Empire or Independence, 1760–1776* (1976); Oliver M. Dickerson, *The Navigation Acts and The American Revolution* (1951); Lawrence H. Gipson, *The Coming of the Revolution* (1954); Jack P. Greene, ed., *The Reinterpretation of the American Revolution, 1763–1789* (1968); George H. Guttridge, *English Whiggism and the American Revolution* (1972); Merrill Jensen, *Founding of a Nation* (1968); Pauline Maier, *From Resistance to Revolution* (1972); Jackson T. Main, *The Social Structure of Revolutionary America* (1965); Richard Merritt, *Symbols of American Community, 1735–1775* (1966); William H. Nelson, *The American Tory* (1961); R. R. Palmer, *The Age of the Democratic Revolution,* (2 vols., 1955–1964); J. R. Pole, *Political Representation in England and the Origins of the American Republic* (1966); John Shy, *A People Numerous and Armed* (1976) and *Toward Lexington* (1965); Willard Wallace, *Appeal to Arms* (1951); Chilton Williamson, *American Suffrage from Property to Democracy, 1760–1860* (1960); Garry Wills, *Inventing America: Jefferson's Declaration of Independence* (1978); Esmond Wright, ed., *Causes and Consequences of the American Revolution* (1966); Alfred Young, ed., *The American Revolutionary* (1976).

The Constitutional Convention 9

When General Washington arrived in Philadelphia on Sunday, May 13, 1787, he went immediately to call on Benjamin Franklin. With the convention that had brought him from Virginia scheduled to begin the next day, Washington had been greeted by chiming bells, an artillery salute, and a procession of soldiers. After that grand entrance into the city, Washington met with the eighty-one-year-old Dr. Franklin at his home off Market Street. Franklin had returned only two years before from Paris, where he had been negotiating for an alliance with the French. There he had impressed his Gallic hosts with his romantic, but contrived, "American" appearance: simple clothing, fur cap, unpowdered gray hair, and spectacles far down his nose. Acclaimed as a citizen of the world, Franklin had an international prestige that was perhaps unmatched by any man of his day.

His high standing, as well as his mostly honorary post as president of Pennsylvania and resident of Philadelphia, placed Franklin in the position of entertaining the delegates arriving for the convention. But Washington and others soon realized that it would be appropriate for Franklin to attend the convention himself, and shortly before it began, Franklin joined the roster of the Pennsylvania delegation by special act of the state legislature. It was perhaps the last great honor bestowed on the doctor. He had never been an effective public speaker (his pen had always done his best "talking"), and at age eighty-one, Franklin's analytic powers had begun to fade. As the great convention wore on, therefore, it became increasingly necessary for another delegate to be present at Franklin's lively dinners to sidetrack the conversation lest the old man inadvertantly reveal secrets of the convention to the guests.

What secrets had to be guarded? Nothing less than a new constitution. The presence of Franklin and Washington at the convention, originally called to correct the flaws in the government under the Articles of Confederation (the loose frame of government adopted for the thirteen sovereign states in 1777 by the Continental Congress), added stature and

James Madison has been called the "master builder of the Constitution." His journals are the main source for later knowledge of proceedings of the convention. (Thomas Gilcrease Institute)

legitimacy to proceedings that undertook the founding of a new government altogether. Delegates from the various states, including James Madison and Alexander Hamilton (Thomas Jefferson and John Adams were in Europe as diplomats representing the United States), drew upon their own experiences in colonial assemblies, town meetings, the Continental Congress, and the Confederation Congress. Many had also participated at conventions that drafted state constitutions and had been active in their state governments. Now these fifty-five men would ponder, debate, disagree, and try to compromise on a new plan for the American national government to safeguard their decade-old revolution.

But Washington and precious few other delegates managed to arrive on time. By May 14, scheduled to be opening day of the meeting, only the Pennsylvania and Virginia delegations were present. Rain had turned the new country's dirt roads into mud, making travel slow and uncertain. Two of Georgia's delegates had to travel over 800 miles under these adverse conditions to reach Philadelphia's State House, where the convention would be held. By the time they arrived, the Virginians had already decided upon fifteen resolves that would eventually stand as fundamental sections of the Constitution.

Proceedings were delayed until May 25, when enough delegates had come from seven states to form a quorum. Even then, only twenty-nine delegates had arrived, and for weeks to come, men straggled into the town of 43,000, then the largest city in the United States, to take part in the gathering. Finally twelve of the thirteen states were represented. Rhode Island alone among the thirteen states refused to send delegates. The state's earlier failure to ratify an amendment to the Articles of Confederation authorizing a 5 percent duty upon imports had contributed to the growing dissatisfaction with the present government. Under the Articles of Confederation, an impossible unanimity was often required before the government could take action. Thus, delegates at a trade convention in Annapolis, Maryland, in 1786 were led to call for

> the Appointment of Commissioners to meet at Philadelphia on the second Monday in May next, to take into Consideration the situation of the United States to devise such further Provisions as shall appear to them necessary to render the Constitution of the Federal Government adequate to the exigencies of the Union. . . .

As a small independent state, Rhode Island feared that a stronger national government would take away the sovereign powers it had exercised since the United States of America (the name took a *plural* form, recognizing state sovereignty) had become a nation. (Even three years after the Philadelphia meeting had concluded and the Constitution had been ratified and implemented, Rhode Island refused to ratify it. The state finally gave in when forced by practical necessity.)

Although Rhode Islanders sulked in their fiercely independent Narragansett Bay towns, the other twelve states sent as delegates a remarkable collection of men. Generally wealthy, influential, imaginative, and intelligent, many of them would later serve in the new national government they were helping to found: two as president, one as vice-president, and five on the U.S. Supreme Court, two of them as chief justice. Aside from the much-lauded George Washington, the Virginia delegates included tall, dignified Governor Edmund Randolph and the younger James Madison, short, slender, and scholar of politics. From Massachusetts came Elbridge Gerry, a signer of the Declaration of Independence who had prospered as a merchant and financier, and the handsome and eloquent Rufus King. Roger Sherman, the mayor of New Haven, Connecticut, excelled in his abilities as a politician, and John Langdon of New Hampshire had made a fortune in commerce and had served as president of his state under the Confederation government. From Pennsylvania came, along with Dr. Franklin, Scottish-born James Wilson, one of America's best and best-known lawyers, sharp-witted Gouverneur Morris, whose crippled arm and wooden leg did little to detract from his great speaking abilities, and English-born Robert Morris, who had served as superintendent of finance for the Confederation from 1781 to 1785 and was probably the richest man in America.

Overshadowing his older colleagues in the New York delegation was thirty-year-old Alexander Hamilton, the arrogant conservative intellectual who had served with Washington in the Revolution, later sitting in his state legislature and in the Continental Congress. The New Jersey delegation, which along with that of Virginia would prove profoundly influential at Philadelphia, included Irish-born William Paterson, long-time attorney general of his state and highly skilled in debate, and Governor William Livingston, a talented wit and writer.

Certainly the delegates had the advantage of a setting historically appropriate to their task. They sat in the east room of the State House,

Independence Hall (then called the Philadelphia State House) was the meeting place of the Continental Congress and the Constitutional Convention. This view, dating from about 1778, shows a cobbled street and the water pumps that served the neighborhood. (Historical Society of Pennsylvania)

site of the first meetings of the Continental Congress and the signing of the Declaration of Independence. The room now served as the meeting place for the Pennsylvania legislature, while the state supreme court met across the hall. The people of Philadelphia clearly had a keener interest in the activities of the legislature and the courts than they did in the curious convocation that now occupied the premises, though city officials tried to accommodate the proceedings. The city commissioner had even spread dirt along Chestnut Street to quiet the noise from passing horses and carriages. By noon the summer sun streamed through the side windows which occupied two walls of the room. New Englanders in woolen suits especially felt the heat and humidity. The windows were nearly always shut for the sake of secrecy, but even when air was let into the room, the delegates were pestered by annoying streams of flies, for the era of window screens had not yet arrived.

Finally the delegates began. After a quorum was achieved, those present went about the business of organizing the convention. The Pennsylvania delegation proposed that George Washington preside, and after the formality of balloting his uncontested nomination, the general was led to the high-backed speaker's chair to serve as president of the Federal

Convention. He modestly bemoaned his lack of experience for the office, but thereafter served with distinction and (all sides agreed) with as much impartiality as possible.

The vast majority of delegates now readily decided that convention proceedings should be kept secret. Such a rule would protect individual members from the pressures of public opinion in their own states and would suppress immediate public outcry over adoption of particularly controversial sections. Even the official secretary of the convention avoided recording any of the discussions and debates. But fortunately for posterity in general, and historians in particular, James Madison sat to the side of the room, faced all the delegates, and wrote down their speeches, debates, and other events of the convention. Others helped the young Madison with this record, which was published after his death in 1840, some fifty-three years later.

The delegates next decided that the Convention should be organized on the basis of state representation, with majority opinion within each delegation counting as one vote. Gouverneur Morris and other Pennsylvania men had argued that states with larger populations should receive greater representation. But Virginia delegates quickly intervened to stop the argument, realizing that it "might beget fatal altercations between the large and small states." It would be just such a conflict that would later bring the convention to its most serious impasse.

As representatives of the largest state both in size and population, the Virginia delegation, headed by Governor Edmund Randolph, now presented its proposals for the new government, drawn up before many of the delegates from other states had yet arrived. Called by some the Randolph Resolutions, the proposals actually seemed to reflect more the ideas of James Madison. They came to be collectively known as the Virginia Plan. Randolph began a long and detailed speech, which pinpointed the crucial weaknesses of the Confederation government. His loose, dark unpowdered hair brushed back from his forehead, Randolph presented not a *revision* of the Articles, which was what most of the delegates expected to hear, but rather fifteen resolves that would create an entirely new government. He "candidly confessed," it was said, "that they were not intended for a federal government—he meant a strong *consolidated* union."

The resolves contained many of the features of the Constitution that we recognize today. The government would be separated into three branches—the legislative, the executive, and the judicial. A legislative branch, which would make the national laws, would consist of two houses. The executive branch would carry out the laws, and national courts would help enforce them.

But the differences between these initial proposals and the final product shaped by many weeks of deliberations proved significant. Under the Virginia Plan the House of Representatives was elected by the people, but the Senate was to be elected—by the House! In both houses, the number of representatives from a state would depend not only on the state's population but also on the *wealth* of its citizentry, measured by the taxes paid. Congressmen would be ineligible for a second term and could be recalled from office by dissatisfied constituents at any time. Congress, in addition to having the power to act whenever the states alone would be incompetent (a vague declaration of power), was given the *absolute* right to veto *any* laws passed by individual states.

Under Randolph's proposals, the roles of executive and judiciary also differed from their modern function. The national executive would be chosen not by the people or the electoral college but by Congress. Instead of *one* president, whom Randolph feared might develop into a tyrannical monarch, the executive would consist of a council of three men, ineligible for a second term. The Supreme Court could join these three in a council of revision, vetoing acts of Congress before they were passed into laws. A veto by the Supreme Court, however, might be overruled by an overwhelming vote in Congress. Other provisions included the admission of new states by a less than unanimous vote, federal guarantee of a republican government to each state and territory, and the requirement that state officers take oaths promising to support the national government.

Randolph's lengthy speech concluded just before the time for that day's adjournment. Delegates decided that these far-reaching resolutions should be debated by all of their number at the next meeting rather than be consigned to committees.

The great debate on the fifteen Virginia Resolves began the next morning with Randolph again calling for a national government with supreme legislative, executive, and judicial branches. Representatives of small states, fearing that under a stronger central government they would lose their influence to the larger states, soon raised their voices in dissent. Pierce Butler of South Carolina and John Dickinson of Delaware argued that the states had no need for a stronger central government and that together they already composed one nation. Pennsylvania's Gouverneur Morris insisted that the states would only be forced to yield to the national government when their powers collided, a statement that only confused many delegates who could not imagine a government in which the state and central governments would share power. Morris's colleague, James Wilson, felt that individuals, not states, should be the focus of government.

One critical question was whether congressional representation should be based on the equality of states, on state populations, or on taxes paid by each states. This question dominated the first half of the convention. Roger Sherman of Connecticut insisted that the state legislatures, rather than people in certain districts, should elect the House of Representatives. This surely would uphold the interests of the states and would center people's interests on the affairs of their state rather than on the national government. The people, Sherman argued, "should have as little to do as may be about the [national] government. They want [i.e., lack] information and are constantly liable to be misled." Charles Pinckney of South Carolina supported Sherman, arguing that election by

Possibly the most distinctive personal presence at the Constitutional Convention was Gouverneur Morris of Pennsylvania: peg-legged, with a crippled arm but always an astute and forceful orator. (Culver Pictures)

state legislature rather than by the people would protect the interests of property from mass assault and thus be "a better guard against bad [i.e., popular] measures." Elbridge Gerry of Massachusetts, however, favored popular election but only because he feared the radicalism of the state legislatures more than that of the people. "The evils we experience," warned Gerry, "flow from the excess of democracy."

Gerry's sentiments, shared by most of the men present, stemmed from actions within the states under the Articles of Confederation. To protect the interests of their debtor farmer constituents, many state legislatures had issued bales of paper money. In some cases the dates for repayment of debts were postponed. In western Massachusetts, mobs of farmers temporarily prevented the collection of debts and protested political *under*representation in what came to be known as Shays's Rebellion.

It was no wonder that the wealthy and powerful delegates to the Federal Convention feared an "excess of democracy." To them the word "democracy" meant tyranny exercised by the uneducated, beastlike mob of common people, threatening their property with high taxes and reducing the debt due to wealthy creditors. Washington exclaimed, "Would to God that wise measures may be taken in time to avert the consequences we have but too much reason to apprehend." Hamilton asserted that "the people seldom judge or determine right." Few delegates to the convention agreed with the sentiments expressed by Thomas Jefferson in a letter from Revolutionary France: "God forbid we should every twenty years be without such a rebellion! What signify a few lives lost in a century or two? The tree of liberty must be refreshed from time to time with the blood of patriots and tyrants. It is its natural manure."

The first votes provided a victory for the Virginia Plan and for the larger states over the smaller ones, which had not yet mounted an organized and united front against the plan. Congress, all agreed, would consist of two Houses, and the people, not the state legislatures, would choose members of the House of Representatives. The authority of Congress over state laws was also approved. But realizing the small states' sensitivity over this issue, Virginia's Madison argued to postpone debate over the clause authorizing the use of federal troops against an offending state. His argument was thought reasonable, considering the widespread fear of executive tyranny among Americans, and the delegates retired to their lodgings by midafternoon on May 31, the initial day of balloting.

When they reassembled the following morning, they temporarily passed over the disputed question of congressional representation and debated, instead, the structure of the executive branch. When James Wilson of Pennsylvania rose to suggest that there be a single executive, silence fell upon the convention. The young nation had been free of royal control for only a few years, and the specter of a single, powerful president seemed (to many of the delegates, at least) to foreshadow creation of another monarch. With his steel-rimmed spectacles hooked on to his powdered wig, Wilson argued that the executive branch was best assigned to a single person to afford energy and speed of decision. This idea was immediately and bitterly opposed by Roger Sherman of Connecticut. Sherman viewed the new executive office as little more than a place from which to enforce the dominant will of Congress. Even Edmund Randolph, who had introduced the Virginia Plan, condemned the idea of a single executive as a fatal step toward monarchy. No doubt worried about the position of the South in a central government with its probable headquarters in Philadelphia or New York, Randolph believed that a single president would always come from the center of population, whereas *three* executives could be drawn from the different sections of the country.

Benjamin Franklin rose, with the slowness of age, to oppose the idea of a special "council of revision" that some had suggested, comprised of the chief executive and a section of the national judiciary, charged with administering the government. From what he had witnessed in Pennsylvania's colonial government, Franklin pointed out, the governor had often threatened to veto a measure unless he received special favors in the form of increased salary, bribes, or increased powers. But a *plural* executive rather than a single person, Franklin argued, serving without pay would guard against these natural tendencies toward ambition and avarice, to which most executives—whether kings, presidents, or governors—succumbed. In the end, however, the delegates voted for a single executive, although it was over two weeks before a decision was reached on the question of a presidential veto power over congressional legislation.

The delegates took up the question of a national judiciary on Tuesday, June 5, while also examining the Virginia Plan's remaining resolves. Should a set of inferior federal courts (beneath the Supreme Court) be created? James Wilson, a Pennsylvania delegate whose interests in western land speculation may account for part of the strength of his nationalist beliefs, argued for their creation with judges to be appointed by the president. But John Rutledge of South Carolina thought that if a single executive appointed the judges, that would too closely resemble a monarchy and that there would be no use for these inferior courts in any case. Roger Sherman—also intent upon limiting the powers of the new federal government—agreed that the existing state courts would serve the same purpose and save the expense of creating separate federal tribunals. Still the delegates voted in favor of the federal court system, although they postponed consideration of the methods of appointing judges. The very touchy issue of whether individual states should be allowed to ratify or reject the new constitution, which was being written without a specific mandate from the states of the Confederation government, was also postponed.

By 1787 Philadelphia had grown from a quaint Pennsylvania town into a thriving cosmopolitan city. The commercial interests of many delegates reflected a number of the concerns felt by influential men in this important market and port city. One Philadelphian had been working for a year on a new invention—the steam engine. Warehouses and vessels lined the waterfront of the Delaware River. Wandering through the city were such diverse people as German-American farmers from the countryside, Indians and frontiersman from the backcountry, and sailors who had come from many foreign nations. In the midst of this energetic urban setting, delegates, when not debating provisions of the new constitution, often enjoyed Philadelphia's convivial atmosphere; one evening, twelve delegates dining in a local tavern managed to consume no less than *sixty* bottles of Madeira port!

Yet there was hardly cause for celebration at that point. Having concluded their preliminary survey of the Virginia Resolves, the delegates now confronted the even more difficult issues presented in creating a new government. This time the small states took the offensive, arguing that the state legislatures and *not* the people should elect the members of the House of Representatives. Charles Pinckney of South Carolina observed that if state legislatures were excluded from participating in the new government or assigned a subordinate role, South Carolina might not ratify the Constitution. John Dickinson of Delaware feared both his small state's losing its independence and an uprising of the people, "the most dangerous influence of those multitudes without property and without principle with which our country, like all others, will soon abound." George Mason, along with Wilson and Madison, argued that at least *one* house should be democratically elected by the people: "The people will be represented; they ought therefore to choose the representatives. The requisites in actual representation are that the representatives should sympathize with their constituents, should think as they think and feel as they feel, and for these purposes should even be residents among them."

Delegates from both small and large states recognized the fundamental issue involved in this debate: how much *power* the new national government would possess. Thus when the subject turned to representation in the Senate, small-state delegates were again the first to respond. John Dickinson moved that senators be chosen by state legislatures, a motion seconded by Roger Sherman. Elbridge Gerry, who, as a Boston merchant, had been greatly frightened by Shays's Rebellion, also argued for election of senators by state legislatures because "the commercial and monied interest would be more secure than in the hands of the people at large."

Such belief in the need for an elitest Senate was widespread among the delegates. Thus James Madison asserted that the Senate should be composed of intelligent, thoughtful men. This idea reflected the sentiments of many delegates who wanted the Senate and the House to become American versions of the British House of Lords and House of Commons. James Wilson suggested that the Senate be elected by the people, but his suggestion was voted down. The delegates agreed that the upper house would *not* be elected by the people. But both sides of the argument had been concerned with the same problem — the need for a national government that would reflect the interests of property holders within the community, that would not permit the unregulated printing of paper money or otherwise threaten the security and stability of property.

Despite certain underlying assumptions such as these, seldom spoken but recognized by all the delegates, large- and small-state representatives continued to debate the proposed powers of the central government. On June 8 Wilson moved that the delegates consider the proposal that Congress have the power to veto *state* laws they judged improper. Gunning Bedford of Delaware worried that such a veto would be still another means by which massive entities such as Virginia and Pennsylvania (two states that contained one-third of the nation's population) could dominate small states such as Delaware (which held about one-ninetieth of the people). South Carolina's Pierce Butler saw the veto as denial of equal justice to states distant from the national capital. But Madison reminded the small states that they would be particularly hurt should the federal union dissolve completely, because of their virtual inability to defend their interests against larger neighbors and foreign countries. When it came to a vote, only the states containing the three largest populations—Virginia, Pennsylvania, and Massachusetts—had majorities in favor of the congressional veto. That idea was dead.

With their first taste of victory, the small states renewed the debate over proportional representation in Congress. David Brearley of New Jersey pondered the dilemma and called for eradicating existing state boundaries and redrawing state lines so that each area would have the same population, a utopian suggestion that died stillborn. His colleague, William Paterson, attacked the very nature of the discussion itself. The convention, Paterson reminded his colleagues, had been called only to consider the revision of the Articles of Confederation. As representatives of various states, he continued, the delegates had no authority to create a government that would annihilate state sovereignty. If the large states decided in favor of a stronger union, Paterson declared, let them go by themselves; they would have no cooperation from smaller states. Tension among the delegates had risen perceptibly as Paterson reached his dramatic conclusion: "I therefore declare that I will never consent to the present system, and I shall make all the interest against it in the state which I represent that I can. Myself or my state will never submit to tyranny or despotism."

Pennsylvania's Wilson jumped to his feet to reply, further accentuating the division. Were not Pennsylvanians equal to citizens of New Jersey? Wilson demanded to know. Why shouldn't his state, then, have a greater representation than New Jersey if it contained more citizens? Wilson threatened that "if the small states will not confederate on this plan, Pennsylvania, and I presume some other states, will not confederate on any other." Heated orations such as Paterson's and Wilson's threatened to tear the convention apart, and after the latter stepped down, the delegates wisely postponed the issue of proportional voting once more and adjourned the meeting.

But they returned on the morning of June 11 still divided on the crucial question. Connecticut's Roger Sherman rose from his chair to offer a compromise. Oddly shaped and awkward, Sherman was nevertheless a very shrewd and able politician. He called for proportional representation in the House and equal state representation in the Senate, thereby offering half a loaf to both large- and small-state delegates. Sherman's suggestion, however, went almost without comment. No other delegate seconded his plan, each side apparently unwilling to modify its stand.

Suddenly everyone began to introduce proposals for representation. John Rutledge and Pierce Butler argued that the vote in the House of Representatives should be according to "quotas of contribution," the original idea of the Virginia Plan. At once Elbridge Gerry of Massachusetts raised the question of slaves—would the Southerners insist that blacks be counted for purposes of representation? Pennsylvania's Wilson moved that a slave be counted as three-fifths of a person, a proposal that had already been made in the Confederation Congress of 1783. At this point, the convention agreed that congressmen should be paid out of the national treasury. More important, there was a majority at hand for the divisive proposal that the Senate as well as the House have representation proportional to a state's population. This final point shocked representatives of small states into concrete, unified action. On June 14 William Paterson of New Jersey demanded an immediate adjournment of the convention and a consideration of an entirely different plan, which he and his supporters wished to substitute for the Virginia Plan.

The next day the nine resolutions of the so-called New Jersey Plan were presented. Unlike the plan Virginia had proposed, the new plan did not create a *national* government but sought to amend the Articles of Confederation. Congress would remain one House with states having equal representation and members being elected by state legislatures. The first step toward reform was the authorization of additional congressional powers. Congress would be allowed to raise revenue through import duties, stamp taxes, and postal rates and to regulate trade and commerce. If more money was needed, Congress would have the power to collect revenue from the states in proportion to their population, counting three-fifths of the slaves. All acts of Congress and treaties entered into by the central government would be binding on all states, and the central Confederation government would be able to use force to require the states to submit in these cases.

The executive, under the New Jersey Plan, would be composed of several persons elected by Congress and would exercise no veto power. But the executive would appoint members of the one federal supreme court. It would handle impeachment cases and review state court decisions dealing with maritime subjects, foreigners, federal treaties, trade regulation, and collection of federal revenue. Had the New Jersey Plan's provisions been adopted by the Confederation government—or even proposed seriously—as late as the previous year, the Philadelphia Convention might never had met.

But now it had met and had gone a significant distance *beyond* simple amendment of the Confederation government toward creation of a new national structure. Paterson might continue to warn the delegates, before he sat down, that they had neither legal authority nor popular support for the creation of a stronger national government. But supporters of the more radical revision, such as Edmund Randolph, reminded their opponents of the perilous times that the United States confronted and for which the Confederation seemed (at least in their eyes) inadequate. Randolph rose to bemoan particularly the weak state of financial affairs that had beset the young nation: "France, to whom we are indebted in every motive of gratitude and honor, is left unpaid the large sums she has supplied us with in the day of our necessity [the Revolution]. Our officers and soldiers, who have successfully fought our battle, and the loaners of money to the public, look up to you for relief. . . ."

When the delegates assembled on Monday morning next, young Alexander Hamilton of New York spoke for six straight hours. But even before he opened his mouth, the delegates knew what to expect: an argument for a powerful national government with considerable safeguards *against* democracy. Hamilton had demonstrated his political skill at the Annapolis, Maryland, Convention the previous year. Designed to be a meeting at which problems of trade between various states would be ironed out, that convention had accomplished little, since only five states sent delegates. Hamilton saved the gathering from total failure by the adoption of his majority report, part of which called for a convention the following year to revise the Articles, a suggestion approved by the Confederation Congress.

Once the Philadelphia Convention opened, however, Hamilton had little use for mere amendment. He argued strongly for a new frame of government in which there would be a single president chosen for life by electors and with an absolute veto. Hamilton would agree to a lower house of Congress elected by the people, but he advocated senators elected for life to check democratic sentiments. The Virginia Plan had not been aristocratic enough for Hamilton's taste. He had only high praise for the House of Lords and the British government generally, which he called "the best in the world." Hamilton wanted a thoroughgoing nationalist regime with strong executive power. All state governors would be appointed by the central government, and each would exercise the power of absolute veto over state legislatures. The people, Hamilton argued, were starting to tire "of an excess of democracy." Even regarding the modified Virginia Plan, he argued: "What even is the Virginia plan, but pork still with a little change of the sauce?" But Hamilton seemed to be alone in his extremist nationalism, and there was no discussion of his proposals at the convention.

Throughout the convention, Luther Martin of Maryland fought strongly for the rights of small states. Martin was a perennially disheveled figure at Philadelphia, noted mainly for his irritatingly long stemwinding speeches. (Culver Pictures)

Worried that Hamilton's ultra-nationalism had driven many delegates into the small-state camp as advocates of merely amending the Articles of Confederation, Madison was on his feet as the meeting opened the next morning. The New Jersey Plan, he argued, would not prevent internal rebellions such as Shays's, nor would it do much to protect the union against foreign powers, either economically or militarily. Madison's eloquence strengthened majority opinion on the question, and the states attending then voted seven to three (with Maryland divided) in favor of the Virginia Plan. Only New Jersey, New York, and Delaware opposed. Had the New Jersey Plan been introduced at the beginning of the convention, it might have fared more successfully. But weeks of discussion of a stronger national government through the Virginia Plan, as well as Madison's pointed closing arguments, helped undercut the notion of simply revising the Articles of Confederation.

By this time, delegates' arguments over proposals often became angry and passionate. Embattled small-state interests now confronted the more nationalistic sections of the Virginia Resolves, including the crucially important issue of congressional representation. John Lansing of New York spoke against a congressional veto of laws passed by state legislatures: "Will the members of the general legislature be competent judges? Will a gentleman from Georgia be a judge of the expediency of a law which is to operate in New Hampshire?" Maryland's Luther Martin, whose sloppy, careless appearance and long-winded hostile speeches annoyed many at the convention, argued that there should be a single house in Congress to represent the state legislatures in the central government. (Martin and William Few of Georgia were the only delegates from a small-farmer background, the class which comprised the great majority of American whites at the time. Thus the many unfavorable comments about Martin's appearance—and the general hostility toward him displayed by other delegates—had a decided tinge of class snobbery about it.) Martin's and other comments revealed that the spirit of the New Jersey Plan remained very much alive, despite the nationalist onslaught.

Unable as yet to agree on the fundamentals of the new government, delegates wisely began to debate and settle lesser issues. Small states won two concessions: the convention did not insist upon paying members of Congress out of the federal treasury, and members of both houses continued to be eligible to hold office in their home states, although they could not hold another federal post simultaneously. Some had favored annual election of members to the lower house, as was done in elections for state legislatures, while others supported a provision in the Virginia Plan that set the term at three years. A compromise of two years was unanimously accepted, with six-year terms for senators. Delegates also voted that senators would be chosen by state legislatures and would have to be at least thirty years old. Clearly the delegates expected the upper house in the national legislature to check "popular" tendencies in the often-elected lower house.

As the heat and humidity of a Philadelphia summer set in upon the already wearied delegates, they sat with the worried expectation that the coming debate over representation and the powers of the national government might create enough anger and dissension to break up the convention. Another long speech by the exasperated and exasperating Luther Martin on June 28 only added to the frustration. Each delegate continued to present his own view, usually well-known by this point, with little or no progress. Madison insisted that the larger states would not conspire to further their particular interests in the national government. The three powerful and populous states of Virginia, Pennsylvania, and Massachusetts were concerned with tobacco, flour, and fish, respectively; what had they in common? Large states, Madison claimed, trying to assuage the fears of small-state delegates, were certainly more apt to become rivals than allies; Britain and France served as the clearest of examples. But Sherman of Connecticut and others continued to insist that bigger states should not have more votes than their smaller brethren.

Worried by the strong possibility of deadlock, Benjamin Franklin rose to urge delegates to display greater tolerance and patience. "The small progress we have made after four or five weeks," he said, "is methinks a melancholy proof of the imperfection of human understanding." Franklin proposed that a member of the Philadelphia clergy be brought in to lead daily prayers each morning. Hamilton and others opposed, believing that such a move might reveal to the public the extent of dissensions within the assemblage. Franklin then observed placidly that such a suspicion among the public might do more good than harm. Finally, Hugh Williamson of North Carolina stated the obvious—that the convention had no money with which to hire a chaplain!

Proceeding without the assistance of divine providence, Oliver Ellsworth reintroduced Connecticut's or Sherman's compromise plan that gave both large and small states an equal vote in the Senate. Madison angrily rejected the idea, charging that Connecticut had not even fully paid its federal requisition of funds during the American Revolution. Ellsworth then jumped to his feet shouting, "the muster rolls will show she had more troops in the field than Virginia!"

Such useless but emotional arguments later led Pennsylvania's Gouverneur Morris to observe that "the fate of America was suspended by a hair." Rufus King of Massachusetts proclaimed he would never listen to the argument that states should have equal representation in the Senate, but Gunning Bedford of Delaware retorted that self-interest blinded the big states: "I do not, gentlemen, trust you." Approval of the Virginia Plan, said Bedford, was not the sole alternative available to the smaller states: "The large states dare not dissolve the confederation. If they do, the small ones will find some foreign ally of more honor and good faith who will take them by the hand and do them justice." The thought had occurred to other small-state delegates at the convention.

The drastic threat of seeking a foreign patron, should the Confederation dissolve, was countered in kind by Gouverneur Morris: "This country must be united. If persuasion does not unite it, the sword will." Another vote on representation in the Senate took place. When Georgia, the final state to be called, divided its vote, the tally in states stood at five to five. All business had come to a standstill.

The deadlock which threatened to destroy the Convention troubled most of the delegates sufficiently to seek some novel means of resolving the apparently intractable disputes. After a few unheeded suggestions, a special committee was formed with one representative from each state to try to break the impasse. While the rest of the delegates adjourned to celebrate the Fourth of July, Franklin suggested that the committee consider a plan based on Sherman's neglected compromise measure. Under this scheme the House would contain one representative for every 40,000 (later reduced to 30,000) citizens, including three-fifths of the slaves. All money bills would originate in the House and could not be amended by the Senate. Each state would have an equal vote in the Senate. Gouverneur Morris strongly disapproved of the compromise, while most members from the small states generally favored the idea, although Paterson of New Jersey thought it conceded too much.

It remained for the delegates to agree on details. They determined that the first House should contain a total of sixty-five representatives distributed according to population. Also, a census should be taken every ten years in order to rearrange representation as needed. An amendment that would have counted black slaves equally with whites for representation was voted down eight states to two. Gouverneur Morris bitterly chided the small states, insisting that their plan would never bring efficient government. His comments so angered Robert Yates and John

Lansing (delegates from a large state, New York, but with localist atti- tudes on the issue) that they packed their bags and left Philadelphia as Alexander Hamilton had done previously (though in Hamilton's case, to attend to private business).

The slavery issue intruded again at this point. Southern states with much of their "property" tied to slavery insisted that enslaved Africans be counted as people for voting purposes. Paterson protested that New Jersey could "regard Negro slaves in no light but as property." Although Pierce Butler and Charles Pinckney of South Carolina moved that *all* slaves be counted for purposes of proportional representation, most Southern delegates asked only that three-fifths of the slaves be counted, a figure that had earlier been used by the Confederation Congress in its frustrating efforts to collect taxes. James Wilson of Philadelphia argued emphatically that this was a different situation, *not* an apportioning of taxes but representation for citizens: "Are the blacks admitted as citi- zens? . . . Then why are they not admitted on an equality with white citi- zens? Are they admitted as property? Then why is not other property ad- mitted into the computation?"

Again a bitterly divisive issue threatened to disrupt the conven- tion. The new quarrel over counting slaves had shifted the argument from large state–small state to North–South. William Davie of North Carolina threatened that his state and perhaps other Southern states would leave unless slaves were counted as three-fifths. Randolph, fearing that North- ern states might someday gain control of Congress and choose to abolish slavery completely, insisted that the slave states needed the security of extra votes in Congress. Gouverneur Morris, objecting not to possible *Northern* influence but to the future role of the *West,* protested the tak- ing of a regular census. Morris feared that population shifts to newly created Western states could threaten the power of the original thirteen. Most delegates, however, recognized the need to compromise on all these issues, and the entire compromise plan as formed in committee passed— though by a margin of only one state. Perhaps the cooler weather had helped cooler heads prevail.

Passage of what would come to be known as the Great Compro- mise seemed a victory for the small states. Their delegates no longer feared that the creation of a stronger central government would lead to oppression by the powerful states. The next discussion of the executive branch proceeded without the strong divisions that had plagued the con- vention earlier. Various proposals for selecting the executive came up: ap- pointment by state executives, direct election by the people, and selec- tion by a system of "electors" chosen by either the people, state legislatures, or Congress. Every possible length of term from four years to life was suggested, but many delegates came to favor the selection of a president by Congress for a single, seven-year term. Although a four-year term was not then adopted, the delegates voted to subject the president to possible impeachment.

The role of the judiciary also figured in debates. Disagreement con- tinued as to whether the executive or the legislative branch should appoint judges. Most delegates agreed that the jurisdiction of national courts should extend "to all cases arising under the national laws and to such other questions as may involve the national peace and harmony."

On July 26, the convention appointed a Committee of Detail composed of Randolph of Virginia, Wilson of Pennsylvania, Nathaniel Gorham of Massachusetts, Ellsworth of Connecticut, and John Rutledge of South Carolina. Their purpose was to organize the various measures, amendments, and proposals the delegates had agreed on into a workable plan of government and to issue a report—in eleven days. The convention adjourned meanwhile, awaiting the plan and report, and delegates had good reason to frequent Philadelphia's taverns in a jovial mood. General Washington, the convention's quiet and stoic president, rode off into the country for some trout fishing with a few friends.

When the convention reassembled on August 6, the Committee of Detail presented an able draft for a plan of government. Wilson of Pennsylvania apparently took portions of a draft by Randolph and augmented it with ideas from the New Jersey Plan and a separate plan drawn up by Charles Pinckney of South Carolina. The influence of the Articles of Confederation and of the various state constitutions was also apparent in this preliminary document. After copies had been distributed, the convention adjourned to give delegates time for study and reflection. The committee's draft would be subjected to intense debate for five more weeks.

In many instances, the committee left questions unanswered for eventual action by the new government once it was in place; in other instances, the committee arrived at new solutions to conform to the governmental structure it was creating. Thus citizenship and residence requirements for membership in Congress were included, while property qualifications, if any, were omitted pending further debate. It was thought best to set suffrage requirements similar to those each state provided for electing the popular house in the state legislature. The more democratic House of Representatives would exercise the power of impeaching public officials, and all criminal prosecutions would be jury trials.

Some of the details worked out by the five members of the Committee of Detail went through without argument; others created prolonged discussion and debate. The delegates eventually voted against the committee's recommendation that members of Congress be paid by their state legislatures, providing instead for payment from the national treasury, a move that would make congressmen more independent from their states. The committee had defined treason, provided for the naturalization process, and granted powers for the levying of taxes and the regulation of commerce. It had also sought to foster greater interstate cooperation by providing for the extradition of criminals, imposing recognition by states of the laws of other states ("full faith and credit"), and granting the citizens of one state the privileges and immunities of citizens in the other states.

The degree to which the delegates at Philadelphia, despite their most heated disagreements, shared a common set of economic interests and political perceptions in forming the new government emerged clearly from the committee's draft. Some of the interests involved, though by no means all, were acutely personal. Many members had speculated in Western land, for example, and were especially concerned that when Western states were admitted to the union, the original states should retain power over them. Although such blatant control was voted down, the delegates did assign Congress the power "to dispose of and make all needful rules and regulations respecting the territory or other property belonging to the United States."

As members of America's economic and political elites, the self-interest of most Founding Fathers can also be traced to money matters. Many of them were creditors, holding bonds and securities that had been issued to fund the Continental Army and state militias during the Revolutionary War. Some delegates had argued that Congress should assume these state debts in order to ensure their repayment, but others realized that this tactic would mainly benefit those who had bought up the bonds from others when they were almost valueless, rather than those who more deservedly had earned compensation for their patriotism. By forbidding the states to print paper money or to alter contractual obligations, the men of the convention were protecting the property of creditors and guarding against the rising power of debtor farmers in state legislatures.

One of the chief defects in the Articles had been the inability of the Confederation Congress to regulate commerce among the several states and with foreign nations. A link between this issue of commerce and another problem soon appeared. Northerners would be greatly helped by the power of Congress to place tariffs on foreign goods and to regulate national trade, which Northern shipping interests dominated. None of this would be of much benefit to Southerners; their wealth lay largely in land and slaves. Pinckney of South Carolina asserted that "the power of regulating commerce is a pure concession on the part of the Southern states."

Southerners demanded some guarantees and safeguards in return. Tempers flared when the South asked that Congress be forbidden to stop the importation of slaves. Gouverneur Morris jumped up to condemn slavery as a "nefarious institution" and "the curse of heaven on the states where it prevails." John Rutledge of South Carolina denied that this was a moral issue, observing that the products of slavery served to enrich the Northern shipping interests. In the end most Northerners echoed the sentiments of Connecticut's Sherman, who said that it would be "better to let the Southern states import slaves than to part with them." The Northern states agreed that Congress could only pass a navigation law by a two-thirds margin in each house, that the import tax on slaves would not be over ten dollars per person, and that for purposes of both taxes and representation, a slave would be counted as three-fifths of a white citizen. In return the Southern states agreed that Congess could terminate all slave importations after 1808.

With the slavery compromise arranged, the hard business of the convention was nearly over. A Committee of Style and Arrangement now went to work on a final draft of the Constitution, an effort that took them only four days. The preamble—in contrast to the Articles of Confederation, which began with "We the undersigned delegates of the States . . ."—now, written by Pennsylvania's Morris, read "We the people of the United States . . ." George Mason of Virginia suggested logically that a national bill of rights should be inserted as a preface to the Constitution. Sherman argued that existing state bills of rights should be sufficient, since they would continue to operate under the new Constitution. The convention voted ten states to none against the adoption of a bill of rights. General Charles Cotesworth Pinckney of South Carolina observed during the debate that bills of rights "generally begin with declaring that all men are by nature born free. Now, we should make that declaration with a very bad grace, when a large part of our property consists in men who are actually born slaves." But the public later demanded that a bill of rights be inserted as one price for ratification of the Constitution.

As the day for signing the document arrived, forty of the fifty-five delegates who had attended at one time or another during the convention were present. Benjamin Franklin urged unanimous approval by the delegates and pleaded with them not to discuss their differences in public. Washington also urged the delegates to sign. By one ironic turn of events, Edmund Randolph's concern with local Virginia politics persuaded the man who had introduced the original Virginia Plan at the meeting's start *not* to sign the final draft. Randolph wished first to observe public reaction, which he believed would be largely negative. Elbridge Gerry of Mas-

The signing of the Constitution as rendered by a twentieth-century artist intent upon capturing an expressive realism for the occasion. (Library of Congress)

sachusetts feared that the Constitution created too strong a central government and might even help foment a civil war during the debate over ratification. He, too, would not sign. George Mason, still unhappy over the convention's refusal to adopt a bill of rights, returned to Virginia to oppose ratification. The remaining thirty-nine men from New Hampshire to Georgia wrote their names on the bottom of the parchment. After dining together at City Tavern, they packed up and returned to their states to renew the debate they had lived with over the past four months —this time with the people.

The signers of the Constitution, despite individual objections, were generally satisfied that they had created a stronger and more workable union of the states. The men who would come to be called Founding Fathers had authorized a new national government with specific powers to collect taxes, coin and borrow money, make treaties with foreign countries, and regulate commerce among the states and with other nations. The Constitution was "the law of the land" and therefore binding on all federal and state courts. The courts, in turn, were empowered to review laws to ensure their conformity with the new document, and the power of the executive and even the militia could enforce the laws made by Congress. Moreover, the new frame of government could not be changed hastily in the heat of public anger. The Constitution could be amended only if two-thirds of both houses of Congress and three-quarters of the state legislatures (or special conventions) agreed.

The delegates at Philadelphia, therefore, could presumably identify with the sentiments that James Madison's notes ascribe to Benjamin Franklin, who watched with evident pleasure as the last of the convention's members signed the new plan of government:

> Doctor Franklin looking toward the Presidents chair, at the back of which a rising sun happened to be painted, observed to a few members near him, that painters had found it difficult to distinguish in their art a rising from a setting sun. I have, he said, often in the course of the session, and the vicissitudes of my hopes and fears as to its issue, looked at that behind the President without being able to tell whether it was rising or setting. But now at length I have the happiness to know that it is a rising and not a setting sun.

IO The New Republic: Establishing a Workable Government

Returning to his home after the signing of the Constitution, Benjamin Franklin had good reason for optimism. He was born in 1706 in New England, some twenty-five years before the colony of Georgia was founded; his life spanned nearly the entire eighteenth century. He moved when young to Pennsylvania. From a small, strongly Quaker community, Franklin's Philadelphia had grown into the commercial and cultural center of the new nation. And Franklin had grown with the town. At the Albany Congress in 1754 (see Chapter 8, pp. 151–154) he had a plan that would have created an assembly with representatives from each colony in proportion to their tax payments, but it had been frustrated by individual colonies' fears of giving up powers and authority. Now that the colonies had become independent states, Franklin and others were not prepared in 1787 to allow a repetition of that disunity.

In the Continental Congress the states had provided the vehicle to raise funds and unite in the revolutionary struggle against Great Britain. By the time of the Declaration of Independence, the first loyalties of almost all the people were toward their particular states. In fact, the Declaration itself had proclaimed the colonies to be "Free and Independent States." When the First Continental Congress met in 1774, it did so in response to the colonial-wide crisis. Acting virtually on their own, without established procedures or obligations to constituents, the members raised an army, issued a continental currency, and conducted foreign relations. But the revolutionary leaders found it expedient to create a more permanent and legitimate government to be called The United States of America. Although in 1777 they drew up the Articles of Confederation, a plan for a loose union of the states, it was not until 1781 that every state approved the plan and the new government could go into operation.

Only six years later the Founding Fathers at Philadelphia's Constitutional Convention decided to replace their nation's first system of government. The convention had seen a heated battle between delegates from small states and those from larger and more powerful ones. The major question of which powers should be exercised by the central government—and which should be denied it—had been a point of contention from the Albany Congress to the Continental Congress, then during the debate over the Confederation government, later at the Annapolis Convention, and finally at the Constitutional Convention in 1787.

Leaders from many states were also worried, however, about growing democratic trends within the states, especially as these sentiments could be detected in the various legislatures. Yet the central government was so weak under the Articles that even a nationwide tariff could not be approved by the required unanimous votes of the states. Was formation of a new constitution and government needed to prevent the union of states from dissolving? Had government under the Articles of Confederation proved a failure? Most important, how did this debate reflect the manner in which Americans thought and acted during the years that followed independence?

COLONIES TO STATES

Even before the Declaration of Independence, the Continental Congress had advised the separate colonies to organize new governments "under the authority of the people." As states sought immediately to create new constitutions, the Congress had begun to create its own successor in the central government: the Articles of Confederation. Resistance to British policies had centered in the colonial legislatures (directed against the royal governors and their councils), and it was the creation of new state governments that preoccupied the minds of most people in the new nation. Between May and December 1776, eight states drew up constitutions. The remainder quickly followed.

American revolutionary theory reflected prevailing ideas of constitutional law in the thirteen colonies at the time. Government derived its powers from the consent of the people. A written constitution drawn up by representatives of the people should embrace the concept of limited government, placing clear restraints upon the powers of executive, legislative, and judicial branches. Most of the new state constitutions also contained bills of rights barring the government from interfering with freedom of speech and conscience and — among other rights — assuring trial by jury and other legal guarantees. The English constitution had never been written down in a single codified document; it remained even in the eighteenth century a collection of laws and customs practiced within the institutions of the realm. But the constitutions of American states provided *written* guidelines. These written guidelines were distinguished from ordinary legislation by their fixed and fundamental nature.

Nonetheless the old, unwritten British constitution with its "balanced government" served as the model for Americans. Power in England, theoretically, was divided or balanced among the monarchy, the aristocracy (in the House of Lords), and the popular electorate (legislating in the House of Commons). In reality, the legislative branch (though growing in power) was probably the weakest of the three at the time of the American Revolution, with the aristocracy wielding significant power in the House of Commons.

The American states sought to correct this tendency by increasing legislative authority and decreasing the influence of state governors. In the colonial period, the greatest political struggles had been those fought between the colonial assemblies, elected by an increasingly higher percentage of the population, and the English royal governors. Now, however, the state legislatures and *not* the governors would have the power to declare war, create new courts, coin money, and raise armies. The Pennsylvania constitution, most radical of the state documents, even eliminated the office of governor entirely, resting the executive power in an elective council of twelve members chosen directly by the people. Since it also made provisions for a single-house legislature, doing away with the upper house, the entire concept challenged the basic idea of government balanced among its branches.

Most states, however, retained their upper houses — state senates whose members were often chosen by the vote of those who could meet higher property qualifications than those required to vote for the lower houses. The state senates had been an outgrowth in the United States of the royal governors' councils, and the new state constitutions generally provided that their power would not be greater than that assigned to the more popularly elected assemblies.

A stronger legislative branch, a weaker executive, and an independent judiciary were ways in which the new states implemented the lessons of the past and the principle of separation of powers, an idea popularized in the mid-eighteenth century by the French political philosopher Montesquieu. Frequent elections, a broad suffrage, and small electoral districts, where constituents could instruct their representatives on how to vote, were practices that gave rise to greater democracy through increased popular participation in government. Unlike the colonial practices of ignoring or underrepresenting new counties in the West, the new state constitutions quickly provided that the western areas be fairly represented in the legislature. Five states provided for periodic adjustments of representation to ensure an equal voice for all areas of the state according to population. Prohibition of plural office holding (occupying more than one political post at a time) would further ensure the separation of powers under the new constitutions, and moderate salaries for public officials to guard against corruption were also featured in many of the documents.

Although legislative power in the states was enlarged nearly to the point of primacy, the executive and judicial branches still exerted a substantial check on the lawmakers' powers. Governors received short and fixed terms. Their vetoes could be overridden, but their power to appoint some officials with legislative assent gave the governors considerable authority. A governor's prestige would also be enhanced by the fact that he entered office by the vote of the people of the entire state. Whereas individual legislators might have widely divergent and narrow interests reflecting the concerns of their constituents, the governor could claim to represent the aspirations of the people as a whole and to pursue the general interest of the state.

An independent judiciary would be nearly free from interference by a powerful legislature or popular governor. After their appointment, judges would serve for long terms or even for lifetime in the new states at salaries that could not be altered at the politicians' whim. Judges had not yet asserted the authoriy to determine the constitutionality of legislation; this power of judicial review would later develop from the need for a higher body, less involved in periodic political controversies, to enforce limits on the power to legislate. When this power evolved, the judiciary's power was further strengthened. These developments within the *state* constitutions—especially the manner in which the constitutions assured both separation of powers and checks and balances within a government—later strongly influenced the delegates to the Philadelphia Convention in their deliberations over creating a new constitution for the entire country.

DEVISING THE ARTICLES OF CONFEDERATION

The organization and structure of state governments, however, did not serve as the model for the new nation's *first* government. The Articles of Confederation were approved by the Continental Congress in 1777 but were not finally approved or ratified by the states until 1781 as the Revolution neared its end. Eight days after the signing of the Declaration of Independence, a committee had submitted the draft of a new government. But congressional approval had been held up by a sixteen-month debate over the apportionment of expenses and voting power under the Articles and over the equally thorny dilemma of Western land policy.

Under the Articles, the states actually surrendered very little of their independence or authority. They continued to enjoy the power to tax and to regulate commerce. In Article 9, Congress was authorized to pursue diplomatic relations, raise and administer military forces and the funds to support them, coin and borrow money, regulate Indian affairs, settle boundary disputes among states, and manage the public lands not yet brought under state control. A simple majority of states was required to decide minor matters, while nine states had to agree on more important questions such as declaring war, adopting treaties, and borrowing or coining money. There was no president or executive branch, although congressional committees were created from time to time in order to serve in an executive capacity. Any amendments to the Articles required the approval of every state.

The crucial powers of commercial regulation, taxation, and ultimate authority (sovereignty) remained within the state governments. The Confederation Congress could merely *request* money from the states; it had no powers of coercion or enforcement. Since the authority of Congress to conduct war and foreign affairs required revenues, the states even helped determine these policies in practice as well as through the payment—or withholding—of requested funds. The spirit of this loose confederation was best illustrated in Article 2, which declared that "each state retains its sovereignty, freedom and independence, and every power, jurisdiction, and right, which is not by this confederation expressly delegated to the United States. . . ."

The apportionment of representatives and taxes, questions that later threatened to break up the Constitutional Convention, became major stumbling blocks to ratification of the Articles. The smaller, less populous states refused to accept representation based upon population, so each state received one vote in the Confederation

Congress. An interesting sectional issue arose over apportioning state revenues to Congress. The New England states had relatively high land values and, therefore, argued that revenues should be raised in proportion to population—and *not* land values. Leaders in the Southern states, which had large populations (including thousands of slaves already counted as three-fifths for representation) but *lower* land values, pushed for taxation on the basis of property values. Supported by representatives from the middle states, Southerners got their way, and property values became the basis for revenue payments under the Articles.

Collecting these taxes from the states would prove far more difficult than agreeing upon the *formula* for collection!

The fact that some states claimed huge areas of Western lands also became a point of contention in approving the Articles. The colonial charters of Georgia, the Carolinas, Virginia, Connecticut, and

In 1787 the first covered wagon left Ipswich, Massachusetts, for new land near Marietta, Ohio. Settlement of the West was a continuing problem for the confederation. (NYPL/Picture Collection)

Massachusetts had claimed land stretching to the Pacific Ocean, while other provincial charters had no such provisions. Those without claims wanted Congress to restrict the western boundaries of the other states and to take control of the Western lands for the entire country. States *with* claims resisted any move to restrict their borders though they argued with one another over *conflicting* claims in the West. Before the Revolutionary War, despite complaints and opposition from Virginia's Ohio Company, speculators from Maryland, Pennsylvania, and New Jersey had purchased lands from Indians in the Ohio Valley. There they hoped to establish the new colony of Vandalia and, after the war, pressed Congress to recognize their project.

Virginia and other states with Western land claims, however, had been able to include a provision in the Articles of Confederation providing that no state would be required to relinquish such claims. Maryland refused to ratify the Confederation government's charter unless Congress took control of these lands, arguing that states with huge holdings in the West would be able to gain so much revenue through land sales that their citizens would pay almost no taxes. This, in turn, would cause many people to move to those states with Western lands and without taxes, leaving "landless" states sparsely populated. As the oldest state, Virginia had the largest land claims. Yet as the Philadelphia Convention would later show, sentiment in Virginia for a stronger central government overcame its more parochial interest in Western lands. When Thomas Jefferson led Virginia to offer Congress all of her land claims north of the Ohio River, Maryland ratified the Articles in the following month.

SOCIETY AND POLITICS IN THE 1780s

War, Social Disorder, and Democracy

The strains of the Revolutionary War had done much to upset the existing economic and social order. Many merchants who had traded under British mercantile patterns now found it hard to adjust to commercial conditions in an independent nation. Beginning in 1776, all govern-

mental power, held previously by British officials, passed to American control, while thousands of administrators and ordinary persons loyal to the crown fled the thirteen states. Over 100,000 of these Tories left for Canada, England, or the West Indies, while others who remained in the United States suffered the loss of wealth, status, and power to the revolutionaries. The new state governments required loyalty oaths and often punished wealthy Tories by confiscating their lands. Merchants, small farmers, and planters alike were forced to adjust to new situations in which their traditional markets and credit sources had been seriously altered. Southern planters lost their normal markets for tobacco, while many of their slaves had escaped to British lines, after receiving promises of liberation (largely broken) from British officials during the Revolution.

This economic disruption proved to have long-range benefits, however, both for upwardly mobile Americans and for the national economy as a whole. The loss of some tobacco markets only encouraged and accelerated the diversification of agriculture in the upper South and led to the establishment of new markets by agrarian entrepreneurs. In Massachusetts, newly prosperous merchant families moved quickly, in Boston and other port cities, to replace the fleeing or discredited Tories, helping to establish with remarkable rapidity a new commercial elite loyal to the Revolution. Operating without some of the British restrictions which had hindered them under the Navigation Acts and the restrictive legislation of the pre-Revolutionary decade and a half, American ships now traded with the West Indies, South America, and even China. The new commercial elite bought the confiscated property of loyalists at greatly reduced prices and speculated in depreciated Revolutionary paper currency. Merchants also used the state and central governments after 1776 to charter banks and other businesses as well as to develop resources for investment purposes. Although land speculators profited most from the outright confiscation of Tory property, the war also helped to eradicate the practice of quitrents, which many farmers had to pay annually to landlords. The Revolution also created a large market for the sale of surplus foodstuffs, which farmers could sell at inflated prices. Although exports remained an important feature of the American economy, interstate and interregional trade soon opened up significant new markets, pointing the direction toward eventual creation of a vast *national* market system within the United States in the century ahead.

The Revolution also intensified patterns of American social development that reached back into the early and mid-eighteenth century. With the British Proclamation of 1763 restricting Western land settlement no longer in effect, for example, and with the withdrawal of most British troops from the United States even before Yorktown, the westward movement of settlement was well under way by the 1780s. Natural increase was responsible for giving that decade the largest percentage growth of population in American history. Nor were the Appalachian Mountains, formidable though they were, proving to be insurmountable. By 1780, twenty thousand settlers occupied the Kentucky territory. The social effects of such movement emerged clearly. A mobile population helped partially to undermine traditional beliefs of social superiority and inferiority along well-defined class lines. The westward movement also brought in its wake "wars" between Indians and American migrants in Georgia, Tennessee, Kentucky, and elsewhere.

The Revolutionary War also encouraged independent religious feeling and weakened the remaining links between church and state within the various states. Denominations that tended to be more democratic and less rigid in their doctrines and rituals spread rapidly, while the older "high status" religious sects lost ground. States that had never known an "official" church during colonial days now wrote strong clauses in their constitutions separating church and state. Some states that had previously "established" the Anglican faith found the affiliation discredited, because of American Anglicanism's close ties to the Church of England, and dropped the official designation. Massachusetts, New Hampshire, and Connecticut retained their Congregationalist established churches into the next century. On the whole, however, people were now free from paying taxes for the church or from attending any designated "state" church, developments that furthered freedom of religion and thought, not only in public action but in the realm of private religious choice.

NORTH AMERICA IN 1783

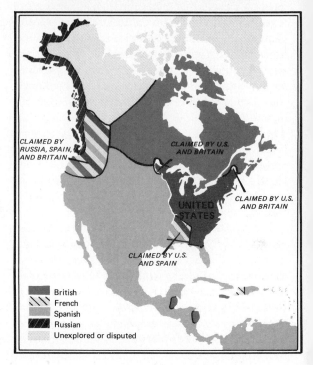

dom of religion and thought, not only in public action but in the realm of private religious choice.

Republican ideology, in addition to furthering developments already under way, also gave rise to growing democratic sentiments as a result of the Revolution. Upwardly mobile middle-class groups in the Northern states especially resented older concepts of deference to the aristocratic class. Membership in private clubs and the wearing of expensive foreign clothing, among other "snobbish" customs, drew criticism from the avidly democratic press. The most ambitious men of the time, however, aimed not at attacking the uneven distribution of income—an unevenness that the Revolution had actually accelerated—but sought instead to gain a higher place within the existing (and changing) economic structure. Social distinctions increasingly became founded more upon wealth and political position after the Revolution than upon association with powerful families from the pre-Revolutionary elite.

Egalitarian values that emerged from the ferment of the American Revolution also stimulated a serious antislavery movement in the new nation. Slavery now stood exposed as a glaring contradiction to the Declaration of Independence's proud assertion that "all men are created equal." As early as 1774, the Continental Congress had urged that the slave trade be abolished, and six state governments soon followed through. Shortly afterward, Philadelphia Quakers organized the world's first antislavery society in 1775, and other societies quickly emerged in both Northern and Southern states. During the war itself, the Continental Army and the militias of the Northern states (and Maryland) promised (and sometimes actually granted) freedom to blacks who enlisted to fight for the Revolutionary cause. Later, the Constitutional Convention would set an 1808 deadline for abolition of the foreign slave trade. In an even more fateful step, Pennsylvania became the first state, in 1780, to pass a statute granting slaves gradual emancipation. By the end of the eighteenth century, most Northern states had either taken similar action or were launched on the process of emancipation. Inevitably, the Southern states began to recognize the emerging distinctions between their social and economic patterns and those of their Northern brethren based upon the continuation—and expansion—of slavery below the Mason-Dixon line.[1]

Politics Within the States

The growth of greater popular participation in government stemmed partly from the extralegal activity of patriots during the Revolution. "Mobs" and groups protesting British actions or patrolling local streets had been a commonly accepted method for enforcing the will of a community upon town or city wrongdoers in colonial days. Al-

though independence reduced the need for such vigilante behavior, many Americans continued to view all official institutions—even their own—with deep distrust. This suspicion was not confined to instructing representatives on how to vote in the state assemblies; citizens often organized committees and conventions appealing to the public as a whole for redress. Mobs helped enforce *economic* standards, for example, when Revolutionary state legislatures were unable to prevent prices from rising rapidly or to control war profiteering. By the mid-1780s, popular associations arose in several states to resist tax collections and judicial actions. State assemblies, by incorporating representatives from the newer Western sections, often included a greater number of small farmers and men of moderate wealth. Significant popular access to government was also achieved by moving several of the state capitals to towns in the interior, by opening assembly meetings to the public, and by reporting legislative debates in the daily and weekly press.

The state legislatures became increasingly the place to introduce laws benefiting local interests and the forum for debates between various interest groups. Older concepts of the public good based upon aristocratic or monarchical premises gave way to the idea of a complex, democratic separation of powers between the branches in which assembly, senate, and governor alike were all responsible—and accountable—to popular demands. Debtor farmers called for low taxes, court delays of debt payments, and printing of inflationary amounts of paper money. Artisan craftsmen wanted price regulation of farm produce, abolition of trade monopolies, and tariffs against competitive foreign imports. Merchant creditors asked for high taxes on land and protection of private contracts. Businessmen sought special legal and economic privileges. All the while, the powers of state legislatures continued to expand. They began to assume duties that belonged in colonial days to the executive or judicial branches by such practices as legislating to overrule judgments and decisions taken by the other branches. More important, however, through such actions as printing great quantities of paper money and delaying settlements against debtor farmers, the legislatures under the

---

[1] To settle a longstanding boundary dispute between Maryland and Pennsylvania, two British astronomers, Charles Mason and Jeremiah Dixon, surveyed the boundary between Pennsylvania and the colonies to the south—including Maryland—from 1763–67. The term "Mason-Dixon line" became a popular phrase in antebellum days for imaginatively dividing free Northern and slave Southern states.

Benjamin Franklin

(Library of Congress)

Americans do not inquire concerning a stranger, *"What is he?* but, *What can he do?"* So Benjamin Franklin commented on the opportunities available to anyone in colonial America. In America, he observed, any industrious young man could become "self-made," rising from poverty and obscurity to fame and wealth. One such individual was Franklin himself. On his deathbed in 1790, he could claim to have been a printer, author, scientist, inventor, philanthropist, and diplomat.

Franklin was born in Boston in 1706, the fifteenth child and youngest son of a family of seventeen children. He left school at the age of ten. First he was an apprentice to his father, a candle- and soapmaker, and then to his brother, a printer. At the age of seventeen he ran away to Philadelphia, with one Dutch dollar and a copper shilling in his pocket. He found employment in a print-shop, and soon demonstrated his ability. Through his brother-in-law, Robert Holmes, he met the eccentric Governor Keith, who sent Franklin off to London, where Franklin found work at Palmer's printing house. After two years in London, he returned to Philadelphia in 1726 and worked as a shop clerk, learning accounts and becoming an "expert in selling."

Within seven years Franklin had bought the weekly newspaper, the *Pennsylvania Gazette,* rescuing it from near bankruptcy. It ran profitably for the next thirty-six years. During these same years Franklin created the overwhelmingly popular *Poor Richard's Almanack,* published yearly from 1732 to 1757. It contained local information for all the colonies, and sayings on the virtues of thrift and hard work. It was "Poor Richard" who said that "A penny saved is a penny earned," "Time is money," and "Little strokes fell great oaks." The *Almanack* sold thousands of copies in America every year and was translated and reprinted in many European countries.

Franklin grew wealthy. He devoted much of his energy to making Philadelphia a better city. He initiated street lighting, police and fire protection, and a colonywide militia. He helped establish a circulating library — the first in the United States — the American Philosophical Society, and the University of Pennsylvania. His scientific and inventive genius, typically American in its practical outlook, produced bifocal eyeglasses, the Franklin stove, a stool that opened up into a ladder, and a rocking chair that fanned the sitter while rocking. By the age of forty Franklin was a distinctly successful man. But, he wrote his mother, he would rather have it said that "he lived usefully," than that "he died rich."

Unquestionably Philadelphia's most prominent citizen, Franklin was sent to London in 1767 to act as agent for Pennsylvania. He emerged as a spokesman for American independence. When he returned home, the Revolution had already broken out. He served in the Second Continental Congress and in 1775 went to France to negotiate for financial and military aid. Franklin charmed the French with his wit, wisdom, and kindness. His personal popularity added much to the success of his diplomatic mission.

When Franklin returned to his beloved Philadelphia, he received a hero's welcome. He was elected president (mayor) of the city. And at the age of eighty-one he became a delegate to the Constitutional Convention in 1787. His interest in the welfare of mankind prompted him to sign a petition to Congress calling for the abolition of slavery. Death claimed him three months later in April 1790. Philadelphia lost its most famous citizen, and the young nation lost a man who embodied its very spirit.

Articles of Confederation incurred the wrath of creditors, capitalists, and merchants—as well as many wealthy landholders—who debated appropriate actions to check what some considered an excess of democracy in the new republic.

THE ACHIEVEMENTS OF THE CONFEDERATION GOVERNMENT

Although the various weaknesses of the Confederation government, perceived or real, led in 1787 to the Philadelphia Convention's attempt to jettison the system, the loose Confederation could still show a respectable number of meaningful achievements. The new government had to face the enormous problems left by the economic and social dislocations created by the war. It also wrestled with the twin dilemmas of establishing viable, legitimate state governments and constructing a central government that could unite the nation while leaving most basic authority with the individual states. In the short time that it wielded power, the Confederation government managed to solve the problem of the Western lands, create an efficient government bureaucracy, and clear away many of the problems wrought by the financing of the war.

Perhaps the Confederation succeeded most impressively in a series of land ordinances culminating in the Northwest Ordinance of 1787. After Virginia relinquished claims to the Ohio country, speculators pressured Congress not to take over the area because they objected to the terms of the cession. When Congress finally gained control, it passed the land ordinances of 1784 and 1785. These ordinances provided for the territory to be surveyed into townships of six miles square along lines running east–west and north–south. Each township was divided into thirty-six lots one mile square. The Confederation government provided for land sales by auction at no less than a dollar an acre, the land to be sold in 640-acre plots (i.e., one square mile). This procedure gave large land companies and speculators a decided advantage over smaller farmers who neither needed 640 acres nor owned six hundred forty dollars. Congress retained four sections and set aside an-

other for the support of public education. The land sales at such a high price (at least for the 1780s) not only kept many low-income settlers from buying their own land but also paved the way for removal of squatter settlers and Indians.

If the terms of sale represented business sense, the terms of the Northwest Ordinance of 1787 were little short of enlightened. It provided for an initial period during which the governor, a secretary, and a three-court judge appointed by Congress would rule the Northwest area. Once the white population of the territory reached five thousand adult males, a representative legislature would be created. The area would be divided into three, four, or five territories, each to be admitted to the union as an equal state when its population reached 60,000. Slavery was forever forbidden. Political and religious freedom were guaranteed and public education encouraged. In creating the future states of Ohio, Indiana, Michigan, Illinois, and Wisconsin, the Confederation government had removed many of the questions regarding the status of new territories acquired by the United States, at least temporarily, thereby encouraging settlement of those and other Western lands. The procedures established in these ordinances also established important precedents for the admission of virtually all the remaining states of the Union.

Another major accomplishment of the Confederation government was the establishment of a federal bureaucracy. Elected by the Confederation Congress and responsible to it, civil servants worked in the departments of war, foreign affairs, finance, and the post office, whether or not Congress was in session. Several men who served in the Confederation's departments continued in their posts after ratification of the Constitution in 1789, notably one gentleman who served as the register of the treasury from 1779 to 1829! Most democratic revolutionaries distrusted such executive power, however, and insisted that congressmen themselves acting in committees should supervise the work of permanent employees.

The Board of Treasury was established to handle the numerous financial problems of the Confederation period. It supervised treasury officials who were settling accounts of military departments. Also, the board oversaw the continen-

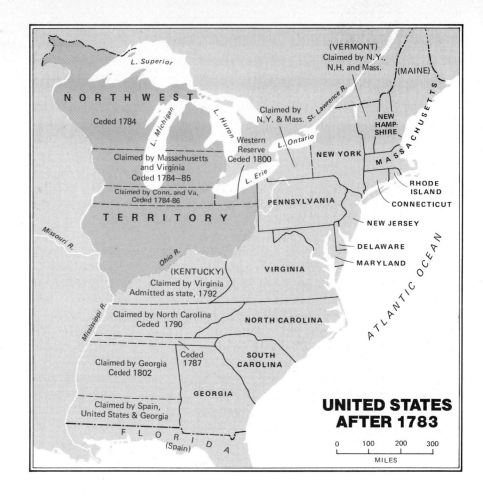

UNITED STATES AFTER 1783

L. Superior

NORTHWEST

Ceded 1784

L. Michigan

L. Huron

Western
Reserve
Ceded 1800

Claimed by Massachusetts
and Virginia
Ceded 1784–85

L. Ontario

L. Erie

Claimed by Conn. and Va.
Ceded 1784-86

T E R R I T O R Y

Missouri R.

Ohio R.

(KENTUCKY)
Claimed by Virginia
Admitted as state, 1792

Mississippi R.

Claimed by North Carolina
Ceded 1790

Ceded
1787

Claimed by Georgia
Ceded 1802

Claimed by Spain,
United States & Georgia

F L O R I D A
(Spain)

Claimed by
N.Y. & Mass. St. Lawrence R.

(VERMONT)
Claimed by N.Y.,
N.H. and Mass.

(MAINE)

NEW
HAMP-
SHIRE

M A S S A C H U S E T T S

NEW YORK

RHODE
ISLAND

CONNECTICUT

PENNSYLVANIA

NEW JERSEY

DELAWARE

MARYLAND

VIRGINIA

ATLANTIC OCEAN

NORTH CAROLINA

SOUTH
CAROLINA

GEORGIA

0   100   200   300
MILES

tal loan officers within the several states as well as those commissioners settling accounts between the United States and various states or individuals. The board reviewed complaints about finance and disbursed payments to troops and civil employees of the government. One member of the board, Arthur Lee, worried over the wealthy speculators who had purchased so many of the Revolutionary War securities: "I am afraid, my dear friend," he wrote at one point, "that we will live to see the noble fabric we have labored so much to rear to liberty, honor, and independence, uprooted from its foundation from the rapacity for speculation which appears to me ascended from commissaries and quartermasters to legislators." Lee's fears would be realized during the first years of the new Confederation government.

PROBLEMS OF THE CONFEDERATION

The experience of many of the new nation's elite in the Continental Congress, Revolutionary War, and Confederation government—when combined with their personal and class perceptions of the situation—fostered a growing feeling of nationalism. The Confederation found itself confronted by tremendous inflation because of the large issues of paper money printed to finance the war, troubled by the states' refusal to pay their alloted requisitions to Congress, and frightened at the threats of mutiny that came from unpaid soldiers in the Continental Army. There occurred, moreover, a marked change in congressional leadership during the Confederation period. Now men as much inter-

A nineteenth-century American artist captures the mood and pedagogical style of a schoolroom in the newly independent United States. Revolutionary America placed great emphasis on the significance of primary and secondary school education. (Library of Congress)

ested in asserting public authority as popular liberty began reaching positions of influence. The Continental Army was intended partly to curb the power of local militias. Single appointees rather than congressional committees now ran the departments of war, foreign affairs, and finance, thereby strengthening the executive function.

By far the most powerful of these men was Robert Morris, a Philadelphia merchant and land speculator who would later argue for a strong nationalist position at the Constitutional Convention. As superintendent of finance, Morris wielded enormous power. In attempting to win support among creditors and merchants for a stronger central government, Morris convinced Congress to recommend to the states that they stop issuing paper money and require all taxes to be raised in coin, or specie. This would help support the value of the new nation's currency, the paper money "continentals," forty dollars of which were worth only one dollar in gold or silver by 1780.

Finance

The key to the nationalist plan was adoption of an amendment to the Articles allowing the Confederation to set a 5 percent tax on imports. This would have given Congress regular funding independent of what the states might see fit to allocate. The Confederation government could then pay back its war debts, thus enhancing the standing of the United States government both domestically and with international creditors. That, in turn, would increase the value of any bonds and securities issued by the Confederation government. The amendment for this tariff passed every state except Rhode Island. But since the Articles required that amendments be ratified by unanimous consent of all the states, the proposal failed.

With the end of the Revolutionary War in 1783, the campaign for a stronger central government, promoted by mercantile and creditor interests among others, received even less support from state governments. A military *coup d'état* had been narrowly averted in 1783, when officers of Washington's army issued an address to Congress and plotted a takeover of the Confederation government. This crisis was prevented only by Washington's personal appearance and plea for restraint.

After the war, however, state autonomy and pride often led the different states to convert federal securities into state bonds, thereby completely subverting the intentions of nationalists like Morris and Alexander Hamilton, who hoped to link the interests of the monied elite closely with those of a stronger central government. Many wealthy individuals with property and interests to protect now looked instead toward their state governments for ultimate redress.

Foreign Relations

Despite the considerable skills of American representatives John Adams in London and Thomas Jefferson in Paris, no amount of diplomatic activity seemed to improve the new nation's standing with the European powers. England refused to surrender its forts in the western lands until Southern planters repaid the debts owed British creditors. The weak Confederation government could not force Southern states to enact the laws needed to comply with this debt repayment, so the British continued to reap the benefits of Western fur trade and retain the allegiance of Indian tribes, despite the pressures of American westward expansion.

In addition to the presence of British troops in the Northwest, the United States faced a Spanish threat in the Southwest. Americans in the Southern states had long eyed the abundant land and fertile soil existing between the Appalachian Mountains and the Mississippi River. Since the

John Jay—like Alexander Hamilton—distrusted the common people and believed that government should be controlled by men of means and education. (Yale University Art Gallery)

Spaniards insisted that no foreign powers could have the right of navigation or settlement on the lower part of the river or its environs, Southern agricultural interests were stymied.

Northern commercial interests met similar frustration at this time. The European governments and their mercantile communities proved reluctant to trade with thirteen virtually independent American states. Meanwhile, competing British goods flooded the American markets, while no American products were admitted—at least none legally—to either the West Indies or any other part of the British Empire. Influenced by Northern merchants, New Yorker John Jay negotiated a treaty with the Spanish minister opening Spain to American trade in return for recognizing Spain's right to refuse American access to the Mississippi. Although seven states voted in favor of ratifying this treaty, the angry South voted in a bloc against it, preventing the three-fourths majority needed to approve it. The incident demonstrated again that a weak Confederation could only advance the legitimate interests of one part of the union by sacrificing those of another, or so it appeared to the nationalists.

Even when American interests were *not* sectionally divided, the structure of the Articles prevented unified action in foreign affairs. Pirates in the Barbary states of North Africa, for example, had seized American ships and sold their crews into slavery for years. Even if Congress had agreed to pay the tribute demanded by the pirates for free navigation into the Mediterranean, there were not enough funds to do so. John Jay, a diplomat to Spain during the Revolution, and others hoped that these humiliating incidents would help mobilize public sentiment for strengthening the central government.

Congress as then set up was ill-equipped to handle any of these problems. It had neither courts nor executive authority with which to coerce states or individuals to obey its various resolutions and recommendations. It had no power to tax or to regulate commerce between the states or with foreign nations. It often took delegates several weeks after a session began to arrive, preventing the quorum needed to decide official business. Delegates were elected annually and prevented from serving more than three years in six. This rapid turnover in membership prevented continuity and experienced leadership from developing, while encouraging confusion and ineffectiveness. The Confederation Congress had met in Philadelphia, in fact, until 1783 when a mutiny in the army barracks there frightened the representatives into leaving the city. After that, Congress could not even decide upon a permanent meeting place, and the delegates wandered in embarrassment from sessions at Princeton to Annapolis to Trenton to New York.

Steps were already well under way by the mid-1780s to shore up the weaknesses of the Confederation. Mechants and land speculators, George Washington among them, helped to organize the Mount Vernon Conference of 1785. They hoped to open up the mouth of the Potomac River to trade with the hinterland. For this, the neighboring states of Maryland and Virginia would have to cooperate by enacting similar commercial legislation. During this period, some states had been taxing the goods arriving from other states as "imports," and boundary disputes occasionally led to armed combat between states. In an attempt to relieve these problems, the Mount Vernon Conference decided to adjourn its meeting and summon a second conference on Confederation problems at Annapolis in 1786. Five states sent delegates to the Annapolis Convention which, though called for the specific purpose of strengthening national authority over commerce, quickly agreed on the necessity of a general revision of the Articles. Through the prodding of Alexander Hamilton and James Madison, *that* convention adjourned even before other states' delegations had arrived. The Confederation Congress, at the request of the Annapolis Convention's sponsors, then summoned yet another convention the following year, this time in Philadelphia, to make "the constitution of the Federal Government adequate to the exigencies of the Union."

Shays's Rebellion

Soon after the delegates had left Annapolis, they received news of a violent episode, which did much to strengthen their cause by persuading Americans of the urgency involved in revising the Articles. As had happened in the western sections of other states, Massachusetts's debtor farmers had taken the law into their own hands. Economic dislocation following the Revolutionary War had caused states to levy new taxes to repay the public debt, thus increasing the debt of already hard-pressed farmers. In western Massachusetts, a number of farmers organized local conventions to demand abolition of the "aristocratic" state senate (which took much of the blame for the high taxes), a lowering of taxes on land, and a reduction in fees charged by lawyers and county courts. Soon after the conventions had ended, mobs stopped the county courts from sitting to prevent mortgage foreclosures at least temporarily while depriving creditors of their rights to collect from debtors. Finally, during the winter of 1786–87, two thousand western Massachusetts farmers rose in armed rebellion. They were led by Daniel Shays, who had served as a captain during the Revolutionary War.

Captain Daniel Shays, a Revolutionary War soldier turned farmer, became the primary leader of "Shays's Rebellion" in western Massachusetts in 1786–87. The two thousand rebel farmers protesting tax and governmental abuses had an even greater impact in states other than Massachusetts, where the prospect of similar "rebellions" stirred support for a stronger central governing authority. (Culver Pictures)

Though Shays's Rebellion was easily put down by the Massachusetts militia, exaggerated reports of armed bands of rebels who conspired to confiscate all private property spread throughout the country. Wealthy merchants like Elbridge Gerry, as well as large landowners, speculators, and creditors throughout Massachusetts—and elsewhere—were horrified by rumors that Shays's men were marching to the federal arsenal at Springfield to seize enough arms to sack Boston and bring down the government of the state. The insurrection struck fear into the hearts of all highly propertied Americans. George Washington's reaction to the stories of spreading rebellion typified the concerns of wealthy slaveholding planters and land speculators everywhere: "I am mortified beyond expression when I view the clouds that have spread over the brightest morn that ever dawned upon any country. . . . Let us have a government by which our lives, liberties and properties will be secured; or let us know the worst at once."

The threat to creditors reached beyond the borders of Massachusetts, especially in Rhode Island where the legislature had made it illegal for anyone to refuse the state's worthless paper money as payment for a debt. Not surprisingly, Rhode Island was the only state that refused to send delegates to the Constitutional Convention, and it only joined the new government reluctantly after all other states had ratified. Perhaps more than any other single factor, Shays's Rebellion convinced the delegates preparing to attend the Philadelphia Convention of the need for overstepping their mandate and creating a new, more powerful central government. Simply revising and strengthening the Articles of Confederation, they reasoned, might not prove sufficiently effective against armed threats to "lives, liberties and properties" by rebellious debtors in other states as well.

RATIFYING THE CONSTITUTION

One of the last debates at the Philadelphia Convention had centered on the method for gaining public approval of the Constitution. In the final committee report, a blank had been left to designate the number of states sufficient for the new government to go into effect. The delegates knew that Rhode Island would not approve of the new document, yet the Articles of Confederation required that amendments receive the unanimous consent of the states.

To agree on less than unanimous consent would be to recognize that the Philadelphia Convention had thoroughly transformed the existing framework of government, which of course it had. James Wilson of Pennsylvania suggested that a simple majority of seven would be sufficient for purposes of ratification. Only the states that chose to approve the new Constitution, Wilson argued, would be bound to it. Pierce Butler of South Carolina sought to support this decision, as well as the delegates' other actions, by claiming the delegates were obedient to a higher law, which allowed for changing the government when the country was poorly governed. After extensive debate, three-quarters or nine states finally became the compromise number agreed upon for ratification.

The final question before the convention was whether the state legislatures or special conventions elected by the people would decide the fate of the new document. With visions of Shays's Rebellion fresh in his mind, Elbridge Gerry declared that the people had "the wildest ideas of government in the world." But many other delegates observed that members of state legislatures sworn to uphold the existing pattern of govern-

ment would be unlikely to support an entirely new government whose creation had never even been authorized. State legislators, moreover, would also feel inclined to vote against the Constitution on grounds of self-interest, perceiving it correctly as creating a new structure of government that undermined the currently dominant influence of the states. A minority of delegates continued to fret that the people should not be allowed to decide ratification through specially elected conventions. There was a "danger of commotions from a resort to the people," cautioned Maryland's Luther Martin, "and to first principles in which the government might be on one side and the people on the other." Nevertheless, in a decision as important as any previously taken, the convention voted nine to one for *popular* ratification through special conventions, and the campaign to win the confidence of the people in the new government began.

Supporters of the new Constitution had enormous advantages, tactically and doctrinally, over their opponents in the ratification controversy. Supporters declared themselves to be Federalists while labeling those opposed to the Constitution anti-Federalists. Since "federalism" describes a government in which both state and central authorities share power, it would have been more accurate, however, to describe those favoring ratification as "nationalists" and those who opposed it as believers in the existing "federalism." Still, the names stuck in the public mind, and the opposition was saddled with a major disadvantage in popular perception. Newspapers, moreover, reflecting the self-interests of urban printers and owners who relied on merchant readers and wealthy advertisers, overwhelmingly supported ratification.

The Federalist supporters of the Constitution worked closely across state lines during the ratification process. They comprised a group whose interests dictated such cohesion, and their frequent exchanges of correspondence dealing with strategy amd tactics during the ratification struggles in various states illustrated their superior organization. Nor did it help the anti-Federalists that the most prestigious Revolutionary leaders — Washington and Franklin among them — supported the Constitution. Such personal endorsements

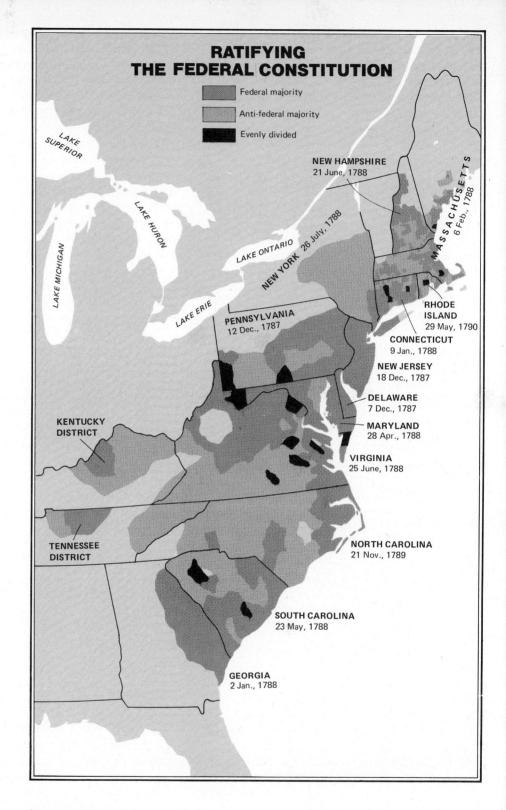

RATIFYING
THE FEDERAL CONSTITUTION

■ Federal majority
▨ Anti-federal majority
■ Evenly divided

LAKE SUPERIOR

LAKE MICHIGAN

LAKE HURON

LAKE ONTARIO

LAKE ERIE

NEW HAMPSHIRE
21 June, 1788

MASSACHUSETTS
6 Feb., 1788

NEW YORK 26 July, 1788

RHODE ISLAND
29 May, 1790

PENNSYLVANIA
12 Dec., 1787

CONNECTICUT
9 Jan., 1788

NEW JERSEY
18 Dec., 1787

DELAWARE
7 Dec., 1787

KENTUCKY DISTRICT

MARYLAND
28 Apr., 1788

VIRGINIA
25 June, 1788

TENNESSEE DISTRICT

NORTH CAROLINA
21 Nov., 1789

SOUTH CAROLINA
23 May, 1788

GEORGIA
2 Jan., 1788

added great strength to Federalist arguments with the electorate. A collection of forceful pro-Constitution essays written by Hamilton, Madison, and John Jay were impressive both as political treatises and as political propaganda. Originally published in newspapers in New York City (and later in Virginia) to influence those states' ratification debates, the essays were later combined and printed as *The Federalist Papers.*

The promise of amendments later to be known as the Bill of Rights helped ease the hesitations of many who had been undecided. Finally, although they opposed the adoption of the Constitution, anti-Federalists disagreed among themselves over how the Articles should be revised. The absence of any genuine alternative or counter-proposal to the new government also served to weaken their opposition.

Those who supported the Constitution often came from a broad sector of American opinion allied to commercial interests. Such people saw the new government's power to regulate commerce as leading to uniform procedures that would encourage stable trade routes, end the bickering between states, and create a climate more likely to stimulate foreign trade. This group included not only merchants but also skilled workers, master craftsmen or independent artisans with small shops. Coopers (barrel makers) and sailmakers, for example, were among those who depended directly upon the prosperity of the shipping industry. Some sold their products to mer-

This superb early-nineteenth-century lady's dressing table made in Baltimore—mahogany and mahogany inlaid with satinwood, with painted and gilt decoration—illustrates (as could many other pieces) the elegance and high quality of American crafts in the late-Revolutionary period. (Maryland Historical Society)

Establishing a Workable Government **207**

chants for export. Many hoped for a protective tariff from the new government to further shield their trade. Even large farmers who produced a sizable surplus crop for export, and ordinary agriculturalists with farms near rivers and streams that produced smaller but easily marketed surpluses, looked for an upsurge in commerce once the new government took power. Anti-Federalists usually had almost no commercial support. Instead, their ranks included many subsistence and debtor farmers in the western sections of states farthest from interstate or foreign markets. These men, like the ones who had marched with Daniel Shays, were more apt to remain suspicious of a new government that threatened to restrain the ability of states to inflate the currency or revise contractual obligations. To the anti-Federalists, such federal restraints smacked of a threat upon individual liberties comparable to the worst English abuses that had led to the Revolution. The anti-Federalists also feared a powerful central government located at some distant but as yet undetermined capital.

Despite Federalist advantages, the noncommercial and small farmer interests often provoked heated ratification battles in the states. Georgia, badly needing federal protection from the Indian tribes surrounding the state, was quick to approve. New Jersey and Connecticut bought goods imported in New York City, which placed a tax on the goods. Their approval reflected (among other things) a belief that though the tax helped to fund New York's debt, under the new Constitution, congressional import duties would use such taxes to fund the national debt as a whole.

The crucial battles were fought in the larger states of Virginia, Pennsylvania, Massachusetts, and New York. Many citizens of these important states were confident that they could continue prospering without a stronger central government. Influential public officials also proved unwilling to lose their power and status by agreeing to the changes incorporated in the Constitution. Despite several cliff-hangers during the ratification process in these states, eventually arguments that the Constitution's checks and balances would preserve states rights adequately—abetted by the shrewd political machinations of powerful Federalists— won by 1789 the votes of the nine states required.

North Carolina and Rhode Island held out briefly, but saw the inevitability of the situation and finally fell into line. The Philadelphia convention's handiwork became the law of the land.

THE BILL OF RIGHTS

In the process of ratifying the Constitution, six states had suggested that amendments be added limiting the power of the new government over popular rights and personal freedoms. James Madison had not considered this necessary during the convention itself, and other delegates shared his opinion. Madison believed at first that such guarantees were superfluous in a republic where the people made the laws on a regular basis and monitored their enforcement through the legislatures. Madison also felt that any declaration of rights in the new Constitution might prove too narrow and thus encourage the violation of rights other than those specified in the amendments. But many of the new government's first Congressional members arrived at the first capital of New York prepared to make good the promise of other Federalists, who had assured their supporters that such constitutional guarantees would be enacted once the new government began its work. Madison, himself, guided the amendments through Congress.

The first ten amendments to the Constitution, known collectively as the Bill of Rights, received ratification by the necessary three-fourths majority of states in 1791. The first nine amendments prohibited Congress from restricting freedom of speech, religion, press, the right to assemble, to petition the government, and to bear arms, while guaranteeing fair trials with due process of law. Also forbidden were general warrants, excessive bail, cruel and unusual punishments, and the quartering of troops in private houses. The Ninth Amendment relieved one of Madison's fears by providing that the simple listing of certain rights in the Constitution did not mean that the government could violate any others presently enjoyed by the people. The Tenth Amendment explicitly reserved to the states all power not delegated to the national government.

With the inauguration of George Washington as president and the establishment of a strengthened Congress equipped with powers to handle the problems confronting the country, the final page in America's book of revolution was closed. At the same time, the opening chapter of the history of a newly revitalized American nation began in that same year, 1789, with the newly empowered Federalists assuming the many unresolved tasks of protecting their young and fragile national identity.

Suggested Readings
Chapters 9-10

The American Revolution

Thomas P. Abernethy, *Western Lands and the American Revolution* (1937); John R. Alden, *The American Revolution, 1775-1783* (1954); Samuel Flagg Bemis, *The Diplomacy of the American Revolution* (1935); Irving Brant, *James Madison: The Virginia Revolutionist* (1941); Wallace Brown, *The King's Friends* (1965); Robert M. Calhoun, *The Loyalists in Revolutionary America, 1760-1781* (1973); Marcus Cunliffe, *George Washington, Man and Monument* (1958); E. P. Douglass, *Rebels and Democrats* (1955); Robert A. East, *Business Enterprise in the American Revolutionary Era* (1938); J. T. Flexner, *George Washington in the American Revolution* (1968); Douglas S. Freeman, *George Washington* (7 vols., 1948-1959); James B. Hedges, *The Browns of Providence Plantation* (1952); Don Higginbotham, *The War of American Independence* (1971); J. Franklin Jameson, *The American Revolution Considered as a Social Movement* (1926); Lawrence S. Kaplan, *Colonies Into Nation: American Diplomacy, 1763-1801* (1972); Bernard Knollenberg, *Washington and the Revolution* (1940); Piers Mackesy, *The War for America* (1964); Jackson Turner Main, *The Sovereign States, 1775-1783* (1973); Dumas Malone, *Jefferson and His Time* (4 vols., 1948-1970); James K. Martin, *Men in Rebellion* (1973); John C. Miller, *Triumph of Freedom, 1775-1783* (1949); Edmund S. Morgan, *The Birth of the Republic, 1763-1789* (rev. ed., 1977) and *The Challenge of the American Revolution* (1976); Samuel Eliot Morison, *John Paul Jones: A Sailor's Biography* (1959); Richard B. Morris, *The Peacemakers: The Great Powers and American Independence* (1965); Mary Beth Norton, *The British-Americans: The Loyalist Exiles in England, 1774-1789* (1972); Howard Peckham, *The War for Independence* (1958); Benjamin Quarles, *The Negro in the American Revolution* (1961); Page Smith, *A New Age Now Begins* (1976); Clarence L. Ver Steeg, *Robert Morris, Revolutionary Financier* (1954); W. M. Wallace, *Appeal to Arms* (1951); Christopher Ward, *The War of the Revolution* (2 vols., 1952); Gordon S. Wood, *The Creation of the American Republic, 1776-1787* (1969); Esmond Wright, *Washington and the American Revolution* (1957); Alfred Young, ed., *The American Revolution: Explorations in the History of American Radicalism* (1976).

The Confederation Period: Government and Politics

H. J. Henderson, *Party Politics in the Continental Congress* (1974); Merrill Jensen, *The American Revolution Within America* (1974), *The Articles of Confederation* (1940), and *The New Nation: A History of the United States During the Confederation, 1781-1789* (1950); Jackson Turner Main, *Political Parties Before the Constitution* (1974) and *The Upper House in Revolutionary America, 1763-1788* (1967); Richard McCormick, *Experiment in Independence: New Jersey in the Critical Period, 1781-1789* (1950); Allan Nevins, *The American States During and After the Revolution* (1924); E. W. Spaulding, *New York in the Critical Period, 1781-1789* (1932); M. L. Starkey, *A Little Rebellion* (1955).

The Constitutional Convention and the American Constitution

Douglass Adair, *Fame and the Founding Fathers* (1974); Charles A. Beard, *An Economic Interpre-*

tation of the Constitution of the United States (1913); Irving Brant, *James Madison the Nationalist, 1780–1787* (1948); Robert Brown, *Charles Beard and the Constitution* (1956); J. E. Cooke, ed., *The Federalist* (1961); Jonathan Elliot, ed., *The Debates in the Several State Conventions on the Adoption of the Federal Constitution* (5 vols., 1876); Max Farrand, *The Framing of the Constitution of the United States* (1913) and *Records of the Federal Convention of 1787* (4 vols., 1911–1937); E. James Ferguson, *The Power of the Purse: A History of American Public Finance, 1776–1790* (1961); Merrill Jensen et al., *The Documentary History of the Ratification of the Constitution* (1976); Cecilia Kenyon, *The Antifederalists* (1966); Leonard Levy, *Essays on the Making of the Constitution* (1969); Staughton Lynd, *Slavery, Class Conflict, and the United States Constitution* (1967); Jackson Turner Main, *The Antifederalists: Critics of the Constitution, 1781–1787* (1961); Forrest McDonald, *E. Pluribus Unum: The Formation of the American Revolution* (1965) and *We the People: The Economic Origins of the Constitution* (1958); J. C. Miller, *Alexander Hamilton: Portrait in Paradox* (1959); Broadus Mitchell and Louise Mitchell, *A Biography of the Constitution of the United States* (1964); Clinton Rossiter, *Alexander Hamilton and the Constitution* (1964) and *1787: The Grand Convention* (1966); Robert A. Rutland, *The Birth of the Bill of Rights, 1776–1791* (1955) and *The Ordeal of the Constitution: The Antifederalists and the Ratification Struggle of 1787–1788* (1966); C. C. Tansill, ed., *Documents Illustrative of the Formation of the Union of the United States* (1927).

The first decades of the American nation proved to be a formidable testing time for the new republic. Although Americans took pride in their new government, and although they quickly accepted the Constitution's basic principles, the national government had to be established and protected. Its future, especially in the earliest years, was by no means assured. Many Americans—and our enemies abroad—asked themselves: Can the fledgling federal republic survive as a unique government in a world of monarchies, most of them autocratic and unfriendly?

The problem of reducing the danger of foreign intrusion into American affairs figured in Thomas Jefferson's bold decision, during his first term as president, to buy from Napoleonic France the massive expanse of western territory that became known as the Louisiana Purchase. Jefferson then directed his private secretary, an army officer named Meriwether Lewis, to explore the new American domain. The expedition led by Lewis and another young officer, William Clark, both advanced and dramatized the westward thrust of exploration and settlement in the new republic. Chapter 11 narrates the Lewis and Clark Expedition. Chapter 12, accompanying this account, examines the passionate political quarrels of the republic's founding decade, the 1790s, which pitted Federalists against Jeffersonian Republicans. After a decade of Federalist rule, which the chapter discusses, the Jeffersonians took power in 1801. The presidencies of Thomas Jefferson and James Madison were both characterized by troubled relations with the leading embattled European powers, England and France, conflicts that led eventually to another American war with Great Britain in 1812.

The United States managed to survive the fierce tangle of domestic and foreign problems that characterized the first generation of American nationhood. In the aftermath of the War of 1812, Americans began a period of relative political calm accompanied by extraordinary economic and geographic expansion. In the 1820s, after a so-called Era of Good Feelings, which followed the decline of Federalist–Jeffersonian arguments, a new brand of politics—and a new political party system—began to emerge. First in the states and then in the federal government, "the people" became supreme through universal white manhood suffrage and through a host of practical and symbolic changes. Symbolizing this process was the election of Andrew Jackson, a "common man" by birth and upbringing, as president in 1828. Chapter 13 describes Jackson's "Road to the White House"—his dramatic life from earliest days and military career to the presidency. Chapter 14 explores the nature of Jackson's political world. It examines the emergence of mass political parties, the growth of the presidency as an institution, and the key issues of this second party system.

The first half of the nineteenth century witnessed not only major political innovation in the United States but also massive economic, social, and cultural changes. The creation of a new factory system and an urban working class, expansion into farming areas (territories soon to become states) in the Southwest and Northwest, and the evolution of a

EXPANDING
AMERICA

UNIT
THREE

modern commercial capitalist economy were accompanied by a host of parallel developments outside the economic realm.

Prominent among these developments was the rise of an entire cohort of devoted social reformers, among them the small number who helped to found the women's rights movement. The first women's rights convention held at Seneca Falls, New York, in 1848 forms the subject of Chapter 15. Other major aspects of antebellum reformist sentiment included the temperance, peace, antislavery, and education movements. The religious developments in this era exercised a profound and complex impact upon the growth of reform concern. New religious groups spread throughout the country, often through revivalist methods, while older churches struggled to maintain their membership and influence. The newer sects ranged from sedate rationalistic Unitarians to more emotional groups like the Millerites holding millennial beliefs. Chapter 16 describes the range of reform and religious activities in American life during the first half of the nineteenth century.

Exploring a Wilderness:
II The Lewis and Clark Expedition

Not every junior officer in the American army received a letter from president-elect Thomas Jefferson that winter, especially not those who served in the distant Ohio territory. But the recently appointed regimental paymaster of American army outposts there, Captain Meriwether Lewis, learned through his commanding officer, General James Wilkinson, that such a letter had arrived for him. Captain Lewis's duties as paymaster took him away from headquarters at Pittsburgh and Detroit to other forts and outposts in the Ohio River Valley, so Jefferson had sent his message through Wilkinson. The February 23, 1801, letter held no ordinary change of assignment or rank for the young officer but offered, instead, a unique opportunity. Jefferson invited Lewis to serve as his private secretary at the recently constructed presidential mansion in Washington, a building not yet commonly known as the White House. Jefferson had special plans ahead for Captain Lewis's work as "private secretary."

Although Lewis rejoiced at the chance to join the president-elect, the opportunity did not come as a complete surprise. Jefferson had long known not only the twenty-six-year-old officer but most of the Lewis family well. Meriwether had been born in 1774 in Albemarle County, Virginia, where his family and the Jeffersons were neighbors. This small tight circle of the Piedmont elite included the Randolphs, Madisons, and other well-placed families, tied together often in kinship relations as well as by economic interests. Lewis's father, William, who died in 1779, had gained some fame and much acclaim by marching against Lord Dunmore, the colony's governor, after the British had seized Virginia's gunpowder supply at the outset of the American Revolution. Young Lewis, fascinated with natural history, settled down and managed his father's plantation for a time in the 1790s. His hard work there while still in his teens earned Jefferson's praise for being "an assiduous and attentive farmer, observing with minute attention all plants and insects he met with." Strong praise indeed from a man who valued both science and agriculture highly.

When the Whiskey Rebellion, a brief Pennsylvania tax revolt, broke out in 1794, Lewis did not hesitate to enroll in the Virginia militia. He never actually fought in the rebellion, but decided to remain with the small army of occupation stationed in Pittsburgh. In 1795 he was transferred to a company of sharpshooters commanded by William Clark (brother of the better-known George Rogers Clark), the man with whom Lewis's name would be linked in his own day and ours. Lewis received a second transfer in 1796, this one to the First U.S. Infantry Regiment, where he served with Indians on Cherokee Nation land, learning their language and culture. Other experiences helped qualify Lewis for his future role as Jefferson's "secretary." He became familiar, for example, with keelboats on the Ohio River while serving as paymaster for troops stationed in wilderness areas.

The president-elect evidently had a broader notion of Lewis's usefulness than merely wielding a secretarial quill pen and similar office duties. In his letter of appointment, Jefferson wrote, "Your knowledge of the Western Country, of the Army, and of all of its interests and relations has rendered it desirable for public as well as private purposes that you should be engaged in that office." Lewis quickly discovered after arriving in Washington what the new president meant by that vague job description.

The new secretary tackled his ordinary duties with customary energy, delivering Jefferson's first message to Congress and making himself totally available for the president's directives. But sometime in 1802 Jefferson and Lewis began to meet in the president's basement study to plan a Western expedition. As a scholar of natural history, and a former vice-president of the American Philosophical Society of Philadelphia, Jefferson had twice tried and twice failed to find a sponsor for an explorer who could catalog flora and fauna while seeking a good commercial overland route to the Pacific from the Eastern United States. American occupation of the upper Missouri country, where such a route lay (Jefferson felt), would achieve several things: it would snatch the North American fur trade away from British control, and it would provide a legacy of land for future generations of American farmers.

Their plans completed by 1803, Jefferson prepared to act. In a message to Congress on January 18, the president masked his true intentions. He argued that an expedition should be funded for the purpose of conferring with Indians from the Ohio country to the Pacific, in order to enlarge the activities of existing trading posts, and to allow purchase of additional Indian lands. Congress, so misadvised, appropriated the twenty-five hundred dollars that Jefferson requested. Lewis, meanwhile, began an intense study of natural science and available maps of the area. He also began recruiting for what now became known as the "Corps of Discovery." But Lewis asked for volunteers without disclosing the expedition's ultimate destination. During late April and May of 1803, the president's secretary went to Pennsylvania to purchase scientific equipment and medical supplies. At the Harpers Ferry landing in Virginia's western mountains, federal arsenal workers labored at constructing a collapsible

iron-framed boat for Lewis's expedition, a vessel that weighed less than one hundred pounds and had been appropriately named the *Experiment*.

By June Lewis had decided on his former commanding officer, Lieutenant William Clark, as the second in command for *his* expedition. Clark proved both eager for the opportunity and delighted to join with a man of his own generation whom he respected from their earlier association. Lewis's letter to Clark about the proposal confided a state secret: that very favorable "expectations are at this time formed by our Govt. that the whole of that immense country watered by the Mississippi and its tributary streams, Missourie inclusive, will be the property of the U. States in less than twelve months from this date." Lewis provided no further word to Clark explaining the mysterious method by which this would happen.

Meriwether Lewis now journeyed to Pittsburgh, where wagons had brought all of the expedition's supplies. The young officer proved impatient with the boatbuilders, who took twelve days to get his oars and poles in place for the journey, describing them as "a set of most incorrigible drunkards" with whom he spent most of his time "alternately persuading and threatening." The equipment eventually loaded on board included astronomical instruments, various kinds of firearms and ammunition (including a new "airgun"), and camping supplies and clothing. The provisions also held many presents for the Indians who would be encountered on the trip, a motley assortment that contained (among other things) three pounds of beads, two dozen earrings, five hundred brooches, seventy-two rings, fifteen pewter looking mugs—and fifteen scalping knives! The total cost of provisions and gifts amounted to slightly over two thousand dollars.

Jefferson's final instructions to Lewis, dated June 20, 1803, took on a very specific and practical tone:

> The object of your mission is to explore the Missouri R. and such principal stream of it as, by its course and communication with the waters of the Pacific Ocean, whether the Columbia, Oregon, Colorado, or any other river, may offer the most direct and practicable water communication across this continent for the purpose of commerce. . . . Should you reach the Pac. Ocean, inform yourself of the circumstances which may decide whether the furs of those parts may not be collected as advantageously at the head of the Missouri . . . as at Nootka Sound, or any other point of that coast, and that trade be consequently conducted through the Missouri and U.S. more beneficially than by the circumnavigation now practiced.

The president also mentioned the importance of soil, plants, animals, and minerals. For Jefferson as head of the American government, rather than as Jefferson the naturalist, however, discovery of a Northwest passage to the Pacific and its commercial advantages had to receive priority.

Lewis's trip down the Ohio began on August 20 and on a frustrating note. The water level was so low that by the time the boat reached Wheeling, Virginia, the men had spent half the trip walking along the riverbed. On September 28, the crew rested at Cincinnati where Lewis gathered specimens of mammoth tusks to send back to Jefferson, only to find out later that they had been lost in a shipwreck. At Louisville, Kentucky, Lewis welcomed his partner, William Clark, aboard. Later that year, on December 8, Clark ran into the expedition's first trouble with America's foreign adversaries, when he presented his compliments to the Spanish governor of Upper Louisiana at St. Louis only to be denied permission to ascend the Missouri River.

The two men worked furiously with their men to prepare for the uncertain journey ahead. Lewis gathered information about the territorial population, number of settlements and social structure, as well as the trading patterns that existed between New Orleans merchants and both the United States and Canada. Clark, meanwhile, supervised the physical labor, keeping his volunteers busy cutting planks for the boats and hammering the craft together. News reached St. Louis at this time that ownership of Upper Louisiana had changed hands. On November 30 the Spanish had turned the keys of the city over to the French.

The following March 1804 Lewis witnessed the formal transfer of the territory from France to the United States, provided for by the Louisiana Purchase agreement negotiated the previous year. Jefferson's secretary took pride in signing the official record that day, and several days later, American soldiers of the First Infantry moved into St. Louis. With the international legal barriers now removed, the expedition was ready to depart.

One Private George Drouillard, who would prove valuable to the project's success, joined the expedition at this point. Drouillard's mother was a Shawnee Indian, and his French father had been a friend of George Rogers Clark. The private himself was a talented scout, Indian interpreter, and hunter. Two French-Canadian members of the expedition also knew various Indian dialects and languages.

The journey began. All the equipment was stowed in three boats: a twenty-two-oared keelboat, a seven-oared Frenchmen's pirogue, and a six-oared soldier's pirogue. The men were divided into three squads under the command of a sergeant, and each received a firearm, gunpowder, and one hundred balls. At 4 P.M. on May 14, 1804, a crowd gathered to give the explorers a send-off, after which Lewis and Clark got under way.

But the intrepid pair did not get very far at first. A rainstorm forced the explorers to stop and make camp only four miles upstream, and there were other problems. The boats had been badly loaded by Clark's soldiers. All the boats were stern-heavy, when they should have been heaviest in the bow so that if a boat hit a snag, it would not ride up on the snag and tear out its bottom.

While the soldiers reloaded the ships, Lewis had a narrow escape. Exploring Indian pictographs around a cave, he slipped and almost fell over a three-hundred-foot cliff. Fortunately, he fell onto a ledge twenty feet below, thereby avoiding certain death. When the journey continued, however, Lewis persisted in exploring the shore, making natural history and astronomical observations. Clark, the better boatsman and navigator, commanded the group of almost fifty men inching their way up the Missouri River.

Danger also lurked in the form of international sabotage. At the French settlement of La Charrette, they met Régis Loisel, a French trader with the Sioux who gave the two American officers much information concerning the country ahead of them. A few days later, Loisel was privately reporting to the Spaniards on the danger of American influence over the Indians and on American land claims to Spanish territory lying farther west. The Spanish governor of west Florida urged that Spanish troops be sent overland from Santa Fé or Chihuahua to capture the party or force it back. Agents actually stalked Lewis and Clark for some time before finally abandoning ideas of stopping them.

As the expedition approached the Platte River, the men began suffering from an outbreak of boils or intestinal upheavals. This forced a stop for several days to cement American friendship with the Oto and Missouri Indian tribes. The explorers told the warriors that they had been sent "by the great Chief of the Seventeen great nations of America" to tell them that their "old fathers the French and Spanish have gone beyond the great lake towards the rising Sun, from whence they never intend returning to visit their former red children in this quarter." The Indians must return French and Spanish flags and medals and receive those of the Americans instead.

In reply, the warriors promised not to injure white traders if the Americans would help them mediate their differences with the Omahas. The Lewis and Clark party then distributed medals, gunpowder, whiskey, and other presents. Soon after passing present-day Council Bluffs, Iowa,

This encounter with Indians in the Dakota country was typical of many such meetings experienced by Lewis and Clark. Most were friendly encounters, but when the situation was threatening, a show of force would normally be made. (The Bettmann Archive)

the explorers came to Pelican Island, covered with birds who had carpeted the surface of all the river with feathers and down. The men soon realized the significance of the sight and, casting out a net, caught over a thousand fish. Still exploring along the banks, Lewis found the remains of a forty-five-foot-long Cretaceous reptile which he ordered sent back to Jefferson.

Fifty or sixty miles above Bismarck, North Dakota, the expedition stopped at Fort Mandan to set up winter quarters. There, on the left bank of the Missouri, downstream from the Mandan villages where the white men could keep a sharp eye on both the Indians and the Canadian traders, the weary party started building a shelter against dampness and cold. Their stockade, completed by Christmas Eve, gave cause for celebration. The white men were amazed both by the aurora borealis, and by the Indians, who played lacrosse stark naked on the ice at 26°F. below zero. The Indians, in turn, were impressed with the skill of Lewis's blacksmith in making iron tools and weapons in the bellows. The Mandans gladly exchanged eight gallons of corn for each piece of metal, which they used to strengthen their weaponry. The Indians were also intrigued with York, Clark's black servant. After continuously trying to wipe the "warpaint" from the big boatsman's skin, they shifted attention to his hard curly hair which continued to fascinate them, a scene that would be repeated time and again with other Western Indians encountered by the expedition.

On November 11, 1804, a pregnant Indian woman, who looked as if she were hardly more than a child, walked into camp. Her name was Sacajawea, a Shoshone who had been captured by a rival tribe and finally

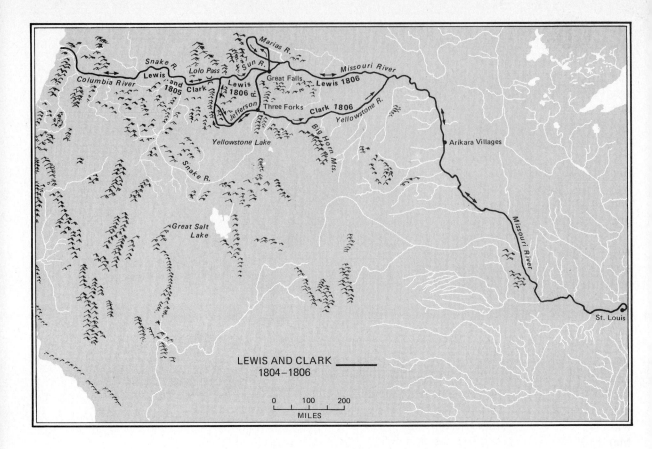

LEWIS AND CLARK
1804–1806

0   100   200
MILES

given to a French trader named Toussaint Charbonneau. The captains realized that Sacajawea and Charbonneau would be valuable when the expedition resumed in the spring. Charbonneau could interpret the languages of the river Indians, while Sacajawea, whose baby was born on February 11, knew the Shoshone tongue. These two would give Lewis and Clark their only chance to communicate with the Rocky Mountain Indians.

Throughout the winter, there was much work to be done. The travelers wove ropes, cured meat, and made battle axes which they exchanged for Indian corn. Lewis compiled Indian vocabularies and worked over his reports, while Clark busied himself with maps, updating his own topographical information by discussions with local Indians.

Most of the men on the expedition were less scientifically preoccupied. The two captains had great difficulty keeping their men away from the Indian villages. Clark noted: "Their womin verry fond of carressing our men &C." An Arikara chief inquired whether there were no women where the white men lived for "one might suppose they had never seen any before." By February 27, 1805, the men had put dalliance aside long enough to cut away the ice that trapped their boats, and about 5 P.M. on April 7, Lewis fired the swivel gun to announce officially their departure. The previous November, the Sioux had voted for a spring war against the whites and had moved to the banks of the Missouri that April but too late to trap the Americans. By then, Lewis and Clark had left.

The Americans had enough on their minds even without the distraction of an Indian war. As the boats continued up the Missouri, it became increasingly necessary for the men to wade in the water, towing the boats and holding up the canoes to escape dangerous waves. One huge wave threatened to scatter the expedition's journals, instruments, books, and medicines. But Sacajawea saved the day, calmly fishing important provisions out of the water. Even the highly skeptical Lewis admitted: "The Indian woman, to whom I ascribe equal fortitude and resolution with any person on board at the time of the accident, caught and preserved most of the light articles which were washed overboard." The men had become trail-hardened by then. Lewis's dog Scammon would catch animals, fish, even wild geese and bring them ashore to his exploring master, who wrote: "The flesh of the beaver is esteemed a delicacy among us. I think the tail a delicious morsel."

The party halted at Loma, Montana, where the river divides. Which stream ran nearest to the headwaters of the Columbia River? Lewis took a group sixty miles up the north fork, where he again barely avoided death, when, after slipping atop a ninety-foot precipice, he managed to grab a handhold. Realizing soon after this incident that he was following a tributary of the Missouri, Lewis named the stream Maria's River after his cousin and sweetheart. After journeying forty miles up the southern stream, Clark realized that he was on the right route. Once reunited, the leaders decided to bury their big red pirogue and much of the heavy baggage before continuing, interring them Indian style to be picked up on the return trip. Lewis had fallen victim to an intestinal illness, but he cured himself by making a concoction from choke cherry twigs that his mother used to administer. He had recovered by the time the party reached the Missouri Falls on June 13. Greatly impressed at the sight, which few, if any, whites had seen before him, Lewis recorded his observation that the spectacular waters "roll and swell into half-formed billows of great height which rise and again disappear in an instant."

The falls were beautiful but costly in time, forcing a detour to a more navigable part of the river. The expedition took a full month to cut a path and move the boats and supplies sixteen miles around the Missouri Falls. Much to Lewis's dismay, the tar substitute on the *Experiment* began to fall off and the collapsible iron ship had to be abandoned. Soon after the boats had been brought back to the water, the explorers came to three forks in the river. Ever conscious of Republican politics, Lewis named the rivers for Jefferson, Secretary of State Madison, and Secretary of the Treasury Albert Gallatin. As the party made its way up the Jefferson River, Sacajawea announced that they were nearing the land of the Shoshone, her own people. Lewis realized that the expedition could not find its way across the Rocky Mountains without someone who knew the trails and without horses to carry their baggage. September was approaching, and the party was not sure of the distance between the headwaters of the upper Missouri and the upper Columbia.

The Shoshone were hesitant about making contact with foreigners. They were a weak Rockies tribe, hemmed in by more powerful Indian nations on all sides, with little knowledge of the white men or access to trade. Their diet was necessarily meager, bordering on subsistence. Though the Americans were for the moment unaware of the Shoshone condition, they were all too familiar with their own. Lewis was suffering from dysentery, while Clark and others had severe attacks of boils. In addition, one of Clark's canoes had sunk in the rapids and another had turned partly over, ruining most of the remaining medical supplies.

The first contact proved helpful to both sides. Lewis spotted and caught up to an old Shoshone woman with a girl of about twelve. The women sat down and lowered their heads, waiting for this new warring tribe to murder them. When instead the explorer loaded them with beads, moccasins, and paint, they ran up to their chief displaying the gifts. The hungry Indians found they could get meat from Lewis's hunters, and they enthusiastically embraced the explorers. Sacajawea suddenly ran excitedly up to the Shoshone chief, discovering that he was her brother! She had also met with another Shoshone woman with whom she had been captured and sold away from the tribe.

The Shoshone realized that they could enjoy future benefits from trading with the whites, who might eventually shield them from their

The help Sacajawea gave to the Lewis and Clark expedition proved essential to its success. (Culver Pictures)

enemies while providing them with firearms to protect and feed themselves. Again, the explorers plied the Indians with gifts, in this case a medal with Jefferson's portrait and a military uniform coat. In return, Lewis seemed to eye the Shoshone horses enviously as when he recorded in an August 14, 1805, diary entry: "Drewyer who had had a good view of their horses estimated them at 400. Most of them are fine horses. Indeed many of them would make a figure on the South side of James River [in Virginia] or the land of fine horses. I saw several with Spanish brands on them, and some mules which they informed me that they had also obtained from the Spaniards." Lewis remained with the Shoshone long enough to rest his men, stock up on supplies, and bury what would be impossible to carry across the mountains. He could not, however, keep his men away from the Shoshone women.

Lewis acquired eleven horses and a mule, not enough for his purposes, but "the Indian women took the balance of the baggage." The expedition struggled down the Lemhi River. At the Bitterroot Mountains the party had to cut its way through with axes, battling also against sleet and snow, especially when crossing Lolo Pass. The men were lucky when they had wolfmeat and crayfish to eat. More often their dinner consisted of soup, snow water, bear grease, dried fish, and camass root flour. Moving down toward the valley known as Ross's Hole in the country of the Selish Indians, the party lost several horses that slipped down the slopes. They were also endangered by falling timber and attacking wasps.

Clark had found a branch of the Columbia River some fifteen or twenty miles ahead on September 22, where he had met with the friendly

Frederic Remington, the greatest artist of the American West, painted from his knowledge of history as well as from his own experience. This drawing shows Lewis and Clark conferring over one of the many decisions to be made (perhaps regarding plans for dividing the party). In the background are Sacajawea and Charbonneau; the men prepare the canoes. (Library of Congress)

Nez Percé tribe. While some sick men rested, others began felling trees for the first *downstream* part of the journey. A local chief and medicine man, Twisted Hair, made a map for the explorers, while the tribe agreed to take care of the animals obtained from the Shoshone. On October 7, four large canoes and one small one carried the party down the Columbia River. The boredom of the journey was spectacularly relieved by the rapids, which smashed two of the boats against the rocks. Bedding, shot pouches, and other important items were lost. During the next two weeks, they saw signs of Indian contact with Europeans: muskets, swords, brass armbands, shirts, and even overalls.

At the Short Narrows of the Columbia River, framed by high and jagged rock walls, many of the men disembarked, while French explorer Peter Cruzat shot the rapids. Afterward he played the violin, while Clark's servant York danced, delighting the local Indian spectators.

As they neared the ocean, the men grew ill from washing their dried fish in the increasingly salty water. Little game could be found. The increasing cold caused great hardship among the American explorers, who found their wet bedding and clothing rotting away from the salt water. Although from the expedition's actual location on November 7, 1805, Clark himself probably could not have seen what he recorded in his diary—the party had indeed almost reached its destination:

> Great joy in camp we are in *view* of the *Ocean,* this great Pacific Ocean which we been so long anxious to see. and the roreing or noise made by the waves brakeing on the rockey shores (as I suppose) may be heard distinctly.

How would the explorers return? If they found trading vessels at the mouth of the Columbia River, this problem would be solved, but if not, the tired men would face a second journey across the North American continent. Jefferson had not sent ships to wait for the party to appear on the river. He was afraid Spain, already disturbed over the French sale of Louisiana, would be angered further by a United States naval vessel so close to her California settlements.

Conditions remained miserable for the explorers. The men had little time and less cause for celebration. Waves were so high that the canoes were in constant danger of overturning, and many men became violently seasick. Camping in Gray's Bay on the north side of the Columbia on November 8, the group had to pile baggage on a tangle of poles to keep it above the tide. One canoe sank before it could be unloaded, and others filled and sank during the night. There was no level ground to lie upon and nothing to eat but dried fish. Indians took their rifles as they slept, although the rifles were later returned. The party moved three miles to the present site of Fort Columbia, opposite Astoria, near a Chinook village. Hunting improved and the Indians were willing to sell food. But they charged such high prices that the supply of trading goods was rapidly disappearing.

The expedition voted almost unanimously to cross the river and look for a winter site on its southern shore. With winter approaching, it made no sense to return to the Rockies without adequate food and clothing. There was also the hope that a ship, any ship, might arrive before spring. Misery continued. Firewood was hard to come by, and there were no deer or elk for meat. The large officers' tent had practically worn out, while the other tent and sails were "so full of holes and rotten that they will not keep anything dry." Although plagued with dysentery, boils, and colds, the men worked in the constant rain to build cabins for winter.

The party rejoiced as best it could that Christmas, but in their exhausted condition, the merrymaking was understandably muted. The scarcity of wild game meant not only a shortage of food, but also a shortage of skins with which to make much-needed clothing. Somehow, through all this suffering, the Indians either deliberately deceived the Lewis and Clark party, or they had not been able to communicate properly the exciting news that the American trade ship *Lydia* lay just off the coast near their encampment! And it did not sail until August 12, 1806, long after the expedition had begun its long homeward trek — overland.

Lewis continued to work throughout the winter, recording each evergreen, shrub, fern, and grass he encountered. He also made observations regarding Indian costumes, canoe building, and domestic animals. There was the now familiar pattern of his men fraternizing with Indian women, and the resulting problem of venereal diseases. Lewis thought it best to ignore a situation he could neither end nor alleviate.

In preparing for the trip home, Lewis had to trade his fine laced uniform coat in order to buy another canoe. He was careful to leave behind, nailed on the fort, a document listing the names of many of his men and the purpose of the expedition. This notice later helped the United States stake out its claim to the Oregon Territory.

Clark, meanwhile, had been spending the winter completing a map from astronomical observations. The two leaders now realized they could save considerable time by traveling directly overland to the falls from the beginning of the Lolo Trail, avoiding the difficult canoe travel along the Missouri's upper waters. Since they now had horses, they could test this route on the way back.

Lewis and Clark knew that they must leave Fort Clatsop on the Pacific and reach the Rockies as soon as the mountain passes opened that spring. Otherwise the Nez Percé might take all their horses for buffalo hunting on the other side of the mountains, leaving the expedition stranded without a way to transport baggage over the Continental Divide. An early departure would also eliminate the need for passing another winter at Fort Mandan. They loaded the canoes, one of which they had stolen from the coastal Indians, and left for home on March 23, 1806. This time, they supplemented their dried salmon diet with game shot in the area.

Once the party reached the Nez Percé, they began scrounging for horses. Charbonneau literally traded the shirt off his back for an animal, not once but twice. One Indian traveler arrived with a number of horses, which he offered to sell or rent. While Clark and some of the men traded

An early pictorial version of the expedition — one of the many meetings with Indians. While Lewis and Clark talk, one of the soldiers (and doubtless the rest) stands, or sits, at the ready, just in case. (Library of Congress)

for horses along the banks of the Columbia, Lewis commandeered the canoes upriver and kept the men busy making saddles and harnesses. Chief Twisted Hair was sorry to report that other chiefs, jealous of his previous meeting with the expedition, had taken the horses and part of the previously buried supplies. By the end of May, however, half of the lost saddles were found and almost all of the horses had been recovered. The whites, especially Clark, won great favor with the Nez Percé for medical services rendered to the tribe; when Clark opened an abscess on a woman's back, she slept so well that her grateful husband gave the Americans a horse. As a partial result of this medical diplomacy, the chiefs agreed to make peace with the impoverished Shoshones and to send emissaries with the party to make peace with the Blackfeet.

The expedition was now ready for a return assault on the Rockies. As the party stood at the foot of the great mountains on June 10, Lewis expressed some doubt: "I am still apprehensive that the snow and the want of food for our horses will prove a serious embarrassment to us, as at least four days' journey of our route in these mountains lies over heights and along a ledge of mountains never entirely destitute of snow." As they set out on the beginnings of the Lolo Trail on June 15, it soon became apparent that many landmarks pointing the way through the pass would be obscured by heavy snow. There was virtually no food for the men or the sixty-six horses, and a hard cold rain soaked everyone. One night many of the party ate the green fungi that grew in some places along the trail but which Lewis described as "truly an insippid taistless food."

After stopping for two hours to consider the crucial decision confronting him, Lewis decided that the situation called for retreat. Both men and horses might starve and freeze to death before the party found the precise paths that would lead them over the Continental Divide. Lewis and Clark would do all in their power to obtain an Indian guide whose knowledge of the terrain might shorten the journey.

Luckily they found such guides, and on June 24 the expedition began struggling up the slopes for a second attempt. In two days they located the equipment they had stored nine months before. The snow-banks were shrinking, and the three Nez Percé guides constantly led the explorers along the fastest route. By this time and at this pace, even bear oil and boiled roots made a tolerable meal. They came out of the snow on June 29 and descended down the northeast side of the mountains. Their Indian guides soon led them to a herd of deer and to a hot springs, where the weary Americans gratefully ate and bathed. Next night, they arrived at "Traveler's Rest" near Missoula, Montana—their old camp on their journey to the Pacific.

After a two-day rest, Lewis and Clark decided to separate and explore different routes to the Missouri River, where they would meet. The captains agreed that Lewis would probe the basin of Maria's River, traveling overland north to the Missouri. Clark, the better boatsman, would go south to the Yellowstone River and follow it down to the Missouri. The two groups split up on July 3. Nez Percé guides showed Lewis two routes to the falls, but after discovering signs of their enemy, the Prairie Minnetares, the Indian guides quickly asked for payment and returned back over the mountains to their own people.

Lewis's party made an easy trip to the falls. The fields were crowded with buffalo, who provided easy and abundant game for the party. Lewis wrote: "The bulls keep a tremendous roaring we could hear them for many miles and there are such numbers of them that there is one continued roar." Upon arriving at the falls on July 13, the men eagerly dug up their buried provisions. But the river had been so high the previous winter that, unfortunately, all of Lewis's bearskins, botanical specimens, and medical supplies had been destroyed. Luckily his damp papers could be dried out, and the chart of the Missouri was rescued unscathed. On July 17, Lewis took some men and headed for Maria's River, while those behind struggled with the job of carrying the expedition's supplies around the falls of the Missouri. This latter group was soon joined by some men from Clark's party, who came floating downriver in canoes, bringing supplies left the previous year at Jefferson's River, which had remained in usable condition.

Lewis and his handful of men found the going considerably rougher by this time. Hunting proved so poor at Maria's River that the group reverted to eating grease with mush made from roots, cooked over a buffalo dung fire in the absence of firewood. One afternoon Lewis scaled a high point. Through his spyglass, he observed a group of Indians looking down at a stream where Lewis's valuable scout and interpreter Drouillard had gone. Although he feared for his men's safety if they came out into the open, Lewis was more afraid of leaving Drouillard to the mercy of the hostile Minnetares. The men made their presence known to the Indians, and after many a wary glance, the Indians invited the Americans to spend the night at their camp.

Then came the most severe conflict with a native tribe during the entire expedition. Near dawn, after trying but failing to steal the whites' rifles, the Minnetares tried to make off with Lewis's horses. The explorers shot two of the Indians, while the others escaped. Fearing pursuit by a large group of Minnetares, Lewis and his men rode hard all day toward the bluffs of the Missouri, covering 120 miles in a little more than 24 hours. There they rejoiced to find the rest of their party and quickly scrambled on board the canoes to make their way downriver.

Meanwhile Clark's party suffered little more than minor mishaps, moving along the Bitterroot, then down Jefferson's River, to the Wisdom River and finally to the Yellowstone. This group found itself under attack, not by Indians, but by swarms of mosquitoes. Since Clark's party did not find Sacajawea's brother or his band of Shoshones, she traveled on with the explorer, who noted she was "of great service to me as a pilot through this country." On July 8, a few days after leaving Lewis, Clark's band found the buried canoes in their old camp. Starting down Jefferson's River on July 10, the expedition covered the same distance in three days downstream that had taken over a week to navigate upstream the year before.

Clark and his men continued to make their way east toward the Missouri, and Sacajawea guided them through Bozeman Pass into the Yellowstone Valley. Clark was alarmed over growing Indian thefts of his horses and directed Sergeant Nathaniel Pryor to take two men and drive the animals directly overland to the Mandan villages. From there Pryor was to head north, giving Canadian fur trader Hugh Heney a letter requesting him to persuade Sioux chiefs to travel to Washington, D.C., with Clark.

These plans were quickly dashed when, the second night out, Indians stole all of Pryor's horses. Pryor and his men then rushed to the Yellowstone River, only to find that Clark's canoes had already passed them. The stranded men began to shoot buffalo and use the skins to make tublike "bull-boats" on which they hoped to float down the Yellowstone to the Missouri. Clark's group reached the Missouri on August 3. Five days later, they were amazed to see the men they had sent on an *overland* mission come *floating* down the Missouri! The only major problem now was to find Captain Lewis and his men.

But the Lewis group was not far behind. The discovery of fresh meat on a pole and a campfire still burning meant to Lewis that Clark was close by. Lewis left the boats one afternoon to hunt for elk, accompanied by the French-Canadian Cruzat, known more for his virtuosity on the violin than his skill as a sharpshooter. The two men went their separate ways until a shot was fired, hitting Lewis "in the hinder part of my right thigh." Believing the shot to have come from the mistaken and nearsighted Cruzat, Lewis cried, "Damn you! You have shot me!" Cruzat was nowhere to be found, and Lewis hobbled toward the river and canoes, ordering his men to search the shore. At last the men found Cruzat, unhurt and apparently surprised at Lewis's misfortune. Although he would never admit the error, it was obvious that Cruzat had mistaken Lewis's leather-clad behind for an elk!

Soon the two groups were reunited. The Lewis party found a note from Clark and later met two white trappers who had just passed Clark's men. Finally, on August 12, the two parties met, and small arms and blunderbusses sounded a sharp salute. Lewis especially welcomed the presence of Clark at this time, since his injury had left him temporarily unable to exercise effective leadership:

> at 1 P.M. I overtook Capt. Clark and party and had the pleasure of finding them all well. as wrighting in my present situation is extreemly painfull to me I shall desist untill I recover and leave to my friend Capt. C. the continuation of our journal.

When they reached the Mandan villages, it was Clark who presided at a council of the Mandans and Minnetares. The Mandans welcomed the explorers warmly.

One of the men, John Colter, decided to travel to the Yellowstone with two passing trappers, where they would stay until they could "make a fortune." Lewis and Clark gave their reluctant consent only after the other men promised to return to St. Louis. After the Minnetare chiefs had refused to send a representative to Washington, Charbonneau announced his intention to stay with the Mandans along with Sacajawea and the baby. Despite their frequent complaints about his services on the journey, Lewis and Clark paid Charbonneau $500.33, while Sacajawea, considerably more valuable to the expedition, received nothing. The friendly Mandans now promised to make war only in self-defense, and one chief agreed to travel with the expedition to St. Louis and later to see the president in Washington.

By the time Lewis and Clark left the Mandans for St. Louis, most Americans had given them up for lost. Now they swept downstream at eighty miles a day. At the mouth of the Vermilion River, they met a fur trader who gave them "the news," including the information that former Vice-President Aaron Burr had killed Alexander Hamilton in a duel in 1804. On September 10, the men gratefully accepted a bottle of whiskey from a group of Frenchmen on their way to the Platte River. This party brought news that American Captain Zebulon Pike had begun an expedition up the Arkansas River, traveling up the Missouri just before the Corps of Discovery had come down. The Lewis and Clark group received cheers and salutes from five Missouri trading boats as they passed La Charrette. When the canoes landed at Fort Bellefontaine, Clark began writing to friends in Kentucky, and Lewis had already composed his report.

Next day, at noon on September 23, 1806, more than three years after the journey had begun, the expedition landed in the center of St. Louis. Clark reported that he allowed his men "to fire off their pieces as a Salute to the Town. We were met by all the village and received a harty welcome from its inhabitants &C."

The expedition had been a resounding success by every standard, accomplishing the goals set out in Jefferson's instructions plus others undreamed of by the president and his private secretary when they plotted the trip in the White House basement. Except for one death from an illness early in the journey, not a single man had perished, despite the many hardships undergone by the Corps of Discovery. While at St. Louis, the returning explorers enjoyed parties and a ball given in their honor. Meriwether Lewis greeted Jefferson in Washington again on December 30, with Clark following two weeks later. The two heroes found themselves feted continuously by Washingtonians during the months that followed.

Of far greater significance to America's destiny than the festivities celebrating the accomplishments of Meriwether Lewis and William Clark, however, was the report Lewis sent to Jefferson upon arriving in St. Louis the previous September. In this message, we can find the growing patriotic self-assurance and passionate optimism that would characterize the generation following Jefferson's. Lewis conveyed to the president his belief in an American manifest destiny to expand across the continent to the Pacific Ocean, stressing the significance of the fur trade and other commercial opportunities available to the United States. He advised the president to erect outposts on the upper Columbia River that could collect furs taken by neighboring trappers and traders while helping transfer goods arriving by ship from Asian ports. Lewis's vision of an American continental presence even included an explicit warning to Jefferson that the United States would have to check British competition in the Northwest if its own ambitions were to succeed, a prophetic warning that foretold British–American conflict over the Oregon Territory four decades later.

Of greatest importance about the lessons that Lewis and Clark drew from their journey, however, was the unswerving belief, held by both men, in the westward march of American society past even the new Louisiana Purchase, across the Rockies and beyond to the Pacific. Less than thirty years after the Declaration of Independence's signing, a president of the founding generation had placed his unique mark on the next century's pattern of development in America, all of which began in the nightly planning sessions between Jefferson and his capable secretary in the tiny basement study of an executive mansion not yet known as the White House.

12 The Embattled Republic: Federalist and Jeffersonian America

The explorations of Lewis and Clark had been a resounding success. President Jefferson was delighted at the diligence with which the two explorers had fulfilled his orders and recorded a great variety of information on the Western territories—natural, ethnological, and political—for use by the new national administration. Yet the Lewis and Clark venture also reflected complex, crucial issues that remained to be resolved. Jefferson, after all, had been forced deliberately to shade his intentions when asking Congress to finance the expedition, realizing that his controversial plan might arouse hostility from his political opponents.

But what sort of opposition, and operating under what guidelines? The Constitution made no mention of political parties. Indeed, most Founding Fathers had opposed the formation of "factions" as contrary to the healthy functioning of a republic. They had hoped, by constructing a government with adequate checks and balances, to minimize the impact of special interests and to encourage the formation of policies based solely on the national interest. The struggle over creation and ratification of the Constitution itself revealed sharply a diversity of interests based upon geography, class, and occupation.

As problems arose during the period from George Washington's Inaugural to Andrew Jackson's victory over the British in 1815—decades when the United States was a young and embattled republic—Americans disagreed profoundly on what constituted "the national interest." By the time of Jefferson's administration, the Lewis and Clark expedition could be seen almost as much as a *political* act, an assertion of Jeffersonian Republican principles, as a triumph of skill and daring.

American national development and domestic politics during this period, perhaps more than in any other, were closely linked to foreign affairs. Jefferson and Lewis had planned their project in secrecy, fearing the reactions of France, Spain, and Britain. A Spanish military detachment had even followed the explorers at the beginning of their journey. Americans argued over the continued European presence and interest in the North American continent and also disagreed over which side to support in the seemingly never ending European wars of that era.

There was also the question of the powers of the national government within the federal system. Did it have the power to create a national bank? Did the United States government have the authority to purchase territory without the direct consent of the existing states? Beyond that, how could the population of such a territory be prevented from creating a nation of its own? Would it even be possible to retain the existing states within one federal union? The extent to which powers had been delegated to the federal government and retained by the states under the Constitution created fundamental disagreements, and the new lands explored by Lewis and Clark intensified those disagreements.

WASHINGTON THE PRESIDENT

The stability of the new constitutional government was greatly enhanced when George Washington, the almost unanimous choice of his countrymen, agreed to serve as the first president of the United States. In leading the colonists to military victory and in his service as president of the Constitutional Convention, Washington had gained a well-deserved reputation for personal integrity. At the urging of Vice-President John Adams, the Senate voted that the president be called "His Highness the President of the United States of America and the Protector of the Rights of the Same." Fortunately, the House of Representatives failed to agree, and that bombastic subtitle was forever discarded. Citizens were confident that the general would not abuse his power to subvert the liberties of Americans. The passage of the Bill of Rights, guided through Congress by James Madison, further reassured people that the ship of state had been launched on a steady course.

Washington's selection of a cabinet also seemed to confirm his political neutrality. He appointed people from different states and different interests to fill federal offices. Alexander Hamilton of New York, who had been the general's personal aide during the Revolution, became secretary of the treasury. Secretary of State Thomas Jefferson and Attorney General Edmund Randolph were Virginia planters. Henry Knox of Massachusetts was chosen as secretary of war. Shortly after his inauguration on April 30, 1789, on a balcony overlooking Wall Street in New York City, the nation's first capital, Washington confided his anxieties in a letter to Knox. The new president believed he faced "an ocean of difficulties, without that competency of political skill, abilities, and inclination, which are necessary to manage the helm. . . . Integrity and firmness are all I can promise."

HAMILTON'S ECONOMIC PROGRAM

Washington brought prestige and stability to the new administration. Alexander Hamilton formulated financial policy in a brilliant and controversial manner, eventually stirring hostilities that would mar Washington's second term and force Hamilton from office. But first came the triumphs.

Born in the West Indies, Hamilton migrated to New York, where he attended King's College, now Columbia University, before becoming an ardent young participant in the Revolution. Hamilton gained status as a member of New York's elite, despite his illegitimate birth, by marrying into one of the state's wealthiest families. Imaginative and ambitious, he saw his role in Washington's cabinet as tantamount to that of "prime minister." At the Constitutional Convention, Hamilton had fought for a powerful central government, a position he advocated forcefully after the convention as one of the authors of the Federalist Papers. Disappointed with the final result, Hamilton viewed the Constitution as transitory, once calling it a "frail and worthless fabric." Now, as secretary of the treasury, he was in a position to rectify what he considered its weaknesses by deliberately strengthening and enlarging the powers of the federal government. His methods were primarily economic: funding and assumption of the national debt, passage of a federal tariff, and creation of the Bank of the United States.

The first business of government was somehow to solve the problem of the nation's debt of fifty-four million dollars—no small sum in those days. In order to defray the costs of fighting the Revolution, the government certificates had been distributed by Congress to soldiers in the Continental army, promising future payment for their services. Since few Americans ever believed the government would pay back the entire debt, however, the certificates declined in value. Soon hard-pressed soldiers in need of ready cash sold their certificates to speculators, who bought them up at well below their face value. Foreigners purchased fully one-fifth of the debt.

Hamilton's twofold debt proposal was unexpected. First, he planned to fund and repay the *entire* debt at face value. Second, the federal government would take over or assume state debts. In this way, the creditors holding bonds would benefit greatly, and their interests would then be bound with those who favored a strong central government (or so Hamilton reasoned). Creditors would not even receive cash but, instead, would be given new government bonds, further cementing the alliance between business and government that Hamilton keenly desired. He also believed this policy would stimulate enterprise and assure the future revenue needs of the government. Although Madison argued in the House that the original bond holders should be compensated, Hamilton insisted

No man wielded more influence in the early days of the American Republic than did Alexander Hamilton. His nationalistic economic policies set the stage for the growth of effective national power. His antidemocratic political policies led to the rise to power of the Jeffersonian Republicans. (Culver Pictures)

that if the creditors were allowed to reap windfall profits by a complete funding of the debt, strong new confidence would be created in the young government. Congress agreed; the debt would be funded in full.

Federal assumption of state debts proved a more controversial plan. Many Northern capitalists had bought up discounted state securities in the South. Also, some Southern states had already taxed their citizens and repaid state debts on the certificates; they now opposed plans that required further taxation. Madison and the Virginia delegation led the opposition to assumption of state debts. Realizing that his plan was close to defeat and that the struggle might split the delicate bonds of union, Hamilton struck a bargain with Secretary of State Jefferson, who had been working closely with Madison on the issue. In exchange for their approval of assumption, Hamilton promised to support the future establishment of the national capital on the Potomac River in the South between

Maryland and Virginia, far from the commercial-minded North. Opposition then diminished and assumption passed in 1790.

Congress would now have to raise money to pay off these debts. The first tariff act of 1789 placed duties on imports to raise revenue. When this proved insufficient, Congress enacted an excise tax on distilled liquors in 1791. As confidence in the stability of the new nation increased, prosperity returned, giving rise to increased imports and greater tariff revenues. Merchants also enjoyed substantial gains by paying lower duties than those on goods brought in by foreign vessels.

Congress also acted in 1791 to satisfy another key element of Hamilton's program by creating the Bank of the United States (BUS). A major political controversy erupted within Congress and elsewhere in the government prior to passage of the bank legislation. Opponents viewed Hamilton's national bank as an unconstitutional extension of congressional authority. Supporters, in turn, argued that the Constitution gave Congress the right to create such an institution. This argument over "strict" versus "loose" construction of the Constitution would recur in every major debate over Hamilton's program.

Capitalized at far more than all of the other existing state banks combined, the new institution provided a stable circulating medium to make trading easier and stimulate economic development. The Bank of the United States was a semiprivate corporation, with the government owning one-fifth of the stock and naming one-fifth of the board of directors. Moveover, BUS stock could be purchased with government bonds, and recently enriched government creditors rushed to buy up shares in the new corporation. The bank's public character allowed the government to hold and disburse funds as it saw fit; yet its control by private individuals on the board gave them significant power in making loans and issuing notes to businessmen. The bank worked just as planned by the secretary of the treasury.

Hamilton continued to press for closer ties between government and business. He admired both British industrial development, then first getting under way, and the mixture of popular and hereditary features in the British government. In his

"Report on Manufactures" of 1791, Hamilton recommended subsidies and protective tariffs to encourage development of American industry, which would make the country less dependent on foreign products. The American economy had not yet reached the stage where such industrialization was feasible, but Hamilton believed it would eventually be possible through a strong government run by a shrewd elite class. The anti-Federalist agrarians and states rights defenders who had dreaded the creation of a new government based upon stronger central control now reacted angrily as they saw some of their worst fears enacted into law through Hamilton's program.

FOREIGN AFFAIRS UNDER WASHINGTON

From the days of the first settlements in Massachusetts, many Americans had felt that they were building a new and better form of society that would serve as an inspiration to the corrupt Old World, a "City upon a Hill," as Puritans had called their experiment. With political independence won, many Americans believed that the United States should set an example in amity for the entire world by trading freely with every country, while remaining independent and uninvolved in disputes between European powers. The policy also reflected practical considerations: the new nation could not hope to become militarily involved in any foreign conflict without suffering severe social and economic dislocation at home, if not outright military defeat. As events would show, however, neither could Americans hope to steer clear of conflicts that struck at the heart of the country's prosperity.

Within months after adoption of the Constitution and Washington's inauguration in 1789, the French Revolution began, sending tremors throughout the European monarchical world. Growing uneasiness with events in France helped persuade Great Britain to recognize and establish full diplomatic relations with the United States in 1791, if only to deflect any possible close links between the two "revolutionary societies" of America and France. By 1793, Britain and France (and many other European nations) were again at war, and this time the French Revolution lent the struggle a particular intensity.

American cabinet meetings soon reflected this passion. Secretary of State Jefferson had been U.S. minister to France in the 1780s and had even watched the beginnings of the French Revolution before returning home in 1789. He had developed a warm sympathy toward the French, and he increasingly supported the goals of their revolution, though he was shaken by the execution of Louis XVI and the ensuing Reign of Terror. Hamilton, on the other hand, saw the destruction of monarchy and aristocracy as the end of civilized society. Along with other American conservatives, he was further shocked when the revolutionists declared the "war of all peoples against all kings," a threat to Britain and Spain.

Attempting to use the crisis to terminate the U.S.–French alliance created under the Treaty of 1778, Hamilton argued that the fall of the French monarchy had nullified the agreement. The United States, he urged, should declare its neutrality and refuse to receive the new French minister, "Citizen" Edmund Genêt. Although agreeing that Americans should remain uninvolved, Jefferson viewed the treaties as still binding and urged that the government refrain from announcing its intentions to remain neutral.

On April 22, 1793, Washington issued a proclamation of neutrality addressed to American citizens, while formally recognizing Genêt and refusing to repudiate the treaties with France. This public announcement disappointed Jefferson, who had hoped that American intentions could be kept secret and used as a bargaining tool to negotiate the withdrawal of British troops, which still occupied parts of the American Northwest and controlled that areas's valuable fur trade. (That issue, the fur trade, would later concern Meriwether Lewis; upon his return from exploring the continent he warned Jefferson of Britain's continuing designs on the fur trade in the Pacific Northwest.) By 1793, Jefferson had seen how little his views counted and decided to quit the cabinet. This was the first major breach in Washington's national coalition government of leaders from the Revolutionary generation.

French Minister Genêt conducted himself foolishly, creating more opposition than support for his country's cause. Although only a foreign envoy, Genêt ignored the proclamation of neutrality and proceeded about his business as if directing a united Franco-American war effort. He commissioned privateers in American ports to fly the French flag and capture British vessels, set up courts to deal with the ships the privateers captured, and organized expeditions to march on Spanish and British territories in North America. Finally, even Jefferson grew disgusted with the French upstart, and Washington demanded Genêt's recall.

Still clinging to idealistic notions of foreign policy, Americans claimed a neutral's right to trade with nations at war. This idea, that "free ships make free goods," quickly ran aground in the summer of 1793, when the British navy began to seize American vessels trading with France and its West Indian possessions. Amid cries for war, Washington decided on calm. He sent John Jay, Chief Justice of the Supreme Court, to negotiate a settlement in London to protect the United States's neutral rights. Other issues, such as the continued presence of British military posts in the Northwest Territory, the British urging Canadian Indians to attack American settlements, and British failing to return American slaves seized during the Revolution, also needed attention.

Jay's mission, however, was marred from the beginning. Hamilton, anxious that peaceful relations be retained with Britain at all costs, had told the British secretly that Americans would do almost anything to avoid war. Bargaining from a weak position, undercut by Hamilton's intrigues, Jay returned with a treaty so one-sided that Washington only reluctantly submitted it to the Senate, which ratified it with equal reluctance. Britain promised to withdraw from posts in the Northwest but with certain conditions. The United States agreed to permit continued British fur trade with the Indians, and although the British agreed to compensate Americans for ships seized in the Caribbean, English creditors would now be allowed to collect pre-Revolutionary debts.

Great Britain clearly gained more than the United States from the Jay Treaty. She continued to refuse to compensate American slaveholders or to halt the seizure of American seamen who were then "impressed" into the Royal Navy. Although some commercial restrictions in England were liberalized, the United States did not gain significantly, since the British would not specifically agree to respect U.S. rights as a neutral. Ratification of the Jay Treaty created further political antagonisms among Americans. Denunciations in the press and popular meetings in Boston, Philadelphia, and New York soon illustrated that in a democratic republic citizens could combine patriotism and active opposition to their government's decisions. Although commonplace today, this idea was startling and revolutionary at the time.

THE DEVELOPMENT OF POLITICAL PARTIES

The division over Hamilton's economic program, the French Revolution, and the war between Britain and France all contributed to growing factionalism within the American government. Many Founding Fathers had feared such factionalism, but they had not been able to prevent it. Jefferson, Madison, and most other Southerners believed that Hamilton's financial measures would benefit bankers and capitalists in Northern seaports at the expense of Southern planters and small farmers in the North. As Jefferson unsuccessfully jockeyed with Hamilton for power in Washington's cabinet, Southerners charged that the secretary of the treasury was in league with Northeastern merchants and speculators in gaining an undue influence over Congress. Also embittered by the administration's pro-British sentiment and by the ratification of Jay's Treaty, Jefferson condemned Hamilton as "not only a monarchist, but for a monarchy bottomed on corruption."

By the 1790s, political differences had gone beyond factionalism to the creation of a pair of distinct political parties, the Republicans and the Federalists. Unlike factions, parties were organized on a more permanent basis for the purpose of seeking votes to elect candidates to office. In developing programs, they often drew different groups together to organize at local, state, and national

The Whiskey Rebellion (1794) was a revolt against the federal excise tax on whiskey. Western Pennsylvania farmers here manhandle the tax collector, burning his cabin and leaving him with a coat of tar and feathers. (Culver Pictures)

levels. They encompassed several issues and sought to be national, rather than sectional, in scope.

Such party organization eventually grew, specifically, from opposition to Hamilton's influence in the Washington administration, and generally, from conflicts over the scope and role of national power. While Jefferson attempted to transfer greater authority to the State Department and away from the Treasury, Madison rallied anti-Hamilton elements in the House. Madison's forces began referring to themselves as the "republican interest," and finally by 1792, as "the Republican party." In 1791, the first Republican newspaper devoted to national issues appeared, and local "Democratic Clubs" began to form in sympathetic imitation of the revolutionary Jacobin societies in France. Although Washington himself was not challenged in the election of 1792, an alliance between New York and Virginia Republicans led North Carolina, Virginia, and New York to cast their second vote for New Yorker George Clinton for vice-president rather than for John Adams.

Supporters of Hamilton and the British continued to refer to themselves as Federalists in order to link their opponents to the anti-Federalists of the preceding decade. This was no longer either accurate or effective, since most Americans realized that the Republican leaders had also supported the Constitution. Madison, after all, had even joined Hamilton in contributing to the Federalist Papers. The struggle over ratification had quickly become history, giving way during the 1790s to more immediate and pressing issues that divided Republicans and Federalists.

The Whiskey Rebellion

Soon Federalist policy received a more direct challenge far from the seat of national government. One of Hamilton's financial measures was to impose a federal excise tax on liquor. Because it was more difficult and more expensive to transport surplus grain over mountainous regions, western Pennsylvania farmers had distilled their corn crops into whiskey. The profit they made in Eastern markets was already small, and the excise tax would reduce it to practically nothing. Thus the tax was largely ignored, and when the United States marshal summoned violators to court, he met strong resistance from Pennsylvania farmers near Pittsburgh.

Their action openly defied national authority, and the Federalists expressed horror at this "rebellion," exaggerating the threat it posed to the government. In Federalist eyes, it was another Shays's Rebellion. Even though the governor of Pennsylvania believed that the courts could handle the situation, Hamilton persuaded Washington that military action was needed. The president himself then led 15,000 soldiers to the disaffected area in October 1794. No one fired a shot; Washington returned to Philadelphia (then the capital); and Hamilton arrested the leaders of the protest movement.

After his return, Washington gave a speech condemning all organized opposition to government policies. He implied that the Republicans and the Democratic Clubs had somehow been responsible for the disturbances. Ignoring the Constitutional right to assemble and to petition government, he urged that such organizations disband. His prestige still remained so great that most of them did dissolve, and Republican opposition suffered a major if temporary setback.

The Election of 1796

Washington's impending retirement in 1796 set the stage for the United States's first contested election. Although Washington's farewell address warned of the dangers of political parties and foreign entanglements, political partisanship grew as arguments concerning the respective merits of British or French policies were hotly debated. The Federalists backed Vice-President John Adams, while Thomas Jefferson ran as the Republican candidate. The two parties also openly endorsed candidates for congressional seats.

The election was understandably bitter and surprisingly close. Federalists called the Republicans anarchists and accused them of trying to disrupt and bring down the government in the manner of the French Jacobins. The Republicans, in turn, denounced Federalist measures as elitist and designed to subvert American liberty as George III and the British Parliament had done. Passions ran remarkably high, inflamed by extreme

John Adams was our second president and the first of the Adams family to distinguish himself in politics. Adams was talented but unpopular, and his administration (1797–1801) witnessed the breakup and defeat of the Federalist party. (Culver Pictures)

and inaccurate charges flung about by both parties. Adams won a close victory over Jefferson, receiving seventy-one electoral votes[1] to sixty-eight for the Virginian. Since he finished second in the electoral vote total, however, Jefferson became vice-president.

THE ADAMS PRESIDENCY

Despite his original intentions to dampen political strife when he took office, John Adams proved incapable of quieting the furious name-

---

[1] The Constitution provided *indirect* election of the president as a means of removing the office from direct popular control. Rather than vote for presidential candidates, voters would vote for "electors"—expected to be prominent men in their states—who would then meet and cast ballots for the president and vice-president. National political parties were not anticipated by the Founders, although they recognized the inevitability of political "factions."

In 1798, Congress was the scene of a brawl between Republican Matthew Lyon, left, and Federalist Roger Griswold, right. In the Speaker's chair sits an amused Jonathan Dayton. (Library of Congress)

calling that had come to characterize both parties. He and Jefferson had been friends during the Revolution, and now the two resolved to reestablish their friendship. Adams again denied the Republican accusation that, because he favored a strong executive, he was a monarchist. He also denied that he felt only hostility toward France. Any moderating influence Adams's Federalist administration might have achieved was soon undermined, however, by the composition of his cabinet. Weak and mediocre, the Adams cabinet remained under the influence of Hamilton, who sent them advice from New York, where he had returned to seeming semi-retirement. Hamilton himself considered Adams too moderate, and he had attempted to manipulate the electoral voting system in 1796 to elect Federalist Thomas Pinckney of South Carolina instead of Adams.

Under Adams, foreign events would continue to exercise a strong influence over American domestic policies. The French responded to the Jay Treaty by attacking American shipping and refusing to receive the American minister. The cabinet, manipulated by Hamilton, convinced President Adams to begin arming merchant ships and to establish an army. When an American three-man negotiating commission went to France to ease tense relations, French Foreign Minister Charles Talleyrand demanded a bribe of $250,000 through three go-betweens designated in official dispatches only as X, Y, and Z. They informed the Americans that the price of a treaty with France would run into millions of dollars.

Aided by French corruption and blackmail, Federalists saw another opportunity to further their own political fortunes. Hamilton believed that a standing army would not only protect the country against a French threat, but could also be used to suppress political opponents. Although he also sided with the British, Adams felt that it was more important to concentrate on building up a navy, since the nation would otherwise be helpless to oppose the British navy. But the Hamiltonians or "High Federalists" demanded a strong army too and a declaration of war against France. They believed that the war with France might eliminate Republican opposition by rallying patriotic feeling around the Federalist administration and, at the same time, permit creation of a strong anti-French alliance with Great Britain.

President Adams remained unwilling to go to war, however, and in 1799 he sent an American minister to Paris to negotiate differences between the two countries. These had led to an undeclared war between the French and American navies in the fall of 1798. Negotiations brought peace with France but split the Federalist party. An agreement in September 1800 finally released the United States from its defunct 1778 alliance with France and compensated Americans for lost ships and goods. Hamilton and his followers, frustrated by peace, again schemed to "dump" Adams, this time in favor of Charles C. Pinckney, the party's vice-presidential candidate.

Federalists of all sentiments had used the anti-French reaction to the XYZ Affair to pass the Alien and Sedition Acts in 1798, an attempt to discredit and eliminate Republican opposition. The Alien Act extended from five to fourteen years the length of the residence requirement for immigrants, who generally favored the Republicans, before they could become voting citizens. The president was also given the temporary authority to deport any alien whom he believed to be dangerous.

The Sedition Act, one of the worst examples of political repression in American history, was also supposed to be temporary, expiring on the day the next president would be inaugurated. It called for fines and imprisonment for those who opposed "any measure or measures of the government of the United States" or anyone who spoke or printed any "false, scandalous and malicious writing against the government of the United States or either house of the Congress or the President." Twenty-five Republicans, including influential newspaper editors, were prosecuted under this law. Even a loiterer outside a New Jersey tavern was sentenced for wishing that the cannon shot fired in honor of Adams had struck the president's posterior!

Spurred by new taxes and by laws inhibiting free expression, Republican opposition grew, with Madison and Jefferson again leading the way. The two drafted the Virginia and Kentucky resolutions as a response by state legislatures to this latest Federalist threat. Both states declared the Alien and Sedition Acts unconstitutional and upheld the right of the states to judge the constitutionality of laws passed by Congress. Although no other states would join in the protest, this action strengthened Republican confidence while raising issues of federal and state authority that would be hotly debated among future generations.

THE ELECTION OF 1800

As the renewal of the contest between Federalist Adams and Republican Jefferson approached in the fall of 1800, bitter divisions within the electorate had developed. Neither Federalists nor Republicans accepted the legitimacy of a political opposition, and both parties considered their chief opponents enemies of constitutional government and the republican system, and bent upon destroying the new Administration.

One *older* elite group supplied much of the leadership, organization, and philosophy for the Republicans. Southern planters who had first felt alienated by Hamilton's pro-commercial economic policies now sought to challenge and obtain national power from New Englander Adams. In order to succeed, they drew support from rising Northern businessmen and from discontented artisans as well as from certain "non-established" ethnic and religious groups. New Englanders tended to favor the Federalists, while most Southern support went to Republicans. Many creditors and urban merchants found much to support in the Hamiltonian system, while many debtor farmers enthusiastically supported Jefferson.

The intensity of the campaign resulted both from increased Republican political organization and from the emotional nature of the issues involved. Jefferson's party had suffered losses in 1798 as a result of French conduct in the XYZ Affair, but a caucus of Republican congressmen set up state committees which supervised creation of powerful local political organizations in 1800. Candidates themselves remained aloof from campaigning by tradition, but newspapers, pamphlets, and public meetings echoed charges, real or imagined. Federalists accused Jefferson of atheism and French Jacobinism which would destroy both religion and property. Republicans called Adams a monarchist and British lackey, criticizing the taxes that Federalists had imposed to support the military buildup. Some Republican newspapermen were arrested and sentenced by Federalist judges, but most editors successfully defied the Sedition Act and lashed out against Federalist policies.

The Republicans won the majority of electoral votes, yet the election went into the House of Representatives. Since the Founding Fathers had not foreseen the formation of political parties, the Constitution had not provided for separate electoral ballots for the offices of president and vice-president. Thus presidential electors in 1800, "the electoral college," had cast seventy-three votes each for Jefferson and Burr, with sixty-five for Adams and sixty-four for Pinckney. So there was Aaron Burr, intended candidate for the vice-presidency, on the same footing with his party chief, Jefferson. When no presidential candidate receives a majority of the *electoral* ballots, then, according to the Constitution, the House of Representatives elects the president.

The Republicans had clearly intended Jefferson to be their presidential candidate, but the Federalists realized that they had been presented another opportunity to keep the "radical" Jefferson out of office by supporting Burr in the House. As usual, however, all Federalists could not agree. Hamilton in particular despised Burr, his political rival in New York City (Burr would later kill Hamilton in a duel in 1804). After thirty-nine House ballots, Hamilton persuaded three Federalist congressmen to submit blank ballots instead of voting for Burr, thereby electing Jefferson president. (The Twelfth Amendment, ratified in 1804, required separate ballots for president and vice-president, thereby eliminating this sort of constitutional problem.) Although the presidential election had been close, Republicans gained large majorities in both the House and the Senate. The elated Jefferson hailed the Republican victory as the "Revolution of 1800."

JEFFERSONIAN REPUBLICANISM

To what extent was the election of 1800 really a "revolution"? Republicans had charged that Adams was an aristocrat with monarchical tendencies, but Jefferson owned thousands of acres of land and several hundred slaves. Even though Jefferson was a member of the Virginia elite, his defense of democratic ideals, his attacks on Federalist "monarchism," his support for religious liberty, and his eloquence as a spokesman for human rights won widespread support. The slaveholding aristocrat brought a more democratic and modest style to the presidency than his predecessor, Adams, despite the latter's humbler personal background.

The election of Jefferson marked a change of emphasis, rather than a drastic change in the nature of American government and society. "We are all Federalists; we are all Republicans," Jefferson announced in his inaugural address. He did not believe in political parties any more than did the Federalist opposition. Still, Jefferson determined (as had Adams) to end political warfare by winning opponents over to his way of thinking rather than by attempting to use political repression (as in the

Jefferson's greatest personal attraction, according to one admirer, was "a countenance beaming with benevolence and intelligence." (White House Collection)

farmer who was economically independent would be the perfect citizen of a republic, since no one could wield economic or social power over him sufficient to control his voting or political opinions. Jefferson, moreover, believed that farmers, freed of the temptations and pitfalls of urban life, had a measure of genuine virtue sufficient to sustain a democratic society interested in advancing the common welfare: "Those who labor in the earth," he declared flatly and sincerely, "are the Chosen people of God."

Those whom Jefferson feared most, on the other hand, were those who had earned their fortunes through commercial and financial speculation in the growing cities and towns: the "perfect" citizens of Alexander Hamilton's ideal republic. These men had largely supported Hamilton's economic program and had benefited from it. Jefferson also saw dangers in industrialization. If American entrepreneurs built factories which attracted men, women, and even children from the surrounding countryside to work in them, then he feared the dreary conditions of industrial society that had already appeared in Europe would reach America, shattering his dream that the New World might someday teach corrupted Europe how to build the just (that is, agrarian) society. The growth of factories would make workers dependent upon their wages from owners, who would then (Jefferson believed) inevitably dictate the workers' voting behavior, a reasonable fear in a day before the existence of either labor unions or the secret ballot.

Jefferson was sworn in as president in the new capital of Washington, certainly a place where the Virginian had no cause to worry about urban decadence—not yet. Despite extravagant planning by a French engineer, Pierre L'Enfant, and despite the best engineering efforts of a black scientist, Benjamin Banneker, to lay out the streets, the new capital was not a city, not even a town. Washington was a clearing in the wilderness with wooden houses here and there. Only one wing of the Capitol building had been completed, and the rotunda had not yet been enclosed. Pennsylvania Avenue, leading from the Capitol to the White House, had been fairly well cleared, but stumps and bushes appeared occasionally in the road. Mosquitoes proved a constant nuisance and even brought malaria to

Alien and Sedition Acts) or outright violence. In this respect, Jefferson's election did constitute a revolution in American government: one group had replaced another at the head of a democratically elected republican government without civil war. A revolutionary movement had succeeded in institutionalizing the peaceful transfer of power from one party to another; few subsequent revolutions in world history could boast of any similar success in this endeavor.

The new administration would be influenced by Jefferson's personal philosophy. Although himself a wealthy planter, he professed to share the interests of small American farmers, who composed the vast majority of the United States population in 1800. Jefferson idealized the agrarian, believing that an ordinary American

The Jeffersonian White House. (Library of Congress)

some. Because much of the federal city remained swampy marshland, congressmen had little choice but to leave their wives at home and move into the crowded boarding houses where they lived for the few months Congress remained in session each year.

The primitive capital proved an appropriate setting for Jefferson to test his political philosophy. Jefferson lived simply, hosting state dinners only rarely. He abandoned the practice of reading his annual message in person because the practice reminded Jefferson too strongly of the British monarch reading a proclamation speech from the throne. Instead, Jefferson sent his secretary, Meriwether Lewis, to deliver it to a congressional clerk. Jefferson ordered that the White House doors be opened every morning and that visitors be accommodated according to the order of their arrival. Foreign dignitaries were often surprised to be greeted by the American president in a faded coat and slippers.

The New Economic Program

Jefferson's new financial policies, with the support of Secretary of the Treasury Albert Galla-

tin, reflected his philosophy of limited government: the new president believed that the government that governed best governed least, especially at the national level. He determined to reduce the public debt, which, as it stood, he felt benefited the wealthy classes at the expense of all other Americans. Republicans had long urged debt reduction, and Jefferson and Gallatin reduced spending and economized wherever possible. The government reduced taxes, and Jefferson persuaded Congress to repeal the much-hated tax on whiskey, which had created great hardship for Western farmers. Increasing revenues from import duties helped Republicans reduce the debt, despite lower taxes, from eighty million to fifty-three million dollars in ten years.

Much of this decrease was made possible by a severe cut of military spending. The regular army was reduced from four thousand to twenty-five hundred men. Naval strength was also diminished, leaving only thirteen ships. The rest were sold to merchants. Jefferson believed that if state militia systems were improved and the U.S. Military Academy was established at West Point, such cutbacks would not seriously threaten national defense.

Republican Gains

Despite this new economic austerity, Jefferson also accepted the need to temper his idealism for purposes of political expediency. He was convinced that through argument and compromise, he could undermine the Federalists and end the two-party system, which he (like most Americans of the period, both Federalist and Jeffersonian) considered "unnatural." Republicans never sought to undo Hamilton's measures of funding and assumption, and they allowed the national bank to exist until its charter expired in 1811. Jefferson even appointed three New Englanders to his cabinet as a gesture toward reconciliation with that Federalist stronghold, and though he continued to believe in the fundamental importance of agriculture, he now admitted the need to make concessions to shipping interests in order to lure them away from the Federalist fold. Yet Jefferson drastically reversed one whole body of Federalist policies: he allowed the Alien Act to expire and quickly obtained the lowering of residence requirements for citizenship from Congress. After the expiration of the Sedition Act, Jefferson refunded all fines and pardoned all who had been imprisoned under the hateful law.

After the 1800 elections, Republicans also sought to undermine the last Federalist stronghold and power base within the national government—the judiciary. Following his defeat, President Adams obtained passage of the Judiciary Act of 1801 and appointed Federalists to sixteen new federal judgeships. These were known as "midnight appointments." Congressional Republicans promptly repealed the act as an unnecessary expenditure, but the political nature of the issue was undeniable. Jefferson had also begun slowly to remove Federalist officeholders from the executive branch and to replace them with Republicans, while trying to avoid an all-out patronage battle with angry Federalists. Meanwhile, Republicans in control of the House came close to impeaching Justice Samuel Chase of the U.S. Supreme Court, an important jurist who had often delivered Federalist harangues while passing judgment on Republican offenders.

Political battles in several states gave reality to the Republican creed by democratizing American life. As competition grew between political elites, it became increasingly necessary to appeal to different classes and groups which before had rarely participated in politics. Popular appeals through newspapers and rallies brought an end to "deference politics," where voters had yielded to the judgment of their better-educated local elite when choosing candidates for office. Political parties encouraged people instead to consider their own self-interest when voting. Parties also exploited existing local and state rivalries, as well as nationally binding symbols, while soliciting support from the different ethnic, economic, and religious groups. Although many Federalists still viewed the Republicans as dangerous revolutionaries, even after Jefferson's first term in office, a majority of Americans soon accepted the value of organized political parties. They especially delighted in the freedom of press arguments and open debate that accompanied enthusiastic partisan campaigning as legitimate means of political expression within a democratic society.

LOUISIANA AND THE WEST

The Louisiana Purchase

Years before Lewis and Clark made their trek across the continent to the Pacific, the American westward movement was well under way. By 1800, nearly a million people lived between the Appalachian Mountains and the Mississippi River. Four new states had entered the Union: Vermont in 1791, Kentucky in 1792, Tennessee in 1796, and Ohio in 1803. Soon American settlers began moving across the Mississippi into Spanish territory. In Pinckney's Treaty of 1795, Spain granted American flatboats the right of navigation on the river down to New Orleans, where they were allowed to leave their goods for shipment elsewhere.

In 1801 Jefferson was shocked to find that the previous year Spain had secretly transferred all of Louisiana to the powerful French government. When, in 1799, Napoleon declared himself dictator, Jeffersonian Republicans lost all sympathy for France. Now Napoleon attempted to re-create the French colonial empire in America that had been lost with the cession of Canada to Great Britain in 1763. Such an empire would serve as a geographic

John Marshall

(NYPL/Picture Collection)

This great American jurist, and Chief Justice of the United States Supreme Court from 1801 to 1835, came from a background remarkably like Thomas Jefferson's—the man who would become his chief adversary in public life. John Marshall was born in Virginia in 1755, the son of a planter, though not one of the colony's wealthiest. Although Marshall spent some time at William and Mary College, for the most part he educated himself in the law. As a young attorney at Richmond, Marshall won recognition as one of Virginia's best legal minds.

Marshall served in the Revolutionary forces, later observing that this experience had reinforced for him a belief in the importance of national unity. A supporter of the Constitution in 1787 and against strong anti-Federalist sentiment in Virginia, Marshall gravitated easily into the Federalist party during the 1790s. He rose in that decade to hold important diplomatic posts, serve in Congress, and finally, to gain appointment as John Adams's secretary of state in 1800. When Marshall was holding this office, at the close of the Federalist era, President Adams named him Chief Justice of the Supreme Court. Marshall had not been Adams's first choice, and many die-hard Federalists distrusted Marshall's nationalist avowals, apparently for no better reason than that he came from the Virginia of Jefferson and Madison.

Once on the Court, Marshall dispelled their unwarranted fears. He proceeded to make the Supreme Court an important factor in the American political process, and for most of the next thirty-four years, Marshall held tight reign over "his" Court. He seldom lost control of the majority, and he himself wrote nearly half of the 1,100 recorded opinions during the 1801–35 period.

Several of Marshall's decisions helped construct the basic fabric of American constitutional law. In *Marbury* v. *Madison*, an 1803 opinion, the Court established the principle of judicial review itself, declaring unconstitutional a 1798 congressional measure and thereby establishing the Court's authority to rule such statutes null and void when in violation of the Constitution. In the landmark *McCulloch* v. *Maryland* decision, Marshall disposed of an attempt by Maryland to tax the local branch of the Second Bank of the United States on the grounds that the attempt represented an unconstitutional state effort to tax a federal agency. Marshall not only asserted the principle of federal supremacy over state authority in this decision but also rebutted Maryland's argument that

limitation upon American expansion, a continuing interest of Jefferson's. Settlers in the Western lands, concerned, for their part, over selling their cash crops to foreign markets, were severely threatened when the French forbade Western farmers from sending their exports down the Mississippi to New Orleans. Alarmed, but wishing to solve the problem peacefully, Jefferson sent James Monroe to France to buy New Orleans and West Florida, authorizing up to ten million dollars for this purpose.

By the time Monroe reached Paris, Napoleon's interests had shifted away from America. In 1803 the emperor faced the threat of losing the

the Bank of the United States itself was unconstitutional, since the Constitution did not explicitly authorize creation of such a bank. "Let the end be legitimate," he wrote, "let it be within the scope of the Constitution, and all means which are appropriate, which are plainly adapted to that end, which are not prohibited, but [are] consist[ent] with the letter and spirit of the Constitution, are constitutional."

Nationalists cheered, while "strict constructionists" reeled as this and other decisions from the Marshall Court expanded federal and judicial powers in a variety of ways: protecting private property through application of the Constitution's contract clause, guaranteeing the right to appeal cases involving federal issues from state to federal courts, broadening "implied powers" under the Constitution, and interpreting federal authority broadly under the Constitution's interstate commerce clause. In the last area, the Court ruled in *Gibbons* v. *Ogden* (1824) that states could not create monopolies in areas under federal jurisdiction. The specific argument involved licenses to run steamboats in New York, but the general problem concerned monopolies on transportation arteries throughout the country. The decision effectively opened the waterways to competitive commerce (within a year after *Gibbons* v. *Ogden*, the number of steamboats sailing New York's inland waters had increased sevenfold).

John Marshall was the most prominent of President Adams's "midnight judges," the Federalists that he appointed to judicial posts with lifetime tenure at the last minute prior to his leaving office in 1801. Jeffersonians had attacked the appointments, but as time passed (and after Republicans had failed to remove Supreme Court justices

through congressional impeachment efforts), they grudgingly came to accept the Federalist judges, including Marshall. They reasoned that, in any event, Jefferson and other Republican presidents would have a chance to appoint their own loyalists to the federal bench and restore a balance. This hope proved to be in vain, since Marshall maintained his nationalist judicial ideas throughout the 1820s despite the presence of Jeffersonian-Republican colleagues. Sometimes, as in the case of Justice Joseph Story, a Jefferson appointee proved to be as nationalist as the Chief Justice.

The Marshall Court's principal contribution was to prevent state power from overwhelming the fragile national government's authority, that would have turned the United States into a loose confederation again despite the new Constitution. Marshall fought hard and regularly to keep the states at bay and to maintain—even expand, where possible—the grants of power to the federal government that he found in the Constitution. He was the supreme "loose constructionist," interpreting the Constitution in a manner that generally allowed the national government to function in any manner that it was not specifically prohibited from doing.

Marshall began to lose his grip on the Court by the end of the 1820s and during his closing years in the 1830s. Dissenters gained a majority more frequently, and the chief justice clashed with President Andrew Jackson regularly, especially over Indian policy. It proved yet another measure of Marshall's greatness and his impact upon the American constitutional system that when he died in 1835, his successor, a strong Jacksonian supporter named Roger B. Taney, modified but never abandoned his predecessor's vision of the Constitution and national power.

French colony of Santo Domingo (now Haiti) through an independence movement of slaves led by Toussaint L'Ouverture. He also feared that he could not obtain enough money to renew his war with Great Britain, and his vision of a restored "New France" in America had faded. When his foreign minister, Talleyrand, therefore, offered the

American negotiators not merely New Orleans but the entire province of Louisiana for fifteen million dollars, the American ministers did not hesitate to accept the offer. They did so despite their lack of any specific authority to make such a purchase, and despite the fact that the price was 50 percent more than their "budget." A bargain was a bargain.

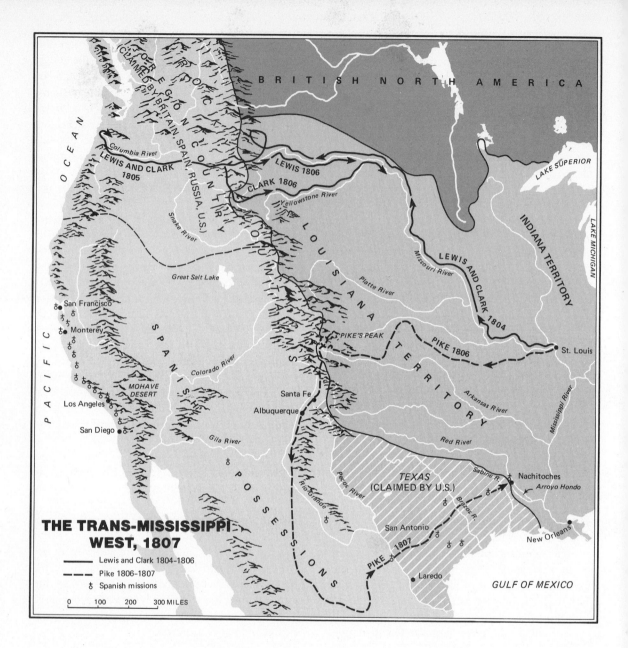

THE TRANS-MISSISSIPPI WEST, 1807

— Lewis and Clark 1804–1806
-- Pike 1806–1807
⚲ Spanish missions

0   100   200   300 MILES

Congressional debate over ratification of the purchase (which, parenthetically, did not stop the Lewis and Clark expedition from proceeding) centered around the question of constitutional authority. New England Federalists believed the new territory would become another Republican stronghold, further undermining the interests of the New England states and irrevocably damaging the Federalists in national politics. Federalists had always believed in a broad interpretation of the Constitution, that the national government had "implied powers" to act in furthering the country's welfare. Republicans adopted a strict construction view, arguing that the central government had only the specific powers delegated in the Constitution and little discretionary authority.

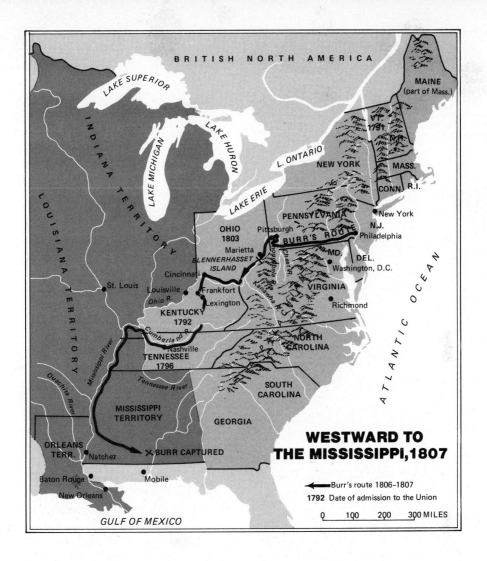

**WESTWARD TO
THE MISSISSIPPI, 1807**

← Burr's route 1806–1807
1792 Date of admission to the Union

0   100   200   300 MILES

The Louisiana Purchase "bargain" dented Republican principles. The Republicans now argued ironically that the federal government did have power to make the agreement, while many Federalists argued the opposite. Jefferson, though reluctant to assert that the government had implied powers that covered the transaction, realized that Napoleon might withdraw the offer if he waited for the long process of a constitutional amendment to ratify the purchase. He, therefore, supported congressional ratification of the treaty which, once achieved, confirmed the Louisiana Purchase.

Jefferson had compromised his constitutional ideals, but he remained consistent in championing the interests of farmers above all others. Within the Louisiana Territory, he believed, lay enough land for any number of farming generations to till, over eight hundred thousand square miles in all. Even before the Lewis and Clark Corps of Discovery had fully explored Louisiana, as early as 1804 in fact, the territory between the Appalachians and Mississippi began filling up with settlers who could purchase 160 acres of Western land from the government with a down payment of eighty dollars. Jefferson even approved of the con-

New Yorker Aaron Burr was a crafty politician, a Jeffersonian Republican who always looked out for Number 1 and almost slid into the White House in 1801. Unhappy as Vice-President, Burr plotted to set up an independent "empire" in the U.S. Southwest and Texas. In 1807, he was tried for treason—Chief Justice John Marshall presiding—and was acquitted. (Culver Pictures)

struction of a national road from Cumberland, Maryland, to Wheeling, Virginia, exercising still another power not explicitly mentioned in the Constitution. This road would cross the Appalachians, making it easier for farmers to transport surplus crops, and thus encourage Western settlement. By 1820, one out of ten Americans lived west of those mountains. After the Lewis and Clark exploring party returned successfully, the vision of westward settlement became fixed in the consciousness of an America fast becoming converted to the gospel of continental expansionism.

The Burr Conspiracy

One major politician of that era needed no encouragement to see the economic and political potential of the newly acquired Western lands. Aaron Burr, brilliant and ever-ambitious, had indicated an interest in promoting his own fortunes

at the expense of his country's in the Louisiana Territory even before stepping down from the vice-presidency in 1805. Burr had approached the British minister, Anthony Merry, asking a half-million-dollar "loan" to help arrange the secession of newly acquired Louisiana from the United States. Although Merry became intrigued with the proposal, his superiors in London dawdled in responding so that Burr turned to other schemes.

He sailed down the Mississippi River in 1806 on a well-equipped flatboat, stopping along the way to visit sympathizers (among them Andrew Jackson) and to propose various elaborate plans for gaining wealth and fortune in the West. Accounts of Burr's proposals differed but, at one point or another, he apparently entertained such disparate schemes as separating several of the Western states (Kentucky and Tennessee among them) from the Union, establishing a Western empire independent of the United States with himself as its president or king, and invading then-Spanish-ruled Mexico with an eye toward "liberating" it.

Burr's presumably treasonous intentions were betrayed to President Jefferson by one of Burr's closest co-conspirators: James Wilkinson, the highest ranking general in the American army and (on the side) a paid agent for the Spaniards. Jefferson ordered Burr's arrest, Burr fled the now-unfriendly Wilkinson's troops, and in February 1807, the former vice-president was finally captured near Mobile. Chief Justice John Marshall presided at Burr's lengthy trial for treason in Richmond, Virginia. After conducting a brilliant defense, much of it as his own attorney, Burr was acquitted. The government failed to produce sufficient evidence—or two witnesses—to show overt treasonous acts on Burr's part. After the not-guilty verdict on September 1, Burr escaped possible further harassment by Jefferson through exiling himself to France for the next four years. He returned to New York City in 1812 where he practiced law, dying there in 1836 at the age of eighty.

THE CRISIS IN AMERICAN SHIPPING

A truce between Great Britain and France, the treaty that Adams obtained with France in

1799, and Napoleon's dictatorship all combined to defuse the foreign issue for Americans, temporarily, and allowed Jefferson to focus attention on domestic policy during most of his first term. Yet as the previous decade had shown, the United States remained dependent on the international trading structure for exporting surplus grain and raw materials while importing manufactured goods. Any significant disturbance in that trade would bring economic dislocation and perhaps social turmoil. This situation would characterize Jefferson's second term in office.

There had already been some trouble early in his administration. Barbary pirates controlling the entrance to the Mediterranean from North Africa demanded periodic tribute from the American government to let our ships proceed. In 1801 Jefferson sent an expedition against one of the North African states, which stopped the pirates' interference and raised American morale and prestige. Yet pirates from other parts of North Africa continued to harass ships, and the American government was forced to pay bribes as late as 1816.

A more serious challenge to future prosperity came in 1803, when England and France went to war again. That war led directly to Napoleon's decision to sell Louisiana, and at first, as in the 1790s, American shipping took advantage of neutrality by importing goods from British and French colonies then reexporting them to the "mother countries" in Europe. The British had previously allowed Americans to deliver these goods to France as long as they first imported the merchandise into the United States. In 1805 an English court denied this right to Americans, and in the next year, Britain proclaimed a partial blockade of French-dominated western Europe. France promptly declared a blockade of England. Both countries began seizing American ships; between 1805 and 1807, the French seized about five hundred vessels, while the British confiscated over one thousand. American rights as a neutral, in short, had again come under sustained attack from both sides.

It quickly became evident that Britain posed the larger danger. Its superior navy had the power to enforce policy far more effectively than the French. The British seized or impressed sailors from American ships, whom they declared to be

The United States and Britain almost went to war in 1807 after the H.M.S. Leopard (right) fired on the U.S.S. Chesapeake (left), then boarded the American warship in search of deserters. (Culver Pictures)

deserters from the Royal Navy. As often as not, however, native-born Americans were taken mistakenly or purposely. Americans responded to this crisis much as they had during the Revolutionary period. Congress passed a Non-Importation Act in 1806 banning the consumption and importation of British goods. This proved to have a negligible effect, and the situation worsened when attempts to negotiate a solution failed in London. It was during this frustrating year that Lewis wrote Jefferson, warning him of British intentions to grab the Northwest trade.

One incident that represented a gross violation of the United States's neutral rights nearly pushed Americans into war. In June 1807 the British frigate Leopard fired on the American frigate Chesapeake in broad daylight as astonished Virginians looked on from the coast. The British captain had demanded to board the *Chesapeake* and search for deserters. The Americans replied that they did indeed have three deserters from the Royal Navy, but that all three were Americans who had escaped impressment! When the search was refused, the *Leopard* opened fire, killing three Americans and wounding eighteen.

The Embargo

After demanding compensation and an apology for the *Chesapeake* incident, Jefferson sought to punish the British in the Embargo Act of 1807. Congress prohibited all U.S. ships from sailing to foreign ports, outlawed all exports from the United States, and refused to import certain British manufactured goods. Jefferson believed that if Britain and France were deprived of their American trade, including goods from their colonies, they would be forced to relax shipping restrictions toward the United States and respect the United States's neutral rights.

The embargo failed miserably. Many American shipowners had no quarrel with British restriction and actually enjoyed higher profits because of the greater risk. Federalists and New England merchants objected, however, using the argument they had employed earlier in the debate over the Louisiana Purchase: that the government did not have the power to curtail trade. Many Republican farmers grew angry when their surplus crops could no longer be sold in the foreign market. Illegal trade with Canada and through Florida helped to subvert the goals of the embargo, leaving Jefferson increasingly frustrated and producing coercive enforcement laws.

But the real reason for its failure was that the embargo hurt Americans far more than it did the British or the French. Public pressure finally forced Congress to repeal the embargo, and Jefferson reluctantly signed this measure in 1809, just days before his good friend, James Madison, was to be sworn in as the next president. One effect of the embargo, curiously, proved more in line with Hamilton's vision of America than Jefferson's. By prohibiting certain British imports, the embargo helped stimulate American industry in ways that, one generation later, would turn Jefferson's vision of an agrarian society into an outdated fantasy.

Causes of the War

After decisively winning the presidential contest and enjoying a brief period of popularity with the embargo's repeal, Madison and the Republicans in Congress passed the Nonintercourse Act in 1809. The law reestablished trade with all countries except Britain and France. For a brief period, when the British minister to the United States violated his instructions in negotiating a treaty, it looked as if the crisis over neutral rights might be resolved. But the agreement was quickly invalidated upon the minister's return to London.

The United States then tried a different tactic. Congress lifted the ban on trade with the two countries in 1810, while authorizing the president to reimpose an embargo on one of the belligerents if the other should relax restrictions. When Napoleon falsely announced that restrictions on American shipping would be lifted, Madison immediately reestablished nonintercourse with Great Britain and severed diplomatic relations soon after. Surrounded by economic hardship and political strife, the British foreign secretary announced on June 23, 1812, that his country would suspend its restrictive maritime policy against American vessels. The move, however, came five days too late. Congress had already declared war on Great Britain.

Americans living in the South and West were the strongest proponents of the war. They had felt most strongly the foreign presence in Louisiana and Florida. They were the most affected by emotional appeals that the United States needed to reassert its independence and strength by successfully challenging Britain, putting an end to impressment and interference with neutral trade. It was also the agrarian South and West that were most keenly threatened by the closing of European markets to American foodstuffs.

Many land-hungry Westerners had also been disturbed by the belief that the British in Canada had been arming Indians to oppose American expansion. No one consulted Indian tribes when Napoleon decided to sell Louisiana to the Americans, and farmers often migrated to new areas before Indian land claims were settled. In the Ohio country, in fact, Thomas Jefferson—celebrator of the "noble savage"—even advised Governor Wil-

The British bombarded Fort McHenry, near Baltimore, throughout the night of September 13–14, 1814. The successful resistance of the Americans inspired a bystander, lawyer Francis Scott Key, to write the verses of "The Star Spangled Banner." (The New-York Historical Society)

liam Henry Harrison on techniques for wheedling the tribes into making treaties that they did not understand! Two Shawnees, Tecumseh and his brother "the Prophet," organized various tribes against further white encroachment. In 1811 they mobilized a large force of warriors until defeated at the Battle of Tippecanoe. Here, thought many, was an example of what British deviousness could accomplish.

When it came, however, the War of 1812 proved one of the most unpopular and controversial conflicts in American history. Every Federalist in Congress voted against war. Even a minority of Republicans, remembering Hamilton's efforts to encourage federal spending for military needs, balked at the idea of taking on a major European power. Many blamed Madison personally for stumbling ineptly into war, and he barely won reelection in 1812 by a margin of one state's electors.

THE WAR OF 1812

The United States entered the war unprepared as well as divided. The government had waited too long to raise funds to build up the navy, and it depended upon volunteer enlistments for the general army and state militias which never came in the hoped-for numbers. Three attempts to conquer Canada ended dismally. The navy fared somewhat better, capturing several British ships on the Atlantic. The American navy also defeated a British fleet on Lake Erie, winning control of the Northwest in 1813. When the British turned the tide against France and defeated Napoleon in 1814, however, they were able to transfer resources and manpower to North America. They successfully blockaded the American coastline. In the gloomiest days of the war, in August 1814, a British fleet sailed up the Chesapeake, landing troops that captured Washington, burning the Capitol and the

THE WAR OF 1812

← U.S. moves ⟵ British moves
★ Battle

0   100   200   300 MILES

The American plan called for attacks against the British from Detroit, Fort Niagara, and Plattsburg, New York. In 1812 William Hull marched from Detroit into Canada. Fearing trouble from Indians on his flank, however, he retreated and surrendered Detroit without a shot. In August the American garrison at Fort Dearborn was wiped out.

In 1813 Americans were more successful. In April Henry Dearborn sailed from Sackets Harbor, New York, across Lake Ontario and burned York (now Toronto). Oliver Hazard Perry's September victory on Lake Erie forced the British to abandon Detroit. William Henry Harrison, who had moved north from Cincinnati, pursued the retreating British into Canada and defeated them at the Battle of the Thames in October.

In 1814 the Creek Indians, allied with the British, attacked Americans along the frontier. Andrew Jackson, moving south through Mississippi Territory, dealt the Creeks a heavy defeat at the Battle of Horseshoe Bend. In September British troops under Robert Ross and Alexander Cochrane sailed up Chesapeake Bay. They burned Washington, D.C., but failed to take Baltimore. That same month a British force under George Prevost moved south from Montreal. Americans led by Thomas Macdonough went north to meet them and won an important victory at the Battle of Lake Champlain. Late in the year a large British fleet commanded by Edward Pakenham moved north from Jamaica. In 1815, in the war's most spectacular battle, Jackson defeated them at New Orleans.

White House. Madison and his government fled ignominiously.

Fittingly, perhaps, the greatest American victory of the war occurred in the Southwest shortly after it had officially ended. On January 8, 1815, with both sides unaware that a peace treaty had already been signed, British Major General Sir Edward Pakenham led a direct frontal assault on New Orleans, keeping his troops in close column formation. His fifty-three hundred men faced an American force of thirty-five hundred composed of militiamen, two battalions of free black troops, disorganized frontiersmen, and pirates, including the notorious Jean Lafitte, all under the direction of General Andrew Jackson, a militia commander from Tennessee. Jackson won an astounding victory, killing two thousand British troops, including General Pakenham and the next two generals in command. Only thirteen Americans died in the action. The victory fired American nationalism, virtually silencing the war's critics, and it made Jackson—"The Hero of New Orleans"—a major overnight figure on the political stage. The war itself decided virtually nothing: on December 24, 1814, the Treaty of Ghent ended the war unconditionally; that is, each side dropped or postponed its demands. Each nation accepted—at least in theory—conditions as they had existed before the war.

Most people in New England continued to oppose the war as they had opposed Jefferson's embargo. Many commercial-minded Federalists viewed the war as one imposed by the South and West at New England's expense, suspecting Madison and the Republicans of trying to use the conflict for partisan political ends and sectional economic motives. It might be recalled that New Englanders had also opposed the Louisiana Purchase and would have opposed appropriations for Lewis and Clark's expedition had Jefferson fully revealed his intentions. Federalist governors opposed the use of state militiamen during the War of 1812, discouraging volunteer enlistments or increasing taxes.

In October 1814, representatives from most New England states gathered at Hartford, Connecticut, to draft a list of grievances and recommendations. Dismayed by their section's waning influence in the policy making of the national government, the Hartford delegates argued that the Constitution had failed to provide equal rights among the states. A few demanded secession from the United States, but the moderate majority proposed a series of constitutional amendments instead. They wanted abolition of the three-fifths compromise which gave greater representation to the Southern states plus a new requirement for a two-thirds vote in Congress either to declare war or to admit new states. With the war's end and Jackson's victory at New Orleans, however, the country was in no mood to listen to disaffected New Englanders. Federalists faced charges of treason from their more patriotic, belatedly pro-war countrymen, and the party never recovered from its opposition to the war. Nothing, other than the Battle of New Orleans, did more to enhance the war's popularity among Americans in all sections than the coming of peace.

Once the war had ended, its unifying effects became more apparent. Even the most remote frontiersman seemed eager to defend the country against foreign attack. Wartime curtailing of trade with Europe had encouraged greater interstate trade and cooperation as well as a growth of domestic industries. The doctrines of the Virginia and Kentucky resolutions (1799) and of the Hartford Convention (1814), one the work of Republicans, the other of Federalists, remained as warnings of what dissatisfied sections might do in the future. The rise of party politics had proved significant by providing, among other things, the means through which such sectional discontent could be channeled and compromised. If serious questions of principle could be resolved through party mechanisms and through the participation in politics of ever-expanding numbers of people, then both national unity and democratic sentiment might grow to an unprecedented degree. Whatever the future held, it seemed clear by 1815, at war's end, that the American republic had withstood successfully the major political and foreign challenges of its early embattled decades. Its energies began shifting toward economic and political expansion, much of it toward the West, thereby beginning to fulfill the promise of continental development foretold in the success of Lewis and Clark's trek through the American wilderness.

Suggested Readings
Chapters 11-12

The Lewis and Clark Expedition and the American Frontier

Thomas P. Abernethy, *The Burr Conspiracy* (1954); John Bakeless, *Lewis and Clark, Partners in Discovery* (1947); John D. Barnhart, *Valley of Democracy: The Frontier Versus the Plantation in the Ohio Valley, 1775–1818* (1953); Paul Russell Cutright, *A History of the Lewis and Clark Journals* (1976); Bernard De Voto, *The Course of Empire* (1952) and *The Journals of Lewis and Clark* (1953); Richard Dillon, *Meriwether Lewis: A Biography* (1965); William H. Goetzmann, *Army Exploration in the American West 1803–1863* (1959); David Freeman Hawke, *Those Tremendous Mountains: The Story of the Lewis and Clark Expedition* (1980); E. Wilson Lyon, *Louisiana in French Diplomacy 1759–1804* (1954); Arthur K. Moore, *The Frontier Mind: A Cultural Analysis of the Kentucky Frontiersman* (1957); Francis Paul Prucha, *American Indian Policy in the Formative Years* (1962); Bernard W. Sheehan, *Seeds of Extinction: Jeffersonian Philanthropy and the American Indian* (1973); Henry Nash Smith, *Virgin Land: The American West as Symbol and Myth* (1950).

The Federalist Era

James M. Banner, Jr., *To the Hartford Convention: The Federalists and the Origin of Party Politics in Massachusetts, 1789–1815* (1969); Morton Borden, *Parties and Politics in the Early Republic, 1789–1815* (1967); Irving Brant, *The Bill of Rights* (1965); James H. Broussard, *The Southern Federalists 1800–1816* (1978); Richard Buel, Jr., *Securing the Revolution: Ideology in American Politics 1789–1815* (1972); William N. Chambers, *Political Parties in a New Nation* (1970); Joseph Charles, *The Origins of the American Party System* (1956); Marcus Cunliffe, *The Nation Takes Shape 1789–1837* (1960); Alexander DeConde, *Entangling Alliance: Politics and Diplomacy Under George Washington* (1958); M. J. Heale, *The Making of American Politics* (1977); Linda K. Kerber, *Federalists in Dissent* (1970); Stephen G. Kurtz, *The Presidency of John Adams* (1957); John C. Miller, *The Federalist Era 1789–1801* (1960); Curtis P. Nettels, *The Emergence of a National Economy 1775–1815*

(1962); Robert V. Remini, *Andrew Jackson and the Course of American Empire 1767–1821* (1977); James M. Smith, *Freedom's Fetters: The Alien and Sedition Laws* (1956); Paul A. Varg, *Foreign Policies of the Founding Fathers* (1963); Leonard D. White, *The Federalists: A Study in Administrative History* (1948).

The Jeffersonians

Thomas P. Abernethy, *The South in the New Nation, 1789–1819* (1961); Henry Adams, *A History of the United States During the Administrations of Jefferson and Madison* (9 vols., 1889–1891); Irving Brant, *The Fourth President: A Life of James Madison* (1970); Roger H. Brown, *The Republic in Peril, 1812* (1964); Harry L. Coles, *The War of 1812* (1965); Noble E. Cunningham, *The Jeffersonian Republicans 1789–1801* (1958) and *The Jeffersonian Republicans in Power* (1963); Richard Ellis, *The Jeffersonian Crisis: Courts and Politics in the New Republic* (1971); David H. Fischer, *The Revolution in American Conservatism* (1965); Reginald Horsman, *Causes of the War of 1812* (1962), *Expansion and American Indian Policy 1783–1812* (1967), *Jefferson and Civil Liberties* (1963), *The Jeffersonian Image in the American Mind* (1960), and *The War of 1812* (1969); L. S. Kaplan, *Jefferson and France* (1967); Ralph Ketcham, *James Madison* (1971); Leonard Levy, *Legacy of Suppression: Freedom of Speech and Press in Early American History* (1960); Dumas Malone, *Jefferson and His Times* (four vols to date, 1948–1969); Bradford Perkins, *Prologue to War: England and the United States 1805–1812* (1961); Merrill D. Peterson, *Thomas Jefferson and the New Nation* (1970); Julius W. Pratt, *The Expansionists of 1812* (1925); Norman K. Risjord, *The Old Republicans: Southern Conservatism in the Age of Jefferson* (1965); Marshall Smelser, *The Democratic Republic 1801–1815* (1968); Burton Spivak, *Jefferson's English Crisis: Commerce, Embargo and the Republican Revolution* (1979); Leonard D. White, *The Jeffersonians 1801–1829* (1951); Charles M. Wiltse, *The Jeffersonian Tradition in American Democracy* (1935); James S. Young, *The Washington Community 1800–1828* (1966).

Andrew Jackson: The Road to the White House 13

The Seminole Indian chiefs stood on the shore and watched the soldiers hang the old man. Almost alone among white men, Alexander Arbuthnot had cared about the Seminoles and had tried to help them. For his pains, the Scottish trader's body now dangled limply from the yardarm of his own schooner under the hot Florida sun in the spring of 1818.

Arbuthnot had been caught up in a war between the United States and the Seminoles, an offshoot of the Creek Indian confederacy who lived mostly in Spanish Florida and occasionally crossed the border to raid American settlements in Georgia and Alabama. The U.S. government, eager to stop the raids and anxious to acquire Florida, sent Major General Andrew Jackson and several thousand men into Spanish Florida. Jackson's forces found few Indians willing to fight, but after several skirmishes he did capture two Seminole leaders, whom he promptly hanged in April 1818. He also ran across two Britons. "My love," the general wrote to his wife Rachel, "I entered the Town of St. Marks on yesterday. I found in St. Marks the noted Scotch villain Arbuthnot . . . I hold him for trial." Farther to the east, American forces encountered Lieutenant Robert C. Armbrister, formerly of His Britannic Majesty's Royal Marines. Both Britons were jailed as allies of the Seminoles.

The War of 1812 had ended only three years earlier, and Americans still believed that the British stirred up the Creeks and Seminoles to raid into the United States. Jackson, acting as commanding general, ordered a court martial for Arbuthnot and Armbrister. His legal basis for trying two British subjects on Spanish soil in an American military court was shaky at best. But when Andrew Jackson felt he was right, technicalities rarely impressed or stopped him.

The case against Arbuthnot, a tall, white-haired, carefully dressed man in his seventies, consisted of one letter, a bill of sale, and two witnesses. Arbuthnot had written the letter to his friend, the Seminole leader Bolecks ("Bowlegs" the American dubbed him), warning him to avoid battle with Jackson's powerful army. Jackson insisted, however, that the letter contained military information and provided advice to the

Indian enemy. The bill of sale listed ten kegs of powder Arbuthnot had sold to the Indians. The witnesses, both personal enemies of the Scotsman, testified to having seen a letter he had written to the Seminoles urging them to attack the Americans. The letter itself was not produced.

Arbuthnot defended himself in a simple but eloquent speech to the court. He denied advising the Seminoles to go to war, since he wished to avoid bloodshed. The sale of a few powder barrels to be used in hunting was, he pointed out, a normal part of a trader's business. How long, after all, would ten kegs have lasted in a war? Arbuthnot pointed to the flimsy nature of the documentary evidence and the hearsay nature of the oral testimony. He swore that he was no agent of the British government.

The case against Armbrister *appeared* to be more serious, though it showed him as pathetic rather than malevolent. The young Royal Marine had been removed from his regiment for dueling with another British officer and had gone to stay with his uncle, the British governor of the Bahama Islands. Armbrister came to Florida on a holiday. To impress the Indians, he said that he was a British agent and that his uncle would be sending them arms and other supplies to use against the Americans. Armbrister was all talk — but the talk was to cost him his life. The very manner of his capture revealed how unthreatening he was. Wandering through the night with an attendant and two slaves, he simply stumbled across the American army!

Armbrister confidently threw himself on the mercy of the court. "I should have no fears, as I am in the hands of Christians," he told his captors. "I know they will not murder me." The tribunal, headed by Jackson's second-in-command, Major General Edmund Gaines, consisted of fourteen American officers. They decided the case rapidly. Alexander Arbuthnot would be hanged as a spy; Lieutenant Robert Armbrister would be shot as a spy. But the court then reconsidered and commuted the young, bumbling Armbrister's sentence to fifty lashes and a year at hard labor.

A courier brought news of the sentences to Jackson for approval. The general, who was with his troops in the field, quickly signed Arbuthnot's death warrant — but he rejected the court's clemency for Armbrister. Instead, he scribbled out an order restoring the original sentence. The ex-marine would be shot.

Jackson, as major general of the United States Army of the South, had bigger things to do than watch the execution of two spies. He marched his army off toward Pensacola, the capital of Spanish Florida. Jackson's aim was to seize the principal Spanish forts and to ship the colonial governor off to Havana, Cuba. He believed (and so, he thought, did President Monroe) that the Seminole threat could never be ended while Spain kept Florida.

Armbrister still could not believe that he was to die. Frantically, he demanded to know whether Jackson had left a pardon before marching away. He had not. Still, it took the dread music of fife and drum summoning the firing squad to convince the ebullient Armbrister of his doom. "I have heard that sound in every corner of the globe," he reflected quietly, "and now I hear it for the last time." The shots rang out a few minutes later; Armbrister collapsed in the dirt; and several soldiers rowed Arbuthnot out to his ship. As the rope went around his neck, the Scotsman swore that Great Britain would avenge his death. The Americans let his body hang for about twenty minutes before cutting it down.

Arbuthnot's threat almost came true. London exploded with anger at the news of the executions. In the streets and in newspaper columns, Jackson and other Americans were damned as murderers. War would have been declared, admitted the foreign secretary, "if the Ministry had but held up a finger." But the British then had more than enough problems in Europe to keep them occupied, and a third war with America was out of the question.

Jackson had more to fear from his own government. When word of the executions, and of his occupation of Spanish Florida, reached Washington, President James Monroe and all but one cabinet member favored relieving Jackson of his command immediately. Fortunately for the general, the lone dissenter, Secretary of State John Quincy Adams, persuaded the others not to admit American fault. Adams, a leading authority on international law (among other things), promised his colleagues that he could justify Jackson's activities and defend the United States position.

"It is an established principle of the laws of nations," Jackson had argued in ordering the executions, "that any individual of a nation making war against the citizens of another nation, they being at peace, forfeits his allegiance, and becomes an outlaw and a pirate." Unfortunately, nobody but Jackson had heard of any such "principle." So Adams's defense had to be a masterpiece of legal distortions and diversions. Rather than defend the lawfulness of Jackson's actions themselves, Adams (like Jackson) went on the attack. He denounced Arbuthnot as a "pretended trader" and argued that anyone who aided "savages" to fight civilized nations could not claim protection under the rules of war. Furthermore, while agreeing *in principle* that all occupied territory in Florida should be returned to Spain (Adams was then negotiating for American purchase of the territory), the secretary refused to admit that Jackson had been wrong to seize the Spanish forts. On the essential points, in short, Adams argued for Jackson's correctness.

After defeating the Seminoles and the Spaniards in Florida, Jackson had returned to the Hermitage, his plantation manor house outside Nashville, Tennessee. There he learned that opponents of the Monroe administration, led by the ambitious Speaker of the House of Representatives, Kentucky's Henry Clay, planned a thorough investigation. Jackson decided to make the long ride to Washington to defend his actions. He had no intention of answering to Congress for his behavior or of letting rival politicians in the capital bandy his name about. If Congress insisted on stirring up the issue, Jackson would make them answer directly to him. This was hardly an idle boast, considering his character, his ambitions, and — especially — his past.

In 1788, Andrew Jackson had crossed the Appalachian Mountains into Tennessee (then part of North Carolina) with a horse, a slave girl he had bought for two hundred dollars, and a commission as traveling prosecutor. The twenty-one-year-old lawyer was accompanying a friend to a new town called Nashville. The friend had been lucky enough to obtain appointment as a judge in the new community, and Jackson tagged along, hoping to secure a good position there also.

His legal training and knowledge were decidedly limited. Jackson had experienced one personal tragedy after another from his earliest days (his father had died shortly before his birth in 1767; his two brothers and his mother had all died of war wounds or epidemic diseases during the Revolution), and he had attended school only irregularly. To the end of his long life—he died in 1845—Jackson might spell a word two or three different ways in the same document or letter. The best that any well-disposed friend could claim for him was that at least he spelled better than either Washington or Napoleon. Jackson had gathered his scant store of legal knowledge by reading law in an attorney's office in western North Carolina for two years. But a good deal of that time had been spent not at study but in taverns and at racetracks; and very early in his young manhood, Jackson had fought the first of his several duels.

Still, to impose the law upon a frontier territory such as Tennessee, determination and physical courage were often more important than legal acumen. Jackson and his fellow lawyers traveled the state with knife and rifle close at hand. And if, at times, he had to *catch* a suspected criminal before he could prosecute, Jackson could handle that as well.

His tall, lanky figure, topped with a shock of red hair and blazing blue eyes, became well known throughout the new state. Men feared his temper but, at the same time, respected his courage and honesty. When Tennessee entered the Union in 1796, Jackson, then a twenty-nine-year-old prosecutor (and protégé of the state's first governor, William Blount), served as delegate to the convention that wrote the Tennessee constitution. He soon became the state's first member of the House of Representatives, a passionate supporter of Jefferson's Democratic-Republican party.

Philadelphia, then the nation's capital, failed to charm the new congressman, and, in turn, even a leader of his own party found him an "uncouth-looking personage, with manners of a rough backwoodsman." An extreme anti-Federalist, Jackson opposed a resolution praising the previous administration and wishing ex-President Washington a pleasant retirement. Jackson also refused to wear a powdered wig, then the fashion, and instead wrapped his long hair in an eel skin. Nor did he care much for all the talk and paperwork of Congress. He soon resigned his House seat, but political duty then dictated that he accept a promotion to the United States Senate. Blount, his benefactor, had been expelled from that body in 1797, so Jackson went back to serve during one Senate session. Again, he resigned as soon as Congress adjourned.

By that time Jackson's personal affairs, both financial and domestic, required his full attention. Although he had rapidly grown wealthy in

Rachel Donelson Robards Jackson, born in Virginia in 1767, migrated with her family to a frontier Kentucky farm and later to Tennessee. After her turbulent early marriage to Lewis Robards, and her two weddings to Andrew Jackson (both before and after her divorce), she managed the Hermitage, from which Jackson was frequently absent, and raised a dozen foster children, mainly the sons of relatives. She died shortly after Jackson's election in 1828. (Library of Congress)

land speculation, a panic in 1795 had wiped away most of his gains and left Jackson with an abiding suspicion of banks and paper money. It would take him nearly nineteen years to climb out of debt.

Jackson had also acquired a wife, in 1791. Rachel Donelson Robards, recalled one contemporary, was "irresistible to men." They admired her figure and her dark eyes, and even forgave her addiction to smoking a corncob pipe. At first meeting, Jackson found her enchanting. He also found her married, although she and her husband, Lewis Robards, already lived apart. Jackson clearly played an important role in making the couple's separation permanent. On hearing that Rachel's husband was approaching Nashville in an unpleasant frame of mind, Jackson escorted Rachel out of danger and down to the Mississippi River port town of Natchez. Frontier social mores were reasonably permissive for their day, but Jackson's three-hundred-mile, unchaperoned trip with another man's wife raised eyebrows and caused gossip. Upon reaching Natchez, the couple heard that Robards had obtained a divorce. Andrew and Rachel were promptly and happily married.

Too promptly, as it turned out. For Rachel's first husband had not yet obtained a final divorce decree; he had only started proceedings for one. For two years before the true situation was uncovered, the Jacksons unwittingly lived in adultery and bigamy. When they discovered the confusion, and after Rachel's divorce from Robards had finally taken effect, Andrew and Rachel went through another marriage ceremony. But even

In a duel fought in 1806, Charles Dickinson meets his match and his fate at the hands of Andrew Jackson. (Granger Collection)

this did not prevent the tangled episode from plaguing the Jacksons for the rest of their lives.

Tennesseans, however, rarely discussed Jackson's marital affairs in public, since the duel still settled many personal disputes in that day. Even the most amusing bit of gossip at Andrew Jackson's expense seemed too costly if it meant a challenge from the hot-tempered Jackson to meet over pistols. Nashville's lack of interest was even more pronounced after Charles Dickinson's experience in 1806.

Jackson's quarrel with Dickinson began over a horse race. But it assumed an uglier dimension when the latter made disparaging allusions to Rachel Jackson. Jackson's second son called on Dickinson and arranged a meeting over pistols at dawn across the border in Kentucky. According to the rules of the dueling code, combatants faced each other twenty-four paces apart and fired once upon command. The seconds then reloaded pistols for another exchange—if necessary.

Charles Dickinson was an accomplished marksman; his seconds rarely had to reload. Dickinson had a reputation as a sure shot and boasted that he would kill Jackson with his first bullet. Jackson, not a quick shooter, decided to let Dickinson fire first. Even if hit, he reasoned, his willpower would sustain him until he had killed the man who had maligned his wife.

The opponents stood and awaited the signal. On the cry of "Fire!" Dickinson's arm flashed out and a gunshot pierced the early morning silence. But Jackson did not fall. He did not even move. His second saw only a puff of dust arise from his jacket.

"Oh God!" cried the horrified Dickinson, stumbling backward. "Can I have missed him?" For answer, he heard only Jackson's second say sharply, "Back to the mark, sir!" Dickinson returned to his position. Jackson carefully sighted along the barrel of his gun and shot his enemy down. The bullet split an artery and Dickinson died that evening.

Only after Dickinson had been carried off to bleed to death did a servant boy notice that Jackson's right boot was full of blood. The victor now opened his coat, and his second saw for the first time where Dickinson's bullet had lodged. It had missed Jackson's heart by inches, breaking two ribs. But Jackson had refused to give his opponent the satisfaction of knowing that he had been hit. "I would have killed him," Jackson swore later, "even if he had shot me through the brain."

Charles Dickinson had many friends and influential allies, so Jackson's revenge proved costly at first to his political ambitions. For the next six years he lived quietly on his cotton plantation. When Congress declared war on Britain in 1812, however, Jackson soon regained his old rank (acquired years earlier) as major general of the Tennessee militia. Although as untrained in war as he had been when starting out as a lawyer, Jackson led three expeditions during the war.

The first campaign, though aborted, helped build his public reputation. Residents of Tennessee and Georgia liked the idea of acquiring Florida from Spain—by force if necessary—and Jackson shared their goal. He assured the secretary of war that his men, unlike certain militia units from Northern states who had refused to cross into Canada, had "no constitutional scruples, and, if the Government orders, will rejoice at the opportunity of placing the American eagle on the ramparts" of Spain's Florida forts.

Thus, by early 1813, Jackson had marched with several thousand volunteer soldiers to Natchez and stood poised to invade eastern Florida. President Madison and Congress decided otherwise. The military authorities in Washington ordered Jackson to dismiss his troops and thank them but said nothing about pay, provisions, or transport for their return home. Jackson was furious and reassured his men that, if necessary, he would march them back "on my own means and responsibility." Although the general's worth as a military strategist was still untested, the combination of devotion to his men with stern enforcement of discipline among them had earned Jackson the affectionate yet appropriate nickname "Old Hickory" (a wood noted for its toughness).

In his second campaign, the quarrelsome major general fought Indians and not American bureaucrats, building a personal legend. Jackson was recovering from wounds received in a brawl with Thomas Hart Benton (later a senator from Missouri) and his brother Jesse. One of the Bentons had put a bullet in Jackson's shoulder, where it remained when Jackson set out in 1813 to fight the Creeks, the only major group of Southern Indians actively hostile to the United States during the War of 1812. On the way into Creek territory (in what is Alabama today) Jackson had to threaten personally to shoot those militiamen whose one-year enlistment period had expired and who wished to return to Tennessee. In March 1814 his troops won a decisive victory over the Creeks at Horseshoe Bend on the Tallapoosa River. Ten times as many Indians as whites died in the battle, and the surviving Creeks fled into Spanish territory.

Jackson's third campaign of the war, against the British at New Orleans, assured him lasting fame. When Andrew Jackson arrived in New

Andrew Jackson's victory over the Creeks at Horseshoe Bend, when he was 46, not only established his national reputation as an Indian fighter, but resulted in his promotion from a Tennessee militia general to commander of the southern division of the regular army. In this climactic battle of the long Creek War, 800 out of 1000 Creek warriors were killed, the greatest number in any Indian battle, although there were few casualties among Jackson's troops and Indian allies.

Orleans in December 1814 with only two thousand troops, chances for additional victories appeared remote. Despite his victory over the Creeks and his commission as a major general in the regular army, many felt that he did not fit the part of a great general. Certainly he did not look it. An aristocratic Creole lady caught one glimpse of Jackson and winced; he resembled a "Kaintuck flatboatman." Worried residents of New Orleans had further cause for complaint: Jackson had divided his forces. The latest messages from Washington had warned the general of a possible British attack at either Mobile or New Orleans. Jackson accepted that estimate until very late in 1814 and, therefore, divided his men between a force at Mobile, and one upriver at Baton Rouge, where they could move toward New Orleans *or* Mobile, depending upon where the British attacked.

Meanwhile, a thousand miles to the southeast, the British had assembled their assault fleet off the West Indian island of Jamaica. Ten thousand sailors manned the ships that would carry almost eleven thousand fighting men, veteran soldiers and marines, many of whom had taken part either in the Napoleonic Wars or in the capture and burning of Washington that spring. Jackson's uncertainty over the scene of battle was realistic, since the British did not decide on New Orleans until late November, a decision made by the admiral of the fleet, not the commanding general, who had not yet arrived. (In matters of mismanagement, disorganization, and upset timetables, the professional British military proved every bit as adept as the amateur Americans.)

The enemy's army commander, Major General Sir Edward Pakenham, had served ably against the French forces in Spain. When he caught up with his armada, he agreed that New Orleans, near the mouth of the Mississippi, represented a far more valuable prize than Mobile. The British also hoped that the French residents of Louisiana, who had been Americans for only a dozen years — that is, since the Louisiana Purchase — would refuse to fight for the Stars and Stripes (the same mistake made by Americans invading Canada in 1812, who had convinced themselves that French Canadians would turn on the British and help the invaders). Pakenham carried with him a royal commission as governor of Louisiana. Once he had pushed out the Americans, he would rule, in trust for Spain, all the territory "fraudulently conveyed by [Napoleon] Bonaparte to the United States."

The British hoped to improve their chances still more by enlisting the help of the pirates of Barataria Bay for the invasion. From this inlet one hundred miles south of New Orleans, Jean Lafitte, himself a landloving businessman (although many called him a "pirate"), directed a very profitable operation against all sorts of shipping. Louisiana's Creole leaders regarded the Baratarians tolerantly, and Lafitte was willing to dicker with all sides. Britain offered him cash (something he always needed), plus amnesty and a Royal Navy commission (neither of which he needed), if he would fight against the Americans.

To make the most of a tangled situation, Lafitte now wrote to the governor of Louisiana. The governor had recently put a $500 price on Lafitte's head — the pirate had responded by offering a $30,000 reward for the governor's. But such acrimony was now behind him. Calling himself "a lost sheep who desires to return to the fold," Lafitte promised, if not to reform, at least to fight the British. When Jackson heard this, he ignored his previous description of the Baratarians as "hellish banditti" in the pay of the British and graciously accepted the pirates as allies. Soon afterward, Lafitte's brother managed somehow to escape from jail.

The general's quick and positive response to Lafitte showed his awareness of his side's weakness. Even with his Tennesseans, the Baratarians, Creole businessmen of the city militia, the Kentucky sharpshooters, and a group of friendly Choctaw Indians, Jackson needed more troops. He agreed to use two battalions of New Orleans free blacks, already organized, as well as a third battalion which was quickly shaped up, to form a regiment. Jackson appointed white officers for the unit, but let the soldiers select their own noncommissioned officers. To an army paymaster reluctant to disburse wages to the new regiment, Jackson sent a curt note: "Be pleased to keep to yourself your opinions upon the policy of making payments to particular corps."

Earlier, Jackson had been undecided about which city the British would attack. Now he faltered briefly in guarding against their invasion route. Although all approaches to New Orleans had been ordered blocked, the Tennessean had not ensured that the job was actually done. Nor had he acquired sufficient supplies for his troops. Two days before Christmas, he first learned that the enemy was encamped nine miles from the city. They had moved two thousand men up through an unguarded bayou. A prudent (and less effective) general might have immediately concentrated on his fortifications. "Gentlemen, the British are below," Jackson announced to his officers. "We will fight them tonight." The ensuing battle, a night attack by the Americans, was a standoff, with about equal casualties on both sides — but it saved New Orleans. Reasoning that Jackson must command overpowering force (fifteen thousand men at least) to come out and attack in that risky fashion, the British commander decided to advance no farther. That gave Jackson two vital weeks to organize his forces.

Preparations for battle continued on both sides over the Christmas holidays. Pakenham brought seventeen heavy cannon from his ships. But he never established superiority in artillery, a mistake that would cost him dearly. On January 4, 1815, a large Kentucky militia contingent marched into the American camp, but few of the men even had rifles. "I don't believe it," Jackson supposedly complained. "I have never seen a Kentuckian without a gun and a pack of cards and a bottle of whiskey in my life." As Jackson rode off to the front line, a New Orleans resident asked him if the women should leave the city. "Say to the ladies not to be uneasy," answered the general. "No British soldier shall enter this city unless over my dead body." The remark seemed, at that moment, as much a prediction of things to come as a promise of safety.

At six o'clock on the morning of January 8, the Americans saw two red rockets streak up from the British lines. This, they knew, signaled an attack. The band of Battalion d'Orleans struck up "Yankee Doodle," as the Americans waited. Except for the artillery, Jackson's troops would hold their fire until the British came within two hundred yards. In the heavy fog and early-morning semidarkness, the defenders, four deep behind their mud and timber wall, could hear the bagpipes of the Ninety-third Highlanders before they could see anything. When the breeze cleared patches in the fog, they began to distinguish the many lines of British troops still off in the distance but approaching at a measured pace. The red-coated British infantry had pushed the French out of North America, twice driven back American invasions of Canada, and just defeated Napoleon. Awaiting the nine thousand advancing Britishers were half as many backwoods farmers, New Orleans businessmen, newly organized free blacks, pirates, Indians, and a very few American army regulars.

Only when Jackson was sure that the redcoats were within range of his men's muskets did he give the command to fire. The American artillery, already very effective, had stopped to let some of the smoke clear from the field. Hundreds of rifles barked out as one, and as the front rank dropped behind to reload, the second came forward to fire. By ranging his troops in four lines, Jackson could maintain a constant wall of flame in the face of the invaders. The Baratarians, the only nonregulars on the American side who could handle cannon, helped blow great holes in the enemy lines.

Soon the advancing British had to step over the bodies of dead and wounded comrades. Their red lines first buckled and then broke under a "leaden torrent no man on earth could face," in the words of one British officer who watched the carnage. There was no lack of valor on the attackers' part, officers or enlisted men. But Jackson held a superb defensive position, with the river on one flank and a swamp on the other. When a

British flanking maneuver on the Mississippi's west bank produced no real results, the frontal attack then under way became suicidal. Pakenham, trying desperately to rally his men, caught two bullets and died on the field, as did the handful of attackers who reached the American parapet. As the troops retreated, some in panic, others more slowly, the commander of the British reserve units saw no point in continuing the slaughter, and he ordered the attack ended.

It all took less than half an hour. Two thousand British soldiers lay on the battlefield, dead or dying. The defending Americans had seven killed and six wounded. Four of the casualties were black soldiers, so eager for battle that they had left their lines to chase the retreating British. Shattered in spirit, the British invaders sailed away eleven days later, after burying their dead. They had time to dig only shallow graves, and that summer the stench of death hovered over New Orleans. The body of Pakenham, who had expected to become His Britannic Majesty's Royal Governor of Louisiana, was returned to London preserved in a barrel of rum.

In mid-February, Jackson, still governing New Orleans under martial law, finally received news from Washington. The British and American governments had signed a peace treaty at Ghent, Belgium, on December 24. The Battle of New Orleans, in short, had been fought fifteen days after the war's end.

But the two-month lag in communications was to prove of enormous benefit to the United States. By January 1815, the Americans were still mired in the war's bad news. The British burning of Washington only confirmed their military dominance in the conflict. True, a few naval victories had interrupted the parade of American defeats, but New England was demanding an end to the war at almost any cost, and talk of secession ran through Massachusetts and Connecticut. When Northerners heard nothing from New Orleans, newspapers accused President Madison of concealing the city's loss. "If an attack has been made on Orleans," despondently reasoned the New York *Post*, "the city has fallen."

Word of Jackson's victory burst upon this gloomy atmosphere, and the country went wild. "GLORIOUS!!! UNPARALLELED VICTORY!" screamed the headlines. Jackson immediately became the nation's hero and made a triumphant return from New Orleans to Nashville. Every state legislature passed a resolution of gratitude. New York's tribute, written by a young state senator named Martin Van Buren, called Jackson's triumph "an event surpassing the most heroic and wonderful achievements which adorn the annals of mankind."

The Battle of New Orleans, by removing the sting from a stalemated, often humiliating war, caught the popular imagination. Volunteers, mainly farmer soldiers, had routed England's professional troops, a fact that seemed to confirm everything Americans liked to believe about republics and democracy. (The country quickly forgot the many times during the War of 1812 when royal forces had smashed republican militiamen.) In the popular mind, Jackson's victory had proved American freemen invincible and, therefore, had demonstrated our national superi-

Andrew Jackson's "almost incredible victory" at the Battle of New Orleans in January 1815 was one of the rare American triumphs in an otherwise bleak war record. Ignoring strategic reasons for the defeat of the more numerous British veterans, grateful Americans credited Jackson's energy, courage, and power, as well as providential intervention. (Culver Pictures)

ority. "The Hunters of Kentucky," a minstrel show ballad about the battle, swept the country, becoming the nation's most popular song.

That a nonprofessional soldier had led the army helped swell the legend considerably. All Americans soon knew the story of Andrew Jackson, a poor orphan who had achieved wealth and influence through his own efforts. It helped considerably that Jackson was a product of the frontier, where American society seemed to be functioning in its most classless and democratic form. That Jackson had come to own a large plantation with many slaves indicated to his many enthusiasts only the extent of opportunity in America.

Jackson's friends in Tennessee watched with great interest the national wave of adulation. The country had once made a military hero president; might it not be persuaded to do so again? Their thoughts ran not to 1816, when Secretary of State James Monroe would probably run for the White House, but to 1824, by which time Monroe would have completed two terms and Jackson would still be only fifty-seven. In 1815, Jackson responded publicly to the proposal with appropriate modesty: "No sir, I know what I am fit for. I can command a body of men in a rough

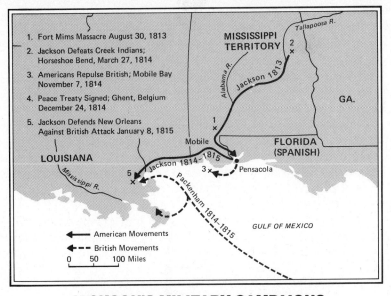

JACKSON'S MILITARY CAMPAIGNS

1. Fort Mims Massacre August 30, 1813
2. Jackson Defeats Creek Indians; Horseshoe Bend, March 27, 1814
3. Americans Repulse British; Mobile Bay November 7, 1814
4. Peace Treaty Signed; Ghent, Belgium December 24, 1814
5. Jackson Defends New Orleans Against British Attack January 8, 1815

way, but I am not fit to be President." But while Jackson, with decreasing sincerity, told this to visitors, two of his close friends published a popular biography of the hero. The Jackson legend grew still further with his conquest of Spanish Florida three years later.

Thus, the angry Jackson who approached Washington in 1819 to face official censure for his high-handed conduct in Florida bore the strengths of a popular idol and the potential of a long-shot presidential candidate. The capital was full of other hopefuls who wanted to see Jackson eliminated. Two of them, Secretary of the Treasury William Crawford and Secretary of War John C. Calhoun, had just voted in the cabinet to recall Jackson in disgrace from Florida. A third, Speaker of the House Henry Clay, would now have his turn.

The House Military Committee, which Clay controlled, had voted without dissent to recommend censure of Jackson, both for hanging Arbuthnot and shooting Armbrister and for seizing Spanish Florida. The House had then begun a twenty-seven-day debate of the censure move. During its deliberations, Jackson arrived in Washington.

The general refused to appear in public at first, remaining in his hotel until the House had voted. Jackson boiled with rage at his accusers, feeling that he had not only done nothing wrong but had carried out the accepted policy of the Monroe administration. Secretary of State Adams tried to calm Jackson, assuring the general that his conduct could be justified by the great theoreticians of international law, Grotius, Vattel, and Puffendorf. "Damn Grotius! Damn Vattel! Damn Puffendorf!" exploded Jackson. "This is a matter between Jim Monroe and myself."

Clay led off the House debate with a long warning of the danger military heroes posed to democracies. He later denied implying that he meant to indict Jackson as a threat to the government, but if Clay's speech did not mean that, it meant nothing. Jackson believed deeply in the Constitution and in democratic civil government. No accusation could have infuriated him more, and from that day Jackson, an unrelenting hater, hated Henry Clay.

But Jackson also had brilliant defenders in the House, led by the Tennessee delegation. The representatives of the Southwest believed, as Jackson did, that only firm action could deal with the Indian menace to settlements on the frontier. On the final vote, the House not only refused, by a vote of 90 to 54, to condemn Jackson for the executions, but, by a 91-to-65 tally, it endorsed his seizure of Florida.

Vindicated, the hero of New Orleans now emerged from his hotel in triumph and journeyed to celebrations in his honor held at Philadelphia and New York. On these occasions, only once did anyone have the temerity to raise the subject of Arbuthnot and Armbrister. "They were spies," answered Jackson coldly. "They ought to have been executed. And I tell you, sir, that I would do the same thing again."

Jackson returned to Washington to find that the Senate had launched its own investigation of his conduct in Florida. But the Senate soon lost interest, and when the United States finally bought Florida from Spain two years later, Monroe sent Jackson there as territorial governor. Jackson accepted the job for a short time—as a symbol of vindication rather than because of any real interest in the post. He returned to Tennessee within a year.

A very different Andrew Jackson appeared in Washington in December 1823 as United States senator and candidate for president. Since spring, he and his friends had been writing amiable, fence-mending letters to political figures in all parts of the country, and Jackson now even spoke and wrote an occasional kind word or two about his old enemies. "General Jackson's manners," admitted an opponent, "are now more presidential than those of any of the candidates." But such niceties were soon forgotten when Jackson suddenly indulged himself in one of those outbursts of temper for which he was famous. The cause this time was political.

Four rivals for the White House, all more experienced in politics than he, now confronted the new senator from Tennessee. William Crawford claimed the support of the old Republicans, including Jefferson himself. John Quincy Adams, son of the only Northern president, counted on the united vote of New England. John C. Calhoun, younger than the rest, would become a major candidate if, as he expected, Pennsylvania lined up with the South on his behalf. Clay of Kentucky represented the young West and a program of high tariffs and government aid to economic development. None of the four professional politicians considered Jackson, although a national hero, to be a major threat. Adams indirectly offered him the vice-presidency, which, Adams suggested, "would offer an easy and dignified retirement to his old age." (The considerate Adams was exactly 118 days younger than Jackson.)

Two events swiftly altered the situation. Crawford, considered to be the front-runner, suffered a stroke. Although his supporters gamely predicted recovery, they found it difficult to press the claims of a man who could neither move nor speak. Then, several months later, a Calhoun meeting in Pennsylvania overruled its chairman and endorsed Jackson. The secretary of war now shelved his dreams of the presidency and announced himself as a vice-presidential candidate under Jackson.

Thus, the hero of New Orleans, without having taken a public stand on any major issue, became almost overnight the leading candidate for the White House. Professional politicians could not understand his popular appeal. But many ordinary Americans saw Jackson as a simple and able person who had already served his country well and now asked only for the chance to serve again—a man of action, not words, who scorned the tangled political world of party machines, caucuses, and Eastern business interests. When skeptics asked where Jackson stood on the issues of the day, his followers replied with rapturous descriptions of the Battle of New Orleans.

In 1824, the states of the Union chose presidential electors on different days and by various methods. But long before the last returns reached Washington from Louisiana (by this time a state), it became clear that no candidate had won a majority. Adams's strength was concentrated in the Northeast; Crawford's in three Southern states; and Clay's in the West. Only Jackson could point to national support, having won eleven states from New Jersey to Illinois and southward to Calhoun's South Carolina. But even with his ninety-nine electoral votes, Jackson had still finished thirty-two short of victory. The House of Representatives would choose the new president.

This should have worked to the advantage of Clay, Speaker and virtual ruler of the House. But the Constitution states that the House can choose only among the top three contenders, and Clay had finished fourth, a few votes behind Crawford. The other candidates quickly recognized that Clay, although he could not himself attain the presidency, would probably determine who among them would gain the office. Emissaries of Adams, Jackson, and Crawford soon besieged the Speaker. Clay enjoyed the attention, but he had vowed that, having missed the presidency this time, he would negotiate primarily with a view to improving his chances for the future.

Every political reason led him to support Adams. Both Clay and Jackson came from the Southwest, but Clay would be more likely to succeed a New Englander like Adams. Even were Jackson, if acclaimed president, to name Clay secretary of state, Calhoun, who had been elected vice-president, would surely press his prior claim to be Jackson's heir. Also, although this probably did not greatly influence the Speaker, his political stance corresponded closely with Adams's beliefs. Finally, Clay did not think that Jackson would make a good president. "I cannot believe," he wrote a friend, "that killing two thousand five hundred Englishmen at

New Orleans qualifies a man for the various difficult and complicated duties of the Chief Magistracy."

Clay met with Adams on January 9, 1825. Communications between cities were slow at the time, but news traveled fast through Washington—then, as it does today. Within hours, the capital knew that Speaker Clay had joined with Secretary of State Adams. Jacksonians fumed indignantly, still hoping that Adams could be stopped. Each state would cast one vote in the House, and Adams needed thirteen for victory. New York, still in doubt, could provide the thirteenth vote. For a month, pro- and anti-Jackson forces worked to gain the New York vote. It boiled down to the decision of a vacillating and aged New York Dutch aristocrat, Steven Van Rensselaer. First Clay and Daniel Webster, then Jackson's supporter Martin Van Buren, extracted promises of support from the eighty-one-year-old congressman. On election day, February 9, Van Rensselaer, confused and undecided, tottered onto the House floor. As tellers passed the ballot box around, he looked upward for heavenly guidance. Receiving none, he hung his head and saw an Adams ballot at his feet. Convinced that the Almighty works in mysterious ways, Van Rensselaer picked up the slip and put it in the box. John Quincy Adams would be president of the United States.

For the second time, the House of Representatives—as in 1801—had chosen the president. The process, though constitutionally correct, produced a national uproar. Jackson and his followers felt deprived, if not defrauded outright. When Adams named Clay his secretary of state, they unleashed a storm of protest. "The Judas of the West has closed the contract," raged Jackson, "and will receive the thirty pieces of silver." Jackson, offended but hardly Christlike, was playing sarcastically upon one of Henry Clay's nicknames, "Harry of the West." In the Senate, Jackson and fourteen others voted unsuccessfully to block Clay's confirmation.

Soon after Adams's inauguration, Jackson resigned from the Senate. The Tennessee legislature had again nominated him for president. Jacksonians in all parts of the country, convinced that their man had been cheated out of the White House, now impatiently awaited the 1828 rematch. While they still boasted of New Orleans, they now also denounced the Adams–Clay "corrupt bargain," in which the presidency had been bought and sold. "Why is Adams on shaky ground?" ran a popular riddle spread by Jackson's friends. The answer: "Because he stands on slippery Clay." Administration members tried vainly to deny the charges —and their denials only gave more currency to the accusation. Politically the issue ruined Clay for years.

Jacksonians received additional assistance from Adams's policy proposals. The president sent to Congress an ambitious national economic program, one calling for a higher tariff, government sponsorship of road and canal construction, and even a national university. Adams also recommended that the federal government operate a chain of observatories, or what he called "lighthouses of the skies." Old-line Jeffersonians, who still believed in limiting the powers and activities of the federal government, reacted in horror. The younger Adams seemed to them as much a Federalist as his father, perhaps more of one, and in 1828 many of the Old Republicans took shelter in Jackson's camp.

The Jackson forces organized efficiently for the next presidential election. They established hard-hitting, sometimes slanderous, newspapers across the country. By denouncing Adams and Clay at countless rallies and ridiculing the president's call for astronomical "lighthouses," they gave a decided anti-intellectual tone to the Democratic campaign. In Congress, led by Martin Van Buren of New York, Jackson men obstructed most administration moves. Many federal officeholders, from the postmaster general on down, worked openly for Jackson, and Adams refused to stop them. The upright New Englander did not believe in firing government officials for political reasons.

But, as the election approached, Clay rallied the administration (National Republican) forces into a semblance of a counterattack. They circulated thousands of copies of the "Coffin Handbill"—a campaign document charging Jackson with the unjust and merciless hanging of six militiamen in 1815. They raked up the story of his duels with Charles Dickinson and others and invented many more incidents of Jackson's mayhem. Worst of all, at least in the candidate's mind, they reopened the subject of Jackson's marriage. "Ought a convicted adulteress," inquired one editor unctuously, "and her paramour husband to be placed in the highest office of this free and Christian land?"

On this subject, Jackson did not have control over his rage. He considered Clay responsible for the attacks and called the secretary of state "the basest, meanest scoundrel that ever disgraced the image of his God." Jackson's advisers kept him, with difficulty, from challenging Clay to a duel, and they lived in fear that Jackson would do something to ruin their carefully planned campaign. "For Heaven's sake, for your country's sake," warned one friend, "do remember that but one man can write you down—and his name is Andrew Jackson."

Politicians who thought they had seen everything watched the campaign of 1828 in shock. Torchlight parades and libelous attacks on opponents would apparently decide the next president. From a thousand stumps and platforms, the Jacksonians denounced the "corrupt bargain" and the "lighthouses of the skies." The old general, they cried, was a man of the people; Adams was a Boston aristocrat who had installed a billiard table in the White House! The supporters of Adams dismissed Jackson as an illiterate and an adulterer, a military chieftain who endangered the liberties of all Americans. Supporters of Jackson retaliated by suggesting that Adams, a former Harvard College professor and professional diplomat, had acted as a pimp for the czar of Russia while serving as minister to St. Petersburg! Both sides resorted time and again to such absurd charges. No slander was too vile or unjust to be rejected by the supporters of either candidate.

Except perhaps for the size of Jackson's majority, the election result surprised few people. The military hero and uncertain speller had swept the West and the South, while also taking Pennsylvania. Adams won only New England, New Jersey, and half of the New York vote. And, in a statistic then calculated for the first time—the popular vote—Jackson led Adams by 150,000. Four times as many men voted in 1828 as had voted four years before, slightly more than half of all those eligible.

At the peak of Jackson's triumph, Rachel Jackson died. Her husband refused to accept that fact and spent an entire night sitting beside her lifeless body. For the rest of his life, Jackson believed that campaign slander had killed his beloved wife. As he had done in 1819 and again in 1823, Jackson began the long trip by horse and flatboat from Nashville to Washington. But the president-elect now journeyed in sorrow. "May God forgive her traducers," he told a friend. "I know that I never shall."

Meanwhile, Washington nervously awaited the coming of its new leader. The capital had known its past presidents well—they had lived there, holding high political offices before moving into the White House. But, except for his brief service in House and Senate, Jackson had not. Washingtonians knew of him mainly by rumors, most of which they hoped were untrue. As one uneasy resident wrote: "General Jackson will be here [about] 15. of Feb—Nobody knows what he will do. My opinion is that when he comes he will bring a breeze with him. Which way it will blow I cannot tell."

14 The Jacksonian Era

Jackson brought more than a breeze with him; within weeks his political enemies were calling it a hurricane. In the eight years before Old Hickory returned to his home at the Hermitage, he permanently remodeled and strengthened the office of the presidency. Moreover, he helped to create a new political party system and to recast the electorate's ideas of what is expected from government.

Before the 1820s, politics in the United States had worked in a relatively genteel fashion. Most states had limited the right to vote to male property owners, and in both the North and the South, wealthy merchants or large landowners had dominated public affairs. Many states had come to be so thoroughly under the control of one party—the Federalist or the Jeffersonian Republican party—that competition hardly existed. Presidential elections in those times were very different from the bitter Jackson–Adams contest of 1828.

This genteel state of affairs had begun to change long before Jackson entered the White House, but the country's first frontier president clearly helped to speed up the process.

THE ERA OF GOOD FEELINGS

At the time that Jackson threw back the British at New Orleans, American politics had already begun to change. The declining Federalists were further weakened by charges of wartime disloyalty because of the Hartford Convention, and by 1820 they had all but disappeared. For nearly ten years a so-called Era of Good Feelings characterized the political scene, with political competitions occurring mainly among groups within the all-powerful Republican party.

This all-inclusive Republican party was not the same one that Jefferson had fashioned. When the war ended, Republicans adopted some of the same measures that they had condemned in the past. This proved especially true with regard to the national bank and the tariff.

The Second Bank of the United States, a corporation with both private and public directors, chartered in 1816, had branches in the major cities and provided most of what little regulation existed of the American financial system. As Jackson rose steadily to power in the 1820s, so did the bank, on a collision course that would provoke the most spectacular political confrontation of the 1830s.

The same war that had made a hero of Jackson had caused the creation of his eventual adversary. The federal government had gone deeply into debt during the war, and it needed more revenue. Dozens of new banks had sprung up after the expiration of the charter of Hamilton's Bank of the United States in 1811. The state banks had operated poorly during the war, and the country now clearly needed a better financial system. The government had to pay off its debts. Moreover, there was growing pressure on it to take a more active role in promoting economic growth. Many Americans wanted federal money to be spent on building a network of roads and canals—internal improvement, as it was then called—especially west of the Appalachian Mountains.

Swallowing pride and party principles, Republicans responded to these pressures by chartering a second national bank. President Madison overcame his previous objections to such a bank. A young South Carolina representative of the Southern planter interest, John C. Calhoun, introduced the bank recharter bill. It passed in 1816, providing for a bank to run until 1836.

Andrew Jackson, seventh president of the United States, and the first president to be born in a log cabin. (Library of Congress)

Next came the tariff. Like the bank issue, debate on the tariff in 1816 began with patriotic statements and a nationwide agreement, but it ended before long in fierce political squabbling. American manufacturers, located mainly in New England, were just then getting started. They wanted higher tariff duties so that Americans would buy fewer foreign goods and more of their own products. They wanted not just a revenue tariff, to bring in funds, but a protective tariff—one set high enough to protect American producers from foreign competition.

In 1816, Calhoun and many other Southerners voted in favor of a higher, protective tariff. They did so not to enrich the New England manufacturers but to bring in the additional revenue then needed by the federal government. National security was one of their primary concerns at the time. Southerners—like Americans in all sections—feared the outbreak of yet another war with Britain, since the War of 1812 had been a standoff. The United States must be better prepared, militarily and financially, argued Southerners, than it had been in 1812.

There was less agreement on internal improvements. The country needed a better transportation system, and Congress passed a bill authorizing national funds. But here, Madison's constitutional conservatism stood in the way. Despite his lapses from Jeffersonianism on the tariff and the bank, Madison could not convince himself that the federal government had the right to spend money in this way. The president vetoed the bill, and for the next two generations each state had to build its own roads and canals.

The Federalists offered little opposition to the candidacy of Secretary of State James Monroe to be Madison's successor. And again, four years later, Monroe received every electoral vote but one for reelection. Throughout his administration, Monroe issued soothing calls for an end to all party divisions. The composition of his cabinet—with the ex-Federalist Adams in the State Department, the Old Jeffersonian Crawford of Georgia in the Treasury, and the Southern nationalist Calhoun as secretary of war—showed that all elements of the political spectrum now coexisted within the Republican party. Harmony had indeed been established in national politics—for a brief moment.

The Panic of 1819

But trouble was already brewing. The first sign was a financial panic. Since the War of 1812, people had been speculating heavily in foreign trade and Western lands. They bought on credit, hoping to reap a large profit before having to pay off their debts. Then, in 1819, the Second Bank— under new management—began calling in loans. As a result, many state banks stopped paying hard money for their notes or closed, and numerous investors went bankrupt.

The Panic of 1819—the first of a series of economic downturns that would continue to occur in the United States at approximately twenty-year intervals until 1929—affected the whole nation, although Western states were the hardest hit.

The national bank, then just three years old, was widely blamed for the hard times. Many Americans attacked the bank as a corrupting agent of aristocracy and privilege, and several state legislatures tried to tax its branches out of existence. The Supreme Court ruled such laws unconstitutional. But the strong antibank feelings that had surfaced never really disappeared. Politicians would capitalize on them throughout the 1820s, and Jackson would find in such feelings a reservoir of political support during the 1830s.

Americans had distrusted banks even during the colonial period—often with good reason, given the high rate of bank failures. In the 1820s, Kentucky and Tennessee witnessed "relief wars," during which debtors organized against creditors. Everywhere, private banking interests were on the defensive. These struggles were a prelude to the Jacksonian battles of the 1830s. They also provided a training ground for several important politicians who would later join Jackson's antibank crusade.

The Missouri Compromise

Another sign that the short-lived Era of Good Feelings (1816–24) had its own tensions came when the always troublesome problem of slavery surfaced again. In the same year as the panic, the issue of statehood for Missouri came to a head. The Missouri Territory was part of the original Louisiana Purchase. Its residents had applied for admission to the Union in 1817. But, at the time, a congressman from New York had demanded that slavery be prohibited in the state as the price of admission. The uneasy sectional truce on the question of slavery quickly evaporated. Congress was deadlocked on the issue for over a year. Southerners had equal voting strength in the Senate, since the nation then had the same number of slave states and free states. Northerners controlled the House of Representatives, however, because the North had acquired a larger population since 1789. Antislavery representatives argued that Congress could and should make prohibition of slavery a condition for admitting new states. Southerners retorted that all states, old or new, were sovereign and could decide the matter of slavery for themselves.

The very mention of the slavery question in Congress terrorized Southerners. As the struggle went on in Congress, Richmond, Virginia, was said to be as "agitated as if affected by all the Volcanic Eruptions of Vesuvius." Southerners, who always suspected that the North wanted to destroy their "peculiar institution" of slavery, now felt their suspicions confirmed. They readied themselves for a long fight on what they considered a life-or-death issue. "To compromise is to acknowledge the right of Congress to interfere and to legislate on the subject," wrote one prominent Southern politician; "this would be acknowledging too much."

Yet compromise they did, when Maine, then a district of Massachusetts, petitioned Congress to become a separate state. Southerners would not admit Maine as a free state unless Missouri joined the Union with the right to permit slavery. Henry Clay, Speaker of the House and a Kentucky slaveholder more identified with the West than with the South, now piloted a three-part compromise through Congress, with a different coalition backing each part. Maine would be admitted as a free state, Missouri as a slave state, and slavery would be banned in the remaining areas of the Louisiana Purchase and in future acquisitions above 36°30' latitude.

The Missouri crisis frightened Americans in the North and West as well as in the South and with good reason. They knew that truly national politics and parties could not exist if slavery became an active issue bitterly dividing the sections of the country. This "momentous question, like a fire-bell in the night, awakened and filled me with terror," wrote Jefferson, in retirement at Monticello. "I considered it once as the knell of the Union . . . this is a reprieve only, not a final sentence." Many other anxious politicians agreed with this analysis, although few were willing to admit it publicly.

The South in particular regarded the compromise uneasily, especially its limitation on the future expansion of slavery. "Instead of joy," one Southern editor mourned, "we scarcely ever recollect to have tasted of a bitterer cup." All three Southerners in Monroe's cabinet advised him that the restriction of slavery was unconstitutional. Sixty percent of the Southern congressmen who voted for the compromise were not returned to the next Congress.

Both Southerners and Northerners now hoped that the slavery issue could be kept quietly localized. The Missouri debates had exposed the deep division between supporters and opponents of slavery. These sectional issues and attitudes had the power to rip the Union apart. Throughout the Age of Jackson, however, politicians would strive to keep the slavery genie bottled up.

In President James Monroe's annual message to Congress on December 2, 1823, he included the principles of foreign policy later known as the Monroe Doctrine. Monroe and his Secretary of State, John Quincy Adams, wanted to clarify the American position in two specific problem areas. They succeeded in a wider sense, as one historian states, by planting their principles "firmly in the national consciousness."

THE MISSOURI COMPROMISE, 1820–1821
AND ADMISSION OF STATES, 1791–1821

Dates indicate entry of states into the Union

Free States   Slave States

The first problem area was the Northwest. Since 1821 Russia had been encroaching on the Oregon country, claimed jointly by Britain and the United States. In October 1823, Adams stated bluntly that "the American continents are no longer subjects for any new European establishments." This principle was repeated in Monroe's speech.

South America was the second problem area. Eight new republics had declared their independence from Spain, but their existence was precarious. Despotic regimes in Europe were successfully crushing revolutions on the Continent, and it was evident that Spain was eager to regain her lost colonies. In August 1823 the English foreign secretary proposed a joint British–American manifesto to warn Europe against intervention. British merchants wanted to retain their profitable new markets in South America, now open to them after the breakup of the Spanish monopoly. And Britain could back up a threat with naval power.

Adams, however, did not want the United States to be "a cockboat in the wake of the British man-of-war." He suspected that the British might restrict American expansion in some way as a price for their support. Also, Britain had not officially recognized the new republics, as the United States was doing. So Adams suggested an independent course of action. Monroe agreed and decided to include a warning in his message to Congress.

Monroe declared that intervention by European monarchies in the democracies of the New World would be judged as "the manifestation of an unfriendly disposition toward the United States." He pledged the United States not to interfere with any existing European colonies in the New World and to keep out of the "internal concerns" of Europe.

The speech was acclaimed at home but viewed abroad as "arrogant." Yet the European powers took no action. Why? Two months earlier, unknown to Adams and Monroe, the English had pressured France to agree not to assist Spain in any invasion of her ex-colonies. Thus the issue had already been defused. Russia, unable to gain support for intervention, withdrew its claims to the Pacific Northwest early in 1824. The South American republics seemed indifferent to the speech. They

President James Monroe, last of the Revolutionary era executives, has gone down in history as the co-author of the Monroe Doctrine and as the man who presided over the demise of the first American political party system. Monroe's years in office were less an "era of good feelings," however, than an era of no national parties and much factional infighting.

were more impressed with "the oaken fleets of Britain" than with "the paper shield of Monroe."

So the significance of Monroe's declaration was widely discounted at first. In years to come, however, its principles were invoked with great reverence by American nationalists, often to rationalize *U.S.* intervention in Latin American affairs.

A RETURN TO PARTY POLITICS

The election of 1824, as we have seen, emphatically closed out the Era of Good Feelings. It also destroyed the method that Americans had first used to select presidential candidates, the congressional caucus or party meeting. The caucus had often been denounced as aristocratic and undemocratic. After Crawford, who was nominated by this means in 1824, lost the election, nobody suggested holding another caucus in the future. Politicians had to find a new process, one that at least *seemed* more democratic.

They found the answer during the next few years in a new nominating device, the convention. Conventions were supposed to be more representative of a party's membership and thus more democratic than the caucus. Only members of the national or state legislature could attend a legislative party caucus. But, in theory, any party member could become a convention delegate. Grass-roots political elements could be represented at a convention, as could groups or factions that had not been able to elect their leaders to Congress.

This change reflected the general movement toward increasing popular participation in the governmental process. Throughout the 1820s, state constitutional conventions revised the old Revolutionary constitutions, lowering or abolishing the property qualifications for voting. More offices were now filled by direct vote of the people; in some states even presidential electors were now chosen by direct vote.

At first, old-line politicians resisted the changeover to conventions. Yet they had little to worry about. Party bosses found that it was not difficult to manipulate convention delegates. On the other hand, conventions gave the *appearance* of equality in an age when political operations were becoming more and more democratized.

For the presidential election that followed the Adams-Clay victory in the House of Representatives, Americans required neither caucus nor convention to indicate the candidates. Jacksonians hungered for their next electoral bout with John Quincy Adams. Only with a brilliantly successful administration could the president hope to fend off their challenge, and for that, Adams was the wrong man at the wrong time.

Like his father, John Adams—another crusty, stubborn, and inflexible man—John Quincy Adams believed in government by the most able and talented. Also like his father, John Quincy Adams learned quickly that such a belief did not make him popular with the majority of his fellow Americans. Adams had been preparing for the presidency all his life, but once in the White House, he found that his hands were tied. He became a minority president, without any real control over Congress. He also lacked the ability to make either himself or his programs popular with the public. Adams was bound to fail, and fail he did.

For four distressing years this very capable individual fussed and floundered. The job called for talents Adams did not possess and could not acquire. He was reserved—a "cold fish" to most people who met him. He was short-tempered with any person he considered a fool, and he claimed to have met many—especially in politics. Most importantly, he was totally unwilling to compromise.

President Adams's expansive first message to Congress, calling for "lighthouses of the skies," ended whatever survival chances his administration might have had. It especially shocked Martin Van Buren, opposition Senate leader, political boss of New York's Albany Regency, and a confirmed Jeffersonian. Van Buren now traveled to Virginia to confer with leaders of the so-called Richmond Junto, the clique that dominated the politics of the state. Van Buren proposed a North–South Republican alliance that would not only oust Adams but prevent Adams's ideas from becoming dominant in the future.

Jackson, Van Buren argued, could accomplish the first end and would be a reasonable president. He was already very popular. He did not support the extreme states' rights position, but neither did he favor a strong national government. Furthermore, Van Buren promised that his Northerners would see that slavery was kept out of national politics. The Southern states would thus be free from antislavery attacks during Jackson's presidency, and presumably afterward as well. In short, after Jackson's victory in 1828, Van Buren wanted to revive the coalition originally formed by Burr of New York and Jefferson and Madison of Virginia. Both the original Jeffersonian group and the new Jacksonian alliance were known as Democratic-Republicans. But the Jeffersonians were more generally referred to as Republicans, while the Jacksonians called themselves Democrats. Anti-Jackson Republicans were first known as National Republicans, later as Whigs.

JACKSON AS PRESIDENT

Few people knew what would happen when Jackson took office. He had been deliberately vague about issues while campaigning, and the Jacksonian Democrats were then more of a faction gathered about a leader than a party with a plat-

form. His inaugural address revealed little except a call for "reform." This word was political shorthand, an indication that Jackson intended to reward his friends and punish his enemies. During the previous generation of one-party, Republican rule, turnover among public officeholders had not been great. The last large-scale shift in government employees had occurred when Jefferson had become president and removed a good many Federalists from office. Since that time a Republican elite, many of them anti-Jackson, had settled cozily into federal jobs, some for a quarter century. Jacksonians understandably demanded that the new president replace these older officials with loyal Jackson supporters.

Although, in fact, Jackson went only about as far as Jefferson had, he and his supporters made more noise about it. He removed about 10 percent of the federal officeholders during his first year as president and a total of about 20 percent in eight years. It was not the clean sweep hoped for by the

Voting day in Philadelphia, as elsewhere in the Jacksonian era, occasioned much rowdy excitement. During this period the number of voters increased, not only because suffrage requirements were eased but also because people took more interest in politics. (Historical Society of Pennsylvania)

Democratic politicos. But the Jacksonians did radically change the nature of federal patronage, in the sense that Jackson openly defended the principle of rotation in office—what came to be known as the spoils system. He agreed with Senator William L. Marcy of New York—an associate of Van Buren— that "to the victor belong the spoils." Jackson acted on the theory (if not always the practice) that, in a democracy, persons of normal intelligence could capably fill most public offices. To Jackson's political opponents this view seemed dangerous. Yet rotation in office, at all levels of

American government, became the standard practice after Jackson and lasted for decades.

Strengthening the Office

Jackson's opponents saw him as a tyrant, an uncouth military man from the West. Obviously, this opinion did not conform to Jackson's vision of himself as an "Old Republican," a true Jeffersonian. But Republicanism had changed significantly since Jefferson's presidency. Jackson hoped to revive what he called the "Republican principles of [17]98." He did not want national power to increase at the expense of the states. Yet his role as a strong president and his ability to dramatize political issues for ordinary people in every section stimulated the growth of national power. Just as Jefferson had strained his principles to purchase Louisiana, Jackson would sometimes find his ideas fairly elastic when put to the test.

Old Hickory's "Old Republicanism" took several forms. In his first annual message, the president criticized the national bank. He also rejected the idea of a high, protective tariff. (Unlike some Southerners, however, he did not deny the tariff's constitutionality.) On the issue of internal improvements, Jackson held views like those of the Republican presidents prior to John Quincy Adams. In 1830 he vetoed the Maysville Road Bill, which would have involved the federal government in a road-building project in the state of Kentucky. He argued that such matters should be left in local hands. He believed, though, that the national government could contribute to interstate projects. This is why he favored national support for the Cumberland Road, an east–west improvement that passed through several states. Jackson received firm support on this question from Martin Van Buren, who was his secretary of state from 1829 to 1831. Van Buren's state, New York, had completed the Erie Canal in 1825 without federal money, and further major internal improvements in the state were unlikely.

Jackson did much to strengthen the American presidency. He was by far the strongest chief executive up to his time and one of the most forceful in American history. Since Jefferson's first term, power had been steadily slipping out of presidential hands and into those of the Congress. Jackson, however, reversed the process.

During his eight years as president, Jackson restored the White House as the focal point of national politics. Where Congress had largely dictated to the last three presidents, Jackson now set out to manage Congress. Working closely with loyal Jacksonians like House Speaker Andrew Stevenson and Senator Thomas Hart Benton—whose bullet the President still carried in his shoulder—he tried to get Congress to support his policies and to defeat bills he did not like. Anti-administration congressmen soon found it difficult to get presidential patronage for constituents hungry for jobs. When his policies failed with Congress, Jackson had no hesitation about vetoing bills. Twelve times he refused his assent to a bill passed by both houses of Congress—three times more than his five predecessors combined. A favorite device of his was the pocket veto—delay in signing a bill until Congress adjourned. Perhaps most important, Jackson vetoed some bills just because he thought them unwise, not necessarily because he regarded them as unconstitutional.

Jackson introduced another innovation into his conduct of the office. Previously, presidents had relied for advice mainly on their cabinets, often consisting of politicians as interested in their own careers as in the nation's problems. Jackson now assembled around him his own personal advisers—a so-called kitchen cabinet that included Van Buren and two newspapermen, Francis Prescott Blair and Amos Kendall. Blair edited the administration newspaper, the Washington *Globe*, and Kendall held a minor job in the Treasury Department, but both were available to advise Jackson on strategy, to consult with party leaders, or to draft Jackson's messages to Congress.

Finally, Jackson was the undisputed head of his party, as well as leader of the government. His power in each role strengthened him in the other, and his extraordinary personal popularity helped him in both. Democrats all over the country followed the administration line as it appeared in the *Globe*, or they soon ceased to be Democrats.

Jackson brought a new concept of the presidency to the White House. Some previous occupants, as well as his political opponents, saw the president's duty as only to administer the government, while Congress, representing the people, made the laws. But Jackson saw himself as the direct representative of the American people, elected by the entire nation, with an obligation to lead the country forcefully.

The "Eaton Affair"

Dramatizing Jackson's concept of the presidency was an intensely personal issue that frayed relations between himself and his vice-president, John C. Calhoun, whose support had helped gain Jackson victory in 1828. Embittered by Jackson's evident preference in assigning cabinet posts for Van Buren and his political allies, Calhoun lost most of his remaining influence in the administration as a result of an episode that came to be known as the "Peggy Eaton affair."

Jackson enjoyed the social company of Peggy O'Neill Eaton, wife of his friend, Tennessee Senator John H. Eaton, whom the president appointed secretary of war. Mrs. Eaton was the daughter of a tavern keeper and a widow at the time she married Eaton, and other Washington wives gossiped incessantly about her morals while spreading rumors that she had engaged in a love affair with John Eaton while her former husband still lived. Once Eaton joined the cabinet, Mrs. Calhoun and other wives of leading Jackson administration officials refused all social contact with the Eatons while continuing their slander mongering.

Nothing could have guaranteed Jackson's anger toward the gossips more easily than what he treated as an obvious comparison to his political enemies' earlier slanders about his beloved dead wife Rachel. The president turned this social flap into a test of political loyalty and insisted that cabinet members deal respectfully with Mrs. Eaton. Caught between their wives and their president, most—including Calhoun—stood ground and continued to question Peggy Eaton's virtue (and virtues). Martin Van Buren, however, a widower, found it easier—and politically useful—to cultivate the Eatons' friendship, something that did not pass unnoticed by Jackson. After many months of battling within the administration over the "Eaton affair," Jackson (with the approval of Van Buren) finally forced the resignation of his entire cabinet in 1831 as a means of reorganizing it with friendlier—and more compliant—figures. Van Buren went to England as American minister where he remained until the Senate voted against his confirmation by a single vote—Calhoun's, casting a tie-breaking ballot as vice-president. The entire episode strengthened Van Buren's claims on Jackson while rupturing the president's personal links to Calhoun.

Nullification

In the crisis over nullification, Jackson most strongly demonstrated his forcefulness and his claim to represent all the American people. Trouble had been brewing over the federal tariff law for many years. In 1828 the South Carolina legislature published an *Exposition and Protest.* It branded protective tariffs as unjust and unconstitutional and termed the 1828 version, supported by Jackson, the Tariff of Abominations. Changes must come, the *Exposition* warned, or South Carolina would act.

Improbably, the man behind the *Exposition* was the vice-president of the United States, John C. Calhoun. Brilliant, ambitious, and totally humorless, Calhoun had begun his political career as a strong nationalist, favoring both a national bank and a protective tariff. But the shifting political sands of South Carolina could no longer support such a stand, and Calhoun now attempted to devise means of protecting his and other states from the national government. Like the rest of the South, he had been profoundly impressed by the Missouri crisis and felt the slave states required strong defenses against a potentially hostile national government. Explained Calhoun, "I consider the Tariff but as the occasion, rather than the real cause of the present state of things."

Calhoun thought he had found a solution in the Virginia and Kentucky resolutions, written by Madison and Jefferson in the late 1790s. He now interpreted them to mean that a state could nullify (refuse to enforce) an act of Congress that it considered unconstitutional. Obviously, the South would find Calhoun's solution extremely useful against any antislavery laws passed by Congress. The aging

Madison denied that the resolutions carried Calhoun's interpretation, but South Carolina accepted that view.

As Southern complaints about the tariff continued, Jackson tried to arrange for a compromise bill to lower import duties. But he never lost sight of the fundamental issue, state defiance of federal law. Jackson rejected nullification totally, vowing to preserve the Union by any means necessary. He applied all the power of the presidency and all the force of his personality to block nullification and denounce John Calhoun.

Nevertheless, South Carolinians went ahead and declared the 1828 tariff "null and void" in their state. What would Jackson do? Though he might compromise on tariff rates, he would not compromise federal authority. "I consider . . . the power to annul a law of the United States, assumed by one state, incompatible with the existence of the Union," he proclaimed in December 1832. South Carolina should not think that it could nullify the Constitution peacefully, and, he warned: "Disunion by armed force is treason." Jackson got Congress to pass a Force Bill reaffirming the president's right to use troops to put down rebellion and enforce the laws. In fifteen days, he wrote a South Carolina Unionist, he could send forty thousand armed troops to South Carolina to put down rebellion; in forty days, two hundred thousand. The Hero of New Orleans would not look far for a general to command them. "I repeat to the Union men, fear not, *the union will* be preserved."

Meanwhile, South Carolina had received no substantial support from other Southern states. The state's isolation left it no real hope of defending itself or nullification. Early in 1833, Clay and Calhoun worked out a compromise bill reducing tariff rates over the next ten years to an acceptable level. The nullification issue collapsed, though to save face, South Carolina declared the Force Bill unconstitutional. An armed clash had been avoided. The Union stood firm. Jackson emerged from the struggle with more strength and greater prestige than before. The president had shown character, political skill, and moral courage—all of which he would need in his next major campaign, the war against the Second Bank of the United States.

The Bank War—and After

Why did Jackson oppose the Second Bank of the United States and come to hate its president, Nicholas Biddle? As an investor, Jackson had lost money in a panic in the 1790s, and he had distrusted banks ever since. As a Jeffersonian, he regarded the bank as a dangerous institution. He thought it was too large and too national in scope. To him, it represented a concentration of economic power, created by the federal government, that endangered states' rights and the rights of the people. The Supreme Court declared the Second Bank of the United States constitutional, but Jackson felt that the president had as much right as the Court to interpret the constitution.

The existence of the bank became the primary issue in the election of 1832. Although the bank's twenty-year charter did not lapse until 1836, Biddle took the advice of Henry Clay and asked for a twenty-year recharter four years early. Clay, running for president as the National Republican candidate, needed an issue on which to challenge Jackson. Clay identified himself totally with the bank and even took on one of its attorneys as his running mate.

Jackson never refused a challenge. After Congress had passed the bank recharter bill, the president vetoed it in a stinging message drafted by Amos Kendall. The powers of the bank, he charged, were "unauthorized by the Constitution, subversive of the rights of the states, and dangerous to the liberties of the people." He called the bank an instrument used by wealthy merchants to oppress the workers and farmers. "It is to be regretted," he warned, with at least one eye on the fall elections, "that the rich and powerful too often bend the acts of government for their own purposes."

The election of 1832 transformed the *Jacksonian* party of 1828 into the *Democratic* party, a coalition with issues and a party constituency. The cementing issue was the Bank of the United States, which symbolized Democratic objections to many other kinds of concentrated government power, such as a high protective tariff and internal improvements.

The Democratic constituency largely reflected the Van Buren–Ritchie agreement of the

Peter Cooper

As an old man looking back, Peter Cooper said that his life had fallen into three parts—thirty years to get started, thirty years to gain a fortune, and thirty years to distribute it wisely. As inventor, manufacturer, and philanthropist, Cooper became a legendary figure. One historian called him "as distinctly an American type as Benjamin Franklin, and as quickly taken to the American heart."

Born in 1791 in New York City, the young Cooper revealed a restless nature and a talent for tinkering. As a boy, he made shoes and hats and even a simple washing machine. For his first child he devised a mechanically rocked cradle attached to a musical instrument, patented as a "Pendulous and Musical Cradle." Some of his ambitious projects, such as propelling ferryboats by compressed air, were grotesque failures. Others, such as an endless chain to haul canal boats, went unrecognized. "I was always fussing and contriving," he wrote, "and was never satisfied unless I was doing something difficult—something that had never been done before, if possible."

He came to a turning point in 1821, when he bought a glue factory in New York. It became the foundation of his fortune. In a few years he had a monopoly in the field and was able to pursue other interests. Cooper invested in real estate and railroads. In 1830, for the Baltimore and Ohio Railroad, he built and piloted the first steam locomotive in the United States, nicknamed "Tom Thumb." With a good sense of the demand for iron in an increasingly industrialized economy, he bought iron mines and ironworks, producing the first structural iron for fireproof buildings. As president of the giant North American Telegraph Company, he supported Cyrus Field in his project for laying the Atlantic cable.

In 1856 Peter Cooper calculated that he was a millionaire. So he turned to the realization of his long-held dream: a workingman's institute in New York City for "the advancement of science and art." He was painfully aware of his own lack of formal education, and yet he was distrustful of much "book learning." Thus he wanted to develop a school "so that the boys and girls of this city who had no better opportunity than I had to enjoy means of information would be enabled to better their condition." Cooper Union opened in 1859, offering free courses in science, technology, art, and design, as well as a library and a museum.

Cooper's public career included reform politics. Some of his ideas were far in advance of his time—controlled currencies, unemployment relief works programs, and government regulation of railroads. In his last years, according to one writer, he became "an unwearied figure for social justice."

Cooper's personal qualities explain the esteem in which the public held him. He had the self-confidence and optimism of the master craftsman. Though hardworking, he was never ruthless. At his funeral in 1883, this tribute was paid: "Here lies a man who never owned a dollar he could not take up to the Great White Throne."

Bank War, Stage I, 1832. President Jackson takes on Biddle's Monster, wielding his bank recharter bill veto sword. (Smithsonian Institution)

previous decade, including most of the South and most urban workers in the North. The latter Democratic constituency was steadily increasing: between 1820 and 1860, three million Irish and two million Germans streamed into the United States, most of them into the ranks of the Democratic party. The Democrats could also count on the support of many backwoods farmers of the West, who supported Jackson and disliked the Eastern bank.

In 1832, workers and farmers both saw the bank as a tool of the rich; they wanted to be paid for their labor and their crops in gold and silver, rather than in banknotes. But Jackson's supporters also included many ambitious entrepreneurs who

disliked the bank for exactly the opposite reason. They felt it was restricting the flow of paper money too tightly, keeping other banks from issuing their own banknotes freely enough to encourage economic growth. But they joined with the other Jacksonians in alleging that the bank only helped to make the rich richer.

Jackson's opposition had an issue and a leader—but not much else. Henry Clay, with only the limited and ineffectual organization of the National Republican party, counted on the bank issue to provide the rest of his votes. For Clay and the National Republicans, the bank stood for many other issues. It was part of Clay's "American system," a plan of positive government action to encourage manufacturing and tie the country together. The system consisted of the bank, a high protective tariff, and extensive internal improvements. For the system, swore Clay, he "would defy the South, the President and the Devil."

The South and the president, at least, defeated Clay roundly in 1832. Whether the bank issue helped or hurt Jackson's campaign is difficult to judge. Although he improved his showing in the electoral college, he was less popular with the voters than when he had run as a fresh and untried candidate in 1828, and his percentage of the popular vote declined. Some Southerners reacted unfavorably to his anti-nullification stand, and a new party in the North called the Anti-Masons siphoned off additional votes. In fighting the bank, Jackson had seemingly raised the threat of class war. Many of his opponents, including wealthy businessmen in New York City and elsewhere, thought that he was trying to set the poor against the rich. All this was more than offset, however, by the incredibly bungled campaign waged by Clay and the National Republicans.

Having gained another four years in the White House, Jackson was convinced that the American people wished him to crush the bank forever. He was also sure that anyone who attacked the bank was for him, and anyone who supported it was against him. Those who wanted to remain Jacksonian Democrats in good standing had to join the antibank crusade. Those who felt they could not support Jackson on this issue switched over completely to the opposition. But Jackson was not a man to let such defections bother him. He would now begin the second battle of the Bank War.

Bank War, Stage II, 1833. Jackson sends the pro-Bank political and economic forces scurrying for safety. He has pulled down the Bank's foundations by ordering removal of U.S. government deposits. (Courtesy, The New-York Historical Society)

Distrusting Biddle, Jackson now wished to remove all government deposits from the bank, to weaken it, and perhaps kill it. By law, only the secretary of the treasury could order the removal of deposits. Jackson found it necessary to replace two men before he found a secretary who would remove the deposits—future Supreme Court Chief Justice Roger B. Taney. The government would now put its money into selected state banks, many of them controlled by Democrats eager to obtain interest-free government deposits. These favored institutions soon acquired the nickname "pet banks."

Biddle now counterattacked. The Philadelphia banker, a man of considerable talent and arrogance, liked to boast that he wielded, as president of the bank, more power than the president of the United States. He would not see that power destroyed without a struggle. He stopped issuing new loans and called in many that the bank had previously granted. The nation immediately plunged into a serious recession. Biddle watched the situation with satisfaction, hoping that he might yet get his recharter. "Nothing but the evidence of suffering," he explained coolly, "will produce any effect on Congress."

Many people felt that Jackson had gone too far and that both the party and the economy had been permanently damaged. Petitions poured into Congress asking for recharter of the bank. Among the thousands of signatures were the names of prominent Democratic merchants, including a sizable number from Northern cities. Some merchants, perhaps a bit braver than the rest, actually went to see Jackson to plead their case. "What do you come to me for?" asked the president, enjoying himself greatly. "Go to Nicholas Biddle. We have no money here, gentlemen. Biddle has all the money."

As calmly as he had once taken physical aim at Charles Dickinson, Jackson had taken political aim at Nicholas Biddle. Any plan aimed at breaking Jackson's will was doomed to failure. Before he would recharter the bank, the president told Van Buren, "I would cut off my right hand from my body."

But would the issue be decided over Jackson's head? Both sides recognized that the congressional elections of 1834 would have an important influence on the outcome of the Bank War. To fight those contests, Jackson's opponents now created a new party, the Whigs. They took their name from the British party that usually opposed the king. After all, they explained, they opposed "King Andrew I." The party consisted mostly of the National Republicans, plus Democrats who had left the party over the bank issue. Apparently, however, not enough had defected. Despite the economic hardships of the winter and spring, Jackson's candidates did well at the polls that year. They even made slight gains in the fall elections for Congress.

Jackson had won the Bank War. The Second Bank of the United States was dead. Biddle later obtained a charter for his bank from the Pennsylvania legislature. But the institution was no longer a national bank, thus it was no longer as powerful as it had been. In 1839 Biddle resigned. In 1841 his bank went bankrupt. He died soon afterward.

Since the mid-1820s the nation had once more prospered, and in the early 1830s the economy began to boom. The government was taking in far more money than it spent. In fact, the national debt completely disappeared during Jackson's tenure—one of the few times in American history that it did so. Speculation in Western lands had become almost a mania. American capitalists were heavily involved, as were European investors. Since the United States was still an underdeveloped, credit-hungry nation, there was a demand for additional capital. Many new banks were chartered. Their promissory notes (written promises to pay a specified sum of money, either on demand or at a certain time) circulated as unofficial paper money.

The speculative boom worried Jackson. In 1836 he issued the Specie Circular, an executive order directing government land agents to accept only gold and silver specie (hard money) as payment. The Deposit Act of that same year included the first federal regulation of the pet banks. But the Whigs added a rider providing that the federal government's surplus revenues should be distributed among the states. This money, in state hands, caused more inflation. Thus it worked against Jackson's Specie Circular.

JACKSON AND THE SUPREME COURT

After the Bank War, Jackson enjoyed one more triumph before leaving the White House. Since 1801, Jeffersonians and Jacksonians had unhappily regarded the Supreme Court under Chief Justice Marshall constantly upholding the power of the federal government and the sanctity of contract. Attempts by anti-Marshall presidents to outnumber Chief Justice Marshall with their own appointments had failed to affect the decisions of the Court.

Jackson had had one serious run-in with Marshall, over a subject to which the president was highly sensitive—Indian policy. The Cherokee Indians in Georgia had developed a modern farming society, with their own written language and their own elected government, based on an 1827 constitution in which the tribe declared itself an independent Cherokee Nation. Georgia officials,

anxious to open Cherokee lands to white settlers, in turn declared state authority over the Indians and ordered the seizure of Cherokee land. White Georgians planned to ship the Cherokees across the Mississippi, as they had done earlier in the case of the Creeks, a course of action approved by Jackson. The Cherokee Nation brought suit, claiming that their treaty with the United States government allowed them to remain unhindered where they were. Marshall spoke for a majority of the Supreme Court in upholding the Cherokees in two cases—*Cherokee Nation* v. *Georgia* (1831) and *Worcester* v. *Georgia* (1832)—directing Georgia state officials to allow the Cherokees to continue running their own affairs and on their own territory. According to Marshall, Georgia's laws did not apply to the Cherokees and white settlers. Even state officials could not enter the Indians' lands without permission from the Cherokees. Georgia ignored the order and proceeded to seize Cherokee lands, while Jackson, for his part, did nothing to

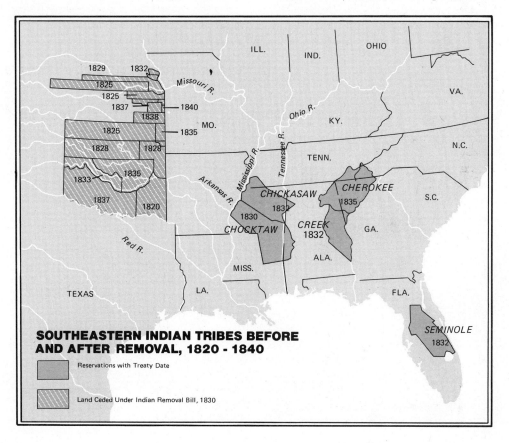

SOUTHEASTERN INDIAN TRIBES BEFORE AND AFTER REMOVAL, 1820 - 1840

Reservations with Treaty Date

Land Ceded Under Indian Removal Bill, 1830

compel state obedience to federal law. "John Marshall has made his decision," he is reputed to have said; "now let him enforce it."

Several years after a small handful of renegade Cherokees signed an 1835 treaty ceding its Georgia lands in exchange for an Indian Territory (later Oklahoma) reservation and a five-million-dollar settlement, Jackson sent an army led by General Winfield Scott to direct the removal of sixteen thousand Cherokees from Georgia. Unwilling to leave their homes, the Cherokees, along with remnants of other tribes, were forced, at rifle and bayonet point, on the arduous trek west during the winter of 1838. Bitter frosts, starvation, and disease took the lives of several thousand Indians before they arrived at the dry wasteland of "Indian Terri-

This later painting of the "trail of tears" portrays the forced removal of the Cherokee Nation in the winter of 1838 from Georgia to Western "Indian Territory," guarded by United States soldiers as the caravan moved along. (Courtesy, Woolaroc Museum, Bartlesville, OK.)

tory." The march became known afterward among American Indians as "the trail of tears." While Jackson's Indian policy led to the removal of most Cherokees, Creeks, Seminoles, Chocktaws, and Chickasaws from the South, similar efforts in the new northwestern states had decimated—and expelled—tribes like the Fox and Sac Indians who stood in the way of white settlement in Illinois and Wisconsin. By the 1840s, most Indian tribes east of the Mississippi River had completely lost control of tribal lands and lapsed into the status of federal (or state) wards, where they had not been physically removed to desolate and unpopulated areas west of the Mississippi.

Several tribes resisted removal forcibly, the most notable instance being the Seminoles led by Chief Osceola in Florida. Pressured to leave for western "Indian Territory" in compliance with an 1833 treaty, the Seminoles revolted, supported by a number of runaway black slaves who had joined the tribe in preceding years. Fighting, for a time, a successful guerrilla-style war against federal troops

sent by Jackson, the Seminoles and blacks held out in the Everglade jungles for several years before their eventual defeat (their leader, Osceola, had been seized deceptively under a flag of truce and shipped off to prison where he died). Whether through actual battle, as in the Seminole War, or through his contemptuous dismissal of Marshall's Supreme Court decisions, Jackson displayed a marked contempt for the rights of Indian Nations. But Jackson was not unique in this view. Rather, he held the attitude toward Indians—that they could not coexist with an expanding white settler civilization—which characterized most of his contemporaries and guided the actions of most nineteenth-century presidents.

In 1835, Marshall died, just in time for Jackson to name his successor. Jackson chose Roger B. Taney, the secretary of the treasury who had finally removed the deposits. Jackson soon saw a difference in the Court's rulings. In the *Charles River Bridge* case (1837), Taney ruled that a state charter, in this case for a bridge, did not constitute an unbreakable monopoly if a second bridge was required by traffic. Property rights were important; but the public, too, had rights. The states must use their powers, ruled Taney, "to promote the happiness and prosperity of the community."

VAN BUREN'S UNHAPPY REIGN

Jackson had been a towering figure as president. But his stature appeared even greater in comparison with the president who preceded him and the one who followed him—both of whom had unfortunate administrations. John Quincy Adams, returning to national politics in the 1830s and 1840s as an antislavery congressman from Massachusetts, must have felt some satisfaction over the difficulties faced by Martin Van Buren, or the Little Magician, as he was called.

The Panic of 1837

Martin Van Buren was Jackson's handpicked choice for the Democratic nomination in the 1836 presidential election. The Whigs could not muster a single strong candidate, and Van Buren won easily over several regional candidates. But even during the campaign, it became clear that economic problems would soon loom large. No sooner had Van Buren been inaugurated in the spring of 1837 than he faced an economic panic, the worst the country had ever known. There were several causes. One was the Specie Circular, which had made much paper money worthless. Another was the fact that British banks raised interest rates and called in loans. In May 1837, New York banks suspended specie payments; that is, they refused to pay out hard cash in exchange for paper money. Other banks soon followed.

All parts of the American business system suffered in the Panic of 1837 and the depression that followed. The price of cotton, America's chief export item, tumbled. Land sales fell from 20 million to 3½ million acres in a year. Merchants found that they could not sell their goods. When sales dropped, factory owners laid off workers. Debtors could not make payments and went bankrupt.

Van Buren responded to the panic by asking Congress to create an independent Treasury system. Like many other Democrats, he had, by then, come to associate the economic crisis with banking itself, whether in the form of a national bank or the pet banks. Van Buren proposed that the United States should simply deposit its funds in "subtreasuries," owned and managed by the government itself. Thus public funds would be separated completely from the private banking structure. Despite three years of successful resistance by Whigs and conservative Democrats, Congress finally enacted the subtreasury plan in 1840. But it did not seriously affect the nation's economic growth, either favorably or otherwise.

The Locofocos

Jacksonian Democrats had attacked the Second Bank of the United States as an undemocratic institution. These attacks went too far for Whig businessmen and politicians, who saw a threat to their economic and political freedom. But they did not go far enough for a small group of radical Democrats called Locofocos, who hated the bank in particular and the wealthy in general.

Most of the Locofocos were artisans, workers, and small businessmen in the urban East.

Many had lost their jobs in the Panic of 1837, displaced by new manufacturing techniques that were part of the growing factory system. They had previously organized themselves into early trade union and local workingmen's parties, many of which achieved some success in winning reforms from state legislatures. Ardently supporting political and economic equality, they hoped to turn the Democratic party into an even more strongly antibank and pro-workingman party than it was under Jackson and Van Buren. Van Buren's own antibank policies had already led many Whigs to brand the entire Democratic party as Locofoco.

Specifically, the Locofocos wanted to prevent private banks from issuing too much paper money and engaging in speculation. Such activities, they felt, had led to the financial panics of 1819 and 1837. Many Jacksonians — workers, farmers, and middle-class Americans — were still reeling from the effects of the recent economic crisis. They hoped to restore a currency system based almost entirely on gold and silver. Some of them even wanted to eliminate paper money altogether.

A HIGH POINT FOR WHIGS

As Van Buren's first term drew to a close, the Whigs marshaled their forces to unseat the Democrats. They had the support of most wealthy Americans, and had recently received a new influx of Democrats who had swallowed Jackson's bank policy but could not endorse Van Buren's. The Whigs also held some appeal for voters among the middle class and working people. Some working people voted Whig out of fear and hatred of the (largely Democratic) immigrants. The Whigs found support in the South among the wealthiest planters, those who had heavy dealings with Eastern businessmen and thus identified with their financial interests. The Whigs also had a hard core of support in the West, among recent settlers from New England, the party's stronghold.

In addition, the Whigs attracted business interests concerned with economic and social expansion. Rejecting Jacksonian fears about panics and paper money, these Whigs argued that the country needed *more* economic development. They wanted more roads, canals, and railroads, and more credit for investors. Government, including the federal government, should play a more active role in spurring development for the benefit of all.

The Whigs smelled victory in the presidential election of 1840. Their factions seemed united at last. Besides, Van Buren, as the president in office, shouldered responsibility for the depression. He had warned that "all communities are apt to look to government for too much." This negative attitude toward federal power did not help in his search for votes.

Van Buren had other problems as the election approached. The "Little Magician" could not make the slavery issue disappear. By trying to keep slavery out of national politics, he was losing votes on both sides. Many Southerners attacked him for refusing to annex Texas after American settlers there had set up an independent republic (see Chapter 20). Many Northerners regarded him as "soft" on slavery and attacked him for refusing to support abolition in the District of Columbia. People like Calhoun and Adams were beginning to destroy the North–South gentleman's agreement, which Van Buren had been instrumental in devising.

Taking advantage of the anti–Van Buren feeling, Whigs decided to mute their own differences. Party managers turned their backs on the Whigs' leading politicians and chose, instead, a candidate with a popular Jacksonian image. He was a military hero and a Westerner, General William Henry Harrison of Ohio.

When a Democratic editor unwisely tried to discredit Harrison as a man content to sit in front of a log cabin drinking hard cider, Whigs turned the slur into a boast. They decorated their floats with log cabins and dispensed hard cider at rallies. They rarely mentioned that Harrison was born in a Virginia mansion belonging to his father, a signer of the Declaration of Independence. Campaigning for Harrison, Daniel Webster actually apologized: "Gentlemen, it did not happen to me to be born in a log cabin; but my elder brothers and sisters were born in a log cabin. Its remains still exist. I make to it an annual visit. I weep."

At the same time, Whigs depicted Van Buren, the son of a small-town tavern keeper, as an

A Harrison campaign poster features a trumpeting angel and includes as well a cheering crowd and the inevitable log cabin and cider barrel. (Benjamin Harrison Home)

Americans—almost 80 percent of those eligible to vote—participated in this national election.

The Whig party had finally arrived, but for how long? When Harrison took over in March 1841, it appeared that the Whigs would remain in power for many years, and that a real two-party system had been established. Even the Whig leaders bypassed as presidential candidates had cause for satisfaction. Daniel Webster became secretary of state. Clay intended to run the administration from the Senate, where he was the most influential Whig, especially since Harrison's inaugural address promised that Congress, not the White House, would lead the way in national affairs. Harrison regarded the veto—so often used by Jackson to browbeat Congress—as a last resort, to be used sparingly, if at all.

But Whiggery's triumph lasted exactly twenty-nine days. Harrison caught cold during his inaugural and died. John Tyler of Virginia became the first vice-president to succeed to the presi-

This early photographic portrait of Daniel Webster, the great Whig senator from Massachusetts, suggests the commanding presence and penetrating gaze which allowed Webster to become one of the most impressive orators of his age. (Library of Congress)

overdressed, would-be aristocrat. They said he lived in luxury, perhaps on dishonestly acquired money. The charges were nonsense, for Van Buren was too smart to be dishonest. Yet, the president's earlier reputation as Jackson's political wirepuller and party chieftain did him no good.

In 1840, the Whigs came of age as a popular party. The National Republicans had previously presented a faintly aristocratic image that was politically damaging. But the new Whig coalition of 1840, which now included hard-fighting political pros from both the Democratic and Anti-Masonic parties, changed all that. The party launched a typically Democratic campaign, with the issues drowned out by songs, rallies, and torchlight parades. One Democratic politician remarked bleakly, "We have taught them to beat us."

The Whigs had learned the lesson well and piled up a Whig landslide. Many states went Whig for the first (and last) time. A record number of

dency. Tyler won a crucial point at the outset. He quickly rejected the suggestion that decisions be made by majority vote of the cabinet. This change —one that Harrison apparently had been considering favorably—would have permanently crippled presidential power. Though not elected to the presidency (his opponents called him His Accidency), Tyler made a vital contribution to maintaining the prestige and power of the office. He established the precedent that a vice-president would inherit the full power of the office, rejecting all attempts to call him *"Acting* president."

Tyler scored lower as a party leader and as a direct representative of the people. A states' rights Southerner, he had been put on the ticket to broaden its appeal. He now demonstrated the dangers of such a policy, infuriating Whig leaders (and damaging the party permanently) by his vetoes of legislation that would have carried out their program. Two national bank bills met with vetoes at Tyler's hands. All of the cabinet except Webster resigned, and the president was officially read out of the Whig party. For a while Tyler hoped he might be vindicated by winning the election of 1844. He tried to build his own organization by offering jobs to cooperative politicians. Except for fellow Virginians and a few hungry office seekers, however, Tyler did not win over many regular Whig party members.

Instead, Tyler devoted much of his "accidental" presidency to foreign affairs. Webster negotiated a treaty with Britain over the boundary between Canada and the northeastern United States. Tyler himself became obsessed with annexing Texas. He ignored warnings that such a move would shatter the fragile sectional truce on slavery. In 1844 he appointed the Democrat John C. Calhoun as secretary of state and ordered the negotiation of a Texas annexation treaty. The Senate rejected the treaty, partly because the South Carolinian had urged it as necessary for the defense of slavery. Calhoun's undiplomatic statement underlined what everyone knew. Slavery, by then, had replaced the Second Bank and related financial concerns as the single most important issue in American political life.

Suggested Readings
Chapters 13-14

Andrew Jackson:
The Road to the White House

James C. Curtis, *Andrew Jackson and the Search for Vindication* (1976); Marquis James, *Andrew Jackson: The Border Captain* (2 vols., 1977); Robert V. Remini, *Andrew Jackson and the Bank War* (1967) and *The Election of Andrew Jackson* (1963).

A Return to Party Politics

James S. Chase, *The Rise of the Presidential Nominating Convention* (1973); Robert G. Gunderson, *The Log-Cabin Campaign* (1957).

Jackson as President

Lee Benson, *The Concept of Jacksonian Democracy: New York As a Test Case* (1961); George Dangerfield, *The Awakening of American Nationalism, 1815–1828* (1965); Michael Feldberg, *The Turbulent Era: Riot and Disorder in Jacksonian America* (1980); William W. Freehling, *Prelude to Civil War: The Nullification Controversy in South Carolina, 1816–1836* (1966); Thomas P. Govan, *Nicholas Biddle* (1959); Bray Hammond, *Banks and Politics in America from the Revolution to the Civil War* (1957); Richard B. Latner, *The Presidency of Andrew Jackson: White House Politics, 1829–1837* (1979); Richard M. McCormick, *The Second American Party System* (1966); Marvin Myers, *The Jacksonian Persuasion* (1957); Sydney Nathans, *Daniel Webster and American Democracy* (1973); Edward Pessen, *Jacksonian America* (1969); Leonard L. Richards, *The Advent of American Democracy, 1815–1848* (1977); Ronald N. Satz, *American Indian Policy in the Jacksonian Era* (1975); Arthur M. Schlesinger, Jr., *The Age of Jackson* (1945); Glyndon G. Van Deusen, *The Jacksonian Era* (1959); John W. Ward, *Andrew Jackson: Symbol for an Age* (1955); Leonard D. White, *Jacksonians: A Study in Administrative History, 1829–1861* (1954).

Jackson and the Supreme Court

Stanley I. Kutler, *Privilege and Creative Destruction: The Charles River Bridge Case* (1971); Michael Paul Rogin, *Fathers and Children: Andrew Jackson and the Subjugation of the American Indian* (1975); Malcolm Rohrbaugh, *The Land Office Business* (1968); Ronald N. Satz, *American Indian Policy in the Jacksonian Era* (1975).

15 Women in Revolt: The Seneca Falls Convention

Tea time on a midsummer Sunday in the upstate New York village of Watertown was normally a quiet occasion, even in 1848 when revolutions seized Europe and antislavery insurgency had begun to spread across America. But this Sunday proved different, at least in Jane Hunt's parlor. Five women sat around an antique mahogany center table that humid July afternoon sipping tea and discussing not only their families but also "things." Confessions seemed in order. Each of the five told of her personal struggle to achieve respect and dignity as an educated woman in the United States. The most impassioned remarks came from Elizabeth Cady Stanton, who had come to Watertown that day for a long-awaited reunion with her friend Lucretia Mott, another guest in the Hunt parlor. Both women were married and had children: Stanton lived in nearby Seneca Falls and Mott in Philadelphia. "I poured out, that day," Stanton later wrote of the July 13 gathering, "the torrent of my long accumulating discontent, with such vehemence and indignation that I stirred myself, as well as the rest of the party to do and dare anything."

Impulsively and without any prior arrangement, the five women decided on the spot to "do and dare" something that had never been done in this country. They decided to organize a women's rights convention, the first ever held in the United States. Nor did they spend much time in preparation. They decided to hold the meeting that week in Stanton's hometown, Seneca Falls. Sitting around the tea table, they wrote a "call" for the occasion to be inserted the following day in the local weekly, the *Seneca County Courier*, and on July 14 New Yorkers throughout the region—many of them doubtless startled by the news—read the following *unsigned* announcement in that paper:

SENECA FALLS CONVENTION

WOMAN'S RIGHTS CONVENTION—A Convention to discuss the social, civil, and religious condition and rights of woman, will be held in the Wesleyan Chapel, at Seneca Falls, N.Y., on Wednesday and Thursday, the 19th and 20th of July, current; commencing at 10 o'clock A.M. During the first day the meeting will be exclusively for women, who are earnestly invited to attend. The public generally are invited to be present on the second day, when Lucretia Mott of Philadelphia, and other ladies and gentlemen, will address the convention.

Lucretia Mott had been one of the five women who prepared the call for the convention. Mrs. Mott's participation in other reform activities, notably abolitionism, had already given her a considerable reputation in the North. In addition to Mrs. Mott and her friend, Elizabeth Cady Stanton (reunited with Mrs. Mott after years of separation), the others at Watertown that day included Mrs. Mott's sister, Martha C. Wright, Mary Ann McClintock, and their hostess, Mrs. Jane Hunt.

No calculated plan, only a casual network of family ties and friendship had brought the women to Watertown that day. Of the five, only Mrs. Mott and Mrs. Stanton had any background in reform activity —though some of the others had also worked in Quaker affairs. Mrs. Mott, in fact, had come to the area originally both to visit her sister, Mrs. Wright, and to attend the Society of Friends' annual meeting in western New York. Western New York had already proved sympathetic to a variety of new religious and social reform movements. Would this prove to be the case with women's rights? None of the five knew if their advertisement would draw a single additional person to the hastily called meeting. Would anyone other than its organizers attend the Seneca Falls Convention on July 19?

For Lucretia Mott and Elizabeth Cady Stanton, the daring notion of that first American women's rights meeting had come eight summers earlier in London, where both women and their husbands attended the World Anti-Slavery Convention. Opponents of slavery demanding immediate "abolition" of the institution had gathered in London that year, 1840, from all parts of Europe and the United States. One of the American delegates, Henry Brewster Stanton, later a prominent lawyer and journalist as well as reformer, had brought his bride, Elizabeth, with him. The Stantons had married in May 1840 at a ceremony in which the word "obey" had been omitted from the traditional vows at Elizabeth's insistence. In London, they met the merchant and Quaker leader James Mott and his wife, Lucretia Coffin Mott, both already well-known in abolitionist circles.

Despite protests by William Lloyd Garrison and other leading American antislavery advocates, the London convention refused to allow women to be seated as official delegates. The ladies were relegated to silence in the spectators' galleries behind a curtained grill. A majority of the convention delegates refused to allow the abolitionist women to participate entirely on grounds of their sex, a circumstance that outraged both Lucretia Mott and Elizabeth Stanton.

Denied access to the proceedings, the two women spent a great deal of time walking through London discussing not only the injustices suffered by slaves but those inflicted upon women. So fierce did Mrs. Mott's opposition become to the convention's exclusion of women that male delegates took to calling her the meeting's "lioness." As the older of

Susan B. Anthony, shown here in an early portrait, was possibly the leading women's rights advocate in nineteenth-century America. She began her lifelong activism on behalf of the movement in the years following Seneca Falls and continued steadily until her death in 1906. Her daring and tactical brilliance led some to call her "the Napoleon of the women's rights movement." (Meserve Collection)

the two women, forty-seven-year-old Lucretia Mott dominated her conversations with Elizabeth Stanton (then twenty-five), and educated her young friend in the problems women encountered when pursuing equal treatment in a male-dominated society.

Lucretia Mott had been raised in the sturdily independent environment of Nantucket, the New England fishing community, and had become first a teacher and then an "acknowledged minister" of the Society of Friends. Long before coming to London, Mrs. Mott had preached on a variety of reform concerns: antislavery, temperance, peace, and women's rights. She had helped to organize the American Anti-Slavery Society and served as president of Philadelphia's separate *female* antislavery society (which she had worked to bring into existence). At the time of the London convention, Mrs. Mott was probably the best-known woman in the American abolitionist movement. Her services as a speaker were prized by reform groups and Quaker meetings alike. Thus Lucretia Mott was the obvious person for the other four organizers to list as the featured speaker in the July 14, 1848, call for a women's rights convention at Seneca Falls.

Elizabeth Cady Stanton had been raised in a Johnstown, New York, household that was far more educated and worldly than the Nantucket

When Elizabeth Cady Stanton was ten, she wanted to take a scissors and cut out of her father Judge Cady's books "all the laws that make women cry." When she grew up, she did everything she could to abolish these laws. She died in 1902, hours after writing to President Theodore Roosevelt urging him to support woman's suffrage. (Brown Brothers)

family in which Lucretia Mott grew to adulthood. Elizabeth's father was a judge and her mother a member of the prominent New York Livingston family. The atmosphere at home was both highly religious and scholarly. Under the tutelage of a Presbyterian minister, Elizabeth studied at the Johnstown Academy, learning Greek, Latin, and mathematics. She then attended Emma Willard's "femle seminary" at Troy, New York, graduating in 1832. In later life, Elizabeth credited her earliest detailed knowledge of women's grievances to the hours spent as a child in her father's law office eavesdropping upon women while they unburdened to Judge Cady the many threads of abuse and discrimination in which they were tangled. Elizabeth also became close to a cousin interested in such matters, Gerrit Smith of Peterboro, New York, later a leading New York merchant and antislavery advocate, before meeting and marrying the reformer Henry Stanton.

As the two committed reformers, Mrs. Mott and Mrs. Stanton, reviewed their exclusion in London from the 1840 conference, they vowed that upon their return to the United States they would organize a women's rights convention. But the project became sidetracked as both women returned to their own communities and resumed their respective lives. At the time, the Stantons lived in Boston, while James and Lucretia

Mott were Philadelphians. Elizabeth began pursuing a career as a reformer, working for both temperance and antislavery groups while also laboring for several years along with other women's rights advocates in New York State to obtain enactment of a statute protecting married women's property rights which was finally passed by the legislature in 1848.

The turning point in Elizabeth Stanton's life came in 1846 when she and her husband moved to the isolated New York village of Seneca Falls, where she was deprived of the lively companionship and social amenities of Boston. Elizabeth, the judge's daughter with a classical education who had married intent upon somehow living in non-coercive domesticity, now found herself overwhelmed in upstate New York by personal isolation and household responsibilities as wife and mother. She watched herself grow daily more embittered by what she later described as a "general discontent" felt with "woman's portion as wife, mother, housekeeper, physician, and spiritual guide . . . [requiring] constant supervision . . . ." For the first time, the dilemmas she confronted as a member of the small educated minority of American women had merged with those of the ordinary, overworked female majority. It was at this point, Elizabeth Cady Stanton recalled, that she identified strongly with these women for the first time.

The sudden appearance in Watertown of her old friend and adviser,

This antifeminist 1851 lithograph, "Two of the Fe'he Males," ridiculed the comfortable, innovative mode of dress—jackets draped over loosely fitted "Turkish" trousers—which was advocated by Amelia Bloomer and other women's rights leaders. (Culver Pictures)

Lucretia Mott, triggered thoughts and feelings that Elizabeth Stanton had kept closely veiled until that unexpected tea time conclave. "My experiences at the World Anti-Slavery Convention, all I had read of the legal status of women, and the oppression I saw everywhere, together swept across my soul, intensified now by many personal experiences," Stanton would later write. "It seemed as if all the elements had conspired to impel me to some onward step. I could not see what to do or where to begin— my only thought was a public meeting for protest and discussion." Now that they had taken the initial step, however, Elizabeth and her four associates realized that they had yet to formulate a clear notion of what they hoped to achieve at the convention—assuming that anyone but their immediate circle actually showed up.

The women met again on Sunday morning, the 16th of July, this time in Mary Ann McClintock's parlor (without Jane Hunt) to draft proposals and resolutions for Wednesday's meeting. Recognizing that they lacked explicit models for organizing women's rights demands, they scanned reports and pamphlets issued by other reform groups—among them the proceedings of antislavery, peace, and temperance conventions—searching for usable examples upon which to pattern a description of the present condition and future aspirations of American women like themselves. In the end, none of the current examples seemed more suitable than the Declaration of Independence, which they then paraphrased skillfully into a "Declaration of Sentiments." The four women labored the entire day on their "Declaration" (see pp. 299–300).

Drafting a series of resolutions which embodied their call for complete equality of the sexes, resolutions that included a demand for women's right to vote, the four organizers concluded their preparations. The Motts planned a brief trip to Philadelphia before the meeting. Elizabeth Stanton and the other two local women returned to their homes, while the *Seneca County Courier*—and word-of-mouth—spread news of the impending convention throughout western New York. Three days remained until the opening session.

Plans for the meeting were suddenly threatened by domestic discord and unexpected illness. When Henry Stanton learned that Elizabeth intended to present the convention with an explicit demand that women receive the right to vote, and not simply with a general set of women's grievances, her normally sympathetic husband balked. Henry Stanton's convictions as a reformer did not extend to the "radical" doctrine of female suffrage, and he threatened to disavow the meeting and leave Seneca Falls for its duration if Elizabeth persisted in demanding the suffrage. When his wife refused to give ground, Stanton followed through on his threat, fleeing the town and returning to his family only after the convention.

When the Motts returned to Philadelphia, meanwhile, James was suddenly taken ill. Lucretia wrote her cohorts in New York explaining that because of this misfortune she and her husband might not be able to

Declaration of Sentiments

When, in the course of human events, it becomes necessary for one portion of the family of man to assume among the people of the earth a position different from that which they have hitherto occupied, but one to which the laws of nature and nature's God entitle them, a decent respect for the opinions of mankind requires that they should declare the causes that impel them to such a course.

We hold these truths to be self-evident: that all men and women are created equal; that they are endowed by their Creator with certain inalienable rights; that among these are life, liberty, and the pursuit of happiness . . .

The history of mankind is a history of repeated injuries and usurpations on the part of man toward woman, having in direct object the establishment of an absolute tyranny over her. To prove this, let facts be submitted to a candid world.

He has never permitted her to exercise her inalienable right to the elective franchise.

He has compelled her to submit to laws, in the formation of which she had no voice.

He has withheld from her rights which are given to the most ignorant and degraded men — both natives and foreigners.

. . . he has oppressed her on all sides.

He has made her, if married, in the eye of the law, civilly dead.

He has taken from her all right in property, even to the wages she earns.

He has made her, morally, an irresponsible being, as she can commit many crimes with impunity, provided they can be done in the presence of her husband.

In the covenant of marriage, she is compelled to promise obedience to her husband, he becoming, to all intents and purposes, her master . . . . He has monopolized nearly all the profitable employments, and . . . closes against her all the avenues to wealth and distinction which he considers most honorable to himself . . . .

He has denied her the facilities for obtaining a thorough education, all colleges being closed against her.

He allows her in Church, as well as State, but a subordinate position . . . .

He has created a false public sentiment by giving to the world a different code of morals for men and women, by which moral delinquencies which exclude women from society, are not only tolerated, but deemed of little account in man.

He has endeavoured, in every way that he could, to destroy her confidence in her own powers, to lessen her self-respect, and to make her willing to lead a dependent and abject life.

Now, in view of this entire disfranchisement of one-half the people of this country, their social and religious degradation — in view of the unjust laws above mentioned, and because women do feel themselves aggrieved, oppressed, and fraudulently deprived of their most sacred rights, we insist that they have immediate admission to all the rights and privileges which belong to them as citizens of the United States.

In entering upon the great work before us, we anticipate no small amount of misconception, misrepresentation, and ridicule; but we shall use every instrumentality within our power to effect our object. We shall employ agents, circulate tracts, petition the state and National legislatures, and endeavour to enlist the pulpit and press in our behalf. We hope this Convention will be followed by a series of Conventions embracing every part of the country.

attend the meeting. Without Mrs. Mott as the featured speaker, the organizers at Seneca Falls lacked a prominent attraction for their conclave. Besides, the women had hoped to use James Mott as chairman of the gathering, both because of his previous experience in such roles and because of their anxiety lest public reaction be overly hostile to a woman as chairman. As it turned out, James recovered in time, and the Motts showed up in Seneca Falls on the eve of the great day. Somewhat to Elizabeth's surprise, Lucretia Mott showed no more enthusiasm for raising the suffrage issue at the meeting than did Henry Stanton. In Mrs. Mott's case, however, the reason was tactical. She urged Mrs. Stanton to tread cautiously, lest the controversial issue of women voting distract public attention from more urgent women's rights problems demanding attention and action. Lucretia stated her complaint to Elizabeth in pithy terms: "Lizzie, thee will make us ridiculous. We must go slowly."

A crowd scene greeted the five delighted organizers at the Wesleyan Chapel on the first day of the convention. Dozens of carriages surrounded the church on the morning of July 19, and many more people, who had walked to attend the proceedings, stood waiting patiently for admission. They had come from every part of western New York. Among those who stood waiting for the meeting to open were a few of the most prominent figures in the reform community, men such as the black abolitionist Frederick Douglass, who published an antislavery newspaper called *The North Star* in the nearby city of Rochester. More than 250 women and at least forty men, the latter drawn to Seneca Falls by sympathy or curiosity, clustered around the chapel. Several of those present later recalled that they had expected to be among the few people daring enough—or foolhardy enough—to risk community disapproval and attend the convention, only to find to their astonishment that the single newspaper "call" had drawn a packed house.

To everyone's surprise, the chapel door proved to be locked, an act that turned out to be one of neglect and not hostility. A nephew of Mrs. Stanton's was hastily called into service, and he climbed through a window to unlock the entry door. The crowd pushed into the church, filling every seat, forcing the Seneca Falls organizers to change their planned format on the spot. They abandoned their earlier plan to bar men from the opening day's proceedings, which "proceeded" with an integrated audience: white and black, male and female. Without further ceremony, the speeches began.

James Mott chaired the meeting wearing his ordinary Quaker garb, his wife and other organizers having agreed (in Mrs. Stanton's words) that "this was an occasion when men might make themselves pre-eminently useful." One of the women, Mary McClintock, was appointed secretary after which Lucretia Mott rose to deliver the keynote oration. Mrs. Mott ranged eloquently on the far-reaching subject of women's "degraded condition . . . the world over," urging that a movement be started to "educate and elevate" women. But the most effective speaker that day proved to be Elizabeth Cady Stanton, despite her inexperience as a platform orator. "I

Y᷉ᴱ MAY SESSION OF Y᷉ᴱ WOMAN'S RIGHTS CONVENTION—Y᷉ᴱ ORATOR OF Y᷉ᴱ DAY DENOUNCING Y᷉ᴱ LORDS OF CREATION.

should feel exceedingly diffident to appear before you at this time, having never before spoken in public," she began, "were I not nerved by a sense of right and duty, did I not feel that the time had come for the question of woman's wrongs to be laid before the public, did I not believe that woman herself must do this work; for woman alone can understand the height, the depth, the length and the breadth of her degradation." (According to one local woman who attended, Mrs. Stanton could hardly be heard at first, so softly did she speak before gaining in confidence—and volume—as her talk continued. So recalled Amelia Bloomer, who then managed the Seneca Falls post office with her husband but who would shortly make her own career as a feminist.)

Mrs. Stanton read the Declaration of Sentiments previously prepared by the organizers plus an accompanying series of resolutions which the five women hoped the convention would adopt. Following her to the pulpit were other speakers who described the property bill for married women that the New York legislature had passed and reviewed the discussion of women's rights at a recently held state constitutional convention. A young law student, Samuel Tillman, "read a series of the most exasperating statutes for women, from English and American jurists, all reflecting the *tender mercies* of men toward their wives, in taking care of their property and protecting them in their civil rights." The audience responded enthusiastically to all the speakers.

This nineteenth-century print satirizes the proceedings at the Seneca Falls convention. (Library of Congress)

The hundreds who jammed into Wesleyan Chapel seemed to agree on every issue but one. When the Declaration of Sentiments was read, the assemblage adopted it with only minor changes in wording. The convention than adopted all but *one* of the resolutions without protest. It went on record urging women's equality in all spheres of society, revision of laws that discriminated against women, opportunities for education and vocational advancement for women, and acceptance of female equality in "capabilities and responsibilities." The Seneca Falls gathering also demanded in those same resolutions that women gain the right to enter the universities, enjoy complete equality within marriage, have control over their property, and equal status in the courts among other rights.

Only Resolution Nine stirred passionate debate during the meeting: "*Resolved,* That it is the duty of the women of this country to secure for themselves their sacred right to the elective franchise." Opponents of the resolution feared that an immediate demand for women's suffrage would provoke public ridicule and stir animosity toward *all* feminist demands, including those that lay within reach more easily. The resolution's main supporters included Mrs. Stanton and Frederick Douglass, whose outspoken speech urging its passage probably swayed a number of those present to favor the resolution. Douglass believed that obtaining the vote would prove decisive in forcing gains on every other women's rights demand. After an extended round of angry debate, Resolution Nine passed by a small majority. At the meeting's conclusion, only one hundred people (sixty-eight women and thirty-two men), one-third of those attending, signed the Seneca Falls Declaration of Principles which incorporated (among other resolutions) the controversial suffrage proposal. Even some of these would later remove their names and disassociate themselves from the declaration, once opponents of women's rights gathered force. Elizabeth Cady Stanton's own father rushed to Seneca Falls after reading about the convention and pleaded with his daughter to disavow her own handiwork. She refused, firmly and absolutely.

Although the two days of discussion and debate at Seneca Falls had continued well into the evenings, the convention adjourned on July 20 without having completed all items on its agenda. The delegates voted to reconvene two weeks later in Frederick Douglass's home city of Rochester. Once the Seneca Falls proceedings were published and distributed, a firestorm of complaints against the actions there filled editorial and letter columns in newspapers throughout the East. In almost every Seneca Falls church as well as in pulpits throughout the state, clergymen denounced the women—and their male supporters—who had arranged the convention. The complaints centered on the efforts by women's rights reformers, in the eyes of their opponents, to "unsex" American females and to destroy the sanctity of traditional women's roles and obligations. Unfortunately for the antifeminists, however, even as they denounced the Seneca Falls convention, they could not help publicizing the work done there—including its now notorious Declaration of Sentiments and the accompanying resolutions. The Declaration of Sentiments was "a most amusing document," explained the New York *Herald.* "The amusing part is the preamble where they asserted their equality." Many women learned for the first time of the new reform movement through journalists' and clergymen's bitter attacks upon its handiwork.

When the convention reassembled at Rochester on August 2, the Unitarian Church which served as its headquarters was as crowded as the Wesleyan Chapel had been at Seneca Falls. At the start, three of the initial contingent of organizers—Mary McClintock, Lucretia Mott, and Elizabeth Stanton—found themselves locked in bitter disagreement with an even bolder and more "radical" stroke taken by a majority of those who arranged the Rochester meeting. The Rochester contingent insisted upon electing a *woman* to chair the convention and an exclusive slate of women to serve in all other official roles at the meeting. Neither Mrs. Mott nor Mrs. Stanton, however, felt persuaded that a woman could prove effective in presiding over such a large, lively, and possibly unruly gathering. "To our great surprise," deadpanned the official "Report" of the Rochester convention, "two or three . . . women, glorious reformers, well deserving the name, coming from a distance to attend the meeting, at first refused to take their seats upon the platform, or otherwise co-operate with the Convention" if Abigail Bush—the person selected as "president" to preside over the meeting—served in that capacity. Lucretia Mott and Elizabeth Cady Stanton actually threatened to leave the convention, a step that would have left the fledgling movement in disarray, but the two women eventually backed down and remained. Before doing so, they listened to some opening remarks by the person whom the Report would describe as "our gentle but heroic President" Bush.

The meeting began with a prayer. The Report continues: "The minutes of the preliminary meeting [at Seneca Falls] were then read by SARAH L. HALLOWELL, at which time much anxiety was manifested concerning the low voices of the women, and whenever reading or speaking was attempted, without giving time for adapting the voice to the size of the house, cries of 'louder,' 'louder,' 'louder,' nearly drowned every other sound." Unlike the Seneca Falls experience, there were clearly some hecklers in the crowd in Rochester, possibly bent upon disrupting the convention.

At that point, although untested in her ability to maintain control over an orderly meeting, President Abigail Bush rose to quell the complainers: "Friends," she began, "we present ourselves here before you, as an oppressed class, with trembling frames and faltering tongues, and we do not expect to be able to speak so as to be heard by all at first, but we trust we shall have the sympathy of the audience, and that you will bear with our weakness, now in the infancy of the movement. Our trust in the omnipotency of right is our only faith that we shall succeed."

Whether Abigail Bush's eloquent opening words stilled the complaints or whether the succeeding speakers managed to pitch their voices louder remains unclear. The remainder of the Rochester meeting proceeded without serious incident, however, though not without an occasional heckler. By now, the speeches must have seemed familiar to veterans of the Seneca Falls meeting. Lucretia Mott rose to defend men against

The photo portrays vividly several generations of women's rights leaders. In the front row are Susan B. Anthony (second from left) and Elizabeth Cady Stanton (fourth from left). (Culver Pictures)

the accusation raised by some women's advocates that they were innately malevolent and oppressive: man, she avowed, "was not a tyrant by nature, but had been made tyrannical by the power which had, by general consent, been conferred upon him." A letter from Elizabeth Stanton's cousin, the abolitionist Gerrit Smith, commending the gathering became part of the official record. Elizabeth read once more the Declaration of Sentiments adopted at Seneca Falls which the Rochester meeting proceeded to adopt as its own. At that point, "a Mr. COLTON, of Connecticut," though miles from his own home, rose to express the hope that woman would remain in *her* home—"her empire and her throne"—rather than try to occupy the pulpit: "He loved the ladies as well as they loved themselves, but he would not have woman exceed her proper sphere . . . engaging in the strife and contention of the political world." Lucretia Mott rose to reply, noting that Colton thought too much of the clergy's pulpit and not enough of the Bible which, she asserted, "had none of the prohibitions in regard to women" as religious teachers. Several speakers complained about allowing women to vote, but Frederick Douglass again delivered an impassioned defense both of women's suffrage and of the feminist struggle for full equality.

Douglass had hardly returned to his seat when a recently married woman named Rebecca M. Sandford stepped forward to the altar and asked whether she might not say a few words. The audience listened attentively as the young bride, who had never before participated in any reform activity, described how she had been on her way west with her husband when she learned of the Rochester convention. The couple had arranged later train transportation so that they could attend the gathering (as she spoke, her husband stood near her and listened with evident approval).

With unstudied eloquence, Rebecca pleaded for both the abolition of slavery and the achievement of women's rights, linking the two "emancipations" as they had been tied in the minds of many American and British reformers. Mrs. Sandford's primary theme was *women's* emancipation:

> Give her the privilege to cooperate in making the laws she submits to, and there will be harmony without severity, and justice without oppression. Make her, if married, a *living being* in the eye of the law — she will not assume beyond duty; give her right of property, and you may justly tax her patrimony as the result of her wages. Open to her your colleges — your legislative, your municipal, your domestic laws may be purified and ennobled. *Forbid her not,* and she will use moderation.

When Mrs. Sandford stepped down, the audience had been stirred as no professional speaker could have done on that occasion. "It was a scene never to be forgotten," Elizabeth Stanton recalled, and it suggested the way in which the cause of women's rights had begun to influence ordinary women normally outside the circles and concerns of avid reformers.

The speeches continued as did the bristling rejoinders by anti-feminists who had come to harass. That evening a Mr. Sulley, for example, demanded to know who would decide matters when husband and wife disagreed, if each family had *two* heads. Did not St. Paul, he demanded to know, "strictly enjoin obedience to husbands, and that man shall be head of the woman?" Mrs. Mott appeared to have been waiting for the inevitable question about St. Paul's instructions, and she plunged into the argument. Among Quakers, Lucretia Mott pointed out, the absence of a promise of *obedience* in the marriage ceremony had never raised difficulties as long as "an appeal to reason" was possible. As for the Apostle Paul, she argued, "many of the opposers of Woman's Rights, who bid us to obey the bachelor, St. Paul, themselves reject his counsel — he advised us not to marry."

But who should hold the property in a family, one Mr. Pickard queried, "and whose name should be retained" after marriage. Elizabeth Stanton responded to Pickard, arguing that the Bible, if "rightly understood, pointed to a oneness of equality, not subordination, and . . . property should be jointly held." She also questioned the appropriateness under all circumstances of taking one's husband's name upon marriage, attacking the custom as a "main reason for woman's inferior status." Fortunately, the exuberant Mrs. Stanton did not attempt to include that argument in any of the convention's resolutions. At the time, it might have provoked debate as heated as a suffrage resolution. Before adjourning, the Rochester gathering endorsed a set of resolves comparable to those adopted at Seneca Falls — again including one that urged the vote for women.

Other women's rights conventions followed in the next few years, spreading from New York State to Massachusetts in 1850, Indiana in 1851, Pennsylvania in 1852, and elsewhere throughout the North. As the

Susan B. Anthony (standing) and Elizabeth Cady Stanton, friends and associates in the women's rights movement, photographed during the early 1890s, after more than four decades of struggle on behalf of their cause. (Library of Congress)

movement spread and gained adherents, so did the anti-feminist opposition become more fervent. When the Massachusetts Women's Rights Convention met at Worcester in 1850 — jeeringly attacked in the press by opponents as the "Hen Convention" — one minister warned his parishioners that he would expel anyone caught attending the meeting. Those who came listened to a number of speakers, among them the militant black abolitionist Sojourner Truth, who demanded direct action to gain equality: "If women want any rights more'n they've got," she exclaimed, "why don't they just take 'em and not be talking about it."

During the 1850s, Sojourner Truth, Susan B. Anthony, Lucy Stone, Elizabeth Cady Stanton, Lucretia Mott, and a growing number of activists spread the gospel of women's rights across the nation through meetings and rallies, mixing their advocacy of equality for women with demands for other reforms, especially the abolition of slavery. None proved so adept, yet direct, in stirring audiences for *both* pivots of American reform — *both* "emancipations" — as Sojourner Truth, as when she stared down into an Akron, Ohio, women's rights gathering in 1851, raised her bare hand in the air, and exclaimed:

Look at my arm! I have ploughed and planted and gathered into barns, and no man could head me — and ain't I a woman? I could work as much and eat as much as a man — when I could get it — and bear the lash as well! And

Abolitionist orator Sojourner Truth, born a slave named Isabella in 1797 in upstate New York, traveled widely as a speaker for antislavery. An itinerant preacher, mystic, and former domestic, she drew great crowds with her statuesque bearing, resonant voice, and fervent denunciation of slavery. (Brown Brothers)

ain't I a woman? I have borne thirteen children, and seen most of 'em sold into slavery, and when I cried out with my mother's grief, none but Jesus heard me—and ain't I a woman?

None of the organizers of that first women's rights convention at Seneca Falls lived to witness the triumph of their disputed Resolution Nine on women's suffrage. Attending that meeting, however, unnoticed by the more prominent persons in the audience, was a nineteen-year-old farm girl named Charlotte Woodward. Attracted by the convention's announcement in the *Seneca County Courier,* Charlotte rode off to the meeting in a farm wagon along with some friends and watched the entire two days' proceedings quietly from a back-row seat. Charlotte never spoke but, at the convention's end, strode forward to sign the Declaration of Sentiments and its accompanying resolutions. Pressures from hostile family members, ministers, and newspaper editorialists in the days that followed the Wesleyan Chapel convention led a number of signers to withdraw their names from the declaration. Not Charlotte. She stood firm and remained committed to women's rights for the remainder of her life. At the close of that life, in 1920, after the Nineteenth Amendment guaranteeing woman's suffrage had been ratified, ninety-one-year-old Charlotte Woodward—the sole survivor of Seneca Falls—finally voted for a president.

16 Religion and Reform in Antebellum America

Religion and the various reform causes were inseparably linked during the decades prior to the Civil War. Often religious motivation explained those individuals who chose to devote themselves to one or another reform activity, as when Lucretia and James Mott expressed their Quaker antislavery convictions through participation in the abolitionist movement. Devout Protestants from all denominations joined the ranks of antislavery, women's rights, temperance, peace, and other reform movements. Reformers regularly cited biblical texts and arguments as justifications for the various social changes they sought—this occurred throughout the Seneca Falls and Rochester conventions—and such arguments were crucial, considering the strong religious orientation of most Americans who fought in the antebellum era for major reforms within their country.

Nor could it be otherwise, at a time when for the great majority of persons, the Bible remained the ultimate and most meaningful moral guide. During the first half of the nineteenth century, Americans paid more serious attention to religion than at any other time in their history except, possibly, in seventeenth-century Puritan New England. Between the Revolution and the Civil War, while American nationality was shaped and institutionalized, Americans (which at the time meant primarily Protestants) grappled with problems of God and country. For many, those problems were inseparable.

As the eighteenth century ended, American religiosity seemed on the wane. Many of the nation's leaders (Jefferson and Franklin, among others), had embraced the religion of Reason. Deism represented an attempt to bypass orthodox forms of religion. It substituted, instead, belief in an imprecise God who had created a very precise universe. To orthodox Christians—whether Congregationalists in New England or Episcopalians in the South—deism meant little more than atheism sugar-coated with spirituality. During the election of 1800, Jefferson's religion (or lack of it) became a campaign issue, though not enough of a negative factor to cost him the presidency.

THE SECOND GREAT AWAKENING

Americans in that era were experiencing a remarkable and wide-ranging religious experience called the Great Revival (or the Second Great Awakening). Beginning in the late 1790s, a wave of religious enthusiasm swept most of the country. Revival meetings, especially those in the frontier states west of the Appalachian Mountains, converted thousands and attracted much attention. In the West, as open a society as then existed in the United States, older, more established religious customs and doctrines gave way to an exuberant religiosity. Preachers stressed a gospel of salvation, and thousands responded with conversions and commitments that, although sometimes short-lived, were nonetheless sincere.

The Great Revival fundamentally altered American Protestantism. Sixty years earlier, during the First Great Awakening, itinerant preachers in countryside and city had been able to rekindle some of the fire of Calvinism, with its doctrine of election and predestination. But by the time of the Great Revival, American Calvinists (found mainly in the Congregationalist and Presbyterian churches by this time) saw doctrinal purity replaced for many of their number by the happier promise of eternal life. Denominations such as the

This highly emotional revival meeting resembled thousands of such meetings that took place throughout the United States during the antebellum era. Many were marked by numerous conversion experiences that increased the membership of newer, evangelical Protestant sects. The great revivals of the early-nineteenth century decreased the influence of older, more established religious groups. (Courtesy, The New York Historical Society)

Baptists and Methodists offered salvation. No longer need one live with the terrible uncertainties of Calvinist damnation hanging over one's head. A positive commitment to God could bring, if not the certainty, then at least the probability of salvation. Men and women could become active instruments of their own salvation. Works, not faith alone, counted for something in the great scoreboard in the sky.

Even more startling, preachers began telling Americans that God *wanted* them to be saved, that God meant love. Hellfire and damnation preaching did not become outdated, as evidenced by the conduct of some evangelical preachers who warned of terrible things in store for those resisting God's message. Yet if hell still existed and eternal damnation still threatened, believers also knew that God was in heaven, gladly awaiting the arrival of the saints.

Unitarianism

The replacement of the Puritan God of wrath by a gentler God of love also helped create several new sects. Though hardly a mass movement, Unitarianism was one of the most important. It began late in the 1700s, in Boston and in outlying Congregationalist churches, and won many followers among well-educated middle-class New Englanders early in the nineteenth century.

In 1803 a Unitarian gained appointment to the professorship of divinity at Harvard College. The struggle for the post clearly revealed the split between religious reformers and the more orthodox Calvinists in New England. Unitarianism included several beliefs that more orthodox Protestants could not accept. First, as their name indicates, Unitarians rejected the Trinity, believing Jesus to be a great religious teacher but not the son of God. Unitarians denied original sin, insisting on mankind's innate goodness and stressing the human capacity for moral improvement. Their most prominent leader, William Ellery Channing of Boston, preached the Unitarian message with a clarity and benevolence that made him a national figure. He was also involved in a variety of reform activities, as were many of the leading Unitarian preachers.

Transcendentalism

The best known of these preachers, Ralph Waldo Emerson, went beyond Unitarianism to expound ideas that made him *the* popular philosopher of nineteenth-century America. Unitarians fostered a belief in the potentially divine character of human life. Beginning with this conviction, Emerson and a number of intellectuals in the Boston area developed the philosophy called transcendentalism, forming a Transcendental Club that remained small in numbers but culturally influential. During the early 1840s Ralph Waldo Emerson, Margaret Fuller, Henry David Thoreau, and other transcendalists published a journal of literature and the arts, The *Dial*, that offered an effective sounding board for these religious and philosophical rebels.

Transcendentalists believed in mankind's natural goodness and perfectibility, and in the active presence of a divine spirit within each human being. God lived within each individual. This meant that everyone remained open to direct moral guidance. In effect, each person became his or her own church. There was no need for actual churches or ministers to mediate in the search for God. "Why should not we enjoy an original relation to the universe?" Emerson wrote in his book *Nature*, published in 1836. "There are new lands, new men, new thoughts. Let us demand our own

works and laws and worship." According to transcendentalist doctrines, each person possessed an "oversoul," an inner soul or spirit, which, when correctly instructed by divine insight, would point the way to perfection and salvation.

Yet, Unitarianism was too geographically restricted and transcendentalism too highbrow to affect the lives of most Americans. Emerson became a successful lecturer and a nationally known personality, but probably no more than a handful of his listeners understood his explanations of the oversoul. A far more numerous group of Americans responded to what today would be called "old-time religion"—a blend of evangelical fervor and strenuous piety, of joyous commitment combined with intolerance toward sin and sinners.

Revivalism

These religious currents converged with spectacular results in New York State's "burned-over district." There, in central and western New York, site of the Seneca Falls convention and many others, evangelical American Protestantism flowered as never before. Starting in the early years of the nineteenth century, when the region was still sparsely settled, revivalism steadily gathered strength. By the 1830s it had peaked in new cities of the area, such as Rochester and Buffalo. The religious ferment of the burned-over district involved a diluting, almost a breaking down, of older organizational forms. In "the district," Presbyterians and Congregationalists joined together in a short-lived merger, and the denominational label of a revivalist preacher counted for less than the force of his message (sometimes *her* message—since a few women were able to break through the sex barrier and do some of the preaching). A Baptist might exhort in a Presbyterian church, and vice versa. Although conservative clergymen were less than happy when the revivalists came to their areas, there was no way to contain the enthusiasm of their congregations.

Among the revivalist preachers were those who believed that Christ was preparing momentarily for his second coming. Ministers who followed this biblical interpretation, sometimes known as Adventism, crisscrossed the northeast-

Charles Grandison Finney was among the best-known and most influential evangelical preachers of the Second Great Awakening. He toured central and western New York in the 1820s, then turned his attention to the cities in the 1830s. (Brown Brothers)

ern United States, attracting between 50,000 and 100,000 Americans—possibly even more—to their vision of the Last Judgment's imminence. Although *most* Adventist ministers avoided assigning a precise date to the event, one controversial group had no uncertainty on this score. They were known as the Millerites, organized by a New York farmer and self-taught preacher named William Miller, assisted by the Reverend Joshua V. Himes. The Millerites became a major force throughout New England and upstate New York during the early 1840s, attracting thousands of followers. But the sect lost most of its adherents after two judgment days that it had predicted—one in 1843 and another the next year—failed to terminate the world. The Adventist movement, however, has remained one of American Protestantism's most vigorous components from that period to the present.

New York's burned-over district produced

the greatest revival preacher of his day, a man named Charles G. Finney. Finney was originally a skeptic. He had decided to study law. But a pious fiancée and a gnawing belief that "lawyering" was not an *honest* profession turned him toward the ministry. He began preaching in the small towns of central and northern New York, riding circuit, just as lawyers did. Finney attracted larger and larger audiences and won many converts. Finney became pastor of the Second Free Presbyterian Church of New York City in 1832 and ran it successfully—gaining many converts—until he withdrew in 1836. The following year, he helped establish a theological department at the antislavery college newly founded at Oberlin, Ohio, where he remained for more than three decades. His was not a fire-and-brimstone approach; it was a hopeful message, though not a simple-minded one. Finney, like many other clerics of his day, tried to retain the pious intensity of Calvinism while discarding some of its more rigid theological doctrines. The attempt was doomed, but the effort shaped the contours of much of modern American Protestantism.

Finney, along with many other evangelical ministers of the nineteenth century, stressed the importance, for churches and their members, of good works and constant involvement in practical morality. Finney himself, like the more decorous Bostonian Reverend Channing, ended his days as a strong antislavery reformer. One of Finney's many converts, Theodore Weld, became a leading abolitionist.

Mormonism

Charles Finney was thoroughly conventional when compared with Joseph Smith, founder of the Mormon church—another product of the burned-over district. Young Smith, born in 1805, became a part-time gold digger, one who could supposedly divine the location of buried gold. Soon, Smith struck it rich beyond his wildest dream. According to Smith, an angel appeared to reveal the location of a book written on gold pages and in a strange script. In the late 1820s Smith translated the text, he said, while fellow believers transcribed what he dictated.

Born in Vermont and raised in New York, Joseph Smith underwent a revelation and founded the Church of Jesus Christ of the Latter Day Saints (Mormon). Persecuted at every turn, Mormons moved west to Ohio, Michigan, Missouri, and Illinois, where Smith was murdered by an anti-Mormon mob in 1844.

The result, the Book of Mormon, is today the sacred text for the Church of Jesus Christ of the Latter-Day Saints, founded in 1830 in Seneca County, New York. Mormons had to withstand the scorn of unbelievers, but in the case of Smith and his followers, opposition was much more extreme. The Mormons left New York in 1831 and, like many thousands of others, went west, first to Ohio, then to Missouri, and, in 1839, established the Mormon town of Nauvoo in Illinois. But there would be no peace even there. With economic rivalry as an underlying cause, and opposition to Smith's next major revelation (polygamy) as the

stated objection, an Illinois mob set upon and murdered Smith in 1844. The Mormons, now led by Brigham Young, then pushed still farther westward and settled in Utah near the Great Salt Lake.

Anti-Catholic Nativism

Mormons were not the only religious minority to fall victim to violence at the hands of rejuvenated, militant Protestant Americans. Although the United States legally proclaimed religious freedom, and although church and state had been separated, toleration did not imply acceptance. At times, even toleration was lacking. The status of Catholics had remained an uneasy one, for example, since colonial times. As more and more Catholic immigrants arrived in the early nineteenth century, Protestants (who, often as not, fought the good fight against one another) could unite temporarily in opposition to Catholics. The idea of a vast Papist conspiracy against Protestant America, which had strong roots in the colonial

Brigham Young took over leadership of the Mormon Church after Smith's death. He led the arduous, but successful, move to the new Mormon Zion near Utah's Great Salt Lake. (The Bettmann Archive)

era's anti-Catholicism, began to spread. During the 1830s, small but insistent "nativist" movements sprang up in Eastern cities. The groups denounced Catholicism as un-American, criticized unrestricted immigration from Catholic countries, and were particularly angered by the ease with which immigrant Americans could gain the vote. Samuel F. B. Morse, better known as the inventor of the telegraph than as a nativist, led one such group in New York City.

For the most part, anti-Catholicism during the 1830s remained nonviolent, with one notable exception: in 1834, the good citizens of the Boston area burned down a Catholic convent in Charlestown. No lives were lost, but the crowd's murderous fury demonstrated once again that religious passion can sometimes lose all restraint. The Charlestown outrage foreshadowed the much more vigorous nativist movement that afflicted America in the 1850s, following the massive Irish and German Catholic immigration of 1847–56. A relatively minor Catholic population in the United States of slightly over 300,000 in 1830 had grown to more than 3 million by 1860, most of the newcomers impoverished and uneducated Irish and Germans who settled in the cities.

Conflicts between the largely working-class Catholic population of the urban North during the 1830–60 period and the Protestant native-born majority focused often on the question of public school education. In state after state, Protestant nativists fought successfully to deny public funding to Catholic denominational schools. These victories had the effect of leaving the public schools nominally nonsectarian but, in fact, strongly Protestant (often evangelical) in moral orientation. Such practices as regular study of and readings from the King James Bible, for example, were common in the nominally "secular" public schools. Catholics proved less successful in gaining a share of tax revenues for schools in which their doctrines would be taught with public funds. Instead, a number of states during the 1840s embarked on a program of developing a privately financed system of parochial school education (based on tuition payments and the contributions of the faithful). This program would provide religious training along with secular teaching—but within schools run by the Catholic church, so that American-born Catholic youths could be shielded in their formative years from the educational influences of the predominately Protestant culture.

SOCIAL CRUSADES OF ANTEBELLUM AMERICA

Background and Motivation of Reformers

What brought the "delegates," men and women alike, to Seneca Falls? What led people to try to change so many of their society's customs and institutions? One important factor was the widespread belief in progress. Many Americans during the antebellum decades came to feel that progress was apparent in all areas of national life. They believed that rapid economic growth could be matched by steady improvement in society and values.

The belief in a divine mission for America had been understood in religious terms by the seventeenth-century Puritans. Eighteenth-century American leaders had thought of it largely in political terms. Now it was seen in social terms by nineteenth-century antebellum reformers. They wanted to liberate Americans by correcting personal defects and eliminating social wrongs. They aimed at achieving *worldly* perfection within the nation itself (not the celestial perfection of evangelical Protestants) and in their own lifetimes. Most reformers believed that, in the struggle to perfect American life, they would also achieve their own moral perfection.

This utopian dream was certainly not confined to the United States at this time. American reformers borrowed ideas from (and corresponded regularly with) their counterparts in Europe. For example, American abolitionists learned much from the British movement to abolish slavery. Many American reformers, especially the Utopians, were influenced by French socialist-communitarian thinkers. Generally, though, the American reformers resembled religious crusaders more than their European counterparts did. American reform was closely connected to the evangelical

Ralph Waldo Emerson

In the history of American writing, the Jacksonian period was a very special moment. In the life span of a single generation, a dazzling new literature burst suddenly into view. The novels of James Fenimore Cooper, Nathaniel Hawthorne, and Herman Melville constituted as fine a body of fiction as was being produced in any nation in the world. Henry David Thoreau's *Walden* and Walt Whitman's *Leaves of Grass* took their places among the most imposing works of art in the English language. Indeed, what Noah Webster and other intellectuals had yearned for so much at the beginning of the century—a new, authentic, and distinctive American culture—was, by mid-century, a flourishing reality.

At the center of this exciting phenomenon stood a quiet, even shy, former Unitarian minister, Ralph Waldo Emerson. He was not as popular a writer as was Cooper. He produced no single work of art as lastingly important as *Leaves of Grass.* But Emerson had a special significance. In his lectures, his essays, and his poems, he brought together all the principal themes and questions that preoccupied the major intellectuals of the period. And because of this, some of his essays became a bible of sorts for young Americans who decided to pursue careers as writers, poets, reformers, or philosophers. Emerson's life—first as a Boston minister, then as a free-lance writer and lecturer living in Concord—was extremely quiet. But he carried on an intense internal struggle—a struggle of ideas and symbols. From this struggle, and from the famous *Journals* where he recorded it, came radical positions on the primary issues of the century—radical positions which themselves soon became a new orthodoxy among writers and artists.

Emerson's radicalism, which he announced in controversial lectures and essays in the 1830s and 1840s, was primarily a radicalism of celebration. He celebrated "Nature" as against "civilization." He was the philosopher and the poet of the "self-reliant" individual. And against the legitimate needs of such an individual, Emerson counted the requirements of society very little. He praised instinct, intuition, experiment, and freedom. He condemned dry logic, routine, and law. He wrote excitedly about whatever was new and young, and he talked constantly of escape from the "sepulchres of the fathers" and the "dry bones of the past." And these commitments led directly and obviously to a celebration of what was "American," and to the repudiation of much of what was "European."

From all this, Emerson's readers could draw a clear and somewhat radical picture of an ideal "American scholar"—as Emerson called the writer. He should plant himself firmly on his own private instincts. He should have no reverence for established customs, and no patience with law. He should be young, and if he could not be young, he should side with the young in almost everything. He should ruthlessly question every rule and institution to see whether they were in tune with "Nature." He should be innovative and daring, always ready to risk public criticism and rejection. And the scholar should do all these things in an acute and continuing consciousness of his identity as an American.

As Emerson put it in his most popular lecture, "Trust thyself: every heart vibrates to that iron string. Whoso would be a man, must be a nonconformist. A foolish consistency is the hobgoblin of little minds, adored by little statesmen and philosophers and divines."

Protestant movements of the day. Nevertheless, although religion and reform were indeed linked, antebellum reform had a distinctly *this*-worldly tone in its concentration on altering existing human institutions or creating new and improved models.

Many Americans lent part-time support to one or another reform activity, but a small number of people devoted their entire lives to the task of achieving social perfection. The dedicated reformer emerged during the 1830s and 1840s as a distinct social type in the United States. Men and women pursued reform as a vocation, especially in New England (no longer Puritan but still puritanical) and to a lesser extent in the Middle Atlantic and Middle Western states. The novelist Nathaniel Hawthorne was once such a reformer. He wrote:

> We were of all creeds and opinions, and generally tolerant of all, on every imaginable subject. Our bond, it seems to me, was not affirmative, but negative. We had individually found one thing or another to quarrel with in our past life, and were pretty well agreed on the futility of lumbering along with the old system any further. As for what should be substituted, there was much less agreement.

Hawthorne raised a question that many have asked about American reformers: Why did some people try to change society while a majority of their countrymen remained content to tolerate existing conditions? What were the reformers' motives? The answers have been as varied as the reform activities themselves. Unfriendly observers and skeptical historians have identified antebellum reform with the personal frustrations or unfulfilled ambitions of the reformers, with psychological or emotional disturbance, even with derangement. Enthusiasts have responded that intense commitment, even fanaticism, is a praiseworthy reaction in the face of evil or in response to obvious social problems.

Although the motivation of each individual reformer can be judged only on its own merits, it is helpful to remember that the antebellum American reform movements occurred during an unsettled period. The economy was undergoing rapid change. A new transportation network of roads, canals, and, later, railroads was opening up the American West to mass settlement. This meant that Western farmers could have access to Eastern or even overseas markets—markets that offered tremendous opportunities for both economic growth and crises, as when the economy plummeted downward in the panics of 1837 and 1857. At the same time industry grew. That growth, in turn, created demands for cheap, reliable labor in the new factories.

At first, Americans naively thought that industrialism could be fostered in a happy, benign atmosphere, free from the horrors of the Industrial Revolution in Britain: the New World would, in this regard as in all others, instruct the Old. The capitalists who owned the textile mills in Lowell, Massachusetts, thought (like Voltaire's Dr. Pangloss) that theirs could be the "best of all possible worlds," with happy young female workers making cotton cloth and happy factory owners making money. It worked for a while, from the 1820s to about the mid-1830s. But economic downturn, wage cuts, strikes, and the replacement of Yankee mill hands with more easily bossed Irish immigrants put an end to the Lowell dream—though not to the growth of industry or profit making.

Antebellum America was a society in motion. Thousands of people were moving westward. Many hundreds of thousands were moving into the fast-growing cities, where social problems, being more concentrated, were also becoming more visible. Boatloads of immigrants, expectant and exploitable, arrived daily during the 1840s and 1850s. Whatever the personal factors involved, whatever the motivation—philanthropy or arrogance—no reforming spirit could remain unaffected by at least some of these developments.

The Cold Water Army

On the night of April 2, 1840, six friends met at a Baltimore tavern, as was their custom, and prepared for a night of hard drinking. Nearby, at a local church, a temperance advocate prepared to deliver a sermon on the evils of alcohol. As a lark, the six decided to attend the lecture—and these sinners who came to scoff remained to pray. Afterward, they organized the Washington Temperance Society, the parent organization of a loose-knit network of prohibition societies that spread to

From a sip to a shot. The inevitable progress of the drinker, as pictured by the temperance advocates. (Fruitlands Museum, Harvard, Massachusetts)

most parts of the country and challenged the legitimacy of "demon rum" eighty years before the prohibition era of the Roaring Twenties.

The fervor of the Protestant crusade of 1800–60, and its potential both as a reforming factor and as a method of social control, is amply illustrated in the crusade for temperance. At first, "temperance" did not necessarily mean prohibition. For one thing, Americans of the colonial and early national periods were a hard-drinking lot. Wheat and rye were plentiful and cheap. So was corn. Rather than let those crops rot once their normal markets had been exhausted, American farmers generally turned them into liquor. The home "still" was as much a part of a well-run American

DEVELOPMENTS IN TECHNOLOGY, 1750-1860
(DATES REFER TO PATENT OR FIRST SUCCESSFUL USE)

YEAR		CONTRIBUTION	IMPORTANCE/DESCRIPTION
1750	Benjamin Franklin	LIGHTNING ROD	Protected buildings against damage from electrical storms.
1775	David Bushnell	SUBMARINE	First American submarine; submerged by taking water into tanks and surfaced when water was pumped out.
1787	John Fitch	STEAMBOAT	First successful American steamboat.
1793	Eli Whitney	COTTON GIN	Simplified process of separating fiber from seeds; helped make cotton a profitable staple of Southern agriculture.
1798	Eli Whitney	JIG FOR GUIDING TOOLS	Facilitated manufacture of interchangeable parts.
1802	Oliver Evans	STEAM ENGINE	First American steam engine; led to manufacture of high-pressure engines used throughout eastern United States.
1813	Richard B. Chenaworth	CAST-IRON PLOW	First iron plow to be made in three separate pieces, thus making possible replacement of parts.
1830	Peter Cooper	RAILROAD LOCOMOTIVE	First steam locomotive built in America.
1831	Cyrus McCormick	REAPER	Mechanized harvesting; early model could cut six acres of grain a day.
1836	Samuel Colt	REVOLVER	First successful repeating pistol.
1837	John Deere	STEEL PLOW	Steel surface kept soil from sticking; farming thus made easier on rich prairies of Middle West.
1839	Charles Goodyear	VULCANIZATION OF RUBBER	Made rubber much more useful by preventing it from sticking and melting in hot weather.
1842	Crawford W. Long	FIRST ADMINISTERED ETHER IN SURGERY	Reduced pain and risk of shock during operations.
1844	Samuel F. B. Morse	TELEGRAPH	Made long-distance communication almost instantaneous.
1846	Elias Howe	SEWING MACHINE	First practical machine for automatic sewing.
1846	Norbert Rillieux	VACUUM EVAPORATOR	Improved method of removing water from sugar cane; revolutionized sugar industry and was later applied to many other products.
1847	Richard M. Hoe	ROTARY PRINTING PRESS	Printed an entire sheet in one motion, vastly speeded up printing process.
1851	William Kelly	"AIR-BOILING PROCESS"	Improved method of converting iron into steel (usually known as Bessemer process because English inventor had more advantageous patent and financial arrangements).
1853	Elisha G. Otis	PASSENGER ELEVATOR	Improved movement in buildings; when later electrified, stimulated development of skyscrapers.
1859	Edwin L. Drake	FIRST AMERICAN OIL WELL	Initiated oil industry in the United States.
1859	George M. Pullman	PULLMAN CAR	First sleeping-car suitable for long-distance travel.

farm as the grist mill. Anyone seeking to control or limit the production and consumption of alcoholic beverages in America obviously would have a difficult task.

Early temperance advocates hoped to rely on persuasion, and they made limited demands. Hard liquor became the prime culprit, with beer and wine apparently exempt from the temperance injunction. Neither high taxes nor horror stories on the evil effects of drink seemed to work, however,

so the temperance forces shifted their line of appeal. The citizens of a godly republic, they argued, must be prepared to discharge their civic and religious duties. But how could a drunken sot vote intelligently for political representatives or pay due homage to God? Obviously, he or she could not.

The American Society for the Promotion of Temperance (founded in 1826) and allied groups, working especially through the churches, urged people to sign a pledge of total abstinence. Many thousands did, and often signing the pledge formed part of a religious conversion. By the mid-1830s the society could claim over a million persons on the temperance (total abstinence) wagon. Still the evils of drink would not go away. Those who refused to give up alcohol, and who thereby polluted society, might have to be coerced into godly behavior.

After the start of the Washington movement in 1840, demands for legal action through state prohibition laws—forbidding the sale of alcoholic beverages—became the hallmark of the antiliquor campaign. But laws must to some extent reflect public opinion; to influence the public, to educate it to the need for prohibition laws, temperance men and women mounted a tremendous publicity campaign—one that resembled in many ways the organized enthusiasm of Harrison's concurrent Whig presidential campaign in 1840.

Rallies, parades, picnics, mass meetings—all marked the efforts of the so-called cold water army. Writers and poets poured (to overfilling) their talents into the crusade. Miss C. B. Porter's *The Silver Cup of Sparkling Drops* included the lines:

> I gazed upon his pallid cheek
> And asked him how his cares begun—
> He sighed, and thus essayed to speak,
> "The cause of all my grief is *rum.*"

Timothy Shay Arthur, a writer who specialized in rum demonology, produced a best seller, *Ten Nights in a Bar Room.* But the heaviest guns of the cold water army were the preachers who inveighed against drink as strenuously and as sincerely as they fought against the devil.

Temperance became a political force to be reckoned with, especially in the Northeast. But its advocates may have overreached themselves and become overconfident on the basis of a few legislative victories. In 1838, Massachusetts had passed a "fifteen gallon" law, stipulating that sales of liquor had to be in amounts of fifteen gallons or more. This obvious discrimination against the poor had one unexpected but understandable effect: a Democrat was elected governor of Massachusetts for the first time. The law was then repealed. Nearby, the state of Maine made legislative history in 1846 by becoming the first state to ban alcoholic bever-

In 1837, Horace Mann dropped a promising career as lawyer and state legislator to become the first State Superintendent of Education in Massachusetts. During his twelve-year tenure, the state's public schools were impressively reformed: teaching standards were raised, the school year was lengthened, state appropriations were doubled, and "Normal Schools" were established to train teachers. (Brown Brothers)

ages altogether. Other states, including some in the West, followed suit; when New York (which had adopted local option in 1845) went for prohibition in 1854, the victory of the temperance advocates seemed an accomplished fact.

It was not. First, the rest of the nation did not rush to emulate Maine's example. Much of the South pretended to be blissfully unaware of the crusade, and the Middle Atlantic states remained ambivalent. Second, some of the prohibition laws had been badly drafted, opening them up to lawsuits. Pre–Civil War temperance suffered perhaps its most severe setback in 1856, when the New York courts ruled that state's prohibition law unconstitutional because it deprived citizens of vested rights in property (their liquor) without due process of law.

Education

Although the movements urging the spread of educational facilities—especially tax-supported primary schooling for all—were not so directly a part of the Protestant crusade as was the temperance movement, the religious factor was present nevertheless. The free primary school—what came to be called "the little red schoolhouse"—was, at first, very definitely a Protestant schoolhouse. Catholics objected that, when public school instruction included Bible readings using the Protestant, King James version of the Bible, then public institutions were being used to serve sectarian purposes. (This was long before anyone in authority paid much attention to the few who objected to having any Bible readings in the public schools at all.)

Diffusion of schooling, it was felt, would wipe out illiteracy, a scourge as bad as alcoholism; at the same time the school system would instill in pupils proper moral attitudes and values. In short, along with its altruistic and humanitarian purposes, advocates of the public school argued that it would provide a superb agency for social control in a society that was becoming increasingly individualistic, unruly, and downright "licentious."

Whatever their definition of "progress," most reformers agreed that the surest road to progress in the United States was through education. They worked to reduce illiteracy. (Although literacy in America was relatively high in compari-son to other societies of that time, it is probable that before the Civil War a majority of Americans could not read or write.) The reformers also tried to improve educational opportunities in a variety of ways. Outside of the South, belief in state-supported primary education for every child became widespread. Public school systems were established throughout the North. In the South, a more limited number of children—mainly from the wealthier classes—continued to attend private academies or to receive instruction from tutors.

The leader of the Northern public school movement was Horace Mann of Massachusetts, ably seconded by Henry Barnard in neighboring Connecticut. The New England common school system, established in colonial times and calling for state aid to towns that established primary schools, had fallen into decay. Many economy-minded small towns had no schools at all; others had ramshackle schoolhouses with poorly paid teachers (mostly males at that time). During the 1830s and 1840s, Horace Mann worked to reorganize his state's school system, raise teacher salaries,

Oberlin College, in Ohio, became a center of controversy because it was coeducational and interracial. Its school of theology was very liberal and heavily supported by prominent Eastern reformers and abolitionists. (Brown Brothers)

and upgrade teacher training. Massachusetts, which doubled its educational budget under Mann's prodding, established the first teacher training institution in 1839. Formal education at the secondary school level also grew in importance. A number of progressive schools—primary and secondary—opened in New England. But it should be stressed that, in the pre–Civil War period, secondary education remained far out of reach of the vast majority of young people, and even primary education was by no means universally available.

Horace Mann, as state secretary of education in Massachusetts, stated his case for education in well-publicized annual reports. Appropriations time brought this warning from Mann:

> In a republic, ignorance is crime. . . . If we do not prepare our children to become good citizens, if we do not develop their capacities, if we do not enrich their minds with knowledge, imbue their hearts with the love of truth and duty, and a reverence for all things sacred and holy, then our republic must go down to destruction.

Mann's well-publicized twelve annual reports (1837–48) as secretary of the state board of education in Massachusetts brought to the attention of reformers and officials throughout the country not only the specific problems of Massachusetts schools but the more general concerns and issues of public education. In 1838, he began editing a magazine called the *Common School Journal* devoted to spreading the gospel—and highlighting the problems—of public school education. Under Mann's leadership in Massachusetts, the salaries of teachers improved significantly, and the number of children enrolled in public schools increased yearly. Elementary school curriculums were modernized, and new methods of teaching reading to the young and the illiterate received his special attention. Mann resigned as secretary in 1848 after being elected to Congress as an antislavery Whig, although not an abolitionist. He became the first president of the newly founded Antioch College at Yellow Springs, Ohio, in 1852, where he taught and administered until his retirement in 1859. Only weeks after retiring, Mann died, still the most influential leader of public education in his generation.

Higher education expanded, too. State universities were established in several Southern and Midwestern states. New private colleges and universities also sprang up. Oberlin College in Ohio, founded in 1833, was the first coeducational college in the country. It was also one of the few schools to admit blacks, and it became a center of antislavery agitation. Antioch College was another antislavery and coeducational institution.

Mount Holyoke in Massachusetts, founded in 1837 as Mary Lyon's Female Seminary, was the first to offer women advanced education. During the period, such opportunities for women increased but at a pitifully slow pace. Women were different, mentally as well as physically, argued the men who dominated American society and who had as little sympathy for the idea of formal education for women as they did for the notion of allowing women to vote. Although men like Horace Mann and Henry Barnard also faced difficulties, the *women* who fought for educational reform—Emma Willard, who started a "female seminary" in Troy, New York (which Elizabeth Cady attended); Mary Lyon, who did likewise in Massachusetts; and Elizabeth Blackwell, who earned and insisted on receiving the first medical degree awarded an American woman—were the ones who fought the hardest fight against prevailing sex prejudice.

Mass education of a more informal kind also flourished in the antebellum period. Breakthroughs in machine technology had resulted in a "printing revolution" that permitted the low-cost production of reading material by steam-powered rotary presses. Hundreds of mass circulation newspapers and magazines, catering to almost every segment of public taste, made their appearance. The famous "penny press" dated from 1833. In that year, the New York *Sun* demonstrated the possibility of profitably increasing readership by cutting its price to one cent. Weekly editions of such leading papers as Horace Greeley's New York *Tribune* (founded in the early 1840s) became the equivalent of the first national magazines for a mass audience. Periodicals such as *Harper's Weekly* and *Godey's Lady's Book* were only two of many serving the apparently insatiable reading appetite of an increasingly literate America.

Schoolteacher Mary Lyon raised the funds to establish Mount Holyoke College by soliciting contributions, door-to-door, from other Massachusetts women. Although the "Seminary" for girls that she founded in South Hadley, Massachusetts, in 1837 was not chartered as a college until 1886, after her death, the level of instruction and entrance requirements from the outset were on a par with those at men's colleges. The pious Miss Lyon also insisted upon a religious atmosphere and, since she believed in the virtue of manual labor, required all students to assist with the housework. (Culver Pictures)

Educator Emma Hart Willard, who was determined to improve women's education—and to prove that women could master as difficult subjects as men—campaigned in New York (unsuccessfully) for the state funding of girls' schools. In 1821, she established the Troy Female Seminary, with financial support from the town, and introduced an advanced curriculum that included math, history, geography, and a wide range of sciences—rather than the hodge-podge of handicrafts usually offered at girls' schools. Mrs. Willard was particularly devoted to teacher preparation and trained two hundred of her graduates to enter the teaching profession. (Culver Pictures)

The most influential form of adult education in this period—again outside the South—was the lyceum movement. It originated in New England in 1826. Lyceums were established by the hundreds throughout the North and Middle West. They were basically lecture halls with small libraries and facilities for discussion and study groups. Lyceums drew a steady stream of well-paid lecturers on regional and even national tours. No better device existed for mass education in a country that still lacked universal literacy but which valued the arts of public speaking and debating.

Almost any cause could gain an attentive audience (and perhaps some converts) easily by sending a speaker to tour the lyceums. Hundreds of reformers—ranging from such rarified philosophers as Emerson to more down-to-earth men and women advocating a variety of nostrums guaranteed to elevate mankind—all followed the lyceum circuit hoping to arouse America to the need for change.

There proved to be no shortage of causes to expound. In addition to temperance and education through formal schooling, reformers called for the end of capital punishment; some demanded changes in the prison system through the establishment of penitentiaries that would rehabilitate and not merely punish; others lectured on spiritualism or the principles of phrenology (character analysis by measuring the contours of the head); still others urged the total renunciation of

war; some wanted the few Jews then living in America converted to Christianity; many demanded equal rights for women; still more demanded the abolition of slavery. Lyceum lectures were not exclusively reform platforms, but the lecture-study circuit never lacked for reformers — those who saw and fretted about the imperfections of a society that they thought should be constantly striving to improve itself. In this connection, note the relative ease with which the women of Seneca Falls quickly organized their convention — and attracted a large audience.

Treatment of the Handicapped

One cause that received a great deal of attention for the first time during the antebellum decades was the manner in which Americans treated

Three writers of the American renaissance 1830–60. (Above) Nathaniel Hawthorne (1804–64), the literary voice of New England's nineteenth-century romantic neo-Puritanism; (below left) Edgar Allan Poe (1809–49), Philadelphia journalist and author, a brilliant and mordant maverick, his

fiery fantasies were at first more admired in Europe than in America; (below right) William Cullen Bryant (1794–1878), poet, editor, and abolitionist, for over half a century New York City's first citizen. (All photos are from The Bettmann Archive)

the mentally ill. Foremost among those responsible for changing public attitudes on this controversial question was Dorothea Dix, a Boston schoolteacher, who spent years studying conditions in the country's insane asylums. Dix found most inmates "confined in cages, closets, cellars, stalls, and pens, where they were chained, naked, beaten with rods, and lashed into obedience." When she exposed these inhuman conditions, all of which she had seen personally, some critics denounced her agitating; but with the help of people like Horace Mann and the young politician Charles Sumner, Dix persisted. Her detailed reports to state legislatures on the hideous conditions, and her long campaign for public recognition of the problem in and outside of Massachusetts, led to many improvements in state-supported mental hospitals.

Among those who helped Dorothea Dix in her campaign to ease the sufferings of mental patients was Dr. Samuel Gridley Howe. A romantic figure, who had fought in the Greek war for independence, Howe was also a very practical reformer. He had concentrated on the education of the deaf and the blind and had succeeded in educating a young woman named Laura Bridgman, a blind deaf-mute. His "feat" in so doing, which attracted a great deal of curiosity and attention, greatly aided Howe in raising money for his Perkins Institute for the Blind. Before he opened his school for the blind, Howe spent several days blindfolded so that he might gain a better understanding of the problems faced by his future pupils.

Other reformers, forerunners of the modern social worker, helped the "neglected poor," the unemployed, the newly arrived immigrant. The work of such individuals as Joseph Tuckerman of Boston and Charles Loring Brace of New York called attention to poverty amid the plenty of the nation's developing cities.

Pacifism

The peace movement gained many followers in the early nineteenth century. A Maine merchant named William Ladd founded the American Peace Society in 1828. It was weakened after a few years, however, when it split into warring factions over the question of whether nations might use force to defend themselves. Some pacifists condemned the use of force under any circumstances, arguing that there was no such thing as a "just" war. Among their leaders was abolitionist William Lloyd Garrison. He led those who believed in absolute pacifism into a much smaller society, the New England Non-Resistance Society, which condemned violence even in self-defense.

Pacifism gradually lost followers as the slavery controversy heated up during the 1840s, and the Mexican War of 1846–48 created a second convulsion within the American Peace Society. A group of dissidents, led by Elihu Burritt, wanted the war condemned. Failing in that, they founded the League of Universal Brotherhood. But the "war" that did the most to undermine organized pacifism was the "war against the slave power." Many of the leading pacifists like Garrison and Burritt were also abolitionists. When faced with the choice of fighting or giving in to slavery, such men renounced pacifism. Thus Garrison ended by praising John Brown's raid on Harpers Ferry and supporting the Civil War.

Woman's Rights

Women were active in almost every progressive cause in antebellum America. In the process of trying to improve conditions for others, they came to recognize the degree to which they themselves were deprived of equal citizenship. The treatment of Elizabeth Stanton, Lucretia Mott, and other women at the World Anti-Slavery Conference in London in 1840 dramatized this fact. They had no political rights, and upon marriage, they lost some of their civil rights, in particular, control over whatever property they had owned. Most of all, women suffered from limited professional and social opportunities. They were refused admission to most secondary schools and universities. Practically all careers but marriage were considered "unfeminine."

Yet women were expected to work. On the nation's farms and in the small towns, where a majority of Americans then lived, women did their share of the work—perhaps more than their share, since they also did most of the work involved in child rearing. But male society threw up powerful barriers against women working outside the home, rural or urban, or participating in public activity.

The woman's rights movement, which began in an organized manner at the Seneca Falls Convention in 1848, next to abolitionism,[1] was the most controversial of antebellum reform crusades. Some male reformers, notably Garrison, Wendell Phillips, Gerrit Smith, and Samuel Gridley Howe, actively supported the feminists. Others, especially clergymen worried about conventional morality, and journalists, looking for a good story, attacked or ridiculed the movement. On one point both clergy and press were united: that the "Bloomer-style" of dress temporarily adopted by leading feminists was shocking. Actually, it was only different, since it consisted of a knee-length jacket over a pair of "Turkish" trousers that were not form fitting. The costume as a whole was no more revealing or provocative than conventional dress. But Bloomerism proved such a handicap to feminism, it evoked so much criticism, that feminists reluctantly returned to less comfortable petticoats and gowns.

Nevertheless, American women made some progress during the pre–Civil War years. Women were allowed to become elementary and then high school teachers. State legislatures began to award married women control over their own property: Mississippi was the first, in 1839; New York followed in 1848 after extensive work by Elizabeth Cady Stanton and other feminists. Girls began attending secondary schools in small numbers, and a few colleges offered higher education to women.

Probably the most important breakthroughs were stubbornly personal. Distinguished careers pursued by individual reformers and intellectuals—such as Blackwell, Dix, Mott, and Stanton—dented the dominant image of woman's mental and emotional unfitness for serious vocations outside the home. In educational institutions like Willard's Female Seminary, which taught mathematics, history, and philosophy, a small percentage of American women began to find themselves intellectually. These reforms came at a time when women were thought incapable of learning much

---

[1] For a full account of abolitionism, see Chapter 22.

besides singing and embroidery and when most women seemed permanently imprisoned by their "circumstance." Susan B. Anthony, an ardent feminist (and abolitionist) who worked to gain the vote for women, once declared that she "would ignore all law to help the slave, and ignore it all to protect an enslaved woman."

Utopian Communities

The idealism and social unrest of the period were perhaps best symbolized by the Utopian communities that sprang up in the antebellum era. From the 1820s through the 1840s more than a hundred colonies were set up. Most were inspired by one or another religious belief, although some were secular, established as proving grounds for new economic or social theories.

The purpose of New Harmony, Indiana, according to its founder, was "to introduce an entire new system of society." He was a successful Scottish industrialist named Robert Owen, who believed that capitalism represented selfishness and that only socialism (communitarian socialism) could bring harmony to society. In 1825 Owen purchased a ready-made colony of 30,000 acres from a German religious group. Within six weeks he had brought together eight hundred colonists. But New Harmony also attracted its share of crackpots and loafers. Quarrels broke out over major and minor issues. And Owen's frequent absences left the group without strong guidance. Within two years, New Harmony was disbanded.

Brook Farm, a few miles west of Boston, operated on a smaller scale but with a more distinguished group of adherents. It began in 1841 as a progressive prep school and cooperative farm, with all pupils and group members sharing daily chores. Its leader, George Ripley, former Unitarian minister and sometime member of the Transcendental Club, believed in "plain living and high thinking." He thought that people could develop more fully when freed from competition. Many intellectuals were associated with Brook Farm. Emerson considered it a nice place to visit, but he did not want to live there. Nathaniel Hawthorne was a group member. (He later satirized the experiment in his novel *The Blithedale Romance*.) When a highly structured, more impersonal working and living system was introduced in 1845 (in other words, when it became more regimented), the farm lost its appeal for many supporters. A fire in 1846 destroyed the main building and brought the experiment to an end. Brook Farm, according to Transcendentalist Orestes Brownson, had been "half a charming adventure, half a solemn experiment."

Less intellectual, and unconcerned with charm, was the Oneida Community in upstate New York, started by John Humphrey Noyes in 1848. Noyes believed that small industry provided a better economic base for a colony than did agriculture. So the community produced and marketed animal traps, furniture, and other consumer goods. Property was owned jointly and distributed equally. Conventional marriage was replaced by "complex marriage," a system in which all group members were considered married to each other. Noyes and his followers believed that no man-made laws could separate them and that they belonged to one another. These doctrines were criticized severely by the outside world. The Oneida Community, like the Mormons, paid the price for their sexual unorthodoxy and financial success. The group finally abolished complex marriage in 1879. Soon afterward, the community itself was dissolved, becoming a joint stock company that specialized in manufacturing silverware.

Most American Utopian communities were unable to become truly self-sufficient or to maintain their cherished isolation from the outside world. Many floundered when it came to putting their high ideals into practice. Yet a few made noteworthy contributions. New Harmony sponsored some important educational innovations—the kin-

The Oneida Community's sexual practices created much controversy. Here, the Oneidans vote on whether to allow the union of two members under their highly regulated scheme of "complex marriage." (Culver Pictures)

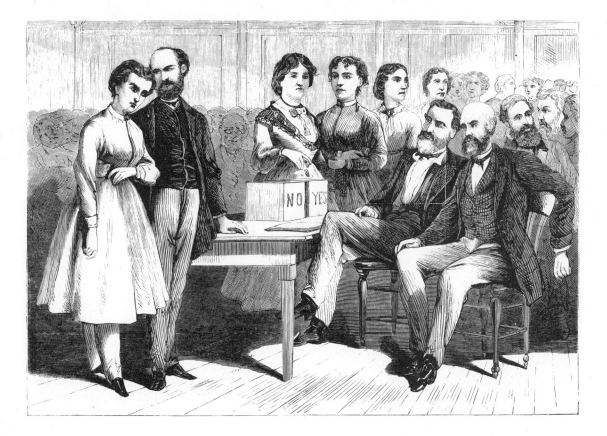

dergarten and the trade school. Brook Farm's combination of work and culture was highly praised, and its school was much admired. As for Oneida, its members pioneered in eugenics and in what, today, would be called encounter sessions.

Most Americans knew about the Utopian communities; but few approved of them, and even fewer actually participated in these early American experiments in communitarianism. Utopian withdrawal offered no solution to a mass society, innovative though some communities might be. To outsiders they appeared, at best, as exotic retreats. Most Americans still believed that piecemeal reform — working to correct gradually the abuses in society as a whole, rather than creating new minisocieties — offered greater hope. Some approached the task of reform with the sour anxiety of a Lyman Beecher, orthodox Congregationalist from Connecticut; others were blessed with the cheerful and optimistic spirit of a William Ellery Channing, the Boston Unitarian. Yet both were clergymen imbued with the belief that mankind could and should better its lot on earth, and approach closer to moral perfection. Such attitudes made the starburst of American reform in the antebellum years a reality and offered a more certain prospect for the future than did the Adventist hopes of William Miller and his followers or the *secular* Utopias.

Origins of the Abolition Movement

Of all the reforms influenced by religion, the one with the closest connections was abolitionism. Certain religious groups had been particularly active in the antislavery movement from its beginning in the eighteenth century. These included the Methodists, Episcopalians, and, particularly, the Quakers, whose opposition continued into the nineteenth century, as evidenced by the activities — among others — of James and Lucretia Mott. Ethical opposition to slavery inspired many leading figures of the Revolutionary period to free their slaves. It also influenced Northern states to abolish slavery gradually by the 1820s.

A leading antislavery organization of the early nineteenth century was the American Colonization Society, founded in 1817. It worked to obtain gradual, compensated emancipation of slaves. After being freed, slaves were to be transported immediately elsewhere, preferably to Africa. The society actually colonized very few blacks. But it did help found Liberia in 1822 as a refuge for ex-slaves. Many Southerners joined the American Colonization Society in an effort to resolve their moral doubts over slavery, but the society lost most of its support in the South after a slave insurrection in 1831 that helped shape attitudes for the next three decades — the Nat Turner Revolt.

Suggested Readings
Chapters 15-16

The Seneca Falls Convention and Early Women's Rights Movement

Lois W. Banner, *Elizabeth Cady Stanton* (1980); Barbara J. Berg, *The Remembered Gate: Origins of American Feminism 1800–1860* (1978); Otelia Cromwell, *Lucretia Mott* (1958); Carl N. Degler, *At Odds: Women and the Family in America, 1776 to the Present* (1980); Ellen DuBois, *Feminism and Suffrage: The Emergence of an Independent Women's Movement in America, 1848–1869* (1978); Eleanor Flexner, *Century of Struggle: The Women's Rights Movement in the United States* (1959); Elinor Rice Hays, *Morning Star: A Biography of Lucie Stone* (1978); Blanche Glassman Hersh, *The Slavery of Sex: Feminist-Abolitionists in America* (1978); Alma Lutz, *Created Equal: A Biography of Elizabeth Cady Stanton* (1940) and *Susan B. Anthony: Rebel, Crusader, Humanitarian* (1959); Keith Melder, *Beginnings of Sisterhood: The American Woman's Rights Movement, 1800–1850* (1977); Judith Nies, *Seven Women: Portraits from the American Radical Tradition* (1977); Elizabeth Cady Stanton, *Eighty Years or More: Reminiscences, 1815–1897* (1898); Elizabeth Cady Stanton, Susan B. Anthony, and Matilda Jocelyn Gage, eds., *History of Woman Suffrage* (Vols. 1–3, 1881–1886).

Religious Reforms

Sydney E. Ahlstrom, *A Religious History of the American People* (1972); Ray A. Billington, *The Protestant Crusade, 1800–1860* (1938); Carl Bode, *The American Lyceum* (1956); Fawn M. Brodie, *No Man Knows My History: The Life of Joseph Smith* (1971); Whitney R. Cross, *The Burned-Over District: Enthusiastic Religion in Western New York, 1800–1850* (1950); Mark Holloway, *Heavens on Earth* (1951); Daniel W. Howe, *The Unitarian Conscience: Harvard Moral Philosophy, 1805–1861* (1970); Ralph L. Lusk, *The Life of Ralph Waldo Emerson* (1949); Perry Miller, ed., *Transcendentalists: An Anthology* (1950); Thomas F. O'Dea, *The Mormons* (1964); Timothy L. Smith, *Revivalism and Social Reform in Mid-Nineteenth Century America* (1965); Bernard A. Weisberger, *They Gathered at the River: The Story of the Great Revivalists and Their Impact Upon Religion in America* (1958).

Social Crusades

Arthur E. Bestor, Jr., *Backwoods Utopias: The Sectarian Origins and the Owenite Phase of Communitarian Socialism in America: 1623–1829* (1950); Peter Brock, *Pacifism in the United States: From the Colonial Era to the First World War* (1968); Michael Fellman, *The Unbounded Frame: Freedom and Community in Nineteenth Century American Utopianism* (1973); Gerald N. Grob, *Mental Institutions in America: Social Policy to 1875* (1973); Michael Katz, *The Irony of Early School Reform: Educational Innovation in Mid-Nineteenth Century Massachusetts* (1968); John A. Krout, *The Origins of Prohibition* (1925); W. David Lewis, *From Newgate to Dannemora: The Rise of the Penitentiary in New York, 1796–1848* (1965); William G. McLoughlin, *The Meaning of Henry Ward Beecher* (1970); Jonathan Messerli, *Horace Mann* (1971); David S. Rothman, *The Discovery of the Asylum* (1971); Harold Schwartz, *Samuel Gridley Howe, Social Reformer* (1956); Ronald G. Walters, *American Reformers, 1815–1860* (1978); Rush Welter, *Popular Education and Democratic Thought* (1962).

Change in American Thought

Rowland Berthoff, *An Unsettled People: Social Order and Disorder in American History* (1971); Daniel Boorstin, *The Americans: The National Experience* (1965); Clifford S. Griffin, *The Ferment of Reform, 1830–1860* (1967); Neil Harris, *The Artist in American Society: The Formative Years, 1790–1860* (1966); Oliver W. Larkin, *Art and Life in America* (1949); F. O. Mathiessen, *American Renaissance: Art and Expression in the Age of Emerson and Whitman* (1941); Perry Miller, *The Life of the Mind in America* (1965); Ernest L. Tuveson, *Redeemer Nation: The Idea of America's Millennial Role* (1968); Alice Felt Tyler, *Freedom's Ferment: Phases of American Social History from the Revolution to the Outbreak of the Civil War* (1964).

Shortly after the Missouri Compromise of 1820, Thomas Jefferson and John Adams, aging patriots, exchanged letters on the one remaining major problem that seemed to threaten the nation's stability. "The real question, as seen in the states afflicted with this unfortunate population," wrote Jefferson in 1821, "is, Are our slaves to be presented with freedom and therefore a dagger? Are we then to see again Athenian and Spartan confederacies? To wage another Peloponnesian War to settle the ascendancy between them?" Adams was equally skeptical. "Slavery in this country," he responded, "I have seen hanging over it like a black cloud for half a century." The "black cloud" was still there when the two Founding Fathers died, in an awesome coincidence, on the same day—July 4, 1826, the fiftieth anniversary of American independence.

During the 1820s and 1830s economic issues such as the Bank War and land policy deflected popular attention from the "black cloud." Only in the 1840s did the landscape once more become overcast with the problem, as Americans grappled with the question of slavery's expansion. Even then, slavery did not completely preoccupy the American people. The nation doubled its population between 1830 and 1850. An industrial factory system began to develop in the North and Middle West. Millions of European immigrants landed on American shores. The country fought a war with Mexico and gained huge new territories in the West. Yet all these events occurred within a society torn by a fundamental and unresolved social problem—the place of blacks and slavery in American life.

The four pairs of chapters that follow examine various phases of the American experience from the 1830s to the 1870s, with special emphasis on changing reactions to the problems of slavery and race. Chapter 17 tells the story of the most important slave revolt in United States history, led by Nat Turner. It serves as a focal point for the discussion of slavery in Chapter 18 which portrays the patterns of Southern society as they affected both slaves and their masters. Chapter 19 deals with the drama of congressional efforts to achieve a compromise over the issue of slavery in the Western territories. The resultant Compromise of 1850 and surrounding events provide a vehicle for exploring, in Chapter 20, three dominant themes of the 1840s and 1850s: Northern economic growth, westward expansion, and the politics of sectional conflict.

John Brown's raid, the subject of Chapter 21, triggered extreme sectional hysteria in both South and North. It can also be understood in relation to a general climate of reform, described in Chapter 22, which characterized the antebellum period. Sectional differences in the United States culminated in civil war and continued in the bitter Reconstruction era that followed. The meaning of the Civil War in human terms is dramatized in Chapter 23 through an account of Sherman's devastating march through Georgia. Chapter 24 describes the major events of the Civil War and Reconstruction—the climactic struggles of a tragic period in our national past.

DIVIDED AMERICA

UNIT FOUR

17 Slaves in Revolt: The Nat Turner Uprising

Six poorly clad black men huddled around their campfire in the woods drinking brandy and barbecuing a pig. They had arrived at this meeting place about noon, started the fire, and waited in silence. Toward mid-afternoon another black man suddenly emerged from the surrounding trees. The six turned to greet him. They had been waiting for this short and stocky figure. His name was Nat Turner. A later description of him reads:

> Five feet 6 or 8 inches high, weighs between 150 and 160 pounds, rather bright complexion, but not a mulatto. Broad shoulders, large flat nose, large eyes. Broad flat feet, rather knockkneed, walks brisk and active. Hair on the top of the head very thin, no beard, except on the upper lip and the top of the chin. A scar on one of his temples, also one on the back of his neck. A large knot on one of the bones of his right arm, near his wrist, produced [by] a blow.

Turner greeted the other blacks and joined them around the campfire. We know his companions only by their first names—Sam, Nelson, Hark, Will, Henry, and Jack.

Turner sat down, stared directly at Will, and demanded to know something he already knew quite well. Why had Will come to his rendezvous? According to Turner's later account, Will replied that "his life was worth no more than others and his liberty was as dear to him." Turner continued the questioning: "I asked him if he thought to obtain his freedom. He said he would, or lose his life."

The seven men spoke further about their plans until some time after sunset. Then, at a command from Turner, they trudged back out of the woods and through ripe tobacco fields to a clearing. Here stood a large, handsome frame house. It belonging to a white man named Joseph Travis, who happened to own Nat Turner. An eighth black, Austin, joined them at the Travis home. Then, as Turner later recounted, "they all went to the cider press and drank, except myself."

About midnight the group gathered in front of the house. Turner climbed through a window, opened the doors to his men, and gave them

guns that had been stored inside. His men now insisted that he "spill the first blood." Armed with a hatchet and accompanied by Will, Turner entered Travis's bedroom and swung wildly at the sleeping man. The blow merely grazed Travis's skull, and he jumped out of bed screaming for his wife. A second later, Will bashed his head in with an ax. Within moments, wielding his ax, Will also killed Mrs. Travis, their three oldest children, and an apprentice, none of whom ever awoke.

The band of black men then searched the house for arms, collecting a half-dozen rifles and several pounds of gunpowder. They left soon afterward and started walking down a road that led to the town of Jerusalem (now Courtland), some fifteen miles away. They had gone only a short distance when someone remembered that the Travises had another child, a baby who slept in a cradle near its parents' bed. "Henry and Will returned and killed it," Nat Turner later observed. He formed the others "in a line as soldiers" and marched his seven-man "army" down the road. With the murder of this one family began the greatest slave revolt in the history of the United States. It started on Sunday, August 21, 1831, in the sleepy Virginia county known as Southampton.

Southampton County, in southeastern Virginia, was an important agricultural area. It had several large farms that employed slave labor and might have been called plantations. Such was the Travis homestead. More common were small farms tilled by poor whites who owned no slaves. The federal census in 1830 showed that Southampton was second among Virginia counties in growing rice and potatoes. A decade later, it led the state in cotton production.

Southampton County's planters might have felt an occasional twinge of concern over their safety. Blacks in the area (most of them slaves) outnumbered whites by almost two to one. Among the 9501 Southampton blacks counted by the 1830 census takers was a thirty-year-old, Bible-reading, visionary slave preacher named Nat Turner.

Turner was born in Southampton County on October 2, 1800. At the time, members of his family were slaves of a man named Benjamin Turner. (It was common for slaves to be given the last name of their master.) When Nat was only three or four years old, he already felt that he had been singled out by God to achieve some great work. As he said later, he thought he "surely would be a prophet." Young Nat certainly seemed a prodigy to his elders. His upbringing was unusual for a slave child, in several ways. At an early age he was taught to read and write by his parents. As a youth, he spent much time at prayer. Also, he was apparently spared much physical labor. Instead, he had free time when he could study schoolbooks belonging to his master's children or simply be alone with his thoughts. He remembered other slaves turning to him for help because of his "superior judgment."

At a very early age, Turner decided to pursue a lonely, almost friendless, life while awaiting the great works for which he believed God had prepared him. "Having soon discovered myself to be great, I must appear so, and therefore studiously avoided mixing in society, and wrapped myself in mystery, devoting my time to fasting and prayer."

Several times as a young man in his twenties, Turner claimed to have divine visions. His reputation as a preacher spread among whites as well as blacks in Southampton County. Yet he appeared aloof and puzzling to most of his fellow slaves. One time he escaped. But, instead of trying to reach shelter in the Great Dismal Swamp—some twenty-five miles away—he stayed in the woods for thirty days. Then he casually returned to his owner. "The Negroes found fault, and murmured against me," Nat later remarked, "saying that if they had my sense they would not serve any master in the world." By this time, however, Nat Turner believed himself destined for a greater role than that of an escaped slave, skulking in swamplands to avoid recapture. "I now withdrew myself as much as my situation would permit, from the intercourse of my fellow slaves, for the avowed purpose of serving the Spirit more fully."

Turner's vision of a divinely inspired slave revolt came to him in 1828, according to his account. "The Spirit instantly appeared to me," he said, and told him of the task ahead: "I should arise and prepare myself, and slay my enemies with their own weapons." A heavenly sign would instruct him when to begin. The signal that triggered his actual plan to revolt was an eclipse of the sun in February 1831. That month, Turner outlined his general scheme to Henry, Hark, Nelson, and Sam, who later brought in Will and Jack. Turner's men began to call him the Prophet because of his mystical statements. The small band of plotters could gather easily at church meetings or barbecues to plan the rebellion, since few whites in the Jerusalem area had the slightest suspicion of an impending uprising.

Nat Turner's master in 1831, Joseph Travis, had acquired him in 1830 after marrying the widow of his former owner. Turner remembered Travis as "a kind master, [who] placed the greatest confidence in me; in fact, I had no cause to complain of his treatment to me." But Travis was a slaveholder. As such, he was marked by "the Prophet" for destruction.

To the very moment of revolt Nat Turner spoke more easily with the God whose commands he believed he was obeying than with his own black followers. After agreeing to meet his six companions in the woods at noon on the fateful Sunday, he joined them instead hours later, for "the same reason that had caused me not to mix with them for years before." However, once the Travis family had been chopped to pieces and the revolt was under way, Turner's aloofness no longer affected them. The killing began in earnest.

Some distance from the Travis house lived Salathiel Francis. His home was the rebels' next stop as they obeyed Turner's command to "carry terror and devastation" along the road to Jerusalem. Their work was aided by the fact that the rebellious slaves knew most of the families in the neighborhood. When they arrived at the Francis house, Sam knocked at the door and shouted that he had a letter to deliver. It was after midnight. Yet the unsuspecting planter opened the door immediately, only to be dragged outside and beaten to death. No one else was home, so Turner and his men marched on to the home of a Mrs. Reese, whose door they found unlocked. They murdered Mrs. Reese in her bed.

By sunrise on Monday other slaves had joined the group. They now numbered fifteen, with nine mounted on horses. Monday morning they arrived at the house of Elizabeth Turner, whom Will killed, along with Sarah Newsome. No woman was raped either then or at any point during Nat Turner's march of destruction. At each stop along the way, however, the rebels destroyed whatever valuable property they found, and they seized money, guns, and ammunition.

From the Turner residence the blacks on horseback rode on to the home of Richard Whitehead, while the others detoured to kill a slave-holding family named Bryant. As the nine armed blacks rode onto his property, Richard Whitehead stared unbelievingly from a nearby cotton patch. The blacks called him, and as he walked toward them, Will's ax dropped him in his tracks. Dismounting, the slaves tore through the house, putting to death the entire family. Here occurred the only murder Nat Turner acknowledged having committed personally during the entire uprising—that of Whitehead's daughter Margaret. Margaret "had concealed herself in the corner. On my approach she fled, but was soon overtaken, and after repeated blows with a sword, I killed her by a blow on the head, with a fence rail."

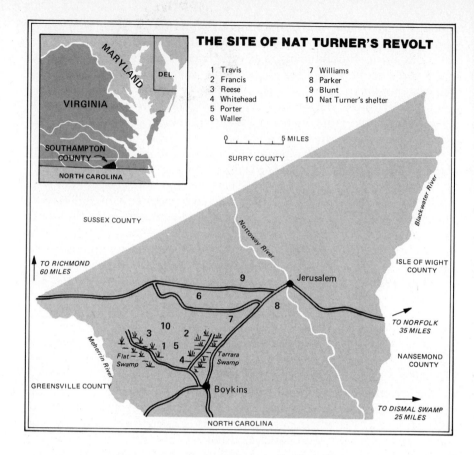

THE SITE OF NAT TURNER'S REVOLT

1 Travis
2 Francis
3 Reese
4 Whitehead
5 Porter
6 Waller
7 Williams
8 Parker
9 Blunt
10 Nat Turner's shelter

By then the six blacks who had detoured to the Bryant home returned, having "done the work of death assigned them." The entire party moved on toward Jerusalem. The mutinous slaves again broke into small bands, since several scattered slaveholding families lay in their path. The main group, led by Turner himself, rode on to Richard Porter's home, only to discover that Porter had escaped with his family. "I understood there," Nat later acknowledged, "that the alarm had already spread, and I immediately returned to bring up those sent to other plantations."

Richard Porter's family was not alone in escaping from Nat Turner's wrath. By dawn on Monday, August 22—less than twelve hours after the revolt began—small numbers of whites began straggling into Jerusalem from the direction of the killings, rousing the town to the threatened black invasion. Within hours, a rider left Jerusalem and headed north for the state capital at Richmond, about seventy miles away. He carried an urgent letter appealing for military help.

Wild rumors spread quickly across the state. In the absence of more accurate information from Southampton, the rumors threw white Virginians into a panic. Thousands of angry slaves, it was said, had banded together to take over the state. According to reports, the rebels were well armed and commanded by soldiers from Haiti.[1] Rumor had it that Northern abolitionists had helped incite the insurrection.

Whole companies of the state militia were hastily called up, and they headed for Jerusalem. By the time the first outside help had arrived, however, the uprising had already been crushed by Southampton County's own militia groups and armed white farmers. They had begun riding out after the small band of black rebels shortly after Richard Porter and others first sounded the alarm.

When he found Porter's family missing, Nat Turner realized the importance of marching as quickly as possible to seize Jerusalem. He knew, too, that he should keep his band together at full strength in the event of an attack. At each house along the way the rebels slaughtered the white inhabitants and urged nearby slaves to join them. By the time Turner and his men reached the home of a Captain Harris, who had also fled with his family, their ranks numbered about forty. Most seemed untroubled by Harris's absence, as they jubilantly destroyed his valuables, drank his liquor, collected his rifles, and rode on.

By this time "General Nat"—as his men reportedly started calling him—had decided on his tactics. He ordered those on horseback to ride ahead, killing whomever they met along the way. This would frighten the remaining whites in the area so that they would flee from their homes, and even abandon Jerusalem to his men. Turner himself remained at the rear, directing his foot soldiers while coaxing the slaves he met to join the rebellion. When General Nat reached a house, its occupants had usually been killed, although he later commented: "I sometimes got in sight in time to see the work of death completed, viewed the mangled bodies as they lay, in silent satisfaction, and immediately started in quest of other victims." In this way, Mrs. Levi Waller and her ten children were killed, then William Williams and his two small boys. Mrs. Williams was caught running away and brought back to her dead husband's side. The rebels ordered her to lie down beside him and shot her. Several other families perished as well. By Monday afternoon the rebel band numbered between fifty and sixty, "all mounted and armed with guns, axes, swords, and clubs." They were only three miles from Jerusalem. Their leader urged them to press on into the town, but several of them insisted on stopping at the plantation of James Parker, where they had relatives. Most of Turner's men rode across the fields toward Parker's house to collect their kinfolk (the Parker family had already escaped), but Turner himself remained at the roadside with seven or eight of his soldiers. This delay proved fatal for the rebels.

A local militia captain, Alexander Peete, had ridden out from Jerusalem at the head of eighteen volunteers. He was probably as startled to find Nat Turner and his small band of blacks in front of the Parker

---

[1] In 1794 blacks in Haiti—led by Toussaint L'Ouverture—had overthrown French rule there. Although the French captured Toussaint, they failed to retake the colony. The success of the black revolt in Haiti frightened American slaveholders for decades afterward.

This crude drawing appeared in a tract called "Horrid Massacre in Virginia," published in 1831. It is a rendering of "Mr. Travis, cruelly murdered by his own slaves." Woodcuts like this satisfied the public taste for a visual record of sensational events, though they were usually far more accurate. (Virginia State Library)

plantation as Turner was to see Peete. Turner coolly ordered his handful of followers to form ranks and prepare to fire. Shots rang out on both sides, and the white militiamen fled. The black insurgents pursued Peete's men until the retreating militiamen ran headlong into another party of armed whites who had left Jerusalem to hunt down the rebels. Turner's small band, now heavily outnumbered, scattered into the surrounding woods. Most of them were wounded. For the rest of Monday afternoon, General Nat backtracked across much of the area of his earlier march. He combed the woods for his men while evading the growing numbers of militiamen who searched for him. By evening he had collected almost forty men, including several new slave recruits. He placed guards around his camp and rested for the night. But the men on patrol panicked, believing the camp under attack. When order was restored, Turner's "army" had been reduced to about twenty.

"The Prophet" set out early on Tuesday morning to continue recruiting the slaves in the area. His group reached the home of Dr. Simon Blunt just before daybreak. Almost immediately, the rebels were fired on by a party of armed whites and by some of Blunt's slaves. Several of Turner's men were killed. The rest retreated to the home of Captain Harris, which earlier had been deserted. This time, another band of militia opened fire on the slaves from within the house. Most of the blacks fled into the woods, where they were quickly rounded up. Only two, Jacob and another slave named Nat, retreated to the woods with General Nat. They waited until evening, when Turner sent his last two followers in search of his original group. They never returned.

Sixty hours after the rebellion had begun, it was crushed. Nat Turner was left alone with the shattered wreckage of his mission. According to Turner's own account, God had not promised him success—only that he would perform the "great work" of "carrying terror and devastation wherever we went." This he had done. In less than three days his men had killed fifty-five whites from Southampton County slaveholding families: eleven men, fourteen women, and thirty children. At least as many blacks were also killed during and after the revolt by white militiamen. These militiamen seldom knew whether their victims had actually taken part in the revolt.

As for Nat Turner himself, he proved more skillful in defeat than in battle. He managed to remain free, eluding thousands of whites, for almost two months. During that period, throughout the country, the black "Prophet" of Southampton County became both famous and infamous.

Just as Virginians of the seventeenth century had studied the omens that foreshadowed Bacon's Rebellion, so did most white Southerners see a train of alarming events leading up to Nat Turner's Revolt. Had not an even more widespread plot among slaves and free blacks been discovered in Charleston, South Carolina, a decade earlier? This conspiracy was led by a free black named Denmark Vesey. It was exposed in 1822, and its leaders were executed. But rumors of such plots cropped up regularly in the years before the Southampton revolt. Had not a militant free black in Boston, David Walker, published a widely distributed *Appeal* in 1829 calling for slave uprisings throughout the South? And, in that same city, had not a journalist and printer named William Lloyd Garrison begun publishing a notorious abolitionist newspaper called *The Liberator*, which demanded immediate and total emancipation of all slaves?

Although Boston was 500 miles from Southampton County, many Southerners blamed the abolitionist writings of Walker and Garrison for stimulating a desire for rebellion in blacks such as Nat Turner. Some even suspected antislavery Northerners of actually plotting the Southampton revolt. Almost every white Virginian, for example, would have agreed with the sentiments of the state's leading newspaper, the Richmond *Enquirer*. Only a few days after the slave rebellion had been crushed, it printed this comment:

> When an appeal is actually made through the press to this unfortunate class of our community, calculated to mislead them, and while it involves us in serious trouble, leads those unhappy creatures to destruction, it is time for us to arouse from an indifference to a conduct which is daily augmenting and becoming worse and worse. To attempt to excite discontent and revolt, or publish writings having this tendency, obstinately and perversely, among us, is outrageous—it ought not to be passed over with indifference. Our own safety—the good and happiness of our slaves, requires it.

This criticism came from a newspaper whose editor, Thomas Ritchie, believed in the gradual emancipation of slaves. Obviously, the reaction of proslavery Southerners was much more hysterical. Thinking about the Nat Turner Revolt, supporters of the "peculiar institution"[2] may have remembered South Carolinian Edward D. Holland's warning at the time of the Vesey conspiracy:

> Let it never be forgotten, that "our NEGROES are truly the *Jacobins*[3] of the country; that they are the *anarchists* and the *domestic enemy,*" *the common enemy of civilized society,* and the barbarians who would, IF THEY COULD, become the DESTROYERS of our race.

Southerners were fearful that Turner's insurrection would inspire other slaves to rebel. They began acting on these fears, often in an incredibly barbaric manner. An antislavery Northern observer, E. A. Andrews, wrote:

> In every town and village, an active and vigilant patrol is abroad at such hours of the night as they judge most expedient, and no Negro dares, after the prescribed hour, to be found at a distance from his quarter. Great cruelty is often practiced by the patrols toward unoffending slaves. The principal object of such visits is to terrify the slaves, and thus secure their good behavior, and especially to prevent their wandering about at night.

---

[2] This term for slavery seems to have been used first by a South Carolina newspaper in the 1850s, which spoke of the dangers then threatening "the peculiar domestic institutions of the South."

[3] The Jacobins were a leftist political group of the French Revolution. Their name became synonymous with extreme and dangerous radicals.

Andrews went south prepared to find such cruelties, and he might therefore be expected to exaggerate. But many similar accounts filled the Southern press itself. The editor of the Richmond *Whig*, a militiaman himself, wrote the following typical account:

> A party of horsemen started from Richmond with the intention of killing every colored person they saw in Southampton County. They stopped opposite the cabin of a free colored man, who was hoeing in his little field. They called out, "Is this Southampton County?" He replied, "Yes, Sir, you have crossed the line by yonder tree." They shot him dead and rode on.

Nowhere was the punishment of innocent slaves for Nat Turner's brief uprising more ruthless than in Southampton County itself. Nathaniel Bacon's men over a century earlier had consoled themselves for failing to find any marauding Indians by slaughtering villages of peaceful ones. In the same manner, roving companies of militiamen and vigilante slave patrols—often drinking from the same stocks that had nourished Nat Turner's band during its brief lifetime—butchered many innocent slaves unlucky enough to fall into their hands. The situation became so offensive to the commander of military forces at Southampton, General Eppes, that he issued an order on September 6 threatening to shoot any of his own men caught mistreating local blacks. Eppes cautioned against further "acts of barbarity and cruelty" on the part of his own troops; but numerous slaves in the area paid with their lives before the carnage ended.

Throughout the South, state legislatures reacted to the acute fear of uprisings by further limiting the already restricted lives of slaves. The Virginia asembly endorsed the widely proclaimed "lesson" of Southampton County (to quote the Richmond *Enquirer*) that "no black man ought to be permitted to become a preacher" by passing a complete ban on "any assembly or meeting, for religious or other purposes" by either slaves or free blacks. Only whites could preach to black congregations, and slaves had to accompany their masters to church. Other new Virginia laws forbade free blacks to carry weapons, increased the penalties for blacks assaulting whites, prohibited the sale of liquor to slaves, and allowed whippings for blacks who expressed "seditious" thoughts.

In every other Southern state, within months after the Nat Turner Revolt, a flood of similar legislation tightened controls over both slaves and free blacks. These actions fulfilled the prediction made by Garrison's *Liberator* concerning the white Southerner's reaction to the Turner uprising. "In his fury against the revolters," wrote the abolitionist editor, "who will remember their wrongs?"

While Nat Turner remained free, the object of Southern fears and fury, forty-six other blacks were brought to trial in Jerusalem for taking part in the revolt. The militiamen had obviously cast their nets too wide, for five free blacks were included among the accused. Sixteen slaves and three freemen died on the gallows for their alleged role in the revolt. Seven more were sentenced to be deported to the harsher conditions of

The capture of Nat Turner. Turner had been hiding in a cave near the Francis farm for almost two months. (NYPL/Picture Collection)

Deep South[4] slavery. The others were acquitted, although several slaves in nearby counties were also convicted as accomplices in the uprising.

Meanwhile, Nat Turner lived a hand-to-mouth existence as a fugitive. After his last supporters had scattered on August 23, he returned to the Travis home and collected some food. In a nearby field he scratched out a shelter under a pile of fence rails. There he remained undetected for six weeks, just a short distance from his former slave cabin. Every evening the hunted rebel would leave briefly to drink water from a nearby stream. As the days wore on, he began to spend the entire night prowling through the neighborhood "gathering little or no intelligence, afraid of speaking to any human being, and returning every morning to my cave before the dawn of day."

One time when he returned, Turner saw a dog leaving his hiding place carrying a piece of meat. His days were now numbered. A few evenings later, two slaves, hunting with the same dog, passed his hideaway. The animal spotted Turner walking nearby and began barking. Turner later recalled:

> Thinking myself discovered, I spoke to the Negroes to beg concealment. On making myself known they fled from me. Knowing then they would betray me, I immediately left my hiding place, and was pursued almost incessantly until I was taken a fortnight afterwards by Mr. Benjamin Phipps, in a little hole I had dug out with my sword, for the purpose of conceal-

---

[4] The term "Deep South" refers to the southeastern states, especially Georgia, Alabama, Mississippi, and Louisiana. The older Southern states such as Virginia and Maryland are often known as the Upper South.

ment, under the top of a falled tree. On Mr. Phipps' discovering the place of my concealment, he cocked his gun and aimed at me. I requested him not to shoot and I would give up, upon which he demanded my sword. I delivered it to him, and he brought me to prison.

Turner was captured on October 30. Once locked in his Jerusalem cell, he was questioned by a white lawyer named Thomas R. Gray. The black insurgent apparently agreed to tell Gray his own story of the revolt. Turner's narrative, edited by Gray, appeared as a pamphlet, *The Confessions of Nat Turner*, early in 1832. At Turner's trial he pleaded not guilty, "saying to his counsel that he did not feel so." His narrative, however, was read to the court and served to convict him. After finding him guilty on November 5, Judge Jeremiah Cobb pronounced the inevitable death sentence, though with added fervor. He sentenced Turner to "be hung by the neck until you are dead! dead! dead!"

In talking to Gray, Nat Turner denied the existence of any widespread slave conspiracy. When he saw the lawyer's skeptical expression he said: "I see, sir, you doubt my word; but can you not think the same ideas might prompt others, as well as myself, to this undertaking?" The prisoner apparently impressed Gray considerably. Despite the attorney's proslavery beliefs, he defended Nat Turner against charges being made in the Southern press that he was an ignorant and cowardly black who had rebelled only to secure enough money to escape northward. "For natural intelligence and quickness of apprehension," Gray wrote, Turner "is surpassed by few men I have ever seen." Furthermore, Turner's Revolt could be understood, the lawyer argued, only as the action of "a complete fanatic warped and perverted by the influence of early impressions." Gray was probably referring to the childhood religious visions "the Prophet" claimed to have had. But elsewhere in the *Confessions*, Gray evoked this fearful image of Turner:

> The calm, deliberate composure with which he spoke of his late deeds and intentions, the expression of his fiend-like face when excited by enthusiasm, still bearing the stains of the blood of helpless innocence about him; clothed with rags and covered with chains; yet daring to raise his manacled hands to heaven, with a spirit soaring above the attributes of man; I looked on him and my blood curdled in my veins.

Most accounts at the time agree on the dignity with which Turner spoke to questioners such as Gray and confronted his final days. "Do you not find yourself mistaken now?" Gray once asked him shortly before his death. "The Prophet" quietly responded, "Was not Christ crucified?" Calmly and without recorded last words, Nat Turner went to his death at noon on November 11, 1831.

One man who was intensely concerned with the whole episode of the Nat Turner Revolt and its aftermath was the governor of Virginia, John Floyd. His diary provides an interesting account of what the insurrection meant to a moderate white Southerner.

Floyd, born in Kentucky, had trained as a surgeon before going into Virginia politics. He had served as a Democratic congressman from 1817 to 1829. Although originally a supporter of Andrew Jackson, he felt increasingly drawn to the views of Jackson's pro-Southern Vice-President, John C. Calhoun. Unlike Calhoun, however, he opposed slavery and advocated gradual emancipation.

Floyd had been governor for only a year when the Nat Turner Revolt occurred. He first heard of the rebellion on Tuesday, August 23, when the rider from Jerusalem reached Richmond. Floyd took immediate charge of preparations for quelling the uprising. Within hours he dispatched several companies of militia to Southampton County. By the end of the week the governor received definite news that the rebellion had been crushed. Yet, on August 29, his diary recorded a request from several other Virginia counties and from the town of Fredericksburg for militiamen to help quell other expected slave revolts. Virginians were obviously uneasy.

Governor Floyd insisted on being kept closely informed about the trials of those blacks accused of taking part in the rebellion. So completely did the Nat Turner Revolt obsess him that his diary in the following months mentions little else but the Jerusalem trials, rumors of other slave conspiracies, and reflections on their meaning. By mid-September, however, Floyd became suspicious of the many reports of black unrest that flowed into Richmond. None of them seemed to materialize once state militia were sent into the area. Of one such rumor he wrote: "I do not exactly believe the report. The slaves are quiet and evince no disposition to rebel."

On several occasions Floyd expressed concern over the fate of those blacks sentenced to be sent to the Deep South. The treatment of slaves was generally much harsher there. Floyd debated whether to commute the sentences rather than "endanger the lives of these Negroes." On other occasions he reprieved some slaves who had been sentenced to death in Jerusalem. Indeed, there is evidence that the governor reviewed personally almost every convicted rebel's trial record.

At the same time, Floyd could not contain his fury at those Northern abolitionists who, he believed, had encouraged the Nat Turner Revolt and similar conspiracies. On September 27 he wrote:

> I have received this day another number of the *Liberator,* a newspaper printed in Boston with the express intention of inciting the slaves and free Negroes in this and the other states to rebellion and to murder the men, women, and children of those states. Yet we are gravely told there is no law to punish such an offense. The amount of it then is this, a man in our states may plot treason in one state against another without fear of punishment, whilst the suffering state has no right to resist by the provisions of the federal Constitution. If this is not checked it must lead to a separation of these states.

When not complaining about the abolitionists, the governor's diary often denounced President Andrew Jackson. Floyd considered him dangerous to Southern interests, especially on such issues as a national tariff policy. After receiving South Carolinian guests returning from an antitariff meeting in Philadelphia, Floyd noted in his diary that the election of Calhoun would "turn out Jackson with all his unworthy officers, men not gentlemen, who lie and slander all men opposed to them to keep themselves in power."

The governor had little time for national politics, however. Requests for men and arms to combat expected slave revolts continued to pour into Richmond from every section of Virginia. Floyd's diary spoke constantly about the "Northern conspirators" who he believed were planning fiendish schemes. As late as October 20, Floyd recorded hearing of a plot by "Northern fanatics" in Philadelphia to stir up a general insurrection throughout Virginia and massacre its white population. Floyd treated the rumors coming from outside his state more seriously than he did those concerning slave conspiracies within Virginia itself, and his diary cautioned that, if the North refused to check the activities of abolitionists, "this Union is at an end as we [in the South] cannot consent to be tied up by the confederacy from doing ourselves justice, when the authorities of these states refuse to check the evil."

Turner's capture and execution only reinforced the determination of antislavery Virginians like John Floyd to prevent such future uprisings, not simply by supervising blacks in the state more closely but also by eliminating the source of discontent itself—that is, slavery. "There are still demands for arms in the lower counties," Floyd's diary commented on November 21. "I could not have believed there was half the fear amongst the people of the lower counties in respect to their slaves."

The problem never seemed to die down, as the governor's subsequent November entries indicate:

> Twenty-third day. I have reprieved for sale and transportation southward several slaves.
> Twenty-sixth day. I have received more applications for arms.
> Twenty-eighth day. I am preparing a message to the General Assembly. It will be ultra states' rights.

By "ultra states' rights" Floyd meant that he would demand that Northern states begin controlling the activities of abolitionists; also he would denounce the federal government for raising tariff duties, in opposition to Southern desires for lower rates.

In his "message to the General Assembly" (the state legislature) the governor also planned to deal with the question of slavery itself. His diary notes: "Before I leave this government, I will have contrived to have a law passed gradually abolishing slavery in this state, or at all events to begin the work by prohibiting slavery on the west side of the Blue Ridge Mountains."

Floyd's plan may sound surprising to us today, but it had the support of many of his fellow Virginians. In large sections of the state slavery had never assumed great economic or social importance. Men like Floyd and Thomas Ritchie of the Richmond *Enquirer* spoke for many Virginians in supporting gradual freeing of the slaves. They favored compensated emancipation—that is, slaveholders would be paid for the slaves who were freed. Most of those who favored this type of emancipation also believed in colonization—resettling former slaves elsewhere. (Africa was the location most commonly thought of.)

Opposition to slavery was particularly strong in the hilly areas and lush valleys west of the Blue Ridge Mountains. There, blacks (whether slave or free) numbered less than 20 percent of the population. In the eastern sections of Virginia, plantation slavery was common and blacks numbered over 50 percent of the total population. Here, supporters of abolition were less numerous.

During the early decades of the nineteenth century, many antislavery voices such as John Floyd's were raised throughout the South. The leading organization devoted to gradual, compensated emancipation—the American Colonization Society—found many of its leaders, and followers, in the region.

When Floyd addressed the state legislature in December 1831, he urged its members to abolish slavery by gradual stages in Virginia. Debate began in January 1832. For three weeks Virginia's legislators wrestled with the problem of abolishing slavery. They engaged in the bluntest and most complete debate on this question ever to take place in the antebellum[5] South. Supporters and opponents of emancipation marshaled

Governor Floyd, though favoring gradual emancipation at the time of the 1831–32 debate in Virginia, soon afterward took a strong proslavery position. (Virginia State Library)

---

[5] "Antebellum" refers to the period prior to the Civil War. The term comes from Latin words meaning "before the war."

their arguments in long speeches detailing the benefits or dangers that would flow from such a policy. Even those who defended the institution did so mainly on the grounds that it was an unavoidable reality rather than a blessing.

A typical defense was that of a delegate named John T. Brown:

> And is there, then, no apology for slavery? Is it a sin of so deep a die that none dare vindicate it? For my own part, I am not the advocate of slavery in the abstract, and if the question were upon introducing it, I should be the very last to agree to it. But I am yet to be convinced that slavery as it exists in Virginia is either criminal or immoral. It was cast upon us by the act of others. It is our lot, our destiny, and whether, in truth, it be right or wrong—whether it be a blessing or a curse—the moment has never yet been when it was possible for us to free ourselves from it. This is enough to satisfy my conscience, and I contend that the happiness of the slave does not call for his emancipation. His condition is better than that of four-fifths of the human family. He enjoys far more of the comforts of life, than the peasantry of many of the nations in Europe. The greater part of mankind must, in the nature of things, be poor and ignorant, toiling anxiously for their daily bread. All cannot be raised to the top of the scale. The Negro, of all others, is the least susceptible of elevation.

The debate ranged over many issues. What might be the economic effects of emancipation? How should colonization be handled? (Both supporters and opponents of abolition were in agreement on the need for this step if blacks were freed.) What was the morality of slaveholding? The specter of Nat Turner hung plainly over the entire proceedings. Few speakers, whatever their views on emancipation, bothered to disguise their anxiety over the prospect of future slave revolts. A typical antislavery speaker, for example, pleaded with his colleagues for support by reversing a standard proslavery argument. James McDowell observed:

> It is true to the letter that there is no laboring peasantry in any other part of the world who, in all external respects, are better situated than our slaves—who suffer less from want—who suffer less from hardship—who struggle less under the toils of life or who have a fuller supply of the comforts which mere physical nature demands. In all these respects the slave shares in the equalizing and benign spirit of our institutions and age.
>
> But it is in this very circumstance, in this alleviated and improved condition, that we have a principal cause of apprehension from the slave. You raise his intelligence with his condition, and as he better understands his position in the world, he were not a man if it did not the more inflame his discontent. That it has this effect we all know. The truth is proverbial: that a slave is the more unhappy as he is the more indulged. He could not be otherwise; he follows the impulse of human nature in being so.

Petitions for and against emancipation reached the legislature from all over Virginia. Debate was halted on January 25. Finally, the legislature voted on a mild measure providing for gradual emancipation over a period of many years. It was defeated by a vote of 73 to 58. The representatives had divided along distinct regional lines. Delegates from west of the Blue Ridge Mountains (who held only 102 slaves among them) supported abolition, 49 to 6. Representatives from the eastern areas (men who together owned 1029 slaves) opposed emancipation by 67 to 9. The eastern counties were overrepresented in the legislature, as they had been since the time of Jamestown, and carried the day for slavery.

Antislavery Virginians such as Governor Floyd felt understandably disheartened. Floyd confided to his diary the thought that Virginia itself would split into states on the question:

> Both sides seem ready to separate the state if any one would propose it. I think that event from appearances highly probable.

Floyd was right, though the creation of a separate state—West Virginia—did not occur for another three decades.

As it turned out, the subject of abolition was never again debated anywhere in the antebellum South. Within months, antislavery Southerners like Governor Floyd shifted their attention to defending what they considered Southern rights over the question of tariff nullification. Yet the rebellion did force many white Southerners to confront their own deepest convictions about the relations between master and slave. Never again would this relationship seem as clear-cut as it had before the August rebellion in Southampton County.

The most lasting result of the Nat Turner Revolt turned out to be increasingly severe Southern control of both slaves and free blacks. Many whites in the region apparently shared the fears (if not the conclusions) of the antislavery Virginia legislator who asked in January 1831:

> Was it the fear of Nat Turner and his deluded and drunken handful of followers which produced or could produce such effects? Was it this that induced distant counties, where the very name of Southampton was strange, to arm and equip for a struggle? No, it was the suspicion eternally attached to the slave himself, the suspicion that a Nat Turner might be in every family, that the same bloody deed could be acted over at any time in any place, that the materials for it were spread through the land and always ready for a like explosion.

A remarkable story was told by a black preacher who was in Virginia during the Nat Turner Revolt. Shortly after the rebellion a Southampton County slaveholder went hunting in the woods with a trusted slave, who carried his master's gun. The black had been with the slaveholder's family for many years, and he had led his master and his family to safety during the uprising. In the forest the bondsman handed the gun to his master, saying that he could no longer live as a slave. He asked his owner either to give him his freedom or to kill him. The white man hesitated for a moment, then took the gun and shot the black man through the heart.

Although this episode might never have occurred, the choice it speaks of was given to white Virginians in the aftermath of the Nat Turner Revolt. Like the slaveholder in the story, they chose to kill the last promise of a peaceful emancipation.

18 Slavery in the Antebellum South

With the wisdom of hindsight, we can say that the issue of slavery was too complex to be resolved—even in one state— by a legislative debate such as that held in Virginia in 1832. The sons of these Virginians would go to war over the "peculiar institution." Their fathers and grandfathers had, after all, wrestled with the problem unsuccessfully since the time of the Revolution.

When news of the Declaration of Independence reached England, even British supporters of the colonial cause complained about one aspect of the American Revolution. The "assigned cause and ground of the rebellion," wrote one Englishman, "is that every man hath an unalienable right to liberty and here the words, as it happens, are not nonsense, but then they are not true; slaves are there in America, and where there are slaves, there liberty is alienated." The practice of slavery in "republican" America seemed a glaring contradiction not only to Englishmen but to the revolutionaries themselves—many of whom owned black slaves. The Declaration of Independence opened with lofty phrases about equality. But the Second Continental Congress cautiously decided to omit a passage in the original draft that denounced human bondage. Some American leaders from Southern colonies, such as Thomas Jefferson and George Washington, expressed concern over maintaining slavery within a democratic republic. But they did so privately.

The thirteen colonies contained about half a million slaves at the time of the Revolution. Every colony had some, but the great majority lived in the South. There were 200,000 in Virginia, 100,000 in South Carolina, and at least 70,000 each in Maryland and North Carolina. In some Southern colonies slaves comprised 50 percent of the population. There were also slaves in the North. New York had 25,000 and New Jersey had about 10,000. Pennsylvania and Connecticut each had about 6,000 slaves. There were about 5,000 in Massachusetts and 4,000 in Rhode Island.

Fear of slave uprisings was common in eighteenth-century colonial America, despite the fact that only a few insurrections actually took place. Boston's Patriots were outraged by the presence of black troops among the occupying British army before the Boston Massacre. They were also angered by rumors that the redcoats were stirring up the city's small black population. Virginians were just as outraged in 1776 when the departing royal governor urged slaves to revolt against their masters and join the British in exchange for their freedom.

Along with fear of blacks went an equal measure of contempt. Most ordinary "free" Americans of the Revolutionary era—even those who favored abolition—believed that blacks were innately inferior to whites. "Comparing them by their faculties of memory, reason and imagination," wrote Jefferson, "it appears to me that in memory they are equal to the whites, in reason much inferior, and in imagination dull and tasteless." Few people of Jefferson's time would have quarreled with his view (although some might have challenged that notion that a black person had a memory—or anything else—equal to a white's).

During the Confederation period, steps were taken to end slavery in large areas of the Republic. In the period between 1783 and 1786, Massachusetts, Connecticut, Rhode Island, New York, and New Jersey either abolished slavery outright or provided for its gradual disappearance. In Virginia the legislature passed an act in 1782 easing the

Slave auctions were regarded as a necessary evil by many slaveowners. After turning some of his "people" over to an auctioneer, one Southerner grieved: "I did not know until the time came what pain it would give me." (Culver Pictures)

process by which owners could emancipate their bondsmen. At Jefferson's direction the Northwest Ordinance of 1787 prohibited slavery in the Northwest Territory. And even though the Constitution made no provision for slavery as an institution, it did provide that the foreign slave trade be abolished after 1808.

But what would happen to slaves who were freed? Since even *moderate* whites feared blacks or looked down on them, very few white Americans were prepared to accept a large free black population living among them. Most schemes for emancipation from the Revolutionary era up to the time of the Virginia legislative debate failed to resolve the underlying problem of freed slaves. Most supporters of gradual emancipation, from Thomas Jefferson to John Floyd, believed in the need for colonization—a policy that was easier to agree on in principle than to achieve in practice.

The task of the North in emancipating its blacks after 1790 was relatively simple. The region contained only 40,000 slaves and 27,000 freed blacks; the white population totaled 1,900,000. Thus roughly 1 out of 28 people was a black. The situation was very different in the South, where there were 1,271,000 whites, 657,000 slaves, and 32,000 free blacks. In other words, over a third of the Southern population was black. By the time of the Nat Turner Revolt, through individual emancipation (a process known as manumission) and increases by birth, there were over 181,000 free blacks in the South.

Fears of an unstable free black population were obviously much greater among Southerners than among Northerners. Many white Southerners sincerely wanted to abolish slavery. But Southern leaders from the time of the Founding Fathers until the Virginia legislative debate of 1832—and beyond—were afraid of even *gradual* emancipation. They thought it would pose a threat to the safety, stability, and "racial purity" of white society. Besides, slavery was profitable.

THE ECONOMICS OF SLAVERY

The antebellum South comprised a million acres of territory. It stretched from Chesapeake Bay to western Texas and from the Ohio River south to the Gulf of Mexico. Although climate and terrain varied considerably in the South, most of the region had rainfall, temperature, and soil conditions adequate for producing a variety of staple cash crops.

During the colonial period, the major crops grown on Southern plantations were tobacco, rice, indigo, and (to a much lesser extent) cotton. In some areas more than one of these crops was important. In Southampton County, for example, farmers grew both rice and cotton on a large scale.

"King Cotton"

Tobacco had been the South's leading export before the Revolution. But after 1800 the Southern economy came to center on cotton. The most important single factor in this change was the cotton gin. ("Gin" is short for "engine.") It was invented in 1793 by a New Englander named Eli Whitney. Before this time, separating cotton fiber from the seeds was done by hand and took a long time. But with Whitney's machine one person could do the work of fifty. At the same time, improvements in technology enabled England's textile industry to process raw cotton into cloth much more efficiently. Thus, early in the nineteenth century, growing cotton became truly profitable in the United States.

Cotton cultivation spread throughout older states such as Georgia and South Carolina. Even more important cotton-growing areas were the sparsely settled regions that eventually became the states of Alabama, Mississippi, Louisiana, Texas, and Arkansas. The United States had exported only 3,000 bales of cotton in 1790. By the time of Nat Turner's Revolt this figure had grown to 805,000 bales. By 1859, on the eve of Civil War, the figure had skyrocketed to 4,500,000 bales. Cotton alone accounted for almost two-thirds of the total export trade of the United States. And the United States—or, more particularly, the American South—had become the world's leading cotton producer. Along with this phenomenal growth went a continuing demand for more slaves to raise the crop.

Tobacco growing remained important in nineteenth-century Virginia, Kentucky, and North Carolina. Rice cultivation prospered along the South Carolina and Georgia seacoasts. Sugarcane production dominated Louisiana agriculture. Elsewhere in the South the main crop was cotton.

Who Owned Slaves

The 1850 census showed that 1,815,000 slaves were employed in cotton production. Some 350,000 worked in the tobacco fields; 125,000 raised rice; 150,000 labored on sugar plantations; and 60,000 produced hemp. Smaller numbers worked as house servants and artisans on plantations. Several thousand labored as workers in the South's few mines and factories.

Throughout the nineteenth century, a constant flow of both white settlers and black slaves shifted millions of Southerners away from the older seaboard regions and into the newer regions of Alabama, Mississippi, Louisiana, Arkansas, and Texas. Older states such as Virginia and Maryland declined in economic importance in the South because they produced relatively little cotton (despite the output of scattered areas such as Southampton County). During the decades between Nat Turner's Revolt and the Civil War, more than 700,000 slaves were sold in the United States, mainly by owners in the Upper South to purchasers in the Deep South.

It would be incorrect to think of the Southern population as divided simply into two groups—white owners and black slaves. Most white South-

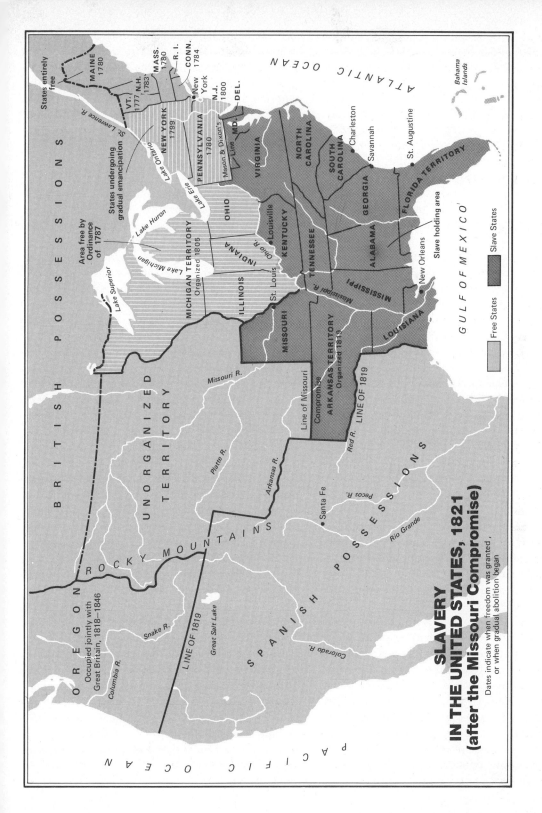

SLAVERY
IN THE UNITED STATES, 1821
(after the Missouri Compromise)

Dates indicate when freedom was granted,
or when gradual abolition began

Free States

Slave States

Slave holding area

States entirely free

States undergoing gradual emancipation

Area free by Ordinance of 1787

Occupied jointly with Great Britain, 1818-1846

BRITISH POSSESSIONS

SPANISH POSSESSIONS

UNORGANIZED TERRITORY

ROCKY MOUNTAINS

OREGON

ATLANTIC OCEAN

PACIFIC OCEAN

GULF OF MEXICO

Bahama Islands

St. Lawrence R.

Lake Ontario

Lake Erie

Lake Huron

Lake Michigan

Lake Superior

MAINE 1780

VT. 1777

N.H. 1783

MASS. 1780

R.I.

CONN. 1784

New York

NEW YORK 1799

N.J. 1800

DEL.

PENNSYLVANIA 1780

MD.

Mason & Dixon's Line

VIRGINIA

NORTH CAROLINA

SOUTH CAROLINA

GEORGIA

Charleston

Savannah

St. Augustine

FLORIDA TERRITORY

OHIO

INDIANA

ILLINOIS

MICHIGAN TERRITORY Organized 1805

Ohio R.

Louisville

KENTUCKY

TENNESSEE

ALABAMA

MISSISSIPPI

LOUISIANA

New Orleans

MISSOURI

St. Louis

Mississippi R.

Missouri R.

Line of Missouri Compromise

ARKANSAS TERRITORY Organized 1819

LINE OF 1819

Red R.

Arkansas R.

Platte R.

Pecos R.

Rio Grande

Santa Fe

LINE OF 1819

Great Salt Lake

Snake R.

Columbia R.

Colorado R.

Slavery in the Antebellum South   **351**

erners owned no slaves at all. Most whites who owned slaves in Southampton County and other regions in the South worked alongside their own bondsmen in the fields.

The entire white population of the South in 1860 numbered approximately 7 million, with the total of white families estimated at 1,400,000. There were 383,635 slaveholders. This meant that almost three out of every four families owned no slaves. Only 2,292 landowners owned more than 100 slaves. Some 46,000 slaveholders owned between 20 and 100. The great majority of slaveholders—those owning fewer than twenty slaves—were not owners of large plantations but simply moderately successful independent farmers. Except in the richest cotton-producing areas, slaveholders generally formed a minority of local landowners.

Before the 1830s, some slaveowners freed their own slaves. Like Governor Floyd, they expected that the policy of a colonized, gradual emancipation would be generally adopted throughout the South. But new laws made the practice of manumission more difficult after the Nat Turner Revolt. In any case, most nineteenth-century slaveholders did not consider the possibility of emancipation very seriously.

SOUTHERN SOCIETY

The social structure of the antebellum South resembled a pyramid. The region's few thousand large planters stood at the top. Beneath them was the larger group of slaveholding whites, who owned enough slaves to staff a small or medium-size plantation. Further down the pyramid stood the majority of slaveholders, who owned fewer than twenty slaves. Below them was the great mass of landowning but nonslaveholding white farmers. Toward the base of the pyramid were the lowest white Southerners, the landless and luckless "poor whites," who generally farmed the region's less fertile hill-country areas. At the base of the pyramid were, of course, the slaves themselves, on whose labor rested the South's entire social and economic structure.

Several groups in the South stood outside the central structure of plantation power and influence. There were professionals and businessmen, people like the journalist Thomas Ritchie or the physician (and governor) John Floyd. Such people were often absorbed into the plantation aristocracy by marriage, political alliance, or slave purchases. There were also free blacks—roughly 228,000 in 1860. Most of them lived in the cities of the Upper South or in New Orleans. Though better off than slaves, they were distrusted and discriminated against by Southern whites.

The plantation gentry were the elite of the South. They and their supporters dominated Southern politics up to the Civil War. Their social events, held in the larger cities and towns, set the tone for Southern society. Their impressive mansions often became centers of social life for the surrounding communities.

Though they might be compared to foreign aristocrats, Southern planters differed from them in at least two ways. (1) They were a working aristocracy. The business records of countless plantations show that the men and women who ran them were constantly concerned with the many problems of cash-crop agriculture. (2) They lived on their lands much of the time, rather than being absentee owners. This direct involvement helps account for the fact that slaveholders in the American South worked out a systematic proslavery argument to justify their holdings (see pages 358–359). They were the only "master class" in the Western Hemisphere to do so.

Susan Dabney Smedes, a planter's wife, once observed that "managing a plantation was something like managing a kingdom." A planter often found himself playing many roles within a brief space of time. He was an absolute ruler of his slaves. He was an aristocrat among fellow planters. He was a democratic politician among white men of all classes. He was a fellow Christian when conducting plantation religious services (often for a mixed audience of family members and slaves). The strains of moving back and forth quickly among such different roles produced anguish among some planters, at least according to their own diary accounts.

Planter Society

The most typical of the South's few cities—as racially mixed and tolerant New Orleans was atypical—was Charleston, South Carolina, the cultural center of the Old South and a prosperous seaport since colonial times. The planters of the area, together with the town merchants, supported concerts, lectures, plays, and libraries when such refinements were unknown elsewhere in the colonies. Charlestonians could point to the following "firsts": public library (1698), theater (1736), symphony orchestra (1762), city college (1770), and museum (1773).

The ebb and flow of social life was governed by the customs of the planters. From May to November, when the rice fields were under irrigation, they lived in the city to avoid the dangers of malaria. The Christmas holidays were usually spent in the countryside. By the end of January, the planters were back in town for a round of races, dinners, balls, and other entertainments.

Fully half the population of the city—the slaves—did not share in these pleasures. They were subject to many restrictions because of their numbers and fears of a revolt. In colonial times, slave uprisings that had broken out in Charleston had been crushed with great severity. In 1822 came the Denmark Vesey plot. Vesey, a one-time West Indian slave who purchased his freedom, was charged with organizing a conspiracy among local slaves to revolt. Fifteen persons were executed and others imprisoned or deported after trials related to the alleged plot. Public gatherings of blacks were forbidden. Black sailors—free elsewhere—were jailed while their ships were in port. In 1815 Charleston had been the leading port for the export of cotton and rice. But, as cotton growing spread into the Deep South, the city gradually lost its importance.

Conditions Favoring Slavery

If only a minority of white Southerners actually owned slaves, why did the whole society support slavery so solidly from the Nat Turner Revolt to the South's secession in 1860? Probably a majority of the volunteer militiamen who had helped to quell Turner's uprising owned no slaves, yet they

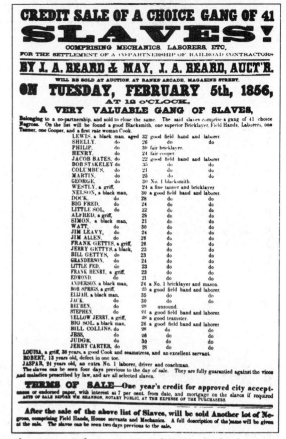

This New Orleans poster of 1856 speaks for itself. (Courtesy, The New-York Historical Society)

seemed passionately committed to maintaining slavery. Why? At least one answer suggests itself immediately in light of the Southampton County experience. Fear of slave insurrections was intense and constant among antebellum white Southerners. As whites rode their nightly slave patrols in the years after the 1831 uprising, many of them must have remembered that Nat Turner's band slaughtered slaveholders and nonslaveholding whites alike. Thus concern for personal and family security helped bind together different economic classes in the South.

Southerners also favored slavery because of its psychological advantages. The existence of a slave class gave all whites—especially poor white landless farmers—some reassurance that they were superior. Black people like Nat Turner and his men had no status within Southern white society. Even the poorest, least educated white person meant more in the eyes of the law and in Southern society than a planter's brightest, most talented slave. Nat Turner acknowledged having received special treatment from his original owner. But Turner had few, if any, rights that any white person was bound to respect.

Belief in the inferiority of blacks was common among almost all Southern (and Northern) whites, whatever their class. This universal sense of white supremacy blurred the sharp contrast between the South's democratic political system and its rigid economic structure, controlled by a few. Planters and poor whites, if they shared nothing else, still felt a common concern for maintaining slavery and the white racial unity it represented.

Slavery influenced status in another way. Nonslaveholding white farmers could aspire to purchase slaves, and some managed to do so; a few even broke into the planter ranks. When this happened, it bolstered the prevailing belief among white Southerners that only an economy run by slave labor could ensure a broad range of economic opportunity.

In this way, anxiety, outright fear, and ambition combined to create a feeling among almost all Southerners that their "peculiar institution" should be retained and, if necessary, defended. One other factor reinforced the consensus. Southerners were subject to fewer outside influences and new ideas than other Americans. For one thing, most white Southerners were native-born and therefore familiar with the customs of their region. Only 4.4 percent of the Southern population in 1860 was foreign born, compared to 18.7 percent elsewhere in the country. Also, there were fewer big cities in the South than in other regions. Even places like Norfolk and Richmond were little more than overgrown country towns. The vibrant, unsettling qualities of urban life affected only a small minority. Most white Southerners lived on farms, on plantations, or in small towns such as Jerusalem. The bulk of the South's free blacks, however, lived in towns and cities—where they were closely watched and their movements rigidly supervised. Cities thus remained the most obvious breeding ground of discontent with the slave system. And free blacks were clearly the most dangerous element within the closed world of slave society.

The Treatment of Slaves

The conditions under which slaves lived varied considerably. They could be treated relatively mildly and with consideration. Nat Turner, for instance, said that he was well treated by both his original owner and his last one. But savagely harsh practices prevailed on rice and sugar plantations in the Deep South. Slaves from other regions of the South were sent there to be punished, as was the case after the Nat Turner Revolt.

Because slaves were valuable property, an owner seldom abused them so cruelly that they died. Short of this, however, a master could treat his slaves much as he pleased. In times of extreme social tension, whites subjected blacks to the most degrading punishment with little fear of legal action or social criticism. Most recent scholars agree, however, that, under ordinary circumstances, slaves in the United States were generally better fed, housed, and clothed than those in Latin America during the same period. The economic condition of many slaves probably compared favorably with that of many industrial workers in the North and elsewhere—as proslavery people argued. (Even black rebels such as Nat Turner did not complain primarily about their *economic* conditions.) Some slaves were allowed to grow crops on private patches and to keep animals, for their own use or for sale. Almost every plantation had a weekly day of rest and special holidays as well. Thus Nat Turner's companions were probably not missed by their owners as they spent that final Sunday eating roast pig, drinking brandy, and scheming rebellion.

Yet, no matter how kindly a master might treat his slaves, the slavery system was brutal, for it rested ultimately on force. "The whole commerce between master and slave," wrote Thomas Jefferson from his own experience, "is a perpetual exercise of the most boisterous passions. The most unremitting despotism on the one part, and degrading submission on the other." Slave codes, such as those strengthened throughout the South following the Nat Turner uprising, gave whites almost

unrestrained physical power over their slaves. A slave master had absolute authority to decide how long his slaves should work and under what conditions. The law permitted the whipping and beating of slaves. Southern newspapers and court records during the antebellum decades contained numerous accounts of how slaves had been mutilated, hanged, shot, starved to death, or even burned alive. (Indeed, the Southern press was the abolitionists' major source for reports on the mistreatment of blacks.)

The law seldom imposed more than minor penalties on whites found guilty of deliberately injuring or killing blacks. Most often, the offenders escaped punishment completely—as did the white militiamen who committed hundreds of atrocities against Southampton County blacks in 1831. Blacks, whether slaves or freemen, were not allowed to testify against whites in Southern courts of law.

It was often impossible for slaves to keep their families together as units. Slave marriages

Although some owners provided good housing for their slaves, much of it was poor, like this ramshackle cabin. Southern physicians often warned planters that they had to provide flooring, windows, and adequate space in order to prevent illness and disease. (Duke University Library)

had no legal status. Slave families were separated, and the members were sold individually as a matter of course. How understandable, then, that the troops of "General Nat" broke ranks at the Parker plantation to collect their missing kinfolk!

ATTITUDES OF BLACKS

Acceptance vs. Resistance

In spite of massive oppression, many slaves appeared to be devoted to their masters, whether from affection, loyalty, or outright fear. This attitude emerges not only from the narratives of slaveholders themselves but from other sources. The slaves who belonged to Dr. Blunt defended their master by firing upon Nat Turner's retreating band. In the Vesey plot and in an 1800 conspiracy in Virginia—led by a slave artisan named Gabriel Prosser—fellow blacks were prominent among those who betrayed the plotters. There are at least two ways of looking at this situation. On the one hand, trusted and indulged slaves such as house servants and artisans had most to lose in any slave uprising—namely, their privileged status. Therefore, they might be expected to place loyalty to their white overlords above any feeling of kinship with rebel slaves. On the other hand, an effective slave rebellion was conceivable only among well-treated bondsmen such as Prosser or Turner. Such people could move easily among other blacks in their areas without arousing the white community's suspicion.

Often in history, those in an oppressed group who have privileged status, but most conscious of their condition, are willing to risk all. So it was with the slave preachers, artisans, house servants, and freed blacks who joined the Prosser, Vesey, and Turner conspiracies. It was easy for Nat Turner's original band of supporters—Will, Hark, Henry, Sam, Nelson, and Jack—to meet with their leader. They plotted rebellion for several months while attending church services and weekend gatherings, and on slave holidays, before finally deciding to strike. Their long period of preparation shows the confidence of slaveholders in the region concerning the loyalty of their most trusted bondsmen.

Slave revolts were relatively uncommon in the antebellum South. Yet blacks used a number of other ways to indicate how much they opposed the system. Many slaves tried to flee from bondage: almost every plantation owner worried about runaways. Some slaves reached freedom in the North, especially after abolitionists organized the "underground railroad" (see page 419). Others simply took off and hid in the woods for a while (as Nat Turner had done), often returning voluntarily as a sign of independence. The huge number of runaways in the antebellum South showed that many slaves silently nursed a keen desire for freedom, despite all the efforts by slaveholders to break the will of their blacks. Sabotage was also common. Blacks burned crops and stole supplies. They sometimes pretended to be sick and found other, often ingenious, ways to express their hatred for the system.

The Role of Religion

In all the efforts by blacks to undermine slavery, the black church and its preachers played a significant role. Most slaves followed the religion of their masters, evangelical Protestantism.[1] It was hardly accidental that, after the Nat Turner Revolt, the Virginia legislature placed a ban on blacks like Turner wandering freely through the countryside preaching the Gospel. Most Southern states tried to restrict the activities of black church meetings from the 1830s on—and with good reason. For one thing, slaves bent on rebellion could plot in safety at such gatherings. For another, the Bible itself—especially the Old Testament—offered to blacks prepared to interpret it that way an ideology that justified resistance. Southern whites may have regarded as strange Nat Turner's claim that a heavenly vision had instructed him to lead his people from bondage and to slaughter their oppressors. But most of his fellow slaves would have immediately understood what he meant.

The spirituals sung by slaves in their churches and elsewhere expressed a great deal. They dwelt on the belief blacks held of themselves as a "chosen" people. "We are the people of God," said one. Another proclaimed: "I'm a child of God, with my soul set free." Such images probably helped keep many slaves from adopting their masters' view of them as submissive children. The spirituals were "sorrow songs," telling of all the troubles and suffering that slaves experienced. They rarely spoke of black inferiority, inadequacy, or unworthiness.

In their religious lives, slaves found more than simply the strength to endure suffering, cer-

---

[1] In general, evangelical Protestants stress the teachings of the Bible rather than the authority of organized church doctrine. They also emphasize the importance of an individual's personal conversion.

John Randolph

John Randolph once said that asking a state to surrender part of its sovereignty was like asking a woman to surrender part of her virtue. This quip is typical of his wit. It also neatly summarizes his passionate belief in the sanctity of states' rights. To this proud, eccentric member of the Randolph family of Virginia, only Republican (anti-Federalist) principles could ensure personal liberty and freedom from the "tyranny" of strong central government. To the end of his life he espoused these principles, sacrificing political friendships and his own promising career for the often-reckless role of congressional gadfly.

In 1799, at the age of twenty-six, Randolph was elected to the House from Charlotte County. For the next thirty years, except for three two-year intervals (a single defeat, sickness, and service as a senator), he represented this district. His appearances on the floor of the House commanded attention. Usually a bit late, he would swagger in, whip in hand, booted and spurred, with one or two of his favorite hunting dogs. He would speak off the cuff in a rambling and theatrical fashion, scattering epigrams right and left. One historian described him as "one of the most brilliant figures that ever strutted and fretted his hour upon the American public stage."

Randolph's high point was his leadership in gaining congressional approval for the Louisiana Purchase in 1803. He did this although he felt that Jefferson was stretching his constitutional powers. Randolph himself believed in a strict interpretation of the Constitution in order to limit the scope of federal power.

His low point came in 1805, when he bungled the politically inspired impeachment trial of a Federalist judge and quarreled with Jefferson. In 1806 Randolph declared himself independent of his party, accusing Jefferson of "pulling Federalism forward." His opposition to the War of 1812, which swelled the power and popularity of the federal government, cost him his congressional seat.

Randolph returned to Congress in 1815 and opposed on principle the Bank of the United States, the tariff, and other nationalistic measures. His eccentric behavior remained unchecked, but he was

(The Bettmann Archive)

no longer a figure of influence. It was the Missouri Compromise of 1820 that brought him back to the limelight—as a spokesman for states' rights and for the Southern way of life. He first linked the ideas that John Calhoun later developed more fully. He also pitted himself against the architect of the compromise, Henry Clay. The two even fought a duel in 1826. According to Clay, Randolph's actions "came near shaking this Union to the center, and desolating this fair land."

Randolph's final position was not altogether congenial to him and to others of his generation who were uneasy about slavery. He regarded himself a friend to blacks. By the terms of his will he freed his four hundred slaves. When once asked whom he considered the greatest orator he had ever known, Randolph replied, "A slave, Sir. She was a mother, and her rostrum was the auction-block."

tain of a reward in heaven. Often, as in the case of Nat Turner, they also discovered the power to resist actively the efforts of those in authority to brutalize and degrade them. Spirituals, and the sermons of black preachers, were often prophetic. They promised a proud vision of betterment, justice, freedom, and personal worth. They taught that slaves could rise above slavery—not only in the next world, but in this one as well. Nat Turner and his fellow black ministers preached that their people could escape from bondage, through their own efforts and with the help of God. Countless deeds of slave resistance were inspired by this vision. It was embedded in the spiritual life of Southern blacks. Nat Turner's Revolt, the most extreme act of resistance by antebellum blacks, can be understood only as the product of such intense religious belief.

JUSTIFYING THE SYSTEM

While blacks found in the Bible a means of enduring slavery, white Southerners turned increasingly to it, and other writings, for evidence to help justify the system. Earlier proslavery advocates —such as those in the 1832 Virginia legislative debate—had apologized for slavery as a "necessary evil" inherited from the past. In the 1830s Southern political figures, led by Calhoun, began aggres- sively defending their peculiar institution. Southerners were disturbed for several reasons. They were shaken by such episodes as the Vesey and Turner revolts. The growth of abolitionism in the North frightened them. So did South Carolina's lonely championing of Southern interests in the nullification crises of 1832–33. In defense, they began arguing that their system of bondage was morally justified on all grounds. In 1837, Calhoun expressed this point of view: "Where two races of different origin, and distinguished by color and other physical differences, as well as intellectual, are brought together, the relation now existing in the slaveholding states between the two is, instead of an evil, a good—a positive good."

Slavery as a Positive Good

The "positive good" argument dominated the thinking of white Southerners between 1832 and the Civil War. The region's leading thinkers went to enormous lengths to devise a rationale for slavery. In doing so, they supported a set of beliefs that differed from the basically optimistic and democratic attitudes held by other Americans elsewhere in the country. These theorists argued that most men are naturally limited in their capacities. They said that human progress and achievement come only at the cost of enslaving peoples that are supposedly suited for such bondage. And they held that human society has always been characterized

An antislavery cartoon, published in 1840, mocks the idea, advanced by many Southerners, that blacks had to be treated like children. Depicting black people as competent and capable was part of the strategy of those who favored abolition. (Courtesy, The New-York Historical Society)

1840.] *Anti-Slavery Almanac.* 29

No indeed! They can' take care of themselves!

by class distinctions. Not even the extreme proslavery advocates during the 1831–32 Virginia legislative debates would have accepted such propositions. Yet, within a decade, they had become the orthodox Southern view of its "peculiar institution."

Governor James H. Hammond of South Carolina insisted that "in all social systems there must be a class to do the menial duties, to perform the drudgery of life." Without such a class, Hammond argued, "you would not have that other class which leads progress, civilization, and refinement." Slavery, then, "constitutes the very mudsill of society and of political government." George Fitzhugh, a brilliant proslavery spokesman, put it in a livelier way. He declared that "some are born with saddles on their backs, and others booted and spurred to ride them—and the riding does them good." These writers argued that whites could not be expected to perform the backbreaking tasks associated with cotton, rice, and tobacco cultivation. Slaves, therefore, became an economic necessity.

Proslavery people used a number of arguments in attempting to prove the virtues of slavery. They found citations in the Bible that justified enslavement, especially instructions that slaves obey their masters. They pointed to the glories of ancient Greece and Rome—both slave societies. They compared, unfavorably, the working conditions of Northern industrial laborers with those of Southern slaves. And, arguing from the false "scientific" theories of their day, they accepted the notion of the innate inferiority of black people.

Such proslavery advocates also glorified planters as an aristocracy of talent and grace. Southern gentlemen were pictured as chivalrous heroes, brave and quick to defend their honor. Southern ladies were portrayed as gentle noblewomen who devoted countless leisure-filled days to such "feminine" pastimes as needlework and music. These romantic images were highly unrealistic. Yet reality and myth agreed on at least one aspect of regional life. Even hostile accounts of the slave South usually acknowledged the longstanding planter traditions of hospitality and generosity toward friend and stranger alike.

Basic to the proslavery defense was a false image of black people. White Southerners insisted on describing blacks as submissive, contented happy-go-lucky children. "A merrier being does not exist on the face of the globe," wrote one Virginian, "than the Negro slave of the United States." This docile image fitted the hopes of Southern slaveholders better than it did the realities of slave life. But Southerners were concerned less with convincing outsiders than with persuading themselves that their proslavery arguments were true. So they harped on the supposed happiness and essential docility of their slaves, despite all evidence to the contrary.

UNCLE CLEM. "Say, Massa Jim, is I wan of them onfortunate Niggers as you was reading about?'
YOUNG GENTLEMAN. "Yes, Uncle Clem, you are one of them."
UNCLE CLEM. "Well, it's a great pity about me.—I'se berry badly off, I is."

Proslavery Americans undoubtedly enjoyed this pictorial jibe at the sometimes overheated arguments of abolitionists. It appeared in Harper's Weekly *in 1861. (Library of Congress)*

SLAVE STATES, 1860
PROPORTION OF WHITE AND BLACK POPULATION
(Figures rounded off to the nearest whole percentage point.)

State	White	Black slaves	Free blacks
SOUTH CAROLINA	42%	57%	1%+
MISSISSIPPI	45%	55%	★
LOUISIANA	50%	47%	3%
ALABAMA	55%	44%	1%+
FLORIDA	55%	44%	1%+
GEORGIA	56%	44%	★
VIRGINIA	56%	39%	5%
NORTH CAROLINA	64%	33%	3%
TEXAS	70%	30%	★
ARKANSAS	74%	26%	★
TENNESSEE	74%	25%	1%+
MARYLAND	75%	13%	12%
KENTUCKY	80%	20%	★
DELAWARE	81%	2%+	17%
MISSOURI	90%	10%	★

White　Black slaves　Free blacks　★ Less than 1 percent free blacks

The End of Moderation

A frank and hard-hitting public debate in the South over the merits of slavery, like the one held in Virginia in 1832, would have been impossible a decade later. Even the idea of gradual emancipation, accompanied by colonization, could not be argued openly in the 1840s. By that time, no Southern state would have elected an emancipationist governor such as John Floyd. Opponents of slavery were driven from positions in Southern churches, universities, and newspapers. Freedom of speech and press on the slavery question no longer existed in the South during the decades before the Civil War. "Southern rights" were to be defended at all costs.

Even before this time, white fears and class tensions had made the South a notoriously violent region. The vengeance taken by militiamen against Southampton County blacks after the Nat Turner uprising did not appear excessive to most white Southerners. The antebellum South was noted for its expert brawlers, marksmen, and duelists. Most Southerners owned guns or at least bowie knives (also known as "Arkansas toothpicks").

Once the "positive good" argument took hold during the 1830s, the level of militancy rose among white Southerners. Planters and their overseers armed themselves, and slave patrols rode regularly through the hot Southern nights. Many plantations became tiny military fortresses, their owners obsessed with thoughts of runaways and rebellions. Southern life became "militarized," not only on the plantations but also in the cities, where militia and town guards watched free blacks closely. By the late 1840s most white Southerners had accepted a view that linked the defense of slavery to every other cherished virtue. The region's leading Presbyterian minister, the Reverend J. H. Thornwell, argued in 1850 that:

> the parties in this conflict are not merely abolitionists and slaveholders—they are atheists, so-

cialists, communists, red republicans, jacobins on one side, and the friends of order and regulated freedom on the other. In a word, the world is the battleground—Christianity and atheism the combatants; and the progress of humanity the stake.

Thornwell probably spoke for the great majority of white Southerners.

The uncharitable, suspicious, and militant South of Thornwell's day seems light years away from the more leisurely, less fearful world of John Floyd and his fellow Virginians. Antislavery Southerners, of either Jefferson's generation or Floyd's, would have found little worth praising in the positive good argument. Yet leaders like Floyd had helped prepare the way for the more aggressive Southerners who followed.

Floyd, after all, supported John C. Calhoun. Like Calhoun, he managed to combine a strong nationalist fervor with an equally passionate belief in Southern rights. He had endorsed South Carolina's attempt at nullification. He opposed slavery, but he had denounced abolitionists and roused public opinion against the "menace" of Northern "agitators." Floyd's generation found it possible to believe strongly in gradual emancipation while at the same time nursing a violent hatred for Northern advocates of immediate abolition.

But the next generation hardened its point of view. One Southerner who would have agreed with Thornwell was John Buchanan Floyd, son of the antislavery Virginia governor. John Buchanan Floyd believed wholeheartedly in slavery. Like his father, he went into politics. He served as secretary of war from 1857 to 1860 in the cabinet of President James Buchanan. While in this post, Floyd transferred an excessive number of arms from Northern to Southern arsenals. His aim was to stockpile military supplies for the sectional conflict everyone expected.

John Buchanan Floyd resigned from the Buchanan cabinet in December 1860, a convinced secessionist. After Virginia joined the Confederacy in May 1861, he volunteered his services to Virginia. Three decades earlier, his father had unsuccessfully urged the Virginia legislature to abolish slavery. Now John Buchanan Floyd accepted a commission from the same legislature. He would become a major general in an army dedicated to preserving the South's "peculiar institution."

Suggested Readings
Chapters 17-18

The Nat Turner Revolt

Herbert Aptheker, *American Negro Slave Revolts* (1943); John B. Duff and Peter M. Mitchell, eds., *The Nat Turner Rebellion: The Historical Event and the Modern Controversy* (1971); William Styron, *The Confessions of Nat Turner* (1967).

Slavery

John W. Blassingame, *The Slave Community* (1972); P. A. Davis, et al., *Reckoning with Slavery* (1976); Robert A. Fogel and Stanley L. Engerman, *Time on the Cross* (2 vols., 1974); John Hope Franklin, *From Slavery to Freedom* (1974); George M. Frederickson, *The Black Image in the White Mind: The Debate on Afro-American Character and Destiny, 1817–1914* (1971); Winthrop D. Jordan, *White Over Black* (1969); Kenneth M. Stampp, *The Peculiar Institution* (1956).

Slavery in America and Elsewhere

David B. Davis, *The Problem of Slavery in Western Culture* (1966); Carl Degler, *Neither Black Nor White: Slavery and Race Relations in Brazil and the United States* (1971); Stanley M. Elkins, *Slavery: A Problem in American Institutional and Intellectual Life* (1959); Lawrence J. Levine, *Black Culture and Black Consciousness: Patterns of Afro-American Folk Thought in the United States* (1976); William Stanton, *The Leopard's Spots: Scientific Attitudes Toward Race in America, 1815–1859* (1960); Allen Weinstein, Frank Otto Gatell, and David Sarasohn, eds., *American Negro Slavery: A Modern Reader* (3rd ed., 1978).

The Negro in the North

Leon Litwack, *North of Slavery: The Negro in the Free States, 1790–1860* (1961); George Rawick, *From Sundown to Sunup: The Making of the Black Community* (1973); Richard Wade, *Slavery in the Cities* (1964).

The Negro in the South

Clement Eaton, *A History of the Old South* (1975) and *The Growth of Southern Civilization, 1790–1860* (1961); Eugene D. Genovese, *Roll, Jordan, Roll* (1974); Herbert G. Gutman, *The Black Family in Slavery and Freedom, 1750–1925* (1976); William Scarborough, *The Overseer: Plantation Management in the Old South* (1966); Robert Starobin, *Industrial Slavery in the Old South* (1970); Charles S. Sydnor, *The Development of Southern Sectionalism, 1819–1848* (1948); William R. Taylor, *Cavalier and Yankee: The Old South and American National Character* (1961).

The Crisis and Compromise of 1850 19

Potomac River breezes chilled the air as legislators returned to Washington, D.C., in December 1849 for the opening of Congress. Senators and representatives tramped through muddy streets past the city's boarding houses, hotels, and half-finished public buildings. An incomplete stone tower jutted out like a bruised silo; when completed several decades later, it would be a monument to George Washington. The Capitol, still topped by a temporary dome, was being repaired and enlarged to make room for the growing number of congressmen who crowded into its corridors with the admission of each new state into the Union.

The mood in Washington when a new Congress convenes is normally charged with excitement. There was special reason, though, for intense feeling in December 1849. Politicians from the North and South feared that the issue of slavery would wreck the approaching Thirty-first Congress. Some brooded anxiously over the possible collapse of the Union itself.

American politicians had deliberately suppressed the slavery question in national politics since the days of the Founding Fathers. No other issue could arouse Americans to such emotion. No other issue had such power to overcome party loyalties. Southerners were particularly troubled. Fearful of abolitionist attacks since the Nat Turner uprising a generation earlier, they warned that Northern interference with slavery could lead to a breakdown of the national party system.

A struggle to elect a Speaker of the House of Representatives began almost from the moment Congress opened on December 3. The difficulty confirmed the fears about sectional political warfare. The Democratic party had dominated national politics since the days of Jackson. There were now 112 Democrats in the House and 109 Whigs. There were also nine members of the newly formed Free Soil party.

Normally the majority party in the House agrees on its candidate for Speaker and then elects him at the opening session. But these were not normal times. The third party representatives held the balance of power, preventing either major party from having a majority.

When this photograph of the Capitol was made in the 1840s, the building was still surmounted by a temporary iron dome. The permanent dome and the House and Senate wings, on either side of the central structure, were added between 1851 and 1865. (Library of Congress)

Bitterness over slavery and sectional issues strained party lines, threatening to break them beyond repair. The Whigs nominated Robert C. Winthrop of Massachusetts, a descendant of the Puritan governor. He opposed the extension of slavery into the Western territories, but he was not an abolitionist. Still, eight Southern Whigs stormed out of the party's caucus. When the Democrats chose Howell Cobb of Georgia, a supporter of slavery, a small but significant minority of Northern Democrats balked at the choice. These defections meant that neither party could exercise control.

Vote followed vote for three weeks. After sixty-two ballots, the House had still failed to select a Speaker. Even the withdrawal of Cobb's and Winthrop's names on various ballots could not break the stalemate. This frustrating inaction immobilized the entire government. Congress was paralyzed. The Senate could not function without the House. President Zachary Taylor could not deliver his annual message.

On December 22 both sides finally recognized the dangers, and they agreed to change the election system itself. House members resolved that, in order to be elected, a Speaker would in future need only a plurality of votes, not a majority. On the sixty-third ballot they finally chose Cobb. Several Northern Democrats who had opposed Cobb voted for him in the end. Some doubtless hoped to ease the tension. Others were simply tired. "Many members," observed Senator Daniel Webster of Massachusetts," wished to go home for the holidays."

The new Speaker was a moderate, genial man, popular with most members. He tried to heal some of the wounds by carefully allotting committee chairmanships to members from all sections of the country. But other quarrels in Congress showed that tensions remained high. Because the speaker was a Southerner, Northerners expected that someone from their section would be chosen clerk of the House, a position of some importance and profit for the holder. Two Northern Democrats in particular wanted the job. Several Democrats from the South broke party lines, however, to help elect a fellow Southerner (though a Whig) from Tennessee. One furious Northerner felt that this action taught a simple lesson. He wrote to his brother, stating angrily that if a Northerner:

> [does not] bow and humble and prostrate himself in the dust before their high mightinesses of the South, he must hope for nothing. My Yankee blood is fairly up in this matter, and I will see the South all d—to everlasting perdition before I will ever open my lips in its defense.

Even the president of the United States came under attack. Zachary Taylor, who owned several plantations and dozens of slaves, should have presented no problem to the South. His career had been devoted entirely to military service. He had never held public office, nor had he even voted. Taylor had never expressed a hostile opinion on slavery—or anything else. During the campaign of 1848 the South had

A cartoon of 1848 pokes fun at Taylor's unwillingness to commit himself on the issues of the day. The two disgruntled men at left have decided to turn to other candidates: John P. Hale, nominated by the Liberty party, and Van Buren ("Matty"), the Free Soil candidate. (Library of Congress)

QUESTIONING A CANDIDATE

clearly seemed more content with Taylor, a Whig, than with his two opponents. One was Lewis Cass of Michigan, a Democrat. He favored popular sovereignty—that is, allowing people in the territories to decide the
slavery question for themselves. Ex-President Martin Van Buren ran on
the Free Soil ticket, opposing the extension of slavery into any territory.

Taylor had encouraged Southern hopes by straddling most embarrassing issues or remaining silent. Attacks on him from antislavery
spokesmen in the North clinched the matter. The South supported
Taylor, and he won the election by a narrow margin.

As president, however, Taylor seemed less acceptable to Southerners. In good Whig fashion he promised to relax the use of the presidential
veto. This position caused concern among Southern Whigs who feared
that he might allow passage of the Wilmot Proviso.[1] In November 1849 a
prominent Southern Whig visited the White House to learn what Taylor
intended to do if Congress adopted the proviso. The president claimed to
be neutral on the matter. But he added ominously that "if Congress sees
fit to pass it, I will not veto it." He opposed the "coercion of the veto" as
undesirable. Taylor had already stated publicly that "the people of the
North need have no apprehension of the further extension of slavery." In
reaction, a group of Southern Whigs vowed once more to leave the Union
before they would accept the Wilmot Proviso.

Two presidential statements in 1849 did little to reassure Southerners. Taylor's message to Congress in December urged all sides to avoid
agitating "exciting topics of a sectional character." But Taylor did just
that. He advised that, since Californians had already decided against slavery, a free California should become a state at once, bypassing entirely
the territorial stage. Southerners found this idea unacceptable. They
regarded as even worse Taylor's observation, in a later speech, that the
New Mexico Territory (present-day New Mexico, Arizona, and part of
Colorado) would probably follow California's lead in framing a state constitution prohibiting slavery. "A good Whig document," said Webster of
the message, "written in a plain and simple style." But to the South it
was evident that Taylor was biased against introducing slavery into
newly acquired territories.

On January 21, 1850, Taylor again pleaded for action on California.
His special message advised, in effect, that the people in California and
New Mexico should enter the Union immediately as states. Avoid
complicating the issue, Taylor seemed to say, by extending the Missouri
Compromise line all the way to the Pacific Ocean. Let the territorial
problem solve itself.

Unfortunately for Taylor's program, the slavery problem in the territories would not go away. Slavery had already reentered national politics to stay. In the summer of 1848, during debates over the Oregon Terri-

---

[1] The Wilmot Proviso was first proposed in 1846. It stated that slavery should be prohibited
in all of the lands acquired from Mexico. Congress did not adopt the provision in 1846, but
many Northern politicians were committed to its passage (the proviso passed the House
twice only to fail both times in the Senate).

tory, Thomas Hart Benton, a Democratic senator from Missouri, had likened the slavery issue to the biblical plague of frogs:

> You could not look upon the table but there were frogs, you could not sit down at the banquet table but there were frogs, you could not go to the bridal couch and lift the sheets but there were frogs! We can see nothing, touch nothing, have no measures proposed, without having this pestilence thrust before us.

Ill feeling over slavery did indeed seem to crop up with every issue. As Congress got under way in 1850, debate in the House seldom rose above the level of name-calling. "For two years," accused Ohio Free-Soiler Joshua Giddings, "the people of the North have been defrauded, deceived, and imposed upon." Georgia's Robert Toombs countered: "I do not hesitate to avow before this House and the country that if by your legislation you seek to drive us from the territories of California and New Mexico and to abolish slavery in this District of Columbia, I am for disunion."

The problem of fugitive slaves brought further trouble. Some Northern states and many Northern citizens had been ignoring or flouting the existing fugitive slave law of 1791. Early in January, Senator James M. Mason of Virginia presented a bill to make the return of captured runaway slaves easier and more certain. William H. Seward, an antislavery Whig from New York and a man close to Taylor, warned that he would try to nullify the effect of a new law by adding a guarantee of trial by local jury for an alleged runaway. The Senate then exploded into a predictable outpouring of sectional complaints and threats. Mississippi's Henry S. Foote branded Seward a fanatic who wished to punish the South. Mason himself, however, defended his proposed bill in reasonable language, and he even agreed to soften parts of it in a bid for Northern votes.

Within a few days two important Democratic senators, Daniel Dickinson of New York and Lewis Cass of Michigan, spoke in favor of milder language and sectional compromise. As tempers cooled, it became possible for someone to step forward and restore calm.

The man who took on this role was Henry Clay. He hoped to engineer the third major compromise of his long career. In 1820, while Speaker of the House, he had helped pass the Missouri Compromise. In 1833, together with John C. Calhoun, he had worked out a compromise tariff bill to lower import duties and thus ease the nullification crisis. The presidency had escaped him three times. But the seventy-three-year-old senator drew consolation from his reputation as a compromiser, and he gloried in the title of "the Great Pacificator" (peacemaker). Clay knew that the conflict of 1850 would be his last major political battle.

On January 29 Clay presented his program for compromise. It consisted of eight points, most of which would soon be joined in one comprehensive, or omnibus, bill. (1) Congress should accept California as a state with a free constitution. (2) In the New Mexico Territory—unfavorable ground for slavery, according to Clay and many others—there should be no congressional restriction or encouragement of slavery. (3) The slave trade should be abolished in Washington, D.C.

These were the pro-North points. Clay's additional proposals were designed to balance things sectionally. (4) The boundary between Texas and New Mexico should be established on a line favoring Texan claims. (5) The federal government should assume responsibility for the debts of Texas before it became a state. (6) Slavery itself was to be guaranteed in the District of Columbia. (7) Congress should pass a tougher fugitive slave law. (8) Congress should formally announce a policy of noninterference with the slave trade among the Southern states. (This eighth and final suggestion, an attempt to sweeten the pill for the South, was later dropped.)

The North stood to gain more from Clay's proposals than the South. Admitting California as a free state would destroy the sectional balance — parity between free and slave states — that still existed in the Senate. (The House already had a Northern majority because the North had more people.) Giving the North a majority in the Senate as well as the House seemed suicidal to proslavery forces.

As for leaving the New Mexico Territory question undecided, Southern extremists feared, with good reason, that free states would eventually emerge from it. Why did this matter to a slaveholder in South Carolina? Because when such states joined the Union, they would elect antislavery congressmen who might vote to abolish slavery. The proposals regarding the Texas boundary and debt would not alter the sectional power balance. And enforcing a new fugitive slave law would depend on Northern cooperation, risky and uncertain at best.

Yet Clay made his appeal primarily to the North, asking for generosity, since the more powerful section had more to give. Northerners, he warned, must be especially understanding about slavery. Although the institution did not figure in their economy or society, slavery was woven into the fabric of Southern society. To talk of abolition threatened the South's "habits, safety, property, life — everything."

Clay expected no help from extremists on the slavery question, and he got none. Northern antislavery advocates had never liked him much, but they bided their time and let Southern extremists voice the first criticisms of his proposals. Eight Southern senators tore into "the Great Pacificator." One angry "fire-eater" (Southern proslavery extremist) denied that Clay had proposed a compromise at all. It was, he said, "cowardly capitulation" to the North.

On February 5 Clay responded with his major speech defending the compromise. In an address which lasted two and a half hours, he ignored the extremists and appealed to Northerners.

> What do you want? What do you want — you who reside in the free states? Do you want that there shall be no slavery introduced into the territories acquired by the war with Mexico? Have you not your desire in California? And in all human probability you will have it in New Mexico also. What more do you want? You have got what is worth more than a thousand Wilmot Provisos.

In the manner of a true compromiser Clay pleaded for moderation.

Let me say to the North and to the South, what husband and wife say to each other. We have mutual faults; neither of us is perfect; nothing in the form of humanity is perfect; let us, then, be kind to each other—forbearing, forgiving each other's faults—and above all, let us live in happiness and peace together.

Henry Clay presents the compromise proposals to a crowded Senate. (The Bettmann Archive)

While Clay looked for votes and worked to generate "spontaneous" meetings, two leading Southerners, representing two generations of proslavery opinion, renewed the attack on his compromise proposals. Senator Jefferson Davis of Mississippi dismissed Clay's plan as misleading if not worthless. He pointed out what many congressmen perhaps chose to ignore in 1850—that no fugitive slave bill, no matter what its provisions, would work if the North chose to sabotage it. Even the Missouri Compromise line, which Davis hinted might be extended to the Pacific Ocean (thus satisfying the South), could not legally bind the states involved.

In the early part of his career, Calhoun followed a nationalistic line, but by the 1830s, when he championed nullification, he had become the South's strongest voice. Abolition, he warned in 1836, "strikes directly and fatally not only at our prosperity, but our existence as a people." (Library of Congress)

According to Davis, Northern aggression had caused the crisis. "I see nothing short of conquest on the one side, or submission on the other." He claimed that the North sought to degrade Southerners, to make them "an inferior class, a degraded caste in the Union." Unless this stopped, warned Davis, Southerners would follow the example of the thirteenth-century English barons who rose up and forced King John to sign the Magna Charta.

The other Southerner who spoke at this time was John C. Calhoun. In contrast to Davis's emotional oration, Calhoun's logical address demanded specific concessions for the South. The South Carolinian had long demanded Southern unity. A year earlier Calhoun had drafted a Southern Address, a strong document of grievance and warning that was signed by forty-eight congressmen.

By 1850 Calhoun was old and sick. He knew that his career and life were almost over. He had already fainted in the Senate lobby several times. On one of these occasions he was carried into the vice-president's office to recuperate. Another South Carolinian, Robert B. Rhett, rushed over. "Ah, Mr. Rhett," Calhoun sighed, "my career is nearly done. The great battle must be fought by you younger men. . . . the South—the poor South!" On March 4 Calhoun presented his speech to the Senate. He did not actually speak, however, because of his feeble health. Senator Mason read his address for him.

Though broken in body, Calhoun remained as firm and uncompromising as ever. He argued that an exact political balance between North and South had to be maintained. No temporary, patchwork solution would do. Compromisers might chant the word "Union!" till doomsday, but it would have no more effect than intoning the word "Health!" over a dying person.

What could be done? As Calhoun saw it, the North had to give slaveholders a chance to settle the West. It had to return runaway slaves and discourage them from fleeing. It had to agree to a constitutional amendment creating a precise balance between Northern and Southern political power in the national government (despite the fact that Northern whites outnumbered Southern whites by more than 2 to 1). If the North could not accept the South on these terms, he concluded, "tell us so, and let the states we both represent agree to separate and part in peace. If you are unwilling we should part in peace, tell us so, and we shall know what to do when you reduce the question to submission or resistance."

Calhoun's defiant stand might represent the views of a minority, but still it demanded some direct response. The South Carolinian had attacked Clay's proposals and momentarily upset the majority's impulse to compromise. The man who accepted Calhoun's challenge was Daniel Webster of Massachusetts.

Webster was scheduled to speak in the Senate on March 7. In those days, a major congressional address was a great public occasion. Congressmen worked for days carefully preparing lengthy speeches. Their fellow legislators sat through the speeches and actually listened. Others, too, wanted to hear. Notice of an important speech on the congressional calendar set off a stampede for seats in the gallery. Spectators would line up for admission to the chamber, even if it meant crowding in the aisles, close-packed with other standees, for four or five hours. The Senate presented just such a picture when Webster gave his famous "Seventh of March" speech.

The portly senator rose, pulled his vest down over his paunch, raised his head, and struck a theatrical pose. "I wish to speak today," Webster began, "not as a Massachusetts man, not as a Northern man, but as an American. I speak today for the preservation of the Union. Hear me for my cause."

Webster traced the history of North–South differences. First, he emphasized the contrast between the North's easy abolition of slavery after the Revolution and the South's commitment to the institution after the invention of the cotton gin and the spread of cotton culture. He did not go so far as to claim that only lack of economic dependence had made slavery seem wrong to the North. But he did argue that his listeners had to bear in mind slavery's significance to the white South. Why then had sectional conflict grown? Because, Webster said, too many radicals in the North now contended that right could be distinguished from wrong "with the precision of an algebraic equation."

Then, Webster denounced both Northern abolitionists and Southern secessionists as dangerous extremists. Abolitionism was harmful, he asserted. The Wilmot Proviso was offensive and unnecessary; no one need "reaffirm an ordinance of nature nor reenact the will of God" by prohibiting slavery in territories "naturally" hostile to its existence. He dismissed the idea of sectional disunion. Secession and peace were mutually exclusive. Finally, Webster argued that, although sectional tensions obviously existed, they could be eased, and major political problems could be settled. Taking Clay's cue, Webster called on the North to keep its part of the basic sectional bargain. It must not harass the South over slavery, however repugnant the slave system. It must obey the law regarding slavery and even approve a new federal law to ensure that Southerners could recapture their fugitive slaves.

When he attacked the secessionists, Webster included Calhoun, the man "who, I deeply regret, is prevented by serious illness from being in his seat today." But Calhoun was there that day, having shuffled into the Senate shortly after Webster started. Calhoun shot back: "The Senator from South Carolina is in his seat." Webster continued with hardly a pause, saying that "peaceable secession is an utter impossibility." When he had finished, the galleries broke into sustained applause. Calhoun tried for the final word: "I cannot agree that this Union cannot be dissolved. Am I to understand that no degree of oppression, no outrage, no broken faith, can produce the destruction of this Union? The Union *can* be broken." These were Calhoun's last words in the Senate.

Webster had more to worry about from Northern reaction to his speech than he did from Calhoun. Webster had opposed slavery, though he was not an abolitionist. Now his call for justice to the South, especially his support for capturing and returning fugitive slaves, infuriated Northern antislavery advocates. They responded predictably and savagely. Horace Greeley, editor of the influential New York *Tribune*, wrote that the speech was "unequal to the occasion and unworthy of its author." William Cullen Bryant wrote a poem about the "fallen angel," the "Godlike Daniel." Theodore Parker, an abolitionist Boston preacher, claimed that he knew "of no deed in American history done by a son of New England to which I can compare this but the act of Benedict Arnold."

Other Americans, however, hailed Webster's speech for what it was—a significant and eloquent statement urging both sides to stop agitating the slavery question. Conservatives, North and South, read it with approval; 120,000 copies had been rushed into print. Even the Charleston *Mercury*, unfriendly to the North and its politics, noted that "with such a spirit as Mr. Webster has shown, it no longer seems impossible to bring this sectional contest to a close." Businessmen overwhelmingly supported the Clay-Webster position. They worried that all the squabbling about slavery would interfere with trade. William W. Corcoran, an important Washington banker, went further. He sent Webster a letter of congratulation with a check for $1000.

With Clay and Webster clearly speaking for an older generation, it remained for a different breed of politician to be heard from. While young Southern fire-eaters continued to regard Calhoun as their mentor (even after his death on March 31), a rising group of Northern politicians looked for new leadership. William H. Seward of New York, who had just arrived in the Senate, became their spokesman.

Seward, a little man of large ambition, had played the political game astutely since the middle 1820s, mainly in his home state. First an Anti-Mason, then a Whig, Seward's election as governor in 1838 broke the Democratic Albany Regency's domination of New York State politics. He knew the value of party organization and party discipline (even at the expense of party principles) far better than most older Whig leaders. He knew also that antislavery and anti-Southern feeling was rising in the North and would soon monopolize American politics.

The leader of the antislavery Whigs, William Seward spoke of a "higher law" than the Constitution. (Library of Congress)

Seward addressed the Senate on March 11. His speech was clearly a reaction to Webster's effort of four days earlier, although there was little similarity between the two in structure, delivery, or content. Seward read a prepared text in a monotone to a sparsely filled chamber. Still, leading senators (even Calhoun) attended because they realized the importance of Seward's views and those for whom he presumably spoke.

In essence, Seward rejected all plans for compromise. Since no real threat of disunion existed, he insisted, why compromise? Slavery, a barbarous relic of earlier and less enlightened times, would die a peaceful and natural death. Why encourage it? Congress could legislate for the territories, and it should prohibit slavery there. "I shall vote for the admission of California directly, without conditions, without qualifications, and without compromise."

Most of Seward's speech followed a Northern hard line on territorial questions, not far removed from President Taylor's stand. But the New Yorker added some statements that made his speech notorious. Did the Constitution protect slavery? "There is a higher law than the Constitution," answered Seward. Slavery must go. A moral question had been raised that transcended the "narrow creeds" of political parties. He dismissed slavery as "temporary, accidental, partial, and incongruous." Freedom, on the other hand, was "perpetual, organic, universal, and in harmony with the Constitution."

Southerners were outraged. Even many Northerners joined in attacking Seward's "higher law" doctrine as anarchy. President Taylor himself, previously close to Seward, ordered his administration newspaper to rap the New Yorker on the knuckles. These quick reactions revealed clearly that Seward, like Calhoun, spoke only for a congressional minority. But, just as clearly, his stand could not be ignored.

Stephen Douglas, Illinois's "Little Giant," was the ultimate mastermind of procompromise strategy. (Library of Congress)

The debate continued. On March 13 another Northerner, Stephen A. Douglas of Illinois, made an important speech. On the surface, Douglas was critical of Clay's proposals. Actually, however, he spent more time attacking Clay's enemies and upholding popular sovereignty, his preferred solution. Douglas regarded the will of local inhabitants in the territories as all-important. He felt that the Missouri Compromise restriction of 1820, which prohibited slavery in the Louisiana Territory north of 36° 30′ latitude, was no restriction at all. Politicians in Washington, he believed, could neither establish nor forbid slavery in a territory. Local laws would prevail. They would inevitably reflect local environment and attitudes. Douglas also added his opinion that slavery could not expand west of the Mississippi beyond where it already existed—that is, Missouri, Arkansas, Louisiana, and Texas. His statement made many Southerners suspicious of Douglas and other so-called National Democrats.

At this point, a Senate fracas indicated how deep the impasse had become. It involved Thomas Hart Benton of Missouri and Henry S. Foote of Mississippi. Both were Democrats, and both wanted a compromise. Beyond this they parted ways. Benton was tall and burly, a polished and often bombastic orator. He had been in the Senate for thirty years, as long as Missouri had been a state. Although he represented a slave state, Benton did not believe in the extension of slavery. Let California join as a free state, he urged, and then solve other disputed sectional matters one by one.

Foote was short, rotund, and animated. Other senators acknowledged his considerable talents yet regarded him as a bit eccentric. Previously, Foote had been close to the Southern extremists. But he now supported Clay's proposals for compromise and strongly urged combining them into an omnibus bill.

On April 17, Benton attacked Clay's omnibus approach as pandering to Southern hysteria. Foote labeled the charge a slander. Benton then rose and headed straight toward his adversary. No match for Benton at

In his last year as a senator, Thomas Hart Benton maintained his moderate views on slavery. (Library of Congress)

Henry Foote's life seemed to embody inconsistency. A Mississippian, he opposed secession. Then he served in the Confederate congress. Still later, he quarreled with Jefferson Davis, resigned his seat, and left the South. (Library of Congress)

coining phrases, Foote decided on another equalizer. He pulled a gun. Other members of the world's greatest deliberative body—as the Senate likes to call itself—quickly moved to avoid catastrophe. As Foote was stopped by a friendly senator, Benton, who rarely let slip the opportunity to add drama to a situation, tore open his shirt front and shouted, "Let the assassin fire! I am not armed. I have no pistols. I disdain to carry arms. A pistol has been brought in to shoot me with—to assassinate me!"

"I brought it here to defend myself," Foote responded lamely, at the same time handing his gun to Senator Dickinson.

"Nothing of the kind, sir," Benton retorted. "It is a false imputation. I carry nothing of the kind, and no assassin has a right to draw a pistol on me."

Foote obviously did not want to shoot Benton; yet the outrageous incident could not be ignored altogether. A special Senate committee investigated. It reported two months later but declined to recommend any disciplinary action against Foote.[2]

Although congressional speechmaking played a more important role in 1850 than it does today, the real work of Congress—then as now—went on in committees. The day after the Benton–Foote confrontation, the Senate attended to more serious business. Foote moved that a select committee chaired by Clay work to resolve the sectional disputes. His resolution passed, 30 to 22. Thirteen senators world serve, seven Whigs and six Democrats. Seven were from slave states, and six were from free states. But only one senator from each section could be labeled an extremist.

For the next three weeks congressional activity creaked to a halt. Even the speechmakers were silent, waiting for Clay's committee to report. Its seven-point recommendation strongly resembled Clay's original plan. There was no minority report.

Few senators seemed satisfied with everything Clay's committee had proposed. When formal debate on the report began on May 13, almost every senator wanted to be heard, some several times.

The compromise faced another challenge—from outside Congress. The Mississippi legislature had called on representatives of the slave states to meet at Nashville, Tennessee, in June 1850 to adopt methods of "resistance to [Northern] aggressions." Calhoun had supported the Mississippi move enthusiastically. His spirit would certainly be present at Nashville. Daniel Webster predicted that if the Southern extremists actually convened at Nashville, Andrew Jackson's body would turn over in its nearby grave.

Nevertheless, the Nashville Convention did take place. But—like New England's Hartford Convention during the War of 1812—it proved a

---

[2] As usual, Benton had the last word. Foote later tried to patch up the quarrel, announcing his intention to write a small book in which Senator Benton would figure prominently. Benton countered with an announcement that he would write a large book that would not even mention Senator Foote. Both men kept their word.

bit of a dud. Only nine of the slave states sent delegates, and not all of them were leaders in their own states. There was a great deal of heated talk. The meeting's final report, drafted by South Carolina fire-eater Robert B. Rhett, honored Calhoun's memory and most of his principles. Yet the convention kept cool. Delegates did not abandon their desire to defend Southern rights. But most still waited for a decision in Congress.

Most Americans observed the Nashville Convention fiasco with satisfaction, and none more so than President Taylor. The general was the nation's most important opponent of Clay's compromise, and he was angry. Clay and other Whig leaders had slighted him. Some had even made fun of him as lacking intelligence. Clay went so far as to heap praise on another general and would-be president, Winfield Scott—Taylor's rival for military glory during the war with Mexico. The president's anger boiled over whenever he heard talk of secession. At one point, a group of worried Southerners had trooped into the White House to ask Taylor if he really meant to maintain the Union at all cost. Eyes blazing (possibly thinking of Andrew Jackson's sternness at such moments), the president swore that he would blockade every Southern port if secessionists took over federal facilities. He promised to head an army of Northern and Western troops to put down any rebellion.

The situation had not yet come to a head, though. In the spring and summer of 1850 the legislative process still seemed the best solution. Yet it looked as if no compromise could jump the hurdle of a presidential veto. Taylor opposed the omnibus bill. When his own newspaper began speaking kindly of Clay, Taylor had the editor replaced by someone who would follow the administration line. Clay argued that his proposals would heal at least some, if not all, of the country's wounds on the slavery question, whereas Taylor's would heal only one, the status of California. The White House responded tartly that the original congressional resolution concerned only California and the New Mexico Territory, with no mention of such inflammatory side issues as fugitive slaves or Texan debts.

Throughout June pro-compromise forces made no progress. Opponents were trying to mutilate the select committee report with amendment after amendment and delay it with parliamentary obstruction. "We shall have a warm summer," Webster predicted. "The political atmosphere will be hot, however the natural may be. I am for it and shall fight it out." Arguments of "no earthly consequence start up from time to time," admitted Clay glumly, "to discourage the stoutest heart." The omnibus was stalled, perhaps permanently.

There matters stood, until Washington heat, gluttony, and divine Providence intervened. On the Fourth of July, President Taylor attended ceremonies at the base of the unfinished Washington monument. Under a broiling sun he dutifully heard the ever-present Henry S. Foote (presumably unarmed this time) deliver the Independence Day oration. As the president got up to leave, aides asked him to stay and witness yet another ceremony. A handful of dust from the tomb of Thaddeus Kosciusko, the Polish hero of the American Revolution, was to be deposited in the monument. Taylor waited, standing exposed to the summer sun for an additional hour.

Back at the White House at last, Taylor refreshed himself with huge quantities of fruits, vegetables, and iced liquids. "Cucumbers and cherries with mush and milk," runs the most bizarre of the many accounts of what he consumed.

Taylor loved to eat—heartily and often. He ignored all danger warnings, verbal or internal, even one that appeared in his own official newspaper: "Do not unnecessarily heat yourselves, but, when heated, drink cold water in moderation. Ice water, in small quantities, is an excellent tonic; but some persons flood the stomach till internal chemistry can no longer overcome its effects." The president's internal chemistry broke down. He was overcome with nausea, stomach cramps, and fever. Taylor lingered on until July 9, when he died of acute gastroenteritis.

Into the White House came Vice-President Millard Fillmore. Like Seward, though always several rungs below him, Fillmore had climbed the ladder of New York Anti-Masonic and Whig politics. New Yorkers of all parties had a history of squabbling and splitting into factions. By 1850 Fillmore and Seward found themselves in warring camps. Taylor might have been on good terms with Seward, but Fillmore had no use for his fellow New Yorker. Where did Fillmore stand on the compromise? Most Southerners distrusted him, since he came from western New York, the most strongly antislavery part of the state. Fillmore's nomination and election to the vice-presidency in 1848 had caused an anxious stir in the slave states. But in that election the South had placed its faith and sectional interests in Taylor's hands.

As late as April 1850, Fillmore had indicated agreement with Taylor's policies. Sometime between April and early July, however, he became a supporter of Clay's compromise. He later claimed that, just before Taylor's death, he had told the president that if the Senate tied the vote on the compromise, he, as vice-president (and president of the Senate), would break the tie with a yes vote. Daniel Webster may have had something to do with Fillmore's conversion. As secretary of state, he emerged as the leading figure of the new administration. He exercised a strong influence over the conscientious but intellectually limited Fillmore. So did Clay, a semiofficial administration spokesman in Congress. Apparently all that remained was to push the omnibus bill through, have the new president sign it, and let peace reign. But this was not to be.

On July 31 the Senate was voting on a complicated series of amendments to the compromise. The omnibus was maneuvered by its opponents into a position where it could be killed. One by one, each of the bill's provisions was rejected by the Senate. The only part to be adopted was a bill granting territorial status to Utah. This passed easily, since the federal government wanted to reassert its authority over the Mormons (see pp. 313–14). Little else remained but disappointment for the pro-compromise forces and delight for Northern and Southern extremists. A reporter for a New York paper described the scene: "Jefferson

Davis's face grinned with smiles. Old Bullion's [Thomas Hart Benton] few hairs actually bristled with delight. *He* had routed *Clay*! *He* had smashed his omnibus to atoms! Seward was dancing about like a little top." The reporter went on to describe other gleeful senators—a Northern supporter of Seward whose "thick sides shook with sporadic spasms"; a Southerner who "looked solemn in solitary glory"; and an Ohio abolitionist shaking hands with a Louisiana fire-eater.

Clay walked out of the Senate chamber humiliated. He had fumbled his last great compromise effort. He soon left Washington for the resort town of Newport, Rhode Island—probably in a huff and surely very tired.

Clay's failure created Douglas's opportunity. Since the omnibus package had fallen to pieces, the energetic Douglas took the logical course of action. He worked on one bill at a time. There were five altogether in addition to the Utah bill.

First was the bill settling the Texan boundary and debt. It passed on August 9. Next came the question of California. Southerners wanted to divide the region into two states—one free and other undecided on slavery. Douglas, however, aimed to have the free-state California constitution adopted as it stood. Jeremiah Clemens of Alabama warned: "I do not know what Alabama may do, but if she determines to resist this bill by force, secession, by any means, I am at her service. If this be treason, I am a traitor—a traitor who glories in the name."

Despite talk of this kind, the Senate passed the California bill on August 13. Next to clear the Senate was the New Mexico territorial bill.

The measure strengthening the fugitive slave laws, which would soon become the weakest link in the compromise chain, passed on

In this bitter comment on the Fugitive Slave Act of 1850, Webster (center) helps a slave catcher chase a fleeing woman and child. In the accompanying caption, Webster is made to say: "Any man can perform an agreeable duty—it is not everyone that can perform a disagreeable duty." (Worcester Art Museum)

August 26. In view of later reactions Northerners were surprisingly calm on the measure, perhaps because several leading antislavery figures had left Washington for cooler parts by that time. Still, twenty-one senators (fifteen of them Northerners) failed to vote on the fugitive slave bill. Had they all responded to the roll call, the bill would probably have been defeated. Douglas had applied strong and effective pressures on his Democratic colleagues in the Senate. The final bill of the compromise was one outlawing the slave trade in Washington, D.C. Clay himself came back to Washington in time to shepherd it through Congress on September 16.

The House of Representatives played second fiddle to the Senate throughout the dramatic 1850 session. Once the bills were through the Senate, the House passed them with little trouble early in September.

The Compromise of 1850 had initially been a Whig venture — or so Clay and Webster saw it, despite their nonpartisan appeals. But it became a reality through a series of bills shepherded through Congress by Stephen A. Douglas, a Democrat who relied largely on the votes of Democratic congressmen. Of eleven senators who supported at least five of the six compromise measures, nine were Democrats. Votes in the House of Representatives revealed the same Democratic concern for compromise. The Democrats, the party of Jefferson and Jackson, had clearly committed themselves to a new version of their old policy — keeping the slavery issue out of national politics.

A Deepening Sectional Conflict 20

Passage of the Compromise of 1850 and its acceptance by most Americans, North and South, seemed to close a dangerous chapter in United States history. Americans felt that they had achieved peace. Or at least they hoped so —with a fervor that showed how afraid they had been. If slavery took root as a national issue, the country itself might split apart. The apparent escape from this danger led to a feeling of elation in 1850. Yet if the past decade was a true indicator of the future, the years ahead would be anything but placid.

Indeed, slavery was already a national issue, even though people might wish to think otherwise. It had become so through its relationship to newly acquired territories in the West—the very question that had led to the Compromise of 1850. Throughout much of American history, disruptive political crises have often been involved with issues of geographic expansion. The slavery controversy was no exception.

EXPANSION INTO THE FAR WEST

Americans have generally believed that they could move freely into unsettled territories wherever available. This belief was never more stoutly held than during the first half of the nineteenth century. In this period some Americans moved into land acquired through the Louisiana Purchase. Even more attractive, however, were Far West regions that did not belong to the United States. The most important of these were the Oregon Country, claimed by Great Britain, and the Mexican-held Southwest and California.

Americans had various reasons for wanting to expand westward. Merchants were attracted to trade possibilities. Oregon, for example, offered not only furs but also a possible base for commerce with Asia. Many Americans were looking for good farming or grazing land. Even those who stayed home in the East took pride in the idea of westward expansion.

Newspapermen and politicians wrote approvingly of national growth. The phrase that best expressed the current attitude was manifest destiny. The term was coined by John L. O'Sullivan, a Democratic editor from New York. He wrote in 1845 that it was the "manifest destiny [of the United States] to overspread and to possess the whole of the continent which Providence has given us for the development of the great experiment of liberty and federated self-government entrusted to us."[1]

In other words, it was manifest (obvious) that fate had destined the United States for an expansionist role. Americans had a God-given mission to establish the Protestant religion, a democratic political system, and a capitalist economy in all the lands from the Atlantic to the Pacific. Many Americans shared this imperial vision in some form.

The Oregon Country

Since the late eighteenth century, many nations had shown an interest in the Oregon Country —the region between the Rockies and the Pacific

---

[1] The term "manifest destiny" was first used in Congress by Robert C. Winthrop, the Whig nominee for Speaker of the House in 1849.

379

coast extending from what is now California northward to Alaska. At various times Spain, Russia, Britain, and the United States had laid claims to all or part of the area.

American merchants en route to the Far East sailed along the Oregon coast. So did traders in search of furs. In 1792 an American named Robert Gray explored and named the Columbia River. Lewis and Clark also explored the Oregon Country. In 1811 New York merchant John Jacob Astor founded a fur-trading post, Astoria, at the mouth of the Columbia River. When the War of 1812 broke out, however, he sold the post to a British company.

By 1825 both Spain and Russia had given up their claims to the Oregon Country. But British fur traders of the Hudson's Bay Company were quite active in the region. There was a spirited three-way rivalry between them, the American traders employed by the Rocky Mountain Fur Company, and Astor's American Fur Company. In 1818, Great Britain and the United States had agreed that the two countries would occupy Oregon jointly until 1827. When the agreement expired, it was extended for an indefinite period.

The settlement of American families in the Oregon Country was stimulated mainly by missionaries, who went to the area in the 1830s. Methodist minister Jason Lee opened a mission in the Willamette Valley near what is now Salem, Oregon. Marcus and Narcissa Whitman, backed by the Congregationalists and Presbyterians, established a mission on the Columbia River near present-day Walla Walla, Washington.

The missionaries' letters described in glowing terms Oregon's fertile soil, magnificent rivers, and excellent climate. Small groups of settlers moved westward in the early 1840s. The first major party of pioneers—a thousand strong—set out from Independence, Missouri, in 1843. The westward migration became so heavy in the late 1840s that it was known as "Oregon fever."

Pioneers made the trip to Oregon along the famous Oregon Trail. From Independence, the trail led northwest and then followed the Platte River, crossing the Rockies at South Pass. Travelers to Oregon proceeded northward through the valleys of the Snake and Columbia rivers.

In 1843, Americans in Oregon organized a provisional government and petitioned Congress for annexation. Settlers from the United States now far outnumbered those from Canada and Britain. The earlier arrangements for joint occupation of the region seemed unsatisfactory—at least to Americans.

Annexation of Oregon was one of the issues in the presidential campaign of 1844. The Whigs nominated Henry Clay, who tried to avoid the

U.S. GROWTH OF POPULATION, 1790-1860

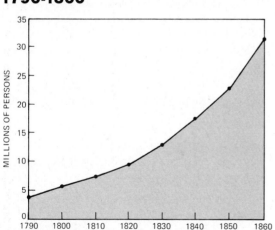

U.S. FOREIGN TRADE, 1790-1860

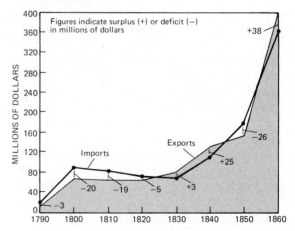

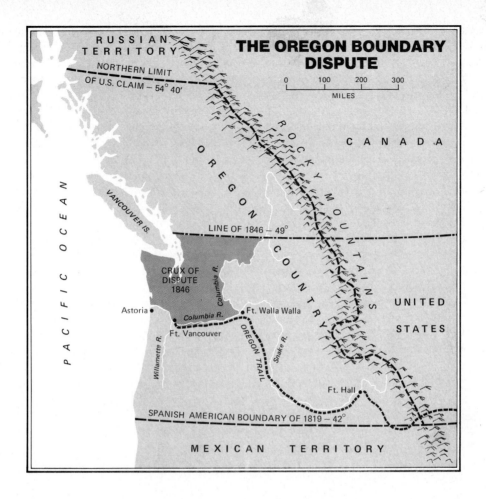

THE OREGON BOUNDARY DISPUTE

RUSSIAN TERRITORY

NORTHERN LIMIT OF U.S. CLAIM — 54° 40'

CANADA

PACIFIC OCEAN

VANCOUVER IS.

LINE OF 1846 — 49°

OREGON COUNTRY

ROCKY MOUNTAINS

UNITED STATES

CRUX OF DISPUTE 1846

Columbia R.

Astoria

Columbia R.

Ft. Walla Walla

Ft. Vancouver

Willamette R.

OREGON TRAIL

Snake R.

Ft. Hall

SPANISH AMERICAN BOUNDARY OF 1819 — 42°

MEXICAN TERRITORY

MILES 0 100 200 300

question of expansion. The Democrats chose James K. Polk, governor of Tennessee and former Speaker of the House of Representatives. Polk was an ardent expansionist, and the Democratic platform stressed "All of Oregon or none." In other words, said Polk, the United States should expand northward to the 54th parallel. The British insisted on the 49th parallel as a more reasonable dividing line, since it continued westward the already existing boundary that divided the rest of the United States from Canada.

After Polk's election, some expansionists demanded war if the British refused to yield to American demands. Their slogan was "54° 40' or Fight!" Other Americans took a calmer view, and in 1846, the Polk administration negotiated a set-

tlement with Britain that established the 49th parallel as the boundary between the western United States and Canada.

An Independent Texas

While American settlement in Oregon led to tension with Britain, expansion into Texas brought on conflict with Mexico. Spain had ceded Florida to the United States in 1819. As part of the bargain, Americans had given up their claim to Texas—a claim they had asserted since the purchase of Louisiana. Americans, however, were already moving into the region. In fact, traders and military adventurers from the United States had helped the Mexicans win independence from Spain in 1821. In return the new Mexican government had confirmed a large land grant previously made by the Spanish to Moses Austin.

Austin, a Missourian, had planned to colonize the Brazos River area with Americans. He died in 1821. Stephen Austin, his son, carried out the plan. In 1822 he planted a colony of three hundred American families at Columbus, Texas. Most were Southerners, small slaveholders or nonslaveholding farmers. They were lured by the promise of practically free farmland for cotton cultivation.

During the next decade American settlers moved steadily into Texas. By 1830 there were at least twenty-five thousand whites and two thousand black slaves. Most of the newcomers remained Protestant despite the terms of the original Austin land grant, which committed American settlers to becoming Roman Catholics. Although Texas formed part of a state in the Mexican republic, the majority of its inhabitants were firmly committed to their American customs and beliefs.

The "invasion" of these American settlers frightened the Mexican government. Its leaders were afraid that the Texans would try to break away and join the United States. Mexico crushed one revolt in 1826. After this, Mexicans tried unsuccessfully to restrict further American immigration. They forbade the importation of slaves into Texas and placed heavy taxes on imported American goods. These efforts proved to be too little and too late. Americans in Texas were already encouraging their fellow countrymen to settle there. They were also agitating with the Mexicans for their own state government.

President Antonio López de Santa Anna decided to tighten Mexican control over Texas. Early in 1836 he led an army of 6000 into the region. On March 2 the Texans met at Washington, Texas, and declared their independence from Mexico. They adopted a constitution legalizing slavery and established a provisional government. As commander of the Texan army they named Samuel

In the last hours of the Alamo garrison Jim Bowie wields the knife named after him as the Texan defenders fight back Santa Anna's attacking Mexican army. (The Bettmann Archive)

Houston, former governor of Tennessee and a friend of Andrew Jackson.

Meanwhile, Santa Anna had begun his siege of the Alamo, a former mission at San Antonio. For twelve days a garrison of 187 Texans led by William B. Travis withstood an attack force of 3000. Finally, on March 6, the Alamo fell. Its defenders—including the famous frontiersman Davy Crockett—were massacred. Later in March 300 Texans were slaughtered in a similar fashion when they surrendered at Goliad. For several weeks Houston had to retreat before Santa Anna's army. Then, on April 21, he made a stand at San Jacinto. Shouting "Remember the Alamo!" and "Remember Goliad!" Houston's men defeated Santa Anna and took the Mexican general prisoner.

Santa Anna signed a treaty (which he later repudiated) recognizing the independence of Texas. In September 1836, Texas voters ratified their new constitution and elected Sam Houston president. At the same time, they indicated their desire for annexation to the United States.

Troubles Over Annexation

The annexation of Texas became a controversial issue. Northern antislavery forces did not want to add another slave state to the Union. President Jackson, who wished to avoid a sectional split, refused to endorse the proposal. So did his successor, Van Buren.

Texans then began to turn to Europe for recognition and aid, showing particular interest in Britain. Southern expansionists were alarmed by the prospect of a close alliance between cotton-hungry Britain and the cotton-producing Republic of Texas. They pressed for a treaty of annexation. So did President Tyler (who had come into office after Harrison's death in April 1841) and Secretary of State John C. Calhoun. A treaty that they negotiated in 1844, however, was rejected overwhelmingly by the Senate.

Texas, like Oregon, was an issue in the presidential campaign of 1844. One of Polk's slogans was a demand for "the reoccupation of Oregon and the reannexation of Texas." (The "re" in each case cleverly implied that the United States had always owned the disputed territories.)

After Polk won, but before he took office, President Tyler exploited the popular support for expansion. He pressed for a joint congressional resolution annexing Texas. Since it was not a treaty, the resolution did not require a two-thirds Senate vote, and thus it squeaked through. Texas ratified the resolution and joined the Union in December 1845.

The Mexican War

When Texas became a state, Mexico broke off diplomatic relations with the United States. This was not the only sore point between the two nations. The United States claimed that the Texan boundary extended to the Rio Grande, whereas Mexico set it at the Nueces River. Another Mexican grievance was the growing number of Americans in California.

Early in 1846 Polk ordered General Zachary Taylor, commanding a force of 1500, to take up a position along the Rio Grande. War fever grew among nationalists in both countries. The Mexicans refused to see John Slidell, an American diplomat sent to Mexico City to negotiate. A minor skirmish between Taylor's forces and the Mexican troops along the Rio Grande gave the eager American president an excuse for war. Polk blamed Mexico for shedding American blood; Congress declared war on May 11; and the House authorized the recruitment of an army of 50,000 volunteers.

The American troops, though fewer in number, were better supplied and better led than the Mexican forces. In fact, the Mexican War served as a training ground for many young officers who later commanded armies during the Civil War. Among them were Robert E. Lee, Ulysses S. Grant, J. E. B. Stuart, George B. McClellan, and "Stonewall" Jackson.

The United States won a series of victories on Mexican soil—at Monterrey, Buena Vista, and Veracruz. In September 1847, Americans took Mexico City itself. The United States also seized New Mexico and California with small military forces supported by American settlers. Mexico had to sue for peace.

The Treaty of Guadalupe Hidalgo ended the war. Mexico gave up California, New Mexico, and the disputed area east of the Rio Grande. In return

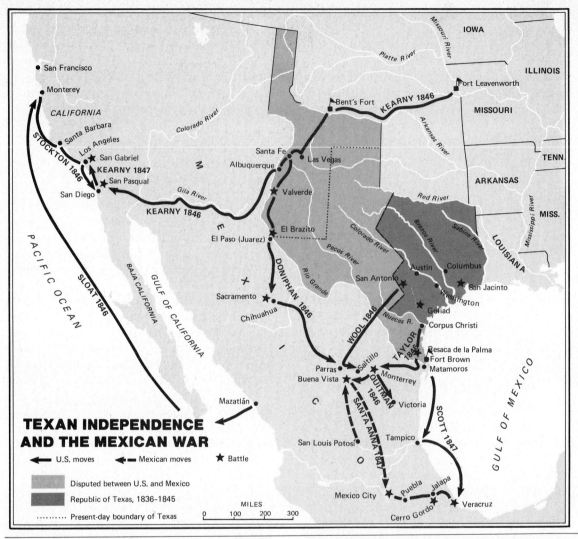

TEXAN INDEPENDENCE AND THE MEXICAN WAR

- ◀ U.S. moves
- ◀- - Mexican moves
- ★ Battle

Disputed between U.S. and Mexico

Republic of Texas, 1836–1845

········· Present-day boundary of Texas

MILES
0   100   200   300

In the spring of **1846,** before war was officially declared, Zachary Taylor engaged the Mexican army in two battles north of Fort Brown, Texas. After Palo Alto (May 8) and Resaca de la Palma (May 9), Taylor drove the Mexicans out of the disputed area between the Nueces River and the Rio Grande. He then crossed the lower Rio Grande and captured Matamoros (May 18) and Monterrey (Sept. 29). Before the end of the year Taylor, aided by John E. Wool, occupied Saltillo, and, along with General A. Quitman, then proceeded south to Victoria.

In the meantime Stephen W. Kearny led an expedition from Fort Leavenworth to Santa Fe (Aug. 15) and proclaimed New Mexico part of the United States. He left part of his army there, sent another detachment under Alexander W. Doni-

phan south to join Taylor, and proceeded to California. Doniphan, on his march from Sante Fe to Chihuahua, defeated the Mexicans at Valverde (Dec. 12) and El Brazito (Dec. 25). Meanwhile, Kearny had arrived in California, where John Sloat had already taken Monterey. After a temporary setback at San Pasqual (Dec. 6) Kearny joined Robert F. Stockton in San Diego.

In **1847** Kearny and Stockton were victorious at San Gabriel (Jan. 8-9). By February the Southwest was in American hands. Doniphan defeated the Mexicans at Sacramento (Feb. 28) and reached his goal, the provincial capital city of Chihuahua, on March 1. Taylor's army drove Mexican forces under Santa Anna out of a narrow mountain pass near the hacienda of Buena Vista (February 22-23).

This print of the American Army taking posses-
sion of the Mexican capital in 1847 appeared in
a history of the war written by George W. Ken-
dall of the New Orleans Picayune. *Kendall was*
one of the first war correspondents ever to ac-
company an army on its campaigns. (Library of
Congress)

In the winter of 1847 Winfield Scott led a force of about 10,000 with orders to take the fortified city of Veracruz. His men landed on the beaches outside the city on March 9, launching the first large-scale amphibious operation in United States military history. On March 29 he captured the city, and began an advance toward the Mexican capital. Near Jalapa, he stormed a mountain pass at Cerro Gordo (April 17-18), routing Santa Anna's army. He reached Puebla in May. Scott badly defeated Santa Anna at Contreras (Aug. 19) and Churubusco (Aug. 20), and captured the hilltop fortress of Chapultepec (Sept. 12). He smashed his way into Mexico City's last defenses on September 14, thus effectively ending the war.

it received $15 million and the Americans' promise to assume their own citizens' outstanding claims against Mexico. The United States acquired an additional 529,000 square miles of territory at a cost of 13,000 American lives, most of them lost as a result of disease. Mexican casualties totaled approximately 14,000 killed or missing in action.

Some rabid expansionists considered even these gains minor. They wanted the United States to pursue its supposed manifest destiny and seize all of Mexico. The Senate prudently disregarded these suggestions, however, and ratified the treaty of peace in March 1848.

Americans in California

Many Americans who moved west from Independence, Missouri, had destinations other than Oregon. At about the same time that Stephen Austin led his settlers into Texas, merchants were opening up the Sante Fe Trail. Year after year their trade caravans left Independence and lumbered south, loaded with goods to be sold in New Mexico. Thousands of Americans started out on the Oregon Trail but turned off before reaching the Oregon Country. One group, the Mormons, went south into Utah (see pp. 313–315). Others pushed farther west on the California Trail; most of them went to either Sutter's Fort (Sacramento) or the Los Angeles area.

Like Texas, California originally belonged to Spain and, after 1821, to Mexico. In the early years of the nineteenth century it attracted relatively few Americans. There were only about seven hundred there in 1845.

Nevertheless, Polk had plans for California. Late in 1845 he wrote Thomas Larkin, the American consul at Monterey, asking him to stir up a revolt and encourage Americans in California to apply for annexation. Larkin received Polk's message in April 1846. At the same time, an explorer and military adventurer named John C. Frémont entered the picture. Moving south from Oregon, he helped lead a revolt of settlers in the Sacramento Valley. On June 14, 1846, at Sonoma, they declared California an independent republic.[2]

Meanwhile, Mexico and the United States had gone to war. American naval forces led by Commodore John Sloat took Monterey on July 7. San Francisco was captured two days later. In August, Commodore Robert Stockton (who replaced the ailing Sloat) declared California annexed to the United States—with himself as governor.

The situation in California was clearly getting out of hand. Polk himself sent in Colonel Stephen Kearny, who had recently taken Sante Fe. When Kearny arrived with a small force in November, he found Stockton and Frémont bickering over who should be in control. Early in 1847 Kearny succeeded in quelling remaining Mexican resistance in the region and in establishing his own authority as governor. California was ceded to the United States in the Treaty of Guadalupe Hidalgo, which ended the Mexican War.

Even before the treaty was ratified, an event occurred that would soon transform California.

<hr />

[2] This event is known as the Bear Flag Revolt because the homemade flag raised by the rebels was adorned with a picture of a grizzly bear.

California goldminers pause for a photograph in 1852. In this type of sluice, water pushed gravel through, while heavier gold sank to the bottom of the trough.

This was the discovery of gold near Sutter's Mill in January 1848. When news reached the East, the Gold Rush was on, and in 1849, the "forty-niners" poured into California. By 1850 there were 100,000 people there, a figure that doubled in the next two years. Most of those who had joined the Gold Rush remained in California, although only a small proportion of them ever struck it rich.

NATIONAL POLITICAL TENSIONS

During the 1830s and 1840s the United States had extended its boundaries to the Pacific Ocean. But these territorial gains brought major political headaches. They were the unwanted and unexpected consequences of manifest destiny. Should Northern or Southern patterns dominate the new Western territories? Should the emerging new states be slave or free? And who would decide the slavery question, Congress or the territories themselves?

National party politics in the 1840s underwent many shifts and changes reflecting the uncertainties of a rapidly growing country. The system in existence at this time was the second American national party system. (The first, which took shape during the early 1800s, pitted the Federalists against the Jeffersonian Republicans.) The second system had arisen in the 1820s out of the struggle for national power between the Jacksonians and the National Republicans. It resulted in two major national parties, the Democrats and the Whigs.

The Democratic party had supporters in both the North and South, and it specifically pledged to keep slavery out of politics. The Whigs promised to do the same. In general Whigs kept this promise. Still, they usually fared better in Northern states, a fact that made them more antislavery in tone than the Democrats. Thus an antislavery politician was more likely to be a Whig than a Democrat.

Some antislavery politicians preferred to work outside the two-party system. Radical abolitionists shunned political parties altogether. Other Americans decided on organized political effort through a third party. In 1840 a small group of moderate abolitionists organized the new Liberty party. They nominated a "reformed" exslaveholder and former Alabaman, James G. Birney, for president. But they polled only seven thousand votes in the 1840 election, which helped to place Harrison in the White House. Four years later the Liberty party again ran poorly. But this time, by taking votes away from Whig candidates in several important states, it helped swing the election in favor of Democrat James K. Polk.

The Wilmot Proviso

Until the mid-1840s, party loyalties generally overcame American sectional differences. A Southern Whig, for example, considered himself a

Whig first and a Southerner second, at least in matters in which party principle played a large role. But things changed, as the slavery issue emerged swiftly in national politics.

One man who helped bring about the change was an obscure Pennsylvania Democratic congressman named David Wilmot. In August 1846 he introduced a proviso (amendment) to an appropriation bill requested by President Polk to buy territory from Mexico. The Wilmot Proviso stated simply that slavery would be forbidden in any states formed out of territory acquired from Mexico.

Both of the major political parties tended to divide along sectional lines in the voting. Southerners—Whigs and Democrats alike—bitterly opposed the Wilmot Proviso. (The proslavery Whigs were sometimes known as "Cotton Whigs.") Some Northern Democrats also opposed the proviso. But many other Northerners—both Democrats and Whigs—favored it. (Northern antislavery Whigs called themselves "Conscience Whigs.")

One antislavery congressman from Illinois—a Whig named Abraham Lincoln—lost his reelection bid in 1848 partly because of his support for the Wilmot Proviso. The growing strength of antislavery feeling in the North can be seen from the fact that the proviso passed the House twice, only to be defeated both times in the Senate, where Southerners enjoyed equal voting strength.

Effects of the Mexican War

Another factor responsible for the growth of sectionalism was the Mexican War. The war was understandably popular in the South, because proslavery people wanted the new territories. Northern opponents of slavery denounced both the war and the prospect that the newly acquired territories might become slave states. Many Northerners saw the war as part of a conspiracy to extend the South's economic base and political power.

Even some thoughtful Southerners recognized the dangers. Calhoun supported the Mexican War, but he warned the Senate that "a deed has been done from which the country will not be able to recover for a long time, if ever. It has closed the first volume of our political history under the Constitution and opened the second."

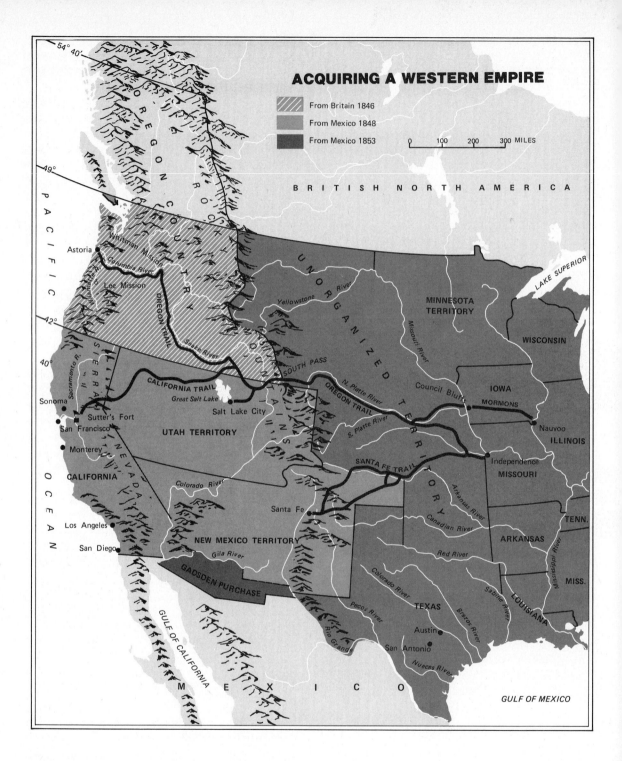

ACQUIRING A WESTERN EMPIRE

- From Britain 1846
- From Mexico 1848
- From Mexico 1853

0   100   200   300 MILES

BRITISH NORTH AMERICA

OREGON COUNTRY

ROCKY

54° 40'

49°

42°

40°

PACIFIC

OCEAN

Astoria

Whitman Mission

Columbia River

Lee Mission

OREGON TRAIL

Snake River

SOUTH PASS

CALIFORNIA TRAIL

Great Salt Lake

Salt Lake City

Sonoma

Sutter's Fort

San Francisco

Monterey

CALIFORNIA

SIERRA NEVADA

Sacramento R.

UTAH TERRITORY

Colorado River

Los Angeles

San Diego

Gila River

NEW MEXICO TERRITORY

Santa Fe

GADSDEN PURCHASE

GULF OF CALIFORNIA

M E X I C O

Yellowstone River

UNORGANIZED TERRITORY

MOUNTAINS

OREGON TRAIL

N. Platte River

S. Platte River

SANTA FE TRAIL

MINNESOTA TERRITORY

Missouri River

Council Bluffs

LAKE SUPERIOR

WISCONSIN

IOWA

MORMONS

Nauvoo

ILLINOIS

Independence

MISSOURI

Arkansas River

Canadian River

Red River

ARKANSAS

TENN.

Colorado River

TEXAS

Austin

San Antonio

Pecos River

Rio Grande

Nueces River

Brazos River

Sabine River

Mississippi River

LOUISIANA

MISS.

GULF OF MEXICO

The Election of 1848

Throughout the North many politicians seemed increasingly willing to sever old party loyalties in order to commit themselves more fully to the antislavery cause. A number of Liberty party abolitionists, antislavery Democrats, and Conscience Whigs banded together in 1848 to form the Free Soil party. They nominated ex-President Martin Van Buren as their candidate for the presidency.

The Free Soil platform cleverly appealed to many different segments of the population. It contained the inevitable antislavery plank. But it also included Whig economic demands, such as support for federally sponsored roads and other internal improvements. In addition it advocated Democratic social values, as in its demand for a federal homestead act that would provide free farms on public lands in the West. "Free Soil, Free Speech, Free Labor, and Free Men" ran the party's motto.

Southerners were now also banding into a party of their own, though it had no name. In Congress, bloc voting on slavery issues created a Solid South that cut across earlier party lines. Thus from 1848 to 1860 Southern Whigs and Democrats usually voted as Southerners on regional questions, particularly slavery.

Despite growing sectionalism, the Whig party managed to elect its 1848 presidential candidate, Mexican war hero Zachary Taylor. Although it had been in existence for only three months, the Free Soil party did well. Its presidential candidate, Van Buren, received 290,000 votes, and the party elected nine congressmen and one senator.

Aftermath of the Compromise

The country soon found itself involved in the crisis over slavery in the new territories that led to the Compromise of 1850. When the sectional crises eased momentarily, tempers cooled. Public opinion in both North and South swung heavily behind such pro-compromise moderates as Stephen A. Douglas and the new president, Millard Fillmore.

Antislavery Northerners, however, continued to demand the exclusion of slavery from the new territories. Like Seward, they believed that "a higher law" had reserved the new lands for free labor. In 1851 Massachusetts sent Charles Sumner, a radical Conscience Whig, to the Senate. Everywhere in the North, abolitionists and their sympathizers denounced the new fugitive slave measure in the Compromise of 1850.

Southern fire-eaters found themselves badly undercut by the Compromise of 1850. Yet they did not give up. After passage of the compromise, a Georgia state convention warned that any further attempt by Congress to exclude slavery from the new territories or interfere with it elsewhere would lead to secession.

In 1852 the nation elected a Democratic president, Franklin Pierce of New Hampshire. Democrats also carried both houses of Congress. These victories were due partly to the fact that the Democrats, unlike the Whigs, had endorsed the Compromise of 1850. The Whig party lost in every section and never again ran a presidential candidate. Even the new Free Soil party suffered because of the general public support for compromise; it received only half as many votes as it had in 1848. In the South the Democrats took effective control of the region's political life. Except for the short-lived Reconstruction period, they were to maintain this monopoly for over a century.

DANGER SIGNALS

A majority of the nation wanted to bury the slavery question and exclude it from political debate. But factors still at work kept the issue alive.

Attempts to enforce the Fugitive Slave Act irritated and angered Northerners. The problem was more symbolic than real, though, since fewer than one in 5000 slaves escaped annually. In 1859 over 500 of the 803 runaways came from border states,[3] where owners displayed little interest in

---

[3] The border states—Delaware, Maryland, Kentucky, Tennessee, and Missouri—were slave states bordering the North that had more moderate views on controlling slaves (and, later, secession) than the rest of the South. West Virginia, which joined the Union in 1863, is usually considered a border state, too.

This daguerreotype of Harriet Beecher Stowe was taken shortly after the publication of Uncle Tom's Cabin. *(The Bettmann Archive)*

recovering their lost property. Only a handful came from the Deep South, which had demanded the tough new law, and where feelings ran highest.

Most of the runaway slaves actually recaptured were caught in the border states and received little attention. But the few slave catchers who roamed New England and the Middle West stirred up a hornets' nest. Abolitionists who stymied the efforts of "slave-nappers" became heroes to their neighbors. Few Northerners objected to the presence of runaway slaves despite their otherwise racist treatment of black people.

Moreover, even Northern moderates who despised abolitionists and endorsed the 1850 compromise reacted emotionally to antislavery appeals. Thousands wept over *Uncle Tom's Cabin*, Harriet Beecher Stowe's best-selling novel. Published in 1851, the book portrayed the sufferings of the fictional Uncle Tom and other slaves at the hands of their masters. Tom, the novel's black hero, was martyred at the end. He represented for Mrs. Stowe the ultimate triumph of the Christian in an evil society. *Uncle Tom's Cabin* probably won hundreds of thousands of sympathizers to the antislavery cause. Translated into twenty languages, the book sold 300,000 copies within a year. Dramatized versions appeared in Northern theaters throughout the 1850s.

President Pierce tried to keep the slavery issue out of politics by pursuing an expansionist foreign policy. During his administration, American ships under Commodore Matthew C. Perry opened Japan to Western trade. The $10 million Gadsden Purchase of land from Mexico rounded out American continental borders in the Southwest. Pierce also pressured China for commercial privileges and agitated for American expansion into Cuba and Central America. Pierce, Douglas, and other Northern Democrats hoped that by stressing the national interests of Americans abroad they could destroy the virus of sectionalism at home. For a time, at least, their policies seemed effective.

But sectional bitterness intruded even into the conduct of foreign affairs. Pierce had directed the American minister to Spain, a Louisianan named Pierre Soulé, to offer Spain $130 million for the island of Cuba, whose purchase many favored both on strategic and economic grounds. Soulé conferred on the matter with the American ambassadors to Great Britain and France (the former was James Buchanan, who himself became president in 1856). The three diplomats sent a confidential dispatch to the State Department after meeting at Ostend, Belgium, urging that—in the event Spain rejected America's offer—the United States should seize the island by force. After the "Ostend Manifesto" was leaked to Congress and the press, antislavery Northerners denounced this proposal as an outrageous bid by Southerners to extend slavery into yet another potential American territory. The controversy put an end to the possibility of acquiring Cuba peacefully.

The Kansas-Nebraska Act

Stephen A. Douglas himself, however, helped to stoke sectional bitterness over slavery and destroy the very compromise he had so skillfully pushed through Congress. In 1854 he introduced a Senate bill to organize the territories of Kansas and Nebraska, a sparsely settled region at that time. Douglas hoped to prevent further congressional furor over the morality of slavery expansion through popular sovereignty, allowing settlers to decide the issue for themselves. Once again, however, as in President Taylor's solution regarding California, it proved easier to devise a practical approach to the slavery issue than to enforce it.

Congress soon found itself embroiled in another quarrel between antislavery and proslavery members. Since Kansas and Nebraska lay within the area of the Louisiana Purchase, the status of slavery there should have been governed by the Missouri Compromise of 1820. This agreement kept slavery out of land that far north. Passage of the Kansas-Nebraska Bill would in effect repeal the Missouri Compromise. This prospect infuriated antislavery Northerners.

Douglas sponsored his bill in order to encourage settlement in the region. This would enable a transcontinental railroad to move across it to the Pacific. The bill's final version included several concessions to Southerners, whose votes Douglas needed. With the support of President Pierce the bill passed in May 1854 after months of furious debate.

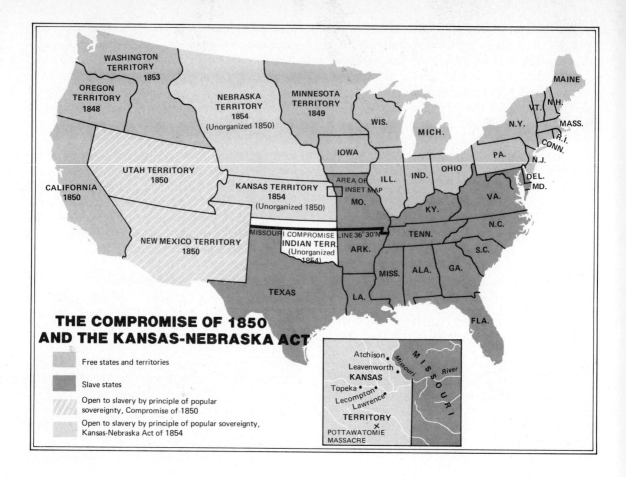

THE COMPROMISE OF 1850
AND THE KANSAS-NEBRASKA ACT

Free states and territories

Slave states

Open to slavery by principle of popular
sovereignty, Compromise of 1850

Open to slavery by principle of popular sovereignty,
Kansas-Nebraska Act of 1854

Two New Parties

Debate over the Kansas-Nebraska Act broke the uneasy truce that had more or less silenced discussions about slavery since 1850. It aroused Northern public opinion against slavery as no previous congressional measure—not even the Fugitive Slave Law of 1850—had ever done. Douglas's concessions to Southerners during the long debate over his measure—and some changes he made to please this camp—were one factor offending the antislavery forces. Another was the possibility, slim, but (in theory) conceivable under the bill's terms, that territories *north* of the 1820 Missouri Compromise line might somehow adopt slavery. Primarily, the measure became a rallying point for (and a symbol of) Northern fears of Southern intentions on the question of slavery's expansion into the Western territories.

Northern outrage at passage of the Kansas-Nebraska Act took concrete form. Throughout the North in 1854 hundreds of thousands of people left the Democratic and Whig parties to join local anti-Nebraska political groups. In a few months these groups united to form the Republican party. It was a much broader coalition of Conscience Whigs, anti-Douglas Democrats, and abolitionists than the Free Soil party had been. The new party demanded complete exclusion of slavery from all remaining federal territories.

The Whig party was dying. Its members sought new political homes. While some became Republicans, others joined the recently formed American party. Members of the party were often

Sam Houston

When Sam Houston arrived in Washington, D.C., in 1846 as a senator from the new state of Texas, he was described as "a magnificent barbarian, somewhat tempered by civilization." He was a stately six-foot-three and had "a lion-like countenance capable of expressing fiercest passions." Flamboyant in speech and manner, he dressed in character. A favorite ensemble included a gold-headed cane, a panther-skin waistcoat, a large sombrero, and a Mexican blanket.

At age fifty-three, the freshman senator was a legend. A runaway youth on the Tennessee frontier, he lived for years with the Cherokees, who dubbed him "the Raven." He was a hero in the War of 1812. A long-time protégé of Andrew Jackson's, he became governor of Tennessee in his mid-thirties. His fame grew as the victorious commander in chief at the Battle of San Jacinto, which won independence for Texas. Twice president of the new republic, he was the prime mover in achieving annexation to the United States.

Texas was a slave state, and Sam Houston himself was a slaveholder. He was, as John F. Kennedy wrote, "a Southerner by birth, residence, loyalty, and philosophy." But he was also "one of the most independent, unique, popular, forceful, and dramatic individuals ever to enter the Senate chamber." He did not bind himself by sectional ties. As he said, "I know neither North nor South; I know only the Union." His was the only Southern vote for all five laws that made up the Compromise of 1850. He and a Tennessean were the only Southern senators to vote against the Kansas-Nebraska Bill.

Houston's staunch defense of the Union cost him his presidential ambitions in 1852 and again in 1856. He denounced "the mad fanaticism of the North" and the "mad ambition of the South," but he was caught between them. His vote against the Kansas-Nebraska Bill resulted in a formal censure by both the Texas legislature and the state Democrats. When he took his case to the people of Texas as an independent candidate for governor in 1857, he was defeated. But he served out his senatorial term and left the capital early in 1859. Still vigorous at age sixty-six, he was determined

(International Museum of Photography at George Eastman House)

to make a comeback. By autumn he had done so, running again for governor and winning handily.

Houston's term of office was cut short, however. The presidential election of 1860 brought on a secessionist crisis in Texas. Pitted against a hostile legislature, Houston delayed—but could not prevent—withdrawal from the Union.

When he refused in March 1861 to take the oath of allegiance to the Confederacy, he was deposed. Gallantly, with sorrow, he bid his farewell: "I have seen patriots and statesmen of my youth one by one gathered to their fathers, and the government which they have reared rent in twain. I stand the last almost of my race, stricken down because I will not yield those principles which I have fought for."

called "Know-Nothings." Their platform was secret, and when asked about it, a party member would answer "I know nothing."

The Know-Nothings were nativists—that is, they felt that immigrants presented a threat to "native Americans." (By "native Americans" the Know-Nothings were referring, not to Indians, but to families who had been in America for two or three generations.)

Know-Nothings were particularly opposed to Roman Catholics. Hundreds of thousands of such newcomers, mainly Irish, had migrated to America in the 1840s after a potato famine in Ireland. Nativists feared the newcomers' religion, and they felt that the Catholics would not fit into American society.

Anti-Catholic sentiment grew at a time when many Americans were fearful of subversive elements in their society, elements plotting in secret to undermine democratic freedoms. Know-Nothings feared a Catholic conspiracy. Slaveholders were afraid of an abolitionist plot. And abolitionists were convinced of a slaveholders' intrigue.

"Bleeding Kansas"

Many people moved to Kansas after passage of the Kansas-Nebraska Act. Most of them were farmers—from both the North and the South. Few seemed to care whether the state became slave or free. Unfortunately, this unconcern did not last.

Antislavery Northerners formed Emigrant Aid Societies, usually under the direction of abolitionists. These societies provided money, guns, and supplies for Northern settlers in Kansas—settlers who were determined that Kansas should be a free state. At the same time, a smaller group of proslavery settlers were backed by neighboring Missourians, who often crossed the border to vote and to fight.

Armed proslavery and antislavery forces clashed frequently and fiercely in what came to be called "Bleeding Kansas." Normal political processes broke down completely. Although a large majority of Kansas settlers voted for a free-state legislature, proslavery forces and Missourians elected their own assembly. Violence ruled the territory, and President Pierce could not maintain order.

The conflict reached Washington. In May 1856, Massachusetts Senator Charles Sumner delivered a fervent antislavery address, "the Crime against Kansas." His speech included an attack on Senator Andrew Butler of South Carolina. Butler's nephew was a hotheaded South Carolina congressman named Preston Brooks. Two days after Sumner's speech, Brooks—determined to avenge his family's honor—marched into the Senate chamber and beat the Massachusetts senator unconscious with a cane. Sumner was injured so severely that he did not reappear in Congress for three years.

As for "Bleeding Kansas," the fighting persisted between proslavery and antislavery irregulars for several more years. One of the antislavery militia leaders, the veteran abolitionist John Brown, would become involved in a dramatic incident in 1859—far from Kansas—that would prove even more significant than the caning of Charles Sumner.

Suggested Readings
Chapters 19-20

Crisis and Compromise in 1850

Holman Hamilton, *Prologue to Conflict: The Crisis and Compromise of 1850* (1964).

Expansion into the Far West

Ray A. Billington, *Westward Expansion* (1974) and *The Far Western Frontier, 1830–1860* (1956); Gene M. Brack, *Mexico Views Manifest Destiny* (1976); Frederick M. Merk, *Manifest Destiny and Mission in American History* (1963); John H. Schroeder, *Mr. Polk's War: American Opposition and Dissent, 1846–1848* (1973); Otis A. Singletary, *The Mexican War* (1960); George Rogers Taylor, *The Transportation Revolution, 1815–1860* (1951); Albert K. Weinberg, *Manifest Destiny* (1935).

National Political Tensions

Gerald M. Capers, *Stephen A. Douglas: Defender of the Union* (1959); Avery Craven, *The Growth of Southern Nationalism, 1848–1861* (1953) and *The Coming of the Civil War* (1963); Bernard DeVoto, *The Year of Decision, 1846* (1943); Don E. Fehrenbacher, *The Dred Scott Case: Its Significance in American Law and Politics* (1978). Eric Foner, *Free Soil, Free Labor, Free Men: The Ideology of the Republican Party Before the Civil War* (1970); Vincent C. Hopkins, *Dred Scott's Case* (1951); Robert W. Johannsen, *Stephen A. Douglas* (1973); Albert J. Kirwan, *John J. Crittenden* (1962); Philip S. Klein, *President James Buchanan* (1962); Allan Nevins, *The Emergence of Lincoln* (2 vols., 1950) and *Ordeal of the Union* (2 vols., 1947); Alice Nichols, *Bleeding Kansas* (1969); David M. Potter, *The Impending Crisis, 1848–1861* (1976); James A. Rawley, *Race and Politics: Bleeding Kansas and the Coming of the Civil War* (1969); Joseph G. Rayback, *Free Soil: The Election of 1848* (1970).

21 John Brown's Raid

The plot seemed so incredible that the secretary of war refused to believe it. John B. Floyd was relaxing at a Virginia resort late in August 1859 when he received an anonymous letter. It warned of a conspiracy to incite a slave uprising throughout the South. " 'Old John Brown,' late of Kansas," according to the writer, had stored a large quantity of arms in a Maryland hideaway. As the head of a "secret association," he planned to attack Virginia first, entering the state at Harpers Ferry, a northwestern border town.[1] The anonymous writer urged Floyd to send federal troops to the town.

The South had experienced no slave rebellion since the Nat Turner Revolt almost thirty years earlier. Floyd (the son of Virginia's governor at the time of the Turner uprising) was a fiery opponent of abolitionism. But he refused to believe that "a scheme of such wickedness and outrage could be entertained by any citizen of the United States." He took no action.

At this time John Brown was fifty-nine years old and a fugitive from justice. President Buchanan himself had authorized a $250 reward for his capture. Brown was wanted in connection with antislavery raids he had conducted in Kansas. It was partly because Brown's name was identified so closely with Kansas that Floyd did not take the Harpers Ferry plot seriously.

In Kansas, Brown had acquired notoriety but little else. In fact, his life was marked by almost total failure. He had struggled constantly to achieve financial security (an understandable goal for the father of twenty children). Brown failed first during the 1830s as an Ohio land speculator. Then, in 1842, he went bankrupt as a sheep rancher. A later career as a wool merchant also ended in failure. In 1855 Brown and his family migrated to the newly opened Kansas Territory. Here Brown soon gained a reputation as a ferocious opponent of slavery.

---

[1] Harpers Ferry and other West Virginia towns mentioned in this chapter were still a part of Virginia at this time; West Virginia did not become a separate state until 1863.

John Brown had always been an abolitionist. Before he moved west, his house had been a station on the underground railroad. In Kansas the situation was violent, with proslavery and antislavery forces struggling for control of the territorial government. Brown and five of his sons took an active role in what was practically a guerrilla war.

Brown was best known for an incident that took place at Pottawatomie, Kansas, in 1856. He led a small band that murdered and mutilated five proslavery settlers. This raid was apparently in retaliation for the burning of Lawrence, Kansas (a free-state town), by slave-state advocates. None of Brown's victims owned slaves. The common thread linking them was their association with a local court that soon would try a case in which Brown was the defendant.

In the fall of 1856 Brown went east with his sons. For the next three years he wandered across the North from Kansas to Massachusetts making speeches and holding private fund-raising meetings. Brown had long toyed with the notion of launching a direct assault on Southern slavery. He knew that this kind of action would frighten moderate abolitionists, so he usually described his aim as a simple raiding expedition southward to rescue a select handful of slaves. By early 1858, however, Brown began revealing his actual plan—"to overthrow slavery in a large part of the country."

Incredibly, Brown told about eighty Northern abolitionists of his scheme. Many had grave doubts about it. One such man was Frederick Douglass, the leading black abolitionist. Another dubious listener was an Iowa Quaker named David J. Gue. Gue had written the anonymous letter to Secretary of War Floyd. He hoped that, if Floyd ordered federal troops to Harpers Ferry, Brown would call off the raid before he and his men were all killed.

Brown could not have gotten as far as he did without the aid of six leading abolitionists, later known as the Secret Six. One was Gerrit Smith, a wealthy landowner in upstate New York. The other five were all from Massachusetts. Franklin B. Sanborn was a Boston schoolteacher. Thomas Wentworth Higginson and Theodore Parker were Unitarian ministers. George Luther Stearns was a prominent merchant and manufacturer of Boston. The sixth member of the group was a physician, Samuel Gridley Howe.

At first the Secret Six, like Brown's other abolitionist supporters, believed that their leader planned some new and dramatic strike against the proslavery forces in Kansas. But then Brown began to reveal his real intentions. Neither political action nor peaceful persuasion had settled the slavery question, he said. Only a slave uprising throughout the South would make slaveholders aware of their moral guilt. God had selected him, Brown continued, to organize and lead such an insurrection. The revolt would begin in Virginia. From there it would quickly spread like a raging brushfire across the entire South. Even if the plot failed, Brown believed that the hysteria that would then sweep the South would provoke a major sectional crisis, dividing a proslavery South and an antislavery North so that civil war might result.

John Brown was fifty-six when this photograph was taken, early in 1857. (Library of Congress)

Gerrit Smith. (Library of Congress)

Franklin B. Sanborn. NYPL/Picture Collection)

Thomas W. Higginson. (Boston Athenaeum)

Theodore Parker. (NYPL/Picture Collection)

George Luther Stearns. (Library of Congress)

Samuel Gridley Howe. (Library of Congress)

Brown asked the Secret Six for financial help. He refused to discuss any tactical and strategic objections they might have. He offered them, as Sanborn later remarked, "only the alternatives of betrayal, desertion, or support." Brown claimed that he now wanted "men of action." What he really wanted—and had in the Secret Six—was a group of people who would raise funds and thus fulfill their private dreams of being something more than mere talkers.

Though some of the six wavered, in the end they all cast their doubts aside and supported Brown. Why should a slave revolt be condemned, they probably reasoned, when the "slave power" had inflicted so much violence on the free states during the previous decade? Hadn't there been undeclared warfare in Kansas? Wasn't there a massive effort by slave catchers to hunt down fugitive slaves? And what about the physical assaults on abolitionists, not to mention the savage beating of Charles Sumner on the floor of the Senate?

By the late 1850s many abolitionists—not only the Secret Six—had become convinced that there could be no peaceful solution to the slavery question. Gerrit Smith wrote the Republican governor of Vermont:

Hitherto I have opposed the bloody abolition of slavery, but now, when it begins to march its conquering bands into the free states, I and ten thousand other peace [movement] men are not only ready to have it repulsed with violence, but pursued even unto death, with violence.

John Brown represented, for Smith and the others among the Secret Six, the obvious instrument of what they believed to be justifiable violence. At the same time, Brown's supporters preferred being kept in the dark concerning his specific plans. They hoped to avoid being identified too closely with the scheme. "I have great faith in the wisdom, integrity, and bravery of Captain Brown," Gerrit Smith wrote Sanborn in July 1858. "Whenever he shall embark on another of his contests with the slave power, I shall again stand ready to help him." The limit on this support became clear only in the final sentences of Smith's note: "I do not wish to know Captain Brown's plans. I hope he will keep them to himself." Or, as

Samuel Gridley Howe put it to Brown himself, "Don't tell me what you are about or where you are going."

Brown's ultimate destination was Harpers Ferry, Virginia, but as a base of operations he chose a farm across the Potomac River in Maryland. Brown, posing as a New York cattle buyer named Isaac Smith, had rented the farm from the Kennedy family in July 1859. He arrived with two of his sons, Owen and Oliver. A third son, Watson, joined them later.

By late August there were fifteen recruits living on the Kennedy farm. Oliver's wife, Martha, and a granddaughter of Brown's, Annie, were brought to the farm to keep house and divert the suspicions of nosy neighbors. Most of the group were young. All but two of Brown's men were under thirty. The oldest, apart from the "commander in chief" himself, was a forty-eight-year-old free black named Dangerfield Newby. He had joined the company hoping to liberate his wife and seven children from a nearby Virginia plantation. As the group waited restlessly through the hot summer, hundreds of weapons reached the farm—200 revolvers, 198 rifles, and 950 iron-tipped pikes destined for use by insurgent slaves.

Several of the recruits still believed that they had come South to rescue a small group of slaves and escort them to safety in Canada. During the summer, though, Brown revealed his actual plan for a full-scale slave revolt that would spread quickly throughout the South.

Brown's men drilled, but their commander made few other preparations for the attack itself. He gathered almost no information about the slaves in the region. He did not even bother to scout the area's roads and hiding places. Nor did he develop a plan of escape in case the assault on Harpers Ferry failed.

The only preparation Brown made for possible failure was a curious effort to ensure that others besides himself would be blamed for the raid. Inside a trunk in the farmhouse, in plain view, Brown left letters that implicated his most prominent Northern supporters, among them the Secret Six.

A final handful of recruits drifted into the "Smith" farm in October. Brown decided to strike. He had already sent Martha and Annie back home and written last-minute notes to Northern relatives and friends.

There were now twenty-one "soldiers": five blacks and sixteen whites. On Sunday, October 16, Brown gathered them together for a final prayer service. He then explained his plan of attack to the newer recruits, three of whom had arrived only the previous day. First his men were to blockade the two bridges into Harpers Ferry. Then they would capture the armory buildings and a rifle factory. They would take hostages to use in the event of attack by federal troops or state militia. Once a sufficient number of blacks from the area had rallied to the invaders, the entire band would retreat toward the nearby mountains and regroup for their march southward.

At eight o'clock that moonless night Brown strode out of the farmhouse followed by eighteen of his men. He posted the remaining three as a rear guard. (One was to go to a nearby schoolhouse on Monday

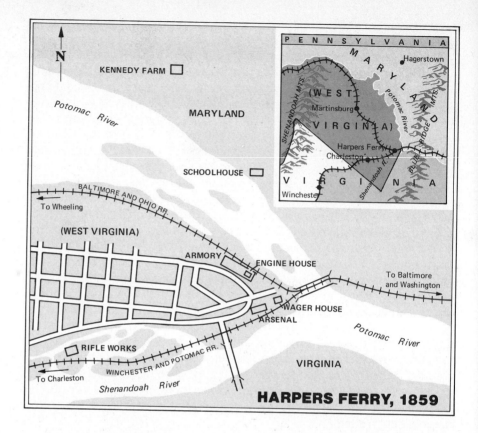

HARPERS FERRY, 1859

to await the escaping slaves who were expected to gather in the area.) Brown then climbed into a wagon filled with the weapons he had collected and rode toward a bridge that led into the silent, sleeping town across the Potomac.

Harpers Ferry was strategically located at the junction of the Potomac and Shenandoah rivers. Baltimore lay eighty miles east by rail and Washington fifty-seven miles by road. The town's main industry was arms manufacture. The federal government maintained a complex of buildings, including a fire-engine house, an armory, and an arsenal. There was also a private rifle works located on an island in the Shenandoah.

The town had a population of slightly more than 2500. Of this total 1251 were free blacks, and only 88 were slaves. Most of the white residents were Northerners employed as skilled craftsmen or government officials in the armory-rifle works complex.

Harpers Ferry was not a typical Southern town. There were no large plantations in the area. Neither cotton nor tobacco was grown there. The few slaveholders in the area owned small farms. Most of the local slaves were house servants. There was no large pool of plantation field hands to be rallied in the immediate area.

Several of Brown's recruits stationed themselves at the two bridges leading into Harpers Ferry. Another group overpowered the single watchman at the government-owned properties and seized control of the armory, the arsenal, and the engine house. They also took over the private rifle works. The invaders herded a small group of prisoners into the engine house as hostages. Now that he controlled millions in government munitions, Brown grew increasingly confident of success. He ordered the telegraph wires cut and dispatched a raiding party to secure more hostages from the nearby countryside. This band returned in the early morning hours of Monday, October 17, with ten freed slaves and three prisoners. Among the latter was the great-grandnephew of George Washington, a minor slaveholder named Lewis W. Washington. Brown had particularly wanted Lewis Washington as a prisoner "for the moral effect it would give our cause having one of your name."

A train whistle signaled the beginning of danger for John Brown's plans. Shortly after midnight an express passenger train from Wheeling reached Harpers Ferry en route to Baltimore. Trainmen found the railroad bridge barricaded and a wounded night watchman shouting warnings of armed night raiders. Brown's raiders began firing, forcing the engineer to back up the train until it was safely out of gunshot range. Just then the Harpers Ferry baggage master, a free black named Hayward Shepherd, wandered down the track. When he tried to run in spite of a raider's command to halt, he was shot down. Shepherd died soon afterward, the first fatality in John Brown's private war against slavery.

By dawn the alarm had sounded throughout the countryside. The residents of Harpers Ferry, except for the handful Brown had taken as hostages or prisoners, armed themselves and fled in panic to a hilltop behind the town. Many of the town's blacks—both slave and free—fled with them. Church bells throughout northwestern Virginia and Maryland tolled the warning signal for slave insurrections. Militia companies began collecting their forces throughout the Blue Ridge towns that bordered on Harpers Ferry, preparing to march on the town.

Up to this point most Virginians who knew of the incident believed that *blacks* had begun a slave uprising at Harpers Ferry much like the one three decades earlier at Jerusalem. Only later in the day would the truth filter out. Brown, amazingly enough, had allowed the Baltimore express train to continue on its way. Thus he ensured that news of his invasion would pass instantly across the telegraph lines from Baltimore to Washington, Richmond, and elsewhere. It is difficult to know whether he was too dazed to act decisively or whether he deliberately wanted to publicize what he had done. In any case, by Monday noon, he and his men had clearly lost the initiative in Harpers Ferry.

Not only did Brown allow the train to proceed. He actually dawdled away the morning. Instead of collecting his hostages and escaping to the nearby mountains, as several of his men urged him to do, he squandered time with his hostages at the engine house. He even ordered breakfast for all of them from a nearby hotel, the Wager House. He divided his

Harpers Ferry at the time of the 1859 raid was a small town in a dramatic setting. In this view, looking southeast, the Potomac curves down from the left and into the far distance; the Shenandoah flows past the church at the right. The government buildings are near the center, not far from the bridge over the Potomac. (Baltimore and Ohio Railroad)

already outnumbered forces, sending several raiders and a few freed slaves across the Potomac to join his rear guard at the schoolhouse.

In the morning, armed townspeople and men from nearby farms got the upper hand. Their rifle fire kept the raiders pinned down to their armory compound. Brown had obviously not expected his opponents to attack so quickly. Yet he remained in the town, either expecting slave reinforcements or perhaps simply making what he believed to be a divinely ordered last stand.

Brown's only means of escape, the two bridges, were retaken by militia late Monday morning. The militia dispersed the few raiders guarding the structures. One of them, the free black Dangerfield Newby, was the first of Brown's men to die in the assault. As he lay dead in the street, townspeople vented their fury at the raid on his body, beating it with sticks.

Brown finally began searching for a way to get out. Some of his men were still across the river in Maryland. Others were trapped in the rifle works. He and most of his raiders, guarding about thirty hostages by now, could not link up with either group. Brown decided to offer an exchange. He would release the hostages in return for a guarantee that he and his men could go free. Will Thompson, the first raider who carried these terms to the militia under a flag of truce, was seized by the crowd and taken away at gunpoint. Brown recognized his predicament at last. He took his remaining men, his few slave recruits, and eleven of his most prominent hostages. They barricaded themselves in the engine house. He then sent out three more people—his son Watson, another raider, and one of the prisoners. They approached the militia under another flag of truce.

The two raiders were shot down, although Watson managed to crawl back to the engine house.

The streets of Harpers Ferry were filled with drunken, hysterical townspeople and militiamen by late Monday afternoon. One group caught an escaping raider near the Potomac, killed him, and then spent hours puncturing his body with bullets. Brown's remaining three men in the rifle works received similar treatment when they were forced to flee toward the river. Two of them fell dead, riddled with bullets. The third, a black named John Anthony Copeland, was rescued from lynching by a local doctor, who protected him from a mob of captors until the arrival of slightly more sober militiamen.

Among the casualties on Monday afternoon was the mayor of Harpers Ferry, a gentle old man named Fontaine Beckham. (His will provided for the emancipation of a slave family owned by him.) He was shot by one of Brown's men. After Beckham's death the town went completely out of control. Residents and local farmers competed with frenzied militiamen in screaming at the raiders while senselessly firing their guns. A mob marched on the Wager House, where Will Thompson remained under guard. They dragged him down to the Potomac, as he shouted: "You may take my life, but eighty thousand will arise up to avenge me, and carry out my purpose of giving liberty to the slaves." The mob peppered his head with bullets before tossing the dead man into the shallow water.

The first word of the leader's identity came late Monday. He sent out yet another note from the engine house repeating his offer to exchange hostages for freedom. It was signed "John Brown." The offer was refused.

The night that followed must have been agonizing for Brown, as he struggled to retain some control over his future despite the obvious failure of his plan. Two of his sons, Oliver and Watson, lay dying. Brown and his four remaining able-bodied men took turns guarding their eleven hostages. Brown spent a good deal of time tending to his prisoners' comfort. Mainly, though, he strode quietly back and forth across the blood-spattered room, alone with his thoughts.

When Brown and his men peered out of their engine-house fortress at dawn on Tuesday, October 18, things had changed. They saw, not Monday's scruffy and jittery mob of local rabbit-shooting militia but a cool, well-dressed company of United States Marines. They were armed with rifles, bayonets, and sledge hammers for the siege that lay ahead. The marines were under the command of Colonel Robert E. Lee, accompanied by Lieutenant J. E. B. Stuart. Brown appeared neither shocked nor unhappy. One of his hostages, Lewis Washington, later observed:

> Brown was the coolest and firmest man I ever saw. With one son dead by his side, and another shot through, he felt the pulse of his dying son with one hand and held his rifle with the other, and commanded his men with the utmost composure, encouraging them to sell their lives as dearly as they could.

In this engine house Brown and his raiders took refuge on October 17. His small band pushed the fire engines up to the doors to impede entry, but Lee's troops broke in, using a heavy ladder as a battering ram. (Baltimore and Ohio Railroad)

Lieutenant Stuart approached the engine house under a flag of truce. He handed a note to Brown demanding unconditional surrender and promising him and his men protection from vigilante justice. Brown refused. He insisted that he would surrender only when he and his men were promised their freedom. Stuart repeated Lee's surrender terms and then, without warning, leaped away from the door waving his cap. While thousands of excited spectators cheered wildly, a party of soldiers began battering at the oak doors of the engine house. Brown's men responded with a volley of shots. Within moments one of the doors had been broken down, and armed marines began dashing into the engine house. The first two were shot. But others swarmed in, overpowering Brown and his four remaining raiders.

Two of the four raiders were quickly bayoneted and died soon afterward. The remaining two, a Quaker youth named Edwin Coppoc and a free black named Shields Green, were captured without being seriously wounded. Brown himself knelt on the floor, his rifle cocked while awaiting the assault. Lieutenant Israel Green, the officer leading the attack on the engine house, entered the building and struck Brown with a light sword before the weary man could fire. Green then tried to run him through with his sword, practically lifting Brown off the ground. Somehow the sword struck either a bone or a belt buckle and failed to inflict a fatal wound. Nevertheless, as Brown collapsed on the ground, Lieutenant

Green continued beating him over the head with his sword until his victim lost consciousness. Finally, the lieutenant regained his self-control. He ordered Brown and his men carried outside and placed on the grass, where their wounds were dressed.

Later that afternoon a detachment of militia confiscated boxes of revolvers and rifles from the Maryland schoolhouse where Brown's recruits had waited vainly for slaves to rally. Another patrol under J. E. B. Stuart occupied the Kennedy farm. By then the rest of Brown's rear guard had fled. They left behind not only hundreds of weapons but also the incriminating letters from the Secret Six and other abolitionists that Brown had abandoned so casually before the raid.

After his wounds had been dressed, Brown was taken to an office in the armory. He was guarded closely, since mobs in the streets of Harpers Ferry wanted to lynch him immediately.

On Tuesday afternoon Brown was visited by a group of politicians, military officers, and newspaper reporters who had just arrived in Harpers Ferry. Among them were Virginia Governor Henry A. Wise and Senator James M. Mason, also of Virginia. Brown did not shirk speaking to the visitors since, as he put it, he wanted "to make himself and his motives clearly understood." It was a new role for the militant man of action, who had often expressed his contempt for mere talkers. In Governor Wise's words, Brown spoke "freely, fluently, and cheerfully." Whether he spoke truthfully, however, is open to question.

Senator Mason asked the old man how he had financed the raid. "I furnished most [of the money] myself," he answered. "I cannot implicate others. It is by my own folly that I have been taken." Brown insisted throughout the interview on accepting completely responsibility for the raid: "No man sent me here; it was my own prompting and that of my Maker, or that of the devil, whichever you please to ascribe it to." (If Brown had sincerely wished to avoid implicating his Northern supporters, though, he might have done so more effectively by not leaving their correspondence in plain view at the Kennedy farm.)

Brown departed most strikingly from the truth when he discussed his motives in attacking Harpers Ferry. He denied any intention of leading a violent slave revolt. He claimed that his purpose had been simply to liberate a group of slaves and lead them to freedom: "We came to free the slaves," he insisted, "and only that."

"Do you consider yourself an instrument in the hands of Providence?" one bystander asked. "I do," Brown replied. "I pity the poor in bondage that have none to help them; that is why I am here; not to gratify any personal animosity, revenge, or vindictive spirit." Brown claimed that only fear for his hostages' safety had prevented his fleeing earlier. He said too that his decision to allow the Baltimore train to proceed stemmed from his concern for the lives of its passengers.

Brown was evidently trying to suggest to his interviewers a dramatic change in personality. His speech was free of the harsh and vindictive rhetoric that he had used formerly in talking of Southern slaveholders. There now emerged the image of a gentle and rather sorrowful agent of Providence. To Senator Mason, he said:

> I think, my friend, [that Southerners] are guilty of a great wrong against God and humanity—I say it without wishing to be offensive. . . . I wish to say, furthermore, that you had better—all of you people at the South— prepare yourselves for a settlement of that question that must come up for settlement sooner than you are prepared for it. . . . You may dispose of me very easily; I am nearly disposed of now; but this question is still to be settled—this negro question I mean—the end of that is not yet.

Brown was directing his words more toward the Northern audience that would read newspaper accounts of the interview than toward his Southern questioners. He was trying to convey to Northern readers the belief that had led him to Harpers Ferry—that slavery could no longer be fought by peaceful means but only by such methods as he had used in his unsuccessful raid.

By late Tuesday afternoon it was possible to tally the results of John Brown's invasion scheme. The slaves he had sent to the Maryland schoolhouse had deserted the previous night and returned to their masters. One unfortunate slave captured with Brown later died in a Charleston prison. Another of his reluctant slave recruits was later found drowned near Harpers Ferry.

Seventeen people were killed during the raid or died soon afterward: the two slaves, three townspeople, one slaveholder, and one marine; and ten of Brown's men, including two of his sons. Five raiders, including Brown, were captured, and the rest escaped into the Maryland mountains. Two others were caught in Pennsylvania a few days later, while five (including Brown's son Owen) fled to safety.

As a military effort, Brown's campaign had failed miserably. Yet, even at its moment of failure, it began to trigger exactly the kind of sectional crisis that Brown had predicted.

Moderates in the North tried to minimize the raid's importance. They dismissed John Brown as a solitary madman whose efforts did not have support among respectable Americans in any section. "It is now well understood," editorialized *Harpers Weekly* in late October 1859, "that the insurrection was merely the work of a half-crazed white." Republican party politicians were especially eager to disassociate their peaceful antislavery views from Brown's violent tactics. "John Brown was no Republican," insisted Abraham Lincoln, and not "a single Republican [has been implicated] in his Harpers Ferry enterprise."

On the other hand, Democrats in both the North and the South denounced the Brown plot as an extension of Republican antislavery agitation. In Virginia itself, a state legislative committee that later investigated the invasion probably spoke for most Southerners when it wrote:

> The whole argument against the *extension* of slavery is soon, by a very slight deflection, made to bear against the *existence* of slavery, and thus the anti-extension idea is merged in that of abolition. . . . The crimes of

John Brown were neither more nor less than practical illustrations of the doctrines of the republican party.

Senator Stephen A. Douglas, the leading Democratic spokesman of the North, called the scheme a "natural, logical, inevitable result of the doctrines and teachings of the Republican party."

More directly concerned, of course, were the Secret Six and Brown's other Northern abolitionist backers. They faced possible arrest and prison terms for their role in the episode. Newspapers throughout the country began reprinting the incriminating letters found at the Kennedy farm. Within a week after Brown's capture Sanborn, Howe, and Stearns had fled to Canada to escape prosecution. Frederick Douglass, after writing an editorial defending the Harpers Ferry raid, sailed to England. Edwin Morton, another of Brown's abolitionist backers, also went to England. (Parker, dying of tuberculosis, had already gone to Europe.)

Gerrit Smith broke down completely. In November friends took him to an asylum for the insane, where he remained until late December, by which time he had "recovered his reason."

Higginson was the only member of the Secret Six to stand his ground. He did not try to deny involvement in the raid. But he did insist that Brown's "acquittal or rescue would not do half as much good as being executed; so strong is the personal sympathy with him."

Higginson's view was shared by most abolitionists. They praised Brown for his actions—and they wanted the South to complete its work of immortalizing their hero. "Let no man pray that Brown be spared!" declared the Reverend Henry Ward Beecher. "Let Virginia make him a martyr!"

Virginia's Governor Wise seemed determined to oblige. Wise decided to charge Brown and his associates, under a Virginia statute, for treason against the state, rather than to hand over the men for trial in a federal court. The governor's position was legally questionable but politically shrewd. Brown's raid on the government arsenal and armory at Harpers Ferry had clearly broken federal laws. Nor did any of the raiders owe allegiance to Virginia. But Wise's action satisfied the general Southern clamor for swift (Southern) vengeance against the raiders. Virginia authorities, fearful that unruly mobs in Harpers Ferry might try to lynch Brown, shifted the trial and the prisoners to Charleston. On October 26 the grand jury indicted Brown and his four accomplices—two whites and two blacks—charging them with the murder of five people, conspiracy to provoke a slave revolt, and treason against the state of Virginia. All of the raiders pleaded not guilty. The judge agreed to separate trials, Brown's being the first.

The trial of John Brown began on October 27, with the defendant reclining on a cot confronting a packed courthouse. Brown's court-appointed lawyer, Virginian Lawson Botts, startled the courtroom audience by immediately producing a telegram from a man in Akron, Ohio. He asserted that Brown and others in his family (which had lived in the Akron area for a number of years) were insane.

At his trial for treason, the wounded Brown had to lie on a cot in the middle of the floor. Governor Wise remarked that the prisoner reminded him of "a broken-winged hawk with talons set." (The New-York Historical Society)

Botts felt that the only way to save his client's life was to have the jury commit him to an insane asylum. But Brown was not interested in saving his life. He wanted to use his trial as a national forum for preaching the antislavery gospel. He did not wish to wither away in obscurity. Finally, because of Brown's objections, his attorneys abandoned the insanity defense.

The trial came rapidly to a conclusion. On October 31, after deliberating only forty-five minutes, the jury found Brown guilty on all charges. Two days later he was carried back into court for sentencing. Before the judge could pronounce his sentence, the prisoner was asked to speak. He talked for five minutes, addressing not the court so much as the country, which would read the text of his speech in newspapers the next day. He spoke slowly and eloquently, defending his actions at Harpers Ferry by distorting the facts and appealing directly—and in the most emotional way—for support from the antislavery North:

> In the first place, I deny everything but what I have all along admitted—the design on my part to free slaves. I intended to do as I did last winter, when I went into Missouri, and there took slaves without the snapping of a gun on either side, moved them through the country, and finally left them in Canada. I designed to have done the same thing again, on a larger scale. That was all I intended. I never did intend murder or treason, or the destruction of property, or to excite or incite slaves to rebellion, or to make insurrection. . . . I see a book kissed here, which I suppose to be the

Trying to recruit a less than enthusiastic disciple to his cause, Brown is ridiculed in this pro-Southern view of the raid. (Library of Congress)

A PREMATURE MOVEMENT.

JOHN BROWN. "Here! Take this, and follow me. My name's Brown."

CUFFEE. "Please God! Mr. Brown, dat is onpossible. We ain't done seedin' yit at our house."

Bible, or at least the New Testament. That teaches me that all things whatsoever I would men should do to me, I should do even so to them. It teaches me further to "remember them that are in bonds, as bound with them." I endeavored to act up to that instruction.

Though Brown lied in his remarks about the plans for a slave revolt, he was truthful about his ultimate intention of liberating the slaves. This distinction was lost not only on many of Brown's Northern admirers but also on the judge, who sentenced him to die on the gallows on December 2. The four other captured raiders were also found guilty at their trials and, like Brown, were sentenced to hang.

In Brown's last month, he continued his efforts to replace his earlier public image as a vengeful border fighter with that of a forgiving yet sternly moral Christian, one who endured his final days as a prisoner with simple dignity. Brown's lawyers worked furiously to collect sworn statements from the condemned man's family and friends testifying to his insanity, in the hope of persuading Governor Wise to commit the condemned man to an asylum. They gathered a large number of such statements, many doubtless from people who were trying to save Brown's life but did not really believe him mad.

At the same time, many people wrote Wise pleading with him to spare Brown and not create an antislavery martyr, thereby increasing sectional tensions. The governor finally rejected the many appeals for clemency, declaring Brown perfectly sane—"cool, collected, and indomitable." "He is a fanatic," Wise wrote, "but firm, truthful and intelligent."

Brown could not have been more delighted at Wise's actions. He wrote: "I am worth inconceivably more to *hang* than for any other purpose."

Brown greeted a procession of visitors in his cell during his last month. Virginia officials also generously (perhaps foolishly) allowed their prisoner to receive and send a steady stream of letters to friends, family, and antislavery associates. These letters helped fix the view of Brown among Northerners as a Christian martyr for the abolitionist cause. The themes he dwelt on in his correspondence were constant: his "cheerful" resignation to death, comparisons of his own death with Christ's, his belief that his death would help achieve his aim of liberating the slaves, and his continued assertion that he served as a messenger of God. In only one month's time Brown made his execution a national event. Thousands now saw him only as a brave Christian going to his death with calm nobility.

On December 1, the afternoon before his execution, Brown received a last visitor, his wife, Mary. She had traveled south, having received Governor Wise's permission to return the bodies of her husband and two sons to their New York farm for burial. Brown and his wife shared supper and discussed family matters. Before going to bed, Brown wrote a final letter to his brother Jeremiah in which he described himself as "quite cheerful and composed."

A sentimental version of Brown on his way to his execution was painted by Thomas Hovenden in 1884. Just before, Brown had stopped by the cell of some of this fellow raiders and spoken to them, parting with the words: "God bless you, my men. May we all meet in Heaven." (MET, Gift of Mr. and Mrs. Carl Stoeckel, 1897)

Brown rose at dawn on December 2, read his Bible briefly, and wrote a final note to Mary. He enclosed his will and gave instructions for his tombstone inscription—simply "John Brown born May 9th 1800 was executed at Charleston, Va., December 2d 1859." Soon afterward his jailers came for him and escorted him down the corridor.

Brown walked briskly down the corridor. Pausing by the cell where the two blacks, Copeland and Green, were being held, he advised them: "Stand up like men, and do not betray your friends." At the cell shared by Cook and Coppoc, the two captured white raiders, Brown engaged in a brief argument with the pair over whether they had made false statements at their trial concerning his conduct. Finally, he shook hands with them both and walked on, shouting: "God bless you, my men. May we all meet in heaven."

Brown stepped out into a street jammed with armed men, observing wryly to his guards: "I had no idea that Governor Wise considered my execution so important." Climbing into a wagon that would take him to the gallows, Brown sat down on his own coffin. He handed one of the guards a last message (punctuated in his own unique style). It was obviously addressed to Americans in every section of the country and read as clearly as a battle order:

> Charleston, Va, 2nd, December, 1859
> I John Brown am now quite *certain* that the crimes of this *guilty, land: will* never be purged *away;* but with Blood. I had *as I now think: vainly* flattered myself that without *very much* bloodshed; it might be done.

At the gallows site 1500 federal troops and state militiamen waited, along with a huge crowd of onlookers. The day itself seemed much too pleasant for a hanging. Looking at the Blue Ridge Mountains in the distance and the cornfields that surrounded them, the doomed John Brown observed: "This *is* a beautiful country. I never had the pleasure of seeing it before."

The prisoner walked quickly up the steps of the scaffold with no hesitation. For ten minutes the officials in charge stumbled about trying to take their assigned positions. Brown himself seemed the most calm and least worried person on the platform. Finally, the preparations were completed, and a hush fell over the spectators as the officials walked off the scaffold, leaving Brown alone and "as motionless as a statue." Moments later, John Brown hung dangling before the huge crowd.

Some of the Southerners present felt, like Edmund Ruffin (a proslavery Virginian), that Brown had gone to his death with "complete fearlessness." Others, like a young actor named John Wilkes Booth, remained too bitter toward the dead man to admire his courage. Several Southern military leaders were present, including "Stonewall" Jackson, later to be a Civil War hero. But it was Colonel J. T. L. Preston's voice that first broke the stillness after Brown's death. "So perish all such enemies of Virginia," Preston exclaimed. "All such enemies of the Union! All such foes of the human race!"

Brown maintained his usual calm to the very moment of his death. A few days earlier he had written to his wife: "I have been whiped, but am sure I can recover all the lost capital occasioned by that disaster; by only hanging a few moments by the neck."

By the time Brown went to his death, he had become a symbol. In the North he had, of course, won the sympathies of convinced antislavery forces. But he had also captured the compassion of many who had previously been either indifferent or opposed to abolitionism. One such person was a prominent New York Democrat and conservative on the slavery issue named George Templeton Strong. A few days after the execution Strong wrote in his diary:

> Old Brown's demeanor has undoubtedly made a great impression—his simplicity and consistency, the absence of fuss, parade and bravado, the strength and clearness of his letters, all indicate a depth of conviction that one does not expect in an abolitionist (who is apt to be a mere talker). Slavery has received no such blow in my time as Brown's strangulation. The supporters of any institution are apt to be staggered and startled when they find that any one man, wise or foolish, is so convinced of its wrong and injustices as to acquiesce in being hanged by way of protest against it. One's faith in anything is terribly shaken by anybody who is ready to go to the gallows condemning and denouncing it.

When Brown died, in fact, few Republicans and Democrats in the North were willing to denounce openly the character and aims of a man whom, only a month earlier, many had attacked as an insane fanatic.

In the South the image of John Brown was naturally a different one. Here he was not the Christian martyr who was becoming increasingly popular in the North. He was, instead, a grim, avenging devil-figure who had tried to start a massive slave revolt. After November 1859, Northerners concentrated on the *words* that had come from John Brown's eloquent tongue and pen after his capture. But Southerners were more concerned with the *deeds* that he and his men had attempted at Harpers Ferry. After the raid several Southern towns had called militia units and vigilante companies into service, declared martial law, and began hunting down conspirators—real or imagined—in their midst. A wave of hysteria sent thousands of fearful whites, many of whom did not own slaves, patrolling their neighborhoods, searching for abolitionist invaders and unruly slaves.

The South mobilized much more quickly and effectively after John Brown's assault than it had after Nat Turner's insurrection three decades earlier. After all, Southerners had been predicting such an assault from the North for more than a generation.

Southerners regarded John Brown even more harshly after the election of Abraham Lincoln as president in November 1860. The impact of John Brown's raid was crucial in provoking what one historian has called a crisis of fear among Southerners concerning Northern-led efforts to stir up slave rebellions. It helped create the climate of intense sectional passion that led to secession and civil war.

Once the South had left the Union, John Brown provided a magnificent symbol for rallying a reluctant Northern public to war. "Fifty years hence," George Templeton Strong confided to his diary in February 1862, "John Brown will be recognized as the Hero or Representative Man of this struggle." He added that "a queer rude song about him seems to be growing popular." The song to which Strong refers was set to the music of another Northern tune, then also growing in popularity—"The Battle Hymn of the Republic"—whose eloquent verses were written by Samuel Gridley Howe's wife, Julia. But Brown would probably have enjoyed the "queer rude song," whose simplicity proved so appealing to the ordinary soldier:

> John Brown's body lies a-mouldering in the grave,
> John Brown's body lies a-mouldering in the grave,
> John Brown's body lies a-mouldering in the grave,
> But his soul goes marching on.

22 The Road to Civil War

Had John Brown launched his raid thirty years earlier, in 1829 instead of 1859, almost all of the North would have joined the South in shock and condemnation. Although Northern states had abolished slavery, and many Northerners viewed the slave system with hostility, few shared the overriding desire of John Brown and the Secret Six to interfere with slavery's operation in the South. Most residents of New England, the Middle Atlantic states, and the Upper Midwest supported the Missouri Compromise and accepted the existence of slavery in the South as a political necessity that cemented the Union of free and slave states.

But between the 1820s and the 1850s, Northern attitudes toward the South and slavery underwent a significant change. A small group of antislavery men and women—stubborn, committed, and intensely religious—could claim a good deal of the credit and assume much of the responsibility for bringing these changes about. At first, the agitators risked social ostracism and even physical injury. Several Southern states offered cash rewards for their arrest and extradition. But slowly these radical antislavery advocates, or abolitionists, gained a hearing for their belief that slavery was morally wrong and should not be subject to political compromise.

The great majority of Northerners never accepted this concept entirely. As late as the eve of the Civil War, the term "abolitionist" was used to smear political opponents. Yet, for various reasons, even the majority of "moderates" in the North began to believe that although slavery could not be snuffed out at once, the institution should not be allowed to extend farther into the new Western territories. Both abolitionists and slaveholders believed that such a policy of restriction would inevitably lead to the end of slavery in the South. So, when the new Republican party won a national victory in 1860 on a slavery restriction platform, Southerners and abolitionists were in agreement on another point: national political compromise on the slavery question had become impossible.

THE ABOLITION MOVEMENT

A leading antislavery (but not abolitionist) organization of the early nineteenth century was the American Colonization Society, founded in 1817. But the Colonization Society, after a promising start, did not prosper. Everybody seemed to have a different notion as to what it stood for and what it might accomplish. Free blacks feared the society as a trap for expatriating them forcibly, and some antislavery people agreed. Thus the society would not end slavery but merely siphon off free blacks. Southerners from the Deep South did not cotton to colonization and took the society's antislavery professions much too seriously. Politicians from such states as South Carolina and Georgia consistently and insistently fought against giving a federal subsidy to the society, an idea opposed by many Northerners too. The shock waves of fear that surged through all of the South in the aftermath of the Nat Turner Revolt in 1831 ended all realistic hopes for strong and widespread Southern support for colonization as a "solution" to the slavery question.

Garrison and His Followers

Abolitionism as an independent movement began in the 1830s. Without doubt its leading fig-

William Lloyd Garrison was stubborn, humorless, and courageous in his crusade for abolition. In 1854 he publicly burned a copy of the Constitution exclaiming, "So perish all compromises with tyranny!" (Courtesy, Dept. of Special Collections, Wichita State University)

ure was William Lloyd Garrison. Born in Massachusetts, he was influenced by a fanatically religious mother. For a time he edited the first temperance paper. Then he turned to the antislavery cause and founded an abolitionist journal, the *Liberator*. It was first published in Boston in 1831. Two years later Garrison organized the American Antislavery Society.

Much of Garrison's support came from free blacks in the North. But the movement quickly grew among white sympathizers as well. By 1837 the American Antislavery Society had 145 local chapters in Massachusetts, 274 chapters in New York, and 213 in Ohio (the Middle Western center of antislavery activity). By 1843 the society had over 200,000 members.

Other abolitionist leaders included Frederick Douglass and Wendell Phillips, Garrison's Boston lieutenant. Prominent figures in New York were Gerrit Smith and the Tappan brothers, Lewis and Arthur. Theodore Weld dominated the Middle West. Among the best-known speakers in the Northeast were Angelina Grimké and her sister, Sarah Grimké Weld.

Garrison and his followers broke deliberately with previous antislavery groups in several ways. First, they demanded the *immediate* rather than *gradual* abolition of slavery. Second, many of the abolitionists opposed the idea of colonization. They believed it was possible for black Americans to be absorbed into American society. Third, the "Garrisonians" abandoned the politeness of earlier antislavery groups. Instead they adopted a militant, aggressive style. Garrison set the tone himself in the first issue of the *Liberator:* "I *will* be as harsh as truth, and as uncompromising as justice. On this subject, I do not wish to think, or speak, or write with moderation. I am earnest—I will not equivocate—I will not excuse—I will not retreat a single inch—AND I WILL BE HEARD."

Changing Tactics

The abolitionists' religious beliefs helped determine their strategy. Most were devout Protestants. They believed that slavery was the country's greatest moral evil, a blot on the United States that had to be erased. Their main objection to slavery was moral. Therefore, they thought, it was essential to convince the mass of Americans, North *and* South, that slavery was immoral and unjust. Abolitionists believed that personal recognition of this fact would result in nationwide demands for an immediate end to slavery. This technique was called moral suasion.

During the 1830s Garrison and his associates made a strong effort to reach slaveholders by mailing hundreds of thousands of abolitionist newspapers and tracts to the South. After the Nat Turner Revolt, the postmaster general, a Southerner, allowed Southern postmasters to refuse to deliver abolitionist propaganda, violating both the law and the senders' civil liberties. Southerners burned antislavery material.

Although Turner's revolt dampened the prospects of colonization as a viable solution to slavery, American blacks continued to emigrate to Africa throughout the nineteenth century. The ship drawn here, a Dutch steamer, left Savannah, Georgia, in 1895 with two hundred blacks bound for Liberia. Founded to provide an African homeland for freed American slaves, Liberia broke away from the fading American Colonization Society in 1847 and established itself as an independent Republic. (Culver Pictures)

By the 1840s abolitionists recognized that moral suasion had failed to win over any significant number of slaveholders. They abandoned this tactic in the South, but they continued to use it in the North.

The abolitionists split into two separate wings—those who opposed Garrison and those who supported him. His opponents objected to him for several reasons. They resented his overbearing leadership. They also disapproved of his demand for equal status for women as abolitionist leaders, and for fusion of the woman's rights campaign with the antislavery movement. They disliked Garrison's constant attacks on the organized churches, many of whose leaders still opposed the drive for emancipation. And they wanted to involve the movement in practical political action. (Garrison wanted to focus on moral agitation.)

In 1840 the anti-Garrisonians withdrew from Garrison's organization and formed the American and Foreign Anti-Slavery Society. Both groups continued their propaganda campaigns to stir up Northern public opinion until the Civil War. But their major energies shifted during the 1840s into direct political agitation at the local, state, and national levels. Abolitionism was now the central concern of all American reformers, whatever their other interests.

Reactions to the Abolitionists

The abolitionists aroused intense feelings that often led to violence. It was dangerous during the 1830s to advocate immediate emancipation, even in the North. Anti-abolitionist mobs, often including prominent community leaders, disrupted abolitionist meetings and destroyed antislavery printing presses. When a leading English abolitionist came to New England in 1835, Bostonians rioted. Garrison was led through the city's streets with a rope around his waist, until police took him into protective custody. (This incident helped convert Wendell Phillips to the abolitionist movement.) That same year in New York City a mob destroyed Lewis Tappan's home, and throughout that stormy decade dozens of anti-abolitionist riots and mobbings took place. Henry B. Stanton, another militant antislavery figure, claimed to have been attacked personally over two hundred times. The worst incident occurred in Alton, Illinois, in 1837. There, Elijah Lovejoy, an abolitionist editor, was shot dead by a mob while defending his home and his press.

Those outside the South who opposed abolitionism feared the reformers almost as much as Southerners feared the slave revolts. To conservative Northerners, the abolitionists seemed to threaten public order, national unity, and established institutions. In fact, race prejudice was as strong in the North as in the South. Certainly free blacks in the North suffered constant abuse and discrimination.

Even white abolitionists could not wholly shed their color prejudice. Only a few treated their black associates as complete equals. Garrison at one point urged the eloquent Frederick Douglass to use more "darky" mannerisms in his speeches. Such attitudes led Douglass to break with the Boston abolitionist.

Although Northerners did not lose their racial prejudices, they gradually became more sympathetic to the abolitionists. Federal interference with antislavery mail to the South won many converts to the abolitionist cause. Even those who did not share abolitionist beliefs disliked the practice of suppressing ideas. A number of Americans who began by defending the abolitionists' civil liberties ended by joining the movement itself.

Other Northerners became aroused by the "gag rule." This resolution, passed by the House of Representatives in 1836, provided that no antislavery petitions would even be considered. Every year a small group of congressmen, led by former President John Quincy Adams, tried to repeal the gag rule. They finally succeeded in ending this flagrant violation of the abolitionists' right of petition in 1844.

THE MOVE INTO POLITICS

The abolitionists' earliest efforts in politics were limited to questioning major party candidates regarding slavery and voting for the individual, if

The murder of editor Elijah Lovejoy made him the first martyr of the abolitionist cause. He aroused controversy by his antislavery principles, first in St. Louis, where his printing office was destroyed, and then across the Mississippi in Alton, Illinois. His murder by an anti-abolitionist mob sent a "shock wave as of an earthquake throughout this continent," according to John Quincy Adams. (Brown Brothers)

Frederick Douglass, born in Maryland, escaped from slavery in 1838. He broke with Garrison, believing in a more political approach to abolition. During the Civil War he organized two black regiments from Massachusetts. Later he served as minister to Haiti. (Nelson Library, Sophia Smith Collection, Smith College)

one could be found, whose answers were satisfactory—or the least unsatisfactory. Needless to say, this went on exclusively in the North. By this method, unpromising though it seemed, abolitionists hoped to hold the balance of power in some Northern districts and states. Only rarely did they succeed.

Many abolitionists yearned for bolder action. James G. Birney was an Alabama plantation owner and slaveholder who had become converted to abolitionism. Finding it unwise and unsafe to advocate abolition in the South, he left for Ohio to establish an antislavery newspaper. Birney had long differed with Garrison on the Boston editor's support for woman's rights and opposition to political action. In 1840, Birney ran for president as the candidate of the new Liberty party.

Both Harrison, the Whig candidate, and Van Buren, the Democrat, he argued, were totally unacceptable to abolitionists, and a new party had to be formed if abolitionists wished to cast a *moral* vote for president. But Garrisonians ridiculed the efforts of Birney and the Liberty party, and abolitionists found little more comfort in the slaveholding Harrison than in Andrew Jackson's hand-picked successor, Van Buren. Of 2.5 million votes cast in 1840, Birney got only seven thousand.

The abolition movement had now split. Garrison maintained headquarters in Boston; the Liberty-ites were headquartered in New York City (where they generated most of their financial support). Although disappointed at their showing in 1840, Liberty party people decided to stay in business. "The fewer we have now," wrote one after the election, displaying strong faith but shaky logic, "the more we have to gain before we carry our point." They continued to work in local and state elections in 1841 and 1842, and increased the party's vote slightly.

Garrison, meanwhile, expanded his antipolitical principles to new and broader dimensions. He had become a moral perfectionist, a pacifist, and a total nonresister, rejecting the use of force under any circumstances. In 1842, he proclaimed "it is morally and politically impossible for a just and equal union to be formed between Liberty and Slavery." By remaining in the Union, Northerners bore as much responsibility for slavery as the South. Only a breakup of the country could ease that guilt. Many who had remained loyal to Garrison up to then could not accept his new demand, or his perfectionism, or his commitment to various other reforms. Garrison for his part wanted no truck with such compromisers. He banished the doubters without a qualm, and forced the shrinking American Antislavery Society to accept his policy.

ABOLITIONIST ACTIVITIES

Antislavery Energies

Despite the bitterness of their split, abolitionists from both wings of the movement engaged in many of the same activities. Both the Garrison and the Liberty party groups maintained newspapers, produced pamphlets, and organized public meetings. They cited the same books and stories detailing atrocities committed against blacks on Southern plantations. And all abolitionists were regarded as equally detestable by slaveholders and conservative Northerners.

Probably no single aspect of the abolitionists' work did more to gain sympathy for them than their efforts to assist fugitive slaves. Black abolitionists made daring raids into the South to rescue some of those in bondage. Other blacks took to podiums to denounce slavery. Outstanding were a famous pair of black women, Harriet Tubman (see p. 421) and Sojourner Truth. A large network of Northern sympathizers, both white and black, maintained the Underground Railroad. In its "stations"—safe havens such as barns and cellars—escaped slaves could hide until "conductors" led them onward to freedom in the North and in Canada.

Many abolitionists actively interfered with slave catchers who came North to recapture runaways. To those who argued that the Constitution gave slaveholders the legal right to reclaim their slave property, people like James Birney replied firmly, "Whatever pledges of noninterference may be given they will be disregarded—at least so long as our body has any life or humanity in it, or any greater fear of God than of man." Even a conven-

The Underground Railroad was neither underground nor a railroad. But somehow it did work to gain freedom from slavery for several thousand blacks. (Library of Congress)

tional major party politician like William H. Seward, the New York Whig, during the Compromise of 1850 debates, warned of a "higher law" than the Constitution—the law of freedom.

The abolitionist attack on slavery also included criticism of the deplorable condition of free blacks in the North. Few Northern states allowed blacks to vote, and the little schooling offered them was substandard and on a rigidly segregated basis. Although white abolitionists found it easier to attack Southern slavery than to rid themselves of prevailing anti-Negro prejudices or to imagine blacks living in equality with whites, the movement still fought against the worst forms of Northern racial discrimination. "No proposition is more true," admitted one Liberty party speaker, "than that the wrongs which the North has done, and continues to do, to its colored people . . . furnish the most influential argument in favor of Southern oppression."

Abolition and Expansionism

By the time the Liberty party rallied for its second national campaign in 1844, the political abolitionists had acquired an issue with national appeal. The giant slaveholding republic of Texas, whose annexation to the United States (possibly as more than one state) the antislavery forces had steadily opposed, was about to be admitted by Congress. Once again, abolitionists organized meetings, printed anti-Texas petitions and newspapers, and tried to pressure Congress to refuse admission. This time, they began to gain support from other Northerners. Many of these did not care about slavery with the same moral intensity as the abolitionists, but they were leery of any action that

Harriet Tubman

The most famous "conductor" on the Underground Railroad was a former slave, Harriet Tubman. In the years 1850 to 1861, from the passage of the Fugitive Slave Act to the outbreak of the Civil War, she made nineteen secret trips into the South rescuing some three hundred people. Offers of rewards for her capture eventually totaled $40,000. But she eluded her enemies successfully and was never caught. In later years she claimed that "on my Underground Railroad, I never ran my train off the track, and I never lost a passenger."

Born in 1820 or 21 on a plantation in Dorchester County, on Maryland's eastern shore, Tubman knew only cruelty as a child. She was one of ten or eleven children born to Benjamin Ross and Harriet Greene. (Her grandparents on both sides had come in chains from Africa.) She received no schooling and thus could not read or write. Because she was found to be too awkward and clumsy for housework, she was made to work as a field hand. When she was about thirteen years of age, an overseer struck her on the head with a two-pound weight and fractured her skull. This resulted in spells of somnolence that affected her for the rest of her life. In 1844, she married a free black named John Tubman, but the marriage did not succeed.

In 1849, Harriet Tubman's master died, and it was rumored that his slaves would be sold. The young woman decided that this was the time to make a break for freedom, which she did with the help of friendly Quakers. She reached Philadelphia and obtained employment in a hotel. There she met the black abolitonist, William Still, who recruited her for the Underground Railroad. He later said of her:

> Harriet was a woman of no pretensions, indeed, a more ordinary specimen of humanity could hardly be found among the most unfortunate-looking farm hands of the South. Yet, in point of courage, shrewdness, and disinterested exertions to rescue her fellowmen, by making personal visits into Maryland among the slaves, she was without her equal.

In December 1850, this single-minded, deeply religious woman began the first of her many trips back into the South to bring out slaves. First, she brought out her brother and his family and later that same year a family of eleven. On one of her most difficult trips, she returned, in 1857, to the eastern shore and brought back her aged parents in a hired wagon. Many tales are told of her tenacity and ingenuity. To inform prospective fugitives that she would be arriving shortly, she sent messages in the "double-talk" that blacks had learned to use in their communications and even in the texts of their songs (spirituals).

Harriet Tubman became well known among abolitionists and sometimes addressed their conventions. But she preferred to remain a woman of mystery whose whereabouts were generally unknown. It was in St. Catharines, Ontario, in April of 1858, however, that she counseled and encouraged John Brown in his plan to take action by force of arms. Only a flareup of her head injury kept her from joining him at Harpers Ferry.

When the Civil War broke out, "General Tubman" (as John Brown had called her) volunteered her services. For three years she worked for the "Union" forces securing information from black informants. She worked as a nurse and a cook, aiding freedmen who had joined the Union Army, supporting herself by selling chickens and eggs. After the war she returned to her farm in Auburn, taking in helpless old black people and black orphans as well. Her farm became the Harriet Tubman Home for Indigent Aged Negroes, which carried on even after her death in 1913.

would so greatly increase the South's size and national political power.

In the election of 1844, the Whigs' Henry Clay, making his last desperate stab at the presidential office he wanted so badly, tried to keep Texas out of the campaign. James K. Polk, the Democratic candidate, openly favored the annexation of Texas and westward expansion generally. Birney, running again on the Liberty party ticket, polled only sixty-five thousand votes, a disappointing total. But had his fifteen thousand votes in New York gone to Clay, Whigs would have carried the state and the election. For the first time, the abolitionists had flexed a small but significant bit of political muscle.

Texas joined the Union shortly after the election, and a year later Polk went to war with Mexico to gain New Mexico and California. Abolitionists opposed the war passionately, first because most of them were pacifists, and second, because they feared that the new territories would be added to the roster of slave states. A few went so far as Henry David Thoreau, who refused to pay his local taxes and spent a night in jail to symbolize his protest. They began to charge that the country was being taken over by an "aggressive slavocracy" (the Slave Power), which intended to crush all criticism of slavery in the North and West, just as it had stamped out dissent in the South. The slavocracy would then embroil the nation in foreign wars to increase its own slave territory and wealth.

Thousands of individuals all over the North, up to now unmoved by the plight of the slaves, rallied to this standard of opposition. "The Mexican War and Slavery," predicted Charles Sumner, a Massachusetts antislavery Whig, "will derange all party calculations." The Whigs of his own Bay State were soon split over the slavery extension issue into "Cotton" and "Conscience" factions. Northern Democrats, unhappy over their party's control by Southerners, now supported the Wilmot Proviso (see Chapter 20). Many Westerners supported it, too; they wanted the land west of the

In this pre-Civil War picture, the great abolitionist Harriet Tubman (far left) stands with a family of slaves, possibly one of the many groups Tubman bravely escorted from the slave South north to freedom. (The Sophia Smith Collection, Smith College)

Advertisements such as these proliferated after the passage of the Fugitive Slave Act of 1850. Despite the stronger law, slaves continued to seek freedom north of the Mason-Dixon line. (NYPL/Picture Collection)

Missouri River for small farms for white settlers, and wanted to keep both slavery and free blacks out of the area.

Although some Liberty men—and, of course, the Garrisonians—warned against accommodating these new allies, most of the party eagerly sought to construct antislavery coalitions. In 1846, New Hampshire Liberty-ites and independent Democrats elected John P. Hale to the U.S. Senate, and a growing number of congressmen openly declared themselves for slavery restriction. Whig Senator William Seward of New York was rapidly becoming the leader of a small group of national political figures committed to antislavery.

In August 1848, at a convention in Buffalo, the Free Soil party emerged—a coalition of Barnburners (antislavery New York Democrats), Conscience Whigs, independent Democrats from the Midwest, and Liberty party members. Both major parties had nominated unacceptable candidates: the Whigs named General Zachary Taylor, a Louisiana slaveholder; and the Democrats, Lewis Cass, widely considered a "doughface"—a Northern man with Southern principles. The new antislavery party adopted a platform opposing the admission of *any* new slave states or allowing slavery to exist in the territories. Yet its presidential nominee was none other than Martin Van Buren, the Jacksonian Democrat who had been so important two decades earlier in forging the "doughface" coalition of Northern and Southern Democrats.

Many abolitionists felt that too much had been conceded. The Free Soil platform said nothing about abolition, or about racial discrimination. Many recalled that only a decade before, Van Buren had been considered the worst of the doughfaces, a Northern president who would make no move to abolish slavery in the District of Columbia or speak out against the gag rule. Gerrit Smith, later of the Secret Six, led a small number of dissidents in forming the Liberty League to uphold the principles of the now disbanded Liberty party. Wendell Phillips, a close ally of Garrison, sneered at the "namby-pamby antislavery" of the Free Soilers.

THE GROWTH OF ANTISLAVERY SENTIMENT

The handful of antislavery men in the Senate, now including Seward, Hale, and a former Liberty-ite from Ohio, Salmon P. Chase, fought hard against the Compromise of 1850. Yet the Compromise, or rather one specific part of it, gave an enormous impetus to the antislavery movement.

The Fugitive Slave Law of 1850 granted almost unlimited power to the federal commissioners appointed to enforce it, and to private slave catchers seeking to profit by it. The latter roamed the Northern states during the 1850s, collecting bounties from Southern planters for capturing and returning blacks who had allegedly escaped from slavery. Some of the victims were indeed runaways; others were not. But commissioners could decide as they pleased—there was little due process and no right of appeal. Northern legislatures, responding to public disgust over the slave catchers, passed what came to be known as "personal liberty laws," to counteract the fugitive slave law. Under the personal liberty laws, state and local officials might delay or withhold help in the distasteful process of returning alleged runaways. Southerners understandably fumed over this Northern betrayal of the Compromise, this Northern version of nullification.

Abolitionists went a step further and actively assisted fugitive slaves. It has been estimated that Boston alone sheltered a minimum of six hundred runaway blacks at any given time. Abolitionists in that city even resorted to violence to keep Negroes out of the hands of slave catchers. Thomas Higginson, for example, led a Boston mob which prevented the return to slavery of a fugitive. Theodore Parker, who often hid runaways in his home, wrote sermons with a pistol within reach of his desk. But when the federal government decided to go into the slave-catching business seriously and with all its power, it usually had its way, as in the case of Anthony Burns of Boston, who was returned to slavery by a massive force of federal troops.

Still, the reaction to such activities showed how attitudes had changed. In the 1830s, Garrison had been led through the streets of Boston with a rope around his body (and placed under "protective custody") for opposing slavery. In the 1850s, when Anthony Burns was returned to the South through those same streets, thousands of protesters lined the streets, and church bells tolled the city's shame.

While persistently agitating the fugitive slave issue, Free Soilers sought to increase their political influence by forming coalitions with members of the major parties. The party might ally with Democrats in one Northern state, Whigs in another; and in yet a third state it might support a Democrat for one office and a Whig for another. Such tactics succeeded in some instances. In the early 1850s, when most Americans, North and South, wished to believe that the Compromise of 1850 had permanently settled the question of slavery, such "deals" may have been necessary to keep antislavery politics alive.

In 1852, both major parties endorsed the Compromise, and most of the Barnburners (Van Buren included) returned to the Democratic party, their natural home. One result of this was to make the Free Soil party decidedly more radical than it had been four years before. Its platform now declared "that slavery is a sin against God and a crime against man . . . and that Christianity, humanity, and patriotism alike demand its abolition." John P. Hale, New Hampshire's non-Compromise senator, became the party's presidential nominee. A natural result of *this* was a falling off in votes. Hale polled about half of Van Buren's total of 1848. Yet the election in 1852 revealed a hard core of 150,000 antislavery votes, a seed for growth should the right issue appear.

That issue was not long in coming. When Stephen A. Douglas introduced the Kansas-Nebraska bill in 1854, reopening the possibility of forming slave states from those and other territories, the North exploded. Free Soilers and other restrictionists formed the new Republican party. "Our position is now rather enviable," wrote one Free Soil congressman, "We lead the hosts of freedom." "Anti-Nebraska" Democrats, as they were known, fielded their own tickets in many states. The American (or Know-Nothing) party, anti-immigrant and anti-Nebraska, made a strong showing. (The two issues did relate to each other, since many immigrants were deeply anti-Negro and also strongly opposed abolitionism.) With the existence of so many parties, shifting coalitions, and candidates with unclear partisan allegiances, finding the winners in the congressional elections of 1854 proved difficult. Despite some doubt as to who had won, those who favored the *expansion* of slavery, under any formula or conditions, had very clearly been the losers.

EMERGENCE OF THE REPUBLICAN PARTY

The Republican party, like most newly formed political organizations, was a complex group. It enrolled virtually all of the Free Soilers, most Northern Whigs (whose party had recently fallen apart), and a significant minority of Northern Democrats for whom the Kansas-Nebraska Act had been too much to swallow. All of these groups united, with varying degrees of commitment, on a single issue: slavery should not expand into the territories. Beyond that, they differed widely. "There are Republicans who are Abolitionists," explained Horace Greeley's New York *Tribune*, "there are others who anxiously desire and labor for the good of the slave, but there are many more whose main impulse is a desire to secure the territories for Free White Labor, with little or no regard for the interests of negroes, free or slave."

Yet, from the start, the party felt the heavy influence of the first group, the "political aboli-

Fugitive Henry Box Brown attempted a most daring escape, after his master refused to purchase Brown's wife and prevent her sale to the South. In a specially constructed crate, 2 feet by 3 feet wide and 2½ feet high, complete with airholes, Brown had himself sent 350 miles by express to Philadelphia, where delighted abolitionists unpacked him. He had spent 27 hours in the box, much of the time upside down, awaiting his "resurrection from the grave of slavery." (Library of Congress)

tionists," who regarded the prevention of slavery's spread as only a first step to total elimination of America's "national sin." They succeeded in getting through a strong antislavery platform at the 1856 Republican convention. But the party's presidential nominee, a professional Western explorer and amateur politican named John C. Frémont, left much to be desired. Even Garrison, however, admitted grudgingly that "as between the three rival parties, the sympathy of every friend of freedom

Dred Scott, the central figure in the celebrated Supreme Court decision of 1857. (Missouri Historical Society)

must be with the Republican party, in spite of its lamentable shortcomings." Frederick Douglass led what little there was of the black vote in the new party, and Gerrit Smith, although running for president himself as the Abolition candidate, donated $500 to the "other" antislavery party.

After only two years of existence, the Republicans ran effectively in 1856. Receiving virtually no votes in the slave states, the new party swept New England and carried New York, Ohio, and several other Western states. The Democratic candidate, James Buchanan, another doughface, carried only five Northern states, some of them mainly because Know-Nothings had voted for their own candidate, ex-President Millard Fillmore. "We are beaten," conceded a leading Republican, "but we frightened the rascals awfully."

Another Weak President

By the time James Buchanan took office as president in March 1857, political parties could no longer appeal to voters on a nationwide basis. Republicans now dominated the North, but they had no following in the South. The Know-Nothing party was dead; so were the Whigs. Southern Democrats generally voted as a bloc. Only Northern Democrats were still trying to bridge the widening gap between the sections. And only an extraordinary, national-minded president, one skilled in the political arts of bullying and compromise, would have stood a chance of repairing all of this political damage. James Buchanan, an elderly, fussy bachelor, quick to please, slow to offend, soon proved the obvious—he was *not* that kind of president.

The Dred Scott Decision

Buchanan's first and only effort at sectional reconciliation produced immediate disaster. The Supreme Court, he stated blandly in his inaugural address, was about to decide the question of slaveholders' rights in the territories. The Court's decision, whatever it turned out to be, should be accepted by all sides, and the opinion should settle the dispute permanently. Dred Scott, a slave, had been taken from Missouri to Illinois and later to Wisconsin. Missouri was a slave state, Illinois a free state, and Wisconsin, at the time, a free territory according to the Missouri Compromise. In 1846, Scott sued for his liberty, claiming that residence in a free state and a free territory had put an end to his slave status. After passing through state courts and lower federal courts, the well-publicized case reached the U.S. Supreme Court.

Even before the decision, antislavery forces had rejected Buchanan's "offer." The Supreme Court of 1857 was controlled by slaveholders and doughfaces. Besides, slavery *did* enjoy protection from the Constitution and laws of the United States; Garrison and other radical abolitionists were right about that. In the twenty years before *Dred Scott* v. *Sandford,* the Supreme Court had upheld both the legality of the interstate slave trade and the rights of slaveowners to retrieve their property forcibly anywhere in the Union. In 1851, six years before *Dred Scott,* in *Strader* v. *Graham,* a case with very similar issues, the court had ruled that a slave going from Kentucky to Ohio remained a slave under the laws of Kentucky, rather than becoming free under the laws of Ohio. Such decisions led John Hale to denounce the Court as "the very citadel of American slavery," an exaggerated but not preposterous allegation.

Moreover, Buchanan's offer of March 1857 was not so generous and open as the president wished people to think. While reading the speech, he already knew (through confidential contacts with one of the justices) how the Court would decide. He had in fact helped persuade a justice from his own state, Pennsylvania, to join the five justices from slave states, so that the Court would not divide along totally sectional lines.

Chief Justice Roger Taney of Maryland, speaking for the majority, ruled against Scott, declaring that the plaintiff had no right to sue since a black could not be a citizen. Taney added gratuitously that white Americans had since colonial times considered blacks inferior human beings, possessing "no rights that a white man was bound to respect." Worst of all, from the North's point of view, Taney and the Court decided that slavery could not be excluded from *any* territory. Slaves, he explained, were property, and according to the Fifth Amendment, persons could not be deprived of property without due process of law.

Opponents of slavery reacted furiously, charging that their warnings about the aggressions of the Slave Power had been confirmed. Not only was the South demanding the possibility of opening all new territories for slavery but the logic of the Court decision could be taken even further. "Does the Constitution make slaves property?" an irate Republican wanted to know. "If so, slavery exists in Ohio today, for the Constitution extends over Ohio, doesn't it?" Northerners, who had considered Kansas-Nebraska too favorable to the South, now felt some of that rage which characterized Southern grievances over nonenforcement of the fugitive slave law. The Buchanan administration, only a week old, was already doomed.

The Emergence of Lincoln

Stephen A. Douglas had helped build the Compromise of 1850—and he had helped to destroy it with the Kansas-Nebraska Act. In 1858 he ran for reelection to the Senate from Illinois. His Republican opponent was a popular former Whig congressman, Abraham Lincoln.

Born in Kentucky in 1809 to poor parents, Abraham Lincoln had moved with his family first to Indiana and then to Illinois. During his early years in these frontier areas the young man educated himself through extensive reading. He managed a general store at New Salem, Illinois, served as a captain of volunteers during a brief Indian war in northern Illinois, and worked as New Salem's postmaster while studying law. Lincoln was admitted to the Illinois bar in 1836. The next year he moved to Springfield and opened a law office.

Lincoln served as a state legislator from 1834 to 1842 while engaged in a private law prac-

The earliest known photograph of Lincoln was taken when he was a congressman—an obscure Whig and unpopular at home because of his opposition to the Mexican War. (Culver Pictures)

tice. He quickly acquired a reputation for his skill as a trial lawyer and his rough frontier humor. Elected in 1846 as a Whig, the young Illinois lawyer served one term in the House. He opposed the Mexican War but remained a member of the Whig party. Like many Northerners, Lincoln was pried loose from former party loyalties only by passage of the Kansas-Nebraska Act in 1854. He denounced the law and, in 1856, joined the newly formed Republican party.

Lincoln's views on slavery were typical of most Northern antislavery moderates. He believed that slavery was "a moral, social, and political wrong." But he denied having any intention of interfering with the institution in the Southern states. Like most Republicans, he felt that it would die out gradually as an unprofitable labor system. He did insist, however, that slavery should be totally excluded from the Western territories.

During a statewide series of public debates Lincoln kept Douglas on the defensive with questions about how, in view of the Dred Scott decision, settlers could legally exclude slavery from a territory under popular sovereignty. Douglas was reduced to arguing that a free-soil majority could simply refuse to enact a slave code, a weak counter to Lincoln's basic point.

In the short run the Lincoln-Douglas debates of 1858 helped to reelect Douglas. But in the long run they damaged him as a national leader. His view that a territory could effectively exclude slavery in spite of the Dred Scott decision gained him votes in Illinois, but it offended Southerners.

As for Lincoln, he emerged as a major national figure in the Republican party. He had dramatized in the debates the basic differences between Douglas Democrats and the Buchanan-Southern Democratic coalition.

Kansas and Collapse

President Buchanan scored no great successes. Perhaps his greatest failure was his Kansas policy, one inherited from fellow Democrat Franklin Pierce to deal with the miniature civil war which raged there. Pressured by Southerners in his cabinet, Buchanan submitted to Congress the "Lecompton Constitution," a document drafted by a proslavery minority in Kansas to serve as the basis for entry into the Union. The Lecompton Constitution legalized slavery, and prohibited agitation against the institution. Congress offered a huge land grant to Kansas if the state would ratify the document, but in 1858 free state settlers voted it down by a 9 to 1 margin. "Ever since the rendition [returning] of Anthony Burns," Thomas Higginson reported with pride, "I have been looking for *men*. I have found them in Kansas. . . . In Kansas, nobody talks of courage, for everyone is expected to exhibit it."

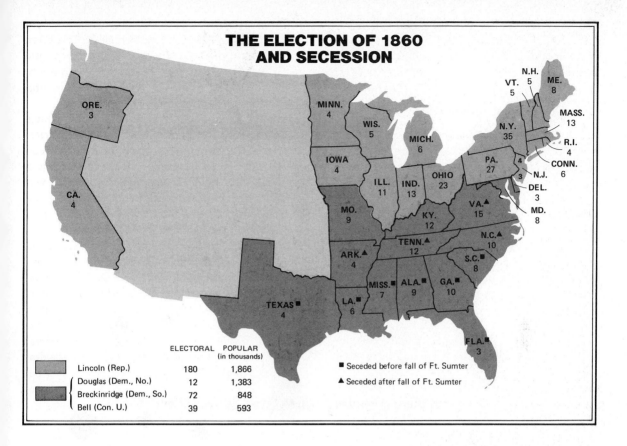

THE ELECTION OF 1860 AND SECESSION

	ELECTORAL	POPULAR (in thousands)
Lincoln (Rep.)	180	1,866
Douglas (Dem., No.)	12	1,383
Breckinridge (Dem., So.)	72	848
Bell (Con. U.)	39	593

■ Seceded before fall of Ft. Sumter
▲ Seceded after fall of Ft. Sumter

On the Lecompton issue, even Douglas, author of the Kansas-Nebraska Act, abandoned ship. Parly due to Lincoln's pressure in Illinois, partly due to obvious irregularities in the framing of the document, Douglas announced, "if this constitution is to be forced down our throats . . . I will resist it to the last." The Democratic party, the last national political institution, now broke in two: Southerners backed Buchanan; most Northerners supported Douglas.

THE FAILURE OF COMPROMISE

The reaction to John Brown's raid showed how fragile the political links between North and South had become. In the North even moderate antislavery advocates were outraged by the South's embittered defense of its "peculiar institution."

They regarded President Buchanan as a turncoat. Though Brown was in fact and by right a federal prisoner, Buchanan had simply handed him over to a Virginia court.

In the South, moderates had lost control of public opinion. People there had already begun preparing for possible secession, if not war. To most Southerners, Buchanan's pro-Southern attitudes no longer seemed adequate protection against "aggressions" (such as the Harpers Ferry raid) that the South believed Northern Republicans were planning. By 1860 armed defense against Northern attack seemed as reasonable to most Southerners as did violent assaults against the slave system to the antislavery North.

What was left to negotiate? How could either section compromise, when each one felt its most vital interests at stake? Brown's raid came at the end of a decade of bitter argument and violent conflict over slavery. It hastened the collapse of normal political life, since democratic politics requires moderation—which no longer had many spokesmen.

Election and Secession

The Democratic party split into sectional wings in 1860. Northern Democrats nominated Stephen A. Douglas for the presidency. The Southerners put forward their own candidate, John C. Breckinridge of Kentucky. He promised to sponsor federal laws that would protect slavery in the territories. The Republicans nominated Abraham Lincoln. A hodgepodge of former Whigs, Know-Nothings, and Democrats formed a new Constitutional Union party. They nominated a fourth candidate, John Bell, also of Kentucky. He pledged mainly to say and do nothing about the slavery question.

But a decade of agitation had eroded the basis for compromise solutions to the slavery question. It was no longer possible to avoid the issue by not talking about it. Douglas and Breckinridge split the Democratic vote. Bell carried three border states. Lincoln won the North. He became president with barely 40 percent of the popular vote, none at all from the Deep South.

Fear swept the South after Lincoln's election. "Secession fever" grew to epidemic proportions within days. South Carolina took the first step. Its legislature passed a secession ordinance on December 20, 1860, climaxing thirty years of leadership in defense of Southern nationalism. By February 1, 1861, six other states—Mississippi, Florida, Alabama, Georgia, Louisiana, and Texas—had adopted similar ordinances. Three days later, these seven states proclaimed the Confederate States of America in Montgomery, Alabama.

Four critical months separated the 1860 election and Lincoln's inauguration in March 1861. The "lame-duck" administration of James Buchanan did little to impede the course of secession. Buchanan condemned Southern actions and demanded obedience to federal laws. But neither he nor his government attempted to interfere as Southerners took control of federal forts, arsenals, and public property in their region.

There were various efforts to end the secession crisis by a political compromise in Congress, similar to the ones of 1820 and 1850. The most important of these was the Crittenden Compromise. It would have extended the Missouri Compromise line across the entire country, legalizing slavery south of it and prohibiting it to the north. By then, however, most Southerners were unprepared to accept any limitation, just as most Republicans opposed any extension, of the system. Lincoln proposed that the North agree to enforce the Fugitive Slave Act and protect Southern slavery by constitutional amendments if necessary. But his belated suggestions seemed inadequate to the secessionists.

Both the Confederate states and the new Republican administration waited in March 1861 to see whether states in the Upper South would also secede. Although fears about Republican intentions were widespread in states like Virginia and North Carolina, especially after John Brown's raid, there were also more Unionists there than in the Deep South.

Lincoln's Inauguration

Lincoln's inaugural address did little to calm the South. The new president promised not to invade the region or interfere with slavery where it already existed. But he made it clear that he believed the Union could not be dissolved at the whim of a state or group of states. He promised "to hold, occupy, and possess the property and places belonging to the federal government" throughout the country, including the South. And he pointed directly to the moral and political issue of slavery (and its extension) as the root of the conflict. "One section of our country," Lincoln said, "believes slavery is right, and ought to be extended, while the other believes it is wrong, and ought not to be extended. This is the only substantial dispute." Finally, he insisted that the question of war and peace was not in his hands but in those of his "dissatisfied fellow countrymen," the secessionists.

Lincoln's promise to maintain control of federal property in the South practically eliminated the possibility of a political compromise with the Confederate states. Lincoln was trapped be-

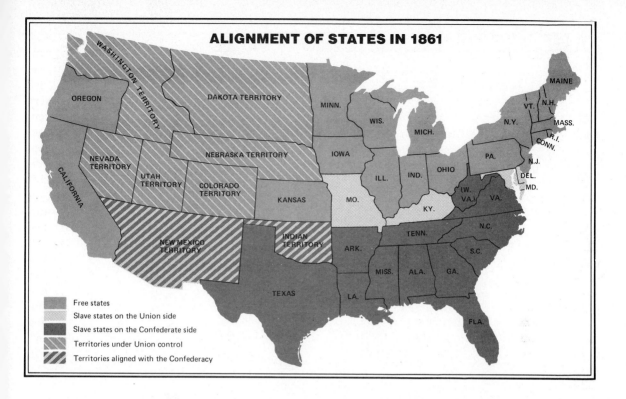

ALIGNMENT OF STATES IN 1861

WASHINGTON TERRITORY
OREGON
DAKOTA TERRITORY
MINN.
WIS.
MICH.
MAINE
VT. N.H.
N.Y.
MASS.
R.I.
CONN.
PA.
N.J.
NEVADA TERRITORY
UTAH TERRITORY
NEBRASKA TERRITORY
IOWA
IND.
OHIO
DEL.
MD.
CALIFORNIA
COLORADO TERRITORY
KANSAS
MO.
KY.
W. VA.
VA.
N.C.
NEW MEXICO TERRITORY
INDIAN TERRITORY
ARK.
TENN.
S.C.
TEXAS
LA.
MISS.
ALA.
GA.
FLA.
ILL.

Free states
Slave states on the Union side
Slave states on the Confederate side
Territories under Union control
Territories aligned with the Confederacy

tween a desire to mediate and a need to maintain national authority, lest it collapse throughout the Upper South as well.

For weeks Lincoln and his cabinet debated their course of action toward the Confederacy. They worried especially about whether to send relief supplies and troops to the few remaining federal posts in the region, such as Fort Sumter in Charleston harbor.

Finally, on April 4, Lincoln dispatched a relief expedition to Sumter. It carried only fresh supplies for the garrison, not reinforcements. Lincoln wanted to avoid the charge that he was making a hostile move toward the Confederacy. He even went so far as to inform the governor of South Carolina about his desire to supply Sumter peacefully. But the Confederate government demanded that the fort be entirely evacuated or, if necessary, destroyed. Charleston's harbor batteries opened fire at Sumter on April 12. Within two days Confederate forces had captured the fort. Virginia, Arkansas, and North Carolina all joined the Confederacy in the weeks that followed. So did Tennessee. Elsewhere in the border states—especially Maryland, Missouri, and Kentucky—Lincoln took firm measures to maintain Union control. "Both parties deprecated war," Lincoln later wrote, "but one of them would *make* war rather than let the nation survive; and the other would *accept* war rather than let it perish. And the war came."

Suggested Readings
Chapters 21-22

John Brown

R. O. Boyer, *The Legend of John Brown: A Biography and History* (1973); Stephen Oates, *To Purge This Land with Blood: A Biography of John Brown* (1970); J. Scott, *The Secret Six* (1979).

Abolitionism and the Antislavery Movement

Martin Duberman, ed., *The Antislavery Vanguard* (1969); Louis Filler, *The Crusade Against Slavery, 1830-1860* (1960); Larry Gara, *The Liberty Line: The Legend of the Underground Railroad* (1961); Aileen S. Kraditor, *Means and Ends in American Abolitionism . . . 1834-1860* (1967); Walter M. Merrill, *Against Wind and Tide: A Biography of William Lloyd Garrison* (1963); Russell B. Nye, *Fettered Freedom: Civil Liberties and the Slavery Controversy, 1830-1860* (rev. ed., 1963); Jane H. Pease and William H. Pease, *They Who Would Be Free: Blacks' Search for Freedom, 1830-1861* (1974); Gerald Sorin, *Abolitionism: A New Perspective* (1972); John L. Thomas, *The Liberator: William Lloyd Garrison* (1963).

Antislavery Politics

Eugene Berwanger, *The Frontier Against Slavery* (1967); F. J. Blue, *The Free Soilers: Third Party Politics, 1848-1854* (1973); S. W. Campbell, *The Slave Catchers* (1968); Avery O. Craven, *The Growth of Southern Nationalism, 1848-1861* (1953); David Donald, *Charles Sumner and the Coming of the Civil War* (1960); Don E. Fehrenbacher, *The Dred Scott Case: Its Significance in American Law and Politics* (1978) and *Prelude to Greatness: Lincoln in the 1850's* (1962); Eric Foner, *Free Soil, Free Labor, Free Men: The Ideology of the Republican Party Before the Civil War* (1970); Harry V. Jaffe, *Crisis of the House Divided: An Interpretation of the Issues of the Lincoln-Douglas Debates* (1959); Robert W. Johannsen, *Stephen A. Douglas* (1973); Roy F. Nichols, *The Disruption of the American Democracy* (1948); David M. Potter, *The Impending Crisis, 1848-1861* (1976); Richard H. Sewell, *Ballots for Freedom: AntiSlavery Politics in the United States, 1837-1860* (1976); Paul Sigelschiffer, *The American Conscience* (1973); Hans Trefousse, *The Radical Republicans* (1969).

The Secession Crisis

Steven A. Channing, *Crisis of Fear: Secession in South Carolina* (1970); David M. Potter, *Lincoln and His Party in the Secession Crisis* (1942); Kenneth M. Stampp, *And the War Came: The North and the Secession Crisis, 1860-1861* (1950).

Sherman's March to the Sea 23

Early on the morning of November 16, 1864, the Union columns headed out of Atlanta, Georgia, bound southeast for the coastal city of Savannah. Northern troops, over sixty thousand strong, with their horses, mules, and wagons, clogged the road. As they reached a hilltop, the soldiers turned to look back toward the town. Their commander, General William Tecumseh Sherman, recalled:

> Behind us lay Atlanta, smoldering and in ruins, the black smoke rising high in the air and hanging like a pall over the ruined city. Away off in the distance, on the McDonough road, was the rear of Howard's column, the gun-barrels glistening in the sun, the white-topped wagons stretching away to the south; and right before us the Fourteenth Corps, marching steadily and rapidly, with a cheery look and a swinging pace, that made light of the thousand miles that lay between us and Richmond. Some band, by accident, struck up the anthem of "John Brown's Body." The men caught up the strain, and never before have I heard the chorus of "Glory, glory, hallelujah!" done with more spirit, or in better harmony of time and place.

On that beautiful day of brilliant sunshine and clean, crisp air, the Civil War, already three and a half years old, seemed exhilarating, if not remote. Sherman later recalled experiencing a "feeling of something to come, vague and undefined, still full of venture and intense interest. Even the common soldiers caught the inspiration, and many a group called out to me — Uncle Billy, I guess Grant is waiting for us at Richmond!"

Although Richmond and victory for the Union were still five months away, Sherman had already made his mark in Georgia. The pall of smoke he and his troops saw above Atlanta came from the fires they had set in the town's railroad depot and machine shops. Flames soon swept into residential areas, destroying hundreds of dwellings. The general's reputation for toughness — "brutality" in the minds of most Southerners — took shape at Atlanta and on the subsequent campaign, his famous march to the sea. "We are not only fighting hostile armies," Sherman believed, "but a hostile people. We must make old and young, rich and poor, feel the hand of war."

Union invasion of the South devastated the Confederate terrain as well as its morale. Marching through Georgia in 1864, General Sherman's troops occupied Atlanta and demolished much of the city—ripping up railroad tracks, destroying the depot, burning down homes, and evacuating the remainder of the residents. The fire-swept shambles behind them, Sherman's men moved on to Savannah. (Culver Pictures)

Sherman, the tough-talking soldier, knew the South well. Born in Ohio in 1820, he attended West Point and, after graduation, spent most of his time on duty in military posts in the South. He resigned from the army in 1853. After working unsuccessfully as a bank manager in California and as a lawyer in Kansas, he tried to get back into the army. Rejected, he had to settle for the job of superintendent of a military academy in Louisiana. The school opened in 1859.

As the sectional crisis deepened, Sherman made it clear that, if Louisiana should secede from the Union, he would resign his post and do all he could to aid the national government. He kept his word when he heard of the Southern attack on Fort Sumter in April 1861. Secession, he thought, was "folly, madness, a crime against civilization." He immediately sought, and gained, reinstatement in the army. It was now more receptive to such applications, since so many regular officers had joined the Confederacy.

Sherman started as a colonel and rose rapidly in the Union high command. He served in the west as one of Grant's most trusted officers. By mid-1864, as a major general, he was assigned the mission of striking from Tennessee into Georgia and seizing Atlanta. The town, though relatively small, was an important railroad center. Confederate troops under General Joseph E. Johnston and, later, General John B. Hood fought hard to hold Sherman back. They were defeated in July at two crucial battles, those of Peachtree Creek and Atlanta. After a siege of several weeks, Atlanta fell.

Sherman's troops entered the city on September 2. Although Hood at first moved south toward safety, he later wheeled northwest toward Tennessee, hoping to harass Sherman's communications so badly that his forces would have to retreat. Inadvertently, Hood's actions may have influenced Sherman in his later decision to move to the sea without regard for communications or established supply lines.

For the time being, however, Sherman wanted to rest his troops and observe Hood's movements. He decided that Hood could be kept at bay by some detachments of his own army, plus Union troops in Tennessee.

Sherman meanwhile undertook some indirect negotiations with the governor of Georgia, Joseph E. Brown. His aim was to separate the state from the Confederacy. There was reason to hope that Georgia might pull out of the war. Brown had already withdrawn his state's militia from the rebel army. And, like many Southern politicians, he had come to detest Jefferson Davis, president of the Confederacy. Davis had stirred bitter reactions because of his insistent demands for troops and supplies from the hard-pressed Southern states. Nothing came of the negotiations, but they may have impressed on Sherman the need for bringing the hardships of war home to the Southern civilian population.

When the war started, Atlanta—not then the state capital—had only twelve thousand inhabitants. Many of them had fled as the Union troops approached. Others followed when Hood abandoned the town. When Sherman entered, he ordered the rest of the civilians to leave, since he did not want them clogging the town and interfering with his lines of communication. He and Hood agreed to a ten-day truce so that these civilians could move out.

By late October, Sherman had decided to march to the sea. On November 2 Grant wired: "I do not really see that you can withdraw from where you are to follow Hood without giving up all we have gained in territory. I say, then, go as you propose."

Sherman gained a reputation as a ruthless commander because of his march through the Confederacy. (Brady Collection, U.S. Signal Corps, National Archives)

Sherman's bold plan called for his army of sixty-two thousand men (five thousand of them cavalry) to move the three hundred miles to Savannah without supply lines and without communications until they reached the Atlantic coast. There the Union navy could provide cover and supplies. Sherman's troops carried enough provisions for twenty or thirty days, but those were considered emergency rations. Food on the march would be "provided" by the farms and plantations along the way—*not*, of course, on a voluntary basis—so Georgia would be made to "howl."

Sherman's Special Field Order #120 detailed the procedure he hoped to establish. Brigade commanders were responsible for organizing foraging parties. Every morning, these would move out from the four main columns under the direction of one or two "discreet officers." Foragers—or "bummers," as they soon came to be called (even by the Yankees themselves)—could seize available livestock and food supplies. They were not supposed to enter houses. Only corps commanders had the authority to order destruction of buildings, and then only in areas of resistance. Foragers for artillery units could take all the animals and wagons they needed.

If possible, foragers were to seize provisions from the rich planters rather than poor farmers. The wealthy were presumed to be more in favor

of the rebellion than their humbler fellow Southerners. (This assumption fitted Northern views of secession as a conspiracy of the elite. It did not square with the facts of Southern political life.)

Sherman's field order directed his men to "forage liberally." They obeyed with a will. Men would go out in the morning on foot, seize a wagon, and then load it with everything valuable and movable they could find. One of Sherman's aides, Major Henry Hitchcock, described a foraging expedition in his diary:

> Plenty of forage along road: corn, fodder, finest sweet potatoes, pigs, chickens, etc. Passed troops all day, some on march, some destroying railroad thoroughly. Two cotton gins on roadside burned, and pile of cotton with one, also burned. Houses in Conyers look comfortable for Georgia village, and sundry good ones along road. Soldiers foraging all along, but only for *forage*—no violence as far as I saw or heard. Laughable to see pigs in feed troughs behind wagons, chickens swinging in knapsacks. Saw some few men—Whites look sullen—darkies pleased.

Stories of Union brutality, supposedly encouraged by Sherman himself, began to circulate. (They continued to circulate for generations.) But his march to the sea, devastating as it was, did not degenerate into an orgy of murder, rape, and arson. Sherman later acknowledged "acts of pillage, robbery, and violence" undoubtedly committed by some of his men. But, he argued, "these acts were exceptional and incidental. I have never heard of any cases of murder or rape; and no army could have carried along sufficient food and forage for a march of three hundred miles; so that foraging in some shape was necessary."

To Sherman, the march became just what he had ordered—harsh but, in the main, well-disciplined. The destruction wrought by his "scorched-earth" policy centered on three main targets: railroads, the few factories on the route, and public buildings that could serve as temporary headquarters for military units.

Sherman marveled at the skill of his men in carrying out his order to "forage liberally." One fact among many proves how proficient they were: Sherman's army started the march driving five thousand head of cattle; they ended it with over ten thousand.

Where were the Confederate forces during these agonizing weeks? Some small cavalry units of the Confederate army did appear from time to time to raid foraging parties. But they had little overall effect. Hood's army had marched northwest to Tennessee and defeat. Since most Georgians of fighting age were serving with the Southern forces, the state militia had been reduced to several thousand old men and young boys. They tried to make a stand at the state capital, Milledgeville, but the Union forces swept them aside. After viewing the casualties, a Northern officer wrote: "I was never so affected at the sight of dead and wounded before. I hope we will never have to shoot at such men again. They know nothing at all about fighting and I think their officers know as little."

Milledgeville fell on November 23. Georgia state officials had fled a short time before. The invading Yankee officers decided to mock the "sovereign state of Georgia." They pretended to hold a session of the state legislature, complete with resolutions and fire-eating oratory. Then they decided to repeal the ordinance of secession. When Sherman heard about these antics, he laughed. Meanwhile, his Milledgeville "legislators" ordered the burning of public buildings in the town.

Sherman's soldiers sliced a path forty to sixty miles wide through central Georgia. Every white family along the way underwent its own particular ordeal and emerged with its own sorrowful story. Tales of the devastation became commonplace: houses broken into and sacked, food and valuables hidden only to be found by the recurrent searches of intruding "bummers," treasured family possessions tossed into the flames, cotton gins and public buildings put to the torch. "Everything had been swept as with a storm of fire," wrote one Macon newspaper. "The whole country around is one wide waste of destruction."

Contrary to Sherman's conception of his foraging troops as restrained and disciplined, most white Southerners in their path regarded them as greedy marauders. The experiences of two Georgia women, a mother and daughter, typified the ordeal. Mary Jones, the widow of a Presbyterian minister, owned three plantations in Liberty County, not far from Savannah. At the time of Sherman's march she and her daughter, Mary Jones Mallard, were living at the plantation known as Montevideo. Their letters and journals vividly portray the impact of war.

Mary Mallard's husband was captured on December 13 by Union cavalry near Montevideo. (Mrs. Mallard was then pregnant and expecting to give birth within days.) The first groups of "bummers" reached the Jones-Mallard household on December 15. They searched the house and made off with a number of family keepsakes. During the next two weeks,

Union raiding parties—sometimes large detachments, sometimes only a few stragglers—arrived almost daily at the home. Each group searched the premises, insulted the two women, and took what food, supplies, or family items remained to be carted away.

Mary Mallard confided unhappily to her journal on December 17.

> The Yankees made the Negroes bring up the oxen and carts, and took off all the chickens and turkeys they could find. They carried off all the syrup from the smokehouse. We had one small pig, which was all the meat we had left; they took the whole of it. Mother saw everything like food stripped from her premises, without the power of uttering one word. Finally they rolled out the carriage and took that to carry off a load of chickens. They took everything they possibly could.

"Everything" included seven of the Jones family's slaves, who—like hundreds of blacks elsewhere along the army's line of march—were pressed into service as porters, laborers, or mule drivers. "So they were all carried off," Mary Mallard grieved, "carriages, wagons, carts, horses and mules and servants, with food and provisions of every kind—and, so far as they were concerned, leaving us to starvation."

Occasionally an officer would apologize for the behavior of his men. One friendly Union soldier, a Missourian, offered to show Mrs. Jones where to hide her things. Mary Mallard noted: "He said he had enlisted to fight for the *Constitution*; but since then the war had been turned into another thing, and he did not approve of this abolitionism, for his wife's people all owned slaves." A few days later, a Virginian told Mrs. Jones that "there was great dissatisfaction in the army on account of the present object of the war, which now was to free the Negroes."

More often than not, however, the raiders stalked through the houses indifferent to its inhabitants. Never knowing whether soldiers coming to the door would behave politely or insolently, the two women lived in constant fear. Several times, "bummers" threatened to return and burn down their house. Yet on other occasions, Union commanders offered them protection and safe-conduct passes to Savannah, which was still in Confederate hands. The women declined to leave, partly because of Mary Mallard's pregnancy. On January 4, 1865, she gave birth to a daughter. Her mother noted in her journal:

> During these hours of agony the yard was filled with Yankees. They were all around the house; my poor child, calm and collected amid her agony of body, could hear their conversation and wild halloos and cursing beneath her windows. After a while they left, screaming and yelling in a most fiendish way as they rode from the house.

Mary Jones's journal makes it clear that Sherman had achieved his major purpose in marching through Georgia—to demoralize beyond repair what remained of the Deep South's fighting spirit. She wrote in January 1865:

> As I stand and look at the desolating changes wrought by the hand of an inhuman foe in a few days, I can enter into the feelings of Job. All our

A Confederate soldier returns to find his home a shambles in the midst of a devastated land. The artist who drew this scene was A. J. Volck, a German-born dentist who lived in Baltimore. He was the best-known satirist to interpret the Civil War from the Southern point of view, (NYPL/Prints Division)

pleasant things are laid low. We are prisoners in our own home. To obtain a mouthful of food we have been obliged to cook in what was formerly our drawing room; and I have to rise every morning by candlelight, before the dawn of day, that we may have it before the enemy arrives to take it from us.... For one month our homes and all we possess have been given up to lawless pillage. Officers and men have alike engaged in this work of degradation. I scarcely know how we have stood up under it. God alone has enabled us to "speak with the enemy in the gates," and calmly, without a tear, to see my house broken open, entered with false keys, threatened to be burned to ashes, refused food and ordered to be starved to death, told that I had no right even to wood or water, that I should be "humbled in the very dust I walked upon," a pistol and carbine presented to my breast, cursed and reviled as a rebel, a hypocrite, a devil.

Troubling Mrs. Jones almost as much as the behavior of Sherman's soldiers was the reaction of her slaves. During the first days of Union occupation, most of them stayed on the plantation, perhaps out of fear, perhaps out of loyalty. But when it became clear that the Northern army firmly controlled the area, a number of slaves left to join the Union columns marching on Savannah. "Many servants have proven faithful," Mrs. Jones wrote in January 1865, "others false and rebellious against all authority or restraint."

Sherman himself pursued an ambiguous policy toward the ex-slaves, who were considered "contraband." He did not want them as soldiers, despite the good record of black regiments in battle when they were

allowed to fight. He rejected the suggestion of General Ulysses S. Grant (by now in charge of all Union forces) that blacks be armed. He felt that his troops would object. And he had another reason. "My aim then," he later wrote, "was to whip the rebels, to humble their pride and make them fear and dread us. I did not want them to cast in our teeth that we had to call on *their* slaves to help us to subdue them."

Nevertheless, Sherman did order the formation of black "pioneer battalions"—construction units—for each army corps. "Negroes who are able-bodied and can be of service to the several columns may be taken along," Sherman instructed, "but each army commander will bear in mind that the question of supplies is a very important one, and that his first duty is to see to those who bear arms." In other words, the army was to keep blacks at a distance, using labor as needed but refraining from becoming a relief organization for ex-slaves who had left their plantations.

Sherman's prejudice against blacks was a crucial factor in his military policy. His brother John was an important antislavery Republican politician from Ohio, but William did not share his views. When still in Louisiana, he had assured Southerners that slavery was best for blacks.

"All the congresses on earth," he said, "can't make the Negro anything else than what he is"—namely a slave, or a second-class noncitizen. In a letter he stated:

> I would not if I could abolish or modify slavery. I don't know that I would materially change the actual political relation of master and slave. Negroes in the great numbers that exist here must of necessity be slaves. Theoretical notions of humanity and religion cannot shake the commercial fact that their labor is of great value and cannot be dispensed with.

Whatever Sherman's own attitudes, it was clear that, from the moment his troops left Atlanta, they sparked the imagination of Georgia's slaves. As Sherman rode through the town of Covington, a day's march from Atlanta, he found that "the Negroes were simply frantic with joy." He later recalled that "Whenever they heard my name, they clustered about my horse, shouted and prayed in their peculiar style, which had a natural eloquence that would have moved a stone."

During the following weeks, as Northern troops foraged their way across Georgia, Sherman witnessed "hundreds, if not thousands, of such scenes." He wrote later that he could still see "a poor girl, in the very ecstasy of the Methodist 'shout,' hugging the banner of one of the regiments."

Thousands of slaves did more than simply greet the liberating Northern army. They joined it, striding alongside or in back of the troop columns. Wrote Mary Jones: "Negroes in large numbers are flocking to them. Nearly all the house servants have left their homes; and from most of the plantations they have gone in a body." The ranks of contraband included strong young men and women in the prime of life, mothers carrying children, and the white-haired elderly.

More than thirty thousand blacks joined Sherman's army at one time or another during its four-week march. Yet only ten thousand remained with its ranks as it entered Savannah. Many had been actively discouraged from remaining by the soldiers. Neither Sherman nor most of his officers and men wished to add the task of foraging to feed a huge contraband population from the food collected each day.

Sherman later remembered personally telling an old black man at one plantation that:

> we wanted the slaves to remain where they were, and not to load us down with useless mouths. We could receive a few of their young, hearty men as pioneers. But if they followed us in swarms of old and young, feeble and helpless, it would simply load us down and cripple us in our great task. I believe that old man spread this message to the slaves, which was carried from mouth to mouth, to the very end of our journey, and that it in part saved us from the great danger we incurred of swelling our numbers so that famine would have attended our progress.

In any case, the thousands of slaves who remained with Sherman's forces did not all passively trudge along waiting to be fed and taken care of. Many played active roles. They carried supplies as porters and mule drivers. Some searched out food, animals, and equipment hidden by Con-

Freed Negroes joining Union lines in North Carolina. (Library of Congress)

federates along the way. Others built roads or repaired bridges so that Sherman's men, equipment, and supply wagons could keep to their ten-mile-a-day pace across the swampy stretches of central Georgia. Still others helped the soldiers to destroy railroads and other strategic targets. A favorite trick was to heat the heavy iron rails and twist them into "Sherman's neckties.")

Local blacks also served as reliable guides behind Confederate lines. One of Sherman's officers, General Oliver O. Howard, ordered one of his men to reach the Union fleet anchored off Savannah. After safely rowing a canoe past enemy posts along the Ogeechee River, the officer and his patrol:

found some Negroes, who befriended him and his men and kept pretty well under cover until evening. Then they went ashore to get a Negro guide and some provisions [after which they passed through Confederate lines]. Soon after this they came to quite a sizable Negro house, went in, and were well treated and refreshed with provisions. When they were eating they were startled by hearing a party of Confederate cavalry riding toward the house. Of course they expected to be instantly captured, but the Negroes, coming quickly to their rescue, concealed them under the floor. The coolness and smartness of the Negroes surprised even Captain Duncan, though he had believed and trusted them. The cavalry stopped but remained only a short time, and the Negroes guided our men back to their boats.

Although few blacks aided the Union side quite so daringly during Sherman's march, the general himself acknowledged that the "large number employed as servants, teamsters and pioneers rendered admirable service."

Sherman's army marched into Savannah on December 21, along with ten thousand blacks marching behind the troops. The general sent a playful telegram to "His Excellency," President Lincoln: "I beg to present you as a Christmas gift the city of Savannah, with one hundred and fifty heavy guns and plenty of ammunition, also about twenty-five thousand bales of cotton."

The message was quickly published throughout the North. Northerners had considered Sherman's army "lost" when the general had broken communication after leaving Atlanta. Sherman and his men instantly became popular heroes. "Our joy was irrepressible," said one high Washington official, "not only because of their safety, but because it was an assurance that the days of the Confederacy were numbered." Even to many Southerners, Savannah's capture seemed to foreshadow final defeat. Given the suffering that Confederate soldiers and civilians had undergone by then, the prospect seemed almost welcome.

Sherman did not order the city's residents to leave, as he had done at Atlanta. With Union ships in the harbor and his troops in control of the surrounding countryside, he felt no useful military purpose would be served by evacuating or burning the city. In fact, Sherman decided to govern Savannah's twenty thousand inhabitants mildly—much to their amazement and that of other Georgians. He gave people the choice of remaining in Savannah or leaving for other cities that were still under Confederate control.

Sherman placed one of his generals in overall command of Savan-

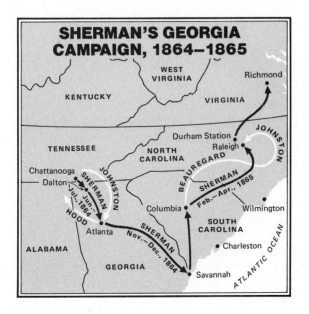

SHERMAN'S GEORGIA CAMPAIGN, 1864–1865

nah, but the Confederate mayor and city council handled most day-to-day matters. Relations between Northerners and Southerners were polite, almost cordial. Only a few hundred citizens left the city. Most people calmly went about their business. Relief ships organized by private citizens in the North arrived regularly in January 1865, bringing much-needed food and clothing. Supplies were distributed to freed blacks and indigent whites. Local markets selling meat, wood, and other necessities reopened under military supervision.

"No city was ever occupied with less disorder or more system than Savannah," Sherman wrote on December 31. "Though an army of sixty thousand men lay camped around it, women and children of an hostile people walk its streets with as much security as they do in Philadelphia." Confederate newspapers raged about the alleged "barbarities" of Sherman's forces on their march from Atlanta, exaggerating the amount of property burned, and the numbers murdered or raped. Meantime the "barbarians" occupied Savannah with little friction.

In Savannah, as on the march from Atlanta, Sherman became a hero to the liberated blacks. He wrote to his wife on Christmas Day: "They flock to me, young and old. They pray and shout and mix up my name with that of Moses and Simon and other scriptural ones as well as 'Abram Linkom'." Hundreds of blacks hurried to see the general, wrote an aide. "There was a constant stream of them, old and young, men, women and children, black, yellow, and cream-colored, uncouth and well-bred, bashful and talkative—but always respectful and behaved—all day long."

It would have come as a great shock to the blacks of Savannah to learn that their hero was at that very moment being attacked in the North for his policy toward ex-slaves. Late in December General Henry W. Halleck wrote Sherman to congratulate him on the march through Georgia and his capture of Savannah. He also warned him that powerful individuals close to the president spoke critically of him, alleging that he "manifested an almost *criminal* dislike" to the Negro. "They say," added Halleck,

> that you are not willing to carry out the wishes of the government in regard to him, but repulse him with contempt! They say you might have brought with you to Savannah more than fifty thousand, thus stripping Georgia of that number of laborers, and opening a road by which as many more could have escaped from their masters; but that, instead of this, you drove them from your ranks, prevented their following you by cutting the bridges in your rear, and thus caused the massacre of large numbers by Wheeler's cavalry.

Sherman defended his decision to discourage slave runaways from joining the march on the grounds that their presence would have overburdened his army and hindered its military success. In responding to Halleck, however, he acknowledged that his sympathy for freed blacks was limited:

Thank God I am not running for an office and am not concerned because the rising generation will believe that I burned 500 niggers[1] at one pop in Atlanta, or any such nonsense. The South deserves all she has got for her injustice to the Negro, but that is no reason why we should go to the other extreme.

It came as no surprise to Sherman, therefore, when Secretary of War Edwin M. Stanton arrived in Savannah on January 9, aboard the Union ship *Nevada.* Stanton was supposedly traveling on a vacation cruise and to supervise the disposition of captured Confederate cotton supplies. Actually he had come to check on Sherman's handling of matters involving blacks. Stanton strongly supported Sherman's military strategy in Georgia. But he disapproved of the general's rumored hostility toward the ex-slave population and of his refusal to use blacks as soldiers.

Sherman denied that any of his officers or troops had been hostile to slaves on their march from Atlanta. But Stanton wanted to hear about Sherman's behavior from the blacks themselves. At his request, therefore, Sherman invited "the most intelligent of the Negroes" in Savannah to come to his rooms to meet the secretary of war. Twenty black men attended the meeting with Sherman and Stanton on January 12, 1865.

Never before had any major American government official met with black leaders to ask what *they* wished for their people. Each man present began by introducing himself with a brief account of his life. The average age was fifty. Fifteen of the men were ministers—mainly Baptist and Methodist—and the other five were church officials of one kind or another. Five of the leaders had been born free. Of the others, three had bought their freedom; most of the rest had been liberated by Sherman's army.

Secretary of War Stanton sat at a table facing the black visitors, making extensive notes on their remarks. Sherman, restless and uneasy over the interview, stood with two of his aides apart from the seated group. He watched the proceedings warily, pacing across the room from time to time during the exchange. The blacks had selected as their spokesman sixty-seven-year-old Garrison Frazier, a Baptist minister. He responded firmly to each of Stanton's questions.

Stanton asked first whether the men were aware of Lincoln's Emancipation Proclamation. Frazier replied that they were.

STANTON: State what you understand by slavery, and the freedom that was to be given by the President's Proclamation.
FRAZIER: Slavery is receiving by irresistible power the work of another man, and not by his consent. The freedom, as I understand it, promised by the Proclamation, is taking us from under the yoke of bondage, and placing us where we could reap the fruit of our own labor, and take care of ourselves, and assist the Government in maintaining our freedom.

---

[1] This term was considered only mildly discourteous in the 1860s. It was commonly used, even by antislavery Northerners.

Stanton then asked how black people could best maintain their new freedom. Frazier suggested that young men should be able to enlist in the army, and that other blacks ought to receive land to farm: "We want to be placed on land until we are able to buy it, and make it our own."

The secretary of war then asked whether the men believed that freed blacks "would rather live scattered among the whites, or in colonies by yourselves?" Frazier answered: "I would prefer to live by ourselves, for there is a prejudice against us in the South that will take years to get over; but I do not know that I can answer for my brethren."

Frazier and his black associates may have considered Stanton's next question offensive. The secretary asked whether the ex-slaves of the South were intelligent enough to sustain their freedom while maintaining good relations with Southern whites. "I think there is sufficient intelligence among us to do so," Frazier replied simply.

The black minister was then asked what he believed were the causes and objectives of the Civil War, and whether blacks generally supported one or the other side. He responded shrewdly and at length. Frazier told Stanton that blacks wished only to help the Union subdue the rebellious Confederacy. He acknowledged that the North's first war aim involved bringing the South back into the Union and that Lincoln had issued the Emancipation Proclamation mainly as a means toward achieving this end. Only the South's refusal to emancipate its slaves "has now made the freedom of the slaves a part of the war." Frazier pointed out that the thousands of runaways who had followed the Union armies, "leaving their homes and undergoing suffering," spoke clearly for the pro-Union sentiments of blacks.

Stanton then indicated that he wanted to ask a question about Sherman. The general—silently furious—left the room. In Sherman's absence, Stanton inquired about "the feeling of the colored people in regard to General Sherman" and whether Negroes regarded "his sentiments and actions as friendly to their rights and interests." Frazier's answer probably surprised Stanton, considering the rumors current in Washington:

> We looked upon General Sherman, prior to his arrival, as a man in the providence of God, specially set apart to accomplish this work, and we unanimously felt inexpressible gratitude to him. Some of us called upon him immediately upon his arrival [in Savannah], and it is probable that he did not meet the Secretary with more courtesy than he met us. His conduct and deportment toward us characterized him as a friend and a gentleman. We have confidence in General Sherman, and think that what concerns us could not be under better hands.

The meeting soon ended, after Stanton had thanked his black visitors for their advice.

Stanton and Sherman spent the next three days discussing problems of policy toward the freedmen. They agreed that Sherman would issue a field order on January 16, the day after Stanton's departure from Savannah.

Special Field Order #15 set aside confiscated or abandoned land along rivers emptying into the Atlantic and on the Sea Islands—nearby islands that lie along the coast from Charleston, South Carolina, to Jacksonville, Florida. These lands were to be used exclusively for settlement by freed blacks. A freedman and his family taking up such land were to be given a "possessory title" to "not more than forty acres of tillable land" until Congress should regulate the title.

Sherman obviously viewed this scheme as a temporary one, needed in order to provide for freedmen and their families in the area during the rest of the war or until Congress acted. "Mr. Stanton has been here," he confidently wrote his wife on the day of Stanton's departure, "and is cured of that Negro nonsense." By now Sherman was impatient to begin his march northward. He appointed General Rufus Saxton as Inspector of Settlements and Plantations for the entire area covered by his field order. On January 21 Sherman's army left Savannah and marched into South Carolina, the symbol of Confederate resistance.

Saxton energetically arranged to transport homeless blacks in Savannah to coastal farms. He wrote urgent letters to Northern sympathizers asking for food and supplies to help sustain the new agricultural settlements. By midsummer of 1865—with the war now over—Saxton and his aides had managed to settle more than forty thousand black people on lands covered in Sherman's order.

The people faced numerous hardships—neglected soil, old equipment (and little of it), poor seed, and shortage of supplies. But the hardworking freedmen, especially those on the Sea Islands of Georgia and South Carolina, successfully grew crops of cotton and various foodstuffs. They received support not only from Saxton and the military but also from Northern white teachers and missionaries, a number of whom traveled into the area to found schools.

Most of the planning and hard work, however, came from the freedmen themselves. Many started out with little more than the clothes on their backs. One party was led by Ulysses Houston, a minister who had been present at the interview with Stanton. Before leaving for Skidaway Island, he wrote a Northern reporter: "We shall build our cabins, and organize our town government for the maintenance of order and the settlement of all difficulties." The reporter later gave this account:

> He and his fellow-colonists selected their lots, laid out a village, numbered their lots, put the numbers in a hat, and drew them out. It was Plymouth colony repeating itself. They agreed if any others came to join them, they should have equal privileges. So blooms the Mayflower on the South Atlantic coast.

The impressive success of this resettlement led many Northerners to urge that Congress enact a general land distribution policy to help all freedmen. Landless ex-slaves also came to expect that, since forty thousand Deep South blacks had quickly and effectively settled new lands, others too would receive their forty acres in the near future. Such hopes were soon dashed.

Andrew Johnson became president after Lincoln was assassinated in April 1865. Many had believed that Johnson would favor a generous land distribution policy once in the White House, since he had been sympathetic to black rights earlier as governor of Tennessee. But a proclamation which he issued in May 1865 completely shattered this belief. Johnson pardoned all former Confederates except those whose taxable property exceeded $20,000 and those who had held high military or civil positions. (Even these groups could apply for special presidential pardon.)

For the great majority of white Southerners, Johnson's proclamation not only restored civil and political rights. It also restored their property—except for slaves—even if previously confiscated as a result of temporary wartime orders such as Sherman's. Not only did the new president omit mentioning the freedmen in his proclamation. He clearly intended them to resume their second-class economic status in the South, although no longer as slaves. Johnson made it plain that he wanted landowning blacks such as those under Saxton's jurisdiction to surrender their newly acquired lands and return to their previous owners.

Saxton now administered the freedmen's new settlements in Georgia, South Carolina, and Florida as assistant director of the Freedmen's Bureau. This agency had been recently established by Congress to coordinate federal relief assistance to ex-slaves. Heading the bureau was Sherman's former subordinate, General Oliver O. Howard. He shared President Johnson's wish to conciliate the South. Unlike the president, though, he did not want to be generous at the expense of the freedmen.

Both Saxton and Howard tried to resist and delay the restoration of black-occupied lands to their former white owners. They were supported by Stanton, who attempted various maneuvers to stave off the move. But Johnson was determined. Sherman's field order was revoked in June 1865. Saxton even traveled to Washington to protest, but without success.

In September the former landholders of Edisto Island, then under Freedmen's Bureau control, petitioned Johnson for the return of their lands. The president directed Howard to visit the island and convince the freedmen to arrange a "mutually satisfactory solution." The president left little doubt that he wanted the blacks to pack up and leave.

Howard unhappily went to Edisto in late October. Trapped between his duty and his sympathies, he met with freed blacks in a local church. They crowded in, furious at the course of events. They refused to quiet down until a woman began the spiritual "Nobody Knows the Trouble I Seen."

The blacks then listened to Howard as he urged them to surrender their farms and return to work for the island's former white landholders. Angry shouts of "no, no" punctuated Howard's talk. One man in the gallery cried out: "Why, General Howard, why do you take away our lands? You take them from us who have always been true, always true to the government! You give them to our all-time enemies! That is not right!"

Howard patiently explained to his audience that their "possessory titles" to the land were not "absolute" or "legal." At his insistence, a committee was formed consisting of three freedmen, three white planters, and three Freedmen's Bureau representatives. It had authority to decide on the island's land ownership. (This practice was also adopted elsewhere on the Sea Islands.)

Howard still hoped to delay restoration of the property until Congress convened late in 1865. But the process of removing blacks from their assigned lands gathered momentum after he left the area to return North.

Saxton was still refusing to dispossess black landholders from the territories under his supervision, so Johnson removed him in January 1866. He was replaced by Davis Tillson, a Freedmen's Bureau official more sympathetic to presidential policy. Tillson issued an order allowing white owners to return to their former Sea Island farms and plantations. Tillson went so far as to charter a boat and accompany the first group, explaining personally to the blacks in residence that they would have to surrender their lands.

Blacks who were willing to sign contracts to work for white owners were allowed to remain. Others were driven from the islands either by Union troops or by white vigilante groups that began to terrorize black landholders throughout the Deep South during this period. One sympathetic New England schoolteacher later wrote of seeing all the freedmen on one Sea Island plantation leaving their newly acquired land with their hoes over their shoulders. "They told us that the guard had ordered them to leave the plantation if they would not work for the owners. We could only tell them to obey orders. After this many of the Sherman Negroes left the island."

For the moment, Howard's policy of delaying restoration had clearly failed. Yet shortly after Congress met in December 1865, the legislators debated the provisions of a new, postwar Freedmen's Bureau Bill designed to protect the rights of ex-slaves in peacetime. The final version of that bill was enacted by Congress over the president's veto in July 1866. It allowed freedmen deprived of their land by Johnson's restoration policy to lease twenty acres of government-owned land on the Sea Islands with an option to buy cheaply within six years. By then, however, almost all of the "Sherman Negroes" had lost their lands.

Also, by this time, Congress and Johnson were struggling bitterly for control of postwar policy toward the South. The outcome of that struggle would determine the nation's response to its millions of newly liberated blacks. Many of them probably shared the anguish of one Sea Island freedman who grieved shortly after his eviction: "They will make freedom a curse to us, for we have no home, no land, no oath, no vote, and consequently no country."

24 Civil War and Reconstruction

On February 23, 1861 (at a time when Sherman had just left his post at the Louisiana military academy), Abraham Lincoln slipped secretly into Washington after an all-night train ride. His aides had planned the night trip, fearing an assassination attempt at a previously scheduled stop in pro-Confederate Baltimore. On his special train the president-elect tried to sleep. But a drunken passenger kept singing the bouncy Southern melody "Dixie" over and over. Lincoln finally muttered to a companion, "No doubt there will be a great time in Dixie by and by." His concern over the impending showdown with the secessionist South was shared by most Northerners.

A thousand miles to the south, the Confederacy's president-elect took a different type of journey to his own inaugural. Lincoln had arrived in the nation's capital, according to one diplomat, "like a thief in the night." Jefferson Davis had traveled from his Mississippi plantation to Montgomery, Alabama—first capital of the rebellious states—like a conquering hero.

Davis was a moderate Southerner who had opposed secession until after Lincoln's election. Now this group had taken charge of the South's new government, replacing many of the zealous fire-eaters who had spread the gospel of disunion during the 1850s. Southern moderates had selected Davis as their president largely because he had declared himself in favor of a peaceful settlement with the North. A West Point graduate, Davis had fought ably in the Mexican War, represented Mississippi in both the House and the Senate, and served as President Pierce's secretary of war.

FIRST STEPS

While Davis pondered his cabinet, the Montgomery convention that had chosen him president wrote a Confederate constitution. For the most part the document copied the provisions of the federal Constitution. It included a bill of rights, and it even prohibited the slave trade. Slavery, of course, was pronounced legal throughout the Confederacy. In a significant speech at Savannah, the vice-president-elect, Alexander Stephens of Georgia, spoke candidly of the new government: "Its foundations are laid, its cornerstone rests, upon the great truth that the Negro is not equal to the white man; that slavery, subordination to the superior race, is his natural and normal condition."

The new Confederate congress began its work by legalizing for the South all Union laws that did not conflict with its new constitution. For two months after Davis's selection as president, the Confederate government waited for some sign of how Lincoln intended to deal with the secession crisis. Then came Sumter—and war.

A "Brothers' War"

When the Civil War began on April 12, 1861, Americans gave it various names. For secessionists it was a "War for Southern Independence" or "the War Between the States." Northerners, on the other hand, considered it "the War of the Rebellion" or simply "the War for the Union." Both sides agreed that, whatever else, it was a "brothers' war," severing links among families, personal friends, and public figures according to their sectional loyalties.

Mississippi politician and Confederate President Jefferson Davis did not provide the kind of flexible leadership the South needed badly during the Civil War. (Brady Collection, U.S. Signal Corps, National Archives)

This deeply painful division reached even into Abraham Lincoln's family. A Kentucky officer named Ben Hardin Helm was the husband of Mary Todd Lincoln's sister. He spent several days at the White House talking to old West Point friends. Some of them were already preparing to head south and join the Confederate army. As Helm—still uncertain—concluded his visit, Lincoln gave him an envelope containing a major's commission in the Union army. The two men grasped hands warmly and exchanged good-byes. A few days later came the news that Helm had chosen the Confederacy.

But another Kentuckian, Fort Sumter's Robert Anderson, accepted Lincoln's promotion to brigadier general that same month. He then left for the front to help keep his native state in the Union.

A third officer, a fervent Unionist, turned down Lincoln's offer to be commander of all Northern troops. Instead, he accepted command of the Confederacy's eastern force, the Army of

Lee was a vigorous fifty-five when the Civil War began. Like Washington, he fought against difficult odds and was much admired by his troops. (Valentine Museum, Richmond, Va.)

Northern Virginia. "If Virginia stands by the old Union, so will I," Robert E. Lee declared. "But if she secedes (though I do not believe in secession as a constitutional right, nor that there is sufficient cause for revolution) then I will follow my native state with my sword and, if need be, with my life."

When Virginia finally broke with the Union, Lee followed.

In many ways the Confederate struggle for independence resembled the American revolt against British rule two generations earlier. Some revolutions are a struggle for colonial independence from a ruling country. Such a revolution occurred in North America in the 1770s. Other revolutions result when one section of a country tries to break away from the whole, leading to an internal war between the nation and the breakaway section. This type of separatist revolt may occur when the people of a particular region feel that their interests and values are directly threatened by those who control the national government. Such was the case in the South after Lincoln's election.[1]

National uprisings, such as the American Revolution, and separatist revolts, such as the Civil War, usually take place only after great soul-searching among those rebelling. The American people do not shift their loyalties easily. Washington, Franklin, and other Revolutionary leaders had served the British Empire faithfully for decades in war and peace. Lee, Davis, and other key Confederate leaders had served the American government

---

[1] More recently, separatist revolts have taken place in Nigeria (where the Ibo province of Biafra revolted unsuccessfully) and in Pakistan (where the Bengali area formerly known as East Pakistan won its independence and became the new country of Bangladesh).

before the South seceded. They finally revolted because they believed the Southern way of life—a culture based upon slavery—was directly threatened by Republican control of the central government.

Mobilization

In the early months of the Civil War most Americans seemed to expect the conflict to be bloody but brief. Few realized what lay ahead. "No casualties yet, no real mourning, nobody hurt," wrote Mary Boykin Chesnut, the wife of a high Confederate officer, in June 1861. "It is all parade, fuss, and fine feathers."

A few leaders believed the situation was more serious. Among them were Lincoln and his generals and their counterparts behind the Southern lines. Mrs. Chesnut noted what Jefferson Davis had told her one evening: "Either way, he thinks it will be a long war, that before the end came we would have many a bitter experience. He said only fools doubted the courage of the Yankees, or their willingness to fight when they saw fit."

Nor did most Southerners underestimate the extent of Northern resources. In almost every respect—population, capital, and raw materials—the Union had the advantage over the Confederacy. Most important, the North could produce endless

RESOURCES OF THE UNION AND THE CONFEDERACY, 1861

	UNION	CONFEDERACY
Population	23,000,000	8,700,000*
Real and personal property	$11,000,000,000	$5,370,000,000
Banking capital	$330,000,000	$27,000,000
Capital investment	$850,000,000	$95,000,000
Manufacturing establishments	110,000	18,000
Value of production (annual)	$1,500,000,000	$155,000,000
Industrial workers	1,300,000	110,000
Railroad milage	22,000	9,000
		*Including 3,500,000 slaves

supplies of guns, ammunition, ships, and other war equipment. The South, on the other hand, had increasing difficulty in keeping its soldiers supplied.

Neither side began with much of an army. There were only eighteen thousand men in the regular army in 1860, with about eleven hundred officers. Only a small number of these had significant combat experience, and most of them resigned to join the Confederate army, so that the South's officer corps was initially better trained than the North's. These officers, Northern and Southern, prepared to fight a conflict far different, in strategy and tactics, from those for which they had been trained.

Both North and South started the war using a system of volunteer enlistments. At first they recruited men for only a few months, since most leaders on both sides believed that the war would be short.

On April 15, the day after the surrender of Sumter, Lincoln issued a proclamation calling up "the militia of the several States of the Union, to the . . . number of seventy-five thousand, in order to suppress [the rebellion] and to cause the laws to be duly executed." The initial news of Sumter's capture outraged Northerners of almost every political persuasion—Douglas Democrats, Constitutional Unionists, Whigs, and Republicans alike. Such unity would prove short-lived. But while it lasted, people as dissimilar as abolitionist ex-pacifists and formerly pro-Southern businessmen all hailed the president's call for troops. Patriotic meetings were held in towns and cities throughout the Union, demanding swift action against the rebellious states. Eager volunteers rushed to join military units in almost every Northern community.

"Before God it is the duty of every American citizen to rally around the flag of the country," shouted an ailing Stephen A. Douglas at a Chicago mass meeting. Douglas, still Lincoln's most influential Northern Democratic opponent, had gone to the White House immediately after Sumter's fall to pledge to Lincoln his complete support in restoring the Union.

As the fighting dragged on, however, it became apparent to both sides that volunteers would not provide enough manpower. Even the cash bounties offered to those who enlisted would not bring in enough volunteers. Casualties mounted in 1862. First the undermanned Confederacy and then the Union turned to drafting soldiers by lottery. Wealthy or influential young men, North and South, could, and often did, avoid going to war. They could provide a paid substitute, who might cost as much as $600. Or they could claim exemption on grounds that their civilian work was essential. (Slaveholders who grew cotton, for example, could avoid service this way.) By the end of the war, the South's troop shortage had become extreme. By then, the Confederacy had begun drafting and training thousands of slaves.

FIGHTING THE CIVIL WAR

Late in May 1861 the Confederate government moved its capital to Richmond. This was done partly because the large Virginia city could accommodate the growing Confederate bureaucracy more easily than Montgomery could. The move also dramatized the Confederacy's promise to defend the Upper South. Besides, Richmond was an important rail and road center. With Northern and Southern capitals and armies now only a hundred miles apart, the area of Virginia and Maryland became, for obvious reasons, the war's pivotal theater of operations.

A thick layer of gloom spread over Washington as Lincoln and his generals prepared for a Southern attack. There was talk that, for the second time in half a century, an American president might be forced to flee the White House, pursued by an invading army.

Southern Strategy

Although a number of important battles were fought during the war, the Confederates resorted to an overall guerrilla strategy that resembled Washington's in the American Revolution. A friend wrote Jefferson Davis complaining of the Confederacy's "purely defensive" strategy and of its reluctance to launch a full-scale attack on the North. Davis replied: "Without military stores, without the workshops to create them, without the power to import them, necessity, not choice, has compelled us to occupy strong positions and everywhere — selecting the time and place of attack — to confront the enemy without reserves." In other words, the South chose to conduct an "offensive defense." It tried to select the time and place for major battles carefully. At other times Southerners harassed Northern armies with cavalry raids led by such intrepid commanders as "Stonewall" Jackson, J. E. B. Stuart, Nathan B. Forrest, and John S. Mosby.

Confederate army commanders realized that it was impossible to prevent Union invasions of the South. They knew too that they had neither the manpower nor the resources to mount a full-scale invasion of the North. So the Confederates worked instead to maintain their armies in the field while fighting back the Union troops thrown against them. They hoped that a war-weary Northern public would finally force Lincoln's government to negotiate a peaceful settlement. Lee and Davis recognized, as Washington did during the 1770s, that a revolutionary army wins by not losing — that is, by displaying the capacity to endure.

Northern Strategy

Recognizing the Southern strategy, Lincoln and his generals committed Northern armies from the beginning to a policy of total war against the

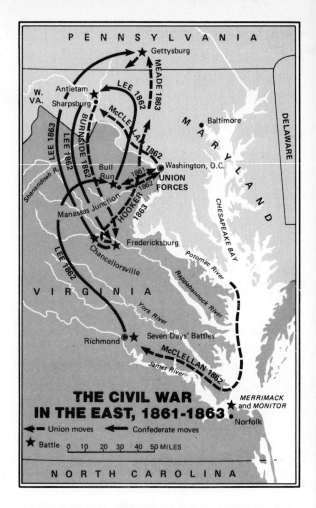

THE CIVIL WAR IN THE EAST, 1861–1863.

◄-- Union moves ◄— Confederate moves
★ Battle   0 10   20   30   40 50 MILES

Fighting broke out on April 12, **1861,** when Confederate batteries opened fire on Fort Sumter in Charleston harbor. The Union quickly began a naval blockade of Confederate shipping. The first major engagement occurred on July 21 at Manassas Junction, Virginia. There an advancing Union army under Irvin McDowell was defeated in the first Battle of Bull Run and driven back to Washington, D.C.

The year **1862** witnessed the first naval battle between ironclads — the Union ship *Monitor* and the Confederate ship *Virginia* (formerly the *Merrimack*) — on March 9 near Norfolk, Virginia. The Union offensives of that year began in March with McClellan's Peninsula Campaign, an attempt to take Richmond from the southeast. He advanced slowly to within a few miles of the city. Confederate forces inflicted heavy casualties on his troops at the end of May. During the subsequent Seven

Days' Battle (June 26–July 2) Lee and Jackson forced McClellan to retreat and abandon the campaign. The Confederate army moved northward to win the second Battle of Bull Run (August 29–30). From there Lee and Jackson advanced into Maryland. Near Sharpsburg, McClellan engaged the Confederates in the Battle of Antietam (September 17). Although militarily the battle was a draw, Lee withdrew to Virginia. McClellan was replaced as Union commander by Burnside, whose overwhelming force was shattered at Fredericksburg (December 13).

In **1863** Hooker took command of the Union army, only to be defeated at Chancellorsville (May 2–4). However, Confederate losses there included "Stonewall" Jackson. Lee marched into Pennsylvania and was defeated at Gettysburg by a Union army under Meade (July 1–3). Lee retreated to Virginia, his second offensive a failure.

South. They were dedicated to the complete destruction of Confederate military power and civil authority by every necessary means. George Templeton Strong wrote in his diary in November 1861:

> Were I dictator at this time, my military policy would be (1) to defend and hold Washington, Western Virginia, Kentucky, Missouri; (2) to support Unionists in North Carolina and in eastern Tennessee; (3) to recover and hold (or destroy with sunken ships) every port and inlet from Hatteras to Galveston.

Strong's proposals resembled the North's actual strategy during the war, which was threefold: (1) to encircle the South in an ever-tightening military net by blockading its ports; (2) to divide the Confederacy in half by seizing control of the Mississippi and Tennessee rivers; (3) to capture Richmond and destroy the main Confederate armies in Virginia, where most Southern troops were concentrated. Strong believed, as did Lincoln and his

Many a Civil War battle exacted enormous tolls in men. Confederate dead lie in a shallow trench at Chancellorsville. Watching a dramatic panorama earlier in the war, Lee had remarked: "It is well that war is so terrible—we would grow too fond of it." (Library of Congress)

officers, that if "the rebels of the South can be locked up and left to suffer and starve," victory would follow.

Superior to the South in its navy, the North was able to impose a blockade of Southern harbors. The Confederates counteracted with fast blockade runners, joined by a number of private merchantmen. In the early years of the war they managed to slip past Union vessels in five out of every six attempts. But the Union blockade became increasingly effective. By 1865 it had choked off Southern cotton exports to Europe, as well as imports of arms and supplies.

Civil War and Reconstruction **455**

In September 1862, President Lincoln visited with General McClellan and his officers at Antietam. (Brown Brothers)

War in the East

The outcome of the Civil War was decided not by naval encounters but by land battles. Northern armies began poorly but improved their performance every year. Confederate forces scored impressive victories at the first and second battles of Bull Run in July 1861 and August 1862. At Fredericksburg, Virginia, in December 1862, the North suffered a crushing defeat, with over twelve thousand casualties.

In May 1863, at Chancellorsville, Maryland, outnumbered Southerners won another victory, though it cost them one of their best generals, "Stonewall" Jackson. They imposed a stalemate on the Virginia front and, several times, threatened to capture Washington itself.

Lincoln searched desperately for Union commanders capable of breaking the stalemate and executing major offensive operations. In the process he appointed a succession of commanding generals—George McClellan, John Pope, McClellan again, Ambrose Burnside, Joseph Hooker, and George Meade. One time, after McClellan had failed to pursue a retreating Confederate force, he reportedly received this letter: "My dear McClellan: If you don't want to use the Army of the Potomac, I should like to borrow it for a while. Yours respectfully, A. Lincoln."

The turning point of the Civil War in the East came in July 1863. Confederate troops under Lee marched into southern Pennsylvania, where they encountered a Union force near Gettysburg. After three days of costly fighting, Lee's invasion was repulsed decisively on July 3.

Each side had over seventy-five thousand troops involved, and the South suffered almost twenty-five thousand casualties. "The results of

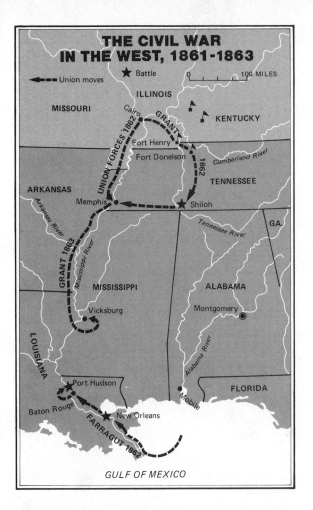

THE CIVIL WAR IN THE WEST, 1861-1863

★ Battle
- - -► Union moves

0   100 MILES

ILLINOIS

MISSOURI

Cairo

KENTUCKY

Fort Henry

Fort Donelson

Cumberland River

TENNESSEE

ARKANSAS

Memphis

Shiloh

GA.

Tennessee River

MISSISSIPPI

Vicksburg

ALABAMA

Montgomery

LOUISIANA

Port Hudson

Baton Rouge

FARRAGUT 1862

New Orleans

Mobile

FLORIDA

Alabama River

Arkansas River

Mississippi River

UNION FORCES 1862

GRANT 1862

GRANT 1863

GULF OF MEXICO

Meanwhile, in the west, the Union won a series of important victories in **1862.** In February Grant captured Fort Henry on the Tennessee River and Fort Donelson on the Cumberland. Moving southward in Tennessee, he was attacked at Shiloh (April 6–7), but Union reinforcements forced the Confederates to withdraw into Mississippi. Union forces also made progress in their drive to gain control of the Mississippi River. Farragut bombarded and captured New Orleans in late April and proceeded up the river to Baton Rouge. To the north, a combined naval and land expedition defeated the Confederate fleet at Memphis on June 6 and captured the city.

In **1863** the Union continued its campaign to secure mastery of the Mississippi. Grant began attacking the Confederate stronghold of Vicksburg in May, and the city surrendered on July 4. With the fall of Port Hudson on July 9, the entire Mississippi was in Union hands and the Confederacy split in two.

this victory are priceless," rejoiced the normally pessimistic Strong. "Philadelphia, Baltimore, and Washington are safe. The rebels are hunted out of the North, their best army is routed, and the charm of Robert Lee's invincibility broken."

War in the West

The South's strategy of tying down and wearing out Union forces worked reasonably well in the East. Elsewhere, however, better-equipped and better-led Union troops won a series of important victories.

In February 1862 federal troops and a gunboat flotilla led by Ulysses S. Grant captured Fort Henry, on the Tennessee River, and Fort Donelson, on the Cumberland River. These moves forced Southern General Albert S. Johnston to abandon Kentucky and parts of Tennessee to the Union.

Admiral Farragut's capture of New Orleans in April 1862 and a series of Northern victories farther up the Mississippi—capped by defeat of the Confederate fleet at Memphis in June—brought most of the river under Union control. Arkansas, Louisiana, and Texas were thus isolated from the rest of the Confederacy.

In the West the decisive point was reached the day after Lee's defeat at Gettysburg. On July 4, 1863, Vicksburg fell. This key Confederate port surrendered after a six-week siege by Union troops. A final Confederate stronghold on the Mississippi—Port Hudson, Louisiana—fell later that same month.

Grant's remarkable success in this western campaign led to his appointment as Lincoln's seventh and last commanding general. Grant appealed to Lincoln for many of the same reasons he did to most Northerners. Wrote one admirer of Grant: "He talks like an earnest businessman, prompt, clearheaded, and decisive, and utters no bosh."

Final Campaigns

Grant took command of the Union forces in the spring of 1864. In May, he and Meade led a Northern force of 100,000 men against Lee's army, which had regrouped in Virginia after its Gettysburg defeat the previous year. It was in the same

Civil War and Reconstruction   **457**

This painting by William H. Overend depicts "An August Morning with Farragut: The Battle of Mobile Bay." (Courtesy, Wadsworth Atheneum, Hartford)

A wood engraving from the Illustrated London News *showing the enlistment of Irish and German immigrants on the Battery in New York City. (Museum of the City of New York)*

U. S. Grant cared less about the cut or condition of his uniform than he did about success in the field. Lincoln said of him: "I can't spare this man—he fights." (Brady Collection, U.S. Signal Corps, National Archives)

month that Union troops led by Sherman began their push to Atlanta.

For the remainder of the war Grant and Sherman pursued the same strategy of wearing down the enemy that Davis and Lee had hoped earlier would win for the Confederacy. No longer did Union forces concentrate on capturing Richmond or other Southern territory for its own sake. Instead, they struck directly at the remaining Confederate armies and resources—as Sherman did in Georgia. They aimed to inflict so heavy a price in casualties and physical devastation, that a war-weary South would be forced to surrender.

Beginning in June 1864, Grant's army tied down most of Lee's forces near Petersburg, Virginia. That fall Sherman led his famous march to the sea from Atlanta to Savannah. From Savannah, Sherman's forces turned north and extended their scorched-earth tactics into South Carolina and North Carolina.

Grant's troops, meanwhile, left their Petersburg trenches for frequent assaults on Lee's thinly manned lines. By early April 1865, Grant had blocked Lee's effort to retreat southward. Lee's army had by then been reduced by death and desertions from fifty-four thousand to thirty thousand men. Lee believed that further fighting was useless and that Confederate defeat was inevitable. He surrendered to Grant at Appomattox, Virginia, on April 9, 1865.

Despite pleas from Jefferson Davis for continued resistance, even if only by guerrilla bands in the Southern hills and forests, the rest of the Confederate armies still in the field surrendered by the end of May. Union troops finally occupied Richmond after Davis and other Confederate officials had fled. For all practical purposes Southern resistance had ended by the time Jefferson Davis was captured on May 10.

A Summing Up

The Civil War has been described as the "first modern war." A number of weapons and tactics associated with later military struggles were first used in its major campaigns. The basic weapon for the infantry, both Union and Confederate, was the single-shot, rifled musket, which had a range and accuracy two or three times greater than earlier, smoothbore guns. Troops could now engage in deadly fire from distances of a quarter to a half mile. Trench warfare, which later dominated much of World War I, came into being, and close-range or hand-to-hand combat was no longer inevitable.

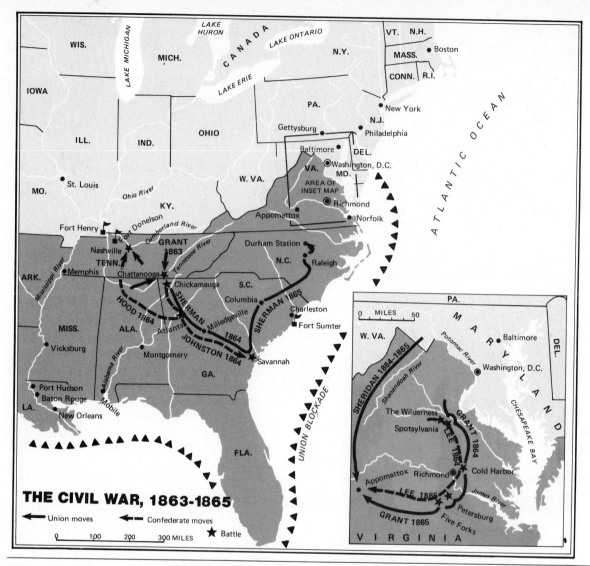

THE CIVIL WAR, 1863-1865

Union moves ⟵
Confederate moves ⟵ - -
★ Battle

0   100   200   300 MILES

The major military actions of the fall of **1863** occurred in the west. On September 9 Union forces maneuvered the Confederates out of Chattanooga, Tennessee, without a battle. Moving south into Georgia, the Union army was stopped at Chickamauga (September 19–20) and driven back into Chattanooga. In October Grant was given command of all the Union's western armies. At the Battle of Chattanooga (November 23–25) he defeated the Confederates in engagements on Lookout Mountain and Missionary Ridge.

In **1864** Grant, now in supreme command of the Union armies, took charge of the Virginia front. He began a campaign to destroy Lee's army and take Richmond. Grant struck again and again; at the Battle of the Wilderness (May 5–6), at Spot-

sylvania (May 8–12), and at Cold Harbor (June 1–3). Lee parried Grant's blows, inflicting heavy casualties on his opponent. In this one-month period the Union army lost approximately sixty thousand men, a number equal to Lee's total strength at the beginning of the campaign. But the North could provide reinforcements of men and supplies; the South lacked reserves of both. Grant pressed on, moving south to Petersburg. He failed to capture it in a bloody four-day battle (June 15–18). However, his subsequent nine-month siege of the town cut Richmond off from the Deep South.

In the west, Union forces under Sherman moved out of Chattanooga in May 1864 to begin their invasion of Georgia. The opposing Confederate general, Joseph E. Johnston, fought a series of

This increased firepower of the infantry threatened both artillery and cavalry. A bank of cannon could no longer offer a solid defense; and the dash of a cavalry charge became mere vainglory when riders could easily be picked off, one by one, from a distance.

The American genius for creating new technology, shown earlier with such peaceful innovations as the cotton gin, was amply demonstrated during the Civil War, when Gatling guns (machine guns), repeating rifles, ironclad ships, and even submarines made their appearance (the latter were, for the most part, failures).

Railroads and telegraph lines revolutionized military communications, particularly for the Northern armies, who sent an estimated 6 million telegrams over fifteen thousand miles of wire set up by the Signal Corps. The most spectacular railroad supply system was that maintained for Sherman during the siege of Atlanta: sixteen hundred tons of supplies arrived daily in sixteen trains from Union depots northwest of the city. European military observers flocked to the United States to study the lessons the New World's "internal war" had to offer the Old World's future struggles.

The Civil War was a modern war in the important sense that it required a break with traditional military thinking in order to achieve victory. Initially most Civil War generals on both sides regarded cities and territories—not enemy armies—as their objectives. They hoped to win by

CIVIL WAR MANPOWER

	UNION	CONFEDERACY
Total serving in armed forces	1,556,678	1,082,119
Killed in battle or died from wounds	110,070	94,000
Died from illness	249,458	164,000
Wounded	275,175	100,000

maneuvering rather than by fighting. By contrast, Lincoln's overall strategy was to move on all fronts simultaneously in order to crush the enemy's forces and gain control of his resources. This warfare of annihilation was a plan that tradition-bound generals scorned. Only in Grant and Sherman did Lincoln find generals who would employ his strategy successfully. They were willing to break the rules to play, and win, a new and deadly game.

Casualties on both sides in the four years of "internal war" totaled almost 40 percent of the armies; several hundred thousand soldiers gave their lives to battle. The South lost its separatist revolt for lack of manpower and equipment. "They are too many for us," Mary Boykin Chesnut despaired two days before Lee's surrender. "Nine tenths of our army are under ground!" she anguished in her diary. "Where is another to come from? Will they wait until we grow one?" Time had run out for the Confederacy, and its will to endure had been crushed.

---

defensive actions but continued falling back toward Atlanta. John B. Hood, who replaced Johnston in July, suffered heavy losses in two pitched battles near Atlanta. It was occupied by Union forces on September 2. After the fall of Atlanta, Hood moved northwest to threaten Tennessee and the Union army's long lines of communication. Sherman sent part of his army to counter Hood's forces. He led the rest of his troops in a virtually unopposed march to the sea from Atlanta to Savannah, which fell on December 22. Meanwhile, Union forces shattered Hood's army at Nashville, Tennessee (December 15–16).

In **1865** Sherman continued his scorched-earth policy as he moved north from Savannah into North Carolina, where Johnston, restored to com-

mand, slowed his advance somewhat. In Virginia the Confederates, outnumbered more than two to one by Grant's reinforced army, were unable to lift the siege of Petersburg. On April 1, Lee's last attack (at Five Forks) was repulsed, and on April 2 he evacuated Petersburg and Richmond, moving westward. A Union army under Philip H. Sheridan, which had marched south through the Shenandoah Valley, blocked his path. Virtually surrounded by an overwhelming force, Lee surrendered to Grant at Appomattox on April 9. On April 18, Johnston surrendered to Sherman at Durham Station, North Carolina. Final Confederate capitulations occurred in Alabama (May 4) and Louisiana (May 26).

In the long run it would have been far cheaper to purchase the abolition of slavery, although such a course was unthinkable to both sides in 1861. Estimates of the war's total cost ran as high as $3 billion for the South and $5 billion for the North. This was three to four times the total estimated value of every slave in the Confederacy. Both the Union and the Confederacy had great difficulty in paying their enormous bills for war equipment, soldiers' salaries, and operating expenses. Both sides resorted to such financial measures as raising taxes, issuing various types of bonds, and printing vast quantities of paper money unsupported by gold or silver reserves.

Crisis in the South

The overriding desire for victory led to sweeping changes in the South. Some affected the master–slave relationship. Southern slaveholders had defended their right to absolute control over their bondsmen in antebellum days. When war came, they watched helplessly as the Confederate government and Southern state governments transferred hundreds of thousands of slaves from private plantations to more urgent labor in the war effort. Slaves even became Confederate soldiers shortly before Appomattox. And throughout the war Southerners relaxed their close supervision of slave movements and activities.

Normal political life also came to a halt in the South during the war. There was no two-party system (as in the North). There was only one all-inclusive ruling, but unruly, "government party." Within the Confederacy there were people who opposed Davis's conduct of the war. They spoke their minds freely. Yet the demands of fighting a separatist revolt prevented any change in government.

The war not only changed master–slave relations and Southern politics, it also altered the Southern economy. The cherished doctrine of states' rights received rough treatment at the hands of Confederate leaders. These men were determined to assume every power they needed to wage war. Davis centralized and nationalized the economy to a remarkable degree. If occasion de-

manded, he interfered freely with the rights of capitalists. The Confederacy did more than seize slaves for war work. It closely regulated foreign commerce. It confiscated food and equipment for the army from private farms. It created government-run industries to produce military equipment. And it tightly controlled what was left of private enterprise.

The Confederacy even created a Cotton Bureau, which took over planters' cotton supplies. The Cotton Bureau paid a set price for the entire crop. By running the Northern blockade, the government acted as the sole Southern salesman in Europe. Government supplies of cotton were used as security for the Confederacy's foreign loans. But the blockade grew daily more effective, and Confederate revenues from European cotton sales—its one important source of revenue—dwindled correspondingly during the war's final years.

In spite of truly heroic effort and sacrifice, the South was destitute by the end of the war. "We have no money, even for taxes, or for their confiscation," wrote Mrs. Chesnut in April 1865. "Our poverty is made a matter of laughing." Millions came close to starving. Confederate officials recommended the nutritional values of such fare as squirrels and rats to make up for the dire shortage of food. At the time of its surrender, Lee's army had enough ammunition to provide each man seventy-five rounds—but no food.

Southern economic devastation by 1865 could be measured in many ways. Compared to 1860, there were 32 percent fewer horses, 30 percent fewer mules, 35 percent fewer cattle, and 42 percent fewer pigs. Cotton crops were destroyed or rotted unpicked in the fields. Few factories remained in operation. There was almost no trade. Only a handful of banks were left, and they were nearly empty.

Prosperity in the North

"We hear they have all grown rich," Mrs. Chesnut complained about Northerners in 1865. "Genuine Yankees can make a fortune trading jackknives!" Industrial growth in the North began before the Civil War, of course. But it was vastly accelerated by wartime demands to equip and sup-

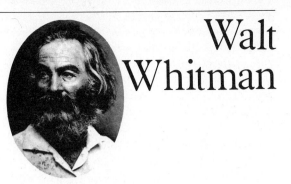

Walt Whitman

(*Library of Congress*)

The poet who was best able to bring together the vitality and idealism of his generation was Walt Whitman. He was born in 1819 in Huntington, Long Island, the son of a carpenter-farmer father with leanings toward Quaker thought, and a sympathetic and understanding mother with very little education. He grew up in a family of nine children of whom both the oldest and the youngest were mentally retarded. Walter, as he was known in the family, left school early in his eleventh year and started a process of self-education that included moving from job to job—as printer's devil, compositor, carpenter, schoolteacher, newspaper writer, and editor.

Whitman's ideas were generated by his childhood in the farming and fishing community on Long Island—his associations with the haymakers and eel fishers, the baymen and pilots—and by the stimulating life of New York, the city in which he worked. He roamed the streets, rode the ferries, and went regularly to the theater and the opera. Early in his life, books had become important to him. He read the Bible, Shakespeare, Ossian, the Greek tragic poets, the ancient Hindu poets, the Nibelungenlied, and the poems of Dante as well as Scott.

Politics were soon a consuming interest. The adult Whitman became an ardent Jacksonian and supporter of the Democratic party. Most of his newspaper jobs were with Democratic journals. The *Democratic Review* was one of the fine literary journals of the time and, through Whitman's work there, he met such literary figures as Hawthorne, Poe, Bryant, Longfellow, Thoreau, and others.

Whitman was especially imbued with the fire of Emerson's transcendentalist ideas. When *Leaves of Grass* appeared, Emerson wrote: "I am not blind to the worth of the wonderful gift of *Leaves of Grass.* I find it the most extraordinary piece of wit and wisdom that America has yet contributed. . . . I greet you at the beginning of a great career." But *Leaves of Grass,* in its first two printings in 1855 and 1856, was not a success. Some readers found it incomprehensible while others found the sexual implications shocking. With the mellowing of the author's language, finally in 1860–61, the volume began to sell.

The Civil War became a critical influence in Whitman's life. Several of his articles at this time dealt with Broadway Hospital where he spent time helping the wounded. Then, in December 1862, he visited his wounded brother, George, a Union soldier, and suddenly realized that he had himself become a part of the war effort. With a part-time job for support, he spent the next three years serving the wounded in hospitals around the city of Washington and sometimes on the battlefields.

In 1865 Whitman published *Drum Taps,* the poems he had written during the war. Some poems are martial outbursts, describing the mobilization of the army. Others are quieter, describing a field hospital or his own lonely vigils with the dying and the dead.

Drum Taps was being printed when the news of Lincoln's assassination reached Whitman. He was inspired to write the dirge that many critics consider his masterpiece. The poem stressed the triumph that peace and beauty achieve in death, for death brings a joining of man and nature. It begins:

When lilacs last in the door-yard bloom'd
And the great star early droop'd
  in the western sky in the night,
I mourn'd—and yet shall mourn
  with ever-returning spring.
O ever-returning spring!
  trinity sure to me you bring;
Lilac blooming perennial
  and drooping star in the west,
And thought of him I love.

ply the army. The number of Northern factories increased from fewer than 140,000 in 1860 to over 250,000 by 1870. Railroad mileage doubled during this decade. Growth in the North was aided not only by government contracts for arms and military supplies. It was helped also by wartime currency inflation, huge federal subsidies to railroads, and protective tariffs for industry.

The result was enormous inflation—high prices but also tremendous profits. There was rapid expansion in industries ranging from wool production to mining, from petroleum to iron manufacturing. Farmers prospered, too, because of the increased demand for every staple crop. Most merchants and shippers shared in the boom. Banking facilities were enlarged greatly after Congress passed several new banking acts. Senator John Sherman wrote his brother General William Sherman about the impact of the war on Northern capitalists: "They talk as confidently of millions as they formerly did of thousands." George Templeton Strong complained that the sedate prewar culture of New York City was being "diluted and swamped by a great flood-tide of material wealth."

A shortage of manpower on Northern farms and in factories stimulated immigration from Europe. In 1865 alone, 180,000 new immigrants arrived on Union soil. In 1866 and 1867 the number spurted to 300,000 yearly.

Perhaps most important in the North, as in the Confederacy, was the role played by the government in stimulating economic growth. Southern Democrats had dominated Congress and the executive branch until the 1850s. They had blocked such measures as the protective tariff, a national banking system, and railroad subsidies. Now the Republicans were in control. They favored industrialization and economic growth. To further their aims, they adopted the Morrill Tariff of 1861, which raised duties. They passed the National Banking Acts of 1863 and 1864, which aided national banks at the expense of state banks. In addition, Congress awarded land-grant subsidies to transcontinental railroads and stimulated Western settlement with the 1862 Homestead Act, which offered land to settlers for nominal sums.

The Republicans changed not only the economic habits of the North but its political life as

well. Lincoln found it no easier than Davis did to govern a country at war. Throughout the conflict the president was attacked from all sides of his wartime government coalition, which was known as the Union party. Abolitionist Republicans (known as Radical Republicans) denounced him for moving too slowly on the question of emancipation, while War Democrats denounced him for moving at all on the problem. Moderate Republicans criticized the lack of military progress by the Northern armies.

Compared to the Confederacy, the North had a poor wartime record in the field of civil rights. In spite of Union victories, many Northerners opposed the war. Lincoln authorized a number of arbitrary military arrests of such civilians, especially Peace Democrats—called "Copperheads" by their enemies. He suspended the privilege of habeas corpus[2] to keep pro-Confederate Northerners in jail once arrested.

In both sections, North and South, the war interfered with civil liberties, but in different ways. Northerners were more likely to be thrown in jail for opposing the war. Southerners were more likely to be punished for resisting government confiscation of their property. These interferences involved of course the civil rights of *white* people. Neither government troubled itself much about the rights of blacks, free or slave.

FREEDOM FOR BLACK PEOPLE

As soon as war broke out, Northern black men tried to enlist in the Union army. They were not allowed to do so, however, until the fall of 1862. Eventually, over 186,000 blacks served as Union soldiers—almost 15 percent of all Northern troops. They were usually led by white officers and they were paid less than white troops. Union commanders were divided in their attitudes toward

---

[2] This privilege, guaranteed by the Constitution, provides that an arrested person can demand that legal authorities show why he or she has been imprisoned. A writ of habeas corpus (Latin words meaning "you have the body") thus protects a person against being held in jail without cause.

using black soldiers. Some welcomed them. Others, like Sherman, did not.

The Emancipation Proclamation

Northern policy toward slavery changed during the war. Many Republicans in the government believed sincerely in emancipation. Lincoln, though, had always regarded it as secondary compared to the overriding importance of winning the war and reuniting the nation.

Like most Americans at the time, Lincoln believed that blacks were inferior. He never felt certain that 4 million ex-slaves could reach full equality with whites in the United States. Throughout the Civil War he tried unsuccessfully to link his moves toward emancipation with efforts to colonize freed blacks. None of these efforts worked out.

Lincoln had been elected on a platform that pledged to restrict slavery but not abolish it. He moved cautiously toward emancipation, mainly because of his military and political problems in conducting the war. Radical Republicans in Congress kept pressuring him for swift abolition. Even many moderate Northerners became fervent converts to emancipation as war casualties mounted, if only to punish the Confederacy. Such Unionists did not change their attitudes toward *black people* (and their supposed inferiority). They only changed their minds about *slavery*.

The situation was complicated by the fact that thousands of runaway slaves took refuge with the Union army. There, they were often treated — as with Sherman's army — as both a help and a hindrance. Thousands of blacks, however, did join Union army ranks. Lincoln, along with most Northerners, grew more sympathetic to emancipation.

Congress took the first step by abolishing slavery in the federal territories in June 1862. Then, in September 1862, Lincoln issued a preliminary proclamation. In it he stated that he would issue a final document on January 1, 1863, freeing the slaves in all states then in rebellion. This final document was the Emancipation Proclamation.

The Emancipation Proclamation actually freed very few people when it was issued. It did not apply to slaves in the border states fighting on the Union side. Nor did it affect slaves in Southern areas already under Union control. Naturally, the states in rebellion did not act on Lincoln's order. But the proclamation did show Americans, and the rest of the world, that the Civil War was now being fought to end slavery.

For all practical purposes the 3½ million black slaves in the South found themselves free within days after Lee's surrender. It was only with final ratification of the Thirteenth Amendment, however, in December 1865, that slavery was ended completely and legally throughout the United States.

Treatment in the North

Though the Union eventually fought to free black people, those who lived in the region faced many difficulties. In 1860 free Northern blacks numbered 225,000. Most of them were restricted to menial jobs. A rigid pattern of segregation in schools, hospitals, transportation, and other public facilities kept blacks and whites separated. Roughly 93 percent of Northern black people lived in states where they could not vote. (Only five New England states allowed blacks to cast ballots in 1865.)

Blacks were the victims of race riots throughout the North during the war. The most destructive took place in New York City in the summer of 1863. There, anger among the city's Irish working class at a new federal draft law exploded into violence during four days and nights of rioting. The new law allowed wealthy citizens to avoid the draft by buying the services of substitute soldiers — something poor laborers clearly could not afford.

Mobs of Irish workers rampaged over Manhattan Island from July 13 to July 16. They burned, looted, and killed. The rioters' main targets were free blacks and, to a lesser extent, white abolitionists and wealthy citizens. The city's outnumbered police force, also composed largely of Irishmen, fought the rioters with great bravery and discipline, finally putting down the rioting with the help of federal troops. By that time, some twelve hundred persons, mostly black, had been killed.

Confederate soldiers, after surrendering and disbanding, begin the journey home. (Culver Pictures)

Many thousands were injured. Property worth millions was damaged or destroyed. Other Northern cities, especially in the Middle West, experienced similar draft riots. Antagonism toward black people ran high throughout the North during the war years.

After the War

The Thirteenth Amendment did not settle the basic questions about the future status of black Americans, especially in the postwar South. Former slaves were now free. But free to *do* what? Free to *be* what? What did freedom mean to someone raised in slavery?

Many ex-slaves simply stayed on their plantations, working for the same masters. Their old habits altered little at first, although now the whites were often as poor as their former bondsmen. "The Negroes seem unchanged," Mrs. Chesnut wrote, referring to her one-time slaves. Other former slaves left their old homes, usually for an uncertain future.

Whatever the fate of individual freed slaves, one characteristic of Southern emancipation was its peaceful nature. Despite the fears of antebellum white Southerners, there were no bloodbaths or vengeful attacks by ex-slaves on their former masters. Black people responded to their new freedom with dignity and grace.

Early in the twentieth century Benjamin Botkin and other folklorists traveled through the United States, recording the recollections of aged ex-slaves. One elderly man recalled:

> The end of the war, it come just like that—like you snap your fingers. Soldiers, all of a sudden, was everywhere—coming in bunches. Everyone was a-singing. We was all walking on golden clouds. Hallelujah! Everybody went wild! we was free. Just like that, we was free. It didn't seem to make the whites mad, either. They went right on giving us food just the same. Nobody took our homes away, but right off colored folks started on the move. They seemed to want to get closer to freedom, so they'd know what it was—like it was a place or a city.

The experience was exciting yet frightening for blacks, people like those who had joined Sherman's army on its march to Savannah. Many of them had never gone beyond the borders of their own farms. One ex-slave commented to Botkin:

> We knowed freedom was on us, but we didn't know what was to come with it. We thought we was going to be richer than the white folks, 'cause we was stronger and knowed how to work, and the whites didn't, and they didn't have us to work for them any more. But it didn't turn out that way. We soon found out that freedom could make folks proud, but it didn't make 'em rich.

As soon as the war was over, blacks began to organize and work for their own advancement. Historians sometimes overlook the fact that, even in 1860, there were 261,000 free blacks in the South. Tens of thousands of them were literate. These men and women—like the leaders who met with Stanton and Sherman—formed an important black leadership base at the end of the war. Many took part in black conventions held in a number of Southern cities in 1865 and 1866. They petitioned the federal government to assist freedom by granting them the franchise, protecting their civil rights, and providing land and economic aid.

THE FIRST YEAR OF RECONSTRUCTION

The basic dilemma of Reconstruction for all those who lived through it, black and white, Southerner and Northerner alike, was its revolutionary nature. Like the Civil War itself, the postwar period had no examples on which to model itself, no constitutional provisions by which policy makers might be guided.

Compared with reconstruction periods that have followed more recent civil wars in Russia, Spain, and China, the American experience was notably mild. Confederate leaders were neither shot nor driven into exile. Indeed, many resumed their careers in American politics. Only a few, such as Jefferson Davis, were imprisoned, and these mainly for a brief period. No Confederate property was confiscated. Nor was any redistribution of wealth forced on the defeated South by the victorious North.

Lincoln's Approach

In Lincoln's second inaugural address, delivered a month before his death, he called for a generous settlement with the defeated South: "With malice toward none, with charity for all . . . let us strive on to finish the work we are in, to bind up the nation's wounds."

As early as 1862 Lincoln had indicated his desire to restore a defeated Confederacy quickly and without revenge against either its leaders or its people. Lincoln suggested a basis for Reconstruction in December 1863. He called for amnesty[3] (except in the case of key leaders) for Southerners who pledged loyalty to the Union. Southern states in which 10 percent of the 1860 electorate took such a loyalty oath and accepted emancipation would be restored immediately to the Union.

Governments in Arkansas, Louisiana, and Tennessee met Lincoln's provisions in 1864. But Congress refused to seat their representatives. The problem was complicated by the fact that Lincoln believed that the executive branch should control

---

[3] Amnesty is a form of pardon for offenses against the government—especially to a group of persons.

Reconstruction, whereas Congress wanted this power for itself. Congressional attitudes were partly a reaction to the vast expansion of presidential authority under Lincoln during the Civil War.

Republicans in Congress were led by Radicals Thaddeus Stevens of Pennsylvania in the House and Charles Sumner of Massachusetts in the Senate. They were afraid that the Democratic party, led by Southern ex-Confederates, would quickly return to national power. So they offered a much tougher Reconstruction plan in a measure known as the Wade-Davis Bill. It provided that a majority of voters in each Southern state take an "ironclad oath" swearing to their *past* as well as to their *future* loyalty. Obviously, if the electorate were composed only of whites, no ex-Confederate state could honestly meet this provision. The bill also required that the Southern states abolish slavery in their constitutions, repudiate the Confederate war debt, and disfranchise Confederate leaders. Congress passed the Wade-Davis Bill on July 4, 1864. Lincoln killed the measure with a pocket veto. Then Congress passed the nonbinding Wade-Davis Manifesto, reasserting the provisions of the earlier bill.

Therefore, by mid-1864, the stage was set for a postwar confrontation between the president and Congress on Reconstruction policy. Was the South to be restored quickly, its new state governments falling into the hands of ex-Confederate whites with a minimum of federal interference? (This is what Lincoln wanted, though he did urge Southern whites to allow at least educated blacks to vote.) Or should the Southern states undergo fundamental political changes before they could rejoin the Union? Should they allow blacks to vote and hold office, while disbarring ex-Confederate leaders and perhaps confiscating their land?

Assassination

With the war almost over, Lincoln's thoughts had turned increasingly to the problem of reconstructing the South. After a trip to Richmond early in April 1865, he spent several days working out various programs.

On the night of April 14, Good Friday evening, President and Mrs. Lincoln went to Ford's Theater in Washington to see a popular play, *Our American Cousin.* Shortly after 10 P.M. a half-crazed Southern sympathizer named John Wilkes Booth shot Lincoln as he watched the play. Booth then stabbed another member of the president's party, leaped onto the stage, rushed from the theater, and rode away. (He was shot down on April 26 by Union troops that had pursued him into Virginia.)

The wounded Lincoln was taken from Ford's Theater to a nearby house. There, family, friends, and government officials kept an all-night vigil. The president remained unconscious until his death at 7:22 the following morning. "Now he belongs to the ages," said Secretary of War Stanton, one of those at his bedside.

Word of Lincoln's assassination spread quickly via the telegraph. The first reaction to the event, shared by most Northerners and even many Southerners, was one of profound shock: "I am stunned," wrote George Templeton Strong, "as by a fearful personal calamity."

For Lincoln was highly popular in the North at the time of his death, a result of Union military victories beginning in 1863 and culminating in Lee's surrender. During the war itself, Southerners—as one might expect—had little affection for "Uncle Abraham." Many Northerners felt the same way, especially in the early years. One such person was Strong, an aristocrat and avowed snob. He never liked Lincoln's often-crude manner of speech and fondness for telling jokes. Yet these very qualities endeared the president to most other Americans. And even Strong, like other Unionists, responded to Lincoln's firm leadership and genuine anguish at the war's increasing toll in human suffering: "It must be referred to the Attorney General," Lincoln once told Strong about a request to pardon a criminal. "But I guess it will be all right, for me, and the Attorney General's very chicken-hearted."

By the war's end, most Northerners probably agreed with Strong's high estimate of Lincoln's wartime achievement. The president's "weaknesses are on the surface," Strong wrote on April 11, 1865. "His name will be of high account fifty years hence, and for many generations thereafter."

Johnson was an honest but tactless man forced to cope with uniquely difficult circumstances. He had to follow Abraham Lincoln in the presidency, and he had to confront the problems of postwar reconstruction. He failed. Jefferson Davis said he had "the pride of having no pride." (Library of Congress)

Johnson's Plan

Lincoln's death placed the burden of reconstructing the South on the shoulders of his former vice-president, Andrew Johnson. Johnson was a War Democrat from Tennessee and a one-time Radical on the Reconstruction issue. Once in the White House, however, he soon adopted Lincoln's basic proposals. Unfortunately, Johnson completely lacked Lincoln's basic sympathy for the problems of freed blacks. Also, he was a dogmatic man. He showed almost none of Lincoln's tact in dealing with political opponents.

Johnson, like Lincoln, believed that Reconstruction was a matter to be handled by the pres-

ident. His position was strengthened by the fact that Congress was not in session for several months after he took office. Johnson readmitted the states of Arkansas, Louisiana, and Tennessee. In May 1865 he issued his own Reconstruction plan. It provided that whites in each Southern state who pledged their future loyalty to the Union could elect delegates to a state convention. This convention had to revoke the ordinance of secession, abolish slavery, and repudiate the Confederate war debt. Then the state would be restored to the Union. Johnson granted amnesty to almost all Confederates who took the oath of allegiance. The exceptions were wealthy people and high officials. Even they could apply for a presidential pardon. By late 1865 all the Southern states except Texas had complied with these provisions. (Texas did so early in 1866.)

Southern Regulation of Blacks

Congress believed that the government had a duty to assist freedmen after the war. So in March 1865 it created the Freedmen's Bureau, a temporary federal assistance agency headed by Oliver O. Howard. The bureau distributed food and medicine to poor blacks (and whites), opened schools, supervised land distribution to freedmen, and tried to defend the civil rights of Southern blacks. (It exercised these functions in helping "Sherman's Negroes" in the resettlement program.)

The Freedmen's Bureau, however, could not protect the physical security of black Southerners without the help of Union troops. This problem was urgent. Brutal riots against blacks occurred in Memphis and New Orleans in 1866, and scattered acts of anti-Negro violence occurred throughout the South.

Yet after Appomattox, Union troops were mustered out of the army at a rapid rate. By the end of 1865 only 150,000 soldiers remained of the million serving six months earlier. Many of these were stationed on isolated Western posts fighting Indians.

Under these conditions it was impossible for Union troops to offer the 4 million Southern blacks, most of them recently freed, any real protection. Most white Southerners had been raised to

Stern, intense, and militant, Thaddeus Stevens called for strict measures to punish the Southern rebels. (Library of Congress)

Charles Sumner, once admonished during an argument, "But you forget the other side," thundered in reply: "There is no other side!" (Library of Congress)

believe that blacks had no civil rights that whites were bound to respect. Killings, beatings, burnings, and other forms of physical terror directed against blacks—mostly to keep them out of politics—began soon after the war's end. Violence against blacks was often carried out by white secret societies. Several were formed after the war, primarily to keep blacks from voting. The most famous, the Ku Klux Klan, was founded in 1866. The turmoil increased during the 1870s.

Many whites in the South adopted other means to reduce black people to a state of virtual enslavement. In every Southern state new govern-

ments were elected by voters according to the provisions of Johnson's Reconstruction plan. But the Johnson state governments, as they were called, allowed no blacks to vote. They adopted so-called Black Codes to regulate the actions and behavior of freedmen. Southern whites claimed that such codes were necessary because of the threat of social disorder as a result of emancipation. There had been no major instance, however, of blacks rioting against whites anywhere in the region.

The Black Codes had some provisions to protect blacks. They legalized marriages between blacks, for instance. They also gave blacks the right to sue and testify in court. But the codes consisted mainly of restrictions. They supervised the movements of blacks, prevented them from carrying weapons, and forbade intermarriage between blacks and whites. Contracts, sometimes for life, forced black people to remain at their jobs. In some states, blacks could not own land or work at any job other than farming without a special license. Black children were forced into certain job apprenticeships.

Reaction in the North

Northern Republicans, both Radicals and moderates, attacked the Johnson state governments. They denounced the Black Codes and called for their immediate repeal. Most Radicals believed that the defeated Southern states should be treated, in Thaddeus Stevens's phrase, like "conquered provinces," until more repentant leaders emerged.

When Congress reconvened in December 1865, representatives and senators elected under the Johnson state governments applied for admission. Republicans in Congress refused to admit them. These Southerners who now claimed loyalty to the Union included fifty-eight former Confederate congressmen, six of Jefferson Davis's cabinet members, and four Southern generals. Most amazing of all was the presence of Alexander Stephens of Georgia, who eight months earlier had been vice-president of the Confederacy!

The 1866 riots in Memphis and New Orleans gave Northerners additional evidence that the white South remained unrepentant. Thus it seemed inevitable that there would be a power struggle between Johnson and congressional Republicans over who would control the Reconstruction process. Who was sovereign in the federal government, the president or Congress? Who could decide?

RADICAL RECONSTRUCTION

Congress answered these questions to its own satisfaction by taking the initiative completely out of Johnson's hands. By 1867 the legislature had won control. It dominated the government for the next ten years.

The Republicans who controlled Congress developed their strategy mainly through the Joint Committee on Reconstruction, which was dominated by the Radicals. This group asserted that Southern states could be readmitted only after meeting congressional requirements. The Joint Committee moved a series of measures through Congress between 1865 and 1867. Most of the bills were vetoed by the hapless Johnson, then repassed by a two-thirds majority.

First, in February 1866, came the new Freedmen's Bureau bill. It expanded the bureau's authority to protect Southern blacks, giving it the right to try in military courts persons accused of violating the civil rights of freedmen.

A Civil Rights Act of April 1866 granted to blacks the same civil rights as those enjoyed by whites. The measure also asserted the right of the federal government to interfere in state affairs to protect a citizen's civil rights.

In order to fortify their position, congressional Republicans in June 1866 adopted and sent to the states the Fourteenth Amendment. In effect, it gave blacks full citizenship. If a state denied the vote to blacks, its representation in the House would be reduced. The amendment also forbade ex-Confederate officials from holding federal or state office again without receiving congressional pardon. The Joint Committee declared that any Southern state wishing readmission would have to ratify the Fourteenth Amendment. The Johnson state governments in the South voted against ratification. (The amendment was eventually ratified in 1868.)

President Johnson hoped his Republican opponents would be defeated in the 1866 congressional election, and he campaigned personally against them. After a wild and bitterly fought campaign, however, anti-Johnson Republicans swept the election. They carried every Union state but three.

A Strong Program

When Congress met after the election, Republicans enacted their program into law. They

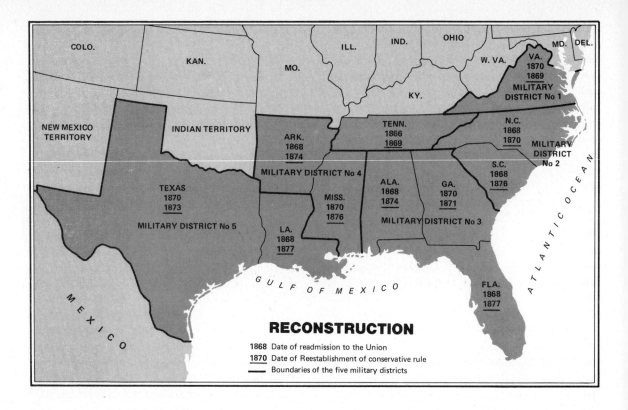

RECONSTRUCTION

1868 Date of readmission to the Union
1870 Date of Reestablishment of conservative rule
—— Boundaries of the five military districts

began with the First Reconstruction Act of March 1867. Significantly, the bill's final form came from a moderate, Republican John Sherman. By this time the moderates agreed with Radicals on most key issues of Reconstruction. This law abolished the existing Johnson state governments. It provided for universal male suffrage—that is, for black as well as white voting.

The First Reconstruction Act also authorized temporary military rule of the South. Ten former Confederate states were still outside the Union. (Tennessee had ratified the Fourteenth Amendment and had been readmitted.) These states were divided into five military districts. To rejoin the Union, a state had to call a constitutional convention elected by universal male suffrage. This body, in turn, had to create a new state government that would ratify the Fourteenth Amendment and guarantee black suffrage. Three subsequent congressional acts strengthened the powers of federal army commanders in the South.

The final act in the congressional drama of Radical Reconstruction involved the effort in 1868 to remove the president through impeachment. Congress had good reason to believe that Johnson would do everything in his power to sabotage the Reconstruction acts. From 1865 to 1868, he had worked to impede every major step Congress had taken to assist Southern blacks or to enforce a harsh settlement upon the white South. In the process, Johnson had systematically interfered with congressional statutes, practically crippling effective operation (for one thing) of the Freedmen's Bureau throughout the South (as in his interference with Sherman's land program) by presidential directives.

Johnson, moreover, had appointed as federal officials in the region (including even provisional governors) ex-Confederates who had not yet even taken the oath of allegiance to the Union. He used his presidential appointment powers ruthlessly to subvert congressional aims on Reconstruction, claiming for himself absolute direction of the process even after Congress had rejected his early effort to form state governments without first obtaining its approval. Johnson's view of presidential authority was a broad, almost modern one (as Lincoln's had been—but during the wartime emergency). But at all times, Johnson lacked his predecessor's tact in dealing with those who disagreed with him—especially in Congress—tact that might have made his view of presidential power more palatable to his political enemies.

Johnson's recurrent efforts to undermine the program of congressional Reconstruction through issuing conflicting orders to federal officials (both military and civil) in the South provoked Republican moderates and radicals to combine in self-defense. An unprecedented special session was called which passed two measures on March 2, 1867.

One of the measures virtually deprived Johnson of command of the American army by requiring him to issue all military orders through the general of the army, Ulysses S. Grant. The second was the Tenure of Office Act. It prohibited the president from removing those officials whose appointments had been made with Senate consent, without again securing Senate approval. This law meant that Johnson could not, for example, arbitrarily fire Secretary of War Stanton. This leading Radical was the man who—along with Saxton and Howard—had tried to block presidential interference with Sherman's land distribution policy. Johnson disregarded the measure and dismissed Stanton. Then the House passed a resolution impeaching Johnson on eleven charges, including alleged violations of the two March 2 bills.

After a Senate trial, the president was acquitted, although even some of his supporters acknowledged that they were less concerned with retaining Johnson—considering him an inept and insensitive chief executive—than they were with upholding the office of the presidency. If Johnson were successfully removed by impeachment, they felt, the process would rupture violently the normal relations between the three coordinate branches of national government. Both sides in the struggle argued from reasonable positions, and the entire impeachment process indicated the under-

lying strength of the constitutional mechanisms, even when tested in the midst of dire political crisis.

A two-thirds majority is needed to convict the president on an impeachment charge. Thirty-five senators voted for his conviction, while nineteen (including seven Republicans) voted for acquittal. Thus Johnson was saved by a one-vote margin.

After his acquittal, Johnson grudgingly complied with the tacit promises made by his supporters to obtain the votes of borderline senators. No longer did he interfere actively—for the brief remainder of his presidency—with enforcement of duly passed congressional statutes on Southern Reconstruction or with those officials charged with enforcing these laws. For the moment, Congress controlled the Reconstruction process.

The effort to unseat Johnson was the most daring episode in the Radicals' Reconstruction plans. A few Radicals such as Stevens tried to push through bills confiscating 394 million acres of land owned by the seventy thousand chief leaders of the Confederacy. (Charles Sumner called the antebellum plantations "nurseries of the Rebellion.") But such measures found little support among the party's moderate majority, and therefore they did not pass.

Most aims of the Radicals were fairly limited. They worked chiefly for Republican political control of the national government. They also hoped that coalitions of black voters and friendly whites would dominate Southern politics, thereby preventing national revival of the Democratic party.

But Republicans did not have any direct social or economic goals. Only a small number of Radicals were committed to complete equality for black Americans. There was no large-scale program to provide landless freedmen with an economic base. Many blacks had been promised "forty acres and a mule." But the thousands resettled on abandoned lands—such as "Sherman's Negroes" of the Deep South—were soon dispossessed.

After the attempt to impeach Johnson, Radicals left the problems of Reconstruction in the hands of federal commanders and new state governments in the South. The quarrel between legis-

Southern black men vote in large numbers for the first time. (The Bettmann Archive)

lative and executive branches over Southern policy ended in 1868, when Republican Ulysses S. Grant was elected president. By then the central drama of Reconstruction had shifted from Washington to the South itself.

The New Radical Governments

Beginning in 1867, so-called Radical state governments were set up according to congressional regulations. New black voters made up a majority of the Radical electorate in five states—Alabama, Florida, Louisiana, Mississippi, and South Carolina. Elsewhere in the South, white Radical majorities were supported by black voters. By 1870 more than 700,000 blacks and 627,000 whites were registered as voters under the Radical state constitutions.[4]

Congress readmitted Louisiana and six other states to the Union under Radical rule in June 1868. By the end of 1870 all ten ex-Confederate states had been readmitted to the Union.

Throughout the South blacks filled public offices for the first time. These were not, however, usually the highest offices. Nor did blacks hold office in proportion to their percentage of voters. Only one state legislature, that of South Carolina, ever had a black majority. No black ever became a Reconstruction Southern governor. (Some states, though, had black lieutenant governors.) There were two black United States senators and fifteen congressmen during the entire period of Radical rule.

Many black political leaders were educated men. Some were among the most distinguished figures in the entire South. Francis L. Cardozo, for example, South Carolina's state treasurer, held degrees from the universities of London and Glasgow, making him perhaps the best-educated politician in the South of either race.

Who were the Radicals in the South? They included many different groups. Some were South-erners, most of whom had been prewar Whigs or secret Union sympathizers during the war. Many Southern businessmen and even a few planters joined the Radicals. They hoped that the new governments would have enough help from Northern capitalists and Republican politicians to rebuild the South's shattered economy. Radicals also included nonslaveholding farmers, who, while they disliked blacks, hated ex-Confederates even more for having led them into what they considered (at least after its loss) "a rich man's war and a poor man's fight." These Southern-born Radicals were called scalawags (an often undeserved term) by former Confederates.

Other Radicals were Northerners. Tens of thousands of them went south after the war for a variety of reasons. Hostile whites referred to them bitterly as carpetbaggers, whose only aim was to fill their luggage with ill-gotten Southern wealth. Yet many were teachers—their carpetbags stuffed only with McGuffey's Readers. Like the people who went to the Sea Islands, their aim was to set up schools for the freedmen. Northern soldiers returned to the South seeking good land; five thousand went to Louisiana alone. Businessmen sought opportunities to invest capital and to profit from the region's economic reconstruction. A number of politically ambitious people did arrive to take part in the Radical governments. But they were by no means all opportunists.

Charges of Corruption

It has often been said that Radical state governments were corrupt. There is some truth to this charge. Legislators in South Carolina, for example, paid $200,000 for $18,000 worth of furniture for the state capitol. Louisiana's Radical governor, H. C. Warmouth, left the state with a personal fortune of half a million dollars, most of it acquired illegally. Similar fortunes were made throughout the South.

Several points should be noted, however, about corruption in the Radical governments. At this time scandals tainted the Grant administration and many Northern state and local governments. The historian John Hope Franklin has termed public dishonesty after the Civil War "bi-

---

[4] The Fifteenth Amendment, adopted in 1870, forbade any state from preventing citizens from voting because of race, color, or "previous condition of servitude." This was a clear effort to eliminate the hypocrisy of some Northern states that demanded suffrage for blacks in the South while continuing to deny it at home.

Louisiana was one of five Southern states to have a majority of black voters. Between 1868 and 1896 the state had 133 black legislators—38 senators and 95 representatives. They were never numerous or strong enough to control political life in Louisiana, though Oscar Dunn (center) did lead a struggle against corruption and extravagance. (Louisiana State Museum)

A black family, most likely sharecroppers, stands in front of their cabin and storehouse. (Brown Brothers)

sectional, bipartisan, and biracial." (Actually, the *blacks* in Congress were not implicated in the Grant scandals, although many of their *white* colleagues were.) State governments everywhere ran up enormous debts. Postwar fortunes in the South were made by Radicals and ex-Confederates, Republicans and Democrats, alike. Given the level of immorality in American politics, North and South, during Reconstruction, it seems fair to say that the Radicals were no more corrupt than other politicians at the time.

In fact, most Radical state funds were spent rebuilding a ruined economy. Somehow, the Radicals managed to begin reconstructing Southern highways, railroads, hospitals, and orphanages.

They also began building schools; many Southern states had had no public school system before the war. The rebuilding had to be done for an additional 3½ million people. These were the ex-slaves, who were now citizens and entitled to the use of public facilities.

An Evaluation

Historians have long debated whether Radical state governments in the South ruled poorly or well. Opinions on this question depend in part on attitudes about whether (or when) blacks should have been allowed the franchise and a role in governing. We tend to forget how short a time Radical governments actually ruled. Tennessee never underwent this type of control. Virginia, North Carolina, and Georgia had returned to conservative hands by 1871. Arkansas, Alabama, and Texas had done so by 1874. And it was all over by 1877.

Some provisions of the Radical state constitutions found approval even among ex-Confederates. The documents ended imprisonment for debt, for example, and did away with property qualifications for voting. Basically, ex-Confederate whites objected less to the corruption of Radical state governments than to their very existence— especially to the presence of blacks on the political slate. Radical rule did not end because of its failure to meet the economic and social problems of the South. Radicals were driven from power because of their insistence on meeting these problems through biracial political cooperation.

THE END OF RADICAL RULE

Two trends put an end to Radical Reconstruction. One was the increasing hostility of white Southerners. The other was the growing indifference of its Northern Republican sponsors.

Southern hostility not only increased. It grew more violent. Thousands of blacks and white Radicals lost their lives to armed bands of whites such as the Ku Klux Klan and local "rifle clubs" that roamed the South during the 1870s. Federal troops and black state militia could suppress only a small number of these groups. Congress passed several Force Bills, making it a national offense to interfere with any citizen's civil rights (including his right to vote). But they had little effect, since only a few thousand federal troops remained in the South to enforce the laws against guerrilla groups like the Klan. To compound the Radicals' problem, Congress repealed its ironclad oath in 1871. No longer did Southerners have to swear that they had always been loyal to the Union. In 1872 a general amnesty restored civil rights (including the right to hold office) to all but about six hundred Confederate officials.

As white terrorists harassed the remaining Radical state governments, Northerners became indifferent. Republicans in Washington grew increasingly weary of the struggle to protect black civil rights. "The whole public," complained President Grant, "is tired of these outbreaks in the South."

The death or retirement of such Radical leaders as Stevens and Sumner helped restore control of Congress to more conservative, business-minded Republicans. A combination of Democrats and reform-minded "Liberal Republicans" nearly won the presidency in 1872 on a platform pledging an end to federal support for Radical regimes in the South. In 1874 the Democrats regained control of the House for the first time since before the war.

Public attention strayed even further away from the South after 1873, when a major depression swept the country. The business slump threw hundreds of thousands out of work and shifted political attention from postwar Reconstruction to the problem of economic recovery.

The Compromise of 1877

In 1876 both presidential candidates, Republican Rutherford B. Hayes and Democrat Samuel B. Tilden, promised even before the election to restore "home rule" to the South. Both pledged to remove federal support for the three remaining Radical state governments—those of Louisiana, South Carolina, and Florida. They implied that Southern whites could now handle all problems connected with blacks, including political rights.

The election ended in a unique stalemate. Two sets of returns arrived from the three states yet in Radical hands. The Radicals claimed that Hayes had won, while Democrats insisted on a Tilden majority. The nineteen doubtful electoral votes (including one disputed Oregon elector) meant the difference between a one-vote Hayes margin and a clear Tilden sweep. Congress finally accepted the recommendation of a specially appointed commission to award all the disputed votes to Hayes, thereby making him president. The South, in turn, received a pledge from Hayes that all remaining federal troops would be removed from the three Radical states, that federal subsidies would be provided for a Southern transcontinental railroad then under construction, and that a Southerner would be appointed to the cabinet.

After Hayes took office, Radical rule promptly collapsed in the three remaining states.

The violence of new vigilante groups, such as the Knights of the Ku Klux Klan, contributed to the overthrow of Republican rule and the demise of Reconstruction. A secret, terrorist society, the Klan formed in 1867 to restore white supremacy by harassing Reconstructionists, intimidating black voters, forcing black officials into resignation, and depriving freedmen of their rights. The tactics of the Klan ranged from pressure, ostracism, and bribery, to arson, beatings, and murder. (Culver Pictures)

This so-called Compromise of 1877 marked the final surrender of the North's promise to defend black political and civil rights against the former white Confederates.

During the decades that followed, Democratic state governments defeated black efforts to participate in Southern politics. In every subsequent election fewer blacks voted.

Violence toward black people increased for the rest of the century. The great majority of Southern blacks farmed other people's lands as tenants or sharecroppers. They were forced into a subordinate place in Southern life, being neither slaves nor completely free persons.

Suggested Readings
Chapters 23-24

Sherman's March

Burke Davis, *Sherman's March* (1980); Lloyd Lewis, *Sherman, Fighting Prophet* (1932); K. P. Williams, *Lincoln Finds a General: A Military History of the Civil War* (4 vols., 1949–56); T. H. Williams, *McClellan, Sherman, and Grant* (1962).

The Civil War

Mark M. Boatner, III, *The Civil War Dictionary* (1959); Bruce Catton, *Centennial History of the Civil War* (3 vols., 1961–63); David Donald, ed., *Why the North Won the Civil War* (1960); Clement Eaton, *A History of the Southern Confederacy* (1954); Shelby Foote, *The Civil War* (3 vols., 1958–74); George Frederickson, *The Inner Civil War* (1965); Paul W. Gates, *Agriculture and the Civil War* (1965); David T. Gilchrust and W. David Lewis, eds., *Economic Change in the Civil War Era* (1965); Harold M. Hyman, *A More Perfect Union: The Impact of the Civil War and Reconstruction on the Constitution* (1973); Mary E. Massey, *Bonnet Brigades: American Women and the Civil War* (1966); Allan Nevins, *The War for the Union* (4 vols., 1959–71); Peter J. Parish, *The American Civil War* (1975); James M. McPherson, *The Negro's Civil War* (1965) and *The Struggle for Equality: Abolitionists and the Negro in the Civil War and Reconstruction* (1964); J. G. Randall and Richard Current, *Lincoln the President* (4 vols., 1945–55); J. G. Randall and David Donald, *The Civil War and Reconstruction* (2nd ed., 1961); Benjamin P. Thomas, *Abraham Lincoln* (1952); Emory Thomas, *The Confederacy as a Revolutionary Experience* (1971); Frank Vandiver, *Their Tattered Flags* (1970).

Reconstruction

W. R. Brock, *An American Crisis* (1963); Robert Cruden, *The Negro in Reconstruction* (1969); John Hope Franklin, *Reconstruction After the Civil War* (1962); Rembert W. Patrick, *The Reconstruction of the Nation* (1964); Kenneth M. Stampp, *The Era of Reconstruction, 1865–1877* (1965); Hans L. Trefousse, *Impeachment of a President* (1975); C. Vann Woodward, *Reunion and Reaction: The Compromise of 1877 and the End of Reconstruction* (1951).

In Congress, July 4, 1776. *The unanimous Declaration of the thirteen united States of America.*

When in the Course of human events, it becomes necessary for one people to dissolve the political bands which have connected them with another, and to assume among the powers of the earth, the separate and equal station to which the Laws of Nature and of Nature's God entitle them, a decent respect to the opinions of mankind requires that they should declare the causes which impel them to the separation. —

We hold these truths to be self-evident, that all men are created equal, that they are endowed by their Creator with certain unalienable Rights, that among these are Life, Liberty and the pursuit of Happiness. —

That to secure these rights, Governments are instituted among Men, deriving their just powers from the consent of the governed, —

That whenever any Form of Government becomes destructive of these ends, it is the Right of the People to alter or to abolish it, and to institute new Government, laying its foundation on such principles and organizing its powers in such form, as to them shall seem most likely to effect their Safety and Happiness. Prudence, indeed, will dictate that Governments long established should not be changed for light and transient causes; and accordingly all experience hath shown, that mankind are more disposed to suffer, while evils are sufferable, than to right themselves by abolishing the forms to which they are accustomed. But when a long train of abuses and usurpations, pursuing invariably the same Object evinces a design to reduce them under absolute Despotism, it is their right, it is their duty, to throw off such Government, and to provide new Guards for their future security. —

Such has been the patient sufferance of these Colonies; and such is now the necessity which constrains them to alter their former Systems of Government. The history of the present King of Great Britain is a history of repeated injuries and usurpations, all having in direct object the establishment of an absolute Tyranny over these States. To prove this, let Facts be submitted to a candid world. —

He has refused his Assent to Laws, the most wholesome and necessary for the public good. —

He has forbidden his Governors to pass Laws of immediate and pressing importance, unless suspended in their operation till his Assent should be obtained; and when so suspended, he has utterly neglected to attend to them. —

He has refused to pass other Laws for the accommodation of large districts of people, unless those people would relinquish the right of Representation in the Legislature, a right inestimable to them and formidable to tyrants only. —

He has called together legislative bodies at places unusual, uncomfortable, and distant from the depository of their public Records, for the sole purpose of fatiguing them into compliance with his measures. —

He has dissolved Representative Houses repeatedly, for opposing with manly firmness his invasions on the rights of the people. —

He has refused for a long time, after such dissolutions, to cause others to be elected; whereby the Legislative powers, incapable of Annihilation, have returned to the People at large for their exercise; the State remaining in the mean time exposed to all the dangers of invasion from without, and convulsions within. —

He has endeavoured to prevent the population of these States; for that purpose obstructing the Laws for Naturalization of Foreigners; refusing to pass others to encourage their migrations hither, and raising the conditions of new Appropriations of Lands. —

He has obstructed the Administration of Justice, by refusing his Assent to Laws for establishing Judiciary powers. —

He has made Judges dependent on his Will alone, for the tenure of their offices, and the amount and payment of their salaries. —

He has erected a multitude of New Offices, and sent hither swarms of Officers to harrass our people, and eat out their substance. —

He has kept among us in times of peace, Standing Armies without the Consent of our legislatures. —

He has affected to render the Military independent of and superior to the Civil power. —

He has combined with others to subject us to a jurisdiction foreign to our constitution, and unacknowledged by our laws; giving his Assent to their Acts of pretended Legislation: —

For quartering large bodies of armed troops among us: —

For protecting them, by a mock Trial, from punishment for any Murders which they should commit on the Inhabitants of these States: —

For cutting off our Trade with all parts of the world: —

For imposing Taxes on us without our Consent: —

For depriving us in many cases, of the benefits of Trial by Jury: —

For transporting us beyond Seas to be tried for pretended offences: —

For abolishing the free System of English Laws in a neighbouring Province, establishing therein an Arbitrary government, and enlarging its Boundaries so as to render it at once an example and fit instrument for introducing the same absolute rule in these Colonies: —

For taking away our Charters, abolishing our most valuable Laws, and altering fundamentally the Forms of our Governments: —

For suspending our own Legislatures, and declaring themselves invested with power to legislate for us in all cases whatsoever. —

He has abdicated Government here, by declaring us out of his Protection and waging War against us. —

He has plundered our seas, ravaged our Coasts, burnt our towns, and destroyed the lives of our people. —

He is at this time transporting large Armies of foreign Mercenaries to compleat the works of death, desolation and tyranny, already begun with circumstances of Cruelty & perfidy scarcely paral-leled in the most barbarous ages, and totally unworthy the Head of a civilized nation. —

He has constrained our fellow Citizens taken Captive on the high Seas to bear Arms against their Country, to become the executioners of their friends and Brethren, or to fall themselves by their Hands. —

He has excited domestic insurrections amongst us, and has endeavoured to bring on the inhabitants of our frontiers, the merciless Indian Savages, whose known rule of warfare, is an undistinguished destruction of all ages, sexes and conditions.

In every stage of these Oppressions We have Petitioned for Redress in the most humble terms: Our repeated Petitions have been answered only by repeated injury. A Prince, whose character is thus marked by every act which may define a Tyrant, is unfit to be the ruler of a free people.

Nor have We been wanting in attentions to our British brethren. We have warned them from time to time of attempts by their legislature to extend an unwarrantable jurisdiction over us. We have reminded them of the circumstances of our emigration and settlement here. We have appealed to their native justice and magnanimity, and we have conjured them by the ties of our common kindred to disavow these usurpations, which would inevitably interrupt our connections and correspondence. They too have been deaf to the voice of justice and of consanguinity. We must, therefore, acquiesce in the necessity, which denounces our Separation, and hold them, as we hold the rest of mankind, Enemies in War, in Peace Friends. —

We, therefore, the Representatives of the united States of America, in General Congress, Assembled, appealing to the Supreme Judge of the world for the rectitude of our intentions, do, in the Name, and by Authority of the good People of these Colonies, solemnly publish and declare, That these United Colonies are, and of Right ought to be, Free and Independent States; that they are absolved from all Allegiance to the British Crown, and that all political connection between them and the State of Great Britain, is and ought to be totally dissolved; and that as Free and Independent States they have full Power to levy War, conclude Peace, contract Alliances, establish Commerce, and to do all other Acts and Things which Independent States may of right do. —

And for the support of this Declaration, with a firm reliance on the protection of divine Providence, we mutually pledge to each other our Lives, our Fortunes and our sacred Honor.

John Hancock
(MASSACHUSETTS)

NEW HAMPSHIRE
Josiah Bartlett
William Whipple
Matthew Thornton

MASSACHUSETTS
Samuel Adams
John Adams
Robert Treat Paine
Elbridge Gerry

DELAWARE
Caesar Rodney
George Read
Thomas McKean

NEW YORK
William Floyd
Philip Livingston
Francis Lewis
Lewis Morris

NEW JERSEY
Richard Stockton
John Witherspoon
Francis Hopkinson
John Hart
Abraham Clark

NORTH CAROLINA
William Hooper
Joseph Hewes
John Penn

MARYLAND
Samuel Chase
William Paca
Thomas Stone
Charles Carroll
  of Carrollton

SOUTH CAROLINA
Edward Rutledge
Thomas Heywood, Jr.
Thomas Lynch, Jr.
Arthur Middleton

RHODE ISLAND
Stephen Hopkins
William Ellery

CONNECTICUT
Roger Sherman
Samuel Huntington
William Williams
Oliver Wolcott

PENNSYLVANIA
Robert Morris
Benjamin Rush
Benjamin Franklin
John Morton
George Clymer
James Smith
George Taylor
James Wilson
George Ross

VIRGINIA
George Wythe
Richard Henry Lee
Thomas Jefferson
Benjamin Harrison
Thomas Nelson, Jr.
Francis Lightfoot Lee
Carter Braxton

GEORGIA
Button Gwinnett
Lyman Hall
George Walton

The Constitution of the United States of America

The preamble establishes the principle of government by the people, and lists the six basic purposes of the Constitution.

W e the People of the United States, in Order to form a more perfect Union, establish Justice, insure domestic Tranquility, provide for the common defence, promote the general Welfare, and secure the Blessings of Liberty to ourselves and our Posterity, do ordain and establish this Constitution for the United States of America.

ARTICLE I • LEGISLATIVE DEPARTMENT

Section 1. All legislative Powers herein granted shall be vested in a Congress of the United States, which shall consist of a Senate and House of Representatives.

Representatives serve two-year terms. They are chosen in each state by those electors (that is, voters) who are qualified to vote for members of the lower house of their own state legislature.

Section 2. The House of Representatives shall be composed of Members chosen every second Year by the People of the several States, and the Electors in each State shall have the Qualifications requisite for Electors of the most numerous Branch of the State Legislature.

No Person shall be a Representative who shall not have attained to the Age of twenty-five Years, and been seven Years a Citizen of the United States, and who shall not, when elected, be an Inhabitant of that State in which he shall be chosen.

The number of representatives allotted to a state is determined by the size of its population. The 14th Amendment has made obsolete the reference to "all other persons"—that is, slaves.

A census must be taken every ten years to determine the number of representatives to which each state is entitled. There is now one representative for about every 470,000 persons.

Representatives and direct Taxes shall be apportioned among the several States which may be included within this Union, according to their respective Numbers, <u>which shall be determined by adding to the whole Number of free Persons, including those bound to Service for a Term of Years, and excluding Indians not taxed, three-fifths of all other Persons.</u> The actual Enumeration shall be made within three Years after the first Meeting of the Congress of the United States, and within every subsequent Term of ten Years, in such Manner as they shall by Law direct. The Number of Representatives shall not exceed one for every thirty Thousand, but each State shall have at Least one Representative; <u>and until such enumeration shall be made, the State of New Hampshire shall be entitled to chuse three, Massachusetts eight, Rhode Island and Providence Plantations one, Connecticut five, New York six, New Jersey four, Pennsylvania eight, Delaware one, Maryland six, Virginia ten, North Carolina five, South Carolina five, and Georgia three.</u>

Source: House Document #529. U.S. Government Printing Office, 1967. [NOTE: *The Constitution and the amendments are reprinted here in their original form. Portions that have been amended or superseded are underlined.*] *The words printed in the margins explains some of the more difficult passages.*

When vacancies happen in the Representation from any State, the Executive Authority thereof shall issue Writs of Election to fill such Vacancies.

The House of Representatives shall chuse their Speaker and other Officers; and shall have the sole Power of Impeachment.

"Executive authority" refers to the governor of a state.

The Speaker, chosen by and from the majority party, presides over the House. Impeachment is the act of bringing formal charges against an official. (See also Section 3.)

Section 3.   The Senate of the United States shall be composed of two Senators from each State, <u>chosen by the Legislature thereof,</u> for six Years; and each Senator shall have one Vote.

The 17th Amendment changed this method to direct election.

Immediately after they shall be assembled in Consequence of the first Election, they shall be divided as equally as may be into three Classes. The Seats of the Senators of the first Class shall be vacated at the Expiration of the second Year, of the second Class at the Expiration of the fourth Year, and of the third Class at the Expiration of the sixth Year, so that one third may be chosen every second Year; and if Vacancies happen by Resignation, or otherwise, <u>during the Recess of the Legislature of any State, the Executive thereof may make temporary Appointments until the next Meeting of the Legislature, which shall then fill such Vacancies.</u>

The 17th Amendment also provides that a state governor shall appoint a successor to fill a vacant Senate seat until a direct election is held.

No Person shall be a Senator who shall not have attained to the Age of thirty Years, and been nine Years a Citizen of the United States, and who shall not, when elected, be an Inhabitant of that State for which he shall be chosen.

The Vice President of the United States shall be President of the Senate, but shall have no Vote, unless they be equally divided.

The Vice President may cast a vote in the Senate only in order to break a tie.

The Senate shall chuse their other Officers, and also a President pro tempore, in the absence of the Vice President, or when he shall exercise the Office of President of the United States.

The president pro tempore of the Senate is a temporary officer; the Latin words mean "for the time being."

The Senate shall have the sole Power to try all Impeachments. When sitting for that Purpose, they shall be on Oath or Affirmation. When the President of the United States is tried, the Chief Justice shall preside: And no Person shall be convicted without the Concurrence of two thirds of the Members present.

Judgment in Cases of Impeachment shall not extend further than to removal from Office, and disqualification to hold and enjoy any Office of Honor, Trust or Profit under the United States: but the Party convicted shall nevertheless be liable and subject to Indictment, Trial, Judgment and Punishment, according to Law.

No President has ever been successfully impeached. In 1868 the Senate fell one vote short of the two-thirds majority needed to convict Andrew Johnson. Twelve other officials—ten federal judges, one senator, and one Secretary of War—have been impeached; four of the judges were convicted.

Section 4.   The Times, Places and Manner of holding Elections for Senators and Representatives, shall be prescribed in each State by the Legislature thereof; but the Congress may at any time by Law make or alter such Regulations, except as to the Place of chusing Senators.

Elections for Congress are held on the first Tuesday after the first Monday in November in even-numbered years.

The Congress shall assemble at least once in every Year, <u>and such Meeting shall be on the first Monday in December,</u> unless they shall by Law appoint a different Day.

The 20th Amendment designates January 3 as the opening of the congressional session.

Section 5.   Each House shall be the Judge of the Elections, Returns and Qualifications of its own Members, and a Majority of each shall constitute a Quorum to do Business; but a smaller number may adjourn from day to day, and may be authorized to compel the Attendance of absent Members, in such Manner, and under such Penalties as each House may provide.

Each House may determine the Rules of its Proceedings, punish its

Each house of Congress decides whether a member has been elected properly and is qualified to be seated. (A quorum is the minimum number of persons required to be present in order to conduct business.) The House once refused admittance to an

Members for disorderly Behavior, and, with the Concurrence of two thirds, expel a Member.

Each House shall keep a Journal of its Proceedings, and from time to time publish the same, excepting such Parts as may in their Judgment require Secrecy; and the Yeas and Nays of the Members of either House on any question shall, at the Desire of one fifth of those Present, be entered on the Journal.

Neither House, during the Session of Congress, shall, without the Consent of the other, adjourn for more than three days, nor to any other Place than that in which the two Houses shall be sitting.

elected representative who had been guilty of a crime. The Senate did likewise in the case of a candidate whose election campaign lent itself to "fraud and corruption."

Section 6. The Senators and Representatives shall receive a Compensation for their Services, to be ascertained by Law, and paid out of the Treasury of the United States. They shall in all Cases, except Treason, Felony and Breach of the Peace, be privileged from Arrest during their Attendance at the Session of their respective Houses, and in going to and returning from the same; and for any Speech or Debate in either House, they shall not be questioned in any other Place.

No Senator or Representative shall, during the Time for which he was elected, be appointed to any civil Office under the Authority of the United States, which shall have been created, or the Emoluments whereof shall have been encreased during such time; and no Person holding any Office under the United States, shall be a Member of either House during his Continuance in Office.

Congressmen have the power to fix their own salaries. Under the principle of congressional immunity, they cannot be sued or arrested for anything they say in a congressional debate. This provision enables them to speak freely.

This clause reinforces the principle of separation of powers by stating that, during his term of office, a member of Congress may not be appointed to a position in another branch of government. Nor may he resign and accept a position created during his term.

Section 7. All Bills for raising Revenue shall originate in the House of Representatives; but the Senate may propose or concur with Amendments as on other Bills.

Every Bill which shall have passed the House of Representatives and the Senate, shall, before it become a Law, be presented to the President of the United States; If he approve he shall sign it, but if not he shall return it, with his Objections to that House in which it shall have originated, who shall enter the Objections at large on their Journal, and proceed to reconsider it. If after such Reconsideration two thirds of that House shall agree to pass the Bill, it shall be sent, together with the Objections, to the other House, by which it shall likewise be reconsidered, and if approved by two thirds of that House, it shall become a Law. But in all such Cases the Votes of both Houses shall be determined by Yeas and Nays, and the Names of the Persons voting for and against the Bill shall be entered on the Journal of each House respectively. If any Bill shall not be returned by the President within ten Days (Sundays excepted) after it shall have been presented to him, the Same shall be a Law, in like Manner as if he had signed it, unless the Congress by their Adjournment prevent its Return, in which Case it shall not be a Law.

Every Order, Resolution, or Vote to which the Concurrence of the Senate and House of Representatives may be necessary (except on a question of Adjournment) shall be presented to the President of the United States; and before the Same shall take Effect, shall be approved by him, or being disapproved by him, shall be repassed by two thirds of the Senate and House of Representatives, according to the Rules and Limitations prescribed in the Case of a Bill.

The House initiates tax bills but the Senate may propose changes in them.

By returning a bill unsigned to the house in which it originated, the President exercises a veto. A two-thirds majority in both houses can override the veto. If the President receives a bill within the last ten days of a session and does not sign it, the measure dies by pocket veto. Merely by keeping the bill in his pocket, so to speak, the president effects a veto.

The same process of approval or disapproval by the President is applied to resolutions and other matters passed by both houses (except adjournment).

Section 8. The Congress shall have Power to lay and collect Taxes, Duties, Imposts and Excises, to pay the Debts and provide for the common Defence and general Welfare of the United States; but all Duties, Imposts and Excises shall be uniform throughout the United States;

To borrow money on the credit of the United States;

To regulate Commerce with foreign Nations, and among the several States, and with the Indian Tribes;

These are the delegated, or enumerated, powers of Congress.

Duties are taxes on imported goods; excises are taxes on goods manufactured, sold, or consumed within the country. Imposts is a general term including both duties and excise taxes.

To establish an uniform Rule of Naturalization, and uniform Laws on the subject of Bankruptcies throughout the United States;

To coin Money, regulate the Value thereof, and of foreign Coin, and fix the Standard of Weights and Measures;

To provide for the Punishment of counterfeiting the Securities and current Coin of the United States;

To establish Post Offices and post Roads;

To promote the Progress of Science and useful Arts, by securing for limited Times to Authors and Inventors the exclusive Right to their respective Writings and Discoveries;

To constitute Tribunals inferior to the supreme Court;

To define and punish Piracies and Felonies committed on the high Seas, and Offenses against the Law of Nations;

To declare War, grant Letters of Marque and Reprisal, and make Rules concerning Captures on Land and Water;

To raise and support Armies, but no Appropriation of Money to that Use shall be for a longer Term than two Years;

To provide and maintain a Navy;

To make Rules for the Government and Regulation of the land and naval Forces;

To provide for calling forth the Militia to execute the Laws of the Union, suppress Insurrections and repel Invasions;

To provide for organizing, arming, and disciplining the Militia, and for governing such Part of them as may be employed in the Service of the United States, reserving to the States respectively, the Appointment of the Officers, and the Authority of training the Militia according to the discipline prescribed by Congress;

To exercise exclusive Legislation in all Cases whatsoever, over such District (not exceeding ten Miles square) as may, by Cession of particular States, and the acceptance of Congress, become the Seat of the Government of the United States, and to exercise like Authority over all Places purchased by the Consent of the Legislature of the State in which the Same shall be, for the Erection of Forts, Magazines, Arsenals, dock-Yards, and other needful Buildings;—And

To make all Laws which shall be necessary and proper for carrying into Execution the foregoing Powers, and all other Powers vested by this Constitution in the Government of the United States, or in any Department or Officer thereof.

Section 9. The Migration or Importation of such Persons as any of the States now existing shall think proper to admit, shall not be prohibited by the Congress prior to the Year one thousand eight hundred and eight, but a tax or duty may be imposed on such Importation, not exceeding ten dollars for each Person.

The privilege of the Writ of Habeas Corpus shall not be suspended unless when in Cases of Rebellion or Invasion the public Safety may require it.

No bill of Attainder or ex post facto Law shall be passed.

No capitation, or other direct, Tax shall be laid, unless in Proportion to the Census or Enumeration herein before directed to be taken.

No Tax or Duty shall be laid on Articles exported from any State.

No Preference shall be given by any Regulation of Commerce or Revenue to the Ports of one State over those of another; nor shall Vessels bound to, or from, one State, be obliged to enter, clear, or pay Duties in another.

No Money shall be drawn from the Treasury, but in Consequence of Appropriations made by Law; and a regular Statement and Account of the Receipts and Expenditures of all public Money shall be published from time to time.

No Title of Nobility shall be granted by the United States: And no Person holding any Office of Profit or Trust under them, shall, without the Consent of the Congress, accept of any present, Emolument, Office, or Title, of any kind whatever, from any King, Prince, or foreign State.

Naturalization is the process by which an alien becomes a citizen.

Government securities include savings bonds and other notes.

Authors' and inventors' rights are protected by copyright and patent laws.

Congress may establish lower federal courts.

Only Congress may declare war. Letters of marque and reprisal grant merchant ships permission to attack enemy vessels.

Militia refers to national guard units, which may become part of the United States Army during an emergency. Congress aids the states in maintaining their national guard units.

This clause gives Congress the power to govern what became the District of Columbia, as well as other federal sites.

Known as the elastic clause, this provision enables Congress to exercise many powers not specifically granted to it by the Constitution.

This clause concerns the slave trade, which Congress did ban in 1808.

The writ of habeas corpus permits a prisoner to appear before a judge to inquire into the legality of his or her detention.

A bill of attainder is an act of legislation that declares a person guilty of a crime and punishes him or her without a trial. An ex post facto law punishes a person for an act that was legal when performed but later declared illegal.

The object of Clause 4 was to bar direct (per person) taxation of slaves for the purpose of abolishing slavery. The 16th Amendment modified this provision by giving Congress the power to tax personal income.

Section 10. No State shall enter into any Treaty, Alliance, or Confederation; grant Letters of Marque and Reprisal; coin Money; emit Bills of Credit; make any Thing but gold and silver Coin a Tender in Payment of Debts; pass any Bill of Attainder, ex post facto Law, or Law impairing the Obligation of Contracts, or grant any Title of Nobility.

No State shall, without the Consent of the Congress, lay any Imposts or Duties on Imports or Exports, except what may be absolutely necessary for executing its inspection Laws: and the net Produce of all Duties and Imposts, laid by any State on Imports or Exports, shall be for the Use of the Treasury of the United States; and all such Laws shall be subject to the Revision and Controul of the Congress.

No State shall, without the Consent of Congress, lay any duty of Tonnage, keep Troops, or Ships of War in time of Peace, enter into any Agreement or Compact with another State, or with a foreign Power, or engage in War, unless actually invaded, or in such imminent Danger as will not admit of delay.

ARTICLE II • EXECUTIVE DEPARTMENT

Section 1. The executive Power shall be vested in a President of the United States of America. He shall hold his Office during the Term of four Years, and, together with the Vice President, chosen for the same Term, be elected, as follows.

Each State shall appoint, in such Manner as the Legislature thereof may direct, a Number of Electors, equal to the whole Number of Senators and Representatives to which the State may be entitled in the Congress: but no Senator or Representative, or Person holding an Office of Trust or Profit under the United States, shall be appointed an Elector.

The Electors shall meet in their respective States, and vote by Ballot for two persons, of whom one at least shall not be an Inhabitant of the same State with themselves. And they shall make a List of all the Persons voted for, and of the Number of Votes for each; which List they shall sign and certify, and transmit sealed to the Seat of the Government of the United States, directed to the President of the Senate. The President of the Senate shall, in the Presence of the Senate and House of Representatives, open all the Certificates, and the Votes shall then be counted. The Person having the greatest Number of Votes shall be the President, if such Number be a Majority of the whole Number of Electors appointed; and if there be more than one who have such Majority, and have an equal Number of Votes, then the House of Representatives shall immediately chuse by Ballot one of them for President; and if no Person have a Majority, then from the five highest on the List the said House shall in like Manner chuse the President. But in chusing the President, the Votes shall be taken by States, the Representation from each State having one Vote; a quorum for this Purpose shall consist of a Member or Members from two thirds of the States, and a Majority of all the States shall be necessary to a Choice. In every Case, after the Choice of the President, the Person having the greatest Number of Votes of the Electors shall be the Vice President. But if there should remain two or more who have equal Votes, the Senate shall chuse from them by Ballot the Vice President.

The Congress may determine the Time of chusing the Electors, and the Day on which they shall give their Votes; which Day shall be the same throughout the United States.

No person except a natural born Citizen, or a Citizen of the United States, at the time of the Adoption of this Constitution, shall be eligible to the Office of President; neither shall any Person be eligible to that Office who shall not have attained to the Age of Thirty-five Years, and been fourteen Years a Resident within the United States.

In Case of the Removal of the President from Office, or of his Death, Resignation, or Inability to discharge the Powers and Duties of the said Office, the same shall devolve on the Vice-President, and the Congress may by Law provide for the Case of Removal, Death, Resignation or Inability, both of the President and the Vice President, declaring what Officer shall then act as President, and such Officer shall act accordingly, until the Disability be removed, or a President shall be elected.

The President shall, at stated Times, receive for his Services, a Compensation, which shall neither be encreased nor diminished during the Period for which he shall have been elected, and he shall not receive within that Period any other Emolument from the United States, or any of them.

Before he enter on the Execution of his Office, he shall take the following Oath or Affirmation: — "I do solemnly swear (or affirm) that I will faithfully execute the Office of the President of the United States, and will to the best of my Ability, preserve, protect and defend the Constitution of the United States."

The Vice President is next in line for the presidency. A federal law passed in 1947 determined the order of presidential succession as follows: (1) Speaker of the House; (2) president pro tempore of the Senate; and (3) Cabinet officers in order in which their departments were created. (So far, death and resignation have been the only circumstances under which a presidential term has been cut short.) This clause has been amplified by the 25th Amendment.

Section 2. The President shall be Commander in Chief of the Army and Navy of the United States, and of the Militia of the several States, when called into the actual Service of the United States; he may require the Opinion in writing, of the principal Officer in each of the executive Departments, upon any subject relating to the Duties of their respective Offices, and he shall have Power to Grant Reprieves and Pardons for Offenses against the United States, except in Cases of Impeachment.

This clause suggests written communication between the President and "the principal officer in each of the executive departments." As it developed, these officials comprise the Cabinet—whose members are chosen, and may be replaced, by the President.

He shall have Power, by and with the Advice and Consent of the Senate, to make Treaties, provided two thirds of the Senators present concur; and he shall nominate, and by and with the Advice and Consent of the Senate shall appoint Ambassadors, other public Ministers and Consuls, Judges of the supreme Court, and all other Officers of the United States, whose Appointments are not herein otherwise provided for, and which shall be established by Law; but the Congress may by Law vest the Appointment of such inferior Officers, as they think proper, in the President alone, in the Courts of Law, or in the Heads of Departments.

Senate approval is required for treaties and presidential appointments.

The President shall have Power to fill up all Vacancies that may happen during the Recess of the Senate, by granting Commissions which shall expire at the End of their next Session.

Without the consent of the Senate, the President may appoint officials only on a temporary basis.

Section 3. He shall from time to time give to the Congress Information of the State of the Union, and recommend to their Consideration such Measures as he shall judge necessary and expedient; he may, on extraordinary Occasions, convene both Houses, or either of them, and in Case of Disagreement between them, with Respect to the Time of Adjournment, he may adjourn them to such Time as he shall think proper; he shall receive Ambassadors and other public Ministers; he shall take Care that the Laws be faithfully executed, and shall Commission all the Officers of the United States.

The President delivers a "State of the Union" message at the opening of each session of Congress. Woodrow Wilson was the first President since John Adams to read his messages in person. Franklin D. Roosevelt and his successors followed Wilson's example.

Section 4. The President, Vice President and all civil Officers of the United States, shall be removed from Office on Impeachment for, and Conviction of, Treason, Bribery, or other high Crimes and Misdemeanors.

ARTICLE III • JUDICIAL DEPARTMENT

Section 1. The judicial Power of the United States, shall be vested in one supreme Court, and in such inferior Courts as the Congress may from time to time ordain and establish. The Judges, both of the supreme and inferior Courts, shall hold their Offices during good Behaviour, and shall, at stated Times, receive for their Services, a Compensation, which shall not be diminished during their Continuance in Office.

Federal judges hold office for life and may not have their salaries lowered while in office. These provisions are intended to keep the federal bench independent of political pressure.

Section 2. The judicial Power shall extend to all Cases, in Law and Equity, arising under this Constitution, the Laws of the United States, and Treaties made, or which shall be made, under their Authority; — to all Cases affecting Ambassadors, other public Ministers and Consuls; — to all Cases of admiralty and maritime Jurisdiction; — to Controversies to which the United States shall be a Party; — to Controversies between two or more States; — between a State and Citizens of another State; — between Citizens of different States; — between Citizens of the same State claiming Lands under Grants of different States, and between a State, or the Citizens thereof, and foreign States, Citizens or Subjects.

This clause describes the types of cases that may be heard in federal courts.

The 11th Amendment prevents a citizen from suing a state in a federal court.

In all Cases affecting Ambassadors, other public Ministers and Consuls, and those in which a State shall be Party, the supreme Court shall have original Jurisdiction. In all the other Cases before mentioned, the supreme Court shall have appellate Jurisdiction, both as to Law and Fact, with such Exceptions, and under such Regulations as the Congress shall make.

The Supreme Court handles certain cases directly. It may also review cases handled by lower courts, but Congress in some cases may withhold the right to appeal to the highest court, or limit appeal by setting various conditions.

The trial of all Crimes, except in Cases of Impeachment, shall be by Jury; and such Trial shall be held in the State where the said Crimes shall have been committed; but when not committed within any State, the Trial shall be at such Place or Places as the Congress may by Law have directed.

The 6th Amendment strengthens this clause on trial procedure.

Section 3. Treason against the United States, shall consist only in levying War against them, or in adhering to their Enemies, giving them Aid and Comfort. No Person shall be convicted of Treason unless on the Testimony of two Witnesses to the same overt Act, or on Confession in open Court.

Treason is rigorously defined. A person can be convicted only if two witnesses testify to the same obvious act, or if he confesses in court.

The Congress shall have Power to declare the Punishment of Treason, but no Attainder of Treason shall work Corruption of Blood, or Forfeiture except during the Life of the Person attainted.

Punishment for treason extends only to the person convicted, not to his or her descendants. ("Corruption of blood" means that the heirs of a convicted person are deprived of certain rights.)

ARTICLE IV • RELATIONS AMONG THE STATES

Section 1. Full Faith and Credit shall be given in each State to the public Acts, Records, and judicial Proceedings of every other State. And the Congress may by general Laws prescribe the Manner in which such Acts, Records and Proceedings shall be proved, and the Effect thereof.

States must honor each other's laws, court decisions, and records (for example, birth, marriage, and death certificates).

Section 2. The Citizens of each State shall be entitled to all Privileges and Immunities of Citizens in the several States.

Each state must respect the rights of citizens of other states.

A Person charged in any State with Treason, Felony, or other Crime, who shall flee from Justice, and be found in another State, shall on demand of the executive Authority of the State from which he fled, be delivered up, to be removed to the State having Jurisdiction of the Crime.

The process of returning a person accused of a crime to the governmental authority (in this case a state) from which he or she has fled is called extradition.

No Person held in Service or Labour in one State, under the Laws thereof, escaping into another, shall, in Consequence of any Law or Regulation therein, be discharged from such Service or Labour, but shall be delivered up on Claim of the Party to whom such Service or Labour may be due.

The 13th Amendment, which abolished slavery, makes this clause obsolete.

Section 3. New States may be admitted by the Congress into this Union; but no new State shall be formed or erected within the Jurisdiction of any other State; nor any State be formed by the Junction of two or more States, or parts of States, without the Consent of the Legislatures of the States concerned as well as of the Congress.

The Congress shall have Power to dispose of and make all needful Rules and Regulations respecting the Territory or other Property belonging to the United States; and nothing in this Constitution shall be so construed as to Prejudice any Claims of the United States, or of any particular State.

A new state may not be created by dividing or joining existing states unless approved by the legislatures of the states affected and by Congress. An exception to the provision forbidding the division of a state occurred during the Civil War. In 1863 West Virginia was formed out of the western region of Virginia.

Section 4. The United States shall guarantee to every State in this Union a Republican Form of Government, and shall protect each of them against Invasion; and on Application of the Legislature, or of the Executive (when the Legislature cannot be convened) against domestic Violence.

A republican form of government is one in which citizens choose representatives to govern them. The federal government must protect a state against invasion and, if state authorities request it, against violence within a state.

ARTICLE V • AMENDING THE CONSTITUTION

The Congress, whenever two thirds of both Houses shall deem it necessary, shall propose Amendments to this Constitution, or, on the Application of the Legislatures of two thirds of the several States, shall call a Convention for proposing Amendments, which, in either Case, shall be valid to all Intents and Purposes, as part of this Constitution, when ratified by the Legislatures of three fourths of the several States, or by Conventions in three fourths thereof, as the one or the other Mode of Ratification may be proposed by the Congress: Provided that no Amendment which may be made prior to the Year One thousand eight hundred and eight shall in any Manner affect the first and fourth Clauses in the Ninth Section of the first Article; and that no State, without its Consent, shall be deprived of its equal Suffrage in the Senate.

An amendment to the Constitution can be proposed (a) by Congress, with a two-thirds vote of both houses, or (b) by a convention called by Congress when two-thirds of the state legislatures request it. An amendment is ratified (a) by three-fourths of the state legislatures, or (b) by conventions in three-fourths of the states. The twofold procedure of proposal and ratification reflects the seriousness with which the framers of the Constitution regarded amendments. Over 6,900 amendments have been proposed; only 26 have been ratified.

ARTICLE VI • GENERAL PROVISIONS

All Debts contracted and Engagements entered into, before the Adoption of this Constitution, shall be as valid against the United States under this Constitution, as under the Confederation.

This Constitution, and the Laws of the United States which shall be made in Pursuance thereof; and all Treaties made, or which shall be made, under the Authority of the United States, shall be the supreme Law of the Land; and the Judges in every State shall be bound thereby, any Thing in the Constitution or Laws of any State to the Contrary notwithstanding.

The supremacy clause means that if a federal and a state law conflict, the federal law prevails.

The Senators and Representatives before mentioned, and the Members of the several State Legislatures, and all executive and judicial Officers, both of the United States and of the several States, shall be bound by Oath or Affirmation, to support this Constitution; but no religious Test shall ever be required as a Qualification to any Office or public Trust under the United States.

Religion may not be a condition for holding public office.

ARTICLE VII • RATIFICATION

The Constitution would become the law of the land upon the approval of nine states.

The Ratification of the Conventions of nine States shall be sufficient for the Establishment of this Constitution between the States so ratifying the Same.

DONE in Convention by the Unanimous Consent of the States present the Seventeenth Day of September in the Year of our Lord one thousand seven hundred and eighty-seven and of the Independence of the United States of America the Twelfth. In Witness whereof We have hereunto subscribed our Names.

G⁰ Washington
Presid* and deputy from
VIRGINIA

Attest: *William Jackson,* Secretary

DELAWARE
Geo: Read
Gunning Bedford, jun
John Dickinson
Richard Bassett
Jaco: Broom

MARYLAND
James McHenry
Dan: of St Thos Jenifer
Danl Carroll

VIRGINIA
John Blair
James Madison Jr.

NORTH CAROLINA
Wm Blount
Richd Dobbs Spaight
Hu Williamson

SOUTH CAROLINA
J. Rutledge
Charles Cotesworth
Pinckney
Charles Pinckney
Pierce Butler

GEORGIA
William Few
Abr Baldwin

NEW HAMPSHIRE
John Langdon
Nicholas Gilman

MASSACHUSETTS
Nathaniel Gorham
Rufus King

CONNECTICUT
Wm Saml Johnson
Roger Sherman

NEW YORK
Alexander Hamilton

NEW JERSEY
Wil: Livingston
David Brearley
Wm Paterson
Jona: Dayton

PENNSYLVANIA
B Franklin
Thomas Mifflin
Robt. Morris
Geo. Clymer
Thos. FitzSimons
Jared Ingersoll
James Wilson
Gouv Morris

AMENDMENT I ● (1791)

Congress shall make no law respecting an establishment of religion, or prohibiting the free exercise thereof: or abridging the freedom of speech, or of the press; or the right of the people peaceably to assemble, and to petition the Government for a redress of grievances.

Establishes freedom of religion, speech, and the press; gives citizens the rights of assembly and petition.

AMENDMENT II ● (1791)

A well regulated Militia, being necessary to the security of a free State, the right of the people to keep and bear Arms, shall not be infringed.

States have the right to maintain a militia.

AMENDMENT III ● (1791)

No Soldier shall, in time of peace, be quartered in any house, without the consent of the Owner, nor in time of war, but in a manner to be prescribed by law.

Limits the army's right to quarter soldiers in private homes.

AMENDMENT IV ● (1791)

The right of the people to be secure in their persons, houses, papers, and effects, against unreasonable searches and seizures, shall not be violated, and no Warrants shall issue, but upon probable cause, supported by Oath or affirmation, and particularly describing the place to be searched, and the persons or things to be seized.

Search warrants are required as a guarantee of a citizen's right to privacy.

AMENDMENT V ● (1791)

No person shall be held to answer for a capital, or otherwise infamous crime, unless on a presentment or indictment of a Grand Jury, except in cases arising in the land or naval forces, or in the Militia, when in actual service in time of War or public danger; nor shall any person be subject for the same offence to be twice put in jeopardy of life or limb; nor shall be compelled in any criminal case to be a witness against himself, nor be deprived of life, liberty, or property, without due process of law; nor shall private property be taken for public use, without just compensation.

To be prosecuted for a serious crime, a person must first be accused (indicted) by a grand jury. No one can be tried twice for the same crime (double jeopardy). Nor can a person be forced into self-incrimination by testifying against himself or herself.

[*The date following each amendment number is the year of ratification.*]

AMENDMENT VI • (1791)

Guarantees a defendant's right to be tried without delay and to face witnesses testifying for the other side.

In all criminal prosecutions, the accused shall enjoy the right to a speedy and public trial, by an impartial jury of the State and district wherein the crime shall have been committed, which district shall have been previously ascertained by law, and to be informed of the nature and cause of the accusation; to be confronted with the witnesses against him; to have compulsory process for obtaining witnesses in his favor, and to have the Assistance of Counsel for his defence.

AMENDMENT VII • (1791)

A jury trial is guaranteed in federal civil suits involving more than twenty dollars.

In suits at common law, where the value in controversy shall exceed twenty dollars, the right of trial by jury shall be preserved, and no fact tried by a jury, shall be otherwise reexamined in any Court of the United States, than according to the rules of the common law.

AMENDMENT VIII • (1791)

Excessive bail shall not be required, nor excessive fines imposed, nor cruel and unusual punishments inflicted.

AMENDMENT IX • (1791)

The listing of specific rights in the Constitution does not mean that others are not protected.

The enumeration in the Constitution, of certain rights, shall not be construed to deny or disparage others retained by the people.

AMENDMENT X • (1791)

Limits the federal government to its specific powers. Powers not prohibited the states by the Constitution may be exercised by them.

The powers not delegated to the United States by the Constitution, nor prohibited by it to the States, are reserved to the States respectively, or to the people.

AMENDMENT XI • (1798)

A state cannot be sued by a citizen of another state in a federal court. Such a case can be tried only in the courts of the state being sued.

The Judicial power of the United States shall not be construed to extend to any suit in law or equity, commenced or prosecuted against one of the United States by Citizens of another State, or by Citizens or Subjects of any Foreign State.

AMENDMENT XII • (1804)

Revises the process by which the President and Vice President were elected (see Article II, Section 1, Clause 3). The major change requires electors to cast separate ballots for President and Vice President. If none of the presidential candidates obtains a majority vote, the House of Representatives—with each state having one vote—chooses a President from the three candidates having the highest number of votes. If no vice

The Electors shall meet in their respective states and vote by ballot for President and Vice-President, one of whom, at least, shall not be an inhabitant of the same state with themselves; they shall name in their ballots the person voted for as President, and in distinct ballots the person voted for as Vice-President, and they shall make distinct lists of all persons voted for as President, and of all persons voted for as Vice-President, and of the number of votes for each, which lists they shall sign and certify, and transmit sealed to the seat of the government of the United States, directed to the President of the Senate;—The President of the Senate shall, in presence of the Senate and House of Representatives, open all the certificates and the votes shall then be counted;—The person having the greatest number of votes for President, shall be the President, if such number be a majority of the whole number of Electors appointed; and if no person have such majority, then from the persons having the highest numbers not exceeding three on the list of those voted for as President, the House of Representatives shall choose immediately, by ballot, the President. But in choosing the President, the votes shall be taken by states, the representation from each state having one vote; a quorum for this purpose shall consist of a member or members from two-thirds of the states, and a majority of all the states shall be necessary to a choice. <u>And if the House of Representatives shall not choose a President whenever the right of choice shall devolve upon them, before the fourth day of March next following, then the Vice-President shall act as President, as in the case of the death or other constitutional disability of the President.</u> — The person having the greatest number of votes as Vice-President, shall be the Vice-President, if such number be a majority of the whole number of Electors appointed, and if no person have a majority, then from the two highest numbers on the list, the Senate shall choose the Vice-President; a quorum for the purpose shall consist of two-thirds of the whole number of Senators, and a majority of the whole number shall be necessary to a choice. But no person constitutionally ineligible to the office of President shall be eligible to that of Vice-President of the United States.

presidential candidate wins a majority, the Senate chooses from the two candidates having the highest number of votes. The portion underlined was superseded by Section 3 of the 20th Amendment.

AMENDMENT XIII • (1865)

Section 1. Neither slavery nor involuntary servitude, except as a punishment for crime whereof the party shall have been duly convicted, shall exist within the United States, or any place subject to their jurisdiction.

Abolishes slavery.

Section 2. Congress shall have power to enforce this article by appropriate legislation.

AMENDMENT XIV • (1868)

Section 1. All persons born or naturalized in the United States, and subject to the jurisdiction thereof, are citizens of the United States and of the State wherein they reside. No State shall make or enforce any law which shall abridge the privileges or immunities of citizens of the United States; nor shall any State deprive any person of life, liberty, or property, without due process of law; nor deny any person within its jurisdiction the equal protection of the laws.

This section confers full civil rights on former slaves. Supreme Court decisions have interpreted the language of Section 1 to mean that the states, as well as the federal government, are bound by the Bill of Rights.

Section 2. Representatives shall be apportioned among the several States according to their respective numbers, counting the whole number of persons in each State, excluding Indians not taxed. But when the right to vote at any election for the choice of electors for President and Vice-President of the United States, Representatives in Congress, the Executive and Judicial officers of a State, or the members of the Legislature thereof, is denied to any of the male inhabitants of such State, being <u>twenty-one</u> years of age, and citizens of the United States, or in any way abridged, except for participation in rebellion, or other crime, the basis of representation therein shall be reduced in the proportion which the number of such male citizens shall bear to the whole number of male citizens twenty-one years of age in such State.

A penalty of a reduction in congressional representation shall be applied to any state that refuses to give all adult male citizens the right to vote in federal elections. This section has never been applied. The portion underlined was superseded by Section 1 of the 26th Amendment. (This section has also been amplified by the 19th Amendment.)

Section 3. No person shall be a Senator or Representative in Congress, or elector of President and Vice-President, or hold any office, civil or military, under the United States, or under any State, who, having previously taken an oath, as a member of Congress, or as an officer of the United States, or as a member of any State legislature, or as an executive or judicial officer of any State, to support the Constitution of the United States, shall have engaged in insurrection or rebellion against the same, or given aid or comfort to the enemies thereof. But Congress may by a vote of two-thirds of each House, remove such disability.

Any former federal or state official who served the Confederacy during the Civil War could not become a federal official again unless Congress voted otherwise.

Section 4. The validity of the public debt of the United States, authorized by law, including debts incurred for payment of pensions and bounties for services in suppressing insurrection or rebellion, shall not be questioned. But neither the United States nor any State shall assume or pay any debt or obligation incurred in aid of insurrection or rebellion against the Unted States, or any claim for the loss or emancipation of any slave; but all such debts, obligations and claims shall be held illegal and void.

Section 5. The Congress shall have power to enforce, by appropriate legislation, the provisions of this article.

AMENDMENT XV ● (1870)

Section 1. The right of citizens of the United States to vote shall not be denied or abridged by the United States or by any State on account of race, color, or previous condition of servitude.

Section 2. The Congress shall have power to enforce this article by appropriate legislation.

AMENDMENT XVI ● (1913)

The Congress shall have power to lay and collect taxes on incomes, from whatever source derived, without apportionment among the several States, and without regard to any census or enumeration.

AMENDMENT XVII ● (1913)

The Senate of the United States shall be composed of two Senators from each State, elected by the people thereof, for six years; and each Senator shall have one vote. The electors in each State shall have the qualifications requisite for electors of the most numerous branch of the State legislature.

When vacancies happen in the representation of any State in the Senate, the executive authority of such State shall issue writs of election to fill such vacancies: *Provided,* That the legislature of any State may empower the executive thereof to make temporary appointments until the people fill the vacancies by election as the legislature may direct.

This amendment shall not be so construed as to affect the election or term of any Senator chosen before it becomes valid as part of the Constitution.

AMENDMENT XVIII ● (1919)

Section 1. After one year from the ratification of this article, the manufacture, sale, or transportation of intoxicating liquors within, the importation thereof into, or the exportation thereof from the United States and all territory subject to the jurisdiction thereof for beverage purposes is hereby prohibited.

Section 2. The Congress and the several States shall have concurrent power to enforce this article by appropriate legislation.

Section 3. This article shall be inoperative unless it shall have been ratified as an amendment to the Constitution by the legislatures of the several States, as provided in the Constitution, within seven years from the date of the submission hereof to the States by the Congress.

AMENDMENT XIX • (1920)

The right of citizens of the United States to vote shall not be denied or abridged by the United States or by any State on account of sex.

Congress shall have power to enforce this article by appropriate legislation.

Gives women the right to vote.

AMENDMENT XX • (1933)

Section 1. The terms of the President and Vice-President shall end at noon on the 20th day of January, and the terms of Senators and Representatives at noon on the 3d day of January, of the years in which such terms would have ended if this article had not been ratified; and the terms of their successors shall then begin.

The "lame duck" amendment allows the President to take office on January 20, and members of Congress on January 3. The purpose of the amendment is to reduce the term in office of defeated incumbents – known as "lame ducks."

Section 2. The Congress shall assemble at least once in every year, and such meeting shall begin at noon on the 3d day of January, unless they shall by law appoint a different day.

Section 3. If, at the time fixed for the beginning of the term of the President, the President elect shall have died, the Vice-President elect shall become President. If a President shall not have been chosen before the time fixed for the beginning of his term, or if the President elect shall have failed to qualify, then the Vice-President elect shall act as President until a President shall have qualified; and the Congress may by law provide for the case wherein neither a President elect nor a Vice-President elect shall have qualified, declaring who shall then act as President, or the manner in which one who is to act shall be selected, and such person shall act accordingly until a President or Vice-President shall have qualified.

Section 4. The Congress may by law provide for the case of the death of any of the persons from whom the House of Representatives may choose a President whenever the right of choice shall have devolved upon them, and for the case of the death of any of the persons from whom the Senate may choose a Vice-President whenever the right of choice shall have devolved upon them.

Section 5. Sections 1 and 2 shall take effect on the 15th day of October following the ratification of this article.

Section 6. This article shall be inoperative unless it shall have been ratified as an amendment to the Constitution by the legislatures of three-fourths of the several States within seven years from the date of its submission.

AMENDMENT XXI • (1933)

Section 1. The eighteenth article of amendment to the Constitution of the United States is hereby repealed.

Repeals the 18th Amendment.

Section 2. The transportation or importation into any State, Territory, or possession of the United States for delivery or use therein of intoxicating liquors, in violation of the laws thereof, is hereby prohibited.

States may pass prohibition laws.

Section 3. This article shall be inoperative unless it shall have been ratified as an amendment to the Constitution by conventions in the several States, as provided in the Constitution, within seven years from the date of the submission hereof to the States by the Congress.

AMENDMENT XXII • (1951)

Limits a President to only two full terms plus two years of a previous President's term.

Section 1. No person shall be elected to the office of the President more than twice, and no person who has held the office of President, or acted as President, for more than two years of a term to which some other person was elected President shall be elected to the office of the President more than once. But this Article shall not apply to any person holding the office of President when this Article was proposed by the Congress, and shall not prevent any person who may be holding the office of President, or acting as President, during the term within which this Article becomes operative from holding the office of President or acting as President during the remainder of such term.

Section 2. This article shall be inoperative unless it shall have been ratified as an amendment to the Constitution by the legislatures of three-fourths of the several States within seven years from the date of its submission to the States by the Congress.

AMENDMENT XXIII • (1961)

By giving the District of Columbia three electoral votes, Congress enabled its residents to vote for President and Vice President.

Section 1. The District constituting the seat of Government of the United States shall appoint in such manner as the Congress may direct:

A number of electors of President and Vice-President equal to the whole number of Senators and Representatives in Congress to which the District would be entitled if it were a State, but in no event more than the least populous State; they shall be in addition to those appointed by the States, but they shall be considered, for the purposes of the election of President and Vice-President, to be electors appointed by a State; and they shall meet in the District and perform such duties as provided by the twelfth article of amendment.

Section 2. The Congress shall have power to enforce this article by appropriate legislation.

AMENDMENT XXIV • (1964)

Forbids the use of a poll tax as a requirement for voting in federal elections.

Section 1. The right of citizens of the United States to vote in any primary or other election for President or Vice-President, for electors for President or Vice-President, or for Senator or Representative in Congress, shall not be denied or abridged by the United States or any State by reason of failure to pay any poll tax or other tax.

Section 2. The Congress shall have power to enforce this article by appropriate legislation.

AMENDMENT XXV • (1967)

Outlines the procedure to be followed in case of presidential disability.

Section 1. In case of the removal of the President from office or of his death or resignation, the Vice-President shall become President.

Section 2. Whenever there is a vacancy in the office of the Vice-President, the President shall nominate a Vice-President who shall take office upon confirmation by a majority vote of both Houses of Congress.

Section 3. Whenever the President transmits to the President pro tempore of the Senate and the Speaker of the House of Representatives his written declaration that he is unable to discharge the powers and duties of his office, and until he transmits to them a written declaration to the contrary, such powers and duties shall be discharged by the Vice-President as Acting President.

Section 4. Whenever the Vice-President and a majority of either the principal officers of the executive departments or of such other body as Congress may by law provide, transmit to the President pro tempore of the Senate and the Speaker of the House of Representatives their written declaration that the President is unable to discharge the powers and duties of his office, the Vice-President shall immediately assume the powers and duties of the office as Acting President.

Thereafter, when the President transmits to the President pro tempore of the Senate and the Speaker of the House of Representatives his written declaration that no inability exists, he shall resume the powers and duties of his office unless the Vice-President and a majority of either the principal officers of the executive department or of such other body as Congress may by law provide, transmit within four days to the President pro tempore of the Senate and the Speaker of the House of Representatives their written declaration that the President is unable to discharge the powers and duties of his office. Thereupon Congress shall decide the issue, assembling within forty-eight hours for that purpose if not in session. If the Congress, within twenty-one days after receipt of the latter written declaration, or, if Congress is not in session, within twenty-one days after Congress is required to assemble, determines by two-thirds vote of both Houses that the President is unable to discharge the powers and duties of his office, the Vice-President shall continue to discharge the same as Acting President; otherwise, the President shall resume the powers and duties of his office.

AMENDMENT XXVI ● (1971)

Section 1. The right of citizens of the United States, who are eighteen years of age or older, to vote shall not be denied or abridged by the United States or any state on account of age.

Lowers the voting age to eighteen.

Section 2. The Congress shall have the power to enforce this article by appropriate legislation.

Few, William, 184
Field, Cyrus, 283
Fifteenth Amendment to the Constitution, 475n
Fillmore, Millard, 376, 426
Finney, Charles G., 313
First Continental Congress, 161, 191
First Reconstruction Act of 1867, 472
Fitzhugh, George, 359
Five Forks, Battle of, 461
Florida, 27, 255–257, 267–268, 430, 475
Floyd, John, 342–345, 347, 352, 360, 361
Floyd, John Buchanan, 361, 396
Foote, Henry S., 367, 373–374, 375
Force Bills, 478
foreign affairs: Adams (John) administration, 238–239; under Articles of Confederation, 202–203; Jefferson administration, 249–250; Madison administration, 250–251, 253; Monroe Doctrine, 276–277; Pierce administration, 391; Tyler administration, 292; Washington administration, 234–235
foreign trade, 1790–1860, c380
Forrest, Nathan B., 454
Fort Donelson, 457
Fort Henry, 457
Fort Sumter, 431, 450, 454
Fort Ticonderoga, 166, 167
Foster, John, 102
Fourteenth Amendment to the Constitution, 471, 472
Fox, George, 119
Fox Indians, 288
France: Adams administration and, 239; in American Revolution, 167; early voyages of exploration, m30; French and Indian War, 151–154; Louisiana Purchase, 212, 217; North American exploration and colonization, 32, 115; Washington administration and, 234–235; XYZ affair, 239, 240
Francis, Salathiel, 335
Francis I, King of France, 18, 32
Franklin, Benjamin, 152–154, 164, 167, 198; at Constitutional Convention, 171, 178–179, 184, 189, 190
Franklin, John Hope, 475
Frazier, Garrison, 445–446
Fredericksburg, Battle of, 454, 456
free blacks, 352, 354, 420, 445–449, 465
Freedmen's Bureau, 448, 449, 469, 472
Free Soil party, 388, 423, 424

Frémont, John C., 386, 425
French and Indian War, 151–154
French Revolution, 234
Frobisher, Martin, m30, 35, 37
Fugitive Slave Act of 1850, 377, 389, 392
fugitive slaves, 367, 368, 377–379, 389, 391
full faith and credit, 187
Fuller, Margaret, 312
fur trade, 32, 215, 230, 380

Gadsden Purchase, 391
Gage, Thomas, 132, 134, 143, 160–163, 166
gag rule, 417
Gaines, Edmund, 256
Gallatin, Albert, 221, 242
Gama, Vasco da, 26, m30
Garrick, Edward, 136–137, 146
Garrison, William Lloyd, 295, 325, 326, 339, 415–417, 419, 424, 425
Gaspée (ship), 159
Gates, Horatio, 169
Gates, Sir Thomas, 52, 54, 55, 57
Gedney, Bartholemew, 102
General Historie of Virginia (Smith), 62
general warrants, 208
Genêt, Edmund, 234–235
George III, King of England, 154, 155, 161, 163–165
Georgia, 76–78, 184–185, 208, 287–288, 430, 433–449, 477
Germantown, Battle of, 167
Gerry, Elbridge, 173, 177, 180, 181, 189, 204, 205
Gettysburg, Battle of, 454
Ghent, Treaty of (1814), 253, 265
Gibbons v. Ogden (1824), 245
Giddings, Joshua, 367
Gilbert, Sir Humphrey, 37
Glorious Revolution, 124
Glover, Goodwife, 88
Godspeed (ship), 42, 45
gold, 27, 31–32, 386
Golden Hind (ship), 36
Goldfinch, Captain, 136, 137
Good, Dorcas, 89
Good, Sarah, 85, 88–91, 93
Good, William, 89
Gorges, Sir Ferdinando, 111
Gorham, Nathaniel, 187
government: under Articles of Confederation, 171–173, 177, 181–183, 191–194, 199–202; colonial, 56–57, 60–62, 105, 106–107, 110, 120, c121, 122, 150–151; Constitution and, 175–190
Grant, Ulysses S., 383, 440, 457, 459–461, 473, 475, 478
Gray, John, 135
Gray, Robert, 380
Gray, Samuel, 141

Gray, Thomas R., 342
Great Awakening, 153
Great Britain: American Revolution, 161–169; colonies, *see* Colonial America; constitution, 192; early voyages of exploration, m30; events leading to American Revolution, 130–161; French and Indian War, 151–154; impressment, 235, 249; Jefferson administration and, 249–250; mercantilism, 149–150; North American exploration and colonization, 34–38, 40–62; Oregon Country, 230, 277, 380–381; post-Revolutionary relations with U.S., 202; War of 1812, 250–253; Washington administration and, 234–235
Great Compromise, 186
Great Revival, 310–315
Greeley, Horace, 372, 425
Green, Israel, 404–405
Green, Shields, 404, 411
Green, William, 135
Green Mountain Boys, 166
Greene, Harriet, 421
Greene, Nathanael, 169
Grenville, George, 155–157
Griggs, William, 86
Grimké, Angelina, 415
Guadalupe Hidalgo, Treaty of 1848, 383, 384, 386
Gue, David J., 397
Guilford Courthouse, Battle of, 169

Habeas corpus, 464
Haida Indians, 24
Hale, John, 86, 102
Hale, John P., 423, 424, 427
Halleck, Henry W., 444
Hallowell, Sarah L., 305
Hamilton, Alexander, 202, 229; Adams administration and, 238, 239; Annapolis Convention and, 203; at Constitutional Convention, 172, 173, 182–183, 186; duel with Burr, 229, 240; economic program of, 232–234, 241; election of 1796, 238; *The Federalist Papers*, 207, 232, 236; foreign intrigues, 234–235; Whiskey Rebellion, 237
Hammond, James H., 359
Hancock, John, 148, 161, 165
Harpers Ferry, Virginia, 396–407, m400
Harrison, William Henry, 250–252; election of 1840, 290–291, 419
Hartford Convention of 1814, 253, 273
Harvard College, 112
Harvey, John, 66
Hathorne, John, 80–82, 88–90, 92, 94, 96, 99

Allen Weinstein is a Professor of History at Smith College, where he directed American Studies for six years and teaches U.S. political and social history. In 1981, he served as the Commonwealth Fund Lecturer in U.S. History at University College, the University of London, and the previous year, he was a Fellow of the Smithsonian's Woodrow Wilson International Center for Scholars in Washington. His book, *Perjury: The Hiss–Chambers Case* (Knopf, 1978; Vintage paperback, 1979), received several awards, most recently a 1979 American Book Awards' finalist nomination in History Paperbacks. He directed The Twentieth Century Fund's study of the Freedom of Information Act's impact upon U.S. intelligence agencies and has lectured and published widely on government information policy. His previous books include *Prelude to Populism* and *American Negro Slavery: A Modern Reader* (with Frank Gatell, 3rd ed., rev., 1980). His articles have appeared in many scholarly periodicals and journals of opinion, both in this country and abroad. He has served on the Editorial Board of *The Journal of American Studies* and presently serves on *The Wilson Quarterly*'s Advisory Board. He has lectured throughout Europe and Israel, twice served as Senior Fulbright Lecturer in Australia, and has taught at Amherst College, Brown University, Hartford College for Women, Teacher's College (Columbia), and the University of Maryland.

Frank Otto Gatell, Professor of History at U.C.L.A., is the author of several books, including *John Gorham Palfrey and the New England Conscience*, and of a number of major articles on the historiography of the Jacksonian period and other subjects. He has taught at Stanford University, the University of Maryland, and the University of Puerto Rico. He has served several times as a Fulbright Professor in Latin America and lectured widely at universities throughout Latin America both in English and Spanish. His many published articles include several on the history of Puerto Rico and other aspects of Latin American history.